Real-Time Rendering
Second Edition

Real-Time Rendering
Second Edition

Tomas Akenine-Möller

Eric Haines

A K Peters
Natick, Massachusetts

Editorial, Sales, and Customer Service Office

A K Peters, Ltd.
63 South Avenue
Natick, MA 01760
www.akpeters.com

Library of Congress Cataloging-in-Publication Data

Möller, Tomas, 1971– /
    Real-time rendering / Tomas Möller, Eric Haines.–2nd edition.
        p. cm.
    Includes bibliographical references and index.
    ISBN 1-56881-182-9
    1. Computer graphics 2. Real-time data processing. I. Haines, Eric, 1958– II. Title.

    T385 .M635 2002
    006.6'773–dc21

                                                                                        2002025151

Printed in the United States of America
06 05 04 03 02   10 9 8 7 6 5 4 3 2

Dedicated to Eva, Felix, and Elina
T. A-M.

Dedicated to Cathy, Ryan, and Evan
E. H.

Contents

Preface

How far the field of real-time rendering has progressed in three years! Vertex or pixel shaders did not exist back then; now these are key abilities of modern graphics accelerators. The first edition of *Real-Time Rendering* discussed multitexturing techniques as the state-of-the-art. This edition has expanded by more than 60%, and includes large amounts of material on curved surfaces, global illumination, non-photorealistic rendering, and many other topics that warranted only a sentence or two in the previous edition.

This book is about algorithms that create synthetic images fast enough that the viewer can interact with a virtual environment. We have focused on three-dimensional rendering and, to a limited extent, user interaction. Modeling, animation, and many other areas are important to the process of making a real-time application, but these topics are beyond the scope of this book.

This field is rapidly evolving and so is a moving target. Graphics accelerators for the consumer market are easily outperforming Moore's Law. Three years pass and accelerators are ten times faster. Graphics libraries appear, evolve, and sometimes die out (e.g., 3dfx's *Glide* API). For these reasons, we have, for the most part, avoided describing specific APIs, chips, buses, memory architectures, etc., except where it serves the goal of informing you about some general concept. We have endeavored to describe algorithms that, by their popularity or lasting value, are likely to be used for some time to come.

We expect you to have some basic understanding of computer graphics before reading this book, as well as computer science and programming. Some of the later chapters in particular are meant for implementers of various complex algorithms. If some section does lose you, skim on through or look at the references. One of the most valuable services we feel we can provide is to at least let you realize what you do not yet know, and to know where to learn about it someday in the future.

This book does not exist in a vacuum; we make a point of referencing relevant material wherever possible, as well as providing a summary of further reading and resources at the end of most chapters. We also spent much time searching for reference locations on the web; most current papers are available there for free. The days have just about come to an end when only those living near a good research library could learn about the newest algorithms.

Because the field is evolving so rapidly, we maintain a web site related to this book at: `http://www.realtimerendering.com/`. The site contains links to tutorials, demonstration programs, code samples, software libraries, book corrections, and more.

Our true goal and guiding light while writing this book was simple. We wanted to write a book that we wished we had owned when we had started out, a book that was both unified yet crammed with details not found in introductory texts. We hope that you will find this book, our view of the world, of some use in your travels.

Acknowledgements

One of the most agreeable aspects of writing this second edition has been working with people and receiving their help. Despite their own pressing deadlines and concerns, many people gave us significant amounts of their time to improve this book. We would particularly like to thank the major reviewers. They are, listed alphabetically: Michael Abrash, Ian Ashdown, Ulf Assarsson, Chris Brennan, Sébastien Dominé, David Eberly, Cass Everitt, Tommy Fortes, Evan Hart, Greg James, Jan Kautz, Alexander Keller, Mark Kilgard, Adam Lake, Dean Macri, Carl Marshall, Jason L. Mitchell, Paul Lalonde, Thomas Larsson, Kasper Høy Nielsen, Jon Paul Schelter, Jacob Ström, Nick Triantos, Joe Warren, Michael Wimmer, and Peter Wonka. Of these, we wish to single out Cass Everitt at NVIDIA and Jason L. Mitchell at ATI Technologies for spending large amounts of time and effort in getting us the resources we needed. Our thanks also go out to Wolfgang Engel for freely sharing the contents of his upcoming book, *ShaderX* [210], so that we could make this edition as current as possible.

From discussing their work with us, to providing images or other resources, to writing reviews of sections of the book, many others helped in creating this edition. They all have our gratitude. These people include: Jason Ang, Haim Barad, Jules Bloomenthal, Jonathan Blow, Chas. Boyd, John Brooks, Cem Cebenoyan, Per Christensen, Hamilton Chu, Michael Cohen, Daniel Cohen-Or, Matt Craighead, Paul Debevec, Joe Demers, Walt Donovan, Howard Dortch, Mark Duchaineau, Phil Dutré, Dave Eberle, Gerald Farin, Simon Fenney, Randy Fernando, Jim Ferwerda, Nickson Fong, Tom Forsyth, Piero Foscari, Laura Fryer, Markus Giegl, Peter Glaskowsky, Andrew Glassner, Amy Gooch, Bruce Gooch, Simon

Green, Ned Greene, Larry Gritz, Joakim Grundwall, Juan Guardado, Pat Hanrahan, Mark Harris, Michael Herf, Carsten Hess, Rich Hilmer, Kenneth Hoff III, Naty Hoffman, Nick Holliman, Hugues Hoppe, Heather Horne, Tom Hubina, Richard Huddy, Adam James, Kaveh Kardan, Paul Keller, David Kirk, Alex Klimovitski, Jason Knipe, Jeff Lander, Marc Levoy, J.P. Lewis, Ming Lin, Adrian Lopez, Michael McCool, Doug McNabb, Stan Melax, Ville Miettinen, Kenny Mitchell, Steve Morein, Henry Moreton, Jerris Mungai, Jim Napier, George Ngo, Hubert Nguyen, Tito Pagán, Jörg Peters, Tom Porter, Emil Praun, Kekoa Proudfoot, Bernd Raabe, Ravi Ramamoorthi, Ashutosh Rege, Szymon Rusinkiewicz, Carlo Séquin, Chris Seitz, Jonathan Shade, Brian Smits, John Spitzer, Wolfgang Straßer, Wolfgang Stürzlinger, Philip Taylor, Pierre Terdiman, Nicolas Thibieroz, Jack Tumblin, Fredrik Ulfves, Thatcher Ulrich, Steve Upstill, Alex Vlachos, Ingo Wald, Ben Watson, Steve Westin, Dan Wexler, Matthias Wloka, Peter Woytiuk, David Wu, Garrett Young, Borut Zalik, Harold Zatz, Hansong Zhang, and Denis Zorin. We also wish to thank the journal *ACM Transactions on Graphics* for continuing to provide a mirror web site for this book.

Alice and Klaus Peters, our production manager Ariel Jaffee, our editor Heather Holcombe, our copyeditor Michelle M. Richards, and the rest of the staff at A K Peters have done a wonderful job making this book the best possible. Our thanks to all of you.

Finally, and most importantly, our deepest thanks go to our families for giving us the huge amounts of quiet time we have needed to complete this edition. Honestly, we never thought it would take this long!

Tomas Akenine-Möller
Eric Haines
May 2002

Acknowledgements for the First Edition

Many people helped in making this book. Some of the greatest contributions were made by those who reviewed parts of it. The reviewers willingly gave the benefit of their expertise, helping to significantly improve both content and style. We wish to thank (in alphabetical order) Thomas Barregren, Michael Cohen, Walt Donovan, Angus Dorbie, Michael Garland, Stefan Gottschalk, Ned Greene, Ming C. Lin, Jason L. Mitchell, Liang Peng, Keith Rule, Ken Shoemake, John Stone, Phil Taylor, Ben Trumbore, Jorrit Tyberghein, and Nick Wilt. We cannot thank you enough.

Many other people contributed their time and labor to this project. Some let us use images, others provided models, still others pointed out important resources or connected us with people who could help. In addition to the people listed above, we wish to acknowledge the help of Tony Barkans, Daniel Baum, Nelson Beebe, Curtis Beeson, Tor Berg, David Blythe, Chas. Boyd, Don Brittain, Ian Bullard, Javier Castellar, Satyan Coorg, Jason Della Rocca, Paul Diefenbach, Alyssa Donovan, Dave Eberly, Kells Elmquist, Stuart Feldman, Fred Fisher, Tom Forsyth, Marty Franz, Thomas Funkhouser, Andrew Glassner, Bruce Gooch, Larry Gritz, Robert Grzeszczuk, Paul Haeberli, Evan Hart, Paul Heckbert, Chris Hecker, Joachim Helenklaken, Hugues Hoppe, John Jack, Mark Kilgard, David Kirk, James Klosowski, Subodh Kumar, André LaMothe, Jeff Lander, Jens Larsson, Jed Lengyel, Fredrik Liliegren, David Luebke, Thomas Lundqvist, Tom McReynolds, Stan Melax, Don Mitchell, André Möller, Steve Molnar, Scott R. Nelson, Hubert Nguyen, Doug Rogers, Holly Rushmeier, Gernot Schaufler, Jonas Skeppstedt, Stephen Spencer, Per Stenström, Jacob Ström, Filippo Tampieri, Gary Tarolli, Ken Turkowski, Turner Whitted, Agata and Andrzej Wojaczek, Andrew Woo, Steve Worley, Brian Yen, Hans-Philip Zachau, Gabriel Zachmann, and Al Zimmerman. We also wish to thank the journal *ACM Transactions on Graphics* for providing a stable web site for this book.

Alice and Klaus Peters and the staff at AK Peters, particularly Carolyn Artin and Sarah Gillis, have been instrumental in making this book a reality. To all of you, thanks.

Finally, our deepest thanks go to our families and friends for providing support throughout this incredible, sometimes grueling, often exhilarating process.

Tomas Möller
Eric Haines
March 1999

Chapter 1
Introduction

Real-time rendering is concerned with making images rapidly on the computer. It is the most highly interactive area of computer graphics. An image appears on the screen, the viewer acts or reacts, and this feedback affects what is generated next. This cycle of reaction and rendering happens at a rapid enough rate that the viewer does not see individual images, but rather becomes immersed in a dynamic process.

The rate at which images are displayed is measured in frames per second (fps) or Hertz (Hz). At one frame per second, there is little sense of interactivity; the user is painfully aware of the arrival of each new image. At around 6 fps, a sense of interactivity starts to grow. An application displaying at 15 fps is certainly real-time; the user focuses on action and reaction. There is a useful limit, however. From about 72 fps and up, differences in the display rate are effectively indetectable.

However, there is more to real-time rendering than interactivity. If this was the only criterion, any application that rapidly responded to user commands and drew anything on the screen would qualify. Rendering in real-time normally means three-dimensional rendering.

Interactivity and some sense of connection to three-dimensional space are sufficient conditions for real-time rendering, but a third element has become a part of its definition: graphics acceleration hardware. While hardware dedicated to three-dimensional graphics has been available on professional workstations for many years, it is only relatively recently that the use of such accelerators at the consumer level has become possible. Many consider the introduction of the 3Dfx Voodoo 1 in 1996 the real beginning of this era [202]. With the recent rapid advances in this market, add-on three-dimensional graphics accelerators are as standard for home computers as a pair of speakers. While it is not absolutely required for real-time rendering, graphics accelerator hardware has become a requirement

1

for most real-time applications. An excellent example of the results of real-time rendering made possible by hardware acceleration is shown in Plate I (following page 274).

1.1   Contents Overview

What follows is a brief overview of the chapters ahead.

Chapter 2, The Graphics Rendering Pipeline. This chapter deals with the heart of real-time rendering, the mechanism that takes a scene description and converts it into something we can see.

Chapter 3, Transforms. Transforms are the basic tools for manipulating the position, orientation, size, and shape of objects and the location and view of the camera.

Chapter 4, Visual Appearance. This chapter covers the definition of materials and lights and their use in achieving a realistic surface appearance. Also covered are other appearance-related topics, such as providing higher image quality through antialiasing and gamma correction.

Chapter 5, Texturing. One of the most powerful hardware-accelerated tools for real-time rendering is the ability to display data such as images on surfaces. This chapter discusses the mechanics of this technique, called texturing, and presents a wide variety of methods for applying it.

Chapter 6, Advanced Lighting and Shading. This chapter discusses the theory and practice of correctly representing materials. One focus is on new hardware features such as vertex and pixel shaders. Global illumination algorithms such as ray tracing and radiosity and their relation to real-time rendering is discussed.

Chapter 7, Non-Photorealistic Rendering. Attempting to make a scene look realistic is only one way of rendering it. This chapter discusses other styles, such as cartoon shading.

Chapter 8, Image-Based Rendering. Polygons are not always the fastest or most realistic way to describe objects or phenomena such as lens flares or fire. In this chapter, alternate representations based on using images are discussed.

Chapter 9, Acceleration Algorithms. After you make it go, make it go fast. Various forms of culling and level of detail rendering are covered here.

Chapter 10, Pipeline Optimization. Once an application is running and uses efficient algorithms, it can be made even faster using various optimization techniques. Finding the bottleneck and deciding what to do about it are the topics covered here.

Chapter 11, Polygonal Techniques. Geometric data comes from a wide range of sources, and sometimes requires modification in order to be rendered rapidly and well. This chapter discusses polygonal data and ways to clean it up and simplify it. Also included are more compact representations, such as triangle strips, fans, and meshes.

Chapter 12, Curves and Curved Surfaces. Hardware ultimately deals in points, lines, and polygons for rendering geometry. More complex surfaces offer advantages such as being able to trade off between quality and rendering speed, more compact representation, and smooth surface generation.

Chapter 13, Intersection Test Methods. Intersection testing is important for rendering, user interaction, and collision detection. In-depth coverage is provided here for a wide range of the most efficient algorithms for common geometric intersection tests.

Chapter 14, Collision Detection. Finding out whether two objects touch each other is a key element of many real-time applications. This chapter presents some efficient algorithms in this rapidly evolving field.

Chapter 15, Graphics Hardware. While graphics-hardware-accelerated algorithms have been discussed in the previous chapters, this chapter focuses on components such as color depth, frame buffers, and basic architecture types. Case studies of a few representative graphics accelerators are provided.

Chapter 16, The Future. Take a guess (we do).

We have included appendices on linear algebra and trigonometry.

1.2 Notation and Definitions

First, we shall explain the mathematical notation used in this book. For a more thorough explanation of many of the terms used in this section, see Appendix A.

1.2.1 Mathematical Notation

Table 1.1 summarizes most of the mathematical notation we will use. Some of the concepts will be described at some length here.

Type	Notation	Examples
angle	lowercase Greek	$\alpha_i, \phi, \rho, \eta, \gamma_{242}, \theta$
scalar	lowercase italic	a, b, t, u_k, v, w_{ij}
vector or point	lowercase bold	$\mathbf{a}, \mathbf{u}, \mathbf{v}_s \ \mathbf{h}(\rho), \mathbf{h}_z$
matrix	capital bold	$\mathbf{T(t)}, \mathbf{X}, \mathbf{R}_x(\rho)$
plane	π: a vector + a scalar	$\pi : \mathbf{n} \cdot \mathbf{x} + d,$ $\pi_1 : \mathbf{n}_1 \cdot \mathbf{x} + d_1$
triangle	$\triangle$ 3 points	$\triangle \mathbf{v}_0\mathbf{v}_1\mathbf{v}_2, \triangle\mathbf{cba}$
line segment	two points	$\mathbf{uv}, \mathbf{a}_i\mathbf{b}_j$
geometric entity	capital italic	A_{OBB}, T, B_{AABB}

Table 1.1. Summary of the notation used in this book.

The angles and the scalars are taken from $\mathbb{R}$, i.e., they are real numbers. Vectors and points are denoted by bold lowercase letters, and the components are accessed as

$$\mathbf{v} = \begin{pmatrix} v_x \\ v_y \\ v_z \end{pmatrix},$$

that is, in column vector format, which is now commonly used in the computer graphics world. At some places in the text we use (v_x, v_y, v_z) instead of the formally more correct $(v_x \ v_y \ v_z)^T$, since the former is easier to read.

In homogeneous coordinates (see Appendix Section A.4), a coordinate is represented by $\mathbf{v} = (v_x \ v_y \ v_z \ v_w)^T$, where a vector is $\mathbf{v} = (v_x \ v_y \ v_z \ 0)^T$ and a point is $\mathbf{v} = (v_x \ v_y \ v_z \ 1)^T$. Sometimes we use only three-element vectors and points, but we try to avoid any ambiguity as to which type is being used. For matrix manipulations, it is extremely advantageous to have the same notation for vectors as for points (see Chapter 3 on transforms and Appendix Section A.4 on homogeneous notation). In some algorithms, it will be convenient to use numeric indices instead of x, y, and z, for example $\mathbf{v} = (v_0 \ v_1 \ v_2)^T$. All of these rules for vectors and points also hold for two-element vectors; in that case, we simply skip the last component of a three-element vector.

The matrix deserves a bit more explanation. The common sizes that will be used are 2×2, 3×3, and 4×4. We will review the manner of accessing a 3×3 matrix $\mathbf{M}$, and it is simple to extend this process to the other sizes. The (scalar) elements of $\mathbf{M}$ are denoted m_{ij}, $0 \le (i, j) \le 2$, where i denotes the row and j the column, as in Equation 1.1.

$$\mathbf{M} = \begin{pmatrix} m_{00} & m_{01} & m_{02} \\ m_{10} & m_{11} & m_{12} \\ m_{20} & m_{21} & m_{22} \end{pmatrix} \tag{1.1}$$

The following notation, shown in Equation 1.2 for a 3×3 matrix, is used to isolate vectors from the matrix $\mathbf{M}$: $\mathbf{m}_{,j}$ represents the jth column vector and $\mathbf{m}_{i,}$ represents the ith row vector (in column vector form). As with vectors and points, indexing the column vectors can also be done with x, y, z, and sometimes w, if that is more convenient.

$$\mathbf{M} = \begin{pmatrix} \mathbf{m}_{,0} & \mathbf{m}_{,1} & \mathbf{m}_{,2} \end{pmatrix} = \begin{pmatrix} \mathbf{m}_x & \mathbf{m}_y & \mathbf{m}_z \end{pmatrix} = \begin{pmatrix} \mathbf{m}_{0,}^T \\ \mathbf{m}_{1,}^T \\ \mathbf{m}_{2,}^T \end{pmatrix} \tag{1.2}$$

A plane is denoted $\pi : \mathbf{n} \cdot \mathbf{x} + d = 0$ and contains its mathematical formula, the plane normal $\mathbf{n}$ and the scalar d. π is the common mathematical notation for a plane. The plane π is said to divide the space into a *positive half-space*, where $\mathbf{n} \cdot \mathbf{x} + d > 0$, and a *negative half-space*, where $\mathbf{n} \cdot \mathbf{x} + d < 0$. All other points are said to lie in the plane.

A triangle can be defined by three points $\mathbf{v}_0$, $\mathbf{v}_1$, and $\mathbf{v}_2$ and is denoted by $\triangle \mathbf{v}_0 \mathbf{v}_1 \mathbf{v}_2$.

Table 1.2 presents a few additional mathematical operators and their notation. The dot, cross, determinant, and length operators are covered in Appendix A. The transpose operator turns a column vector into a row vector and vice versa. Thus a column vector can be written in compressed form in a block of text as $\mathbf{v} = (v_x \ v_y \ v_z)^T$. Operator 4 requires further explanation: $\mathbf{u} \otimes \mathbf{v}$ denotes the vector $(u_x v_x \ u_y v_y \ u_z v_z)^T$, i.e., component i of vector $\mathbf{u}$ and component i of vector $\mathbf{v}$ are multiplied and stored in component i of a new vector. In this text, this operator is used exclusively for color vector manipulations. Operator 5, introduced in *Graphics Gems IV* [359], is a unary operator on a two-dimensional vector. Letting this operator work on a vector $\mathbf{v} = (v_x \ v_y)^T$ gives a vector that is perpendicular to $\mathbf{v}$, i.e., $\mathbf{v}^\perp = (-v_y \ v_x)^T$. We use $|a|$ to denote the absolute value of the scalar a, while $|\mathbf{A}|$ means the determinant of the matrix $\mathbf{A}$. Sometimes, we also use $|\mathbf{A}| = |\mathbf{a} \ \mathbf{b} \ \mathbf{c}| = \det(\mathbf{a}, \mathbf{b}, \mathbf{c})$, where $\mathbf{a}$, $\mathbf{b}$, and $\mathbf{c}$ are column vectors of the matrix $\mathbf{A}$. The ninth operator, factorial, is defined as shown below, and note that $0! = 1$.

$$n! = n(n-1)(n-2) \cdots 3 \cdot 2 \cdot 1 \tag{1.3}$$

	Operator	Description
1:	$\cdot$	dot product
2:	$\times$	cross product
3:	$\mathbf{v}^T$	transpose of the vector $\mathbf{v}$
4:	$\otimes$	piecewise vector multiplication
5:	$\perp$	the unary, perp dot product operator
6:	$\mid \cdot \mid$	determinant of a matrix
7:	$\mid \cdot \mid$	absolute value of a scalar
8:	$\parallel \cdot \parallel$	length (or norm) of argument
9:	$n!$	factorial
10:	$\binom{n}{k}$	binomial coefficients

Table 1.2. Notation for some mathematical operators.

The tenth operator, the binomial factor, is defined as shown in Equation 1.4:

$$\binom{n}{k} = \frac{n!}{k!(n-k)!}. \qquad (1.4)$$

Further on, we call the common planes $x = 0$, $y = 0$, and $z = 0$ the *coordinate planes* or *axis-aligned planes*. The axes $\mathbf{e}_x = (1 \ \ 0 \ \ 0)^T$, $\mathbf{e}_y = (0 \ \ 1 \ \ 0)^T$, and $\mathbf{e}_z = (0 \ \ 0 \ \ 1)^T$ are called *main axes* or *main directions* and often the x-axis, y-axis, and z-axis. This set of axes is often called the *standard basis*. Unless otherwise noted, we will use orthonormal bases (consisting of mutually perpendicular unit vectors; see Appendix Section A.3.1).

The notation for a range that includes both a and b, and all numbers in between is $[a, b]$. If you want all number between a and b, but not a and b themselves, then we write (a, b). Combinations of these can also be made, e.g., $[a, b)$ means all numbers between a and b including a but not b.

The C-math function `atan2(y,x)` is often used in this text, and so deserves some attention. It is an extension of the mathematical function $\arctan(x)$. The main differences between them are that $-\frac{\pi}{2} < \arctan(x) < \frac{\pi}{2}$, that $0 \leq \mathtt{atan2(y, x)} < 2\pi$, and that an extra argument has been added to the latter function. This extra argument avoids division by zero, i.e., $x = \mathtt{y/x}$ except when $\mathtt{x} = 0$.

We use a right-hand coordinate system (see Appendix Section A.2) since this is the standard system for three-dimensional geometry in the field of computer graphics.

Colors are represented by a three-element vector, such as (*red, green, blue*), where each element has the range [0, 1].

1.2.2 Geometrical Definitions

The basic rendering primitives (also called drawing primitives) used by most graphics hardware are points, lines, and triangles[1].

Throughout this book, we will refer to a collection of geometric entities as either a *model* or an *object*. A *scene* is a collection of models comprising everything that is included in the environment to be rendered. A scene can also include material descriptions, lighting, and viewing specifications.

Examples of objects are a car, a building, and even a line. In practice, an object often consists of a set of drawing primitives, but this may not always be the case; an object may have a higher kind of geometrical representation, such as Bézier curves or surfaces, subdivision surfaces, etc. Also, objects can consist of other objects, e.g., we call a car model's door an object or a subset of the car.

Further Reading and Resources

The most important resource we can refer you to is the website for this book: http://www.realtimerendering.com/. It contains links to the latest information and websites relevant to each chapter. The field of real-time rendering is changing with real-time speed. In the book we have attempted to focus on concepts that are fundamental and techniques that are unlikely to go out of style. On the website we have the opportunity to present information that is relevant to today's software developer and we have the ability to keep up-to-date.

---

[1] The only exceptions we know of are Pixel-Planes [244], which could draw spheres, and the NVIDIA NV1 chip, which could draw ellipsoids.

Chapter 2
The Graphics Rendering Pipeline

"A chain is no stronger than its weakest link."
–Anonymous

This chapter is concerned with presenting the core of real-time graphics, namely, the *graphics rendering pipeline*, hereafter referred to as the rendering pipeline or simply the pipeline. The main function of the pipeline is to generate, or *render*, a two-dimensional image, given a virtual camera, three-dimensional objects, light sources, lighting models, textures, and more. The rendering pipeline is thus the underlying tool for real-time rendering. The process of using the pipeline is depicted in Figure 2.1. The locations and shapes of the objects in the image are determined by their geometry, the placement of the camera in the environment, and the characteristics of that environment. The appearance of the objects is affected by material properties, light sources, textures, and lighting models.

The different stages of the rendering pipeline will be discussed and explained here, with focus on the function and not on the implementation. This is because some of the implementation details will be dealt with in later chapters, but also because some stages are taken as givens. For example, what is important to someone using lines are characteristics such as vertex data formats, colors, and pattern types, and whether, say, depth cueing is available, not whether lines are implemented via Bresenham's line-drawing algorithm [101] or via a symmetric double-step algorithm [829]. Often most of these pipeline stages are implemented in hardware, which makes it impossible to optimize or improve on the implementation. Details of basic draw and fill algorithms are covered in depth in books such as Rogers's [657]. What we can optimize is how and when we use the given implementations.

9

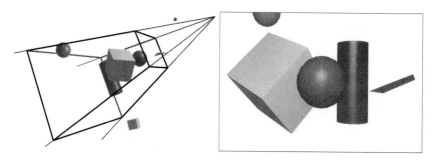

Figure 2.1. In the left image, a virtual camera is located at the tip of the pyramid (where four lines converge). Only the primitives inside the view volume are rendered. For an image that is rendered in perspective (as is the case here), the view volume is a frustum, i.e., a truncated pyramid with a rectangular base. The right image shows what the camera "sees." Note the bottommost cube in the left image is not in the rendering to the right because it is located outside the view frustum. Also, the triangle in the left image is clipped against the smaller (*near*) plane of the frustum, which results in a quadrilateral.

The goal of this chapter is thus to provide a detailed understanding of the function of the rendering of images, while omitting discussion of implementation issues.

2.1   Architecture

In the physical world, pipelines appear in many different forms, from oil pipelines to factory assembly lines to ski lifts. They also appear in graphics rendering.

A pipeline consists of several stages [354]. In the case of the oil pipeline, oil cannot move from the first stage of the pipeline to the second until the oil already in that second stage has moved on to the third stage, and so forth. This implies that the speed of the pipeline is determined by its slowest pipeline stage, no matter how fast the other stages may be.

Ideally, a nonpipelined construction that is divided into n pipelined stages should give a speed-up of a factor of n, which is the reason to use it. For example, a ski chairlift containing only one chair is inefficient; adding more chairs creates a proportional speed-up in the number of skiers brought up the hill. The pipeline stages execute in parallel, but they are stalled until the slowest stage has finished its task. For example, if the steering wheel attachment stage on a car assembly line takes three minutes and every other stage takes two minutes, the best rate that can be achieved is one car made

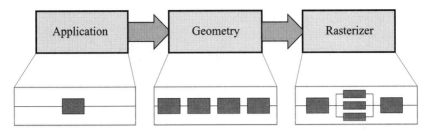

Figure 2.2. The basic construction of the rendering pipeline, consisting of three stages: application, geometry, and the rasterizer. Each of these stages may be a pipeline in itself, as illustrated below the geometry stage, or a stage may be (partly) parallelized as shown below the rasterizer stage. In this illustration, the application stage is a single process, but this stage could also be pipelined or parallelized.

every three minutes; the other stages must be idle for one minute while the steering wheel attachment is completed. For this particular pipeline, the steering wheel stage is the *bottleneck*, since it determines the speed of the entire production.

This kind of pipeline construction is also found in the context of real-time computer graphics. A coarse division of the real-time rendering pipeline into three *conceptual stages* is shown in Figure 2.2. The stages are called *application*, *geometry*, and *rasterizer*. This structure is the core— the engine of the rendering pipeline —which is used in real-time computer graphics applications, and is thus an essential base for discussion in subsequent chapters. Each of these stages is usually a pipeline in itself, which means that it consists of several substages. We differentiate between the conceptual stages (application, geometry, and rasterizer), functional stages, and pipeline stages. A functional stage has a certain task to perform, but does not specify the way that task is executed in the pipeline. A pipeline stage, on the other hand, is executed simultaneously with all the other pipeline stages. A pipeline stage may also be parallelized in order to meet high performance needs. For example, the geometry stage may be divided into five functional stages, but it is the implementation of a graphics system that determines its division into pipeline stages. A given implementation may combine two functional stages into one pipeline stage, while it divides another, more time-consuming, functional stage into several pipeline stages, or even parallelizes it.

It is the slowest of the pipeline stages that determines the *rendering speed*, the update speed of the images. This speed may be expressed in frames per second (fps), that is, the number of rendered images per second, or in Hz (which is simply the notation for $1/second$, i.e., the frequency). Since we are dealing with a pipeline, it does not suffice to add up the time it takes for all the data we want to render to pass through the entire pipeline. This, of course, is a consequence of the pipeline construction, which allows the stages to execute in parallel. If we could locate the bottleneck, i.e., the slowest stage of the pipeline, and measure how much time it takes data to pass through that stage, then we could compute the rendering speed. Assume, for example, that the bottleneck stage takes 20 ms (milliseconds) to execute, then the rendering speed would be $1/0.020 = 50$ Hz. However, this is true only if the output device can update at this particular speed; otherwise, the true output rate will be slower. In other pipelining contexts, the term *throughput* is used instead of rendering speed.

EXAMPLE: RENDERING SPEED Assume that our output device's maximum update frequency is 60 Hz, and that the bottleneck of the rendering pipeline has been found. Timings show that this stage takes 62.5 ms to execute. The rendering speed is then computed as follows. First, ignore the output device, which gives us a maximum rendering speed of $1/0.0625 = 16$ Hz. Second, adjust this value to the frequency of the output device: 60 Hz implies that rendering speed can be 60 Hz, $60/2 = 30$ Hz, $60/3 = 20$ Hz, $60/4 = 15$ Hz, $60/5 = 12$ Hz, and so forth. This means that we can expect the rendering speed to be 15 Hz, since this is the maximum speed the output device can manage that is less than 16 Hz.   □

As the name implies, the application stage is driven by the application and is therefore implemented in software. This stage may, for example, contain collision detection, acceleration algorithms, animations, force feedback, etc. The next step, implemented either in software or in hardware, depending on the architecture, is the geometry stage, which deals with transforms, projections, lighting, etc. That is, this stage computes what is to be drawn, how it should be drawn, and where it should be drawn. Finally, the rasterizer stage draws (renders) an image with use of the data that the previous stage generated. These stages and their internal pipelines will be discussed in the next three sections.

2.2 The Application Stage

The developer has full control over what happens in the application stage, since it always executes in software. Therefore, the developer can change the implementation in order to change performance. In the other stages, it is harder to change the implementation, since parts or all of those stages are built upon hardware. However, it is still possible to affect the time consumed by the geometry and the rasterizer stages, by, for example, decreasing the number of triangles to be rendered during the application stage.

At the end of the application stage, the geometry to be rendered is fed to the next stage in the rendering pipeline. These are the rendering primitives, i.e., points, lines, and triangles, that might eventually end up on the screen (or whatever output device is being used). This is the most important task of the application stage.

A consequence of the software-based implementation of this stage is that it is not divided into substages, as are the geometry and the rasterizer stages.[1] However, this stage could be executed in parallel on several processors in order to increase performance. In CPU design, this would be called a *superscalar* construction, since it is able to execute several things at the same time in the same stage. In Section 10.5, two different methods for utilizing multiple processors will be presented.

One process commonly implemented in this stage is collision detection. After a collision is detected between two objects, a response may be generated and sent back to the colliding objects as well as to a force feedback device. The application stage is also the place to take care of input from other sources, such as the keyboard, the mouse, a Virtual Reality (VR) helmet, etc. Depending on this input, several different kinds of actions may be taken. Other processes implemented in this stage include texture animation, animations via transforms, geometry morphing, or any kind of calculations that are not performed in any other stages. Acceleration algorithms, such as hierarchical view frustum culling, among others (see Chapter 9), are also implemented here.

2.3 The Geometry Stage

The geometry stage is responsible for the majority of the per-polygon operations or per-vertex operations. This stage is further divided into the functional stages shown in Figure 2.3. Note again that, depending on the implementation, these functional stages may or may not be equivalent to pipeline stages. In some cases, a number of consecutive functional stages

---

[1]Of course, since it probably executes on a pipelined CPU, you could say that the application stage is further subdivided into several pipeline stages, but this is not relevant here.

Figure 2.3. The geometry stage subdivided into a pipeline of functional stages.

form a single pipeline stage (which runs in parallel with the other pipeline stages). In other cases, a functional stage may be subdivided into several smaller pipeline stages.

For example, at one extreme, all stages in the entire rendering pipeline may run in software, and then you could say that your entire pipeline consists of one pipeline stage. At the other extreme, each functional stage could be subdivided into several smaller pipeline stages, and each such pipeline stage could execute on a designated floating point processor.

Also note that the geometry stage performs a very demanding task. With a single light source, each vertex requires approximately 100 individual precision floating point operations [9].

2.3.1   Model and View Transform

On its way to the screen, a model is transformed into several different *spaces* or *coordinate systems*. Originally, a model resides in its own *model space*, which simply means that it has not been transformed at all. Each model can be associated with a *model transform* so that it can be positioned and oriented. It is possible to have several model transforms associated with the same model. This allows several copies (called *instances*) of the same model to have different locations, orientations, and sizes in the same scene, without requiring replication of the basic geometry.

It is the vertices and the normals of the model that are transformed by the model transform. The coordinates of an object are called *model coordinates*, and after the model transform has been applied to these coordinates, the model is said to be located in *world coordinates* or in *world space*. The world space is unique, and after the models have been transformed with their respective model transforms, all models exist in this same space.

As mentioned previously, only the models that the camera (or observer) sees are rendered. The camera has a location in world space and a direction, which are used to place and aim the camera. To facilitate projection and clipping, the camera and all the models are transformed with the *view transform*. The purpose of the view transform is to place the camera at

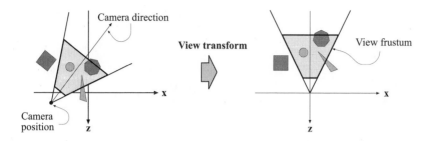

Figure 2.4. In the left illustration, the camera is located and oriented as the user wants it to be. The view transform relocates the camera at the origin looking along the negative z-axis, as shown on the right. This is done to make the clipping and projection operations simpler and faster. The light gray area is the view volume. Here, perspective viewing is assumed, since the view volume is a frustum. Similar techniques apply to any kind of projection.

the origin and aim it, to make it look in the direction of the negative z-axis,[2] with the y-axis pointing upwards and the x-axis pointing to the right. The actual position and direction after the view transform has been applied is dependent on the underlying Application Program Interface (API). The space thus delineated is called the *camera space*, or more commonly, the *eye space*. An example of the way in which the view transform affects the camera and the models is shown in Figure 2.4. Both the model transform and the view transform are implemented as 4×4 matrices, which is the topic of Chapter 3. For efficiency reasons, these are usually concatenated into one matrix before transforming the models. If they are concatenated in this way, however, the world space is not available—one moves directly to eye space.

More elaborate transforms can happen at this stage. *Vertex blending* (Section 3.4) can be done to smoothly join rigid parts (e.g., making a hand and arm join cleanly at the wrist). Transforms performed by a *vertex shader* further on down the pipeline can also modify the geometry of the surface (see Section 6.5).

2.3.2 Lighting and Shading

In order to lend models a more realistic appearance, the scene can be equipped with one or more light sources. One may choose whether or not the lights affect the appearance of the geometry. The geometric models

---

[2]We will be using the $-z$ axis convention; some texts prefer looking down the $+z$ axis. The difference is mostly semantic, as transform between one and the other is simple.

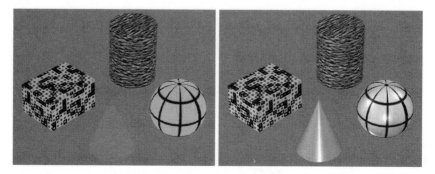

Figure 2.5. A scene without lighting is on the left; a lit scene on the right.

may also have a color associated with each vertex, or a texture (an image) "glued onto" them. Figure 2.5 gives an example. Notice how a texture gives the surface a three-dimensional effect without lighting, but solid colors are unconvincing.

For those models that are to be affected by light sources, a *lighting* equation is used to compute a color at each vertex of the model. This equation approximates the real-world interaction between photons and surfaces. In the real world, photons are emitted from light sources and are reflected or absorbed by surfaces. In real-time graphics, not much time can be spent on simulating this phenomenon. For example, true reflections and shadows normally are not part of this equation. Also, models are normally represented graphically by triangles, as these are the geometric primitives used by most graphics hardware. The color at each vertex of the surface is computed using the location of the light sources and their properties, the position and the normal of the vertex, and the properties of the material belonging to the vertex. Then the colors at the vertices of a triangle are interpolated over the triangle when rendering to the screen. This interpolation technique is called *Gouraud shading* [285]. The lighting equation and shading are treated in more detail in Chapter 4. To simulate more elaborate lighting effects, *pixel shading* techniques (Section 6.6) are employed further down the pipeline, during rasterization.

Normally, lighting is calculated in world space, but if the light sources are transformed with the view transform, the same lighting effect is obtained in eye space. This is because the relative relationships between light sources, the camera, and the models are preserved if all entities that are included in the lighting calculations are transformed to the same space, namely the eye space.

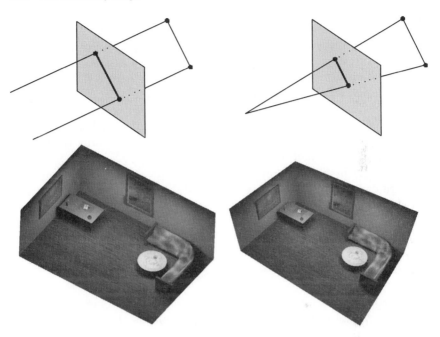

Figure 2.6. On the left is an orthographic, or parallel, projection; on the right is a perspective projection.

2.3.3   Projection

After lighting, rendering systems perform *projection*, which transforms the view volume into a unit cube with its extreme points at $(-1, -1, -1)$ and $(1, 1, 1)$.[3] The unit cube is called the *canonical view volume*. There are essentially two projections methods, namely *orthographic* (also called *parallel*) [4] and *perspective* projection. See Figure 2.6.

The view volume of orthographic viewing is normally a rectangular box, and the orthographic projection transforms this view volume into the unit cube. The main characteristic of orthographic projection is that parallel lines remain parallel after the transform. This transformation is a combination of a translation and a scaling.

---

[3]Different volumes can be used, for example $0 \le z \le 1$. Blinn has an interesting article [74] on using other intervals.

[4]Actually, orthographic is just one type of parallel projection. There is also an oblique parallel projection method [328], which is much less common.

The perspective projection is a bit more complex. In this type of projection, the farther away an object lies from the camera, the smaller it appears after projection. In addition, parallel lines may converge at the horizon. The perspective transform thus mimics the way we perceive objects' size. Geometrically, the view volume, called a *frustum*, is a truncated pyramid with rectangular base. The frustum is transformed into the unit cube as well. Both orthographic and perspective transforms can be constructed with 4×4 matrices (see Chapter 3), and after either transform, the models are said to be in *normalized device coordinates*.

Although these transformations transform one volume into another, they are called projections because after display the z-coordinate is not stored in the image generated.[5] In this way, the models are projected from three to two dimensions.

2.3.4 Clipping

Only the primitives wholly or partially inside the view volume need to be passed on to the rasterizer stage, which then draws them on the screen. A primitive that lies totally inside the view volume will be passed on to the next stage as is. Primitives totally outside the view volume are not passed on further, since they are not rendered. It is the primitives that are partially inside the view volume that require *clipping*. For example, a line that has one vertex outside and one inside the view volume should be clipped against the view volume, so that the vertex that is outside is replaced by a new vertex that is located at the intersection between the line and the view volume. Due to the projection transformation, the transformed primitives are clipped against the unit cube. The advantage of performing the view transformation and projection before clipping is that it makes the clipping problem consistent; primitives are always clipped against the unit cube. The clipping process is depicted in Figure 2.7. In addition to the six clipping planes of the view volume, the user can define additional clipping planes to visibly chop objects.

2.3.5 Screen Mapping

Only the (clipped) primitives inside the view volume are passed on to the screen mapping stage, and the coordinates are still three-dimensional when

---

[5]Rather, the z-coordinate is stored in a Z-buffer. See Section 2.4.

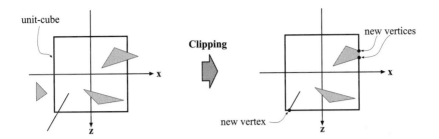

Figure 2.7. After the projection transform, only the primitives inside the unit cube (which correspond to primitives inside the view frustum) are desired for continued processing. Therefore, the primitives outside the unit cube are discarded, primitives totally inside are kept, and primitives intersecting with the unit cube are clipped against the unit cube, and thus new vertices are generated and old ones are discarded.

entering this stage. The x- and y-coordinates of each primitive are transformed to form *screen coordinates*. Screen coordinates together with the z-coordinates are also called *window coordinates*. Assume that the scene should be rendered into a window with the minimum corner at (x_1, y_1) and the maximum corner at (x_2, y_2), where $x_1 < x_2$ and $y_1 < y_2$. Then the screen mapping is a translation followed by a scaling operation. The z-coordinate is not affected by this mapping. The new x- and y-coordinates are said to be screen coordinates. These, along with the z-coordinate $(-1 \leq z \leq 1)$, are passed on to the rasterizer stage. The screen mapping process is depicted in Figure 2.8.

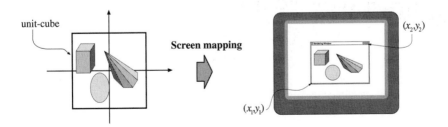

Figure 2.8. The primitives lie in the unit cube after the projection transform, and the screen mapping procedure takes care of finding the coordinates on the screen.

2.4   The Rasterizer Stage

Given the transformed and projected vertices, colors, and texture coordinates (all from the geometry stage), the goal of the rasterizer stage is to assign correct colors to the pixels[6] to render an image correctly. This process is called *rasterization* or *scan conversion*, which is thus the conversion from two-dimensional vertices in screen space—each with a z-value (depth-value), one or two colors, and possibly one or more sets of texture coordinates associated with each vertex—into pixels on the screen.[7] Unlike the geometry stage, which handles per-polygon operations, the rasterizer stage handles per-pixel operations. The information for each pixel is stored in the *color buffer*, which is a rectangular array of colors (a red, a green, and a blue component for each color). For high-performance graphics, it is critical that the rasterizer stage be implemented in hardware. Akeley and Jermoluk [8] and Rogers [657] offer more information on scan conversion.

To avoid allowing the human viewer to see the primitives as they are being rasterized and sent to the screen, *double buffering* is used. This means that the rendering of a scene takes place off screen, in a *back buffer*. Once the scene has been rendered in the back buffer, the contents of the back buffer are swapped with the contents of the *front buffer* which was previously displayed on the screen. The swapping occurs when the electron gun of the monitor cannot disturb the display.

This stage is also responsible for resolving visibility. This means that when the whole scene has been rendered, the color buffer should contain the colors of the primitives in the scene which are visible from the point of view of the camera. For most graphics hardware, this is done with the Z-buffer (also called *depth buffer*) algorithm [116].[8] A Z-buffer is the same size and shape as the color buffer, and for each pixel it stores the z-value from the camera to the currently closest primitive. This means that when a primitive is being rendered to a certain pixel, the z-value on that primitive at that pixel is being computed and compared to the contents of the Z-buffer at the same pixel. If the new z-value is smaller than the z-value in the Z-buffer, then the primitive that is being rendered is closer to the camera than the primitive that was previously closest to the camera at

---

[6]Short for *picture elements*.

[7]Pipeline diagrams sometimes depict this stage in two parts. The first is called *triangle setup*, in which the various differentials and other data for the triangle's surface are computed, and the second part is called rasterization, in which the pixels are checked and filled.

[8]When a Z-buffer is not available, a BSP tree can be used to help render a scene in back-to-front order. See Section 9.1.2 for information about BSP trees.

that pixel. Therefore, the z-value and the color of that pixel are updated with the z-value and color from the primitive that is being drawn. If the computed z-value is greater than the z-value in the Z-buffer, then the color buffer and the Z-buffer are left untouched. The Z-buffer algorithm is very simple, has $O(n)$ convergence (where n is the number of primitives being rendered), and works for any drawing primitive for which a z-value can be computed for each (relevant) pixel. Also note that this algorithm allows the primitives to be rendered in any order, which is another reason for its popularity. However, partially transparent primitives cannot be rendered in just any order. They must be rendered after all opaque primitives, and in back-to-front order (Section 4.5). For more information on different buffers and buffering methods, see Section 15.1.

Texturing is a technique used to increase the level of realism in a rendered three-dimensional world, and it is treated in more detail in Chapter 5. Simply put, texturing an object means "gluing" an image onto that object. This process is depicted in Figure 2.9. The image may be one-, two-, or three-dimensional, with two-dimensional images being the most common. The target object can be a set of connected triangles, but may be a set of lines, quadrilaterals, spheres, cylinders, parametric surfaces, etc.

We have mentioned that the color buffer is used to store colors and that the Z-buffer stores z-values for each pixel. However, there are other

Figure 2.9. A cow model without textures is shown on the left. The two textures in the middle are "glued" onto the cow, and the result is shown on the right. The top texture is for the eyes, while the bottom texture is for the body of the cow. *(Cow model reused courtesy of Jens Larsson.)*

buffers that can be used to create some different combinations of images. The *alpha channel* is associated with the color buffer and stores a related opacity value for each pixel (Section 4.5). The *stencil buffer* is part of OpenGL, and usually contains from one to eight bits per pixel. Primitives can be rendered into the stencil buffer using various functions, and the buffer's contents can then be used to control the rendering into the color buffer and Z-buffer. As an example, assume that a filled circle has been drawn into the stencil buffer. This can be combined with an operator that allows rendering of subsequent primitives into the color buffer where only the circle is present. The stencil buffer is a powerful tool for generating special effects.

The *frame buffer* generally consists of all the buffers on a system, but it is sometimes used to mean just the color buffer and Z-buffer as a set. In 1990, Haeberli and Akeley [300] presented another complement to the frame buffer called the *accumulation buffer*. In this buffer, images can be accumulated using a set of operators. For example, a set of images showing an object in motion can be accumulated and averaged in order to generate motion blur. Other effects that can be generated include depth of field, antialiasing, soft shadows, etc.

When the primitives have reached and passed the rasterizer stage, those that are visible from the point of view of the camera are displayed on screen. These primitives are rendered using an appropriate shading model, and they appear textured if textures were applied to them.

2.5   Through the Pipeline

Points, lines, and triangles are the rendering primitives from which a model or an object is built. Here we will follow a model through the entire graphics rendering pipeline, consisting of the three major stages: application, geometry, and the rasterizer. In this example, the model includes both lines and triangles, and some of the triangles are textured by a two-dimensional image. Moreover, the model is being lit by one light source, and the scene is rendered with perspective into a window on the screen.

Application

Here, the user can interact with the models in the scene if the application so allows. Say that the user has selected a subset of the scene, and moves it using the mouse. The application stage must then see to it that the model transform for that subset of the models is updated to accommodate for the translation. Another example: The camera moves along a predefined path, and the camera parameters, such as position and view direction, must then be updated by the application. At the end of the application stage, the primitives of the model are fed to the next major stage in the pipeline— the geometry stage.

Geometry

The view transform was computed in the previous stage, and there it was also concatenated with the model transform for a certain model. In the geometry stage the vertices and normals of the model are transformed with this concatenated matrix, putting the models into eye space. Then lighting at the vertices is computed using material properties, textures, and light source properties, followed by projection-transforming the model into a unit cube, and all primitives outside the cube are discarded. All primitives intersecting the unit cube are clipped against the cube in order to obtain a set of primitives that lies totally inside the unit cube. The vertices then are mapped into the window on the screen. After all these per-polygon operations have been performed, the resulting data is passed on to the rasterizer—the final major stage in the pipeline.

Rasterizer

In this stage, all primitives are rasterized, i.e., converted into pixels in the window. Those primitives that have been associated with a texture are rendered with that texture (image) applied to them. Visibility is resolved via the Z-buffer algorithm.

Summary

The rest of this book builds upon the graphics pipeline structure. The place in this pipeline where software leaves off and acceleration hardware takes over is constantly shifting, with the trend being that commonly used software algorithms become part of the hardware. Trade-offs in price, speed, and quality are some of the major factors in this equation. Historically, hardware graphics acceleration has started at the end of the pipeline, first performing rasterization of a triangle's scanline. Successive generations of hardware have then worked back up the pipeline, to the point where some higher level application stage algorithms are being committed to hardware. Hardware's only advantage over software is speed, but for real-time rendering speed is critical.

We will focus on providing methods to increase speed and improve image quality, while also describing the features and limitations of hardware acceleration algorithms and graphics APIs. We will not be able to cover every topic in depth, so our goal is to introduce concepts and terminology, give a sense of how and when various methods can be applied, and provide pointers to the best places to go for more in-depth information.

Further Reading and Resources

Blinn's book *A Trip Down the Graphics Pipeline* [76] is a great resource for learning about the subtleties of the rendering pipeline as well as software implementation tips and tricks. This book's website: (`http://www.realtimerendering.com/`) gives links to hundreds of software rendering implementations.

Chapter 3
Transforms

"What if angry vectors veer
Round your sleeping head, and form.
There's never need to fear
Violence of the poor world's abstract storm."
–Robert Penn Warren

For the computer graphics practitioner, it is extremely important to master transforms. With them, you can position, reshape, and animate objects, lights, and cameras. You can also ensure that all computations are carried out in the same coordinate system, and project objects onto a plane in different ways. These are only a few of the operations that can be performed with transforms, but they are sufficient to demonstrate the importance of the transform's role in real-time graphics, or, for that matter, in any kind of computer graphics.

This chapter will begin with the most essential, basic transforms, in the form of 4×4 matrices. These are indeed *very* basic, and this section could be seen as a "reference manual" for simple transforms. More specialized matrices are then described, followed by a discussion and description of quaternions, a powerful transform tool. Finally, projection matrices are described. Most of these transforms, their notations, functions, and properties are summarized in Table 3.1. We use homogeneous notation, denoting points and vectors in the same way (using bold lowercase letters). A vector is represented as $\mathbf{v} = (v_x \ v_y \ v_z \ 0)^T$ and a point as $\mathbf{v} = (v_x \ v_y \ v_z \ 1)^T$. Throughout the chapter, we will make extensive use of the terminology and homogeneous notation explained in Appendix A. You may wish to review this appendix now.

Transforms are a basic tool for manipulating geometry. Most graphics Application Programming Interfaces (APIs) include matrix operations that implement many of the transforms discussed in this chapter. However, it is still worthwhile to understand the real matrices and their interaction

Notation	Name	Characteristics
$\mathbf{T}(\mathbf{t})$	translation matrix	Moves a point. Affine.
$\mathbf{R}_x(\rho)$	rotation matrix	Rotates ρ radians around the x-axis. Similar notation for the y- and z-axes. Orthogonal & affine.
$\mathbf{R}$	rotation matrix	Any rotation matrix. Orthogonal & affine.
$\mathbf{S}(\mathbf{s})$	scaling matrix	Scales along all x-, y-, and z-axes according to $\mathbf{s}$. Affine.
$\mathbf{H}_{ij}(s)$	shear matrix	Shears component i by a factor s, with respect to component j. $i, j \in \{x, y, z\}$. Affine.
$\mathbf{E}(h, p, r)$	Euler transform	Orientation matrix given by the Euler angles head (yaw), pitch, roll. Orthogonal & affine.
$\mathbf{P}_o(s)$	orthographic projection	Parallel projects onto some plane or to a volume. Affine.
$\mathbf{P}_p(s)$	perspective projection	Projects with perspective onto a plane or to a volume.
$\texttt{slerp}(\hat{\mathbf{q}}, \hat{\mathbf{r}}, t)$	slerp transform	Creates an interpolated quaternion with respect to the quaternions $\hat{\mathbf{q}}$ and $\hat{\mathbf{r}}$, and the parameter t.

Table 3.1. Summary of most of the transforms discussed in this chapter.

behind the function calls. Knowing what the matrix does after such a function call is a start, but understanding the properties of the matrix itself will take you further. For example, such an understanding enables you to discern when you are dealing with an orthogonal matrix, whose inverse is its transpose (see page 730), making for faster matrix inversions. Knowledge like this can lead to accelerated code.

3.1 Basic Transforms

This section describes the most basic transforms, such as translation, rotation, scaling, shearing, transform concatenation, the rigid-body transform, normal transform (which is not so normal), and computation of inverses. For the experienced reader, this can be used as a reference manual for simple transforms, and for the novice, it can serve as an introduction to the subject. This material is necessary background for the rest of this chapter and for other chapters in this book.

All translation, rotation, scaling, reflection, and shearing matrices are affine. The main characteristic of an affine matrix is that it preserves the parallelism of lines, but not necessarily lengths and angles. An affine transform may also be any sequence of concatenations of individual affine transforms. We start with the simplest of transforms—the translation.

3.1.1 Translation

A change from one location to another is represented by a translation matrix, $\mathbf{T}$. This matrix translates an entity by a vector $\mathbf{t} = (t_x, t_y, t_z)$. $\mathbf{T}$ is given below by Equation 3.1.

$$\mathbf{T}(\mathbf{t}) = \mathbf{T}(t_x, t_y, t_z) = \begin{pmatrix} 1 & 0 & 0 & t_x \\ 0 & 1 & 0 & t_y \\ 0 & 0 & 1 & t_z \\ 0 & 0 & 0 & 1 \end{pmatrix} \tag{3.1}$$

An example of the effect of the translation transform is shown in Figure 3.1. It is easily shown that the multiplication of a point $\mathbf{p} = (p_x, p_y, p_z, 1)$ with

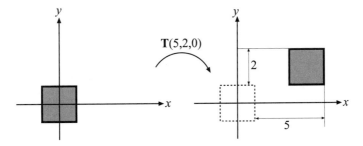

Figure 3.1. The square on the left is transformed with a translation matrix $\mathbf{T}(5, 2, 0)$, whereby the square is moved 5 distance units to the right and 2 upwards.

$\mathbf{T}(\mathbf{t})$ yields a new point $\mathbf{p}' = (p_x + t_x, p_y + t_y, p_z + t_z, 1)$, which is clearly a translation. Notice that a vector $\mathbf{v} = (v_x, v_y, v_z, 0)$ is left unaffected by a multiplication by $\mathbf{T}$, because a direction vector cannot be translated. In contrast, both points and vectors are affected by the rest of the affine transforms. The inverse of a translation matrix is $\mathbf{T}^{-1}(\mathbf{t}) = \mathbf{T}(-\mathbf{t})$, that is, the vector $\mathbf{t}$ is negated.

3.1.2   Rotation

A more elaborate set of transforms is represented by the rotation matrices, $\mathbf{R}_x(\phi)$, $\mathbf{R}_y(\phi)$, and $\mathbf{R}_z(\phi)$, which rotate an entity ϕ radians around the x-, y-, and z-axes respectively. They are given by Equations 3.2–3.4.

$$\mathbf{R}_x(\phi) = \begin{pmatrix} 1 & 0 & 0 & 0 \\ 0 & \cos\phi & -\sin\phi & 0 \\ 0 & \sin\phi & \cos\phi & 0 \\ 0 & 0 & 0 & 1 \end{pmatrix} \qquad (3.2)$$

$$\mathbf{R}_y(\phi) = \begin{pmatrix} \cos\phi & 0 & \sin\phi & 0 \\ 0 & 1 & 0 & 0 \\ -\sin\phi & 0 & \cos\phi & 0 \\ 0 & 0 & 0 & 1 \end{pmatrix} \qquad (3.3)$$

$$\mathbf{R}_z(\phi) = \begin{pmatrix} \cos\phi & -\sin\phi & 0 & 0 \\ \sin\phi & \cos\phi & 0 & 0 \\ 0 & 0 & 1 & 0 \\ 0 & 0 & 0 & 1 \end{pmatrix} \qquad (3.4)$$

For every 3×3 rotation matrix,[1] $\mathbf{R}$, that rotates ϕ radians around any axis, the sum of the diagonal elements is constant independent of the axis. This sum, called the *trace* [478], is:

$$\mathrm{tr}(\mathbf{R}) = 1 + 2\cos\phi. \qquad (3.5)$$

The effect of a rotation matrix may be seen in Figure 3.4 on page 33. What characterizes a rotation matrix, $\mathbf{R}_i(\phi)$, besides the fact that it rotates ϕ radians around axis i, is that it leaves all points on the rotation axis, i, unchanged. Note that $\mathbf{R}$ will also be used to denote a rotation matrix around any axis. All rotation matrices are orthogonal (easily verified using the

---

[1]If the bottom row and rightmost column is deleted from a 4×4 matrix, a 3×3 matrix is obtained.

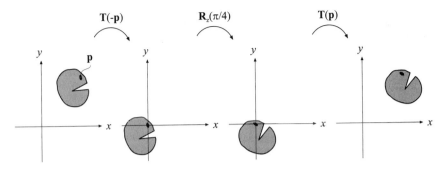

Figure 3.2. Example of rotation around a specific point **p**.

definition of orthogonal matrices given on page 730 in Appendix A), which means that $\mathbf{R}^{-1} = \mathbf{R}^{T}$. This also holds for concatenations of any number of these transforms. But there is also an additional way to obtain the inverse, $\mathbf{R}_i^{-1}(\phi) = \mathbf{R}_i(-\phi)$, that is, rotate in the opposite direction around the same axis. Also, the determinant of a rotation matrix is always one.

EXAMPLE: ROTATION AROUND A POINT Assume that we want to rotate an object by ϕ radians around the z-axis, with the center of rotation being a certain point, **p**. What is the transform? This scenario is depicted in Figure 3.2. Since a rotation around a point is characterized by the fact that the point itself is unaffected by the rotation, the transform starts by translating the object so that **p** coincides with the origin, which is done with $\mathbf{T}(-\mathbf{p})$. Thereafter follows the actual rotation: $\mathbf{R}_z(\phi)$. Finally, the object has to be translated back to its original position using $\mathbf{T}(\mathbf{p})$. The resulting transform, $\mathbf{X}$, is then given by:

$$\mathbf{X} = \mathbf{T}(\mathbf{p})\mathbf{R}_z(\phi)\mathbf{T}(-\mathbf{p}). \qquad (3.6)$$

□

3.1.3 Scaling

A scaling matrix, $\mathbf{S}(\mathbf{s}) = \mathbf{S}(s_x, s_y, s_z)$, scales an entity with factors s_x, s_y, and s_z along the x-, y-, and z-directions respectively. This means that a scaling matrix can be used to enlarge or diminish an object. The larger the s_i ($i \in \{x, y, z\}$), the larger the scaled entity gets in that direction. Setting any of the components of **s** to 1 naturally avoids a change in scaling in that direction. Equation 3.7 shows **S**.

$$\mathbf{S(s)} = \begin{pmatrix} s_x & 0 & 0 & 0 \\ 0 & s_y & 0 & 0 \\ 0 & 0 & s_z & 0 \\ 0 & 0 & 0 & 1 \end{pmatrix} \tag{3.7}$$

Figure 3.4 on page 33 illustrates the effect of a scaling matrix. The scaling operation is called *uniform* if $s_x = s_y = s_z$ and *nonuniform* otherwise. Sometimes the terms *isotropic* and *anisotropic* scaling are used instead of uniform and nonuniform. The inverse is $\mathbf{S}^{-1}(\mathbf{s}) = \mathbf{S}(1/s_x, 1/s_y, 1/s_z)$.

Using homogeneous coordinates, another valid way to create a uniform scaling matrix is by manipulating matrix element at position $(3,3)$, i.e., the element at the lower right corner. This value affects the w-component of the homogeneous coordinate, and so scales every coordinate transformed by the matrix. For example, to scale uniformly by a factor of 5, the elements at $(0,0)$, $(1,1)$, and $(2,2)$ in the scaling matrix can be set to 5, or the element at $(3,3)$ can be set to $1/5$. This is shown below.

$$\mathbf{S} = \begin{pmatrix} 5 & 0 & 0 & 0 \\ 0 & 5 & 0 & 0 \\ 0 & 0 & 5 & 0 \\ 0 & 0 & 0 & 1 \end{pmatrix} = \begin{pmatrix} 1 & 0 & 0 & 0 \\ 0 & 1 & 0 & 0 \\ 0 & 0 & 1 & 0 \\ 0 & 0 & 0 & 1/5 \end{pmatrix} \tag{3.8}$$

Setting the element at the lower right (position $(3,3)$) to generate a uniform scaling may be inefficient, since it involves divides in the homogenization process; if the element is 1, no divides are necessary. Of course, if the system always does this division without testing for 1, then there is no extra cost.

A negative value on one or three of the components of **s** gives a *reflection matrix*, also called a *mirror matrix*.[2] If only two scale factors are -1, then we will rotate π radians. Reflection matrices usually require special treatment when detected. For example, a triangle with vertices in a counter-clockwise order will get a clockwise order when transformed by a reflection matrix. This order change can cause incorrect lighting and back-face culling to occur. To detect whether a given matrix reflects in some manner, compute the determinant of the upper left 3×3 elements of the matrix. If the value is negative, the matrix is reflective.

---

[2] According to some definitions of a reflection matrix, the negative component(s) must equal -1.

EXAMPLE: SCALING IN A CERTAIN DIRECTION The scaling matrix **S** scales along only the x-, y-, and z-axes. If scaling should be performed in other directions, a compound transform is needed. Assume that scaling should be done along the axes of the orthonormal, right-oriented vectors $\mathbf{f}^x$, $\mathbf{f}^y$, and $\mathbf{f}^z$. First, construct the matrix **F** as below.

$$\mathbf{F} = \begin{pmatrix} \mathbf{f}^x & \mathbf{f}^y & \mathbf{f}^z & \mathbf{0} \\ 0 & 0 & 0 & 1 \end{pmatrix} \tag{3.9}$$

The idea is to make the coordinate system given by the three axes coincide with the standard axes, then use the standard scaling matrix, and then transform back. The first step is carried out by multiplying with the transpose, i.e., the inverse, of **F**. Then the actual scaling is done, followed by a transform back. The transform is shown in Equation 3.10.

$$\mathbf{X} = \mathbf{FS(s)F}^T \tag{3.10}$$

$\square$

3.1.4 Shearing

Another class of transforms is the set of shearing matrices. These can, for example, be used in games to distort an entire scene in order to create a psychedelic effect or to create fuzzy reflections by jittering (see Section 6.10.2). There are six basic shearing matrices,[3] and they are denoted $\mathbf{H}_{xy}(s)$, $\mathbf{H}_{xz}(s)$, $\mathbf{H}_{yx}(s)$, $\mathbf{H}_{yz}(s)$, $\mathbf{H}_{zx}(s)$, and $\mathbf{H}_{zy}(s)$. The first subscript is used to denote which coordinate is being changed by the shear matrix, while the second subscript indicates the coordinate which does the shearing. An example of a shear matrix, $\mathbf{H}_{xz}(s)$, is shown in Equation 3.11. Observe that the subscript can be used to find the position of the parameter s in the matrix below; the x (whose numeric index is 0) identifies row zero, and the z (whose numeric index is 2) identifies column two, and so the s is located there:

$$\mathbf{H}_{xz}(s) = \begin{pmatrix} 1 & 0 & s & 0 \\ 0 & 1 & 0 & 0 \\ 0 & 0 & 1 & 0 \\ 0 & 0 & 0 & 1 \end{pmatrix}. \tag{3.11}$$

---

[3] Actually, there are *only* six shearing matrices, because we shear in planes orthogonal to the main axes. However, a general shear matrix can shear orthogonally to any plane.

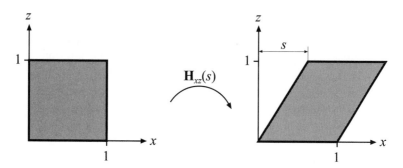

Figure 3.3. The effect of shearing the unit square with $\mathbf{H}_{xz}(s)$. Both the y- and z-values are unaffected by the transform, while the x-value is the sum of the old x-value and s multiplied by the z-value, causing the square to be tilted.

The effect of multiplying this matrix with a point $\mathbf{p}$ yields a point: $(p_x + sp_z \ p_y \ p_z)^T$. Graphically, this is shown for the unit square in Figure 3.3. The inverse of $\mathbf{H}_{ij}(s)$ (shearing the ith coordinate with respect to the jth coordinate, where $i \neq j$), is generated by shearing in the opposite direction, that is, $\mathbf{H}_{ij}^{-1}(s) = \mathbf{H}_{ij}(-s)$.

Some computer graphics texts [235, 234] use a slightly different kind of shear matrix:

$$\mathbf{H}'_{xy}(s,t) = \begin{pmatrix} 1 & 0 & s & 0 \\ 0 & 1 & t & 0 \\ 0 & 0 & 1 & 0 \\ 0 & 0 & 0 & 1 \end{pmatrix}. \tag{3.12}$$

Here, however, both subscripts are used to denote that these coordinates are to be sheared by the third coordinate. The connection between these two different kinds of descriptions is $\mathbf{H}'_{ij}(s,t) = \mathbf{H}_{ik}(s)\mathbf{H}_{jk}(t)$, where k is used as an index to the third coordinate. The right matrix to use is a matter of taste and API support.

Finally, it should be noted that since the determinant of any shear matrix $|\mathbf{H}| = 1$, this is a volume preserving transformation.

3.1.5 Concatenation of Transforms

Due to the noncommutativity of the multiplication operation on matrices, the order in which the matrices occur matters. Concatenation of transforms is therefore said to be order-dependent.

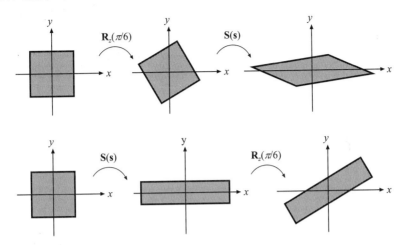

Figure 3.4. This illustrates the order dependency when multiplying matrices. In the top row, the rotation matrix $\mathbf{R}_z(\pi/6)$ is applied followed by a scaling, $\mathbf{S}(\mathbf{s})$, where $\mathbf{s} = (2, 0.5, 1)$. The composite matrix is then $\mathbf{S}(\mathbf{s})\mathbf{R}_z(\pi/6)$. In the bottom row, the matrices are applied in the reverse order, yielding $\mathbf{R}_z(\pi/6)\mathbf{S}(\mathbf{s})$. The results are clearly different. It generally holds that $\mathbf{MN} \neq \mathbf{NM}$, for arbitrary matrices $\mathbf{M}$ and $\mathbf{N}$.

As an example of order dependency, consider two matrices, $\mathbf{S}$ and $\mathbf{R}$. $\mathbf{S}(2, 0.5, 1)$ scales the x-component by a factor two and the y-component by a factor 0.5. $\mathbf{R}_z(\pi/6)$ rotates $\pi/6$ radians counter-clockwise around the z-axis (which points outwards from the paper). These matrices can be multiplied in two ways, with the results being totally different. The two cases are shown in Figure 3.4.

The obvious reason to concatenate a sequence of matrices into a single one is to gain efficiency. For example, imagine that you have an object that has several thousand vertices, and that this object must be scaled, rotated, and finally translated. Now, instead of multiplying all vertices with each of the three matrices, the three matrices are concatenated into a single matrix. This single matrix is then applied to the vertices. This composite matrix is $\mathbf{C} = \mathbf{TRS}$. Note the order here: The scaling matrix, $\mathbf{S}$, should be applied to the vertices first, and therefore appears to the right in the composition. This ordering implies that $\mathbf{TRSp} = (\mathbf{T}(\mathbf{R}(\mathbf{Sp})))$.[4]

---

[4] Another valid notational scheme sometimes seen in computer graphics uses matrices with translation vectors in the bottom row. In this scheme, the order of matrices would be reversed, i.e., the order of application would read from left to right. Vectors and matrices in this notation are said to be in *row-major* form since the vectors are rows. In this book, we use *column-major* form.

3.1.6 The Rigid-Body Transform

When a person grabs a solid object, say a pen from a table, and moves it to another location, perhaps to her shirt pocket, only the object's orientation and location change, while the shape of the object generally is not affected. Such a transform, consisting of concatenations of only translations and rotations, is called a *rigid-body transform* and has the characteristic of preserving lengths and angles.

Any rigid-body matrix, $\mathbf{X}$, can be written as the concatenation of a translation matrix, $\mathbf{T}(\mathbf{t})$, and a rotation matrix, $\mathbf{R}$. Thus, $\mathbf{X}$ has the appearance of the matrix in Equation 3.13.

$$\mathbf{X} = \mathbf{T}(\mathbf{t})\mathbf{R} = \begin{pmatrix} r_{00} & r_{01} & r_{02} & t_x \\ r_{10} & r_{11} & r_{12} & t_y \\ r_{20} & r_{21} & r_{22} & t_z \\ 0 & 0 & 0 & 1 \end{pmatrix} \tag{3.13}$$

The inverse of $\mathbf{X}$ is computed as $\mathbf{X}^{-1} = (\mathbf{T}(\mathbf{t})\mathbf{R})^{-1} = \mathbf{R}^{-1}\mathbf{T}(\mathbf{t})^{-1} = \mathbf{R}^T\mathbf{T}(-\mathbf{t})$. Thus, to compute the inverse, the upper left 3×3 matrix of $\mathbf{R}$ is transposed, and the translation values of $\mathbf{T}$ change sign. These two new matrices are multiplied together to obtain the inverse. Another way to compute the inverse of $\mathbf{X}$ is to consider $\mathbf{R}$ (making $\mathbf{R}$ appear as 3×3 matrix) and $\mathbf{X}$ in the following notation.

$$\bar{\mathbf{R}} = \begin{pmatrix} \mathbf{r}_{,0} & \mathbf{r}_{,1} & \mathbf{r}_{,2} \end{pmatrix} = \begin{pmatrix} \mathbf{r}_{0,}^T \\ \mathbf{r}_{1,}^T \\ \mathbf{r}_{2,}^T \end{pmatrix}$$

$$\mathbf{X} = \begin{pmatrix} \overset{\Longrightarrow}{\bar{\mathbf{R}}} & \mathbf{t} \\ \mathbf{0}^T & 1 \end{pmatrix} \tag{3.14}$$

Here, $\mathbf{0}$ is a 3×1 column vector filled with zeros. Some simple calculations yield the inverse in the expression shown in Equation 3.15.

$$\mathbf{X}^{-1} = \begin{pmatrix} \mathbf{r}_{0,} & \mathbf{r}_{1,} & \mathbf{r}_{2,} & -\bar{\mathbf{R}}^T\mathbf{t} \\ 0 & 0 & 0 & 1 \end{pmatrix} \tag{3.15}$$

3.1.7 Normal Transform

A single matrix can be used to consistently transform points, lines, polygons, and other geometry. The same matrix can also transform vectors following along these lines or on the surfaces of polygons. However, this matrix cannot always be used to transform one important geometric property, the surface normal (and also the vertex lighting normal). Normals must be transformed by the transpose of the inverse of the matrix used to transform geometry [319] (see Turkowski's gem [757] for a proof and applications in backface culling and shading). So, if the matrix used to transform geometry is called $\mathbf{M}$, then we must use the matrix, $\mathbf{N}$, below to transform the normals of this geometry.

$$\mathbf{N} = (\mathbf{M}^{-1})^T \tag{3.16}$$

Figure 3.5 shows what can happen if the proper transform is not used.

In practice, we do not have to compute the inverse if we know the matrix is orthogonal, e.g., that it was formed from only rotations. In this case, the matrix itself can be used to transform normals, since the inverse of an orthogonal matrix is its transpose. Two matrix transposes cancel out, giving the original rotation matrix. Furthermore, translations do not affect vector direction, so any number of translations can be performed without affecting the normal. After transformation, we can also avoid the step of renormalizing the normals (i.e., making their lengths 1 again). This is because length is preserved by a matrix formed with just rotations and translations (see Section 3.1.6 on rigid-body transforms). So the original matrix can be used to transform the normal.

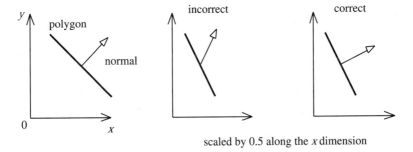

Figure 3.5. On the left is the original geometry, a polygon and its normal shown from the side. The middle illustration shows what happens if the model is scaled along the x-axis by 0.5 and the normal uses the same matrix. The right figure shows the proper transform of the normal.

If, in addition, one or more uniform scaling matrices are also used to form the matrix, the inverse still does not need to be computed. Such scalings affect only the length of the transformed normal, not its direction. In this case, the matrix transforms the normals, then the normals have to be renormalized. If the overall uniform scaling factor applied to the matrix is known or derived, it can be used to renormalize the normals. For example, if we know that a series of scalings were applied that makes the object 5.2 times larger, then normals transformed by this matrix are renormalized by dividing them by 5.2.

Even if it turns out that the full inverse must be computed, only the transpose of the *adjoint* (see Section A.3.1) of the matrix's upper left 3×3 is needed. The adjoint of the matrix is similar to the inverse, except that the matrix computed is not divided by the original matrix's determinant. The adjoint is therefore faster to compute than the inverse. We do not need to divide by the determinant, since we know we will have to normalize the transformed normal anyway.

Note that normal transforms are not an issue in systems where after transformation the surface normal is derived from the triangle (e.g., using the cross product of the triangle's edges). However, it is often the case that triangle vertices contain normal information for lighting, and so normal transformation must be addressed.

3.1.8   Computation of Inverses

Inverses are needed in many cases, for example, when changing back and forth between coordinate systems. Depending on the available information about a transform, one of the following three methods of computing the inverse of a matrix can be used.

- If the matrix is a single transform or a sequence of simple transforms with given parameters, then the matrix can be computed easily by "inverting the parameters" and the matrix order. For example, if $\mathbf{M} = \mathbf{T}(\mathbf{t})\mathbf{R}(\phi)$, then $\mathbf{M}^{-1} = \mathbf{R}(-\phi)\mathbf{T}(-\mathbf{t})$.

- If the matrix is known to be orthogonal, then $\mathbf{M}^{-1} = \mathbf{M}^T$, i.e., the transpose is the inverse. Any sequence of rotations is orthogonal.

- If nothing in particular is known, then the adjoint method (Equation A.37 on page 728), Cramer's rule, LU decomposition, or Gaussian elimination could be used to compute the inverse (see Section A.3.1). Cramer's rule and the adjoint method are generally preferable, as they have fewer branch operations; "if" tests are good to avoid on modern architectures.[5] See Section 3.1.7 on how to use the adjoint to inverse transform normals.

The purpose of the inverse computation can also be taken into account when optimizing. For example, if the inverse is to be used for transforming vectors, then only the 3×3 upper left part of the matrix normally needs to be inverted (see the previous section).

3.2 Special Matrix Transforms and Operations

In this section, a number of matrix transforms and operations that are essential to real-time graphics will be introduced and derived. First, we present the Euler transform (along with its extraction of parameters), which is an intuitive way to describe orientations. Then we touch upon retrieving a set of basic transforms from a single matrix. Finally, a method is derived that rotates an entity around an arbitrary axis.

3.2.1 The Euler Transform

This transform is an intuitive way to construct a matrix to orient yourself (i.e., the camera) or any other entity in a certain direction. Its name comes from the great Swiss mathematician Leonard Euler (1707–1783).

First, some kind of default view direction must be established. Most often it lies along the negative z-axis with the head oriented along the y-axis, as depicted in Figure 3.6. The Euler transform is the multiplication of three matrices, namely the rotations shown in the figure. More formally, the transform, denoted $\mathbf{E}$, is given by Equation 3.17.[6]

$$\mathbf{E}(h, p, r) = \mathbf{R}_z(r)\mathbf{R}_x(p)\mathbf{R}_y(h) \qquad (3.17)$$

Since $\mathbf{E}$ is a concatenation of rotations, it is also clearly orthogonal. Therefore its inverse can be expressed as $\mathbf{E}^{-1} = \mathbf{E}^T = (\mathbf{R}_z\mathbf{R}_x\mathbf{R}_y)^T = \mathbf{R}_y^T\mathbf{R}_x^T\mathbf{R}_z^T$, although it is, of course, easier to use the transpose of $\mathbf{E}$ directly.

---

[5]Intel has shown that on a Pentium III, Gaussian elimination takes 1074 cycles, Cramer's rule 846, and Cramer's rule with Intel's Streaming SIMD Extensions 210 cycles [384].

[6]Actually, the order of the matrices can be chosen in 24 different ways [710], but we choose this one because it is commonly used.

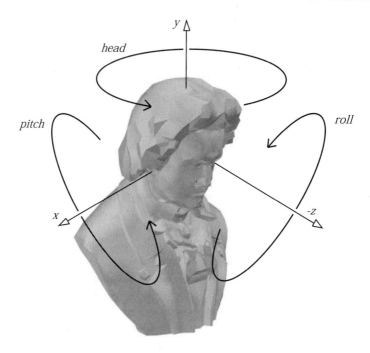

Figure 3.6. Depicting the way, in terms of the Euler transform, you turn your *head,* *pitch,* and *roll.* The default view direction is shown, looking along the negative z-axis with the head oriented along the y-axis.

The Euler angles h, p, and r represent in which order and how much the head, pitch, and roll should rotate around their respective axes.[7] This transform is intuitive and therefore easy to discuss in layperson's language. For example, changing the head angle makes the viewer shake his head "no," changing the pitch makes him nod, and rolling makes him tilt his head sideways. Rather than talking about rotations around the x-, y-, and z-axes, we talk about altering the head, pitch, and roll. Note that this transform can orient not only the camera, but also any object or entity as well.

When you use Euler transforms, something called *gimbal lock* may occur [707, 793]. This happens when rotations are made so that one degree of freedom is lost. For example, start with $h = 0$, i.e., we do not rotate

---

[7]Sometimes the angles are all called "rolls," e.g., our "head" is the "y-roll" and our "pitch" is the "x-roll". Also, "head" is sometimes known as "yaw," for example, in flight simulation.

around the y-axis. This should then be followed by a rotation around the x-axis. Say we rotate $\pi/2$ radians (90°) around the x-axis. Finally, we would like to rotate around the world z-axis, but due to our previous rotation, our rotation matrix around the z-axis at this point would actually be a rotation around the y-axis. The conclusion is that we have lost one degree of freedom—we cannot rotate around the world z-axis. Quaternions (see Section 3.3) do not have this defect.

Another way to see that one degree of freedom is lost is to set $p = \pi/2$ and examine what happens to the Euler matrix $\mathbf{E}(h, p, r)$:

$$\mathbf{E}(h, \pi/2, r) = \begin{pmatrix} \cos r \cos h - \sin r \sin h & 0 & \cos r \sin h + \sin r \cos h \\ \sin r \cos h + \cos r \sin h & 0 & \sin r \sin h - \cos r \cos h \\ 0 & 1 & 0 \end{pmatrix}$$

$$= \begin{pmatrix} \cos(r+h) & 0 & \sin(r+h) \\ \sin(r+h) & 0 & -\cos(r+h) \\ 0 & 1 & 0 \end{pmatrix}. \tag{3.18}$$

Since the matrix is dependent on only one angle $(r+h)$, we conclude that one degree of freedom has been lost.

3.2.2 Extracting Parameters from the Euler Transform

In some situations, it is useful to have a procedure that extracts the Euler parameters, h, p, and r, from an orthogonal matrix. This procedure is shown in Equation 3.19.[8]

$$\mathbf{F} = \begin{pmatrix} f_{00} & f_{01} & f_{02} \\ f_{10} & f_{11} & f_{12} \\ f_{20} & f_{21} & f_{22} \end{pmatrix} = \mathbf{R}_z(r)\mathbf{R}_x(p)\mathbf{R}_y(h) = \mathbf{E}(h, p, r) \tag{3.19}$$

Concatenating the three rotation matrices in Equation 3.19 yields:

$$\mathbf{F} = \begin{pmatrix} \cos r \cos h - \sin r \sin p \sin h & -\sin r \cos p & \cos r \sin h + \sin r \sin p \cos h \\ \sin r \cos h + \cos r \sin p \sin h & \cos r \cos p & \sin r \sin h - \cos r \sin p \cos h \\ -\cos p \sin h & \sin p & \cos p \cos h \end{pmatrix}. \tag{3.20}$$

---

[8]The 4×4 matrices have been abandoned for 3×3 matrices, since the latter provide all the necessary information for a rotation matrix; i.e., the rest of the 4×4 matrix always contains zeros and a one in the lower right position.

From this it is apparent that the pitch parameter is given by $\sin p = f_{21}$. Also, dividing f_{01} by f_{11}, and similarly dividing f_{20} by f_{22}, gives rise to the following extraction equations for the head and roll parameters.

$$\frac{f_{01}}{f_{11}} = \frac{-\sin r}{\cos r} = -\tan r$$
$$\frac{f_{20}}{f_{22}} = \frac{-\sin h}{\cos h} = -\tan h$$
(3.21)

Thus, the Euler parameters h (head), p (pitch), and r (roll) are extracted from a matrix $\mathbf{F}$ using the function $\mathtt{atan2(y,x)}$ (see page 6 in Chapter 1) as in Equation 3.22.

$$\begin{aligned} h &= \mathtt{atan2}(-f_{20}, f_{22}) \\ p &= \arcsin(f_{21}) \\ r &= \mathtt{atan2}(-f_{01}, f_{11}) \end{aligned}$$
(3.22)

However, there is a special case we need to handle. It occurs when $\cos p = 0$, because then $f_{01} = f_{11} = 0$, and so the $\mathtt{atan2}$ function cannot be used. That $\cos p = 0$ implies that $\sin p = \pm 1$, and so $\mathbf{F}$ simplifies to:

$$\mathbf{F} = \begin{pmatrix} \cos(r \pm h) & 0 & \sin(r \pm h) \\ \sin(r \pm h) & 0 & -\cos(r \pm h) \\ 0 & \pm 1 & 0 \end{pmatrix}.$$
(3.23)

The remaining parameters are obtained by arbitrarily setting $h = 0$ [749], and then $\sin r / \cos r = \tan r = f_{10}/f_{00}$, which gives $r = \mathtt{atan2}(f_{10}, f_{00})$.

Note that from the definition of arcsin (see Section B.1), $-\pi/2 \le p \le \pi/2$, which means that if $\mathbf{F}$ was created with a value of p outside this interval, the original parameter cannot be extracted. That h, p, and r are not unique means that more than one set of the Euler parameters can be used to yield the same transform. More about Euler angle conversion can be found in Shoemake's 1994 article [710]. The simple method outlined above can result in problems with numerical instability, which is avoidable at some cost in speed [617].

EXAMPLE: CONSTRAINING A TRANSFORM Imagine you are holding a wrench snapped to a screw bolt and to get the screw bolt in place you have to rotate the wrench around the x-axis. Now assume that your input device (mouse, VR gloves, space-ball, etc.) gives you an orthogonal transform for the movement of the wrench. The problem that you encounter is that you do not want to apply that transform to the wrench, which supposedly should rotate around only the x-axis. So to restrict the input transform, called **P**, to a rotation around the x-axis, simply extract the Euler angles, h, p, and r, using the method described in this section, and then create a new matrix $\mathbf{R}_x(p)$. This is then the sought-after transform that will rotate the wrench around the x-axis (if **P** now contains such a movement). □

3.2.3 Matrix Decomposition

Up to this point we have been working under the assumption that we know the origin and history of the transformation matrix we are using. This is often not the case: For example, nothing more than a concatenated matrix may be associated with some transformed object. The task of retrieving various transforms from a concatenated matrix is called *matrix decomposition*.

There are many reasons to retrieve a set of transformations. Uses include:

- Extracting just the scaling factors for an object.

- Finding transforms needed by a particular system. For example, VRML [781] uses a *Transform* node (see Section 3.1.5) and does not allow the use of an arbitrary 4×4 matrix.

- Determining whether a model has undergone only rigid-body transforms.

- Interpolating between keyframes in an animation where only the matrix for the object is available.

- Removing shears from a rotation matrix.

We have already presented two decompositions, those of deriving the translation and rotation matrix for a rigid-body transformation (see Section 3.1.6) and deriving the Euler angles from an orthogonal matrix (Section 3.2.2).

As we have seen, it is trivial to retrieve the translation matrix, as we simply need the elements in the last column of the 4×4 matrix. We can also determine if a reflection has occurred by checking whether the determinant of the matrix is negative. To separate out the rotation, scaling, and shears takes more determined effort.

Fortunately, there are a number of articles on this topic, as well as code available online. Thomas [749] and Goldman [270, 271] each present somewhat different methods for various classes of transformations. Shoemake [709] improves upon their techniques for affine matrices, as his algorithm is independent of frame of reference and attempts to decompose the matrix in order to obtain rigid-body transforms.

3.2.4 Rotation about an Arbitrary Axis

Sometimes it is convenient to have a procedure that rotates an entity by some angle around an arbitrary axis. Assume that the rotation axis, $\mathbf{r}$, is normalized and that a transform should be created that rotates α radians around $\mathbf{r}$.

To do this, first find two more arbitrary axes of unit length that are mutually orthogonal with themselves and with $\mathbf{r}$, i.e., orthonormal. These then form a basis.[9] The idea is to change bases (Section A.3.2) from the standard basis to this new basis, and then rotate α radians around, say, the x-axis (which then should correspond to $\mathbf{r}$) and finally transform back to the standard basis [155]. This procedure is illustrated in Figure 3.7.

The first step is to compute the orthonormal axes of the basis. The first axis is $\mathbf{r}$, i.e., the one we want to rotate around. We now concentrate on finding the second axis, $\mathbf{s}$, knowing that the third axis, $\mathbf{t}$, will be the cross product of the first and the second axis, $\mathbf{t} = \mathbf{r} \times \mathbf{s}$. A numerically stable way to do this is to find the smallest component (in absolute value) of $\mathbf{r}$,

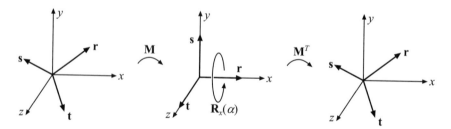

Figure 3.7. Rotation about an arbitrary axis, $\mathbf{r}$, is accomplished by finding an orthonormal basis formed by $\mathbf{r}$, $\mathbf{s}$, and $\mathbf{t}$. We then align this basis with the standard basis so that $\mathbf{r}$ is aligned with the x-axis. The rotation around the x-axis is performed there, and finally we transform back.

---

[9]An example of a basis is the standard basis, which has the axes $\mathbf{e}_x = (1,0,0)$, $\mathbf{e}_y = (0,1,0)$, and $\mathbf{e}_z = (0,0,1)$.

and set it to 0. Swap the two remaining components, and then negate the first[10] of these. Mathematically, this is expressed as [377]:

$$\bar{\mathbf{s}} = \begin{cases} (0, -r_z, r_y), & \text{if } |r_x| < |r_y| \text{ and } |r_x| < |r_z| \\ (-r_z, 0, r_x), & \text{if } |r_y| < |r_x| \text{ and } |r_y| < |r_z| \\ (-r_y, r_x, 0), & \text{if } |r_z| < |r_x| \text{ and } |r_z| < |r_y| \end{cases}$$

$$\mathbf{s} = \bar{\mathbf{s}}/\|\bar{\mathbf{s}}\|$$

$$\mathbf{t} = \mathbf{r} \times \mathbf{s} \tag{3.24}$$

This guarantees that $\bar{\mathbf{s}}$ is orthogonal (perpendicular) to $\mathbf{r}$, and that $(\mathbf{r}, \mathbf{s}, \mathbf{t})$ is an orthonormal basis. We use these three vectors as the rows in a matrix as below.

$$\mathbf{M} = \begin{pmatrix} \mathbf{r}^T \\ \mathbf{s}^T \\ \mathbf{t}^T \end{pmatrix} \tag{3.25}$$

This matrix transforms the vector $\mathbf{r}$ into the x-axis ($\mathbf{e}_x$), $\mathbf{s}$ into the y-axis, and $\mathbf{t}$ into the z-axis. So the final transform for rotating α radians around the normalized vector $\mathbf{r}$ is then:

$$\mathbf{X} = \mathbf{M}^T \mathbf{R}_x(\alpha)\mathbf{M}. \tag{3.26}$$

In words, this means that first we transform so that $\mathbf{r}$ is the x-axis (using $\mathbf{M}$), then we rotate α radians around this x-axis (using $\mathbf{R}_x(\alpha)$), and then we transform back using the inverse of $\mathbf{M}$, which in this case is $\mathbf{M}^T$ because $\mathbf{M}$ is orthogonal.

Another method for rotating around an arbitrary, normalized axis $\mathbf{r}$ by ϕ radians has been presented by Goldman [268]. Here, we simply present his transform:

$$\mathbf{R} =$$

$$\begin{pmatrix} \cos\phi + (1-\cos\phi)r_x^2 & (1-\cos\phi)r_x r_y - r_z\sin\phi & (1-\cos\phi)r_x r_z + r_y\sin\phi \\ (1-\cos\phi)r_x r_y + r_z\sin\phi & \cos\phi + (1-\cos\phi)r_y^2 & (1-\cos\phi)r_y r_z - r_x\sin\phi \\ (1-\cos\phi)r_x r_z - r_y\sin\phi & (1-\cos\phi)r_y r_z + r_x\sin\phi & \cos\phi + (1-\cos\phi)r_z^2 \end{pmatrix}.$$

$$\tag{3.27}$$

In Section 3.3.2, we present yet another method for solving this problem, using quaternions. Also in that section are more efficient algorithms for related problems, such as rotation from one vector to another.

---

[10]In fact, either of the nonzero components could be negated.

3.3   Quaternions

Although quaternions were invented back in 1843 by Sir William Rowan Hamilton as an extension to the complex numbers, it was not until 1985 that Shoemake [707] introduced them to the field of computer graphics. Quaternions are a powerful tool for constructing transforms with compelling features, and in some ways, they are superior to both Euler angles and matrices, especially when it comes to rotations and orientations. For example, they are represented very compactly, and they can be used for the stable interpolation of orientations.

A quaternion has four components, so we choose to represent them as vectors, but to differentiate them, we put a hat on them: $\hat{\mathbf{q}}$. We begin with some mathematical background on quaternions, which is then used to construct interesting and useful transforms.

3.3.1   Mathematical Background

We start with the definition of a quaternion.

Definition.   A quaternion $\hat{\mathbf{q}}$ can be defined in the following ways, all equivalent.

$$
\begin{aligned}
\hat{\mathbf{q}} = & \ (\mathbf{q}_v, q_w) = iq_x + jq_y + kq_z + q_w = \mathbf{q}_v + q_w, \\
\mathbf{q}_v = & \ iq_x + jq_y + kq_z = (q_x, q_y, q_z), \quad\quad\quad\quad\quad (3.28) \\
i^2 = & \ j^2 = k^2 = -1, \ jk = -kj = i, \ ki = -ik = j, \ ij = -ji = k
\end{aligned}
$$

The variable q_w is called the real part of a quaternion, $\hat{\mathbf{q}}$. The imaginary part is $\mathbf{q}_v$, and i, j, and k are called imaginary units.   □

For the imaginary part, $\mathbf{q}_v$, we can use all the normal vector operations, such as addition, scaling, dot product, cross product, and more. Using the definition of the quaternion, the multiplication operation between two quaternions, $\hat{\mathbf{q}}$ and $\hat{\mathbf{r}}$, is derived as shown below. Note that the multiplication of the imaginary units is noncommutative.

Multiplication :

$$\hat{q}\hat{r} = (iq_x + jq_y + kq_z + q_w)(ir_x + jr_y + kr_z + r_w)$$
$$= i(q_y r_z - q_z r_y + r_w q_x + q_w r_x)$$
$$+ j(q_z r_x - q_x r_z + r_w q_y + q_w r_y) \qquad (3.29)$$
$$+ k(q_x r_y - q_y r_x + r_w q_z + q_w r_z)$$
$$+ q_w r_w - q_x r_x - q_y r_y - q_z r_z =$$
$$= (\mathbf{q}_v \times \mathbf{r}_v + r_w \mathbf{q}_v + q_w \mathbf{r}_v, \; q_w r_w - \mathbf{q}_v \cdot \mathbf{r}_v)$$

As can be seen in the above equation, we use both the cross product and the dot product to compute the multiplication of two quaternions.[11] Along with the definition of the quaternion, the definitions of addition, conjugate, norm, and an identity are needed:

Addition : $\hat{q} + \hat{r} = (\mathbf{q}_v, q_w) + (\mathbf{r}_v, r_w) = (\mathbf{q}_v + \mathbf{r}_v, q_w + r_w)$

Conjugate : $\hat{q}^* = (\mathbf{q}_v, q_w)^* = (-\mathbf{q}_v, q_w)$

Norm : $n(\hat{q}) = \hat{q}\hat{q}^* = \hat{q}^*\hat{q} = \mathbf{q}_v \cdot \mathbf{q}_v + q_w^2 = q_x^2 + q_y^2 + q_z^2 + q_w^2$

Identity : $\hat{i} = (\mathbf{0}, 1)$

$$(3.30)$$

When $n(\hat{q}) = \hat{q}\hat{q}^*$ is simplified (result shown above), the imaginary parts cancel out and only a real part remains. The norm is sometimes denoted $||\hat{q}||^2 = n(\hat{q})$ [511]. A consequence of the above is that a multiplicative inverse, denoted by $\hat{q}^{-1}$, can be derived. The equation $\hat{q}^{-1}\hat{q} = \hat{q}\hat{q}^{-1} = 1$ must hold for the inverse (as is common for a multiplicative inverse). We derive a formula from the definition of the norm:

$$n(\hat{q}) = \hat{q}\hat{q}^* \qquad (3.31)$$
$$\Longleftrightarrow \qquad (3.32)$$
$$\frac{\hat{q}\hat{q}^*}{n(\hat{q})} = 1 \qquad (3.33)$$

This gives the multiplicative inverse as shown below.

$$\textbf{Inverse :} \quad \hat{q}^{-1} = \frac{1}{n(\hat{q})}\hat{q}^* \qquad (3.34)$$

---

[11] In fact, the quaternion multiplication is the origin of both the dot product and the cross product.

The formula for the inverse uses scalar multiplication, which is an operation derived from the multiplication seen in Equation 3.29: $s\hat{q} = (\mathbf{0}, s)(\mathbf{q}_v, q_w) = (s\mathbf{q}_v, sq_w)$, and $\hat{q}s = (\mathbf{q}_v, q_w)(\mathbf{0}, s) = (s\mathbf{q}_v, sq_w)$, which means that scalar multiplication is commutative: $s\hat{q} = \hat{q}s = (s\mathbf{q}_v, sq_w)$.

The following collection of rules are simple to derive from the definitions.

Conjugate rules: $(\hat{q}^*)^* = \hat{q}$

$$(\hat{q} + \hat{r})^* = \hat{q}^* + \hat{r}^* \qquad (3.35)$$

$$(\hat{q}\hat{r})^* = \hat{r}^*\hat{q}^*$$

Norm rules: $n(\hat{q}^*) = n(\hat{q})$

$$n(\hat{q}\hat{r}) = n(\hat{q})n(\hat{r}) \qquad (3.36)$$

Laws of Multiplication:

Linearity: $\hat{p}(s\hat{q} + t\hat{r}) = s\hat{p}\hat{q} + t\hat{p}\hat{r}$

$$(s\hat{p} + t\hat{q})\hat{r} = s\hat{p}\hat{r} + t\hat{q}\hat{r} \qquad (3.37)$$

Associativity: $\hat{p}(\hat{q}\hat{r}) = (\hat{p}\hat{q})\hat{r}$

A unit quaternion, $\hat{q} = (\mathbf{q}_v, q_w)$, is such that $n(\hat{q}) = 1$. From this it follows that $\hat{q}$ may be written as

$$\hat{q} = (\sin\phi\,\mathbf{u}_q, \cos\phi) = \sin\phi\,\mathbf{u}_q + \cos\phi, \qquad (3.38)$$

for some three-dimensional vector $\mathbf{u}_q$, such that $||\mathbf{u}_q|| = 1$, because

$$n(\hat{q}) = n(\sin\phi\,\mathbf{u}_q, \cos\phi) = \sin^2\phi(\mathbf{u}_q \cdot \mathbf{u}_q) + \cos^2\phi = \sin^2\phi + \cos^2\phi = 1, \qquad (3.39)$$

if and only if $\mathbf{u}_q \cdot \mathbf{u}_q = 1 = ||\mathbf{u}_q||^2$. As will be seen in the next section, unit quaternions are perfectly suited for creating rotations and orientations in a most efficient way. But before that, some extra operations will be introduced for unit quaternions.

For complex numbers, a two-dimensional unit vector can be written as $\cos\phi + i\sin\phi = e^{i\phi}$. The equivalent for quaternions is:

$$\hat{q} = \sin\phi\,\mathbf{u}_q + \cos\phi = e^{\phi\mathbf{u}_q}. \qquad (3.40)$$

The log and the power functions for unit quaternions follow from Equation 3.40:

Logarithm : $\log(\hat{\mathbf{q}}) = \log(e^{\phi\mathbf{u}_q}) = \phi\mathbf{u}_q,$

Power : $\hat{\mathbf{q}}^t = (\sin\phi\mathbf{u}_q + \cos\phi)^t = e^{\phi t\mathbf{u}_q} = \sin(\phi t)\mathbf{u}_q + \cos(\phi t).$

$$(3.41)$$

3.3.2 Quaternion Transforms

We will now study a subclass of the quaternion set, namely those of unit length, called *unit quaternions*. The most important fact about unit quaternions is that they can represent any three-dimensional rotation, and that this representation is extremely compact and simple.

Now we will describe what makes unit quaternions so useful for rotations and orientations. First, put the four coordinates of a point or vector $\mathbf{p} = (p_x\ p_y\ p_z\ p_w)^T$ into the components of a quaternion $\hat{\mathbf{p}}$, and assume that we have a unit quaternion $\hat{\mathbf{q}} = (\sin\phi\mathbf{u}_q,\ \cos\phi)$. Then

$$\hat{\mathbf{q}}\hat{\mathbf{p}}\hat{\mathbf{q}}^{-1} \qquad (3.42)$$

rotates $\hat{\mathbf{p}}$ (and thus the point $\mathbf{p}$) around the axis $\mathbf{u}_q$ by an angle 2ϕ. Note that since $\hat{\mathbf{q}}$ is a unit quaternion, $\hat{\mathbf{q}}^{-1} = \hat{\mathbf{q}}^*$. This rotation, which clearly can be used to rotate around any axis, is illustrated in Figure 3.8.

Any nonzero real multiple of $\hat{\mathbf{q}}$ also represents the same transform, which means that $\hat{\mathbf{q}}$ and $-\hat{\mathbf{q}}$ represent the same rotation. That is, negating the axis, $\mathbf{u}_q$, and the real part, q_w, creates a quaternion which rotates exactly

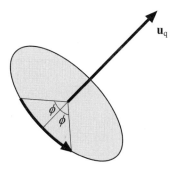

Figure 3.8. Illustration of the rotation transform represented by a unit quaternion, $\hat{\mathbf{q}} = (\sin\phi\mathbf{u}_q,\ \cos\phi)$. The transform rotates 2ϕ radians around the axis $\mathbf{u}_q$.

as the original quaternion does. It also means that the extraction of a quaternion from a matrix can return either $\hat{q}$ or $-\hat{q}$.

Given two unit quaternions, $\hat{q}$ and $\hat{r}$, the concatenation of first applying $\hat{q}$ and then $\hat{r}$ to a quaternion, $\hat{p}$ (which can be interpreted as a point $\mathbf{p}$), is given by Equation 3.43.

$$\hat{r}(\hat{q}\hat{p}\hat{q}^*)\hat{r}^* = (\hat{r}\hat{q})\hat{p}(\hat{r}\hat{q})^* = \hat{c}\hat{p}\hat{c}^* \tag{3.43}$$

Here, $\hat{c} = \hat{r}\hat{q}$ is the unit quaternion representing the concatenation of the unit quaternions $\hat{q}$ and $\hat{r}$.

Matrix Conversion

Since some systems have matrix multiplication implemented in hardware and the fact that matrix multiplication is more efficient than Equation 3.42, we need conversion methods for transforming a quaternion into a matrix and vice versa. A quaternion, $\hat{q}$, can be converted into a matrix $\mathbf{M}^q$, as expressed in Equation 3.44 [707, 708].

$$\mathbf{M}^q = \begin{pmatrix} 1 - s(q_y^2 + q_z^2) & s(q_xq_y - q_wq_z) & s(q_xq_z + q_wq_y) & 0 \\ s(q_xq_y + q_wq_z) & 1 - s(q_x^2 + q_z^2) & s(q_yq_z - q_wq_x) & 0 \\ s(q_xq_z - q_wq_y) & s(q_yq_z + q_wq_x) & 1 - s(q_x^2 + q_y^2) & 0 \\ 0 & 0 & 0 & 1 \end{pmatrix} \tag{3.44}$$

Here, the scalar is $s = 2/n(\hat{q})$. For unit quaternions, this simplifies to:

$$\mathbf{M}^q = \begin{pmatrix} 1 - 2(q_y^2 + q_z^2) & 2(q_xq_y - q_wq_z) & 2(q_xq_z + q_wq_y) & 0 \\ 2(q_xq_y + q_wq_z) & 1 - 2(q_x^2 + q_z^2) & 2(q_yq_z - q_wq_x) & 0 \\ 2(q_xq_z - q_wq_y) & 2(q_yq_z + q_wq_x) & 1 - 2(q_x^2 + q_y^2) & 0 \\ 0 & 0 & 0 & 1 \end{pmatrix}. \tag{3.45}$$

Once the quaternion is constructed, *no* trigonometric functions need to be computed, so the conversion process is efficient in practice.

The reverse conversion, from an orthogonal matrix, $\mathbf{M}^q$, into a unit quaternion, $\hat{q}$, is a bit more involved. Key to this process are the following differences made from the matrix in Equation 3.45:

$$\begin{aligned} m_{21}^q - m_{12}^q &= 4q_wq_x, \\ m_{02}^q - m_{20}^q &= 4q_wq_y, \\ m_{10}^q - m_{01}^q &= 4q_wq_z. \end{aligned} \tag{3.46}$$

The implication of these equations is that if q_w is known, the values of the vector $\mathbf{v}_q$ can be computed, and thus $\hat{q}$ derived. The trace, $\text{tr}(\mathbf{M})$, of a matrix, $\mathbf{M}$, is simply the sum of the diagonal elements of the matrix. The trace of $\mathbf{M}^q$ is calculated by:

$$\text{tr}(\mathbf{M}^q) = 4 - 2s(q_x^2 + q_y^2 + q_z^2) = 4\left(1 - \frac{q_x^2 + q_y^2 + q_z^2}{q_x^2 + q_y^2 + q_z^2 + q_w^2}\right)$$
$$= \frac{4q_w^2}{q_x^2 + q_y^2 + q_z^2 + q_w^2} = \frac{4q_w^2}{n(\hat{\mathbf{q}})}.$$
(3.47)

This result yields the following conversion for a unit quaternion:

$$q_w = \frac{1}{2}\sqrt{\text{tr}(\mathbf{M}^q)} \qquad q_x = \frac{m_{21}^q - m_{12}^q}{4q_w}$$

$$q_y = \frac{m_{02}^q - m_{20}^q}{4q_w} \qquad q_z = \frac{m_{10}^q - m_{01}^q}{4q_w}$$
(3.48)

To have a numerically stable routine [708], divisions by small numbers should be avoided. Therefore, first, set $t = q_w^2 - q_x^2 - q_y^2 - q_z^2$, from which it follows that:

$$\begin{aligned}
lm_{00} &= t + 2q_x^2, \\
m_{11} &= t + 2q_y^2, \\
m_{22} &= t + 2q_z^2, \\
u &= m_{00} + m_{11} + m_{22} = t + 2q_w^2,
\end{aligned}$$
(3.49)

which in turn implies that the largest of m_{00}, m_{11}, m_{22}, and u determine which of q_x, q_y, q_z, and q_w is largest. If q_w is largest, then Equation 3.48 is used to derive the quaternion. Otherwise, we note that the following holds:

$$\begin{aligned}
4q_x^2 &= +m_{00} - m_{11} - m_{22} + m_{33}, \\
4q_y^2 &= -m_{00} + m_{11} - m_{22} + m_{33}, \\
4q_z^2 &= -m_{00} - m_{11} + m_{22} + m_{33}, \\
4q_w^2 &= \text{tr}(\mathbf{M}^q).
\end{aligned}$$
(3.50)

The appropriate equation of the ones above is then used to compute the largest of q_x, q_y, and q_z, after which Equation 3.46 is used to calculate the remaining components of $\hat{\mathbf{q}}$. Luckily, there is code for this—see the *Further Reading and Resources* at the end of this chapter.

Spherical Linear Interpolation

Spherical linear interpolation is an operation that, given two unit quaternions, $\hat{\mathbf{q}}$ and $\hat{\mathbf{r}}$, and a parameter $t \in [0, 1]$, computes an interpolated quaternion. This is useful for animating objects, for example. It is not as useful for interpolating camera orientations, as the camera's "up" vector can become tilted during the interpolation, usually a disturbing effect [235].

The algebraic form of this operation is expressed by the composite quaternion, $\hat{\mathbf{s}}$, below:

$$\hat{\mathbf{s}}(\hat{\mathbf{q}}, \hat{\mathbf{r}}, t) = (\hat{\mathbf{r}}\hat{\mathbf{q}}^{-1})^t \hat{\mathbf{q}}. \qquad (3.51)$$

However, for software implementations, the following form, where slerp stands for spherical linear interpolation, is much more appropriate:

$$\hat{\mathbf{s}}(\hat{\mathbf{q}}, \hat{\mathbf{r}}, t) = \text{slerp}(\hat{\mathbf{q}}, \hat{\mathbf{r}}, t) = \frac{\sin(\phi(1-t))}{\sin\phi}\hat{\mathbf{q}} + \frac{\sin(\phi t)}{\sin\phi}\hat{\mathbf{r}}. \qquad (3.52)$$

To compute ϕ, which is needed in the equation above, the following fact can be used: $\cos\phi = q_x r_x + q_y r_y + q_z r_z + q_w r_w$ [159]. For $t \in [0,1]$, the slerp function computes (unique[12]) interpolated quaternions that together constitute the shortest arc on a four-dimensional unit sphere from $\hat{\mathbf{q}}$ ($t = 0$) to $\hat{\mathbf{r}}$ ($t = 1$). The arc is located on the circle that is formed from the intersection between the plane given by $\hat{\mathbf{q}}$, $\hat{\mathbf{r}}$, and the origin, and the four-dimensional unit sphere. This is shown in Figure 3.9. The computed rotation quaternion rotates around a fixed axis at constant speed. A curve such as this, that has constant speed and thus zero acceleration, is called a *geodesic* curve [181].

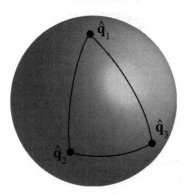

Figure 3.9. Unit quaternions are represented as points on the unit sphere. The function slerp is used to interpolate between the quaternions, and the interpolated path is a great arc on the sphere. Note that interpolating from $\hat{\mathbf{q}}_1$ to $\hat{\mathbf{q}}_2$ and interpolating from $\hat{\mathbf{q}}_1$ to $\hat{\mathbf{q}}_3$ to $\hat{\mathbf{q}}_2$ are not the same thing, even though they arrive at the same orientation.

---

[12]If and only if $\hat{\mathbf{q}}$ and $\hat{\mathbf{r}}$ are not opposite.

The `slerp` function is perfectly suited for interpolating between two orientations. This procedure is not as simple with the Euler transform, because when several Euler angles need to be interpolated, gimbal lock (see Section 3.2.1) can occur.

When more than two orientations, say $\hat{q}_0, \hat{q}_1, \ldots, \hat{q}_{n-1}$, are available, and we want to interpolate from $\hat{q}_0$ to $\hat{q}_1$ to $\hat{q}_2$, and so on until $\hat{q}_{n-1}$, `slerp` could be used in a straightforward fashion. Now, when we approach, say, $\hat{q}_i$, we would use $\hat{q}_{i-1}$ and $\hat{q}_i$ as arguments to `slerp`. After passing through $\hat{q}_i$, we would then use $\hat{q}_i$ and $\hat{q}_{i+1}$ as arguments to `slerp`. This will cause sudden jerks to appear in the orientation interpolation, which can be seen to the left in Figure 3.9. This is similar to what happens when points are linearly interpolated; see the upper right part of Figure 12.1 on page 484. Some readers may wish to revisit the following paragraph after reading about splines in Chapter 12.

A better way to interpolate is to use some sort of spline. We introduce quaternions $\hat{a}_i$ and $\hat{b}_{i+1}$ between $\hat{q}_i$ and $\hat{q}_{i+1}$. Surprisingly, these are computed as shown below [199][13]:

$$\hat{a}_i = \hat{b}_i = \hat{q}_i \exp\left[-\frac{\log(\hat{q}_i^{-1}\hat{q}_{i-1}) + \log(\hat{q}_i^{-1}\hat{q}_{i+1})}{4}\right]. \tag{3.53}$$

The $\hat{q}_i$, $\hat{a}_i$, and $\hat{b}_i$ will be used to spherically interpolate the quaternions using a smooth cubic spline, as shown in Equation 3.54.

$$\begin{aligned} &\texttt{squad}(\hat{q}_i, \hat{q}_{i+1}, \hat{a}_i, \hat{a}_{i+1}, t) = \\ &\quad \texttt{slerp}(\texttt{slerp}(\hat{q}_i, \hat{q}_{i+1}, t), \texttt{slerp}(\hat{a}_i, \hat{a}_{i+1}, t), 2t(1-t)) \end{aligned} \tag{3.54}$$

As can be seen above, the `squad` function is constructed from repeated spherical interpolation using `slerp` (see Section 12.1.1 for information on repeated linear interpolation for points). The interpolation will pass through the initial orientations $\hat{q}_i$, $i \in [0, \ldots, n-1]$, but not through $\hat{a}_i$—these are used to indicate the tangent orientations at the initial orientations.

Rotation from One Vector to Another

A common operation is transforming from one direction **s** to another direction **t**. The mathematics of quaternions simplifies this procedure greatly. First, normalize **s** and **t**. Then compute the unit rotation axis, called **u**, which is computed as $\mathbf{u} = (\mathbf{s} \times \mathbf{t})/\|\mathbf{s} \times \mathbf{t}\|$. Next, $e = \mathbf{s} \cdot \mathbf{t} = \cos(2\phi)$ and $\|\mathbf{s} \times \mathbf{t}\| = \sin(2\phi)$, where 2ϕ is the angle between **s** and **t**. The quaternion that represents the rotation from **s** to **t** is then $\hat{q} = (\sin\phi\mathbf{u}, \cos\phi)$. In

---

[13]Shoemake [707] gives another derivation.

fact, simplifying $\hat{q} = (\frac{\sin\phi}{\sin 2\phi}(s \times t), \cos\phi)$, using the half-angle relations (see page 746) and the trigonometric identity (Equation B.9) gives [541]:

$$\hat{q} = (q_v, q_w) = \left(\frac{1}{\sqrt{2(1+e)}}(s \times t), \frac{\sqrt{2(1+e)}}{2} \right). \tag{3.55}$$

Directly generating the quaternion in this fashion (versus using the cross product $s \times t$) avoids numerical instability when s and t point in nearly the same direction [541]. Stability problems appear for both methods when s and t point in opposite directions, as a division by zero occurs. When this special case is detected, any axis of rotation perpendicular to s can be used to rotate to t.

Sometimes we need the matrix representation of a rotation from s to t. After some algebraic and trigonometric simplification of Equation 3.45, the rotation matrix becomes [563]:

$$\mathbf{R}(s, t) = \begin{pmatrix} e + hv_x^2 & hv_xv_y - v_z & hv_xv_z + v_y & 0 \\ hv_xv_y + v_z & e + hv_y^2 & hv_yv_z - v_x & 0 \\ hv_xv_z - v_y & hv_yv_z + v_x & e + hv_z^2 & 0 \\ 0 & 0 & 0 & 1 \end{pmatrix}. \tag{3.56}$$

In the above equation, we have used the following intermediate calculations:

$$\begin{aligned} v &= s \times t, \\ e &= \cos(2\phi) = s \cdot t, \\ h &= \frac{1 - \cos(2\phi)}{\sin^2(2\phi)} = \frac{1 - e}{v \cdot v}. \end{aligned} \tag{3.57}$$

As can be seen, all square roots and trigonometric functions have disappeared due to the simplifications, and so this is an efficient way to create the matrix.

Note that care must be taken when s and t are parallel or near parallel, because then $\|s \times t\| \approx 0$. If $\phi \approx 0$, then we can return the identity matrix. However, if $2\phi \approx \pi$, then we can rotate π radians around *any* axis. This axis can be found as the cross product between s and any other vector that is not parallel to s (see Section 3.2.4). Möller and Hughes use Householder matrices to handle this special case in a different way [563].

EXAMPLE: POSITIONING AND ORIENTING A CAMERA Assume that the default position for a virtual camera (or viewpoint) is $(0\ 0\ 0)^T$ and the default view direction v is along the negative z-axis, i.e., $v = (0\ 0\ -1)^T$.

Now, the goal is to create a transform that moves the camera to a new position $\mathbf{p}$, looking in a new direction $\mathbf{w}$. Start by orienting the camera, which can be done by rotating the default view direction into the destination view direction. $\mathbf{R}(\mathbf{v}, \mathbf{w})$ takes care of this. The positioning is simply done by translating to $\mathbf{p}$, which yields the resulting transform $\mathbf{X} = \mathbf{T}(\mathbf{p})\mathbf{R}(\mathbf{v}, \mathbf{w})$. In practice, after the first rotation another vector-vector rotation will most likely be desired to rotate the view's up direction to some desired orientation. $\qquad\qquad\square$

3.4 Vertex Blending

Imagine that an arm of a digital character is animated using two parts, a forearm and an upper arm, as shown to the left in Figure 3.10. This model could be animated using rigid-body transforms (Section 3.1.6). However, then the joint between these two parts will not resemble a real elbow. This is because two separate objects are used, and therefore, the joint consists of overlapping parts from these two separate objects. Clearly, it would be better to use just one single object. However, static model parts do not address the problem of making the joint flexible.

Vertex blending is one possible solution to this problem [457, 458, 468, 492, 822]. This technique has several other names, such as skinning, enveloping, and skeleton-subspace deformation. While the exact origin of the algorithm presented here is unclear, defining bones and having a skin react to changes is an old concept in computer animation [510]. In its simplest form, the forearm and the upper arm are animated separately as before, but at the joint the two parts are connected through an elastic "skin." So, this elastic part will have one set of vertices that are transformed by the forearm matrix and another set that are transformed by the matrix of the upper arm. This results in triangles whose vertices may be transformed by different matrices, in contrast to using a single matrix per triangle. See Figure 3.10. This basic technique is sometimes called *stitching* [822].

By taking this one step further, one can allow a single vertex to be transformed by several different matrices, with the results weighted and blended together. This is done by having a skeleton of bones for the animated object, where each bone's transform may influence each vertex by a user-defined weight. Since the entire arm may be "elastic", i.e., all vertices may be affected by more than one matrix, the entire mesh is often called a skin (over the bones). See Figure 3.11, and Plates II and III (following page 274)

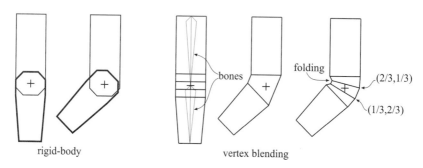

Figure 3.10. An arm consisting of a forearm and an upper arm is animated using rigid-body transforms of two separate objects to the left. The elbow does not appear realistic. To the right, vertex blending is used on one single object. The next-to-rightmost arm illustrates what happens when a simple skin directly joins the two parts to cover the elbow. The rightmost illustrates what happens when vertex blending is used, and some vertices are blended with different weights: $(2/3, 1/3)$ means that the vertex weighs the transform from the upper arm by $2/3$ and from the forearm by $1/3$. This figure also shows a drawback of vertex blending in the rightmost illustration. Here, folding in the inner part of the elbow is visible. Better results can be achieved with more bones, and more carefully selected weights.

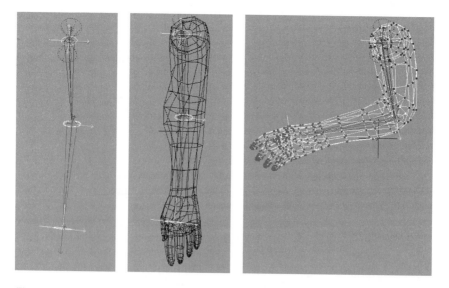

Figure 3.11. A real example of vertex blending. The left image shows the two bones of an arm, and the middle shows the skin of the arm in resting position. On the right, the forearm has moved, and vertex blending has been applied, most notably at the elbow. *(Images courtesy of Jeff Lander.)*

for examples. Many commercial modeling systems have this same sort of skeleton-bone modeling feature. Tombesi discusses how to retrieve the data needed for vertex blending from the 3DS MAX modeler [751].

Mathematically, this is expressed in Equation 3.58, where $\mathbf{p}$ is the original vertex, and $\mathbf{u}(t)$ is the transformed vertex whose position depends on the time t. There are n bones influencing the position of $\mathbf{p}$, which is expressed in world coordinates. The matrix $\mathbf{M}_i$ transforms from the initial bone's coordinate system to world coordinates. Typically a bone has its controlling joint at the origin of its coordinate system. For example, a forearm bone would move its elbow joint to the origin, with an animated rotation matrix moving this part of the arm around the joint. $\mathbf{B}_i(t)$ is the i:th bone's world transform that changes with time to animate the object, and is typically a concatenation of a number of matrices, such as the hierarchy of previous bone transforms and the local animation matrix. One method of maintaining and updating the $\mathbf{B}_i(t)$ matrix animation functions is discussed in depth by Woodland [822]. Finally, w_i is the weight of bone i for vertex $\mathbf{p}$. The vertex blending equation is:

$$\mathbf{u}(t) = \sum_{i=0}^{n-1} w_i \mathbf{B}_i(t) \mathbf{M}_i^{-1} \mathbf{p}, \quad \text{where} \quad \sum_{i=0}^{n-1} w_i = 1, \quad w_i \geq 0. \tag{3.58}$$

The matrix $\mathbf{M}_i$ is not explicitly shown in some discussions of skinning, but rather is considered as being a part of $\mathbf{B}_i(t)$. We present it here as it is a useful matrix that is almost always a part of the matrix concatenation process.

In practice, the matrices $\mathbf{B}_i(t)$ and $\mathbf{M}_i^{-1}$ are concatenated for each bone for each frame of animation and the resulting matrix is used to transform the vertices. The vertex $\mathbf{p}$ is transformed by the different bones' concatenated matrices, and then blended using the weights w_i—thus the name *vertex blending*. The weights are nonnegative and sum to one[14], so what is occurring is that the vertex is transformed to a few positions and then interpolated amongst them. As such, the transformed point $\mathbf{u}$ will lie in the convex hull of the set of points $\mathbf{B}_i(t)\mathbf{M}_i^{-1}\mathbf{p}$, for all $i = 0 \ldots n - 1$ (fixed t). The normals should also be transformed using Equation 3.58 with the exception that the transpose of the inverse of the $\mathbf{B}_i(t)\mathbf{M}_i^{-1}$ should be used, as shown in Section 3.1.7. Remember, though, that the transpose of the inverse is not needed in cases where only rotations and translations are

---

[14]In fact, the API normally requires summation to one, as the last weight for a vertex is never specified directly, but rather is assumed to be one minus the sum of the other weights.

used (i.e., not scaling or shearing). This fact can be used to optimize vertex shader code for vertex blending in order to be able to use more bones [468].

Vertex blending can be done by the host CPU, but if the application is the bottleneck, then it is worth doing this operation on the graphics hardware, if possible (see Chapter 10). Some graphics hardware can do vertex blending directly. Also, hardware with a vertex shader can be programmed to perform vertex blending. A single model can have a large number of interconnected bones, with each vertex influenced by a few different bones. It is easiest if the model's whole set of bone matrices can be used together; otherwise the model must be split up and some bones replicated.[15]

DirectX 8 allows skinning through a choice of either of two pipelines, the fixed function path, or through the vertex shader (see Section 6.5). The fixed function pipeline supports a 256 matrix palette for vertex blending, though not all hardware has support for this many matrices. Each vertex can use a maximum of four of these matrices. In practice, there are few cases where a single vertex is influenced by more than four bones [468]. This system is called "indexed vertex blending."

However, this matrix palette system cannot be used in conjunction with the vertex shader, as it is part of an entirely different pipeline.[16] The fixed function matrix palette system can be emulated to some extent with vertex shaders. Lander describes how up to about 29 bones can be handled at once while using vertex shaders [468]. The obvious advantage to using vertex shaders for skinning is that vertex shading effects can be done and accelerated by hardware. Another advantage is that if a system has vertex shader hardware support, there is a solid minimum number of matrices (e.g., about 29) that are available in the palette, versus the indeterminate number under the fixed function system. Note however, that this number will increase as the hardware gets more sophisticated; DirectX 9 specifies vertex shaders that have enough memory for about 82 bones. Also, when using vertex shaders, it is possible to specify sets of weights that are outside the range $[0, 1]$ or do not sum to one (which makes sense only if some other blending algorithm is being used). Another advantage of using vertex shaders over a matrix palette system, is that they can easily be combined with per-pixel lighting effects, such as bump mapping.

If accurate collision detection (see Chapter 14) is desired on vertex blended models, then the blending has to take place on the CPU in order to get access to the transformed vertices. This often also holds when silhou-

---

[15] DirectX provides a function `ConvertToIndexedBlendedMesh` to perform such splitting.

[16] In fact, NVIDIA recommends never using the fixed-function matrix palette system, as even software vertex shaders are faster.

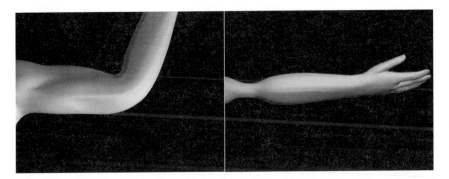

Figure 3.12. Problems with vertex blending. The left image shows folding at the elbow, and the right shows how the area around the joint twists as the forearm rotates. *(Images courtesy of Nickson Fong [492].)*

ette generation is done when creating shadows using the shadow volume method presented in Section 6.12.3. Another drawback of vertex blending is that unwanted folding, twisting, and self-intersection can occur [492]. See Figure 3.12. Correcting these problems can be difficult, and good solutions can be expensive to compute. One solution is presented by Lewis et al. [492].

3.5 Projections

Before one can actually render a scene, all relevant objects in the scene must be projected onto some kind of plane or into some kind of simple volume. After that, clipping and rendering are performed (see Section 2.3).

The transforms seen so far in this chapter have left the fourth component, the w-component, unaffected. That is, points and vectors have retained their types after the transform. Also, the bottom row in the 4×4 matrices has always been (0 0 0 1). *Perspective projection matrices* are exceptions to both of these properties: The bottom row contains vector and point manipulating numbers, and, the homogenization process is often needed (i.e., w is often not 1, so a division by w is needed to obtain the nonhomogeneous point). *Orthographic projection*, which is dealt with first in this section, is a simpler kind of projection that is also commonly used. It does not affect the w component.

In this section, it is assumed that the viewer is looking along the negative z-axis, with the y-axis pointing up and the x-axis to the right. This is a right-handed coordinate system. Some texts and software, e.g., DirectX, use a left-handed system in which the viewer looks along the positive z-axis. Both systems are valid, and in the end, the same effect is achieved.

3.5.1 Orthographic Projection

A characteristic of an orthographic projection is that parallel lines remain parallel after the projection. Matrix $\mathbf{P}_o$, shown below, is a simple orthographic projection matrix that leaves the x- and y-components of a point unchanged, while setting the z-component to zero, i.e., it orthographically projects onto the plane $z = 0$.

$$\mathbf{P}_o = \begin{pmatrix} 1 & 0 & 0 & 0 \\ 0 & 1 & 0 & 0 \\ 0 & 0 & 0 & 0 \\ 0 & 0 & 0 & 1 \end{pmatrix} \tag{3.59}$$

The effect of this projection is illustrated in Figure 3.13. Clearly, $\mathbf{P}_o$ is non-invertible, since its determinant $|\mathbf{P}_o| = 0$. In other words, the transform drops from three to two dimensions, and there is no way to retrieve

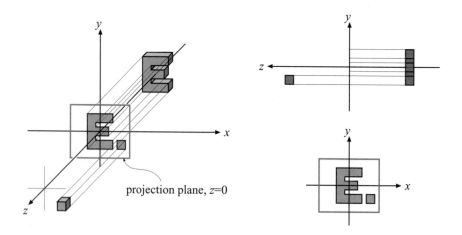

Figure 3.13. Three different views of the simple orthographic projection generated by Equation 3.59. This projection can be seen as the viewer is looking along the negative z-axis, which means that the projection simply skips (or sets to zero) the z-coordinate while keeping the x- and y-coordinates. Note that objects on both sides of $z = 0$ are projected onto the projection plane.

the dropped dimension. A problem with using this kind of orthographic projection for viewing is that it projects both points with positive and points with negative z-values onto the projection plane. It is usually useful to restrict the z-values (and the x- and y-values) to a certain interval, from, say n (near plane) to f (far plane).[17] This is the purpose of the next transformation.

A more common matrix for performing orthographic projection is expressed in terms of the six-tuple, (l, r, b, t, n, f), denoting the left, right, bottom, top, near, and far planes. This matrix essentially scales and translates the AABB (*Axis-Aligned Bounding* Box; see the definition in Section 13.2) formed by these planes into an axis-aligned cube centered around the origin. The minimum corner of the AABB is (l, b, n) and the maximum corner is (r, t, f). It is important to realize that $n > f$, because we are looking down the negative z-axis at this volume of space. Our common sense says that the near value should be a lower number than the far. OpenGL, which also looks down the negative z-axis, presents their input near value as less than far in the orthographic matrix creation call glOrtho, then internally negates these two values. Another way to think of it is that OpenGL's near and far values are (positive) distances along the view direction (the negative z-axis), not z eye coordinate values.

The axis-aligned cube has a minimum corner of $(-1, -1, -1)$ and a maximum corner of $(1, 1, 1)$. This cube is called the *canonical view vol-*

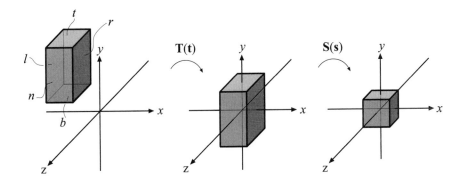

Figure 3.14. Transforming an axis-aligned box on the canonical view volume. The box on the left is first translated, making its center coincide with the origin. Then it is scaled to get the size of the canonical view volume, shown at the right.

---

[17]The near plane is also called the *front plane* or *hither*; the far plane is also the *back plane* or *yon*.

ume, and the coordinates in this volume are called *normalized device co-ordinates.*[18] The transformation procedure is shown in Figure 3.14. The reason for transforming into the canonical view volume is that clipping is more efficiently performed there, especially in the case of a hardware implementation.

After the transformation into the canonical view volume, vertices of the geometry to be rendered are clipped against this cube. The geometry not outside the cube is finally rendered by mapping the remaining unit square to the screen. This orthographic transform is shown here:

$$
\mathbf{P}_o = \mathbf{S(s)T(t)} = \begin{pmatrix} \dfrac{2}{r-l} & 0 & 0 & 0 \\ 0 & \dfrac{2}{t-b} & 0 & 0 \\ 0 & 0 & \dfrac{2}{f-n} & 0 \\ 0 & 0 & 0 & 1 \end{pmatrix} \begin{pmatrix} 1 & 0 & 0 & -\dfrac{l+r}{2} \\ 0 & 1 & 0 & -\dfrac{t+b}{2} \\ 0 & 0 & 1 & -\dfrac{f+n}{2} \\ 0 & 0 & 0 & 1 \end{pmatrix}
$$

$$
= \begin{pmatrix} \dfrac{2}{r-l} & 0 & 0 & -\dfrac{r+l}{r-l} \\ 0 & \dfrac{2}{t-b} & 0 & -\dfrac{t+b}{t-b} \\ 0 & 0 & \dfrac{2}{f-n} & -\dfrac{f+n}{f-n} \\ 0 & 0 & 0 & 1 \end{pmatrix}.
$$

(3.60)

As suggested by the above equation, $\mathbf{P}_o$ can be written as the concatenation of a translation, $\mathbf{T(t)}$, followed by a scaling matrix, $\mathbf{S(s)}$, where $\mathbf{s} = (2/(r-l), 2/(t-b), 2/(f-n))$, and $\mathbf{t} = (-(r+l)/2, -(t+b)/2, -(f+n)/2)$. This matrix is invertible.[19], i.e., $\mathbf{P}_o^{-1} = \mathbf{T(-t)S}((r-l)/2, (t-b)/2, (f-n)/2)$

In computer graphics, a left-hand coordinate system is most often used after projection—i.e., for the viewport, the x-axis goes to the right, y-axis goes up, and the z-axis goes into the viewport. Because the far value is less than the near value for the way we defined our AABB, the orthographic transform will always include a mirroring transform. To see this, say the original AABBs is the same size as the goal, the canonical view volume. Then the AABB's coordinates are $(-1, -1, 1)$ for (l, b, n) and $(1, 1, -1)$ for (r, t, f). Equation 3.60 yields

---

[18]Some APIs use other canonical volumes, such as an AABB from $(-1, -1, 0)$ to $(1, 1, 1)$.

[19]If and only if $n \neq f$, $l \neq r$, and $t \neq b$; otherwise, no inverse exists.

$$\mathbf{P}_o = \begin{pmatrix} 1 & 0 & 0 & 0 \\ 0 & 1 & 0 & 0 \\ 0 & 0 & -1 & 0 \\ 0 & 0 & 0 & 1 \end{pmatrix}, \qquad (3.61)$$

which is a mirroring matrix. It is this mirroring that converts from the right-handed viewing coordinate system (looking down the negative z-axis) to left-handed normalized device coordinates.

Some systems, such as DirectX, also map the z-depths to the range $[0, 1]$ instead of $[-1, 1]$. This can be accomplished by applying a simple scaling and translation matrix applied after the orthographic matrix, that is:

$$\mathbf{M}_{st} = \begin{pmatrix} 1 & 0 & 0 & 0 \\ 0 & 1 & 0 & 0 \\ 0 & 0 & 0.5 & 0.5 \\ 0 & 0 & 0 & 1 \end{pmatrix}. \qquad (3.62)$$

So the orthographic matrix used in DirectX is:

$$\mathbf{P}_{o[0,1]} = \begin{pmatrix} \dfrac{2}{r-l} & 0 & 0 & -\dfrac{r+l}{r-l} \\ 0 & \dfrac{2}{t-b} & 0 & -\dfrac{t+b}{t-b} \\ 0 & 0 & \dfrac{1}{f-n} & -\dfrac{n}{f-n} \\ 0 & 0 & 0 & 1 \end{pmatrix}. \qquad (3.63)$$

which is normally presented in transposed form, as DirectX uses a row-major form for writing matrices.

3.5.2 Perspective Projection

A much more interesting transform than orthographic projection is perspective projection, which is used in the majority of computer graphics applications. Here, parallel lines are generally not parallel after projection; rather, they may converge to a single point at their extreme. Perspective more closely matches how we perceive the world, i.e., objects further away are smaller.

First, we shall present an instructive derivation for a perspective projection matrix that projects onto a plane $z = -d$, $d > 0$. We derive from world space to simplify understanding of how the world-to-view conversion proceeds. This derivation is followed by the more conventional matrices used in, for example, OpenGL [601].

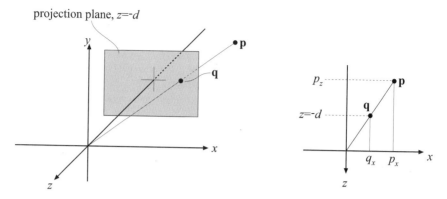

Figure 3.15. The notation used for deriving a perspective projection matrix. The point **p** is projected onto the plane $z = -d$, $d > 0$, which yields the projected point **q**. The projection is performed from the perspective of the camera's location, which in this case is the origin. The similar triangle used in the derivation is shown for the x-component at the right.

Assume that the camera (viewpoint) is located at the origin, and that we want to project a point, **p**, onto the plane $z = -d$, $d > 0$, yielding a new point $\mathbf{q} = (q_x, q_y, -d)$. This scenario is depicted in Figure 3.15. From the similar triangles shown in this figure, the following derivation, for the x-component of **q**, is obtained:

$$\frac{q_x}{p_x} = \frac{-d}{p_z} \qquad \Longleftrightarrow \qquad q_x = -d\frac{p_x}{p_z}. \tag{3.64}$$

The expressions for the other components of **q** are $q_y = -dp_y/p_z$ (obtained similarly to q_x), and $q_z = -d$. Together with the above formula, these give us the perspective projection matrix, $\mathbf{P}_p$, as shown here:

$$\mathbf{P}_p = \begin{pmatrix} 1 & 0 & 0 & 0 \\ 0 & 1 & 0 & 0 \\ 0 & 0 & 1 & 0 \\ 0 & 0 & -1/d & 0 \end{pmatrix}. \tag{3.65}$$

That this matrix yields the correct perspective projection is confirmed by the simple verification of Equation 3.66.

$$\mathbf{q} = \mathbf{P}_p \mathbf{p} = \begin{pmatrix} 1 & 0 & 0 & 0 \\ 0 & 1 & 0 & 0 \\ 0 & 0 & 1 & 0 \\ 0 & 0 & -1/d & 0 \end{pmatrix} \begin{pmatrix} p_x \\ p_y \\ p_z \\ 1 \end{pmatrix} = \begin{pmatrix} p_x \\ p_y \\ p_z \\ -p_z/d \end{pmatrix} \Rightarrow \begin{pmatrix} -dp_x/p_z \\ -dp_y/p_z \\ -d \\ 1 \end{pmatrix}$$

(3.66)

The last step comes from the fact that the whole vector is divided by the w-component (in this case $-p_z/d$), in order to get a 1 in the last position. The resulting z value is always $-d$ since we are projecting onto this plane.

Intuitively, it is easy to understand why homogeneous coordinates allow for projection. One geometrical interpretation of the homogenization process is that it projects the point (p_x, p_y, p_z) onto the plane $w = 1$.

As with the orthographic transformation, there is also a perspective transform that, rather than actually projecting onto a plane (which is non-invertible), transforms the view frustum into the canonical view volume described previously. Here the view frustum is assumed to start at $z = n$ and end at $z = f$, with $0 > n > f$. The rectangle at $z = n$ has the minimum corner at (l, b, n) and the maximum corner at (r, t, n). This is shown in Figure 3.16.

The parameters (l, r, b, t, n, f) determine the view frustum of the camera. The horizontal field of view is determined by the angle between the left and the right planes (determined by l and r) of the frustum. In the same manner, the vertical field of view is determined by the angle between the top and the bottom planes (determined by t and b). The greater the field of view, the more the camera "sees." Asymmetric frustums can be created by $r \neq -l$ or $t \neq -b$. Asymmetric frustums are, for example, used for stereo viewing (see Section 15.1.5) and in CAVEs [152].

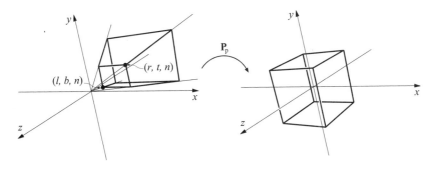

Figure 3.16. The matrix $\mathbf{P}_p$ transforms the view frustum into the unit cube, which is called the canonical view volume.

The field of view is an important factor in providing a sense of the scene. The eye itself has a physical field of view compared to the computer screen. This relationship is:

$$\phi = 2\arctan(w/(2d)) \tag{3.67}$$

where ϕ is the field of view, w is the width of the object perpendicular to the line of sight, and d is the distance to the object. For example, a 21-inch monitor is about 16 inches wide, and 25 inches is a minimum recommended viewing distance [20], which yields a physical field of view of 35 degrees. At 12 inches away, the field of view is 67 degrees; at 18 inches, it is 48 degrees; at 30 inches, 30 degrees. This same formula can be used to convert from camera lens size to field of view, e.g., a standard 50mm lens for a 35mm camera (which has a 36mm wide frame size) gives $\phi = 2\arctan(36/(2*50)) = 39.6$ degrees.

Using a narrower field of view compared to the physical setup will lessen the perspective effect, as the viewer will be zoomed in on the scene. Setting a wider field of view will make objects appear distorted (like using a wide angle camera lens), especially near the screen's edges, and will exaggerate the scale of nearby objects. However, a wider field of view gives the viewer a sense that objects are larger and more impressive, and has the advantage of giving the user more information about the surroundings.

The perspective transform matrix that transforms the frustum into a unit cube is given by Equation 3.68.[20]

$$\mathbf{P}_p = \begin{pmatrix} \dfrac{2n}{r-l} & 0 & -\dfrac{r+l}{r-l} & 0 \\ 0 & \dfrac{2n}{t-b} & -\dfrac{t+b}{t-b} & 0 \\ 0 & 0 & \dfrac{f+n}{f-n} & -\dfrac{2fn}{f-n} \\ 0 & 0 & 1 & 0 \end{pmatrix} \tag{3.68}$$

After applying this transform to a point, we will get another point $\mathbf{q} = (q_x, q_y, q_z, q_w)^T$. The w-component, q_w, of this point will (most often) be nonzero and not equal to one. To get the projected point, $\mathbf{p}$, we need to divide by q_w: $\mathbf{p} = (q_x/q_w, q_y/q_w, q_z/q_w, 1)^T$. The matrix $\mathbf{P}_p$ always sees to it that $z = f$ maps to $+1$ and $z = n$ maps to -1. After the perspective transform is performed, clipping and homogenization (division by w) is done to obtain the normalized device coordinates.

---

[20]The far plane can also be set to infinity. See Equation 6.35 on page 266 for this form.

To get the perspective transform used in OpenGL, first multiply with $\mathbf{S}(1, 1, -1)$, for the same reasons as for the orthographic transform. This simply negates the values in the third column of Equation 3.68. After this mirroring transform has been applied, the near and far values are entered as positive values, with $0 < n' < f'$, as they would traditionally be presented to the user. However, they still represent distances along the world's negative z-axis, which is the direction of view. For reference purposes, here is the OpenGL equation:[21]

$$\mathbf{P}_{OpenGL} = \begin{pmatrix} \dfrac{2n'}{r - l} & 0 & \dfrac{r + l}{r - l} & 0 \\ 0 & \dfrac{2n'}{t - b} & \dfrac{t + b}{t - b} & 0 \\ 0 & 0 & -\dfrac{f' + n'}{f' - n'} & -\dfrac{2f'n'}{f' - n'} \\ 0 & 0 & -1 & 0 \end{pmatrix}. \quad (3.69)$$

Some APIs (e.g., DirectX) map the near plane to $z = 0$ (instead of $z = -1$) and the far plane to $z = 1$. In addition, DirectX uses a left-handed coordinate system to define its projection matrix. This means DirectX looks along the positive z-axis and presents the near and far values as positive numbers. Here is the DirectX equation:

$$\mathbf{P}_{p[0,1]} = \begin{pmatrix} \dfrac{2n'}{r - l} & 0 & \dfrac{r + l}{r - l} & 0 \\ 0 & \dfrac{2n'}{t - b} & \dfrac{t + b}{t - b} & 0 \\ 0 & 0 & \dfrac{f'}{f' - n'} & -\dfrac{f'n'}{f' - n'} \\ 0 & 0 & 1 & 0 \end{pmatrix}. \quad (3.70)$$

DirectX uses row-major form in its documentation, so this matrix is normally presented in transposed form.

One effect of using a perspective transformation is that the computed depth value does not vary linearly with the input p_z value. For example, if $n' = 10$ and $f' = 110$ (using the OpenGL terminology), when p_z is 60 units down the negative z axis (i.e., the halfway point) the normalized device coordinate depth value is 0.885, not 0. Figure 3.17 shows the effect of varying the distance of the near plane from the origin. Placement of

---

[21]So, to test that this really works in the z-direction, we can multiply $\mathbf{P}_{OpenGL}$ with $(0, 0, -n', 1)^T$. The z-component of the resulting vector will be -1. If we instead use the vector $(0, 0, -f', 1)^T$, the z-component will be $+1$, as expected. A similar test can be done for $\mathbf{P}_{[0,1]}$.

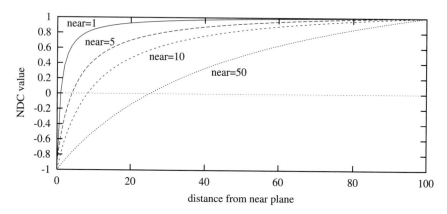

Figure 3.17. The effect of varying the distance of the near plane from the origin. The distance $f' - n'$ is kept constant at 100. As the near plane becomes closer to the origin, points nearer the far plane use a smaller range of the normalized device coordinate depth space. This has the effect of making the Z-buffer less accurate at greater distances.

the near and far planes affects the precision of the Z-buffer. This effect is discussed further in Section 15.1.3.

Further Reading and Resources

One of the best books for building up one's intuition about matrices in a painless fashion is Farin and Hansford's *The Geometry Toolbox* [225]. Another useful reference is Rogers's *Mathematical Elements for Computer Graphics* [656]. For a different perspective, many computer graphics texts, such as Watt and Watt's [793], Hearn and Baker's [328], and the two books by Foley et al. [235, 234], also cover matrix basics. The *Graphics Gems* series [29, 261, 333, 431, 610] presents various transform-related algorithms and has code available online for many of these. Golub and Van Loan's *Matrix Computations* [274] is the place to start for a serious study of matrix techniques in general. See: http://www.realtimerendering.com/ for code for many different transforms, including quaternions. More on skeleton-subspace deformation/vertex blending and shape interpolation can be read in Lewis et al.'s SIGGRAPH paper [492].

Pletinckx [628] and Schlag [683] present different ways of interpolating smoothly between a set of quaternions. Vlachos and Isidoro [774] derive formulae for C^2 interpolation of quaternions. Related to quaternion interpolation is the problem of computing a consistent coordinate system along a curve. This is treated by Dougan [184].

Chapter 4
Visual Appearance

"Light makes right."
–Andrew Glassner

When you render images of three-dimensional models, the models should not only look correct geometrically, they should also have a realistic visual appearance. This is usually accomplished via a combination of techniques, such as associating a material with each surface, applying various kinds of light sources, adding textures, using fog, transparency, and antialiasing techniques, compositing, and more. We will deal with many of these methods in this chapter. Texturing, advanced lighting and shading, and stylistic rendering will be covered in the chapters that follow.

4.1 Light Sources

Humans can see an object because photons bounce off (or are emitted from) the surface of the object and reach the eyes of the viewer. These photons may come from other objects or from *light sources*. In this context, there are three different types of light sources—*directional lights*, *point lights*, and *spotlights*, which are illustrated in Figure 4.1. The ways in which the parameters of the different types of light sources interact with the properties of a surface are described in Section 4.3.

A directional light is considered to be positioned essentially infinitely far away from the objects that are being lit. An example of such a light is the sun. Point and spotlights are called *positional lights* because they each have a location in space. A positional light can be thought of as a single point that emits photons. In contrast, real light sources have an area or volume, and so cast shadows with soft edges (see Section 6.12). In Figure 4.2, the three different light source types illuminate a square.

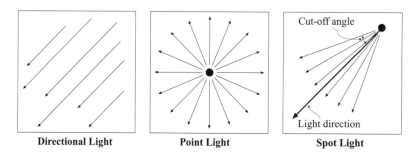

Figure 4.1. Three different types of light sources. A directional light is positioned infinitely far away, and the light rays from such a light source are therefore parallel when they arrive at an object. A point light has a position in space and sends light rays uniformly in every direction from that position. A spotlight is like a point light, but it emits light only within the volume of a cone, defined by a cut-off angle and a light direction. An example of a spotlight is a flashlight's beam.

All three light source types have intensity parameters in common. Each light source normally has an intensity and sometimes a color to it. Color is normally described as a set of red, green, and blue values (a.k.a., RGB). In theory this vector could have more than 3 values; see Hall's book [316] for more on color representation. A light can be further subdivided and have an ambient, diffuse, and specular intensity (these terms will be defined later on). These qualities are summarized in Table 4.1, where the **s** is short for *source*, in order to avoid confusion with the light vector, **l**, used later on. This kind of division is not physically accurate (real lights have just a single intensity and color), but it gives the user of a real-time graphics application

Figure 4.2. Here a square, subdivided into $100 \times 100 \times 2$ triangles, is lit by a directional light source (left), a point light source (middle), and a spotlight (right).

Notation	Description
$\mathbf{s}_{amb}$	Ambient intensity color
$\mathbf{s}_{diff}$	Diffuse intensity color
$\mathbf{s}_{spec}$	Specular intensity color
$\mathbf{s}_{pos}$	Light source position (four elements)

Table 4.1. Table of common light source parameters for directional, point, and spotlights.

more control over scene appearance. This table shows the common light source parameters for the light sources in OpenGL [601] and DirectX [180]. Some graphics APIs describe the intensities with fewer parameters.

A spotlight has a few more parameters. First, it has a direction vector, which is where the spotlight points. This parameter is denoted $\mathbf{s}_{dir}$. It also has a *cut-off angle*, s_{cut}, which is half the angle of the spotlight cone. Then, to control attenuation within the cone, it has a *spot exponent*, s_{exp}, which can be used to concentrate the light distribution in the center of the cone, and let it fall off from the center. The light direction and the cut-off angle parameters are shown at the right in Figure 4.1. Other parameters are possible for spotlight control; for example, the edge of the spotlight's effect can be softened so it does not drop off so sharply.

In the real world, a light drops off with the square of the distance from it. In the area of real-time rendering, the norm is that lights do not drop off with distance. Such lights are generally easier to control (because there is no need to worry about the effect of distance), and their effects may be computed more quickly. Directional light sources have no drop-off effects by definition, since they are infinitely far away. However, positional light sources sometimes allow control of their intensity based on distance. For example, OpenGL has three parameters, s_c, s_l, and s_q, that are used to control the attenuation which is proportional to some function of the distance from the light source. These parameters are described in more detail in Section 4.3.4.

4.2 Material

In real-time systems, a material consists of a number of material parameters, namely ambient, diffuse, specular, shininess, and emissive. The color of a surface with a material is determined by these parameters, the parameters of the light sources that illuminate the surface, and a lighting model. This interaction is explained in the next section.

Notation	Description
$\mathbf{m}_{amb}$	Ambient material color
$\mathbf{m}_{diff}$	Diffuse material color
$\mathbf{m}_{spec}$	Specular material color
m_{shi}	Shininess parameter
$\mathbf{m}_{emi}$	Emissive material color

Table 4.2. Table of material constants.

Plate IV (following page 274) gives a feel for how these values affect the appearance of the material.

4.3 Lighting and Shading

Lighting is the term that is used to designate the interaction between material and light sources, as well as their interaction with the geometry of the object to be rendered. As will be seen in the subsequent sections in this chapter, lighting can also be used with colors, textures, and transparency. All these elements are combined into a visual appearance on the screen.

Shading is the process of performing lighting computations and determining pixels' colors from them. There are three main types of shading: flat, Gouraud, and Phong. These correspond to computing the light per polygon, per vertex, and per pixel. In flat shading, a color is computed for a triangle and the triangle is filled with that color. In Gouraud shading [285], the lighting at each vertex of a triangle is determined, and these lighting samples (i.e., computed colors) are interpolated over the surface of the triangle. In Phong shading [621], the shading normals stored at the vertices are used to interpolate the shading normal at each pixel in the triangle. This normal is then used to compute the lighting's effect on that pixel. The effect of these three methods on the same lighting and materials is shown in Figure 4.3.

Flat shading runs fast and is simple to implement. While it does not give a smooth look to curved surfaces as Gouraud shading does, this can be an advantage; sometimes the user wants to see the underlying facets making up the model. Most graphics hardware implement Gouraud shading because of its speed and much improved quality. It is about as fast as flat shading, because the effect of lighting is computed only at the triangle vertices. A problem with this technique is that the shading is highly dependent

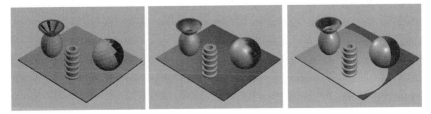

Figure 4.3. The same scene is shown with flat, Gouraud, and Phong shading, respectively (the flat shaded image has no specular highlighting component computed).

on the level of detail of the objects that are rendered. This problem is illustrated in Figure 4.5. Problems with Gouraud shading include missing highlights, failure to capture spotlight effects, and Mach banding [264, 316] (see Figure 4.3). As we will discuss in Section 5.7.2, these limitations can be partially overcome by using textures to represent lighting effects. Phong shading avoids these problems by interpolating the surface normal and computing the lighting at each pixel. Because per-pixel lighting is more complex and much more costly than per-vertex lighting, Phong shading is currently rare in commercial graphics hardware. The difference between flat, Gouraud, and Phong shading is illustrated in Figure 4.4. As will be seen in Chapter 6, textures have become a popular way of simulating per pixel shading.

Gouraud shading can achieve essentially the same shading result as Phong shading by subdividing a surface into triangles smaller than a pixel. This algorithm can be quite slow in practice, but it is a way in which Gouraud shading hardware can be coerced into acting more like a Phong shader. The concept of subdividing a surface into tiny fragments, rendering each of these, and then blending the results is powerful (though rarely used in real-time systems). For example, it is the basis of Pixar's RenderMan system [142, 761, 22], which is used in film production.

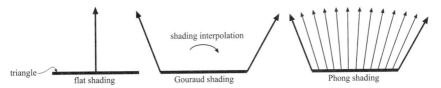

Figure 4.4. Flat shading is shown to the left (one color per polygon). The middle shows Gouraud shading, where the shading is computed at the vertices and interpolated over the polygons. Phong shading is shown to the right, where the normal is interpolated over the triangle, and shading computed at each pixel.

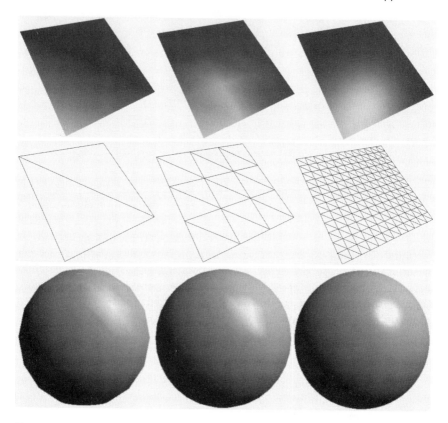

Figure 4.5. Shading is affected by the drawing primitives' size and location. The top row shows three squares with 2, 18, and 288 triangles. The middle row shows the wire frames of those shapes. The image at the right, with the highest triangle density, has the best shading. The bottom row shows how the quality of shading (and the silhouette quality) of approximations of spheres increases with the number of triangles. The spheres contain (left to right) 256, 1024, and 16,384 triangles.

The illumination at the vertices (or at all pixels for Phong shading) is computed using a *lighting model*. For real-time graphics purposes, all of these models are very similar, and each can be divided into three major parts, namely the *diffuse*, the *specular*, and the *ambient* components. These parts and their sum are illustrated in Figure 4.13, on page 81.

In the following sections, we will review each lighting model component and then see how these are combined into a lighting equation. It should be mentioned that this sort of lighting model is not based on much physical theory, but the result is still fairly good and relatively easy to control. For good or ill, many graphics accelerators and APIs use the type of lighting model we will describe. It is possible for application writers to substitute a different model and simply send down their own color per vertex when Gouraud shading. Vertex and pixel shading support lets the programmer put custom shaders onto the hardware itself. More accurate models describing the interaction of light and material are discussed in Chapter 6. Also, *Non-Photorealistic Rendering* (NPR) techniques, discussed in Chapter 7, include lighting models that are designed to provide different artistic effects or ways of presenting data. So, the lighting model presented here is commonly supported in hardware, but is in no way the only option available.

From a user interface perspective, the parameters in the equations that follow do not need to be exposed directly to the user as they stand. For example, Strauss [735] discusses more intuitive user controls for setting material values.

4.3.1 Diffuse Component

This part of the lighting model is the one with most connection to physical reality and the interaction between light and surfaces. This is because it is based on the geometric property called Lambert's Law, which states that for surfaces that are ideally diffuse (totally matte, without shininess), the reflected light is determined by the cosine between the surface normal **n** and the light vector l. The light vector goes from the surface point **p** to the light source. See Figure 4.6.

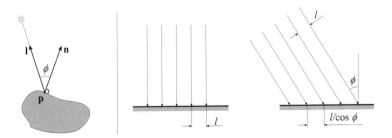

Figure 4.6. The diagram on the left shows the geometry for diffuse lighting. The illustration on the right shows light hitting a surface straight on and at an angle.

Specifically, the effect of the light is

$$i_{diff} = \mathbf{n} \cdot \mathbf{l} = \cos \phi, \tag{4.1}$$

where both $\mathbf{n}$ and $\mathbf{l}$ are normalized. Note that diffuse lighting is zero if the angle $\phi > \pi/2$, i.e., the surface faces away from the light.

The right side of Figure 4.6 shows a geometric interpretation of Lambert's Law. First, the light rays are shown hitting the surface perpendicularly. These rays are a distance l apart. The intensity of the light is related to this distance; the intensity decreases as l becomes greater. On the far right, the light rays are shown coming from a different direction. They make an angle ϕ with the normal of the plane. The distance between the light rays where they hit the surface is $l/\cos \phi$. Since the intensity is inversely proportional to this distance, this means that the diffuse lighting must be proportional to $\cos \phi$.

When a photon arrives at a diffuse surface, it is momentarily absorbed in that surface. Depending on the color of the photons from the light source and the color of the material, the photons may be totally absorbed or they may be sent away in an arbitrary reflection direction. Valid reflection directions are those that make an angle with the normal that is less than $\pi/2$ radians (i.e., those above the surface plane, not through it). For diffuse reflection, the probability for the new reflection direction is then equal for every direction. This means that the diffuse component of the lighting equation is independent of the camera's position and direction. In other words, the diffuse component is *view-independent*; the surface being lit looks the same from any angle. This can be seen in the equation itself, as the viewer's location does not play a part in it.

To make use of the diffuse color of the light source, $\mathbf{s}_{diff}$, and the diffuse color of the material, $\mathbf{m}_{diff}$, Equation 4.1 is redefined into Equation 4.2, where $\mathbf{i}_{diff}$ is the color of the diffuse contribution.

$$\mathbf{i}_{diff} = (\mathbf{n} \cdot \mathbf{l})\mathbf{m}_{diff} \otimes \mathbf{s}_{diff} \tag{4.2}$$

Remember that the $\otimes$ operator performs componentwise multiplication (see Section 1.2). Incorporating the fact that the diffuse lighting is zero if the angle between $\mathbf{n}$ and $\mathbf{l}$ is greater than $\pi/2$ radians gives Equation 4.3.

$$\mathbf{i}_{diff} = \max((\mathbf{n} \cdot \mathbf{l}), 0)\mathbf{m}_{diff} \otimes \mathbf{s}_{diff} \tag{4.3}$$

EXAMPLE: DIFFUSE COMPONENT The color vector $\mathbf{m}_{diff} \otimes \mathbf{s}_{diff}$ of Equation 4.2 is used to express the fact that photons of some wavelengths of light are absorbed by the material.[1] For example, if a light sends out the diffuse light $\mathbf{s}_{diff} = (1.0, 1.0, 1.0)$, which represents white light, and the material of an object has the diffuse parameter $\mathbf{m}_{diff} = (1.0, 0.0, 0.0)$, which represents red, then $\mathbf{m}_{diff} \otimes \mathbf{s}_{diff} = (1.0, 0.0, 0.0)$, which means that the diffuse component can be at most $(1.0, 0.0, 0.0)$. If, instead, the color of the light source is cyan, $(0.0, 1.0, 1.0)$, and the color of the material is magenta, $(1.0, 0.0, 1.0)$, the result will blue, $(0.0, 0.0, 1.0)$.

Assume that we have a blue light source, $\mathbf{s}_{diff} = (0.0, 0.0, 1.0)$, and a red material, $\mathbf{m}_{diff} = (1.0, 0.0, 0.0)$; then $\mathbf{m}_{diff} \otimes \mathbf{s}_{diff} = (0.0, 0.0, 0.0)$. This means that a red surface cannot reflect blue light. □

4.3.2   Specular Component

While the purpose of the diffuse component is to catch the behavior of matte surfaces, the purpose of the specular component is to make a surface look shiny by creating highlights. Highlights help the viewer understand the surface's curvature, as well as determine the direction and locations of light sources [287]. The effect of using highlights is shown in Figure 4.7. One model used in hardware graphics to simulate the effects of highlights is expressed in Equation 4.4, where $\mathbf{v}$ is the vector from the surface point $\mathbf{p}$ to the viewer, and $\mathbf{r}$ is the reflection of light vector $\mathbf{l}$ around the normal $\mathbf{n}$.

$$i_{spec} = (\mathbf{r} \cdot \mathbf{v})^{m_{shi}} = (\cos \rho)^{m_{shi}} \tag{4.4}$$

Figure 4.7. Left: object without specular component, i.e., without highlights. Right: object with highlights.

---

[1] What follows is a simplified way of discussing color. See Section 6.2 for the wavelength-based approach.

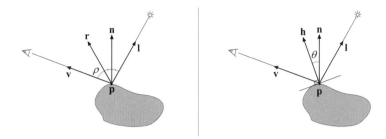

Figure 4.8. This figure shows the geometry for the two different specular lighting equations described in the text. In the left illustration, the light vector $\mathbf{l}$ is reflected around $\mathbf{n}$, which yields the reflection vector $\mathbf{r}$. The formula for the specular attenuation factor is then $(\mathbf{r} \cdot \mathbf{v})^{m_{shi}}$, which is dependent on the view vector $\mathbf{v}$ from the point $\mathbf{p}$ to the viewer. The right figure shows the geometry for another specular lighting equation. There, the half vector is $\mathbf{h} = (\mathbf{l} + \mathbf{v})/\|\mathbf{l} + \mathbf{v}\|$, and the specular attenuation factor is instead $(\mathbf{n} \cdot \mathbf{h})^{m_{shi}}$, which is also dependent on $\mathbf{v}$. OpenGL and DirectX use the specular lighting equation shown on the right.

This is called the *Phong lighting equation* [621] (not to be confused with Phong shading, which has to do with interpolating normals and lighting per pixel). It is used to describe the fact that for shiny surfaces, incident photons tend to bounce off in the reflection direction $\mathbf{r}$. In practice, Equation 4.4 means that the specular contribution gets stronger the more closely aligned the reflection vector $\mathbf{r}$ is with the view vector $\mathbf{v}$. The geometry of the specular component is depicted on the left in Figure 4.8.

The light vector, $\mathbf{l}$, is reflected around the normal, $\mathbf{n}$, which yields the reflection vector $\mathbf{r}$. This is calculated by

$$\mathbf{r} = 2(\mathbf{n} \cdot \mathbf{l})\mathbf{n} - \mathbf{l}, \qquad (4.5)$$

where $\mathbf{l}$ and $\mathbf{n}$ are assumed to be normalized, and therefore $\mathbf{r}$ is normalized too. If $\mathbf{n} \cdot \mathbf{l} < 0$, then the surface faces away from the light and a highlight normally is not computed. The reflection vector geometry is shown in Figure 4.9.

Turning back to Equation 4.4, we see that this term is at maximum when $\mathbf{r}$ and $\mathbf{v}$ are equal, which means that if we look at a surface and the reflection vector of a light source points directly back at us, then the specular component is maximized, and thus produces a highlight there. As the angle between the viewer and the reflection direction increases, the specular component drops off. While the diffuse term is view-independent, the specular term is view-dependent, since the highlights change position

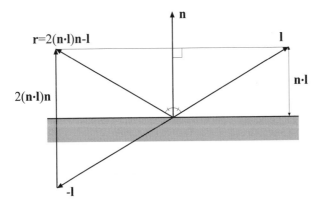

Figure 4.9. This figure shows how the reflection vector **r** can be computed using simple linear algebra. The light vector **l** is reflected around the normal **n** in order to generate **r**. First, **l** is projected onto **n**, and we get a scaled version of the normal: $(\mathbf{n} \cdot \mathbf{l})\mathbf{n}$. Then **l** is negated, and if we add two times the projection vector, the reflection vector is obtained: $\mathbf{r} = 2(\mathbf{n} \cdot \mathbf{l})\mathbf{n} - \mathbf{l}$.

on the surface if the viewer moves. A popular variation of Equation 4.4 was first presented by Blinn [69]:

$$i_{spec} = (\mathbf{n} \cdot \mathbf{h})^{m_{shi}} = (\cos \theta)^{m_{shi}}, \qquad (4.6)$$

where **h** is the normalized half vector between **l** and **v**:

$$\mathbf{h} = \frac{\mathbf{l} + \mathbf{v}}{||\mathbf{l} + \mathbf{v}||}. \qquad (4.7)$$

This geometry is depicted in the right part of Figure 4.8. The rationale behind Equation 4.6 is that **h** is the normal of the plane through the point **p** that reflects the light from the light source (which comes from direction **l**) perfectly into the eye of the viewer, i.e., the camera. So the term $\mathbf{n} \cdot \mathbf{h}$ is maximized when the normal **n** at **p** coincides with the half-vector **h**. The factor $\mathbf{n} \cdot \mathbf{h}$ decreases when the angle between **n** and **h** increases. One reason to use this equation is so that the underlying API does not need to compute a reflection vector, and so can be faster. If a directional light and an orthographic (parallel) view is used (or if a nonlocal viewer is used— see Section 10.3.2), then the light direction and view direction are both constants, and **h** is then constant for the entire scene.

The approximate relationship between these two kinds of specular lighting is shown below [232].

$$(\mathbf{r} \cdot \mathbf{v})^{m_{shi}} \approx (\mathbf{n} \cdot \mathbf{h})^{4m_{shi}} \qquad (4.8)$$

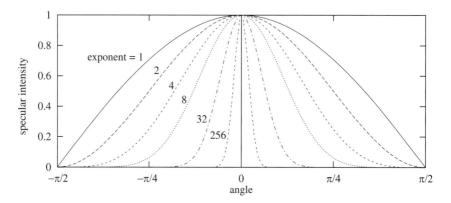

Figure 4.10. The shininess parameter, m_{shi}, raises the dot product of two vectors to a power. The dot product is the cosine of the angle between these two vectors, so for $m_{shi} = 1$ a cosine curve is produced. As m_{shi} increases, the curve is pulled in, making for a tighter highlight and a shinier impression.

As with the diffuse case, to make this equation take into account the material parameters of the surface at $\mathbf{p}$ as well as the light source parameters, the specular attenuation factor from Equation 4.6 is multiplied with the color vector $\mathbf{m}_{spec} \otimes \mathbf{s}_{spec}$, which describes the photons from a light source that could be specularly reflected off a surface with the material parameter $\mathbf{m}_{spec}$. In this way, Equation 4.9 is obtained. OpenGL and Direct3D implementations use this formula.

$$\mathbf{i}_{spec} = (\mathbf{n} \cdot \mathbf{h})^{m_{shi}} \mathbf{m}_{spec} \otimes \mathbf{s}_{spec} \qquad (4.9)$$

If the angle between $\mathbf{n}$ and $\mathbf{h}$ is greater than $\pi/2$, then the specular contribution is zero. This is expressed in the equation below.

$$\mathbf{i}_{spec} = \max((\mathbf{n} \cdot \mathbf{h}), 0)^{m_{shi}} \mathbf{m}_{spec} \otimes \mathbf{s}_{spec} \qquad (4.10)$$

Also, as with the diffuse contribution, if $\mathbf{n} \cdot \mathbf{l}$ is less than zero (i.e., the light is below the surface), then the specular term is zero. The parameter m_{shi} describes the *shininess* of the surface—the greater m_{shi}, the more shiny the surface appears. Figure 4.10 shows how increasing m_{shi} has the effect of narrowing the area in which the highlight is rendered.

Using m_{shi} to raise the contribution to a power is just one way of controlling the way in which reflected intensity drops off. Phong's illumination model has little physical validity; it just looks reasonable under most circumstances. See Figure 4.11 for an example of a situation in which the Phong model looks unrealistic when per-pixel shading is used [821].

Figure 4.11. When the shininess component, m_{shi}, is low and the light is beyond the object, Phong highlighting can produce artifacts as the shading algorithm improves. Here the shininess is about 7, and $\mathbf{n} \cdot \mathbf{h}$ Phong/Blinn highlighting is used, with two light sources. On the left is a Gouraud shaded sphere with little tessellation. In the middle the Gouraud shaded sphere is highly tessellated. On the right, the sphere is per-pixel shaded, with an unnatural line the most visible. This occurs because $\mathbf{n} \cdot \mathbf{l}$ goes to less than zero at this silhouette edge, so i_{spec} suddenly drops to zero.

It is perfectly reasonable to use other specular highlight functions. For example, Schlick [685] gives an alternate approximation to Phong's equation that is normally faster to compute. Using the terminology from Equation 4.4, Schlick's approximation is:

$$t = \cos \rho,$$

$$\mathbf{i}_{spec} = \frac{t}{m_{shi} - tm_{shi} + t} \mathbf{m}_{spec} \otimes \mathbf{s}_{spec}. \tag{4.11}$$

More physically based terms can be added to the basic specular equation. Blinn uses microfacets (tiny angled surfaces to simulate roughness, treated statistically) to include a term for self-shadowing and masking of the surface [69, 265, 316, 793]. That is, as light comes in or the surface is viewed at a shallow angle, the bumpiness of the surface itself can block light from getting to the eye. Other physically based factors, such as the Fresnel reflectance, can also be included in the specular equation [50, 345]. These topics are covered in Chapter 6).

An example of a simple function that is considerably different from the standard model is:

$$\mathbf{i}_{spec} = \lceil \max(\mathbf{n} \cdot \mathbf{h}, 0) - t \rceil \mathbf{m}_{spec} \otimes \mathbf{s}_{spec} \tag{4.12}$$

where t is some threshold value. That is, if $\max(\mathbf{n} \cdot \mathbf{h}, 0)$ is greater than t, use 1, else use 0 as the multiplier. Two examples are shown in Figure 4.12. This equation gives a specular highlight that gives the appearance of an area

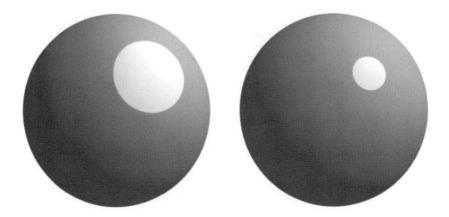

Figure 4.12. The specular formula from Equation 4.12 is used for these examples. The left image uses $t = 0.35$, while the right uses $t = 0.7$.

light reflected on a mirror surface. In this case, t affects the apparent size of the light being reflected. The light reflection gives a uniformly bright spot. This sort of function is more useful when doing per-pixel shading (since Gouraud shading will not show the sharp fall-off to 0), but almost no graphics hardware directly supports such shading. However, as will be discussed in Section 5.7.4, we can use environment mapping to give similar, arbitrarily complex specular effects.

4.3.3   Ambient Component

In our simple lighting model, lights shine directly on surfaces, but nothing else does. In contrast, in the real world, light emanating from a light source might bounce off a wall and then reach an object. The light from the wall would not be accounted for in either the diffuse or the specular component. See Sections 6.4.2 and 6.13.1 for techniques that do account for such illumination. To attempt to simulate this indirect lighting, the lighting model includes the ambient term, which is usually just some combination of material and light constants, as shown in Equation 4.13.

$$\mathbf{i}_{amb} = \mathbf{m}_{amb} \otimes \mathbf{s}_{amb} \qquad (4.13)$$

Adding this constant term means that an object will receive some minimum amount of color, even if not directly illuminated. In this way, surfaces facing away from a light will not appear entirely black.

Most APIs support a global ambient value, as is discussed in the next section. OpenGL also supports an ambient value per light, so when a light is turned off, its ambient contribution automatically is removed.

Using an ambient term as the only method of illuminating surfaces that face away from all lights is often found to be unacceptable. Such areas are all given the same color, and the three-dimensional effect is lost. A better approach is to implement some form of *fill lighting*, to simulate light from the sky or reflected from other objects [63]. One solution is to make sure objects all receive at least a little direct illumination by strategically placing lights in a scene. Another common technique is to use a *headlight* [781], which is a point light attached to the viewer's location. As the viewer moves, so does the light, and the light provides all surfaces with varying degrees of brightness. The specular component of the fill light is sometimes turned off to make it less distracting.

4.3.4 Lighting Equation

In this section, the total lighting equation will be put together step–by–step. This equation determines how light sources interact with the material parameters of an object, and thus, it also (partly) determines the colors of the pixels that a particular object occupies on the screen.

This lighting model is a *local lighting model*, which means that the lighting depends only on light from light sources, not light from other surfaces. From the preceding sections, it could be guessed that the lighting is determined by the ambient, diffuse, and specular components. In fact, the total lighting intensity, called $\mathbf{i}_{tot}$, is the sum of those components, as shown in Equation 4.14 and illustrated in Figure 4.13.

$$\mathbf{i}_{tot} = \mathbf{i}_{amb} + \mathbf{i}_{diff} + \mathbf{i}_{spec} \tag{4.14}$$

Figure 4.13. The basic lighting equation is illustrated for a teapot by adding (from the left) the ambient, the diffuse, and the specular components. The resulting lighting is shown at the right. *(Tea cup model is reused courtesy of Joachim Helenklaken.)*

The way in which the lighting changes when varying material parameters is shown in Plate IV (following page 274).

Now, light intensity in the real world is inversely proportional to the square of the distance from the light source, and this kind of attenuation has not been taken into account yet. This attenuation holds only for positional light sources, and only the diffuse and specular component are affected by it. To give us some more parameters to play with, the following formula is often used to control attenuation by distance.

$$d = \frac{1}{s_c + s_l||\mathbf{s}_{pos} - \mathbf{p}|| + s_q||\mathbf{s}_{pos} - \mathbf{p}||^2} \qquad (4.15)$$

Here, $||\mathbf{s}_{pos} - \mathbf{p}||$ is the distance from the light source position, $\mathbf{s}_{pos}$, to the point $\mathbf{p}$ that is to be shaded; s_c is a term that controls *constant* attenuation; s_l controls *linear* attenuation; and s_q controls *quadratic* attenuation. For physically correct distance attenuation, set $s_c = 0$, $s_l = 0$, and $s_q = 1$. Equation 4.16 modifies Equation 4.14 in order to take the distance attenuation into account.

$$\mathbf{i}_{tot} = \mathbf{i}_{amb} + d(\mathbf{i}_{diff} + \mathbf{i}_{spec}) \qquad (4.16)$$

Figure 4.2 on page 68 shows how a spotlight illuminates the scene in a different way. A factor denoted c_{spot} is used to represent this effect. If the vertex that is about to be shaded is outside the spotlight cone, then $c_{spot} = 0$, which means that the light rays from the spotlight does not reach that vertex. If the vertex is inside the cone, then the following formula is used:

$$c_{spot} = \max(-\mathbf{l} \cdot \mathbf{s}_{dir}, 0)^{s_{exp}}. \qquad (4.17)$$

Here, $\mathbf{l}$ is the light vector, $\mathbf{s}_{dir}$ is the direction of the spotlight (i.e., a vector that points from the light source position along the center line of the spotlight cone), and s_{exp} is an exponentiation factor used to control the fall-off from the center of the spotlight. All vectors are assumed to be normalized. If the light source is not a spotlight, then $c_{spot} = 1$. The modified lighting equation is shown below.

$$\mathbf{i}_{tot} = c_{spot}(\mathbf{i}_{amb} + d(\mathbf{i}_{diff} + \mathbf{i}_{spec})) \qquad (4.18)$$

Spotlights in Direct3D are specified differently, with an inner and outer cone angle. Light is the same intensity up to the border of the inner cone's area, falling off to darkness at the edge of the outer cone. The way the light falls off from the inner to outer cone is typically linear, but can be modified.

As discussed in Section 4.2, the material has an emissive parameter called $\mathbf{m}_{emi}$. This is another ad-hoc parameter. It describes how much light a surface emits. Note that other surfaces are not affected by this light emission; it is essentially a method for adding a solid color to a surface without having the lighting affect it.

In OpenGL, Direct3D, and most other APIs, there is also a global ambient light source parameter, $\mathbf{a}_{glob}$, that approximates a constant background light coming from everywhere. It is componentwise multiplied with the ambient material parameter, $\mathbf{m}_{amb}$. The incorporation of these parameters into the lighting equation is shown in Equation 4.19, and as can be seen, the new parameters are simply added to the original lighting equation.

$$\mathbf{i}_{tot} = \mathbf{a}_{glob} \otimes \mathbf{m}_{amb} + \mathbf{m}_{emi} + c_{spot}(\mathbf{i}_{amb} + d(\mathbf{i}_{diff} + \mathbf{i}_{spec})) \qquad (4.19)$$

This equation applies only when *one* light source is used. Say that there are n light sources, each identified by an index k (superscript). The lighting equation for multiple light sources is shown in Equation 4.20.

$$\mathbf{i}_{tot} = \mathbf{a}_{glob} \otimes \mathbf{m}_{amb} + \mathbf{m}_{emi} + \sum_{k=1}^{n} c_{spot}^k(\mathbf{i}_{amb}^k + d^k(\mathbf{i}_{diff}^k + \mathbf{i}_{spec}^k))$$

$$= \mathbf{a}_{glob} \otimes \mathbf{m}_{amb} + \mathbf{m}_{emi}$$

$$+ \sum_{k=1}^{n} \max(-\mathbf{l}^k \cdot \mathbf{s}_{dir}^k, 0)^{s_{exp}^k} \Big(\mathbf{m}_{amb} \otimes \mathbf{s}_{amb}^k$$

$$+ \frac{\max((\mathbf{n} \cdot \mathbf{l}^k), 0)\mathbf{m}_{diff} \otimes \mathbf{s}_{diff}^k + \max((\mathbf{n} \cdot \mathbf{h}^k), 0)^{m_{shi}}\mathbf{m}_{spec} \otimes \mathbf{s}_{spec}^k}{s_c^k + s_l^k||\mathbf{s}_{pos}^k - \mathbf{p}|| + s_q^k||\mathbf{s}_{pos}^k - \mathbf{p}||^2} \Big)$$

$$(4.20)$$

Lighting computations usually take more time with an increasing number of light sources. Also, the sum of light source intensity contributions may be greater than 1, and the resulting lighting color is usually clamped to $[0, 1]$ when rendered. However, clamping overflow can result in color shifts. To avoid this problem, some systems scale overflowing color by the largest component. There are also even more elaborate systems, such as limiting how much any given component (diffuse, specular, etc.) can contribute to the total color.

EXAMPLE: CLAMPING VERSUS SCALING Due to lighting and materials that were too bright, a bright orange of $(2.5, 1.5, 0.5)$ is computed. It will turn into yellow, $(1.0, 1.0, 0.5)$, when clamped to the range $[0, 1]$. By instead scaling the original color by $1/2.5$, we can change the color displayed to $(1.0, 0.6, 0.2)$, maintaining the original orange hue and saturation. □

Overflows often cause the loss of geometric detail, as the entire overflow area takes on the same color. Having the same color results in the visual effect of flatness. A similar problem when using bump mapping [70] is that bumpy surfaces with too much light will lose their bumps, as the darker and brighter areas will all have the same shade. The best solution to the problem is simply to avoid creating lighting that is too bright.

4.4 Aliasing and Antialiasing

Imagine a large black triangle moving slowly across a white background. As a screen grid cell is covered by the triangle, the pixel value representing this cell should smoothly drop in intensity. What actually happens is that the moment the grid cell's center is covered, the pixel color immediately goes from white to black. See the leftmost column of Figure 4.14.

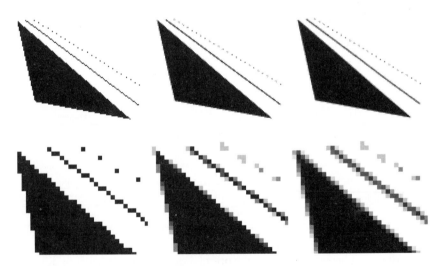

Figure 4.14. The upper row shows three images with different levels of antialiasing of a triangle, a line, and some points. The lower row images are magnifications of the upper row. The leftmost column uses only one sample per pixel, which means that no antialiasing is used. The middle column images were rendered with four samples per pixel (in a grid pattern), and the right column used eight samples per pixel (in a 4 × 4 checkerboard). All images were rendered using InfiniteReality graphics [568].

This, in fact, is precisely how most hardware-accelerated real-time rendering takes place by default. Polygons show up in pixels as either there or not there. Lines drawn have a similar problem. The edges have a jagged look because of this, and so this visual artifact is called "the jaggies," that turn into "the crawlies" when animated. More formally, this problem is called *aliasing*, and efforts to avoid it are called *antialiasing* techniques.[2]

The subject of sampling theory and digital filtering is large enough to fill a book [277, 636, 813]. As this is a key area of rendering, the basic theory of sampling and filtering will be presented. Then, we will focus on what currently can be done in real time to alleviate aliasing artifacts.

4.4.1 Sampling and Filtering Theory

The process of rendering of images is inherently a sampling task. This is so since the generation of an image is the process of sampling a three-dimensional scene in order to obtain color values for each pixel in the image (an array of discrete pixels). To use texture mapping (see Chapter 5), texels have to be resampled to get good results under varying conditions. To generate a sequence of images in an animation, the animation is often sampled at uniform time intervals. This section is an introduction to the topic of sampling, reconstruction, and filtering. For simplicity, most material will be presented in one dimension. These concepts extend naturally to two dimensions as well, and can thus be used when handling two-dimensional images.

Figure 4.15 shows how a continuous signal is being sampled at uniformly spaced intervals, that is, discretized. The goal of this *sampling* process is

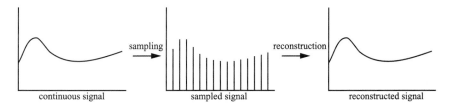

Figure 4.15. A continuous signal (left) is sampled (middle), and then the original signal is recovered by reconstruction (right).

---

[2]Another way to view this problem is that the jaggies are not actually due to aliasing—it is only that the edges are "forced" into the grid formed by the pixels [793, 795].

Figure 4.16. The top row shows a spinning wheel. This is inadequately sampled in the bottom row, making it appear to move in the opposite direction. This is an example of aliasing due to a too low sampling rate.

to represent information digitally. In doing so, the amount of information is reduced. However, the sampled signal needs to be *reconstructed* in order to recover the original signal. This is done by *filtering* the sampled signal.

Whenever sampling is done, aliasing may occur. This is an unwanted artifact, and we need to battle aliasing in order to generate pleasing images. In real life, a classic example of aliasing is a spinning wheel being filmed by a movie camera [260]. Because the wheel spins much faster than the camera records images, the wheel may appear to be spinning slowly (backwards or forwards), or may even look like it is not rotating at all. This can be seen in Figure 4.16. The effect occurs because the images of the wheel are taken in a series of time steps, and so is called *temporal aliasing*. Common examples of aliasing in computer graphics are the "jaggies" of a rasterized line, and when a texture with a checker pattern is minified (see Section 5.2.2).

Aliasing occurs when a signal is being sampled at too low a frequency. The sampled signal then appears to be a signal of lower frequency than the original. This is illustrated in Figure 4.17. For a signal to be sampled prop-

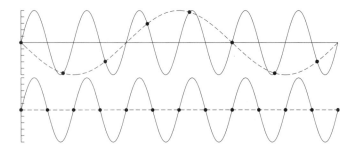

Figure 4.17. The solid line is the original signal, the circles indicate uniformly spaced sample points, and the dashed line is the reconstructed signal. The top figure shows a too low sample rate. Therefore, the reconstructed signal appears to be of lower frequency. The bottom shows a sampling rate of exactly twice the frequency of the original signal, and the reconstructed signal is here a horizontal line. It can be proven that if the sampling rate is increased ever so slightly, perfect reconstruction is possible.

erly (i.e., so that it is possible to reconstruct the original signal from the samples), the sampling frequency has to be more than twice the maximum frequency of the signal to be sampled. This is often called the *sampling theorem*, and the sampling frequency is called the *Nyquist*[3] *rate* [636, 813] or *Nyquist limit* [795]. The fact that the theorem uses the term "maximum frequency" implies that the signal has to be *bandlimited*, which simply means that there are not any frequency content above a certain frequency. Put another way, the signal has to be smooth enough relative to the spacing between neighboring samples.

A three-dimensional scene is normally never bandlimited when rendered with point samples. Edges of polygons, shadow boundaries, and other phenomena produce a signal that changes discontinuously and so produces frequencies that are essentially infinite. Also, no matter how closely packed the samples are, objects can still be small enough that they do not get sampled at all. Thus, it is impossible to entirely avoid aliasing problems when using point samples to render a scene. However, at times it is possible to know when a signal is bandlimited. One example is when a texture is applied to a surface. It is possible to compute the frequency of the texture samples compared to the sampling rate of the pixel. If this frequency is lower than the Nyquist limit, then no special action is needed to properly sample the texture. If the frequency is too high, then schemes to bandlimit the texture are used (see Section 5.2.2).

Reconstruction

Given that a bandlimited signal has been sampled, we will now discuss how the original signal can be reconstructed from the sampled signal. To do this, a filter can be used. Three commonly used filters are shown in Figure 4.18. Note that the area of the filter should always be one, otherwise the signal can appear to grow or shrink.

In Figure 4.19, the box filter (nearest neighbor) is used to reconstruct a sampled signal. This is the worst filter to use, as the resulting signal is a noncontinuous stair case. Still, it is often used in computer graphics because of its simplicity. As can be seen in the illustration, the box filter is placed over each sample point, and then scaled so that the topmost point of the filter coincides with the sample point. The sum of all these scaled and translated box functions is the reconstructed signal shown to the right.

The box filter can be replaced with any other filter. In Figure 4.20, the tent filter, also called the triangle filter, is used to reconstruct a sampled signal. Note that this filter implements linear interpolation between

---

[3] After Harry Nyquist [1889-1976], Swedish scientist, who discovered this in 1928.

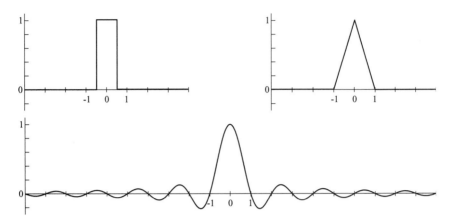

Figure 4.18. The top left shows the box filter, and the top right the tent filter. The bottom shows the sinc filter (which has been clamped on the x-axis here).

neighboring sample points, and so it is better than the box filter, as the reconstructed signal now is continuous.

However, the smoothness of the reconstructed signal using a tent filter is not very good; there are sudden slope changes at the sample points. This has to do with the fact that the tent filter is not a perfect reconstruction filter. To get perfect reconstruction the ideal lowpass filter has to be used.

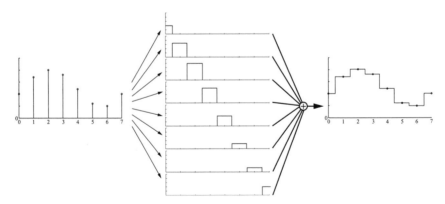

Figure 4.19. The sampled signal (left) is reconstructed using the box filter. This is done by placing the box filter (see Figure 4.18) over each sample point, and scaling it in the y-direction so that the height of the filter is the same as the sample point. The sum is the reconstruction signal (right).

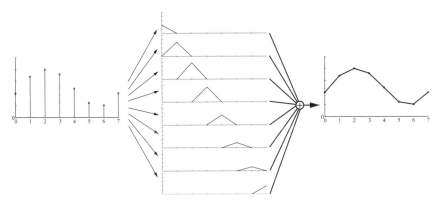

Figure 4.20. The sampled signal (left) is reconstructed using the tent filter. The reconstructed signal is shown to the right.

A frequency component of a signal is a sine wave: $\sin(2\pi f)$, where f is the frequency of that component. Given this, a lowpass filter removes all frequency components with frequencies higher than a certain frequency defined by the filter. Intuitively, the lowpass filter removes sharp features of the signal, i.e., the filter blurs it. The ideal lowpass filter is the sinc filter (Figure 4.18 bottom):

$$\text{sinc}(x) = \frac{\sin(\pi x)}{\pi x}. \tag{4.21}$$

Using the sinc filter to reconstruct the signal gives a smoother result, as shown in Figure 4.21. The reasons why an ideal lowpass filter must be used, and why the sinc filter is ideal, are buried in the theory of Fourier analysis [636].[4] What can be seen is that the sampling process in Figure 4.15 introduces high frequency components (abrupt changes) in the signal, and the task of the lowpass filter is to remove these. In fact, the sinc filter eliminates all sine waves with frequencies higher than $1/2$ the sampling rate. The sinc function, as presented in Equation 4.21, is the perfect reconstruction filter when the sampling frequency is 1.0 (i.e., the maximum frequency of the sampled signal must be smaller than $1/2$). More generally,

---

[4]Briefly, the reason is that the ideal lowpass filter is a box filter in the frequency domain. That is, all frequencies above the width of this filter in this domain are removed. This is related to the fact that the signal in the frequency domain is multiplied with the box filter. Transforming the box filter from the frequency domain to the spatial domain gives a sinc function. At the same time, the multiplication operation is transformed into the *convolution* function, which is what we have been using in this section, without actually pointing it out.

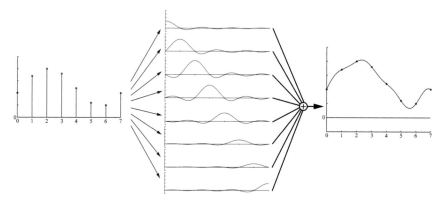

Figure 4.21. Here, the sinc filter is used to reconstruct the signal. The sinc filter is the ideal lowpass filter.

assume the sampling frequency is f_s, that is, the interval between neighboring samples is $1/f_s$. For such a case, the perfect reconstruction filter is $\text{sinc}(f_s x)$, and it eliminates all frequencies higher than $f_s/2$. This is useful when resampling the signal (next section). The filter width of the sinc is infinite and also is negative at times, so it is impractical.

After using the sinc filter, a continuous signal is obtained. However, in computer graphics we cannot use continuous signals, but we can use them to resample the continuous signal to another size, i.e., either enlarge the signal, or diminish it. This is discussed next.

Resampling

Resampling is used to magnify or minify a sampled signal. Assume that the original sample points are located at integer coordinates $(0, 1, 2, \ldots)$, that is, with unit intervals between samples. Furthermore, assume that after resampling we want the new sample points to be located uniformly with an interval a between samples. For $a > 1$, minification (downsampling) takes place, and for $a < 1$, magnification (upsampling) occurs.

Magnification is the simpler case of the two, so let us start with that. Assume the sampled signal is reconstructed as shown in the previous section. Intuitively, since the signal now is perfectly reconstructed and continuous, all that is needed is to resample the reconstructed signal at the desired intervals. This process can be seen in Figure 4.22.

However, this technique does not work when minification occurs. The frequency of the original signal is too high for the sampling rate to avoid aliasing. Instead it has been shown that a filter using $\text{sinc}(ax)$ should be

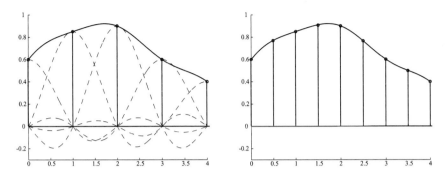

Figure 4.22. On the left is the sampled signal, and the reconstructed signal. On the right, the reconstructed signal has been resampled at half the sample rate, that is, magnification has taken place.

used to create a continuous signal from the sampled one [636, 716]. After that, resampling at the desired intervals can take place. This can be seen in Figure 4.23. Said another way, by using $sinc(ax)$ as a filter here, the width of the lowpass filter is increased, so that more of the signal's higher frequency content is removed. As shown in the figure, the filter width (of the individual sinc's) is doubled in order to decrease the resampling rate to half the original sampling rate. Relating this to a digital image, this is similar to first blurring it (to remove high frequencies) and then resampling the image at a lower resolution.

With the theory of sampling and filtering available as a framework, the various algorithms used in real-time rendering to reduce aliasing are now discussed.

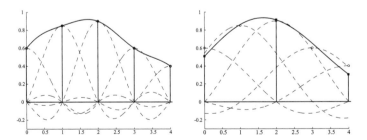

Figure 4.23. On the left is the sampled signal, and the reconstructed signal. On the right, the filter width has doubled in order to double the interval between the samples, that is, minification has taken place.

4.4.2   Screen-Based Antialiasing

Edges of polygons produce noticeable artifacts if not sampled and filtered well. Shadow boundaries, specular highlights, and other phenomena where the color is changing rapidly can cause similar problems. The algorithms discussed in this section help improve the rendering quality for these cases. They have the common thread that they are screen-based, i.e., that they operate only on the output samples of the pipeline and do not need any knowledge of the objects being rendered.

There are antialiasing schemes that are focussed on particular rendering primitives. Two special cases are texture aliasing and line aliasing. Texture antialiasing is discussed in Section 5.2.2. Line antialiasing can be performed in a number of ways. One method is to treat the line as a quadrilateral one pixel wide that is blended with its background; another is to consider it an infinitely thin, transparent object with a halo; a third is to render the line as an antialiased texture [536]. These ways of thinking about the line can be used in screen-based antialiasing schemes, but special-purpose line antialiasing hardware can provide rapid, high-quality rendering for lines. For a thorough treatment of the problem and some solutions, as well as source code on the web, see Nelson's two articles [583, 584].

In the black triangle example in Figure 4.14, one problem is the low sampling rate. A single sample is taken at the center of each pixel's grid cell, so the most that is known about the cell is whether or not the center is covered by the triangle. By using more samples per screen grid cell and blending these in some fashion, a better pixel color can be computed.[5]

The general strategy of screen-based antialiasing schemes is to use a sampling pattern for the screen and then weight and sum the samples to produce a pixel color, **p**:

$$\mathbf{p}(x, y) = \sum_{i=1}^{n} w_i \mathbf{c}(i, x, y). \qquad (4.22)$$

where n is the number of samples taken for a pixel. The function $\mathbf{c}(i, x, y)$ is a sample color and w_i is a weight, in the range $[0, 1]$, that the sample will contribute to the overall pixel color. The sample position is taken based on which sample it is in the series $1 \ldots n$, and the function optionally also uses the integer pixel location (x, y). In other words, where the sample is taken on the screen grid is different for each sample, and optionally the sampling

---

[5]Here we differentiate a pixel, which consists of an RGB color triplet to be displayed, from a screen grid cell, which is a geometric area on the screen centered around a pixel's location. See Smith's memo [717] to understand why this is important.

pattern can vary from pixel to pixel. Samples are normally point samples in real-time rendering systems (and almost all rendering systems, for that matter). So the function $\mathbf{c}$ can be thought of as two functions. First a function $\mathbf{f}(i, n)$ retrieves the floating-point (x_f, y_f) location on the screen where a sample is needed. This location on the screen is then sampled, i.e., the color at that precise point is retrieved. In practice, this process is locked in place at the beginning of the frame. The sampling scheme is chosen and the rendering pipeline configured to compute the samples at the proper subpixel locations.

The other variable in antialiasing is w_i, the weight of each sample. These weights sum to one. Except for the Quincunx algorithm, all methods used in real-time rendering systems give a constant weight to their samples, i.e., $w_i = \frac{1}{n}$. Note that the default mode for graphics hardware, a single sample at the center of the pixel, is the simplest case of the antialiasing equation above. There is only one term, the weight of this term is one, and the sampling function $\mathbf{f}$ always returns the center of the pixel being sampled.

All antialiasing algorithms that take more than one sample per pixel are called *supersampling* methods. Conceptually simplest, *Full-Scene Antialiasing* (FSAA) renders the scene at a higher resolution and then averages neighboring samples to create an image. For example, say an image of 500×400 pixels is desired. If you render an image of 1000×800 off-screen and then average each 2×2 area on the screen, the desired image is generated with 4 samples per pixel. This is a common method used in consumer level hardware. It is costly, as all subsamples must be fully shaded and filled, but has the advantage of simplicity. Other, weaker versions of this method sample at twice the rate on only one screen axis, and so are called 1×2 or 2×1 supersampling.

A related method is the *accumulation buffer* [300, 514]. Instead of one large off-screen buffer, this method uses a buffer that has the same resolution as, and usually more bits of color than, the desired image.[6]. To obtain a 2×2 sampling of a scene, 4 images are generated, with the view moved half a pixel in the screen x- or y- direction as needed. Essentially, each image generated is for a different sample position within the grid cell. These images are summed up in the accumulation buffer. After rendering, the image is averaged (in our case, divided by 4) and sent to the display. Accumulation buffers are a part of OpenGL and many hardware systems support their use [11, 808]. They can also be used for such effects as

---

[6]Even if the system does not have an accumulation buffer, one can be simulated by blending separate images together using pixel operations [558] The quality will suffer, however, because the low-order bits of each image will be lost when blending, potentially causing color banding.

motion blur, where a moving object appears blurry, and *depth of field*, where objects not at the camera focus appear blurry. However, the additional costs of having to rerender the scene a few times per frame and move the result to the screen makes this algorithm costly for real-time rendering systems.

The T-buffer is a variant of the accumulation buffer. It consists of a set of 2, 4, or more image and Z-buffers, each of which can be used for rendering. There is a mask that determines where a triangle gets sent. At the end of the pipeline is some video logic that combines the set of buffers to display a single, averaged image. So, for motion blur and depth of field, you send down each triangle a number of times, changing the mask as you change the position or view. Triangles that do not need these effects can be sent just once, to all buffers.

The T-buffer's real strength is for antialiasing. Data can be sent to all the buffers at the same time. Screen x and y offsets can be set individually for each buffer. So instead of doing multiple passes, you can send each triangle once and have it processed in parallel to the set of buffers, with each buffer having a slightly different viewing offset. Combining these images gives an antialiased image. An advantage of this approach over the accumulation buffer is that antialiasing can be done by default for existing applications without needing any programming changes, since only a single pass is needed. It is just a matter of setting the graphics driver to be in antialiasing mode. Memory is used to obtain speed: Separate buffers are needed for each view, but only one pass is needed.

An advantage that both the accumulation buffer and T-buffer have over FSAA (and over the A-buffer, which follows) is that sampling does not have to be a uniform orthogonal pattern within a pixel's grid cell. Each pass is independent of the others, so alternate sampling patterns are possible. Sampling in a rotated square pattern such as $(0, 0.25)$, $(0.5, 0)$, $(0.75, 0.5)$, $(0.25, 0.75)$ gives more vertical and horizontal resolution within the pixel. Sometimes called *Rotated Grid SuperSampling* (RGSS), this pattern gives more levels of antialiasing for nearly vertical or horizontal edges, which usually are most in need of improvement. Figure 4.24 shows how the sampling pattern affects quality.

Another algorithm that is used to increase the sampling rate per pixel is Carpenter's A-buffer [113], sometimes called *multisampling*. This algorithm is commonly used in software for generating high-quality renderings, but at noninteractive speeds. Instead of rendering at a higher resolution or using multiple passes, the A-buffer computes a polygon's approximate coverage of each grid cell. A multisampling algorithm, in general, is one that takes more than one sample per pixel in a single pass, and (unlike FSAA and

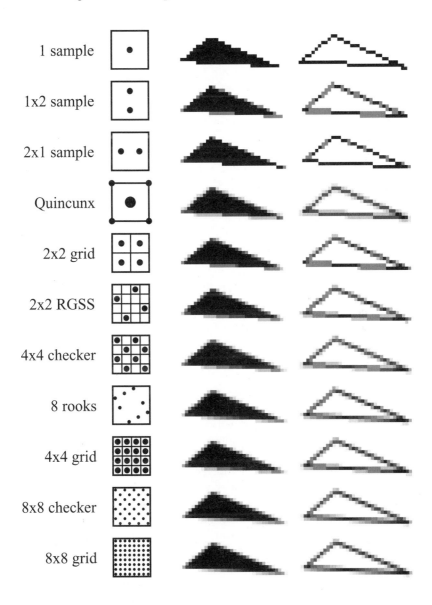

Figure 4.24. A comparison of various pixel sampling schemes. The Quincunx scheme needs an average of two samples per pixel, as the corner samples are divided evenly among the four neighboring pixels. The 2 × 2 rotated grid captures more gray levels for the nearly horizontal edge than a straight 2 × 2 grid. Similarly, the 8 rooks pattern captures more gray levels for such lines than a 4 × 4 grid, despite using fewer samples.

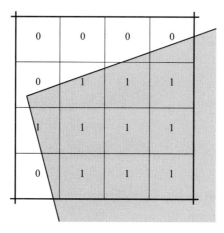

Figure 4.25. The corner of a polygon partially covers a single screen grid cell associated with a pixel. The grid cell is shown subdivided into a 4×4 subgrid and those cells that are considered covered are marked by a 1. The 16-bit mask for this cell, read from left to right and top to bottom, is 0000 0111 1111 0111.

the accumulation and T-buffer) shares computations among the samples for a grid cell. In the case of a hardware A-buffer, the lighting values are typically computed once per surface for the grid cell and shared by all the surface's samples. This lower rate of illumination sampling helps save on computation cost, but means that antialiasing of textures and shadows cannot be performed by the basic A-buffer. The A-buffer's focus is on edge antialiasing and properly rendering transparency (see Section 4.5).

In the A-buffer, each polygon rendered creates a *coverage mask* for each screen grid cell it fully or partially covers. See Figure 4.25 for an example of a coverage mask. The shade for the polygon associated with this coverage mask is (typically) computed as its shade at the center of the grid cell. The z-depth is also computed at the center. Some systems compute a pair of depths, a minimum and maximum. Others also retain the slope of the polygon, so that the exact z-depth can be exactly derived at any subgrid location, which allows interpenetrating polygons (i.e., fragments that pierce one another) to be rendered properly [397]. The coverage mask, shade, z-depth, and other information make up a *fragment*.

A screen grid cell can have any number of fragments. As they collect, fragments can be discarded if they are hidden. For example, if an opaque fragment A has a coverage mask that fully covers fragment B, and fragment A has a maximum z-depth less than the minimum z-depth of B, then fragment B can be safely discarded. Coverage masks can also be merged and used together. For example, if one opaque fragment covers one part of a pixel and another opaque fragment another, their masks can be logically OR:ed together and the larger of their maximum z-depths used to form a larger area of coverage. Because of this merging mechanism, fragments are often sorted by z-depth. Depending on the design, such merging can happen when a fragment buffer becomes filled or as a final step before shading and display.

Once all polygons have been sent to the A-buffer, the color to be stored in the pixel is computed. This is done by determining how much of the mask of each fragment is visible, and then multiplying this percentage by the fragment's color and summing the results. See Figure 4.14 for an example of multisampling hardware in use. Transparency effects, one of the A-buffer's strengths, are also folded in at this time.

Though this sounds like an involved procedure, many of the mechanisms for rendering a triangle into a Z-buffer can be reused to implement the A-buffer in hardware [808]. Storage requirements are certainly much lower than for the high-resolution technique, and the procedure requires far fewer passes than the accumulation buffer technique. The overall processing power necessary is less than in either previous method, as shading and z-depth computations are done only once for each pixel that a polygon covers. See Mammen [514], Schilling & Straßer [681], Winner et al. [808], Jouppi & Chang [397], and Waller et al. [787] for more on hardware implementations of this class of algorithms.

Another approach from Matrox performs an A-buffer algorithm, storing a list of Z-sorted fragments with 4x4 masks per edge pixel. It conserves memory by creating and linking in fragments as needed, i.e., only when an edge crosses a pixel. This is in comparison to previous hardware schemes that must allocate space for all the fragments in advance. This hardware solution does not have enough depth to perform transparency ordering, but does provide a high quality solution for edge antialiasing.

While all of these antialiasing methods result in better approximations of how each polygon covers a grid cell, they have some limitations. One limit is simply the size of the coverage mask. Even at 8×8 (64 bits), aliasing can still be visible for edges that are nearly horizontal or vertical. This is because with such edges there are effectively 9 levels of coverage (i.e., 0 bits, 8 bits, ..., 64 bits) that are used the most, versus 65 levels for an arbitrary edge. Horizontal and vertical edges turn a two-dimensional sampling pattern into a one-dimensional sampler, so losing resolution.

Another limitation is that a box filter is often used for simplicity in combining the samples. Box filtering means adding up the samples in a grid cell without regard for position, and with samples in one cell having no effect on the color of other, neighboring pixels. As discussed in the previous section, this is a terrible filter but it will be with us for a long time because of its simplicity. The sinc filter was presented as the ideal filter, but a problem with it is that it goes off into infinity. The box filter treats the pixel as a little square. It is important to keep in mind that a pixel is actually not a little square [717], and that samples outside the pixel's grid cell can (and should) influence the pixel's color.

There are a wide range of practical filters that allow samples to affect more than one pixel that are used for higher-quality reconstruction of samples on a screen and of a texture [813]. All of these filter functions have some approximation to the sinc function, but with a limit on how many pixels they influence, and no negative lobes. Sometimes these filters are referred to generically as Gaussian filters, as many of them are based on some form of the Gaussian (bell curve) equation when computing them. Some workstations support the OpenGL 1.2 Imaging Subset in hardware, making some digital filtering effects directly available.

One real-time antialiasing scheme that lets samples affect more than one pixel is NVIDIA's Quincunx method [591], also called *High Resolution Antialiasing* (HRAA). "Quincunx" means an arrangement of five objects, four in a square and the fifth in the center, such as the pattern of five dots on a six-sided die. In this multisampling antialiasing scheme, the sampling pattern is a quincunx, with four samples at the pixel cell's corners and one sample in the center (see Figure 4.24). Each corner sample value is distributed to its four neighboring pixels. So instead of weighting each sample equally (as most other real-time schemes do), the center sample is given a weight of $\frac{1}{2}$, and each corner sample has a weight of $\frac{1}{8}$. Because of this sharing, an average of only two samples are needed per pixel for the Quincunx scheme, and the results are considerably better than 2 sample FSAA methods. This pattern approximates a two-dimensional tent filter, which, as discussed in the previous section, is superior to the box filter. One important feature of all filters is something also mentioned in the previous section: All samples are given the same overall effect on the image. The Quincunx scheme fulfills this requirement, as the corner samples influence four pixels at one-fourth the strength that center samples have on only one pixel. The extra samples needed are generated just before storing the result in the frame buffer, so eliminating fill rate costs. Also, texels are fetched only once per fragment instead of for each sample, so reducing memory bandwidth costs. This sharing introduces some error, however, as the texel sample is taken at the center of the pixel and shared with the northwest corner sample. NVIDIA's Accuview technology, introduced with the GeForce4, reduces overall error by shifting both the Quincunx pattern and the texel sample's location [592]. Accuview also includes a new sampling mode called "4xS," though information is sparse as to what exactly this mode does.

A final factor that leads to poor antialiasing is a lack of gamma correction. Edges of polygons often look as if they represent twisted rope instead of straight lines. This problem is discussed in Section 4.7.

As discussed in the previous section, a scene can be made of objects that are arbitrarily small on the screen, meaning that no sampling rate can ever perfectly capture them. So, a regular sampling pattern will always exhibit some form of aliasing. One approach to avoiding aliasing is to distribute the samples randomly over the pixel, with a different sampling pattern at each pixel. This is called *stochastic sampling*, and the reason it works better is that the randomization tends to replace repetitive aliasing effects with noise, to which the human visual system is much more forgiving [260].

The most common kind of stochastic sampling is *jittering*, a form of *stratified sampling*, which works as follows. Assume that n samples are to be used for a pixel. Divide the pixel area into n regions of equal area, and place each sample at a random location in one of these regions.[7] See Figure 4.26. The final pixel color is computed by some averaged mean of the samples. N-rooks sampling is another form of stratified sampling, in which n samples are placed in an $n \times n$ grid, with one sample per row and column [704]. Incidently, a form of N-rooks pattern is used in the InfiniteReality [397, 568] (see Section 15.3.7), as it is particularly good for capturing nearly horizontal and vertical edges. For this architecture, the same pattern is used per pixel and is subpixel-centered (not randomized within the subpixel), so it is not performing stochastic sampling.

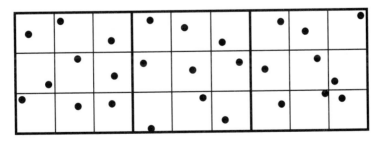

Figure 4.26. A typical jitter pattern for three pixels, each divided into a 3 × 3 set of subcells. One sample appears in each subcell, in a random location.

---

[7]This is in contrast to accumulation buffer screen offsets, which can allow random sampling of a sort, but each pixel has the same sampling pattern.

The SuperScene hardware antialiasing scheme from 3Dlabs [1] uses jittered sample patterns per pixel. This is significant, as normally in real-time hardware, a single sampling pattern is used for all pixels. Details are sketchy, but its multisampling method appears to be related to the *A*-buffer, and allows up to 16 samples per pixel. Dynamic sample allocation is done depending on the number of objects overlapping a pixel, meaning that less memory is needed overall.

AT&T Pixel Machines and Silicon Graphics' VGX, and more recently ATI's SMOOTHVISION scheme, use a technique called *interleaved sampling*. In ATI's version, the antialiasing hardware allows up to 16 samples per pixel, and up to 16 different user-defined sampling patterns that can be intermingled in a repeating pattern (e.g., in a 4×4 pixel tile, with a different pattern in each). The sampling pattern is not different for every pixel cell, as is done with a pure jittering scheme. However, Molnar [564], as well as Keller and Heidrich [415], found that using interleaved stochastic sampling minimizes the aliasing artifacts formed when using the same pattern for every pixel. See Figure 4.27. This technique can be thought of as a generalization of the accumulation buffer technique, as the sampling pattern repeats, but spans several pixels instead of a single pixel.

There are still other methods of sampling and filtering. One of the best sampling patterns known is *Poisson disk sampling*, in which nonuniformly distributed points are separated by a minimum distance [141, 179]. Molnar presents a scheme for real-time rendering in which unweighted samples are arranged in a Poisson disk pattern with a Gaussian filtering kernel [564].

Molnar also presents a sampling pattern for performing adaptive refinement [57]. This is a technique where the image improves over time by increasing the number of samples taken. This scheme is useful in interactive applications. For example, while the scene is changing, the sampling

Figure 4.27. On the left, antialiasing with the accumulation buffer, with four samples per pixel. The repeating pattern gives noticeable problems. On the right, the sampling pattern is not the same at each pixel, but instead patterns are interleaved. *(Images courtesy of Alexander Keller and Wolfgang Heidrich.)*

rate is kept low; when the user stops interacting and the scene is static, the image improves over time by having more and more samples taken and the intermediate results displayed. This scheme can be implemented using an accumulation buffer that is displayed after certain numbers of samples have been taken.

In summary, there are a wide range of schemes for antialiasing edges, with tradeoffs of speed, quality, and manufacturing cost. No solution is perfect, nor can it be, but hardware-supported methods such as the Quincunx algorithm offer a reasonable answer at relatively little extra cost, and jittered multisampling gives an even higher quality result by breaking up pattern repetition. Undoubtedly, graphics accelerators will offer even better sampling and filtering schemes as time goes on.

4.5 Transparency, Alpha, and Compositing

Transparency effects in real-time rendering systems are relatively simplistic and limited. Effects normally unavailable include the bending of light (refraction), attenuation of light due to the thickness of the transparent object, and reflectivity and transmission changes due to the viewing angle, to name a few. That said, a little transparency is better than none at all, and real-time systems do provide the ability to render a surface as semi-transparent, blending its color with the object behind it. It turns out that this simple form of transparency is a powerful tool for a variety of techniques (see Chapter 8).

One simple method for giving the illusion of transparency is called *screen-door transparency* [575]. The idea is to render the transparent polygon with a checkerboard fill pattern. That is, every other pixel of the polygon is rendered, thereby leaving the object behind it partially visible. Usually the pixels on the screen are close enough together that the checkerboard pattern itself is not visible. The problems with this technique include:

- A transparent object can be only 50% transparent. Fill patterns other than a checkerboard can be used, but in practice these are usually discernable as shapes themselves, detracting from the transparency effect.

- Only one transparent object can be convincingly rendered on one area of the screen. For example, if a transparent red object and transparent green object are rendered atop a blue object, only two of the three colors can appear on the checkerboard pattern.

That said, one advantage of this technique is its simplicity. Transparent objects can be rendered at any time, in any order, and no special hardware (beyond fill pattern support) is needed.

What is necessary for more general and flexible transparency effects is the ability to blend the transparent object's color with the color of the object behind it. For this, the concept of *alpha blending* is needed [103, 187, 630]. When an object is rendered on the screen, an RGB color and a Z-buffer depth are associated with each pixel. Another component, called alpha (α), can also be generated and, optionally, stored. Alpha is a value describing the degree of opacity of an object for a given pixel. An alpha of 1.0 means the object is opaque and entirely covers the pixel's area of interest; 0.0 means the pixel is not obscured at all.

To make an object transparent, it is rendered on top of the existing scene with an alpha of less than 1.0. Each pixel covered by the object will receive a resulting RGBα (also called RGBA) from the rendering pipeline. Blending this value coming out of the pipeline with the original pixel color is done using the **over** operator, as follows:

$$\mathbf{c}_o = \alpha_s \mathbf{c}_s + (1 - \alpha_s)\mathbf{c}_d \quad [\textbf{over } \text{operator}]. \qquad (4.23)$$

where $\mathbf{c}_s$ is the color of the transparent object (called the *source*), α_s is the object's alpha, $\mathbf{c}_d$ is the pixel color before blending (called the *destination*), and $\mathbf{c}_o$ is the resulting color due to placing the transparent object **over** the existing scene. In the case of the rendering pipeline sending in $\mathbf{c}_s$ and α_s, the pixel's original color $\mathbf{c}_d$ gets replaced by the result $\mathbf{c}_o$. If the incoming RGBα is, in fact, opaque ($\alpha_s = 1.0$), the equation simplifies to the full replacement of pixel's color by the object's color.

To render transparent objects properly into a scene usually requires sorting. First, the opaque objects are rendered, then the transparent objects are blended on top of them in back-to-front order. Blending in arbitrary order can produce serious artifacts, because the blending equation is order-dependent. See Figure 4.28 and Plate X. The equation can also be modified so that blending front-to-back gives the same result. For the special case where only two transparent surfaces overlap and the alpha of both is 0.5, the blend order does not matter and so no sorting is needed [580]. If sorting is not possible or only partially done, it is often best to use Z-buffer testing but no z-depth replacement for rendering the transparent objects. In this way, all transparent objects will at least appear. Other techniques such as turning off culling, or rendering transparent polygons

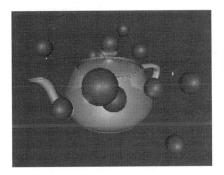 

Figure 4.28. The left shows some of the problems with rendering transparent surfaces in arbitrary depth order. On the right, the surfaces are correctly rendered back to front, using depth peeling in hardware. Note in particular the differences on the closest two spheres. *(Images courtesy of Cass Everitt, NVIDIA Corp.)*

twice while toggling Z-buffer depth testing and write enable, can work in some situations, but nothing is generally foolproof beyond sorting [580].

One method that requires no sorting entails simplifying Equation 4.23 to:

$$\mathbf{c}_o = \alpha_s \mathbf{c}_s + \mathbf{c}_d. \qquad (4.24)$$

Draw order can then be arbitrary, as the alphas of the transparent objects do not affect the destination. However, this does not look natural, as the opaque surfaces simply have color added to them instead of appearing filtered through the use of blending [536].

Other methods of correctly rendering transparency without the application itself needing to sort are possible. An advantage to the A-buffer multisampling method described on page 94 is that the fragments can be combined in sorted order by hardware to obtain high quality transparency. Normally an alpha value for a fragment represents either transparency, the coverage of a pixel cell, or both. A multisample fragment's alpha represents purely the transparency of the sample, since it stores a separate coverage mask.

Transparency can be computed using two or more depth buffers and multiple passes [173, 416, 514]. First, a rendering pass is made so that the opaque surfaces' z-depths are in the first Z-buffer. Now the transparent objects are rendered. On the second rendering pass, the depth test is modified to accept the surface that is both closer than the depth of the first buffer's stored z-depth, and the farthest among such surfaces. Doing so renders the backmost transparent object into the frame buffer and the z-depths into a second Z-buffer. This Z-buffer is then used to derive the next-closest transparent surface in the next pass, and so on. Currently, no commercial graphics hardware has two dedicated depth buffers. However, hardware supporting pixel shading can be used to compare z-depths in a similar fashion and so perform *depth peeling*, where each visible layer is found in turn [216]. While effective, such an approach is slow, as each layer peeled is a separate rendering pass. Mark and Proudfoot [516] discuss a hardware architecture extension they call the "F-buffer" that solves the transparency problem by storing and accessing fragments in a stream.

There are a number of other blending operators besides **over** [103, 630], but these are not as commonly used in real-time applications. The **over** operator can also be used for antialiasing edges. As discussed in the previous section, a variety of algorithms can be used to find the approximate percentage of a pixel covered by the edge of a polygon. Instead of storing a coverage mask showing the area covered by the object, an alpha can be stored in its place. In fact, a variety of algorithms can generate alpha values that approximate the coverage of an edge, line, or point.

As an example, say an opaque polygon is found to cover 30% of a screen grid cell. It would then have an alpha of 0.3. This alpha value is then used to blend the object's edge with the scene, using the **over** operator. While this alpha is just an approximation of the area an edge covers, this interpretation works fairly well in practice if generated properly. An example of a poor way to generate alphas is to create them for every polygon edge. Say two adjacent polygons fully cover a pixel, with each covering 50% of it. If each polygon generates an alpha value for its edge, the two alphas would combine to cover only 75% of the pixel, allowing 25% of the background to show through. This sort of error is avoided by using coverage masks or by blurring the edges outwards, as discussed in the previous section.

To summarize, the alpha value can represent transparency, edge coverage, or both (if one multiplies the two alphas together).

EXAMPLE: BLENDING A teapot is rendered onto a background using antialiasing techniques. Say at some pixel the shade of the surface is a beige, $(0.8, 0.7, 0.1)$, the background is a light blue, $(0.7, 0.7, 0.9)$, and the surface is found to cover 0.6 of the pixel. The blend of these two colors is:

$$0.6(0.8, 0.7, 0.1) + (1 - 0.6)(0.7, 0.7, 0.9),$$

which gives a color of $(0.76, 0.7, 0.42)$.   □

The **over** operator turns out to be useful for blending together photographs or synthetic renderings of objects. This process is called *com-*

positing [103, 718]. In such cases, the alpha value at each pixel is stored along with the RGB color value for the object. The alpha channel is sometimes called the *matte*, and shows the silhouette shape of the object. See Figure 5.19 on page 149 for an example. This RGBα image can then be used to blend it with other such *elements* or against a background.

The most common way to store RGBα images are with *premultiplied alphas* (also known as *associated alphas*). That is, the RGB values are multiplied by the alpha value before being stored. This makes the compositing **over** equation more efficient:

$$\mathbf{c}_o = \mathbf{c}'_s + (1 - \alpha_s)\mathbf{c}_d. \tag{4.25}$$

where $\mathbf{c}'_s$ is the premultiplied source channel. Also important, premultiplied alphas allow cleaner theoretical treatment [718].

In fact, computers generate three-dimensional synthetic images as premultiplied RGB values. For example, say we render a semi-transparent beige polygon, color $(0.8, 0.7, 0.1)$ and alpha 0.6, against a black background. The product of these two is $(0.48, 0.42, 0.06)$, so what is computed is an RGBα of $(0.48, 0.42, 0.06, 0.6)$. If we view this image, the polygon will be displayed with a color of $(0.48, 0.42, 0.06)$, i.e., the alpha is simply ignored. Note that with premultiplied RGBα values, the RGB components can never normally be greater than the alpha value.

Another way images are stored is with *unmultiplied alphas*, also known as *unassociated alphas* (or, *nonpremultiplied alphas*). An unmultiplied alpha is just what it says: the RGB value is not multiplied by the alpha value. This is rarely used in synthetic image storage, since the final color we see at a pixel is not the shade of the polygon; it is the shade multiplied by alpha, blended with the background. For some two-dimensional applications, an unassociated alpha is used to mask a photograph without affecting the underlying image's data. Image file formats that support alpha include TIFF (both types of alpha) and PNG (unassociated alpha only) [577].

A concept related to the alpha channel is *chroma-keying* [103]. This is a term from video production, in which actors are filmed against a blue, yellow, or (increasingly) green screen and blended with a background. In the film industry this process is called *blue-screen matting*. The idea here is that a particular color is designated to be considered transparent; where it is detected, the background is displayed. This allows objects to be given a shape by using just RGB colors—no alpha needs to be stored. One drawback of this scheme is that the object is either entirely opaque or transparent at any pixel, i.e., alpha is effectively only 1.0 or 0.0. As an example, the GIF format allows one color (actually, one palette entry; see

Section 15.1.2) to be designated as transparent. Though available in some APIs, DirectX 9 is phasing out this concept.

4.6 Fog

For real-time computer graphics, *fog* is a simple atmospheric effect that can be added to the final image. Fog can be used for several purposes. First, it increases the level of realism for outdoor scenes. Second, since the fog effect increases with the distance from the viewer, it helps the viewer of a scene to determine how far away objects are located. Third, if used properly, it helps to provide smoother culling of objects by the far plane. If the fog is set up so that objects located near the far plane are not visible due to thick fog, then objects that go out of the view frustum through the far plane seem to fade away into the fog. Without fog, a popping effect is experienced as the object is clipped by the far plane. Fourth, fog is often implemented in hardware, so it can be used with little or no additional cost. Examples of images rendered with fog are shown in Figure 4.29.

The color of the fog is denoted $\mathbf{c}_f$ (which the user selects), and the *fog factor* is called $f \in [0, 1]$, which decreases with the distance from the viewer. Assume that the color of a shaded surface is $\mathbf{c}_s$, then the final color of the pixel, $\mathbf{c}_p$, is determined by

$$\mathbf{c}_p = f\mathbf{c}_s + (1 - f)\mathbf{c}_f. \tag{4.26}$$

Note that f is somewhat nonintuitive in this presentation; as f decreases, the effect of the fog increases. This is how OpenGL and DirectX present

Figure 4.29. The left image shows a scene rendered without fog and the right image shows the same scene rendered with linear fog. *(The duck model is reused courtesy of Jens Larsson.)*

the equation, but another way to describe it is with $f' = 1 - f$. The main advantage of the approach presented here is that the various equations used to generate f are simplified. These equations follow.

Linear fog has a fog factor that decreases linearly with the depth from the viewer. For this purpose, there are two user-defined scalars, z_{start} and z_{end}, that determine where the fog is to start and end (i.e., become fully foggy) along the viewer's z-axis. If z_p is the z-value (depth from the viewer) of the pixel where fog is to be computed, then the linear fog factor is

$$f = \frac{z_{end} - z_p}{z_{end} - z_{start}}. \tag{4.27}$$

There are also two sorts of fog that falls off exponentially, as shown in Equations 4.28 and 4.29. These are called *exponential fog*:

$$f = e^{-d_f z_p}, \tag{4.28}$$

and *squared exponential fog*:

$$f = e^{-(d_f z_p)^2}. \tag{4.29}$$

The scalar d_f is a parameter that is used to control the density of the fog. After the fog factor, f, has been computed, it is clamped to $[0, 1]$, and Equation 4.26 is applied to calculate the final value of the pixel. Examples of what the fog fall-off curves look like for linear fog and for the two exponential fog factors appear in Figure 4.30.

Tables are sometimes used in implementing these fog functions in hardware accelerators. That is, for each depth, a fog factor f is computed and stored in advance. When the fog factor at a given depth is needed, the fog factor is read from the table (or linearly interpolated from the two nearest table entries). Any values can be put into the fog table, not just those in the equations above. This allows interesting rendering styles in which the fog effect can vary in any manner desired.

In theory, that is all there is to the fog effect: The color of a pixel is changed as a function of its depth. However, there are a few simplifying assumptions that are used in some real-time systems which can affect the quality of the output.

First, fog can be applied on a vertex level or a pixel level [180]. Applying it on the vertex level means that the fog effect is computed as part of the illumination equation and the computed color is interpolated across the polygon using Gouraud shading. Pixel-level fog is computed using the depth stored at each pixel. All other factors being equal, pixel-level fog gives a better result.

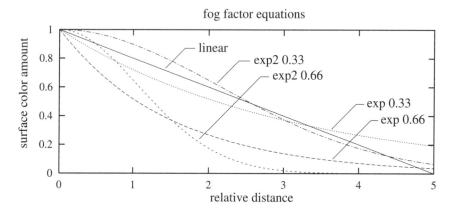

Figure 4.30. Curves for fog fall-off: linear, exponential, and squared-exponential, using various densities.

The fog factor equations use a value along the viewer's z-axis to compute their effect. In traditional software rendering pipelines and many graphics accelerators, the z-values are computed in a nonlinear fashion (see Section 15.1.3). Using these z-values directly in the fog-factor equations gives results that do not follow the actual intent of the equations. For this reason, some graphics hardware supports *eye-relative depth* for correctly computing the depth. This is accomplished by undoing the effect of the perspective transformation so that the depth values change in a linear fashion.

Another simplifying assumption is that the distance along the viewing axis is used as the depth for computing the fog effect. This depth is computed on modern hardware as an *eye-relative depth*. Since the z-depth varies nonlinearly (Section 15.2), a linear $1/w$ depth along the view direction is calculated. However, a more accurate way to compute fog is to use the true distance from the viewer to the object. This is called *radial fog*, *range-based fog*, or *Euclidean distance fog* [344]. Figure 4.31 shows what happens when radial fog is not used. The highest-quality fog is generated by using pixel-level radial fog.

Other types of fog effects are certainly possible. Dietrich [174] presents a per-pixel method of producing fog by using texture mapping. Fog effects can also be produced by overlaying sets of semitransparent billboard images. Legakis [482] introduced a method for producing images with fog in multiple layers, where the density depends on the height from the ground, and is computed via look-up tables. This can produce effects such as fog in a valley. Heidrich et al. [344] show how layered fog can be implemented so

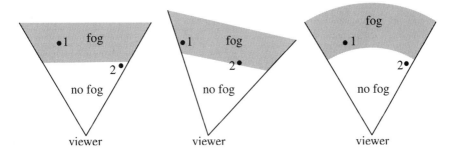

Figure 4.31. Use of z-depth versus radial fog. On the left is one view of two objects, using view-axis-based fog. In the middle, the view has simply been rotated, but in the rotation, the fog now encompasses object 2. On the right, we see the effect of radial fog, which will not vary when the viewer rotates.

as to perform all computations in hardware. The basic idea behind these volumetric fog techniques is to compute how much of some volume of space is between the object and the viewer, and then use this amount to change the object's color by the fog color [199]

4.7 Gamma Correction

Once the pixel values have been computed, we need to display them on a monitor. There is a physical relationship between the voltage input to an electron gun in a *Cathode-Ray Tube* (CRT) monitor and the light output by the screen. This relationship is a power function:

$$I = a(V + \epsilon)^\gamma. \tag{4.30}$$

where V is the input voltage, a and γ (gamma) are constant for each monitor, ϵ is the black level (brightness) setting for the monitor, and I is the intensity generated [328, 631]. The gamma value for a particular CRT ranges from about 2.3 to 2.6. See the left side of Figure 4.32. Values considerably different from this range are often claimed, but the largest source of error in gamma computation is caused by poor black level (brightness) settings [631]. While 2.5 is usually given as a good average monitor value, there is also a perceptual effect that is often factored into this equation. This is the *surround effect*, which depends on the viewing environment (assumed to be dark for television viewing, for example). The net effect is

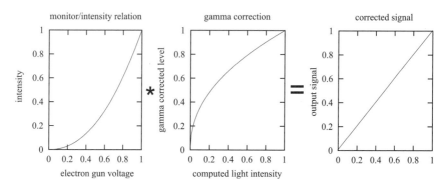

Figure 4.32. On the left is the normalized relation of voltage to intensity for an electron gun in a CRT. In the middle is the gamma correction curve needed to convert a computed intensity value to the displayed pixel value. The two curves multiplied together give a linear relationship, shown to the right.

that a composite gamma of 2.2 is used by NTSC, the color TV encoding scheme; Rec. 709 for HDTV uses a value of 1/0.45 (about 2.222) [631]. The value of 2.2 has been proposed as part of a standard color space for computer systems and the Internet, called *sRGB* [732]. Another color space that will influence graphics hardware design is Microsoft's higher quality *scRGB* proposal (formerly called sRGB64), which has 16 bits of precision per channel and a gamma of 1.0.

It turns out that, by coincidence, the CRT response curve nearly matches the inverse of light sensitivity of the human eye [631]. This has the effect of endowing the CRT with a near-optimal set of luminance values for displaying images. However, this nonlinearity causes a problem within the field of computer graphics. Lighting equations compute intensity values that have a linear relationship to each other. For example, a computed value of 0.5 is expected to appear half as bright as 1.0. To ensure that the computed values are perceived correctly relative to each other, *gamma correction* is necessary. At its simplest, assuming the black level ϵ is zero, the computed color component c_i is converted by:

$$c = c_i^{1/\gamma}, \tag{4.31}$$

for display by the CRT (see Figure 4.32). For example, with a gamma of 2.2 and $c_i = 0.5$, the gamma-corrected c is 0.73. So, if the electron gun level is set at 0.73, an intensity level of 0.5 is displayed. Computed colors need to be boosted by this equation to be perceived properly with respect to one another when displayed on a CRT monitor.

This is the basic idea behind gamma correction; see Poynton's book and web site [631] for a thorough treatment of the subject. In practical terms, gamma correction is important to real-time graphics in a few areas:

- Cross-platform compatibility

- Color fidelity, consistency, and interpolation

- Dithering

- Line and edge antialiasing quality

- Alpha blending and compositing

- Texturing

Cross-platform compatibility affects all images displayed, not just scene renderings. SGI and Apple Macintosh computers have gamma correction mechanisms built into their machines, though each has its own, different, gamma power value that they aim for [631]. CRT monitors all have a gamma of around 2.5; the way manufacturers choose to adjust for gamma differ. What this means is that, if gamma correction is ignored, models authored and rendered on, say, an SGI machine will display differently when moved to a Macintosh or a PC. This problem instantly affects any images or models made available on a web server, since currently there is no standard gamma value for web browsers [732]. Some sites have employed the strategy of attempting to detect the platform of the client requesting information and serving up images or models tailored for it.

Even if an application is limited to platforms using the same gamma mechanism, there are still problems with failing to perform gamma correction. One is color fidelity: The appearance of a color will differ from its true hue. Another problem is color consistency: Without correction, intensity controls will not work as expected. If a light or material color is changed from $(0.5, 0.5, 0.5)$ to $(1.0, 1.0, 1.0)$, the user will expect it to appear twice as bright, but it will not. Another place where consistency is violated is when using lights with a distance-squared fall-off. Without gamma correction, these fade out to darkness much faster than they would in reality. Shadows of objects, multiple light sources, and fog will also not combine in an expected manner [547]. A third problem is color interpolation: A surface that goes from dark to light will not appear to increase linearly in brightness across its surface. Again, without gamma correction, the midtones will appear too dark.

Lack of gamma correction also adversely affects *dithering* algorithms. In dithering, two colors are displayed close together and the eye combines

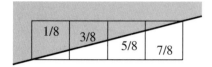 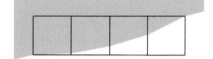

Figure 4.33. On the left, four pixels covered by the edge of a white polygon on a black (shown as gray) background, with true area coverage shown. If gamma correction is not done, the edge will be perceived similarly to the figure on the right, as the midtones are darkened.

them and perceives a blend of the two. Without accounting for gamma, the dithered color can be perceptibly different from the color that is to be represented. Similarly, using screen-door transparency will result in a different perceived color from the blended transparency color (see Section 4.5).

Dithering problems have faded as graphics hardware moves away from using less than 24-bit color (see Section 15.1.2). However, as the use of line and edge antialiasing in real-time rendering increases, gamma's effect on the quality of these techniques will be more noticeable. For example, say a polygon edge covers four screen grid cells (Figure 4.33). The polygon is white; the background is black. Left to right, the cells are covered $\frac{1}{8}$, $\frac{3}{8}$, $\frac{5}{8}$, and $\frac{7}{8}$. So if we are using a box filter, we want the pixels to appear as 0.125, 0.375, 0.625, and 0.875. If the system has a gamma of 2.2, we need to send values of 0.389, 0.640, 0.808, and 0.941 to the electron guns. Failing to do so will mean that the perceived brightness will not increase linearly. Sending 0.125 to the guns, for example, will result in a perceived relative brightness of only 0.010; 0.875 will be affected somewhat less and will be perceived as 0.745.

This nonlinearity causes an artifact called *roping*, because the edge looks somewhat like a twisted rope [78, 583]. Figure 4.34 shows this effect. It is worth noting that *Liquid-Crystal Displays* (LCDs) often have different voltage/luminance response curves.[8] Because of this different response curve, lines that look antialiased on CRTs may look jagged on LCDs, or vice versa.

Similarly, alpha blending and compositing should be done in a linear space and the final result should be gamma-corrected. This can lead to difficulties, as pixel values stored in the color buffer are likely to be gamma-corrected. Bits of accuracy are lost as values are transferred from one computational space to another. Blinn [78] discusses this problem in depth.

---

[8]Some LCD monitors have additional hardware to make the LCD display act in the same fashion as CRT monitors [221]. In this way, color fidelity can be maintained.

Figure 4.34. On the left, the set of antialiased lines are gamma-corrected; in the middle, the set is partially corrected; on the right, there is no gamma correction. *(Images courtesy of Scott R. Nelson.)*

Texturing is another area where problems can occur. Images used as textures are normally stored in gamma-corrected form for some particular type of system, e.g., a PC or Macintosh. When using textures in a synthesized scene, care must be taken to gamma-correct the texture a sum total of only one time. As noted in Section 5.2.2, mipmap generation must also take gamma correction into account. Gamma correction for pixel shaders is a concern, as blending and texturing are commonly used within this part of the pipeline. DirectX 9 and later are expected to address these concerns, so that pixel shaders can perform their operations in a gamma-corrected space.

There are a number of hardware solutions if gamma correction is determined to be necessary. One technique on inexpensive hardware is to take eight-bit color component values generated by the rendering equation and use a look-up table to convert these to their gamma-corrected equivalent. Converting from eight-bits in linear space to eight-bits in gamma-corrected space loses precision. For example, while input color $\frac{0}{255}$ maps to output color $\frac{0}{255}$, input color $\frac{1}{255}$ maps to $\frac{21}{255}$, so output levels 1 to 20 never get used with this scheme; more precision on the input side is needed to access these output levels. For a gamma of 2.2, using such a table causes only about 184 of the 256 hardware output levels (72%) to get used. Unfortunately, this has the effect of causing what are called *banding* or *contouring* artifacts, as nearby colors jump to different hardware color values.[9]

A better solution, implemented in some hardware, is to compute the pixel value at some higher precision and use a larger look-up table to convert

---

[9]Contouring artifacts among the darker shades are possible even when gamma correction is done properly and 24 bits of color are used. Dithering can be used to avoid these artifacts. The point here is that $8 \rightarrow 8$ gamma correction will give much more serious contouring artifacts.

(e.g., using 12 bits, the look-up table has 2^{12}, or 4096, entries). This topic is covered by Blinn [73].

However, if the presence of gamma-correction hardware cannot be guaranteed, other solutions must be explored. About the only practical real-time solution is to attempt to perform gamma correction earlier on in the pipeline. For example, we could gamma-correct the illumination value computed at the vertex, then Gouraud shade from there. This solution partially solves the cross-platform problem, though it does not address the other rendering problems detailed previously. It is also difficult if not impossible to use with multipass and pixel shader rendering methods (see Section 5.4).

Another approach taken by many applications is to ignore the gamma correction problem entirely and not do anything about it. Unless gamma correction hardware support is commonly available or speed is not an issue, doing nothing is sometimes the only solution. Even if the issues you encounter cannot be fixed, it is important to understand what problems are caused by a lack of gamma correction.

A final warning: Some software applications (e.g., games) include a control for "gamma correction" to modify the contrast or brightness of the scene. By now it should be clear that this control is not actually performing gamma correction, but rather is a method of responding to varying monitor settings and user preferences. Gamma correction is not a user preference; it is something that can be designed into an application to allow cross-platform consistency and to improve image fidelity and rendering algorithm quality.

Further Reading and Resources

A thorough treatment of lighting, lights, materials, color, and signal processing can be found in Glassner's two-volume work *Principles of Digital Image Synthesis* [264, 265]. Hall's book [316] also gives a comprehensive treatment of lighting models, shading techniques, and color science.

Wolberg's book [813] is an exhaustive guide to sampling and filtering for computer graphics. Foley et al. cover the topic in some depth in a section of their classic book [235]. Blinn's *Dirty Pixels* book [77] includes some good introductory articles on filtering and antialiasing, as well as articles on alpha, compositing, and gamma correction. Shirley has a useful summary of sampling patterns used in computer graphics [704]. A summary of practical antialiasing methods for consoles and PCs is provided by Mitchell [558].

This article also touches on solutions to problems caused by interlaced television displays. A good quick read that helps correct the misconception that a pixel is a little square is Smith's article on the topic [717]. Poynton's *A Technical Introduction to Digital Video* [631] gives solid coverage of gamma correction in various media, as well as other color-related topics.

On this book's website (`http://www.realtimerendering.com/`) are pointers to Java applets that let you see the effects of the various lighting model components, as well as links to other web resources.

Chapter 5
Texturing

"All it takes is for the rendered image to look right."
–Jim Blinn

A surface's texture is its look and feel—just think of the texture of an oil painting. In computer graphics, texturing is a process that takes a surface and modifies its appearance at each location using some image, function, or other data source. As an example, instead of precisely representing the geometry of a brick wall, a color image of a brick wall is applied to a single polygon. When the polygon is viewed, the color image appears where the polygon is located. Unless the viewer gets close to the wall, the lack of geometric detail (e.g., the fact that the image of bricks and mortar is on a smooth surface) will not be noticeable. Huge modeling, memory, and speed savings are obtained by combining images and surfaces in this way. Color image texturing also provides a way to use photographic images and animations on surfaces.

However, some textured brick walls can be unconvincing for reasons other than lack of geometry. For example, if the bricks are supposed to be shiny, whereas the mortar is not, the viewer will notice that the shininess is the same for both materials. To produce a more convincing experience, a specular highlighting image texture can also be applied to the surface. Instead of changing the surface's color, this sort of texture changes the wall's shininess depending on location on the surface. Now the bricks have a color from the color image texture and a shininess from this new texture.

Once the shiny texture has been applied, however, the viewer may notice that now all the bricks are shiny and the mortar is not, but each brick face appears to be flat. This does not look right, as bricks normally have some irregularity to their surfaces. By applying bump mapping, the surface normals of the bricks may be varied so that when they are rendered, they do not appear to be perfectly smooth. This sort of texture wobbles the direction of the polygon's original surface normal for purposes of computing lighting.

These are just three examples of the types of problems that can be solved with textures. In this chapter, texturing techniques are covered in detail. First, a general framework of the texturing process is presented. Next, we focus on using images to texture surfaces, since this is the most popular form of texturing used in real-time work. The various techniques for improving the appearance of image textures are detailed, and then methods of getting textures to affect the surface are explained.

5.1 Generalized Texturing

Texturing, at its simplest, is a technique for efficiently modeling the surface's properties. One way to approach texturing is to think about what happens for a single sample taken at a vertex of a polygon. As seen in the previous chapter, the color is computed by taking into account the lighting and the material, as well as the viewer's position. If present, transparency also affects the sample, and then the effect of fog is calculated. Texturing works by modifying the values used in the lighting equation. The way these values are changed is normally based on the position on the surface. So, for the brick wall example, the color at any point on the surface is replaced by a corresponding color in the image of a brick wall, based on the surface location. The specular highlight texture modifies the shininess value, and the bump texture changes the direction of the normal, so each of these change the result of the lighting equation.

Texturing can be described by a generalized texture pipeline. Much terminology will be introduced in a moment, but take heart: Each piece of the pipeline will be described in detail. This full texturing process is not performed by most current real-time rendering systems, though as time goes by, more parts of the pipeline will be incorporated. Once we have presented the entire process, we will examine the various simplifications and limitations of real-time texturing.

A location in space is the starting point for the texturing process. This location can be in world space, but is more often in the model's frame of reference, so that as the model moves, the texture moves along with it. Using Kershaw's terminology [418], this point in space then has a *projector* function applied to it to obtain a set of numbers, called parameter-space values, that will be used for accessing the texture. This process is called *mapping*, which leads to the phrase *texture mapping*.[1] Before these

---

[1]Sometimes the texture image itself is called the texture map, though this is not strictly correct.

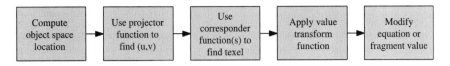

Figure 5.1. The generalized texture pipeline for a single texture.

new values may be used to access the texture, one or more *corresponder* functions can be used to transform the parameter-space values to texture space. These texture-space values are used to obtain values from the texture, e.g., they may be array indices into an image texture to retrieve a pixel. The retrieved values are then potentially transformed yet again by a *value transform* function, and finally these new values are used to modify some property of the surface, such as the material or shading normal. Figure 5.1 shows this process in detail for the application of a single texture. The reason for the complexity of the pipeline is that each step provides the user with a useful control.

Using this pipeline, this is what happens when a polygon has a brick wall texture and a sample is generated on its surface (see Figure 5.2). The (x, y, z) position in the object's local frame of reference is found; say it is $(-2.3, 7.1, 88.2)$. A projector function is then applied to this position. Just as a map of the world is a projection of a three-dimensional object into two dimensions, the projector function here typically changes the (x, y, z)

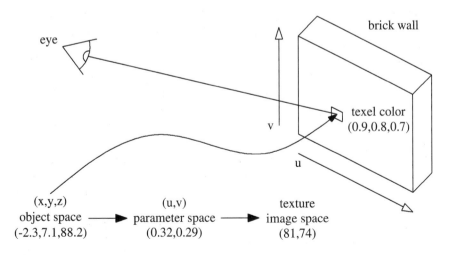

Figure 5.2. Pipeline for a brick wall.

vector into a two-element vector (u, v). The projector function used for this example is an orthographic projection (see Section 2.3.3), acting essentially like a slide projector shining the brick wall image onto the polygon's surface. To return to the wall, a point on its plane could be transformed into a pair of values ranging from 0 to 1. Say the values obtained are $(0.32, 0.29)$. These parameter-space values are to be used to find what the color of the image is at this location. The resolution of our brick texture is, say, 256×256, so the corresponder function multiplies the (u, v) by 256 each, giving $(81.92, 74.24)$. Dropping the fractions, pixel $(81, 74)$ is found in the brick wall image, and is of color $(0.9, 0.8, 0.7)$. The original brick wall image is too dark, so a value transform function that multiplies the color by 1.1 is then applied, giving a color of $(0.99, 0.88, 0.77)$. This color modifies the surface properties by directly replacing the surface's original diffuse color, which is then used in the illumination equation.

The first step in the texture process is obtaining the surface's location and projecting it into parameter space. Projector functions typically work by converting a three-dimensional point in space into texture coordinates. Projector functions commonly used in modeling programs include spherical, cylindrical, and planar projections [59, 418, 465]. Other inputs can be used to a projector function. For example, the surface normal can be used to choose which of six planar projection directions is used for the surface. Other projector functions are not projections at all, but are an implicit part of surface formation; for example, parametric curved surfaces have a natural set of (u, v) values as part of their definition. See Figure 5.3. The texture coordinates could also be generated from all sorts of different parameters, such as the view direction, temperature of the surface, or anything else imaginable. The goal of the projector function is to generate texture coordinates. Deriving these as a function of position is just one way to do it.

Noninteractive renderers often call these projector functions as part of the rendering process itself. A single projector function may suffice for the whole model, but often the artist has to use tools to subdivide the model and apply various projector functions separately [611]. See Figure 5.4.

In real-time work, projector functions are usually applied at this modeling stage, and the results of the projection are stored at the vertices. This is not always the case; for example, OpenGL's glTexGen routine provides a few different projector functions, including spherical and planar. Having the accelerator perform the projection on the fly has the advantage that texture coordinates then do not have to be sent to the accelerator, thereby saving bandwidth. Some rendering methods, such as environment mapping (see Section 5.7.4), have specialized projector functions of their own

Figure 5.3. Different texture projections. Spherical, cylindrical, planar, and natural (u, v) projections are shown left to right. The bottom row shows each of these projections applied to a single object (which has no natural projection).

that are evaluated per vertex or per pixel. More generally, vertex shaders (Section 6.5) can be used to compute a near-infinite variety of complex projector functions on the graphics accelerator itself.

The spherical projection casts points onto an imaginary sphere centered around some point. This projection is the same as used in Blinn and Newell's environment mapping scheme (Section 5.7.4), so Equation 5.4 on page 154 describes this function. This projection method suffers from the same problems of vertex interpolation described in that section.

Cylindrical projection computes the u texture coordinate the same as spherical projection, with the v texture coordinate computed as the distance along the cylinder's axis. This projection is useful for objects that have a natural axis, such as surfaces of revolution. Distortion occurs when surfaces are near-perpendicular to the cylinder's axis.

The planar projection is like an x-ray slide projector, projecting along a direction and applying the texture to all surfaces. It uses orthographic projection (Section 3.5.1). This function is commonly used to apply texture maps to characters, treating the model like it was a paper doll by gluing separate textures on to its front and rear.

As there is severe distortion for surfaces that are edge-on to the projection direction, the artist often must manually decompose the model into

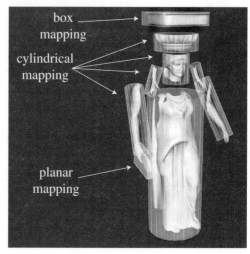

Figure 5.4. How various texture projections are used on a single model. *(Images courtesy of Tito Pagán.)*

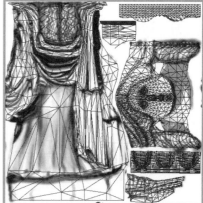

Figure 5.5. A number of smaller textures for the statue model saved in two larger textures. The right figure shows how the polygonal mesh is unwrapped and displayed on the texture to aid in its creation. *(Images courtesy of Tito Pagán.)*

near-planar pieces. There are also tools that help minimize distortion by unwrapping the mesh, or creating a near-optimal set of planar projections, or otherwise aid this process. The goal is to have each polygon be given a fairer share of a texture's area, while also maintaining as much mesh connectivity as possible to ease the artist's work [465, 611]. Figure 5.5 shows the workspace used to create the statue in Figure 5.4. Eckstein et al. [204] give a brief overview of research to date, and give a way of fixing features (such as eyes and mouth texture locations) onto a mesh while otherwise minimizing distortion. Work such as "lapped textures", done by Praun et al. holds promise for applying material textures to surfaces in a convincing fashion [632].

Texture coordinate values are sometimes presented as a three-element vector, (u, v, w), with w being depth along the projection direction. Other systems use up to four coordinates, often designated (s, t, r, q) [600]; q is used as the fourth value in a homogeneous coordinate (see Section A.4) and can be used for spotlighting effects [694]. To allow each separate texture map to have its own input parameters during a rendering pass, APIs allow multiple sets of texture coordinates (see Section 5.5 on multitexturing). However the coordinate values are applied, the idea is the same: These parameter values are interpolated across the surface and used to retrieve texture values. Before being interpolated, however, these parameter values are transformed by corresponder functions.

Corresponder functions convert parameter-space values to texture-space locations. They provide flexibility in applying textures to surfaces. One example of a corresponder function is to use the API to select a portion of an existing texture for display; only this subimage will be used in subsequent operations.

Another corresponder is an optional matrix transformation. The use of a 4×4 matrix is supported explicitly in OpenGL, and is simple enough to support at the application stage under any API. This transform is useful for the sorts of procedures that transforms normally do well at: It can translate, rotate, scale, shear, and even project the texture on the surface.[2]

Another class of corresponder functions controls the way an image is applied. We know that an image will appear on the surface where (u, v) are in the $[0, 1)$ range. But what happens outside of this range? Corresponder functions determine the behavior. In OpenGL, this type of corresponder

---

[2] As discussed in Section 3.1.5, the order of transforms matters. Surprisingly, the order of transforms for textures must be the reverse of the order one would expect. This is because texture transforms actually affect the space that determines where the image is seen. The image itself is not an object being transformed; the space defining the image's location is being changed.

function is called the "wrapping mode"; in Direct3D, it is called the "texture addressing mode."[3] Common corresponder functions of this type are:

- **wrap** (DirectX), **repeat** (OpenGL), or **tile** – The image repeats itself across the surface; algorithmically, the integer part of the parameter value is dropped. This function is useful for having an image of a material repeatedly cover a surface, and is often the default.

- **mirror** – The image repeats itself across the surface, but is mirrored (flipped) on every other repetition. For example, the image appears normally going from 0 to 1, then is reversed between 1 and 2, then is normal between 2 and 3, then is reversed, etc. This provides some continuity along the edges of the texture.

- **clamp** (DirectX) or **clamp to edge** (OpenGL) – Values outside the range $[0,1)$ are clamped to this range. This results in the repetition of the edges of the image texture. This function is useful for avoiding accidentally taking samples from the opposite edge of a texture when bilinear interpolation happens near a texture's edge [600].[4]

- **border** (DirectX) or **clamp to border** (OpenGL) – Parameter values outside $[0,1)$ are rendered with a separately defined border color or using the edge of the texture as a border. This function can be good for rendering decals onto surfaces, for example, as the edge of the texture will blend smoothly with the border color. Border textures can be used to smoothly stitch together adjoining texture maps, e.g., for terrain rendering. The texture coordinate is clamped to half a texel inside $[0,1)$ for clamp-to-edge and half a texel outside $[0,1)$ for clamp-to-border.

See Figure 5.6. These corresponder functions can be assigned differently for each texture axis, e.g., the texture could repeat along the u axis and be clamped on the v axis.

---

[3]Confusingly, Direct3D also has a feature called "texture wrapping," which is used with Blinn environment mapping. See Section 5.7.4.

[4]OpenGL's original GL_CLAMP was not well-specified prior to version 1.2. As defined, points outside of the texture's border are a blend of half the border color and half the edge pixels during bilinear interpolation. GL_CLAMP_TO_EDGE was introduced as its replacement in OpenGL 1.2 to rectify this problem, and GL_CLAMP_TO_BORDER_ARB properly always samples only the border beyond the texture's boundaries. However, much hardware does not support borders, so implements GL_CLAMP as if it were GL_CLAMP_TO_EDGE. Newer hardware (e.g., the GeForce3) implements GL_CLAMP correctly, but the result is normally not what is desired. The gist: Use GL_CLAMP_TO_EDGE unless you know you need a different clamping behavior.

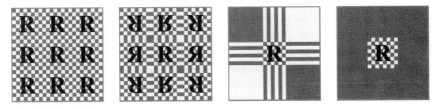

Figure 5.6. Image texture repeat, mirror, clamp, and border functions in action.

DirectX 8.0 also includes a **mirror once** texture addressing mode that mirrors the texture once, then clamping to the range $(-1, 1)$. As of the end of 2001, only ATI supports this corresponder function in hardware. The motivation for mirror once is for three-dimensional texture light maps.

For real-time work, the last corresponder function applied is implicit, and is derived from the image's size. A texture is normally applied within the range $[0, 1)$ for u and v. As shown in the brick wall example, by multiplying parameter values in this range by the resolution of the image, one may obtain the pixel location. The pixels in the texture are often called *texels*, to differentiate them from the pixels on the screen. The advantage of being able to specify (u, v) values in a range of $[0, 1)$ is that image textures with different resolutions can be swapped in without having to change the values stored at the vertices of the model.

The set of corresponder functions uses parameter-space values to produce texture coordinates. For image textures, the texture coordinates are used to retrieve texel information from the image. This process is dealt with extensively in Section 5.2. Two-dimensional images constitute the vast majority of texture use in real-time work, but there are other texture functions. A direct extension of image textures is three-dimensional image data that is accessed by (u, v, w) (or (s, t, r) values). For example, medical imaging data can be generated as a three-dimensional grid; by moving a polygon through this grid, one may view two-dimensional slices of this data.

Covering an arbitrary three-dimensional surface cleanly with a two-dimensional image is often difficult or impossible [59]. As the texture is applied to some solid object, the image is stretched or compressed in places to fit the surface. Obvious mismatches may be visible as different pieces of the texture meet. A solid cone is a good example of both of these problems: The image bunches up at the tip, while the texture on the flat face of the cone does not match up with the texture on the curved face. One solution is to synthesize texture patches that tile the surface seamlessly while minimizing distortion. Performing this operation on complex surfaces is technically challenging and is an active area of research. See Turk [756] for one approach and an overview of past research.

The advantage of three-dimensional textures is that they avoid the distortion and seam problems that two-dimensional texture mappings can have. A three-dimensional texture can act as a material such as wood or marble, and the model may be textured as if it were carved from this material. The texture can also be used to modify other properties, for example changing (u, v) coordinates in order to creating warping effects [536].

Three-dimensional textures can be synthesized by a variety of techniques. One of the most common is using one or more noise functions to generate values [201]. See Figure 5.7. Because of the cost of evaluating the noise function, often the lattice points in the three-dimensional array are precomputed and used to interpolate texture values. There are also methods that use the accumulation buffer or color buffer blending to generate these arrays [536]. However, such arrays can be large to store and often lack sufficient detail. Miné and Neyret [550] use lower resolution

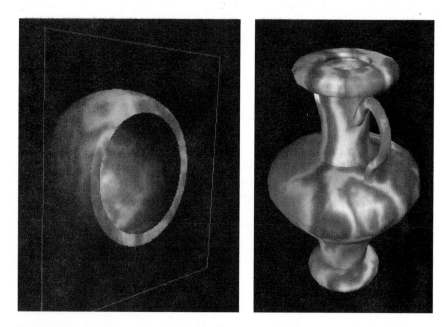

Figure 5.7. Two examples of real-time procedural texturing using a volume texture. The marble texture is continuous over the surface, with no mismatches at edges. The object on the left is formed by cutting a pair of spheres with a plane and using the stencil buffer to fill in the gap. *(Images courtesy of Evan Hart, ATI Technologies Inc.)*

three-dimensional Perlin noise textures and combine them to create marble, wood, and other effects. Hart has created a pixel shader that computes Perlin noise on the fly, albeit slowly (it takes 375 passes on a GeForce2, though surprisingly, this still gives a display rate of faster than a frame a second) [325]. Hart et al. have also done other research on hardware solutions for procedural textures [324].

Two-dimensional texture functions can also be used to generate textures, but here the major advantages are some storage savings (and bandwidth savings from not having to send down the corresponding image texture) and the fact that such textures have essentially infinite resolution and potentially no repeatability.

It is also worth noting that one-dimensional texture images and functions have their uses. For example, these include contour lines [301, 600] and coloration determined by altitude (e.g., the lowlands are green; the mountain peaks are white). Also, lines can also be textured; one use of this is to render rain as a set of long lines textured with a semitransparent image.

The texture is accessed and a set of values is retrieved from it. When performing Gouraud interpolation, the texture coordinates are not linearly interpolated, as this will cause distortions [330]. Instead, perspective correction is performed on the texture coordinate values. This process is discussed further in Section 15.2.

The most straightforward data to return from a retrieval is an RGB triplet that is used to replace or modify the surface color; similarly, a single grayscale value could be returned. Another type of data to return is RGBα, as described in Section 4.5. The α (alpha) value is normally the opacity of the color, which determines the extent to which the color may affect the pixel. There are certainly other types of data that can be stored in image textures, as will be seen when bump-mapping is discussed in detail (Section 5.7.5).

Once the texture values have been retrieved, they may be used directly or further transformed. The resulting values are used to modify one or more surface attributes. Recall that almost all real-time systems use Gouraud shading, meaning that only certain values are interpolated across a surface, so these are the only values that the texture can modify. Normally, we modify the RGB result of the lighting equation, since this equation was evaluated at each vertex and the color is then interpolated. However, other values can be modified. For example, as will be discussed in Section 5.7.5, values such as the light's direction can be interpolated and combined with a texture to make the surface appear bumpy.

Most real-time systems let us pick one of a number of methods for modifying the surface. The methods, called *combine functions* or *texture blending operations*, for gluing an image texture onto a surface include:

- **replace** – Simply replace the original surface color with the texture color. Note that this removes any lighting computed for the surface, unless the texture itself includes it.

- **decal** – Like **replace**, but when an α texture value is available, the texture is blended with the underlying color but the original α value is not modified. As the name implies, it is useful for applying decals (see Section 5.7.1).

- **modulate** – Multiply the surface color by the texture color. The shaded surface is modified by the color texture, giving a shaded, textured surface.

These two are the most common methods for simple color texture mapping. Using **replace** for texturing in an illuminated environment is sometimes called using a *glow texture*, since the texture's color always appears the same, regardless of changing light conditions. There are other property modifiers, which will be discussed as other texture techniques are introduced.

Modulating the entire shade of a surface by a texture can be unconvincing, because the texture will dim both the diffuse and specular terms. In reality, a material can reflect a highlight even if its diffuse color is dark. So, on some systems the diffuse and specular shading colors can be interpolated separately, with only the diffuse shade being modified by the texture. See Plate V (following page 274).

Revisiting the brick wall texture example, here is what happens in a typical real-time system. A modeler sets the (u, v) parameter values once in advance for the wall model vertices. The texture is read into the renderer, and the wall polygons are sent down the rendering pipeline. A white material is used in computing the illumination at each vertex. This color and (u, v) values are interpolated across the surface. At each pixel, the proper brick image's texel is retrieved and modulated (multiplied) by the illumination color and displayed. In our original example, this texture was multiplied by 1.1 at this point to make it brighter; in practice, this color boost would probably be performed on the material or texture itself in the modeling stage. In the end, a lit, textured brick wall is displayed.

5.2 Image Texturing

In image texturing, a two-dimensional image is effectively glued onto the surface of a polygon and rendered. We have walked through the process with respect to the polygon; now we will address the issues surrounding the image itself and its application to the surface. For the rest of this chapter, the image texture will be referred to simply as the texture. In addition, when we refer to a pixel's cell here, we mean the screen grid cell surrounding that pixel. As mentioned in Section 4.4.2, a pixel is actually a displayed color value that can (and should, for better quality) be affected by samples outside of its grid cell.

The texture image size used in hardware accelerators is usually restricted to $2^m \times 2^n$ texels, or sometimes even $2^m \times 2^m$ square, where m and n are nonnegative integers.[5] Graphics accelerators have different upper limits on texture size.

Assume that we have an image of size 256×256 pixels and that we want to use it as a texture on a square. As long as the projected square on the screen is roughly the same size as the texture, the texture on the square looks almost like the original image. But what happens if the projected square covers ten times as many pixels as the original image contains (called *magnification*), or if the projected square covers only a fraction of the pixels (*minification*)? The answer is that it depends on what kind of sampling and filtering methods you use for these two separate cases.

5.2.1 Magnification

In Figure 5.8, a texture of size 32×64 texels is textured onto a rectangle, and the rectangle is viewed rather closely with respect to the texture size, so the underlying graphics system has to magnify the texture. The most common filtering techniques for magnification are *nearest neighbor* (the actual filter is called a box filter—see Section 4.4.1) and *bilinear interpolation*.[6]

In the left part of Figure 5.8, the nearest neighbor method is used. One characteristic of this magnification technique is that the individual texels may become apparent. This effect is called *pixelation*, and occurs because the method takes the value of the nearest texel to each pixel center when magnifying, resulting in a blocky appearance. While the quality of

---

[5] One exception to the powers-of-two rule is NVIDIA's *texture rectangle* extension, which allows any size texture to be stored and used. See Section 6.6.

[6] There is also *cubic convolution*, which uses the weighted sum of a 4×4 array of texels, but it is currently not commonly available.

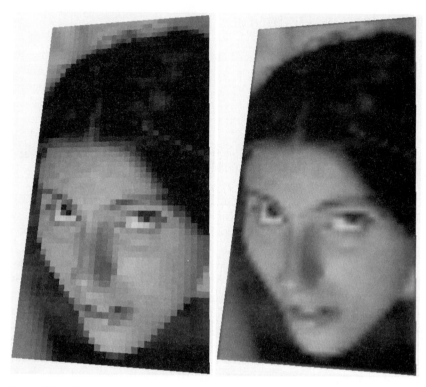

Figure 5.8. Texture magnification. Here, a texture of size 32 × 64 was applied to a rectangle, which was viewed very closely (with respect to texture size). Therefore, the texture had to be magnified. On the left, the nearest neighbor filter is used, which simply selects the nearest texel to each pixel. Bilinear interpolation is used on the rectangle on the right. Here, each pixel is computed from a bilinear interpolation of the closest four neighbor texels.

this method is sometimes poor, it requires only one texel to be fetched per pixel.

In the right part of the same figure, bilinear interpolation (sometimes called *linear interpolation*) is used. For each pixel, this kind of filtering finds the four neighboring texels and linearly interpolates in two dimensions to find a blended value for the pixel. The result is blurrier, and much of the jaggedness from using the nearest neighbor method has disappeared.[7]

Returning to the brick texture example on page 120: Without dropping the fractions, we obtained $(p_u, p_v) = (81.92, 74.24)$. These fractions are

---

[7]Looking at these images with eyes squinted has approximately the same effect as a low-pass filter, and reveals the face a bit more.

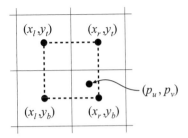

Figure 5.9. Notation for bilinear interpolation. The four texels involved are illustrated by the four squares.

used in computing the bilinear combination of the four closest pixels, which thus range from $(x_l, y_b) = (81, 74)$ to $(x_r, y_t) = (82, 75)$. See Figure 5.9 for notation. First, the decimal part is computed as: $(u', v') = (p_u - \lfloor p_u \rfloor, p_v - \lfloor p_v \rfloor)$. This is equal to $(u', v') = (0.92, 0.24)$ for our example. Assuming we can access the texels' colors in the texture as $\mathbf{t}(x, y)$, where x and y are integers, the bilinearly interpolated color $\mathbf{b}$ at (p_u, p_v) is:

$$\mathbf{b}(p_u, p_v) = \begin{aligned} & (1 - u')(1 - v')\mathbf{t}(x_l, y_b) + u'(1 - v')\mathbf{t}(x_r, y_b) \\ & + (1 - u')v'\mathbf{t}(x_l, y_t) + u'v'\mathbf{t}(x_r, y_t). \end{aligned} \tag{5.1}$$

Which filter is best typically depends on the desired result. The nearest neighbor can give a crisper feel when little magnification is occurring, but bilinear interpolation is usually a safer choice in most situations.

5.2.2 Minification

When a texture is minimized, several texels may cover a pixel's cell, as shown in Figure 5.10. To get a correct color value for each pixel, you should integrate the effect of the texels influencing the pixel. However, it is difficult to determine precisely the exact influence of all texels near a particular pixel, and it is effectively impossible to do so perfectly in real time.

Because of this limitation, a number of different methods are used in real-time work. One method is to use the nearest neighbor, which works exactly as the corresponding magnification filter does, i.e., it selects the texel which is visible at the very center of the pixel's cell. This filter may cause severe aliasing problems. In Figure 5.11, nearest neighbor is used in the top figure. Towards the horizon, artifacts appear because only one of

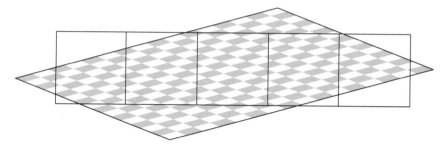

Figure 5.10. A view of a checkerboard-textured polygon through a row of pixel cells, showing how a number of texels affect each pixel.

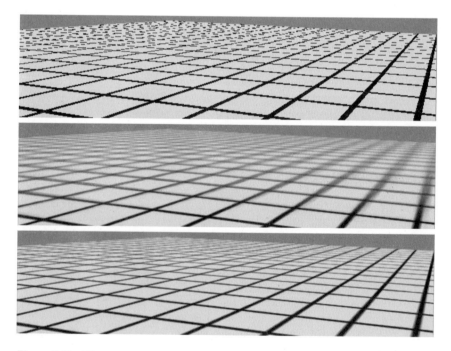

Figure 5.11. The top image was rendered with point sampling (nearest neighbor), the center with mipmapping, and the bottom with summed area tables.

the many texels influencing a pixel is chosen to represent the surface. Such artifacts are even more noticeable as the surface moves with respect to the viewer, and are one manifestation of what is called *temporal aliasing*.

Another filter often available is bilinear interpolation, again working exactly as in the magnification filter. This filter is only slightly better than the nearest neighbor approach for minification. It blends four texels instead of using just one, but when a pixel is influenced by more than four texels, the filter soon fails and produces aliasing.

Better solutions are possible. As discussed in Section 4.4.1, the problem of aliasing can be addressed by sampling and filtering techniques. The signal frequency of a texture depends upon how closely spaced its texels are on the screen. Due to the Nyquist limit, we need to make sure that the texture's signal frequency is no greater than half the sample frequency. For example, say an image is composed of alternating black and white lines, a texel apart. The wavelength is then 2 texels wide (from black line to black line), so the frequency is $\frac{1}{2}$. To properly display this texture on a screen, the frequency must then be at least $2 \times \frac{1}{2}$, i.e., at least one pixel per texel. So, for textures in general, there should be at most one texel per pixel to avoid aliasing.[8]

To achieve this goal, either the pixel's sampling frequency has to increase or the texture frequency has to decrease. The antialiasing methods discussed in the previous chapter give ways to increase the pixel sampling rate. However, these give only a limited increase in sampling frequency. To more fully address this problem, various texture minification algorithms have been developed.

The basic idea behind all texture antialiasing algorithms is the same: to preprocess the texture and create data structures that will help compute a quick approximation of the effect of a set of texels on a pixel. For real-time work, these algorithms have the characteristic of using a fixed amount of time and resources for execution, which implies that for each texture, a fixed number of samples are taken per pixel. A single sample will retrieve the effects of one or more texels.

Mipmapping

The most popular method of antialiasing for textures is called *mipmapping* [802]. It is implemented in some form on even the most modest graphics accelerators now produced. "Mip" stands for *multum in parvo*, Latin for "many things in a small place"—a good name for a process in which the original texture is filtered down repeatedly into smaller images.

---

[8]More correctly, one texel per sample, since supersampling schemes use more samples per pixel.

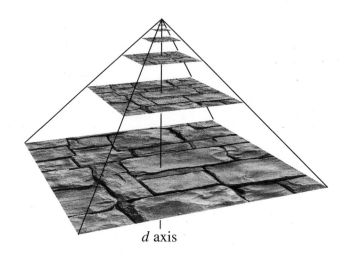

d axis

Figure 5.12. A mipmap is formed by taking the original image (level 0), at the base of the pyramid, and averaging each 2 × 2 area into a texel value on the next level up. The vertical axis is the third texture coordinate, d. In this figure, d is not linear; it is a measure of which two texture levels a sample uses for interpolation.

When the mipmapping minimization filter is used, the original texture is augmented with a set of smaller versions of the texture before the actual rendering takes place. The texture (level zero) is downsampled to a quarter of the original area, with each new texel value often computed as the average of the four neighbor texels. The new, level-one texture is sometimes called a *subtexture* of the original texture. The reduction is performed recursively until one or both of the dimensions of the texture equals 1 texel. This process is illustrated in Figure 5.12.

Two important elements in forming high-quality mipmaps are good filtering and gamma correction. The common way to form a mipmap level is to take each 2 × 2 set of pixels and average them to get the mip value. The filter used is then a box filter, one of the worst filters possible. This can result in poor quality, as it has the effect of blurring low frequencies unnecessarily, while keeping some high frequencies that cause aliasing [92]. It is better to use a Gaussian, Lanczos, Kaiser, or similar filter; fast, free source code exists for the task [92, 691]. See also Section 4.4.1 on sampling and filtering. That said, care must be taken filtering near the edges of textures, paying attention to whether the texture repeats or is a single copy.

By ignoring gamma correction, the overall perceived brightness of the mipmap level will be different than the original texture [93]. As you get

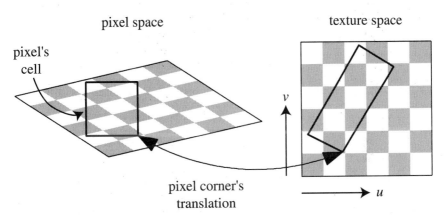

pixel space   texture space

pixel's cell

pixel corner's translation

Figure 5.13. On the left is a square pixel cell and its view of a texture. On the right is the projection of the pixel cell onto the texture itself.

farther away from the object and the uncorrected mipmaps get used, the object can look darker overall, and contrast and details can be affected.

The basic process of accessing this structure while texturing is straightforward. A screen pixel encloses an area on the texture itself. When the pixel's area is projected onto the texture (Figure 5.13), it includes one or more texels.[9] The goal is to determine roughly how much of the texture influences the pixel. There are two common measures used to compute d (which OpenGL calls λ, and which is also known as the level of detail). One is to use the longer edge of the quadrilateral formed by the pixel's cell to approximate the pixel's coverage [802]; the other is to use as a measure the largest absolute value of the four differentials $\partial u/\partial x$, $\partial v/\partial x$, $\partial u/\partial y$, and $\partial v/\partial y$ [430]. Each differential is a measure of the amount of change in the texture coordinate with respect to a screen axis. For example, $\partial u/\partial x$ is the amount of change in the u texture value along the x-screen-axis for one pixel. Because mipmapping is standard in hardware, the precise computations are not covered in depth here. See Williams's original article [802] or Flavell's presentation [233] for more about these equations. McCormack et al. [531] discuss the introduction of aliasing by the largest absolute value method, and they present an alternate formula. Ewins et al. [219] analyze the hardware costs of several algorithms of comparable quality.

The intent of computing the coordinate d is to determine where to sample along the mipmap's pyramid axis (see Figure 5.12). The goal is

---

[9]Using the pixel's cell boundaries is not strictly correct, but is used here to simplify the presentation. Texels outside of the cell can influence the pixel's color; see Section 4.4.1.

a pixel-to-texel ratio of at least 1:1 in order to achieve the Nyquist rate. The important principle here is that as the pixel cell comes to include more texels and d increases, a smaller, blurrier version of the texture is accessed. The (u, v, d) triplet is used to access the mipmap. The value d is analogous to a texture level, but instead of an integer value, d has the fractional value of the distance between levels. The texture level above and the level below the d location are sampled. The (u, v) location is used to retrieve a bilinearly interpolated sample from each of these two texture levels. The resulting sample is then linearly interpolated, depending on the distance from each texture level to d. This entire process is called trilinear interpolation and is performed per pixel.[10] Some hardware performs weaker versions of this algorithm, e.g., per polygon, nearest neighbor, bilinear interpolation on the closest texture level, dithered per pixel between two bilinear samples, or other combinations. Because trilinear interpolation uses two mipmap accesses (versus bilinear, where a single subtexture is accessed), it is twice as expensive to perform on some hardware.

One user control on the d coordinate is the *Level of Detail bias (LOD bias)*. This is a value added to d, and so it affects the relative perceived sharpness of a texture. If we move further up the pyramid to start (increasing d), the texture will look blurrier. A good LOD bias for any given texture will vary with the image type and with the way it is used. For example, images that are somewhat blurry to begin with could use a negative bias, while poorly filtered (aliased) synthetic images used for texturing could use a positive bias. When a textured surface is moving, it often requires a higher bias to avoid temporal aliasing problems.

The result of mipmapping is that, instead of trying to sum all the texels which affect a pixel individually, precombined sets of texels are accessed and interpolated. This process takes a fixed amount of time, no matter what the amount of minification. However, mipmapping has a number of flaws [233]. A major one is *overblurring*. Imagine a pixel cell that covers a large number of texels in the u direction and only a few in the v direction. This case commonly occurs when a viewer looks along a textured surface nearly edge-on. In fact, it is possible to need minification along one axis of the texture and magnification along the other. The effect of accessing the mipmap is that square areas on the texture are retrieved; retrieving rectangular areas is not possible. To avoid aliasing, we choose the largest measure of the approximate coverage of the pixel cell on the texture. This results in the retrieved sample often being relatively blurry. This effect can

---

[10]Mipmapping and filtering in general can also be applied to three-dimensional image textures, in which case an additional level of interpolation is used.

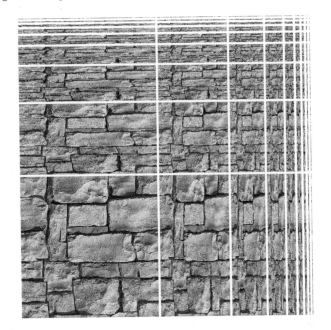

Figure 5.14. The ripmap structure. Note that the images along the diagonal from the lower left to the upper right are the mipmap subtextures.

be seen in the mipmap image in Figure 5.11. The lines moving into the distance on the right show overblurring.

Ripmapping

There are a number of techniques to avoid some or all of this overblurring. One method is the *ripmap* (Hewlett-Packard's term). The idea is to extend the mipmap to include downsampled rectangular areas as subtextures that can be accessed [330]. Figure 5.14 shows the ripmap subtexture array. Four coordinates are used to access this structure: the usual two (u, v) values to access each subtexture, and two for a location in the ripmap array; these indicate the four subtextures among which to interpolate. These last two coordinates are computed using the pixel cell's u and v extents on the texture: The more texels included along an axis, the more downsampled the map that is used [536].

Summed-Area Table

Another method is the *summed-area table* [151]. To use this method, one first creates an array that is the size of the texture but contains more bits

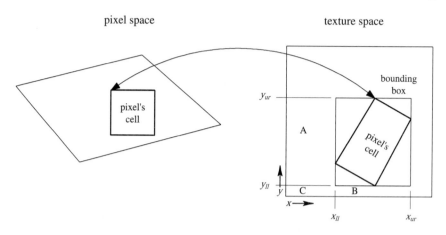

Figure 5.15. The pixel cell is back-projected onto the texture, bound by a rectangle, and the four corners of the rectangle are used to access the summed-area table.

of precision for the color stored (e.g., 16 bits or more for each of red, green, and blue). At each location in this array, one must compute and store the sum of all the corresponding texture's texels in the rectangle formed by this location and texel $(0,0)$ (the origin). During texturing, the pixel cell's projection onto the texture is bound by a rectangle. The summed-area table is then accessed to determine the average color of this rectangle, which is passed back as the texture's color for the pixel. The average is computed using the texture coordinates of the rectangle shown in Figure 5.15. This is done using the formula given in Equation 5.1.

$$\mathbf{c} = \frac{\mathbf{s}[x_{ur}, y_{ur}] - \mathbf{s}[x_{ur}, y_{ll}] - \mathbf{s}[x_{ll}, y_{ur}] + \mathbf{s}[x_{ll}, y_{ll}]}{(x_{ur} - x_{ll})(y_{ur} - y_{ll})} \tag{5.2}$$

Here, x and y are the texel coordinates of the rectangle and $\mathbf{s}[x, y]$ is the summed-area value for that texel. This equation works by taking the sum of the entire area from the upper right corner to the origin, then subtracting off areas A and B by subtracting the neighboring corners' contributions. Area C has been subtracted twice, so it is added back in by the lower left corner. Note that (x_{ll}, y_{ll}) is the upper right corner of area C, i.e., $(x_{ll} + 1, y_{ll} + 1)$ is the lower left corner of the bounding box.

The results of using a summed-area table are shown in Figure 5.11. The lines going to the horizon are sharper near the right edge, but the diagonally crossing lines in the middle are still overblurred. Similar problems occur with the ripmap scheme. The problem is that when a texture is viewed along its diagonal, a large rectangle is generated with many of the texels situated nowhere near the pixel being computed. For example, imagine a long, thin rectangle representing the pixel cell's back-projection lying diagonally across the entire texture in Figure 5.15. The whole texture rectangle's average will be returned, rather than just the average within the pixel cell.

Ripmaps and summed-area tables are examples of what are called *anisotropic filtering* algorithms [330]. Such algorithms are schemes that can retrieve texel values over areas that are not square. However, they are able to do this most effectively in primarily horizontal and vertical directions. Ripmaps were used in high-end Hewlett-Packard graphics accelerators in the early 1990s. To our knowledge, summed-area tables have never seen implementation in hardware. Both schemes are memory intensive. While a mipmap's subtextures take only an additional third of the memory of the original texture, a ripmap's take an additional three times as much as the original. Summed-area tables take at least two times as much memory for textures of size 16×16 or less, with more precision needed for larger textures. Texture memory is a relatively precious commodity, not to be squandered.

Unconstrained Anisotropic Filtering

For current graphics hardware, the most common method to further improve texture filtering is to reuse existing mipmap hardware. The basic idea is that the pixel cell is back-projected, and this quadrilateral (quad) on the texture is then sampled a number of times, and the samples are combined. As outlined above, each mipmap sample has a location and a squarish area associated with it. Instead of using a single mipmap sample to approximate this quad's coverage, the algorithm uses a number of squares to cover the quad. The shorter side of the quad is used to determine d (unlike in mipmapping, where the longer side is often used); this makes the averaged area smaller (and so less blurred) for each mipmap sample. The quad's longer side is used to create a *line of anisotropy* parallel to the longer side and through the middle of the quad. When the amount of anisotropy is between 1:1 and 2:1, two samples are taken along this line (see Figure 5.16). At higher ratios of anisotropy, more samples are taken along the axis.

This scheme allows the line of anisotropy to run in any direction, and so does not have the limitations that ripmaps and summed-area tables had. It also requires no more texture memory than mipmaps do, since it uses the mipmap algorithm to do its sampling. For example, a graphics accelerator may have a dual-pipe architecture that allows it to obtain two

pixel space   texture space

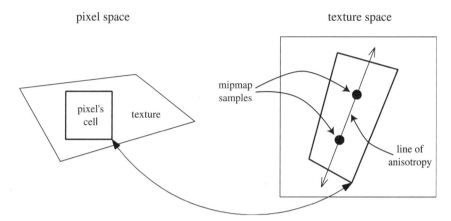

Figure 5.16. Anisotropic filtering. The back-projection of the pixel cell creates a quadrilateral. A line of anisotropy is formed between the longer sides.

mipmap samples in parallel. This architecture can then perform 2:1 anisotropic filtering in real time. As higher numbers of parallel pipes appear in chip sets, the maximum anisotropic ratio that can be used increases. Also, higher ratios can be obtained by having the hardware repeatedly sample. For example, an NVIDIA GeForce3 can perform 8:1 anisotropic filtering. Implementations of anisotropic filtering normally take only as many trilinear samples as are needed. Some implementations, such as the ATI Radeon 8500, perform anisotropic filtering only if the pixel footprint on the texture is nearly vertical or horizontal. An example of anisotropic filtering is shown in Figure 5.17.

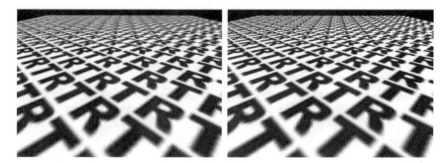

Figure 5.17. Mipmap versus anisotropic filtering. Trilinear mipmapping has been done on the left, 16:1 anisotropic filtering on the right, both at a 640 × 450 resolution, using ATI Radeon hardware. Towards the horizon anisotropic filtering provides a sharper result with minimal aliasing.

This idea of sampling along an axis was first introduced by Schilling et al. with their Texram dynamic memory device [682]. Barkans describes the algorithm's use in the Talisman system [46]. A similar system called Feline is presented by McCormack et al. [532]. Texram's original formulation has the samples along the anisotropic axis (also known as *probes*) given equal weights. Talisman gives half weight to the two probes at opposite ends of the axis. Feline uses a Gaussian filter kernel to weight the probes. These algorithms approach the high quality of software sampling algorithms such as the Elliptical Weighted Average (EWA) filter, which transforms the pixel's area of influence into an ellipse on the texture and weights the texels inside the ellipse by a filter kernel [330].

5.3   Texture Caching and Compression

A complex application may require a considerable number of textures. The amount of fast texture memory varies from system to system, but the general rule is that it is never enough. There are various techniques for *texture caching*, where a balance is sought between speed and minimizing the number of textures (or parts of textures) in memory at one time. For example, for textured polygons that are initially far away, the application may load only the smaller subtextures in a mipmap, since these are the only levels that will be accessed [2, 90]. Each system has its own texture management tools and its own performance characteristics (e.g., 256×256 textures are optimized on some accelerators [180]).

Some general advice is to keep the textures small—no larger than is necessary to avoid magnification problems—and to try to keep polygons grouped by their use of texture. Even if all textures are always in memory, such precautions may improve the processor's cache performance. Another method, called *tiling* or *mosaicing*, involves combining a few smaller (non-repeating) textures into a single larger texture image in order to speed access by avoiding switching textures [180, 536]. See Figure 5.5 on page 122 for an example. Subimages do not have to be a power of two along their edges, so can be used for mapping video input, for example [600]. However, if mipmapping is used, then care must be taken to avoid having the images bleed into each other at higher subtexture levels [825]. Some APIs allow limits to which mipmap levels are generated and used, which helps avoid this problem.

A *Least Recently Used* (LRU) strategy is one commonly used in texture caching schemes, and works as follows. Each texture loaded into the graph-

ics accelerator's memory is given a time stamp for when it was last accessed
to render an image. When space is needed to load new textures, the texture
with the oldest time stamp is unloaded first. DirectX and OpenGL also
allow a priority to be set for each texture, which is used as a tie-breaker: if
the time stamps of two textures are the same, the lower priority texture is
unloaded first. Setting priorities can help in avoiding unnecessary texture
swapping [825].

If managing your own texture manager, one useful strategy suggested
by Carmack [247] is to check the texture being swapped out. If it was
used in the current frame, then thrashing is occurring. LRU is a terrible
strategy under these conditions, as every texture will be swapped in during
each frame. Under this condition, change to *Most Recently Used* (MRU)
until such a time as no textures are swapped out during a frame, then
switch back to LRU.

Loading a texture costs a noticeable amount of time. In a demand-
driven system, where a texture is loaded when it is accessed by a polygon
in view, the number of textures loaded in each frame can vary considerably.
The need for a large number of textures to be loaded in a single frame
makes it difficult to maintain a constant frame rate. One solution is to use
prefetching, where future needs are anticipated and the texture loading is
then spread over a few frames [90].

For flight simulators and geographical information systems, the image
datasets can be huge. The traditional approach is to break these images
into smaller tiles that hardware can handle. Tanner et al. [568, 741] present
an improved data structure called the *clipmap*. The idea is that the entire
dataset is treated as a mipmap, but only a small part of the lower levels of
the mipmap is required for any particular view. For example, if the viewer
is flying above terrain and looking off into the distance, a large amount
of the entire texture may be seen. However, the texture level 0 image is
needed for only a small portion of this picture. Since minification will take
place, a different portion of the level 1 image is needed further out, level 2
beyond that, and so on. By clipping the mipmap structure by the view,
one can identify which parts of the mipmap are needed. An image made
using this technique is shown in Plate IX (following page 274).

Other methods to perform texture caching and improve performance are
discussed by Blow [90] and Wright [825]. Dumont et al. have researched
perceptual rules for weighting how textures are cached [188].

One solution that directly attacks the memory and bandwidth problems and caching concerns is fixed-rate texture compression [54]. By having hardware decode compressed textures on the fly, a texture can require
less texture memory and so increase the effective cache size. At least as

significant, such textures are more efficient to use, as they consume less memory bandwidth when accessed. There are a variety of image compression methods used in image file formats such as JPEG and PNG [546, 577], but it is costly to implement decoding for these in hardware. S3 developed a scheme called S3 Texture Compression (S3TC) [666], which was chosen as a standard for DirectX and called DXTC. It has the advantages of creating a compressed image that is fixed in size, has independently encoded pieces, and is simple (and therefore fast) to decode. Given a particular image type and resolution, we know in advance how much space is needed for the compressed version. This is useful for texture caching, as we know that any image of the given resolution can reuse this image's memory. Each compressed part of the image can be dealt with independently from the others; there are no shared look-up tables or other dependencies, which simplifies decoding. Compressed textures can save memory, but also can be used to provide higher resolution images for the same memory cost. For example, an application could use a 256×256 uncompressed texture. With a compression ratio of 4:1, a 512×512 compressed texture could be used in its place. Using the compressed, higher resolution texture would reduce magnification artifacts that can occur when the viewer is close to the texture.

The DXTC image compression scheme is relatively simple. First the image is broken up into 4×4 pixel blocks, called *tiles*. For opaque images (i.e., those with no alpha channel), each 16-pixel block is encoded by storing two colors and 16 two-bit values. The two colors are represented by 16 bits (5 bits red, 6 green, 5 blue) and are chosen to bound the color range of the pixel block. Given these two colors, the encoding and decoding processes derive two other colors that are evenly spaced between them. This gives four colors to choose from, and so for each pixel, a 2-bit value is stored as a selection of one of these four colors. Thus, a 16-pixel block is represented by a total of 64 bits, or an average of 4 bits per pixel. Given that an image is often originally stored with 16 or 24 bits per pixel, the scheme results in a 4:1 or 6:1 texture compression ratio. Similar schemes are used for images with 1-bit or 8-bit alpha channels [527, 180]. The technique also can be applied to three-dimensional textures.

The main drawback of this compression scheme is that it is *lossy*. That is, the original image usually cannot be retrieved from the compressed version. Only four different color values are used to represent 16 pixels, so if a tile has more than four colors in it, there will be some loss. In practice, the compression scheme generally gives acceptable image fidelity. However, normal maps, used in bump mapping, do not compress well under this scheme.

One of the problems with S3TC is that all the colors used for a block lay on a straight line in RGB space. For example, S3TC cannot represent the colors red, green, and blue in one block. Ivanov and Kuzmin [388] present a similar scheme called *color distribution* that attacks this problem. Essentially, they use the colors from the neighbors' blocks in order to achieve more colors. However, it appears that this scheme needs more memory accesses during decompression, so it is thus slower to unpack, or at least uses more memory bandwidth.

5.4   Multipass Texture Rendering

In computer graphics theory, all illumination equation factors are evaluated at once and a sample color is generated. In practice, the various parts of the lighting equation can be evaluated in separate passes, with each successive pass modifying the previous results. This technique is called *multipass rendering* [173, 568]. There are a wide variety of effects that are done with multiple passes, such as motion blur, depth of field, antialiasing, soft shadows, planar reflections, and more. Here the goal is more modest: to use more elaborate surface lighting equations.

Hardware accelerators are able to significantly improve performance over software renderers for various operations; however, they do not have the flexibility to provide arbitrarily complex lighting models in a single pass. As a simple example, consider the diffuse and specular parts of the lighting equation. Imagine that your hardware can apply only one texture to a surface as it is rendered, and interpolates only one color channel. This is primitive hardware by today's standards, but we want to keep the example simple. There is always some upper limit to the number of textures that hardware can apply in a single pass to a surface, so multipass rendering will always be needed to handle this complexity.

Say you wish to have the diffuse color modulated (multiplied) by a texture, and want the specular highlight to be unmodified by the texture. As shown in Plate V after page 274, this gives a more convincing look. Even with the basic hardware outlined above, this is possible using two passes. In the first pass, compute and interpolate the diffuse illumination contribution and modulate it by the texture. Then compute and interpolate the specular part and render the scene again. This result would then be added to the existing diffusely lit, textured image. Since diffuse and specular components can be treated independently (see Equation 4.14 in Chapter 4), it is perfectly acceptable to compute the lighting in this way.

In a single pass the texture modifies the surface by operations such as **replace**, **decal**, and **modulate**, discussed on page 128. At the end of the texturing pipeline, the texture and surface have formed a fragment, a bundle of color (RGBα) and geometric information (such as the z-depth, and possibly a stencil value or pixel coverage mask) that is applied to the pixel. In normal Z-buffer rendering of opaque surfaces, this fragment replaces the existing pixel data or is discarded, depending on whether it is currently visible or not. In multipass rendering, however, two different functions are commonly used to fold this fragment into the existing image:

- **add** – Add the previous pixel color and the fragment color. Subtracting the fragment color is also possible.

- **blend** – As explained in Section 4.5, two color values can be blended by an alpha value. This alpha value can come from the stored pixel information, from the texture, from a constant alpha sent down the pipeline, or from vertices (in which each vertex is given an alpha value and the alpha is interpolated across the surface).

As will be seen, the alpha channel can be used for a variety of effects beyond transparency and antialiasing.

The basic idea behind multipass rendering is that each pass computes a piece of the lighting equation and the frame buffer is used to store intermediate results. By using off-screen storage and compositing images, arbitrarily complex lighting equations can be evaluated (though not necessarily quickly) [619, 624], as will be seen in Section 6.7.

Multipass rendering is useful when one wants to enable a rendering system to work on a variety of hardware. For example, an early design of the *Quake III* engine uses 10 passes. From Hook's notes [148]:

- (passes 1–4: accumulate bump map)

- pass 5: diffuse lighting

- pass 6: base texture (with specular component)

- (pass 7: specular lighting)

- (pass 8: emissive lighting)

- (pass 9: volumetric/atmospheric effects)

- (pass 10: screen flashes)

On the fastest machine, up to 10 passes are done on some objects to render a single frame. However, if the graphics accelerator cannot maintain a reasonable frame rate, various passes (those in parentheses) can be eliminated. For example, removing the bump-mapping passes reduces the lighting model to 6 passes. The quality of the image is lower, but the real-time experience is maintained. A rendering system is said to be *scalable* if it has this ability to work in some reduced form on various platforms. Pallister and Macri [614] discuss other techniques to make a system scalable.

5.5   Multitexturing

Most graphics hardware today allows two or more textures to be applied in a single rendering pass. This process is called *multitexturing* [180, 695]. To combine the results of these texture accesses, a *texture blending cascade* (a pipeline) is defined that is made up of a series of *texture stages* [180], also called texture units [695]. The first texture stage combines two texture (or interpolated vertex) values, typically RGB and perhaps α (alpha), and this result is then passed on to the next texture stage. Second and successive stages then blend another texture's or interpolant's values with the previous result. This is illustrated in Figure 5.18. Another way to think of this process is that the texture units form a series like a pipeline. The triangle's interpolated vertex values enter the pipeline. Then, each texture in turn is applied to the set of values. After applying the texture, the color and alpha values may be combined (e.g., added). The result is passed onto the next texture stage.[11] The color leaving the last texture stage then optionally has the separate specular color contribution added to it. The final RGB and alpha values then replace or blend with the stored values in the frame buffer [695]. As will be seen in Section 6.6, this simple linear model of the texture pipeline has changed in recent years, as more power and flexibility is added to successive generations of hardware.

In addition to saving rendering passes, multitexturing actually allows more complex shading models than does the application of a single texture per pass. For example, say you want to use a lighting model with expression $AB + CD$, where each variable represents a different color texture's value. This expression is impossible to evaluate without multitexturing or using

---

[11] In DirectX 8 the results from a texture stage may alternately be stored in a separate temporary register, which can then be accessed by any later texture stage.

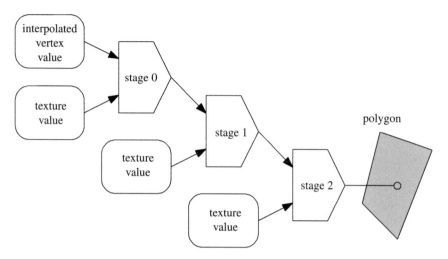

Figure 5.18. The result from a texture is combined with an interpolated value in stage 0, and the result of that combination is then combined with another texture in stage 1. This result of that combination is combined with yet another texture in stage 2 and then applied to the polygon.

off-screen rendering.[12] A multipass algorithm could combine AB in two passes and add C in the next, but it could not fold in D because C would already have been added to AB. There is no place to keep C separate from AB, since only one color can be stored in the color buffer. With multitexturing, the first pass could compute AB. Then the second pass could compute CD and add this result to the AB in the color buffer.

Section 5.7.4 gives an example of how multitexturing can be used for a more elaborate lighting model. Multitexturing and multipass rendering are two of the basic mechanisms used to build up complex lighting equations, and this area is covered in depth in Section 6.6.

5.6 Texture Animation

The image applied to a surface does not have to be static. For example, a video source can be used as a texture that changes from frame to frame.

The texture coordinates need not be static, either. In fact, for environment mapping, they usually change with each frame because of the way

---

[12]Off-screen rendering can be used to store images that can then be combined later.

they are computed (see Section 5.7.4). The application designer can also explicitly change the texture coordinates from frame to frame. Imagine that a waterfall has been modelled and that it has been textured with an image that looks like falling water. Say the v coordinate is the direction of flow. To make the water move, one must subtract an amount from the v coordinates on each successive frame. Subtraction from the texture coordinates has the effect of making the texture itself appear to move forward.

More elaborate effects can be created by modifying the texture coordinates. Linear transformations such as zoom, rotation, and shearing are possible [536, 823]. Image warping and morphing transforms are also possible [813], as are generalized projections [301]. Transforms can in most cases be carried out by using the texture matrix, a part of most graphics pipelines.

By using texture blending techniques, one can realize other animated effects. For example, by starting with a marble texture and fading in a flesh texture, one can make a statue come to life [555].

5.7 Texturing Methods

With the basic theory in place, we will now cover various other forms of texturing beyond gluing simple color images onto surfaces. The rest of this chapter will discuss the use of alpha blending in texturing, reflections via environment mapping, and rough surface simulation using bump mapping, among others. The two chapters that follow will also frequently draw upon texturing methods.

5.7.1 Alpha Mapping

The alpha value can be used for many interesting effects. One texture-related effect is *decaling*. As an example, say you wish to put a picture of a flower on a teapot. You do not want the whole picture, but just the parts where the flower is present. By assigning an alpha of 0 to a texel, you make it transparent so that it has no effect. So, by properly setting the decal texture's alpha, you can replace or blend the underlying surface with the decal. Typically, a clamp or border corresponder function is used with a transparent border to apply a single copy of the decal (versus a repeating texture) to the surface.

Another application of alpha is in making cutouts. Say you make a decal image of a tree, but you do not want the background of this image to affect the scene at all. That is, if an alpha is found to be fully transparent, then the textured surface itself does not affect that pixel. In this way, you can render an object with a complex silhouette using a single polygon.

In the case of the tree, if you rotate the viewer around it, the illusion fails since the tree has no thickness. One answer is to copy this tree polygon and rotate it 90 degrees along the trunk. The two polygons form an inexpensive three-dimensional tree, sometimes called a "cross tree" [545], and the illusion is fairly effective when viewed from ground level. See Figure 5.19. In Section 8.3, we discuss a method called billboarding, which is used to reduce such rendering to a single polygon.

Providing this texture effect means a slight extension of the rendering pipeline. Before testing and replacing the Z-buffer value, there needs to be a test of the alpha value. If alpha is 0, then nothing further is done for the pixel. If this additional test is not done, the tree's background color will not affect the pixel's color, but will potentially affect the z-value, which can lead to rendering errors.

Combining alpha blending and texture animation can produce convincing special effects, such as flickering torches, plant growth, explosions, atmospheric effects, etc.

Figure 5.19. On the left, the tree texture map and the 1-bit alpha channel map below it. On the right, the tree rendered on a single polygon; by adding a second copy of the polygon rotated 90 degrees, we form an inexpensive three-dimensional tree.

5.7.2 Light Mapping

Phong shading was presented in Section 4.3. This technique yields more precise lighting evaluation by computing the illumination at each pixel. But since Gouraud shading is the norm in graphics hardware, short of meshing surfaces finely in order to capture the lighting's effect more finely, it appears that general Phong shading is not possible in a fixed function pipeline. However, for static lighting in an environment, the diffuse component on any surface remains the same from any angle. Because of this view-independence, the contribution of light to a surface could be captured in a texture structure attached to a surface. An elaborate version of this concept was first implemented by Arvo [26] and later by Heckbert [331] in order to capture global illumination information, i.e., light bouncing around the environment.

Carmack realized that this sort of method could be applied to real-time work in lieu of using lighting equations during rendering [2]. By using a separate, precomputed texture that captured the lighting contributions, and multiplying it with the underlying surface, one can achieve Phong-like shading (see Plate XX, following page 274). As Hook points out, this technique is more accurately termed "dark mapping," because the original surface actually decreases in intensity [363]. To make light mapping a bit easier to use and to maintain brightness, DirectX provides texture blending operations that boost the output intensity by a factor of two or four. Values above 1.0 are clamped to 1.0. While multiplying the two textures has a connection with how physical reality works, for a different look another lighting model could be used, such as adding or blending the two textures together.

If the lighting will never change, or will only change in overall brightness, the light texture can simply be multiplied by the surface's material texture during the modeling stage, and the single resulting texture can be used [362]. However, a number of advantages accrue by using light mapping in a separate stage. First, the light texture can generally be low-resolution. In some cases, the brightness of lighting changes slowly across a surface, so the resolution of the texture representing the light can be quite small compared to the surface texture's size. Minimal processing is needed to modify or swap such light textures on the fly. Lighting situations can be reused with a variety of environments, and color textures can be tiled and have different lighting on each tile. Using texture coordinate animation techniques (Section 5.6), light textures can be made to move on walls—e.g., a moving spotlight effect can be created. Also, light maps can be recalculated on the fly for dynamic (changing) lighting. In summary, the flexibility of using separate light textures often outweighs the cost of a separate pass or additional texture stage. See Plate XI following page 274.

Using textures to represent shadows is related to the idea of light mapping. See Section 6.12.1 for more about this method.

Projective textures [536, 694, 823] are also related to light maps, providing a more flexible method of creating lighting such as that made by a slide projector (Figure 5.20). See Section 6.12.2 for projective mapping being used in a similar way to cast shadows.

Image light maps are typically used on diffuse surfaces, and so are sometimes called diffuse light maps. The specular component can also be affected by light mapping, but here the effect is sometimes a little more involved. A diffuse light map simulates the illumination on a diffuse surface. This works because a diffuse surface looks the same regardless of the angle at which it is viewed. The specular component varies with the view direction, and so a simple substitution of light by a light map cannot be done.

It is possible to capture the specular component by meshing the surface, and then use a light map to capture effects such as spotlight falloff or cone cutoff. However, usually the specular highlight varies rapidly across a surface, so a mesh will have to be so fine that there is little to gain in using a light map along with it.

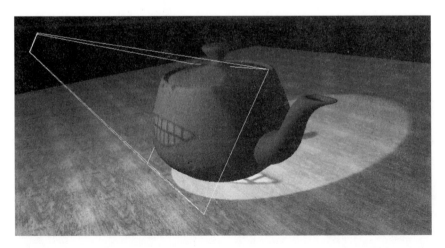

Figure 5.20. Projective texturing. The texture is projected onto the teapot and ground plane. Note that the teapot does not cast a shadow; the projective texture is applied to all surfaces it encounters. *(Image courtesy of NVIDIA Corp.)*

As discussed in Section 5.7.4, one method of rendering shininess on a surface for directional lights is to use environment mapping, as this technique gives a per-pixel specular highlight.

An extension to image texture light maps is three-dimensional texture light maps, where actual beams of light are stored throughout the volume [174, 258, 536]. Though memory-intensive (as are all three-dimensional textures), this method is advantageous because the light is actually there in space. If the light's volume of effect is symmetrical along the three axes, the memory footprint can be reduced eightfold by using the mirror-once corresponder function (see page 125). The three-dimensional texture is applied whenever an object overlaps the light's volume. If the light drops off in a spherical pattern, the volume can be represented by combining a two-dimensional and a one-dimensional texture map [174].

5.7.3 Gloss Mapping

Not all objects are uniformly shiny over their surface. The wooden statue's eyes are made of obsidian, the tile floor is worn in places, and the jet's steel wings have letters painted on in flat paint. These phenomena can be simulated by using a technique called *gloss mapping*, and the texture that makes this happen is called a *gloss map*. See Figure 5.21.

A gloss map is a texture that varies the contribution of the specular component over the surface. For example, imagine a brick wall with shiny bricks and dull mortar. The gloss map would then be white where the bricks are located and black where the mortar is. The surface of the wall itself would have to be tessellated to properly catch the specular highlight.

Figure 5.21. A shiny metal sheet. On the right, a gloss map is added to give the effect that the surface is corroded. *(Images courtesy of NVIDIA Corp.)*

The lighting equation per pixel is:

$$\mathbf{o} = \mathbf{t}_{diff} \otimes \mathbf{i}_{diff} + t_{gloss}\mathbf{i}_{spec}, \tag{5.3}$$

where $\mathbf{t}_{diff}$ is the RGB diffuse surface texture map that gives the bricks and mortar their color, $\mathbf{i}_{diff}$ is the interpolated diffuse lighting color, t_{gloss} is the single-value gloss map, and $\mathbf{i}_{spec}$ is the interpolated highlight from the vertex. The effect is that the bricks will have a specular highlight while the mortar will not. The shininess exponent of the surface is not affected, rather the brightness of the highlights is modulated by the gloss map.

The key idea here is that all material (and for that matter, light) properties can be supplied by textures rather than by constants or per-vertex values. This theme will be explored further in Section 6.6 on pixel shaders.

5.7.4 Environment Mapping

Environment Mapping (EM), also called reflection mapping, is a simple yet powerful method of generating approximations of reflections in curved surfaces. This technique was introduced by Blinn and Newell [68]. All EM methods start with a ray from the viewer to a point on the reflector. This ray is then reflected with respect to the normal at that point. Instead of finding the intersection with the closest surface, as ray tracing does [260, 705], EM uses the direction of the reflection vector as an index to an image containing the environment. This is conceptualized in Figure 5.22.

The environment mapping approximation assumes that the objects and lights being reflected with EM are far away, and that the reflector will not reflect itself. If these assumptions hold, then the environment around the reflector can be treated as a two-dimensional projection surrounding it.

The steps of an EM algorithm are:

- Generate or load a two-dimensional image representing the environment (this is the environment map).

- For each pixel that contains a reflective object, compute the normal at the location on the surface of the object.

- Compute the reflection vector from the view vector and the normal.

- Use the reflection vector to compute an index into the environment map that represents the objects in the reflection direction.

- Use the texel data from the environment map to color the current pixel.

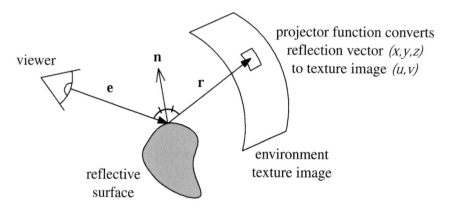

viewer

projector function converts
reflection vector *(x,y,z)*
to texture image *(u,v)*

environment
texture image

reflective
surface

Figure 5.22. Environment mapping. The viewer sees an object, and the reflection vector **r** is computed from **e** and **n**. The reflection vector accesses the environment's representation. The access information is computed by using some projector function to convert the reflection vector's (x, y, z) to (typically) a (u, v) value, which is used to retrieve texture data.

The term *reflection mapping* is sometimes used interchangeably with environment mapping. However, this term has a specific meaning. When the surface's material properties are used to modify an existing environment map, a reflection map texture is generated. A simple example: To make a red, shiny sphere, the color red is multiplied with an environment map to create a reflection map. Reflection mapping techniques are discussed in depth in Section 6.4.2.

There are a variety of projector functions that map the reflection vector into one or more textures. Blinn and Newell's algorithm and Greene's cubic environment mapping technique are classic mapping methods, and so are covered first. The sphere map technique is presented next. Finally, Heidrich and Seidel's paraboloid mapping method is explained.

Blinn and Newell's Method

In 1976, Blinn and Newell [68] developed the first environment mapping algorithm. For each environment-mapped pixel, they compute the reflection vector and then transform it into spherical coordinates (ρ, ϕ). Here ϕ, called longitude, varies from 0 to 2π radians, and ρ, called latitude, varies from 0 to π radians. (ρ, ϕ) is computed from Equation 5.4, where $\mathbf{r} = (r_x, r_y, r_z)$ is the normalized reflection vector.

$$
\begin{aligned}
\rho &= \arccos(-r_z) \\
\phi &= \texttt{atan2}(r_y, r_x)
\end{aligned}
\tag{5.4}
$$

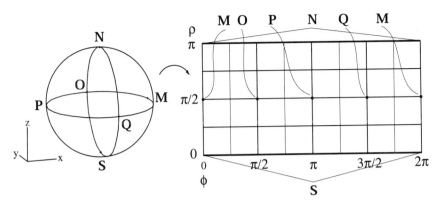

Figure 5.23. Illustration of Blinn and Newell's environment map. The sphere on the left is unfolded into the rectangle (the environment map) on the right. The key points **N, S, M, O, P,** and **Q,** mentioned in the text, are also shown.

See page 6 for a description of `atan2`. The viewer's reflection vector is computed similarly to the light's reflection vector (see Section 4.3.2):

$$\mathbf{r} = \mathbf{e} - 2(\mathbf{n} \cdot \mathbf{e})\mathbf{n}, \tag{5.5}$$

where $\mathbf{e}$ is the normalized vector from the eye to the surface location, and $\mathbf{n}$ is the surface normal at that location.

The spherical coordinates (ρ, ϕ) are then transformed to the range $[0, 1)$ and used as (u, v) coordinates to access the environment texture, producing a reflection color. Since the reflection vector is transformed into spherical coordinates, the environment texture is an image of an "unfolded" sphere. Essentially, the texture covers a sphere that surrounds the reflection point. This projector function is sometimes called a latitude-longitude mapping, since v corresponds to latitude and u to longitude. This mapping is shown in Figure 5.23.

Some key points are displayed in this table:

name	coordinate	angles
N (north pole)	$(0, 0, 1)$	$\rho = \pi, \phi$ is undefined
S (south pole)	$(0, 0, -1)$	$\rho = 0, \phi$ is undefined
M	$(1, 0, 0)$	$\rho = \pi/2, \phi = 0$
O	$(0, 1, 0)$	$\rho = \pi/2, \phi = \pi/2$
P	$(-1, 0, 0)$	$\rho = \pi/2, \phi = \pi$
Q	$(0, -1, 0)$	$\rho = \pi/2, \phi = 3\pi/2$

Although easy to implement, this method has some disadvantages. First, there is a border at $\phi = 0$, and second, the map converges at the poles. An image used in environment mapping must match at the seam along its vertical edges (i.e., must tile seamlessly) and needs to avoid distortion problems near the top and bottom edges.

This method computes an index into the environment map for each visible point on the objects that should have reflections. Its computations are therefore on a per-pixel basis, which implies that it is not normally feasible for real-time graphics. This is because lighting equations are normally evaluated at the vertices, not per pixel.

For real-time work, Equation 5.4 can be used to compute indices into the environment map at the vertices, and then these coordinates can be interpolated across the triangle. However, errors will occur if the vertices of a triangle have indices to the environment map that cross the poles. As discussed in Section 11.2.1, texture coordinate problems at the poles are difficult to avoid when using triangles for interpolation.

Errors can also occur if the endpoints span the seam where the vertical edges of the environment textures meet. For example, imagine a short line that has one u coordinate at 0.97 and the other u coordinate at 0.02. An error results if we interpolate from 0.97 to 0.02 without paying attention to the seam, as the interpolation would travel through 0.96 on down. Interpolation should go up to 0.98, 0.99, then wrap to 0.0, 0.01, 0.02. One solution to this problem is to find the absolute value of the difference between the coordinates (0.95 = 0.97 − 0.02 for the example). If this value is greater than 0.5, then 1.0 is added to the smaller coordinate and the texture is repeated. For the example, the range would then be 0.97 to 1.02 [465]. Some APIs have direct support to avoid seam problems. For example, DirectX supports what it calls "texture wrapping" (not to be confused with its "wrap texture address mode"; see Section 5.1).

In general, this method sees little use as an environment mapping technique. It is described here in part for historic reasons, and because the spherical projector function is commonly used in texture mapping in general. The next three methods are those that currently find use for EM.

Cubic Environment Mapping

In 1986, Greene [287] introduced another EM technique. This method is far and away the most popular EM method implemented in modern graphics hardware, due to its speed and flexibility. The *cubic environment map* (a.k.a. em cube map) is obtained by placing the camera in the center of the environment and then projecting the environment onto the sides of a cube positioned with its center at the camera's location. The images of the cube are then used as the environment map. In practice, the scene is rendered six times (one for each cube face) with the camera at the center of the cube, looking at each cube face with a 90-degree view angle. This type of environment map is shown in Figure 5.24. In Figure 5.25, a typical cubic environment map is shown.

A great strength of Greene's method is that environment maps can be generated by any renderer relatively easily (versus Blinn and Newell's method, which uses a spherical projection), and can be generated in real time. See Plate XII, following page 274, for an example. It also has more uniform sampling characteristics. In contrast, Blinn and Newell's method has an excessive number of texels near the poles as compared to the equator.

The direction of the reflection vector (which does not have to be normalized) determines which face of the cube to use. The reflection vector coordinate with the largest magnitude selects the corresponding face (e.g., the vector $(-3.2, 5.1, -8.4)$ selects the $-Z$ face). The remaining two coordinates are divided by the absolute value of the largest magnitude coordinate, i.e., 8.4. They now range from -1 to 1, and are simply remapped to $[0, 1]$ in order to compute the texture coordinates. For example, the coordinates $(-3.2, 5.1)$ are mapped to $((-3.2/8.4+1)/2, (5.1/8.4+1)/2) \approx (0.31, 0.80)$.

In the same manner as Blinn and Newell's method, this technique is per-pixel based. If two vertices are found to reflect onto different cube faces, steps need to be taken to interpolate correctly between them. One application-side method is to subdivide the problematic polygon along the EM cube edge [301], so that all interpolation happens on a single cube face. The solution that modern hardware implements is to put the reflection

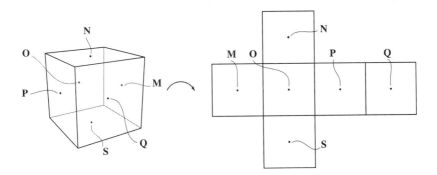

Figure 5.24. Illustration of Greene's environment map, with key points shown. The cube on the left is unfolded into the environment map on the right.

Figure 5.25. A typical cubic environment map. *(Image courtesy of Ned Greene/NYIT.)*

vector interpolation and face computation in the accelerator. By doing so, the EM lookup can be done per pixel. Cubic maps have no singularities, and are *view-independent*, i.e., they can be used for any view direction. However, because they need special purpose hardware, other solutions were developed that can work on any accelerator with texturing (in other words, any accelerator).

Sphere Mapping

First mentioned by Williams [802], and independently developed by Miller and Hoffman [548], this was the first environment mapping technique supported in general commercial graphics hardware. The texture image is derived from the appearance of the environment as viewed orthographically in a perfectly reflective sphere, so this texture is called a sphere map. One way to make a sphere map of a real environment is to take a photograph of a shiny sphere, such as a Christmas tree ornament. See Plate XXIV, following page 274, for an example. This resulting circular image is also sometimes called a *light probe*, as it captures the lighting situation at the sphere's location [162]. Sphere map textures for synthetic scene can be generated using ray tracing or by warping the images generated for a cubic environment map [536]. See Plate VI (following page 274) for an example of environment mapping done with sphere maps.

The sphere map has a basis (see Appendix A) that is the frame of reference in which the texture was generated. That is, the image is viewed along some axis $\mathbf{f}$ in world space, with $\mathbf{u}$ as the up vector for the image and $\mathbf{h}$ going horizontally to the right (and all are normalized). This gives a basis matrix:

$$\begin{pmatrix} h_x & h_y & h_z & 0 \\ u_x & u_y & u_z & 0 \\ f_x & f_y & f_z & 0 \\ 0 & 0 & 0 & 1 \end{pmatrix}. \tag{5.6}$$

To access the sphere map, first transform the surface normal, $\mathbf{n}$, and the vector, $\mathbf{e}$, from the current eye position to the vertex using this matrix. This yields $\mathbf{n}'$ and $\mathbf{e}'$ in the sphere map's space. The reflection vector is then computed to access the sphere map texture:

$$\mathbf{r} = \mathbf{e}' - 2(\mathbf{n}' \cdot \mathbf{e}')\mathbf{n}', \tag{5.7}$$

with $\mathbf{r}$ being the resulting reflection vector, in the sphere map's space.

What a reflective sphere does is show the entire environment on just the front of the sphere. It maps each reflection direction to a point on the two-dimensional image of this sphere. Say we wanted to go the other direction, that given a point on the sphere map we would want the reflection direction. To do this, we would get the surface normal at the sphere at that point and so generate the reflection direction. So, to reverse the process and get the location on the sphere, we need to derive the surface normal on the sphere, which will then yield the (u, v) parameters needed to access the sphere map.

The sphere's normal is the half-angle vector between the reflection direction $\mathbf{r}$ and the direction to the eye, which is $(0, 0, 1)$ in the sphere map's space. See Figure 5.26. This normal vector $\mathbf{n}$ is simply the sum of the eye and reflection vectors, i.e., $(r_x, r_y, r_z + 1)$. Normalizing this vector gives the unit normal:

$$m = \sqrt{r_x^2 + r_y^2 + (r_z + 1)^2}, \tag{5.8}$$

$$\mathbf{n} = \left(\frac{r_x}{m}, \frac{r_y}{m}, \frac{r_z + 1}{m} \right). \tag{5.9}$$

If the sphere is at the origin and its radius is 1, the unit normal's coordinates are then also the location $\mathbf{h}$ of the normal on the sphere. We do not need

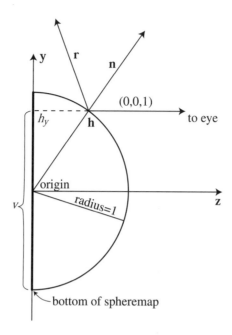

Figure 5.26. Given the constant view direction and reflection vector **r** in the sphere map's space, the sphere map's normal **n** is halfway between these two. For a unit sphere at the origin, the intersection point **h** has the same coordinates as the unit normal **n**. Also shown is how h_y (measured from the origin) and the sphere map texture coordinate v are related.

h_z, as (h_x, h_y) describes a point on the image of the sphere, with each value in the range $[-1, 1]$. To map this coordinate to the range $[0, 1)$ to access the sphere map, divide each by two and add a half, as shown below.

$$m = \sqrt{r_x^2 + r_y^2 + (r_z + 1)^2} \tag{5.10}$$

$$u = \frac{r_x}{2m} + 0.5 \tag{5.11}$$

$$v = \frac{r_y}{2m} + 0.5 \tag{5.12}$$

In practice, this equation can be computed using the texture matrix [827].

Sphere mapping is an improvement over Blinn and Newell's method in a number of ways. There is no texture seam to interpolate across and only one singularity, located around the edge of the sphere map. This singularity rarely causes problems, as all valid texture locations are inside the circle it forms and so its border cannot be crossed. Because of this, the technique can be implemented on any graphics hardware that supports texture mapping, since the texture coordinates can be computed by the application. This texture projector function is also simple to add to graphics hardware, and can be implemented using the texture matrix.

There are some disadvantages to the sphere map. First, moving between two points on the sphere map is not linear. As in Blinn and Newell's method, linear interpolation on the texture is just an approximation, and errors become more serious toward the edge of the map. The sphere map is valid for only a single view direction, so even if the view changes direction, the same mapping gets used. For example, if you use the same sphere map as you moved around a reflective object in empty space, the object will look like it is moving instead of you. The sphere map does capture the entire environment, so it is possible to compute the EM texture coordinates for the new eye viewing direction in the application stage for each frame. However, doing so can result in visual artifacts, as small parts of the sphere map become magnified due to the new view, and the singularity becomes a problem. If the viewer is to be allowed to change view direction, it is better to use a view-independent EM, such as cubic mapping, if available, or paraboloid mapping, explained next.

Paraboloid Mapping

Heidrich and Seidel [342, 345] propose using two environment textures to perform paraboloid environment mapping. The idea is similar to that of sphere mapping, but instead of generating the texture by recording the reflection of the environment off a sphere, two paraboloids are used. Each paraboloid creates a circular texture similar to a sphere map, with each covering an environment hemisphere. See Figure 5.27.

As with sphere mapping, the reflection ray is computed with Equation 5.7 in the map's basis. The sign of the z-component of the reflection vector is used to decide which of the two textures to access. Then the access function is simply:

$$u = \frac{r_x}{2(1+r_z)} + 0.5 \qquad (5.13)$$

$$v = \frac{r_y}{2(1+r_z)} + 0.5 \qquad (5.14)$$

for the front image, and the same with sign reversals for r_z for the back image.

Paraboloid mapping works on hardware that supports proper projective texture coordinate transformation and interpolation [410]. The texture

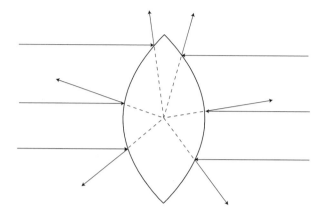

Figure 5.27. Two paraboloid mirrors that capture an environment using diametrically opposite views. The reflection vectors all extend to meet at the center of the object, the foci of both paraboloids.

transformation matrix is set and used as follows:

$$\begin{pmatrix} 1 & 0 & 1 & 1 \\ 0 & 1 & 1 & 1 \\ 0 & 0 & 0 & 0 \\ 0 & 0 & 2 & 2 \end{pmatrix} \begin{pmatrix} r_x \\ r_y \\ 1 \\ r_z \end{pmatrix}. \tag{5.15}$$

The authors present an OpenGL implementation for this method. The problem of interpolating across the seam between the two textures is handled by accessing both paraboloid textures. If a sample is not on one texture, it is black, and each sample will be on one and only one of the textures. Summing the results (one of which is always zero) gives the environment's contribution.

There is no singularity with the paraboloid map, so interpolation can be done between any two reflection directions. The paraboloid map has more uniform texel sampling of the environment compared to the sphere map and even the cubical map. For these reasons, paraboloid mapping, like cubic mapping, is view-independent. As with sphere maps, paraboloid mapping can be done on any graphics hardware that supports texturing. The main drawback of paraboloid mapping is in making the maps themselves. Cubic maps are straightforward to make for synthetic scenes and can be regenerated on the fly, and sphere maps of real environments are relatively simple to photograph, but paraboloid maps have neither advantage. Paraboloid maps have to be created by either warping images or by using ray tracing.

Lighting Using Environment Mapping

An important use of environment mapping techniques is generating specular reflections and refractions [555, 802]. As discussed in Section 4.3, Gouraud shading can miss highlights (reflections of lights) because a light's effect is assessed only at the vertices. Environment mapping can solve this problem by representing the lights in the texture. By doing so, we can simulate highlighting on a per-pixel basis for any number of lights, at a fixed cost (see Plate VI, following page 274). Lights do not have to be points, but can be any size and shape.

Recursive reflections of objects in a scene can be performed using environment mapping [173, 536]. For example, imagine a red and a blue mirrored ball some distance from each other. Generate an EM for the red sphere, then generate an EM for the blue while using the red sphere's EM during its creation. The blue sphere now includes a reflection of the red sphere, which in turn reflects the world. This recursion should in theory go on for several steps (until we cannot make out any differences), but this is expensive. A cheaper version of this computes only one environment map per frame using the environment maps from the previous frame [238]. This

Figure 5.28. Recursive reflections, done with environment mapping. *(Image courtesy of Kasper Høy Nielsen.)*

gives approximate recursive reflections. Figure 5.28 shows some examples using this technique. Hakura et al. [314] show how a set of EMs can be used to capture local interreflections, i.e., when a part of an object is reflected in it self. Such methods are very expensive in terms of texture memory. Rendering a teapot with ray tracing quality required 100 EMs of 256×256 resolution.

Other material effects, such as ambient and diffuse, can be computed quickly using environment mapping. Some background in radiometry theory is needed before delving into these techniques. This background is presented in Section 6.1, and the techniques themselves are then presented in Section 6.4.2.

A potential stumbling block of EM is worth mentioning. Flat surfaces usually do not work well when environment mapping is used. The problem with a flat surface is that the rays that reflect off of it usually do not vary by more than a few degrees. This results in a small part of the EM texture's being mapped onto a relatively large surface. Normally, the individual texels of the texture become visible, unless bilinear interpolation is used; even then, the results do not look good, as a small part of the texture is extremely magnified. We have also been assuming that perspective projection is being used. If orthographic viewing is used, the situation is much worse for flat surfaces. In this case, all the reflection vectors are the same, and so the surface will get a constant color from some single texel. Other real-time techniques such as planar reflections (Section 6.10.1) may be of more use for flat surfaces.

EXAMPLE: DIFFUSE, GLOSS, AND REFLECTION MAPPING Various texturing effects can be combined. One example from Bushnell and Mitchell is to use reflection mapping with gloss and diffuse color texturing [107]. The pear shown in Plate XIII (following page 274) is rendered using this lighting model, which looks like this:

$$\mathbf{o} = \mathbf{t}_{diff} \otimes \mathbf{i}_{diff} + t_{gloss}\mathbf{r}_{spec}, \qquad (5.16)$$

where $\mathbf{t}_{diff}$ is the RGB texture, $\mathbf{i}_{diff}$ the interpolated diffuse lighting, t_{gloss} the monochrome gloss texture, and $\mathbf{r}_{spec}$ the reflection map's RGB specular highlight. One texture has four channels and is set up so that the RGB values are the diffuse pear skin texture, $\mathbf{t}_{diff}$, and the alpha value is actually the gloss intensity, t_{gloss}. The alpha channel is not used in the traditional way here; it is not meant to affect the opacity of the RGB values. Rather, the alpha channel is an efficient place to store the gloss texture. The reflection map represents how a light creates a specular highlight on a surface (see Section 6.4.2 for more about this type of reflection map).

This lighting model can be computed using two texture stages. Each texture stage has up to two RGB color inputs and up to two alpha inputs. In the first stage, the interpolated diffuse color and the pear skin's RGB texture are the two color inputs. These are multiplied together (a.k.a. modulated) to give the first term $\mathbf{t}_{diff} \otimes \mathbf{i}_{diff}$ of the equation. There is one alpha channel input, the gloss map texture's value, which is stored in the alpha channel of the texture. See Figure 5.29.

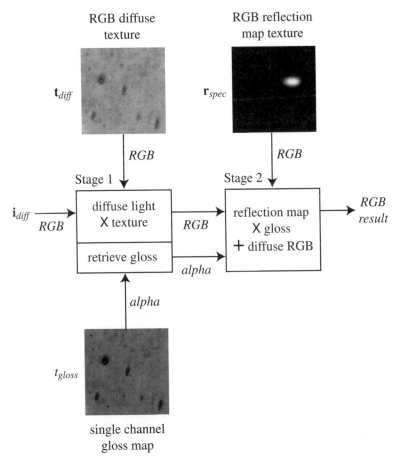

Figure 5.29. Multitexture example. The first texture consists of an RGB texture $\mathbf{t}_{diff}$ of the pear's skin color and a gloss map t_{gloss} stored in the alpha channel. The reflection map $\mathbf{r}_{spec}$ has a single bright patch represent the reflected light. *(Images courtesy of J.L. Mitchell, ATI Technologies Inc.)*

These color and alpha results from the first texture stage are inputs to the second stage. The other input is the color retrieved from the reflection map. A special operator is used in this stage. It multiplies a color by an alpha and adds in the other color. This operator is used here to multiply the reflection map's specular highlight $\mathbf{r}_{spec}$ term by the first stage's t_{gloss} value stored in alpha. The result is added to the first term and the final result is as shown in Equation 5.16. □

5.7.5 Bump Mapping

Introduced by Blinn in 1978 [70], *bump mapping* is a technique that makes a surface appear uneven in some manner: bumpy, wrinkled, wavy, etc. See Figure 5.30 for an example. Bump maps can simulate features that would otherwise take many polygons to model, e.g., folds in clothes or musculature on animals [673]. See Plate XXXVIII (following page 562). The basic idea is that, instead of using a texture to change a color component in the illumination equation, we access a texture to modify the surface normal. The geometric normal of the surface remains the same; we merely modify the normal used in the lighting equation. This operation has no physical equivalent; we perform changes on the surface normal, but the surface itself remains smooth in the geometric sense. Just as having a normal per vertex gives the illusion that the surface is smooth between polygons, modifying the normal per pixel changes the perception of the polygon surface itself.

 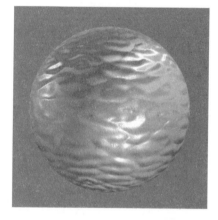

Figure 5.30. A wavy heightfield bump image and its use on a sphere, rendered with per-pixel illumination.

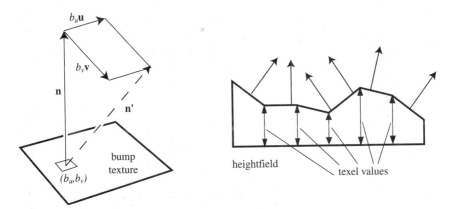

Figure 5.31. On the left, a normal vector **n** is modified in the **u** and **v** directions by the (b_u, b_v) values taken from the bump texture, giving **n'** (which is unnormalized). On the right, a heightfield and its effect on shading normals is shown.

One bump texturing technique stores in a texture two signed values, b_u and b_v, at each point. These two values correspond to the amount to vary the normal along the **u** and **v** image axes. That is, these texture values, which typically are bilinearly interpolated, are used to scale two vectors that are perpendicular to the normal. These two vectors are added to the normal to change its direction. The two values b_u and b_v describe which way the surface faces at the point. See Figure 5.31. This type of bump map texture is called an *offset vector bump map* or *offset map*.

Another way to represent bumps is to use a *heightfield* to modify the surface normal's direction. Each monochrome texture value represents a height, so in the texture white is a high area and black a low one (or vice versa; a signed value is used to scale or negate the values in bump maps in still-image rendering systems). This is a common format used when first creating or scanning a bump map. The heightfield is used to derive u and v signed values similar to those used in the first method. This is done by taking the differences between neighboring columns to get the slopes for u, and between neighboring rows for v [684]. A variant is to use a Sobel filter, which gives a greater weight to the directly adjacent neighbors [258].

Per-pixel bump mapping is extremely convincing, and offers an inexpensive way to add the effect of geometric detail. One place the illusion breaks down is around the silhouettes of objects. At these edges, the viewer notices that there are no real bumps, just smooth outlines. Another artifact of using bump mapping is that the bumps do not cast shadows onto their own surface, which can look unrealistic. More advanced real-time rendering methods can be used to provide self-shadowing effects. Sloan and Cohen encode the height of the shadowing horizon at each point on the bump map for eight cardinal directions, then generate and access a series of textures to determine the amount of self-shadowing for a given lighting situation [715]. Heidrich et al. use ellipses to approximate the effect of the horizon, as well as illumination from the interreflection of light on the surface [347]. Microsoft similarly stores cones of influence in a texture to encode the amount a surface is self-shadowed [547]. Malzbender et al. [513] present a method of encoding illumination for a set of images into a texture consisting of polynomial coefficients that capture bumpiness, self-shadowing, and interreflection effects.

For static scenes, lighting can (and should) be precomputed. For example, if a surface has no specular highlights and the lights do not move with respect to the surface, then the bumpy shading could be computed once and the result used as a color texture map for that surface. Similarly, if the surface, light, and eye all are fixed relative to each other, a shiny bumpy surface needs to be rendered only once. All of the bump mapping algorithms that follow are for dynamic lighting situations, though of course these can be used to precompute static lighting.

In classical bump mapping, the normal is varied per pixel and used in a full illumination equation. This flexibility to evaluate any equation is beyond the capabilities of almost all real-time systems. Instead, what we do is to solve specific, simpler versions of the general illumination equation. The parts of the simpler equation that change per pixel are retrieved from or computed using textures. Note that for the bump mapping techniques in this section there is an assumption that a square piece of the bump map is being applied to a square patch of the surface. In other words, the texture being applied is assumed to have its u-axis perpendicular to the v-axis (the texture is not sheared) and the axes have similar scales (the texture is not stretched). Breaking the square patch assumption can lead to rendering artifacts [175, 422].

Emboss Bump Mapping

One of the first methods used for real-time bump mapping employs a technique borrowed from two-dimensional image processing. Called *embossing* [684], it is a way to give a chiselled look to an image. To obtain an embossed effect, the height field image is copied, shifted slightly, and subtracted from its original. See Figure 5.32.

This same embossing technique can be used with three-dimensional surfaces. The basic algorithm is as follows [536, 612]:

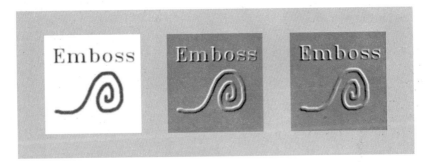

Figure 5.32. Embossing. The original image is on the left; the center shows the image embossed as if lit from the upper left; the right shows it as if lit from the upper right.

1. Render the surface with the heightfield applied as a diffuse monochrome texture.

2. Shift all the vertex (u, v) coordinates in the direction of the light.

3. Render this surface with the heightfield again applied as a diffuse texture, subtracting from the first-pass result. This gives the emboss effect.

4. Render the surface again with no heightfield, diffusely illuminated and Gouraud-shaded. Add this shaded image to the result.

The involved part of the procedure is determining how much to shift the vertex (u, v) values in Step 2. What we need to do is add to these vertex values the light's direction relative to the surface. This process is shown in Figure 5.33.

To find the light's direction relative to the surface, we need to form a coordinate system at the vertex and transform the light into this system (similar to Equation 5.6). First, retrieve the shading normal $\mathbf{n}$ at the vertex. Then, find a surface vector $\mathbf{t}$ that follows one of the two texture coordinate axes $\mathbf{u}$ or $\mathbf{v}$; $\mathbf{t}$ is perpendicular to $\mathbf{n}$ and tangent to (i.e., travels along) the surface. Finally, create a third vector $\mathbf{b}$, the binormal, which is mutually perpendicular to $\mathbf{n}$ and $\mathbf{t}$ and runs in the direction of the other texture coordinate axis (the one not used when forming $\mathbf{t}$). This vector is found by simply computing the cross product: $\mathbf{b} = \mathbf{n} \times \mathbf{t}$. Normalize all these vectors and form a basis matrix:

$$\begin{pmatrix} t_x & t_y & t_z & 0 \\ b_x & b_y & b_z & 0 \\ n_x & n_y & n_z & 0 \\ 0 & 0 & 0 & 1 \end{pmatrix}. \tag{5.17}$$

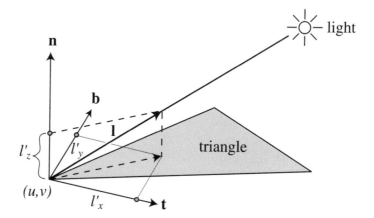

Figure 5.33. The light's direction **l** is transformed so that it is expressed as **l′** in terms of the triangle vertex's normal **n**, tangent vector **t**, and binormal **b**. The light's direction is then cast upon the triangle's plane by setting $l'z$ to zero. This resulting vector is scaled and added to the vertex's texture coordinates.

This matrix is used to transform the light direction **l**, the normalized vector from the vertex to the light. The resulting light vector is then in the vertex's *tangent space* [175, 422]. See Figure 5.34. This basis matrix creation and shift computation must be performed separately at each vertex for curved surfaces and for flat surfaces where the light vector noticeably changes. The resulting vector (l'_x, l'_y) gives the direction in which to shift (u, v). For example, if **t** follows the **u** axis, then l'_x is multiplied by some

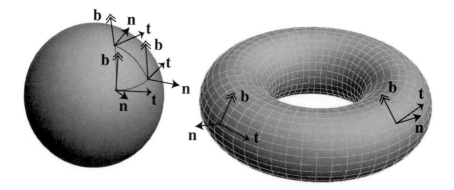

Figure 5.34. A spherical triangle is shown with its tangent space basis shown at each corner. Shapes like a sphere and torus have a natural tangent space basis, as the latitude and longitude lines on the torus show.

value and added to texture coordinate u, and l'_y is multiplied by the same scale value and added to v.[13]

The value used to multiply l'_x and l'_y varies depending on the height-field's characteristics and the effect desired. A good start is to resize the shift to be the width of a texel. That is, normalize the vector (l'_x, l'_y) and divide by r, where r is the bump texture's resolution [536].

There are a number of serious limitations and problems with the emboss method of bump mapping. The technique applies only to diffuse surfaces; specular highlights are not possible. When the light is directly over a surface, no offset occurs, so the bumps disappear entirely. The basic embossing algorithm does not handle bumps that face away from the light on surfaces that are illuminated. The technique also does not allow mipmap filtering of the bump map, as the algorithm is based on shifting approximately one texel. As smaller mipmap levels are used, not enough shifting occurs and the surface goes flat. Though the technique can be used on almost any system, it is not robust and has failed to be adopted in applications. We discuss it here because forming a tangent space surface basis and transforming the light vector to it is a key component of the dot product method, discussed next.

Dot Product Bump Mapping

An algorithm that is conceptually simple is the dot product method, sometimes called *dot3 bump mapping*. This is the primary method of performing bump mapping on modern graphics hardware. Instead of storing heights or slopes, the actual normals for the surface are stored as (x, y, z) vectors in a *normal map* [131, 174, 258, 342, 345, 422]. The 8 bit values are mapped to $[-1, 1]$, e.g., for the x-axis the value 0 represents -1.0 and 255 represents 1.0 .[14] To compute the effect of a light source, the positional light source's location (or directional light's direction) is transformed to the surface's tangent space basis at each vertex, in the same fashion as for embossing (see the previous section). The coordinates of each vertex's light vector are interpolated across the surface. In other words, instead of a color or depth value, a vector to the light is interpolated. This vector is typically passed in as a vertex color. In practice, it is best to interpolate among the unnormalized light vectors, and normalize the resulting vector, which

---

[13] For this algorithm, the vector **n** does not affect the calculations, and so it does not have to be placed in the basis matrix 5.17. All that is actually needed is the upper left 2×3 matrix.

[14] Note that 16-bit (HILO) values can be used for representing normal maps. These have the advantage of filtering better when mipmapping. However, most bump mapping artifacts are due to quantization of the original height data the normal map is derived from, not the quantization of the normals [547].

is converted to 8-bit values in the range $[-1, 1]$. By using a specially built cubic environment map, any vector can be quickly renormalized [258, 422]. The unnormalized vector's direction is used to access the cube map. The normalized values for each direction are stored in this cube map as 8-bit signed values. Note that all vectors pointing in the same direction will access the same cube map location, regardless of the lengths of the vectors. The vector is automatically normalized by retrieving the normalized direction from the cubic environment map.

The bump texture, which consists of normals, is then combined with the interpolated light vector at each pixel. These are combined by taking their dot product, which is a special texture-blending function provided precisely for this purpose. An example is shown in Plate XIV (following page 274). DirectX supports this specialized texture-blending operation as D3DTOP_DOTPRODUCT3, but that does not mean that hardware necessarily supports this function. Computing the dot product of the normal and the light vector is exactly how the diffuse component is calculated (see Section 4.3.1), so this results in a bumpy-looking surface that will change appearance as it moves with respect to the light.

An advantage of normal maps is that they can also be used for computing specular highlights on bumps in a straightforward manner. Instead of using the vector to the light, interpolate the half angle vector that is a part of Blinn's lighting model (see Section 4.3.2). Using pixel shading techniques, the $\mathbf{n} \cdot \mathbf{h}$ specular term can be raised to the 8th power (i.e., the shininess is 8).[15] When using this technique, it is good to force the specular contribution to zero when the unperturbed shading normal faces away from the half-angle vector [422]. See Figure 5.35 and Plate XV following page 274. Plate XVII also uses this technique.

Filtering bump maps is a difficult problem compared to filtering color textures. The bump maps represent surface normals, and using an average normal to represent a set of normals is often invalid, as the normal is used in a nonlinear illumination equation. Imagine looking at stairs made of blocks of shiny white marble. At some angles, the tops or sides of the stairs catch the light and reflect a bright specular highlight. However, the average normal for the stairs is at, say, a 45-degree angle; it will capture highlights from entirely different directions than the original stairs. Olano and North [594] summarize previous work and propose a scheme of storing Gaussian distributions of normals. Most proposed schemes are currently

---

[15]This term can be raised to any power by using a dependent texture read, discussed in the example on page 226, or by directly using the power function provided in later versions of the pixel shading language.

Figure 5.35. Diffuse and specular bump mapping. The color texture is modulated by the diffuse contribution computed using a normal bump map. The specular contribution is computed with a normalized version of the normal map and added in. *(Images courtesy of NVIDIA Corp.)*

not practical for real-time hardware, but performing at least some sort of filtering is important, as it avoids aliasing artifacts. In mipmapping, the texel on the next level up is formed from the average of the four corresponding texels associated with it. Kilgard notes that averaging the four signed normals works reasonably well [422]. These average normals do not have to be renormalized when used with diffuse surfaces. Not normalizing just tends to dim the object in places where bumps exist as it moves away from the viewer. This dimming matches the behavior found in some experiments by Kilgard. For specular highlights using normal maps, the normalization of the normal map mipmap levels should be done [422, 619]. Otherwise, nonnormalized vectors will give results that, when raised to a power, dim down considerably from what should be seen.

For rigid bodies, the tangent space basis can be computed once and stored for each vertex. See the *md2shader demo* [590] and the articles by Dietrich [175] and Kilgard [422] for how to compute these tangent vectors. During creation, care must be taken that the basis is formed properly, i.e., that all three vectors are pointing in the right direction. For example, in Figure 5.33, the binormal is assumed to be going in the general direction of the **v** texture coordinate axis; if this axis is, in fact, going the opposite direction, the computed binormal's direction should then be negated.

Environment Map Bump Mapping

One way to give the appearance of bumpiness to a shiny surface is *Environment Map Bump Mapping* (EMBM). The idea is to perturb (u, v) environment-mapping coordinates by u and v differentials found in the bump texture. This gives the effect of wobbling the reflection vector, thereby distorting the look of the reflected surface [422, 612].

The original version of this algorithm, introduced with DirectX 6, allows only a single planar environment map to be defined. Essentially, it is something like defining a cube map with only one face. After accessing the offset bump map, a user-defined 2×2 matrix is applied in order to rotate and scale the differentials before they are added. This matrix controls the perceived bumpiness of the map. Figure 5.36 shows how the technique works.

There are a few advantages to this technique. First, it requires only two texture accesses, regardless of the number of lights. When used in conjunction with planar reflections (see Section 6.10.1), EMBM can reflect a dynamically changing scene. This algorithm is limited by its lack of an environment map that encompasses the whole world, and the difficulty of controlling the effect on curved surfaces. EMBM is often used to render

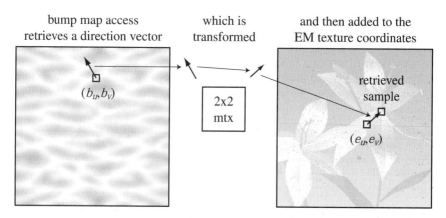

| bump map access retrieves a direction vector | which is transformed | and then added to the EM texture coordinates |

Figure 5.36. One texture coordinate, (b_u, b_v), accessed the offset bump map, which consists of two channels of signed values. The vector retrieved is transformed by a matrix, then added to another texture coordinate, (e_u, e_v). The resulting coordinate is used to access the environment map.

Figure 5.37. The left half of the image shows a planar reflection of the environment, the right shows the addition of environment map bump mapping. *(Image courtesy of ATI Technologies Inc.)*

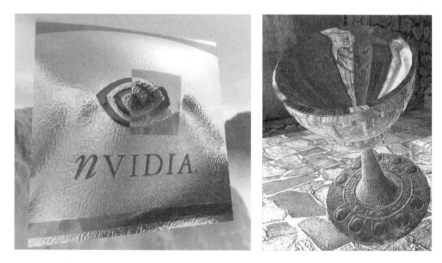

Figure 5.38. Examples of normal mapping combined with cubic environment mapping, giving a shiny, bumpy surface that reflects the environment. *(Left image courtesy of NVIDIA Corp. Right image courtesy of ATI Technologies Inc.)*

reflections across bodies of water or other flat surfaces. Figure 5.37 shows an image made using this technique, as does Plate XIX.

Historically, EMBM is important in that it marks the first use of a *dependent texture read* in consumer level graphics hardware. A dependent read is where the results from accessing one texture modifies the texture coordinates of a later access. This is a powerful feature, and its use will be discussed further in Section 6.6. Using pixel shader control along with dot product bump mapping and cubic environment mapping allows a more general EMBM scheme to be used, along the lines of research by Bennebroek et al. [55]. The concept fully integrates bump and environment mapping. The normal map is accessed and a reflection direction generated, which is then used to look up the color for the environment. See Figure 5.38 and Plate XVI (following page 274).

Other Techniques

Hardware-supported bump mapping is an active area of research. Miller et al. [549] discuss ways of combining current hardware with table lookups and parameter caching to increase performance and functionality. Ernst et al. [212], Schilling et al. [682], Peercy et al. [618], and Ikedo & Ma [383] all propose new schemes for bump mapping and hardware support. Ernst et al. [213] give a summary of many different bump mapping techniques and propose their own Gouraud-based method. For efficiency, Tarini et al. [742] quantize normal maps into, for example, 2048 normals, compute the shade for each normal once for the scene, then use the quantized mapping to obtain the shade during surface rendering. This approach works well for terrain rendering, where there are many vertices with the same lighting situation [362]. Heidrich et al. [344, 345] show how normal maps can be combined with spherical and paraboloid environment maps. Kautz et al. [409] describe a technique for generating bump maps for close-up detail from existing shininess functions. Kilgard [422] summarizes much work to date, gives derivations of the underlying equations, and presents in-depth analysis of and code for practical real-time bump mapping techniques. Ginsburg and Gosselin [258] discuss dot product bump mapping, including a per-pixel spotlighting technique.

A new primitive introduced with DirectX 9 is made using *displacement mapping*. Originally mentioned by Cook [140], this idea was first used commercially in RenderMan [761]. Normally, a heightfield bump map affects the shading normal on a surface, but not the geometry itself. In displacement mapping, the heightfield actually affects the geometry. See Plate XVIII following page 274. The idea is to first tessellate the surface, then sample the heightfield to find the amount of displacement, and then

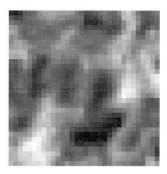 

Figure 5.39. The heightfield on the left is used to displace the vertices of a mesh. Combined with a normal map and color texture, this transform gives the image on the right. *(Images courtesy Juan Guardado, Matrox Graphics Inc.)*

displace each vertex along its normal. This process is described for more general subdivision surfaces in Section 12.6.6. Guardado at Matrox has invented a fractional tessellation scheme for triangles, which is used in their displacement mapping hardware. See Section 12.3.3.

Displacement mapping can be done on the CPU since it just involves moving vertices along normals, but highly tessellated meshes can be expensive to send across the bus, and a major point of displacement mapping is to avoid that bus traffic. Hardware can accelerate this process by providing a tessellation unit that generates triangles on the unperturbed surface. For each of the vertices on these triangles, the heightfield is sampled and an interpolated height is provided to the vertex shader. The vertex position is then shifted by this height along the vertex normal. Such functionality is supported in DirectX 9, and companies such as Matrox have hardware to accelerate this task. The advantages are that this frees the CPU from doing this task, and the amount of information sent across the bus to the accelerator is massively reduced. Instead of sending, say, a vertex with a normal and texture coordinates, 8 floats (32 bytes), only a single byte from the heightfield texture is needed. See Figure 5.39 for an example. The tessellation rate of each patch can be varied per edge, and be fractional, as described in Section 12.3.3. This allows displacement mapped surfaces to smoothly change in level of detail. That is, as an object moves farther away, fewer polygons are generated for it.

5.7.6 Other Texturing Techniques

This chapter has covered some of the uses of texturing. There are many others potentially useful in real-time work, including:

- Detail textures, which are used in, for example, flight simulators. Terrain data seen up close will give a slowly varying and unrealistic look, so another less-magnified texture is blended in to provide visual detail [536].

- Antialiased lines and text rendered as rectangles with smooth edges by using alpha-blended transparency [301].

- Cylinder mapping, a form of environment mapping that reflects horizontal tube lights, useful in curved body visualization and anomaly detection [602].

- Line integral convolution, a technique for visualizing vector fields [344].

- Photorealistic rendering, done by using a variety of techniques to access one or more environment maps in order to approximate the reflective characteristics of the material [343, 345, 410, 530]. These techniques are discussed in Section 6.4.

- Non-photorealistic rendering, in which the goal is to present an artistic style or accentuate particular features of the model. See Chapter 7.

- Volume rendering, by rendering a set of image texture slices with alpha values in back-to-front order and blending these [301, 536]. See Section 8.12.

This is only a small number of possible applications of texturing, more are discussed in the next chapter, and undoubtedly there are more still that remain to be discovered. Because of its speed and versatility, texturing is the basic mechanism that is used in real-time rendering to shade per pixel.

Further Reading and Resources

Heckbert has written a good survey of texture mapping [329] and a more in-depth report on the topic [330]; both are available on the web, and the URLs appear in this book's bibliography. Wolberg's book [813] is another good work on image textures, particularly in the areas of sampling and filtering. Watt's books [793, 794, 795, 796] and Rogers' *Procedural Elements* book [657] are general texts on computer graphics that have more information about texturing.

The SIGGRAPH OpenGL Advanced Techniques course notes [536] have extensive coverage of texturing algorithms and are available on the web.

While RenderMan is meant for high-quality still images, the *RenderMan Companion* [761] has some good material on texture mapping and on procedural textures. For extensive coverage of three-dimensional procedural textures, see *Texturing and Modeling: A Procedural Approach* [201].

Visit this book's website, `http://www.realtimerendering.com/`, for many other resources.

Chapter 6
Advanced Lighting and Shading

"If it looks like computer graphics,
it is not good computer graphics."
    –Jeremy Birn

New graphics accelerator capabilities have made it possible to represent new materials and lighting situations in real time. In the previous chapter, texturing techniques such as light maps, environment maps, and bump mapping have added considerable realism to surfaces. This chapter focuses on how the lighting model has been extended by using more elaborate multitexture methods, vertex shaders, and pixel shaders. In order to do so, the first part of the chapter is devoted to laying down a strong foundation of how light interacts with matter. Vertex and pixel shaders, along with languages for controlling shading, are then discussed. Sections then follow on advanced techniques such as motion blur, depth of field, reflections, refractions, and shadows. The chapter closes with a discussion of global illumination algorithms such as radiosity and ray tracing and how they are used for real-time rendering.

The Gouraud shading model was invented in 1971 [285]. Phong's specular highlighting equation was introduced around 1975 [621]. Applying textures to surfaces was presented a year later by Blinn and Newell [68]. These algorithms have been the mainstay of graphics accelerators for years. Some specialized graphics accelerators have been made to implement true Phong shading, where the surface normal is interpolated and used to compute the shade at each pixel [55]. However, creating a hardware pipeline with full, general shading occurring per pixel is an expensive proposition. Instead, Gouraud interpolation and multitexturing were used to implement more realistic lighting equations.

The next step in this evolution has been the addition of vertex and pixel shaders. Until their introduction, the standard hardware graphics accelerator used a *fixed-function* pipeline. The graphics API could turn functionality on and off and set parameters. The vertex shader replaces part of the fixed-function vertex processing pipeline with a unit that the user can program to do a set of operations on each vertex. Similarly, the pixel shader provides a more flexible set of texturing operations that can be controlled with a programming language or a more flexible API. With the additional ability of being able to render to a texture, increasingly complex lighting models and other graphical operations become possible in real time.

6.1   Radiometry and Photometry

When using the simple lighting models presented in the previous chapters, concepts of physics and measurement are usually ignored. The diffuse and specular terms are computed with respect to some numbers that are relative to the output brightness levels desired. A light has a value of, say, 0.7, because that is how much the scene's designer wants this light to affect the surfaces' appearance. The lighting model is simple enough that directly changing a value in the equation has a fairly clear effect within the scene: Dim the light and object is darker, turn up the specular highlight power and the object looks shinier.

The basic lighting model is a simple approximation of how the real world works. In computer graphics scenes, often a light source has the same brightness regardless of its distance from the object, which is at odds with physical reality—imagine a house light having the same effect from 2 kilometers as from 2 meters. With this simple model, objects appear to be painted with flat paint (purely diffuse), or look like shiny plastic (when the specular color is the light's color) or metal (when the specular color also includes the object's color).

To portray a wider range of material types, it is necessary to have a better understanding of how light works and is measured. Using the mental model of photons as particles works well for the most part. Wavelength-related phenomena such as polarization, phosphorescence, and fluorescence are usually disregarded by even high-quality batch rendering systems, and so for the most part are disregarded here as well [664]. At its simplest, photons are generated at an emitter (i.e., a light source) and eventually some arrive at our eyes. The path each photon takes can vary: Some photons come directly from the light, while most others bounce off one or more surfaces before arriving. Along the way, emitted photons are absorbed, often depending on the wavelength—this is how objects take on colors. For example, a blue object absorbs everything but "blue" wavelengths, or combinations of wavelengths that look blue. Each color we perceive is not related to an individual wavelength, but rather to how a collection of photons with a spectral distribution is interpreted by our eyes. In fact, an infinite variety of spectral distributions are interpreted by our eyes as being the same color. In most rendering systems, wavelength distribution is ignored and only the resulting RGB color[1] of a material is recorded.

Some definitions from the fields of radiometry and photometry follow. Radiometry deals with the measurement of radiation throughout the electromagnetic spectrum. Historically, the field of radiometry has been concerned with optical radiation in the frequency range between 3×10^{11} and 3×10^{16} Hertz, which corresponds to wavelengths from 1000 to 0.01 micrometers (μm). This range includes the infrared, visible, and ultraviolet regions of the electromagnetic spectrum. Photometry is like radiometry except that it weights everything by the sensitivity of the human eye. Therefore, photometry deals with only the visible spectrum, also called the *visible band*, a wavelength range of about 380 to 780 nanometers (nm). A wavelength of 450 is blue, 540 nm is green, and 650 nm is red. However, photometry does not deal with the perception of color itself, but rather the perceived strength of various wavelengths. For example, green light appears considerably brighter to the eye than red or blue light.

The results of radiometric computations are converted to photometric units by multiplying by the *CIE photometric curve*,[2] a bell-shaped curve centered around 555 nm that represents the eye's response to various wavelengths of light [30, 133, 711, 265]. See Figure 6.1. There are many other factors, physical, psychological, and physiological, that can affect the eye's response to light, but photometry does not attempt to address these. Photometry is based on the average measured response of the human eye when the observer has adapted to normal indoor lighting conditions. The conversion curve and the units of measurement are the only difference between the theory of photometry and the theory of radiometry.

---

[1] The RGB color actually represents the combination of three spectral bands. This is discussed in detail in the next section, on colorimetry.

[2] The full and more accurate name is the "CIE photopic spectral luminous efficiency curve." The word "photopic" refers to lighting conditions brighter than 3.4 candelas per square meter—twilight or brighter. There is a corresponding "scotopic" CIE curve, centered around 507 nm, that is for when the eye has become dark adapted to below 0.034 candelas per square meter—a moonless night or darker.

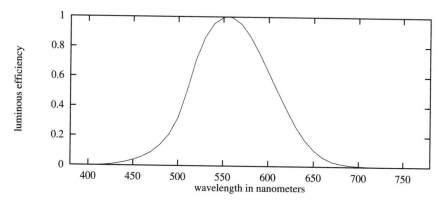

Figure 6.1. The photometric curve.

In radiometry, *radiant energy*, Q, is the basic unit of energy, measured in *joules* (abbreviated "J"). Each photon has some amount of radiant energy, equal to Planck's constant (6.62620×10^{-34} joule-seconds) times the speed of light (2.998×10^8 meters/second) divided by the wavelength of the photon. Equivalently, the number of photons per joule is 5.034×10^{15} multiplied by the photon wavelength; for example, at a wavelength of 550 nm, there are about 2.77×10^9 photons per joule.

The *radiant flux* or *radiant power*, Φ or P, of a light source is equal to the number of joules per second emitted (i.e., dQ/dt). The *watt* (W) is another term for joules per second.

After photons leave a light source, the next step is to measure how they arrive at a surface. *Radiant flux density* is the radiant flux per unit area on a surface, and is measured in terms of watts per square meter. The concept of radiant flux density can be applied to any surface, real or imaginary. That is, it can be measured anywhere in space. Visualize a square in space; the radiant flux density for the square is proportional to the rate that photons from all directions travel through it each second, divided by its area. In theory, we can make the area infinitesimally small and so measure the radiant flux density at a point:

$$u = \frac{d\Phi}{dA} \qquad (6.1)$$

where Φ is the radiant flux passing through the point and dA is differential area. If the flux over a finite area is uniform, it can be computed simply as $u = \Phi/A$.

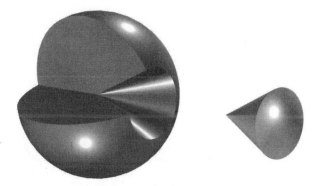

Figure 6.2. A cone with a solid angle of one steradian removed from a cutaway view of a sphere.

Radiant flux density is referred to by other names in specific circumstances. The term *irradiance*, E, is used when flux arrives at a surface. The *radiant exitance*, M, also called the *radiosity*, B, is the amount of flux leaving a surface, and uses the same units as irradiance.

In computer graphics, lights and viewers are often treated as points. Measurements in terms of areas do not apply. Instead, solid angles are used. Solid angles are measured in *steradians* (abbreviated "sr"). The solid angle is the concept of a two-dimensional angle extended to three dimensions [265]. In two dimensions, an angle of 2π radians covers the whole unit circle. Extending this to three dimensions, a solid angle of 4π steradians would cover the whole area of the unit sphere. See Figure 6.2.

The most important radiometric unit for computer graphics is the *radiance L*. The reason is that radiance is what we store in a pixel. A simple way to think about incoming radiance is to imagine a narrow laser beam hitting a surface. The amount of radiant flux coming from that direction and hitting the surface at a given point is the radiance. Unlike irradiance and exitance, radiance can refer to light either arriving at or leaving a surface, i.e., can be incoming or outgoing. The incoming radiance at a surface is [30]:

$$L_{surf} = \frac{d^2\Phi}{dA(d\omega\cos\theta)} \tag{6.2}$$

which is measured in terms of watts per square meter per steradian. The term $d\omega$ is the differential solid angle—imagine an infinitesimally narrow cone, essentially a ray. The angle of the incoming light compared with the

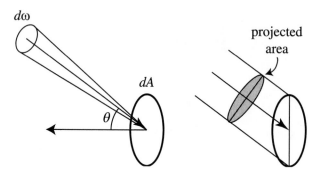

Figure 6.3. Radiance is power per unit projected area per unit solid angle.

surface's normal is denoted θ. See Figure 6.3. Radiance is defined as the amount of power (watts) per unit area, per unit solid angle.

The equation above is useful for integrating the incoming radiance to compute the irradiance at a surface. Though we are often interested in the radiance reaching a surface, the radiance value is independent of the surface. That is, it is a value that is measured for any point in space for some given direction. Radiance is defined as being with respect to the power per unit solid angle per unit *projected* area, as shown on the right in Figure 6.3. The cosine term in the equation above represents the projected area of the surface along the ray. Recall Lambert's Law from Section 4.3.1. Using this law, the radiant flux is distributed over a larger area as its angle to the surface increases. So a surface-independent way to think about radiance is that it is a fixed amount of power (i.e., photons per second) coming from a given direction. The angle of the surface affects this radiance only in that radiance is measured for a differential area perpendicular to its direction of movement. A surface-independent form of the radiance equation is:

$$L = \frac{d^2\Phi}{dA d\omega} \tag{6.3}$$

in which the previous equation's surface attenuation term is set to one (i.e., the angle θ is always zero). In this way, the radiance is a fixed amount for a given direction and location. The location can be any point in space (e.g., at the eye), not just at a surface.

The radiance in an environment can be thought of as a function of five variables (or six, including wavelength), called the *radiance distribution* [133]. Three of the variables specify a location, the other two a direction. This function then describes all light travelling anywhere in space. One way to think of the rendering process is that the eye and screen define a point and a set of directions (e.g., a ray going through each pixel), and this function is evaluated at the eye for each direction. Another way to think of this function is that, for a given location, an environment map of everything in the scene represents the incoming radiance for all directions. The radiance distribution is then the set of all possible environment maps for a scene [535]. Image-based rendering, discussed in Section 8.2, commonly uses a related concept, called the *light field* for an object. This is a four-dimensional space instead of five; one dimension can be eliminated by assuming nothing blocks the view of the object. One way to understand how this assumption leads to four dimensions is to think of the set of all orthographic views of an object. This set is defined by varying the altitude and azimuth angles, for two dimensions, and the location on the view plane of each view gives another two dimensions. Image-based rendering also uses the *plenoptic function* [535], which is the radiance distribution with time added as another variable.

An object's radiance value is not affected by distance (ignoring atmospheric effects such as fog). In other words, a surface will have the same luminance regardless of its distance from the viewer. This seems in contradiction to the basic law that a light's intensity drops off with the square of the distance, so it deserves some explanation. Imagine looking at a square panel one meter square that is emitting light uniformly across its surface, such as closely spaced fluorescent tubes behind frosted glass. Say you view the panel at 10 meters and then at 20 meters away. Your eyes will receive about one quarter the rate of photons per second at 20 meters than at 10, in keeping with the inverse square law. However, instead of explaining this lower rate as a pure distance effect, it can also be explained as occurring because the light covers about one quarter the solid angle that the viewer can see at 20 meters versus 10. Think of making a digital photo of the light at each distance (and assume that the camera avoids overexposure). At 10 meters, the light panel covers, say, 4000 pixels; at 20 meters, it covers about 1000. The radiance at each light pixel is constant (ignoring atmospheric effects): It is only the number of pixels that changes in relationship to the distance from the light.

In fact, the inverse square law for lighting is an approximation, meant to be used when the light is sufficiently far away. Lambert's *Photometria* [456] from 1760 first presents the "five-times" rule of thumb. If the distance from the light source is five times or more that of the light's width, then the inverse square law is a reasonable approximation and so can be used. Closer than this and the solid angle the light covers will vary noticeably different from an inverse square relationship. In such cases, radiosity techniques can be used to determine more precise illumination values (see Section 6.13.1).

Similarly, any object we view in a scene has a radiance that does not change, regardless of how far we move away from it. It may have a smaller overall contribution, "cover less pixels," as we move away from it, but its radiance remains constant. The idea of radiance is that we are measuring light in a direction. It does not matter if the light is from emission, reflection, refraction, scattering, or other means.

In photometry, there are comparable units to those in radiometry, with the addition of being weighted by the response of the eye. The *candela* (abbreviated "cd") is a measure of luminous power per unit solid angle, in a given direction. The *lumen* (lm) is analogous to the watt in radiometry, and is derived from the candela. *Luminous energy* corresponds to *radiant energy*, and is measured in *talbots*. *Illuminance* denotes the luminous flux density, corresponding to irradiance. The metric unit for illuminance is called *lux* (lx), lumens per square meter.[3] This property is what most light meters measure, and it is important in illumination engineering. *Luminance* is analogous to radiance. The unit used is candelas per square meter, sometimes called the *nit*. Luminance is often used to describe the brightness of flat surfaces. For example, a typical laptop computer display screen ranges from 100 to 250 nits, and CRT monitors from 50 to 125 nits.

6.2 Colorimetry

Light is perceived in the visible band, from 380 to 780 nanometers (nm). Light from a given direction consists of a set of photons in some distribution of wavelengths. This distribution is called the light's spectrum. See Figure 6.4 for an example.

Humans can distinguish about 10 million different colors. The eye works by having three different types of cone receptors in the retina, with each type of receptor responding differently to various wavelengths. So for a given spectrum the brain itself then receives only three different signals from these receptors. This is why just three numbers can be used to represent any spectrum seen.

But what three numbers? A set of standard conditions for measuring color was proposed by the CIE (*Commission Internationale d'Eclairage*),

---

[3]In North America, lighting designers use the deprecated Imperial unit of measurement, called the foot-candle (fc).

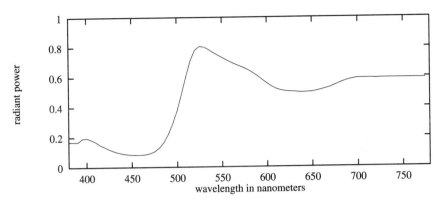

Figure 6.4. The spectrum for a ripe brown banana under white light [265].

and color matching experiments were performed using them. In color matching, three colored lights are projected on a white screen so that their colors add together and form a patch. A test color to match is projected next to this patch. The test color patch is of a single wavelength from the spectrum. The observer can then change the three colored lights using knobs calibrated to a range weighted $[-1, 1]$ until the test color is matched. A negative weight is needed to match some test colors, and such a weight means that the corresponding light is instead added to the test color patch. One set of test results for three lights called r, g, and b, is shown in Figure 6.5. The lights were almost monochromatic: $r = 645$ nm, $g = 526$ nm, and $b = 444$ nm.

What these curves give is a way to convert a spectrum to three values. Given a single wavelength of light, the three colored light settings can be read off the graph, the knobs set, and lighting conditions created that will give an identical sensation from both patches of light on the screen. Given an arbitrary spectrum, these curves can be multiplied by the spectrum and the area under the resulting curve (i.e., the integral) gives the relative amounts to set the colored lights to match the perceived color produced by the spectrum. Very different spectra can resolve to the same three weights; in other words, they look the same to an observer. Matching spectra are called *metamers*.

The three weighted r, g, and b values cannot directly represent all visible colors, as there are negative weights for various wavelengths. The CIE proposed three different hypothetical light sources that did not use monochromatic light. These are denoted $\overline{x}(\lambda)$, $\overline{y}(\lambda)$, and $\overline{z}(\lambda)$, and their spectra

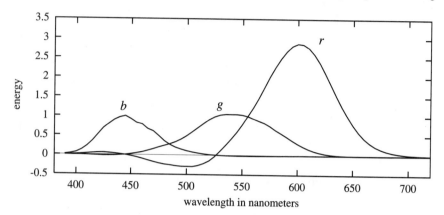

Figure 6.5. The r, g, and b 2-degree color matching curves, from Stiles & Burch (1955). Values are shown in terms of energy, not the $[-1, 1]$ knob range.

are shown in Figure 6.6. Given a surface reflectance and light source, their product defines a color function $C(\lambda)$, i.e., a spectrum. By multiplying this function by a color matching curve and integrating, a single value is computed for each curve:

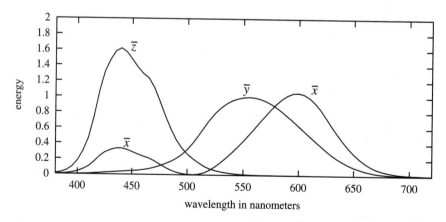

Figure 6.6. The Judd-Vos-modified CIE (1978) 2-degree color matching functions. Note that the two $\overline{x}$'s are part of the same curve.

$$X = \int_{380}^{780} C(\lambda)\overline{x}(\lambda)d\lambda,$$

$$Y = \int_{380}^{780} C(\lambda)\overline{y}(\lambda)d\lambda, \qquad (6.4)$$

$$Z = \int_{380}^{780} C(\lambda)\overline{z}(\lambda)d\lambda.$$

These X, Y, and Z *tristimulus values* are weights that define a color in CIE XYZ space. This three-dimensional space is awkward to work in, so the plane where $X + Y + Z = 1$ is used. See Figure 6.7. Coordinates in this space are called x and y, and are computed as follows:

$$x = \frac{X}{X + Y + Z},$$

$$y = \frac{Y}{X + Y + Z}, \qquad (6.5)$$

$$z = \frac{Z}{X + Y + Z} = 1 - x - y.$$

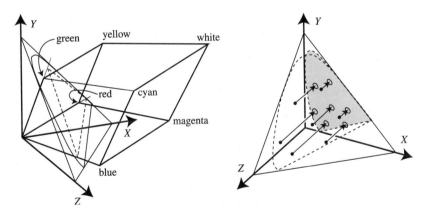

Figure 6.7. On the left, the RGB color cube is shown in XYZ space, along with its gamut projection and chromaticity diagram onto the $X + Y + Z = 1$ plane. Lines radiating from the origin have a constant chromaticity value, varying only in luminance. On the right, seven points on the plane $X + Y + Z = 1$, and so in xyz coordinates, are projected onto the XY plane (by dropping the z value). The chromaticity diagram outline is shown for both planes, with the resulting diagram shown in gray.

The z value gives no additional information, so is normally omitted. The plot of the *chromaticity coordinates* x and y values is known as the CIE chromaticity diagram. See Plate XXI (following page 274). The curved line in the diagram shows where the colors of the spectrum lie, and the straight line connecting the ends of the spectrum is called the *purple line*. Illuminant E, the equal energy spectrum, is often used to define white, at the point $x = y = z = \frac{1}{3}$. For a computer monitor, the *white point* is the combination of the three color phosphors at full intensity, i.e., the brightest white.

Given a color point (x,y), draw a line from the white point through this point to the spectral line. The relative distance of the color point compared to the distance to the edge of the region is the *saturation* of the color. The point on the region edge defines the *hue* of the color. The chromaticity diagram describes a plane; the third dimension needed to fully describe a color is the Y value, which is called the xyY coordinate system. The color matching function $\overline{y}(\lambda)$ is, in fact, one and the same as the photometric curve (see page 184), as radiance is converted to luminance with this curve.

The chromaticity diagram is important in understanding how color is used in rendering, and the limits of the rendering system. A computer monitor presents colors by using some settings of R, G, and B color values. Each color channel controls some physical phenomenon, e.g., exciting a phosphor, which in turn emits light in a particular spectrum. By exciting three phosphors, three spectra are emitted, which are added together and create a single spectrum that the viewer perceives. The eye's three types of cones also each have their own color matching functions, i.e., each cone responds to the incoming spectrum and sends a signal to the brain.

The display system is limited in its ability to present different colors by the spectra of its three channels. An obvious limitation is in luminance, as a computer monitor is only so bright, but there are also limits to saturation. As seen earlier, the r, g, and b color matching system needed to have negative weights for some of the spectrum colors to be matched. These colors with negative weights are colors that could not be displayed by a combination of the three lights. Video displays and printers are limited in a similar fashion.

The triangle in the chromaticity diagram represents the *gamut* of a typical computer monitor. The three corners of the triangle are the most saturated red, green, and blue colors the monitor can display. An important property of the chromaticity diagram is that these limiting colors can be joined by straight lines to show the limits of the monitor as a whole. The straight lines represent the limits of colors that can be displayed by mixing these three primaries.

Conversion from RGB to XYZ space (or vice versa) is linear and can be done with a matrix [194, 235]. A common conversion is to transform an RGB color to a grayscale luminance value:

$$Y = 0.2125R + 0.7154G + 0.0721B. \tag{6.6}$$

A few words are in order about this equation. First, in older texts, it is often given as $Y = 0.30R + 0.59G + 0.11B$. Poynton [631] discusses how this form is based on older NTSC phosphors; the equation given above is based on modern CRT and HDTV phosphors. This brings us full circle to the photometric curve shown on page 184. This curve, representing how a standard observer's eye responds to light of various wavelengths, is multiplied by the spectra of the three phosphors and each resulting curve is integrated. The three resulting weights are what form the luminance equation above. So, the reason that a grayscale intensity value is not equal parts red, green, and blue is because the eye has a different sensitivity to various wavelengths of light.

The gamut affects the rendering process in a number of ways. The gamuts and white point locations of monitors vary, both because of the physical makeup and due to the adjustment of brightness and contrast, meaning that how a color looks on one monitor will not be the same as another's. The gamuts of printers differ more still from monitors, so that there are colors that can display well on one device, but not another. Scanners also have a gamut of colors they can record, and so have similar mismatches and limitations. Monitor gamuts are always triangles, by the nature of how they produce colors. Film, print, and other media have gamuts that are roughly triangular, but with curved edges or other irregularities, due to the characteristics of the chemicals or inks used to capture color.

The CIE XYZ system is useful for precise description, but there are many other color spaces with different strengths and uses. For example, CIE LUV and CIE LAB define color spaces that are more perceptually uniform. Color pairs that are perceptibly different by the same amount can be up to 20 times different in distance in CIE XYZ space.

CIE LUV improves upon this, bringing the ratio down to a maximum of four times. Other color systems common in computer graphics include HSB (*Hue, Saturation, Brightness*) and HLS (*Hue, Lightness, Saturation*) [235]. CMYK (*Cyan, Magenta, Yellow, blacK*) is for the inks used in standard four-color printing. YIQ is used for television. Dawson [161] gives a good overview of color display and perception issues concerning real-time applications and television.

Though colorimetry has strong mathematical underpinnings, the basis is the perception of color by some set of observers under controlled conditions. Even under these conditions, observers' genetic, physical, and mental states affect results. In the real world, there are many more variables that affect human perception of a color patch, such as the lighting conditions, the surrounding colors, and past conditions. Some of these perceptual effects can be put to good use. For example, using red lettering on a blue background has long been a way to grab attention, because the blue surrounding color further accentuates the perceived brightness of the red. Another important effect for computer graphics is that of *masking* [230]. A high-frequency, high-contrast pattern laid on something tends to hide flaws. In other words, a texture such as a Persian rug will help disguise color banding and other shading artifacts, meaning that less rendering effort needs to be expended for such surfaces.

A computer screen has a certain useful luminance range, while a real image has a potentially huge luminance range. *Tone reproduction* (also called *tone mapping*) is the process of fitting a wide range of illumination levels to within the screen's limited gamut [192, 755]. The fact that the eye takes time to adjust to rapidly changing lighting conditions can be simulated in real-time rendering by artificially changing the perception of light. For example, for a person coming out of a tunnel in a virtual world the scene could be made to appear bright and washed out for a second and then fade to normal light and color levels. This would mimic the perceived feeling of coming out of a real tunnel into the light [616].

There are many other cases where tone reproduction plays a part. As a demonstration, take a CD jewel case and look down on it. Aim it to reflect a ceiling light. By the Fresnel effect, discussed beginning on page 199 of the next section, the reflection from the CD case is only about 4% the power of the light itself. Our eyes rapidly adjust when shifting from the CD to the light and so we do not notice this wide disparity.

This section has touched on only the basics of color science, primarily to bring an awareness of the relation of spectra to color triplets and to discuss the limitations of devices. Stone's set of course notes [734] is a good place to start to understand more about digital color, with excellent pointers to resources. Glassner's *Principles of Digital Image Synthesis* [264, 265] discusses color theory and perception. Ferwerda's more recent tutorial discusses vision research relevant to computer graphics [230].

6.3 BRDF Theory

The term BRDF stands for *Bidirectional Reflectance Distribution Function* [585]. As its name implies, it is a function that describes how light is

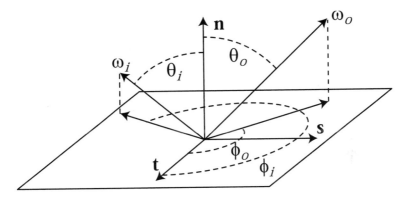

Figure 6.8. The BRDF. Azimuth angles ϕ_i and ϕ_o are given with respect to a given tangent vector **t**.

reflected from a surface. Thus, it is used to describe material properties. The inputs to this function are incoming and outgoing azimuth and elevation angles, as measured on the surface (see Figure 6.8). Another input that is part of a BRDF is the wavelength of the incoming light (which we represent with RGB color). Though some materials change color depending on the incoming and outgoing directions, a simplifying assumption is often made that the hue and saturation of a material remains constant. The result from a BRDF is a unitless value that is the relative amount of energy reflected in the outgoing direction, given the incoming direction. Another way to think about this function is in terms of photons. The BRDF gives the probability that an incoming photon will leave in a particular direction.

The BRDF describes how incoming and outgoing radiance is related, but does not explain how materials themselves physically interact with light. For example, in reality, plastic has a substrate that is white, with embedded pigment particles. Specularly reflected light tends to stay white, as it does not penetrate into the material; diffuse light from the material is from light that has penetrated and interacts with the pigments. Metals conduct electricity, so some electromagnetic waves stimulate the electrons, which cause these waves to reflect. This behavior causes specular highlights to pick up a color of the surface (which can change with the angle of incidence), while also minimizing the diffuse component, as little light bounces around inside the surface [138, 139]. The response and wavelength dependence of metals and plastics are considerably unlike each other, but these are expressed simply as different BRDFs.

A BRDF has a few important properties. *Helmholtz reciprocity* means that the input and output angles can be switched and the function value will be the same. The BRDF must also be *normalized,* which means that the total amount of outgoing energy must always be less than or equal to incoming energy.

The BRDF is a powerful abstraction for describing how light interacts with a surface, but it is an approximation of a more general equation. This equation is the *Bidirectional Surface Scattering Reflectance Distribution Function* (BSSRDF) [585]. The BRDF describes how light comes from above a surface and leaves the surface at the same point. This description does not include the scattering of light within the surface, as seen in marble and other materials [393]. The general BSSRDF encompasses these phenomena by adding incoming and outgoing locations as inputs to the function. The BSSRDF describes the relative amount of light that travels along the incoming direction, then from one point to the other of the surface, then along the outgoing direction. Note that this function also captures the idea that a surface is not necessarily uniform; as the position changes, the reflectance can also change. In real-time rendering, the position on the surface is used to access color textures, gloss and bump maps, etc. Even the general BSSRDF, as complex as it is, still leaves off other variables that can be important in the physical world, such as the polarization of the light [664]. Also, transmission of light through a surface is not handled, only reflection [265]. To handle transmission, two BRDFs and two BTDFs ("T" for "Transmittance") are defined for the surface, one for each side, and so make up the BSDF ("S" for "Scattering").

Given a BRDF and an incoming radiance distribution, the *reflectance equation* determines the outgoing radiance for a given viewing direction, relative to the surface. It does this by integrating the incoming radiance from all directions on the hemisphere above the surface [409]:

$$L(\theta_o, \phi_o) = \int \int_\Omega f(\theta_o, \phi_o, \theta_i, \phi_i) L(\theta_i, \phi_i) cos(\theta_i) d\sigma(\theta_i, \phi_i). \qquad (6.7)$$

Subscripts i and o are the incoming and outgoing (view) directions. The function L is the radiance travelling in a given direction. The function f is the BRDF. The double integral and σ notation at the end means to integrate over the hemisphere Ω. So, what this equation means is that for all directions on the hemisphere over the surface, determine the incoming radiance, multiply it by the BRDF for this direction and the outgoing direction, scale by the incoming angle to the surface, and integrate. The result is then what radiance (essentially, pixel brightness) is seen for that

viewing direction. This equation is evaluated separately for the three color
channels.

To determine the effect of a single point light source, the equation simplifies to:

$$L(\theta_o, \phi_o) = f(\theta_o, \phi_o, \theta_i, \phi_i)L(\theta_i, \phi_i)cos(\theta_i) \tag{6.8}$$

where θ_i, ϕ_i is the light source direction. To simplify the notation, the normalized vectors ω_i and ω_o can be used to replace the azimuth and elevation
angles.[4] Furthermore, the cosine term for the light can be computed by
using the surface normal $\mathbf{n}$:

$$L(\omega_o) = f(\omega_o, \omega_i)L(\omega_i)(\mathbf{n} \cdot \omega_i). \tag{6.9}$$

The $L(\omega_i)$ function is the light source's incoming radiance (brightness).
This is modified by the BRDF and the angle of the surface to the light.
To evaluate the effect of more than one light in the scene, the radiance
contribution of each light is computed and summed together.

For a diffuse surface, the BRDF is trivial: It always returns some constant value. For Blinn's form of Phong highlighting the function is, in
simplified form:

$$f_{phong}(\omega_o, \omega_i) = \frac{k_s(\mathbf{n} \cdot \mathbf{h})^{m_{shi}}}{\mathbf{n} \cdot \omega_i}. \tag{6.10}$$

See Equation 4.6 for the notation used. The term k_s controls the intensity of the specular contribution. BRDFs will exist for each RGB color
channel. The $\mathbf{n} \cdot \omega_i$ term is present to cancel out its existence in Equation 6.9. In other words, the Phong specular term is a bit odd in that its
BRDF cancels out the reflectance equation's cosine term from the angle of
incidence. This occurs because the Phong highlighting model is ad hoc and
ignores the effect of the projected area.

One way to understand a BRDF is to visualize it with the input direction held constant. See Figure 6.9. For a given direction of incoming light,
the distribution of outgoing energy is displayed. The spherical part around
the point of intersection is the diffuse component, since outgoing energy
has an equal chance of reflecting in any direction. The ellipsoidal piece is a
reflectance lobe, and is from the specular component. Naturally, such lobes
are in the reflection direction from the incoming light, with the thickness of
the lobe corresponding to the fuzziness of the reflection. By the principal

---

[4]In this text, we normally use bold Roman letters for vectors, but ω is the standard
way of presenting this direction vector, so we use it here.

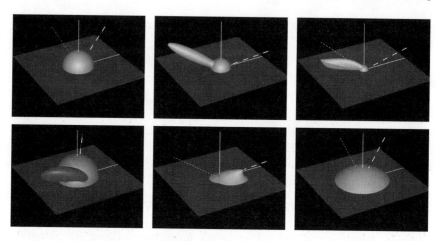

Figure 6.9. Example BRDFs. The line with long dashes is the incoming light direction, and the short dash line is the ideal reflection direction. In the top row, the left figure shows a diffuse surface (a simple hemisphere). The middle figure shows Phong/Blinn highlighting added to the diffuse term. The right figure shows the Torrance-Sparrow model [753]. Note how the Fresnel term comes into play at grazing angles, and how the specular highlight is not strongest in the reflection direction. In the bottom row, the left figure shows a close-up of Ward's anisotropic model. In this case, the effect is to tilt the specular lobe. The middle figure shows the Hapke/Lommel-Seeliger "lunar surface" BRDF [321], which has strong retroreflection. The right figure shows Lommel-Seeliger scattering, in which dusty surfaces scatter light toward grazing angles. *(Images courtesy of Szymon Rusinkiewicz, from his "bv" BRDF browser.)*

of reciprocity, these same visualizations can also be thought of how much each different incoming direction contributes to a single outgoing direction.

Over the years, various theoretical models for BRDFs have been developed, and a few key concepts are used by many of these to describe how surfaces behave. One idea is that a surface can be modelled by using *microfacets* [32, 316]. Each microfacet is a tiny, flat mirror on the surface, with a random size and angle. See Figure 6.10. In these models, the microfacets

Figure 6.10. A magnified cutaway of a surface composed of microfacets.

are often given a Gaussian distribution of sizes and angles, as Gaussians are simpler to work with mathematically. Specular reflection can be described by direct reflections from some microfacets, and diffuse reflection as interreflection off several facets or as scattering within the surface material itself. Microfacets can shadow each other (i.e., one facet can cast a shadow onto another for a given light direction) or mask each other (i.e., one facet can be in front of another facet for a given viewing direction). Another surface representation technique is called *height correlation*, where microfacets have sizes near the wavelength of the light, so that effects such as interference come into play and so phenomena such as diffraction can be simulated [728].

A physically based factor that is important to take into account is *Fresnel reflectance*. This term is particularly important for nonconductive, or *dieletric*, materials such as plastic, glass, and water. The effect is that when a dielectric is looked at along a grazing angle, it is more reflective. In comparison, metals vary relatively little due to the angle. All materials become fully reflective at the shallowest grazing angle. This effect is simple to see: Hold this book so that you are looking at a very shallow angle along a page, and look toward a light source (a computer monitor is good). At an extremely shallow angle, the page is shiny and you can see reflections from the screen. This effect is one reason shiny metals look metallic and shiny plastics look as they do.

The full Fresnel formula is dependent on the index of refraction, the coefficient of extinction, and the incident angle, and can compute polarized or unpolarized values for the light. In computer graphics, polarization is normally ignored, so the average of the two polarizations is used. Note that opaque surfaces have an index of refraction, contrary to how the term is normally thought about. A good working index of refraction for dielectric materials is 1.5. Finally, the coefficient of extinction can be set to zero if not known [138, 139, 265, 316]. This results in the follow equation:

$$F = \frac{1}{2} \frac{(g-c)^2}{(g+c)^2} \left(1 + \frac{[c(g+c)-1]^2}{[c(g-c)+1]^2} \right) \qquad (6.11)$$

where

$$c = \mathbf{v} \cdot \mathbf{h} \qquad (6.12)$$

is a measure of the viewer's and light's angle of incidence, and where

$$g = \sqrt{n^2 + c^2 - 1} \qquad (6.13)$$

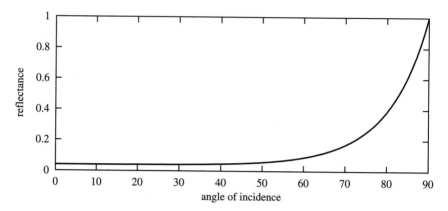

Figure 6.11. The Fresnel reflection for a surface with an index of refraction of 1.5. The angle is relative to both the eye and light, as it is formed by the view (or light) vector and the half angle, which is the angle halfway between the viewer and light directions. When this angle nears 90 degrees, the eye and light vectors point in nearly opposite directions, i.e., the eye is looking along the surface toward the light.

with **v** being the vector from the surface to the viewer,[5] **h** being the half angle vector (see Equation 4.7 on page 77), and n the index of refraction. This value F describes the reflectance of a given surface at various angles. See also Equation 6.21 on page 231 for a faster approximation. Figure 6.11 shows an example curve.

Microgeometry and the Fresnel effect are key elements in such BRDF models as Cook-Torrance [138, 139] and Ashikhmin et al. [32]. The HTSG BRDF model [327], which uses height correlation, is good at simulating many physical phenomena and is probably the most complete BRDF model currently available, but is very costly to compute. Oren and Nayar [604] present a realistic model for nonreflective surfaces such as unglazed clay, plaster, and sand, which are not purely Lambertian surfaces. Readers are referred to Glassner [265] for detailed information about older theoretical models, and to Ashikhmin [32] and McCool [530] for overviews of relevant newer work. Dutré's compendium [194] is a good reference for summaries of BRDF models.

A limitation of some BRDF theoretical models is that they do not account for *anisotropy*. See Figure 6.12. If the viewer and the light source do not move and a flat sample of the material changes its appearance when it is rotated about its normal, the material is anisotropic. Surfaces such as

---

[5]The vector to the light can be used in place of **v**; the result is equivalent.

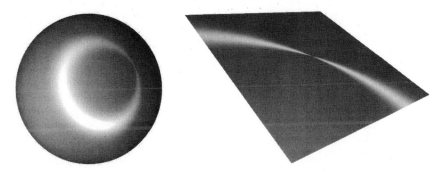

Figure 6.12. Anisotropic surfaces, rendered using general cosine lobe basis functions by Lafortune et al. [451].

brushed metal, varnished wood, and woven cloth, as well as fur and hair, have a definite directional component to them. This difference between isotropic and anisotropic surfaces has an important effect on how BRDFs are evaluated. With anisotropic BRDFs, the azimuth angle (i.e., the angle around the axis) compared to the surface itself is important, so both ϕ_i and ϕ_o are needed to evaluate the BRDF. This means the BRDF must be evaluated in terms of four angles, the two elevations and two azimuths. For isotropic surfaces, which do not vary with the rotation of the surface, only three values are needed to evaluate the surface. The azimuth angles ϕ_i and ϕ_o can be combined into one relative angle $\phi = \phi_i - \phi_o$.

Ward [791] points out that there are two types of models for BRDFs, those based on physical theory and those that are designed to empirically fit a class of surface types. Theoretical BRDF models that include anisotropy, such Poulin-Fournier [622] and HTSG [327], are complex to evaluate and so currently find little direct application within real-time rendering. Because of its simplicity, Banks' empirical model [38] is useful for giving the impression of anisotropy. The direction of the grooves or fur [487] is represented by a tangent vector perpendicular to their direction. One form of the specular portion of this anisotropic BRDF is [343, 408]:

$$f = m_{spec}(\sqrt{1 - (\mathbf{l} \cdot \mathbf{t})^2}\sqrt{1 - (\mathbf{v} \cdot \mathbf{t})^2} - (\mathbf{l} \cdot \mathbf{t})(\mathbf{v} \cdot \mathbf{t}))^{m_{shi}} \tag{6.14}$$

where m_{spec} is the material's specular coefficient for one color band, m_{shi} is the shininess exponent, $\mathbf{l}$ is the direction to the light, $\mathbf{v}$ the direction to the viewer, and $\mathbf{t}$ the tangent vector. The resulting BRDF value f is clamped to zero, i.e., if it is negative, it is set to zero. As usual, this BRDF

f value is multiplied by the incoming light's radiance and the cosine term, $\mathbf{l} \cdot \mathbf{n}$ (again clamped to zero), to compute the outgoing radiance:

$$L_o = L_i(\mathbf{l} \cdot \mathbf{n})f. \qquad (6.15)$$

Ward's empirical model [791] for anisotropic surfaces is more involved, but is designed with simplicity in mind and has been implemented with a type of pixel shader [408].

A problem with theoretical models is that they are not necessarily useful for representing some given material sample. Another approach is to acquire BRDF data from the actual surface. Goniometers, imaging bidirectional reflectometers, and image-based methods have been used to obtain the reflectance measurements over the incoming and outgoing angles. Some of these databases are public and available online, such as those from Cornell University [144] and Columbia-Utrecht [137]. Ward [791], discusses measurement in depth, Kautz et al. [409] give an overview of current acquisition techniques, and Marschner et al. [519] discuss previous work and their own image-based method for measuring BRDFs.

Another way to represent BRDFs is with basis summation techniques. These are focused on representing the shape of the BRDF itself. Look again at Figure 6.9: For a given incoming direction, a surface is formed that represents the reflectance at any outgoing direction. The BRDF surface is generally changing in a smooth fashion, with few places where it changes rapidly. Basis summation techniques endeavor to capture the BRDF's surface as the weighted sum of a set of functions. In a sense, the Phong/Blinn lighting model represents the BRDF by just two functions, a diffuse component and a specular lobe. More realistic precomputed BRDFs have been represented with a summation of spherical harmonics, Ward or generalized cosine lobes, and spherical wavelets, to name a few bases [451, 530, 664]. Such methods are less computationally demanding than complex theoretical models such as HTSG, and avoid the noise problems and data storage requirements of acquired data. While suitable for software implementation, these techniques often do not easily translate to hardware's capabilities.

6.4   Implementing BRDFs

A straightforward way to use any BRDF model or dataset is to compute the vertex color and pass this on down the pipeline. One disadvantage is the same as anything rendered with Gouraud shading: If the BRDF's reflectance changes rapidly over a few pixels (e.g., on a glossy highlight), linear interpolation will miss or overemphasize these changes, depending where the vertices lay. One solution is to finely tessellate the surface. This solution can quickly become an extremely expensive bottleneck on performance. Another disadvantage of using this vertex color approach is that it can represent the effect of only point or directional lights. Nonetheless, evaluating BRDF models is a valid method, and can be acceptable for those BRDFs without sharp specular lobes. Vertex shaders, discussed in Section 6.5, can make this technique faster by using the graphics hardware accelerator to compute the BRDF values.

Pixel shaders can also be used to evaluate BRDF models. This approach will be discussed in Section 6.6. In lieu of having pixel shader functionality available, other less hardware-intensive approaches have been devised to represent BRDFs, and are the subject of this section.

To save on computation, it is possible to store data for a large number of elevations and azimuths in an array and access and interpolate the BRDF value needed from it. Similarly, empirically acquired BRDF data could be accessed in this fashion. For isotropic surfaces, the BRDF needs only three variables, so, in fact, a three-dimensional texture map or its equivalent can be used to store the BRDF directly. However, this approach can be memory-intensive. Also, care needs to be taken, as measured data is usually noisy and have gaps in the set (such as at shallow angles and at the incoming light direction, where measurements are difficult to obtain). A compact representation of the BRDF data for a given material that could be accessed quickly would have a number of advantages. It would avoid the evaluation costs for precise theoretical models, and the storage requirements and noisiness of acquired datasets. Two approaches that are used in real-time work to compactly represent BRDFs are factorization and environment map filtering.

6.4.1 Factorization

One way to represent a BRDF is not as a sum of weighted basis functions, but rather as a sum of products, with each product consisting of two terms. The idea is to convert a BRDF into a set of pairs of two-dimensional textures. Each pair of textures is accessed by the four-dimensional set of BRDF incoming and outgoing angles, the two retrieved texture values are retrieved and multiplied together, and then the results of these multiplications are summed to get a pixel color. In practice, it has been found that for many surfaces, just a single pair of two textures is sufficient to give reason-

ably convincing results for many materials [405]. The basic factorization
algorithm and its implementation is explained thoroughly and clearly by
Kautz et al. [410] and Wynn [828]. We recommend these articles and the
related source code to interested readers, and so will only briefly discuss
the ideas behind the algorithm here. McCool et al. [530] present a newer
factorization technique with some advantages over the basic factorization
algorithm, and also provide code.

The original BRDF has two direction vectors, incoming and outgoing. Factorization, or separable decomposition, starts by representing the
BRDF as the summation of a simpler pair of functions:

$$f(\boldsymbol{\omega}_i, \boldsymbol{\omega}_o) \approx \sum_{j=1}^{n} p_j(\boldsymbol{\omega}_i) q_j(\boldsymbol{\omega}_o). \tag{6.16}$$

It is possible to create these two sets of functions p and q such that
they compute essentially the same value as f for all possible input vectors.
The catch is that the number of terms n in the summation may have to be
very large.

The idea behind factorization is to map the incoming and outgoing directions to pixels on the textures in such a way that the BRDF function
is separated in as few significant terms as possible, and that a direction
vector can be interpolated linearly across the textures. The textures accessed are of the same form as those used for environment mapping: sphere,
paraboloid, and cubic maps, with cubic maps offering the highest quality.
The goal is to form texture pairs; one texture is accessed by the incoming
direction, the other by the outgoing. See Figure 6.13 and Plate VII following page 274. We will call these the incoming and outgoing textures of
the pair.

Figure 6.13. Factorization of a BRDF for gold, using the Cook-Torrance surface
model [138]. The two textures are accessed with the incoming light and outgoing view directions, and are multiplied together at each pixel to generate the teapot's illumination.
(Images from a program by Chris Wynn, NVIDIA Corp.)

The *uv*-coordinates of each texel on an incoming texture represents an incoming direction, and likewise with the outgoing texture. For example, the *u* coordinate could be mapped to the azimuth angle and the *v* coordinate to the elevation angle. In practice such a parameterization would give a poor factorization, resulting in the need for a large number of texture pairs to be summed to approximate the BRDF. It also does not linearly interpolate well, so would result in serious errors interpolating the texture across a triangle. Picking a good reparameterization of the directions depends on the type of material, and is not an exact science. As an example, the BRDF for velvet has been found to separate well when the directions are recast into surface tangent space, as done for embossed bump mapping in Section 5.7.5.

To compute the texture pairs a large matrix is formed. Each texel in the incoming texture (i.e., each incoming direction) represents a row index in the matrix, and each texel in the outgoing texture a column index in this matrix. Each element in this matrix is a reflectance from the BRDF, computed using these incoming and outgoing directions. *Singular Value Decomposition* (SVD) or *Normalized Decomposition* (ND) is performed on this matrix, which creates pairs of column and row vectors; these vectors are then the values stored in the texture pairs. Normalized decomposition is not as accurate, but has the advantages that it is less complex and memory intensive as SVD, and the texture values are all positive values.

Forming the texture pairs is an offline process, done in advance. To access the texture pairs during rendering, the incoming and outgoing direction vectors are evaluated at each vertex of the model and two pairs of texture coordinates are generated using the same reparameterization. These texture coordinates are then used to access the textures on the surface and multiply the two resulting pixel colors together. Successive pairs of textures are multiplied in the same fashion and added to the final pixel color. See Figure 6.13 for a typical pair of textures and a resulting image.

The separable decomposition can be thought of as a form of data compression [410]. The four-dimensional BRDF is converted to pairs of textures, and the graphics hardware performs the decompression. Since the textures can be represented by sphere and paraboloid maps, this technique of rendering can work on all graphics hardware. See Plate VIII, following page 274, for some results. If available, cubic maps give better results for interpolating across the textures, especially for anisotropic BRDFs and at shallow angles. Mipmapping can be used on the textures, which provides antialiasing of specular highlights.

While this technique is useful, it has limitations. Rendering artifacts and interpolation can cause some problems, though these are usually minor [410]. The main drawback of the approach is that at least two texture accesses are needed for every light source in the scene. Also, only point and directional light sources can be used. The radiance coming from area lights, the sky, or other surrounding objects cannot be captured. The next technique for representing BRDFs is complementary to factorization, and both techniques can be used together when rendering.

6.4.2   Environment Mapping Filtering

As discussed in Section 5.7.4, an environment map can be used to render a perfectly shiny surface. This concept can be extended to glossy and diffuse surfaces. To simulate a different degree of roughness for a surface, the environment's representation in the texture can be filtered [287]. By blurring the environment map (EM) texture, we can present a rougher-appearing specular reflection. This is sometimes called a reflection map, as it multiples the reflectance of the surface by the EM. In theory, such blurring should be done in a nonlinear fashion; that is, different parts of the texture should be blurred differently. However, the eye tends to be fairly forgiving, because the general effect of the reflection is usually more important than the exact reflection itself. So a lazy way to obtain fuzzy reflections is to just uniformly blur the environment maps and hope for the best (care still needs to be taken around the edges of the maps, though).

A more physically realistic method is to use the Phong specular equation to filter the environment map. See Figure 6.14. The specular lobe

Figure 6.14. The left figure shows an eye ray reflecting off an object to retrieve a perfect mirror reflection from the surrounding environment. The middle figure shows a reflection ray's specular lobe, which is used to sample the environment map. The right figure shows summing the cosine weighted hemisphere above the same surface location to obtain the incoming light contribution for the diffuse component. This sum is view-independent.

determines which texels on the EM to sample and how much to weight each texel's relative contribution. Heidrich and Seidel [345] use a single reflection map in this way to simulate the blurriness of a surface.

The idea here is that the EM is thought of as a sphere around the object. Each texel in the EM represents a different (and different sized) area on this sphere, which is constant and so can be computed once. The quadrilateral formed by a texel actually describes a spherical quadrilateral, but approximating these with the areas of two flat triangles is simpler to compute and acceptable for small areas on a sphere. To create a map that simulates the blurriness of a surface, first perform a preprocess to compute the normalized directions of the texel corners and the area of the texel:

```
For each texel n on the EM :
  Retrieve the four corners of the texel, c_{n,1}, ..., c_{n,4}
  Compute and store the normalized directions
      d_{n,1}, ..., d_{n,4} of the texel corners on the EM
  a_n = sum of areas of the two triangles
      Δd_{n,1}d_{n,2}d_{n,3} and Δd_{n,1}d_{n,3}d_{n,4}
next n
```

The corners of the texels are shared, so in practice this loop can be made more efficient. The main code for creating the filtered reflection EM is:

```
For each texel color c on the reflection map :
  r = normalized reflection direction of texel for the EM
  q = (0, 0, 0)
  For each texel n on the EM :
    p = 0
    s = 0
    For each texel corner i of d_{n,1}, ..., d_{n,4}:
      e = (r · d_{n,i})
      if (e > 0)
        p += e^{m_{shi}}    [shininess]
    next i
    f = color of texel n
    q += a_n p f
    s += a_n p
  next n
  Set color of texel c = q/s
next c
```

What this code does for each reflection direction is to find how much every EM texel contributes relative to this direction. Imagine some light coming in from near a given reflection direction. Light directly from the reflection direction will give the largest contribution, dropping off as the direction to the incoming light increasingly differs from the reflection direction. The area of the EM texel multiplied by the texel's BRDF contribution gives the relative effect of this texel. This weighted contribution is multiplied by the color of the EM texel, and the results summed to compute $\mathbf{q}$. The sum of the weighted contributions, s, is also computed. The final result $\mathbf{q}/s$ is the overall color integrated over the reflection direction's lobe.

This reflection map works well for metallic surfaces. To account for the Fresnel term for nonmetallic objects, one approach is to store this term in a table that is accessed by the angle between the viewer and surface normal. The Fresnel term can then be retrieved and stored in the alpha channel during rendering, and then blended with the color information. Heidrich and Seidel [345] present two different blending equations:

$$\mathbf{c}_o = \mathbf{c}_d + f\mathbf{c}_r \tag{6.17}$$

and

$$\mathbf{c}_o = (1 - f)\mathbf{c}_d + f\mathbf{c}_r \tag{6.18}$$

where $\mathbf{c}_d$ is the diffuse color, $\mathbf{c}_r$ the reflected color, $\mathbf{c}_o$ is the output color, and f is the Fresnel term. The second equation simulates diffuse surfaces with a transparent coating.

For a view-independent EM such as a cubic or paraboloid map, the color stored is valid for all mirror reflections in that direction, regardless of the viewer's location. The EM, in fact, stores radiance values of the incoming illumination—it does not matter how this data is accessed. A variety of eye and surface orientations can generate the same reflection direction, for example. In each case, the radiance in that direction is the same.

However, this same independence does not hold when the EM is filtered to create a reflection map. A single reflection map is sufficient only if all viewing and surface directions that yield the same reflection direction have the same shaped specular lobe. This is never the case for anything but perfect mirror surfaces. Think about viewing a shiny (not mirror) sphere from in front and nearly behind it. When in front, a ray reflecting from the sphere that goes straight back may have, say, a symmetric Phong lobe. From nearly behind, a ray reflecting the same direction must in reality have a piece of its lobe cut off. See Figure 6.15. The filtering scheme presented earlier assumes all lobes for a given reflection direction are the

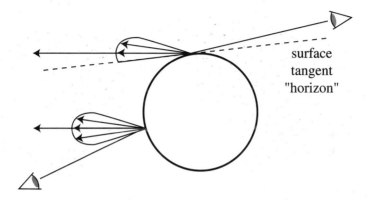

Figure 6.15. A shiny sphere is seen by two viewers. Separate locations on the sphere give the same reflection directions for both viewers. The left viewer's surface reflection samples a symmetric lobe. The right viewer's reflection lobe must be chopped off by the horizon of the surface itself, since light cannot reflect off the surface below its horizon.

same shape and height. In fact, this means the lobes also have to be radially symmetric. Beyond the problem at the horizon, most BRDFs do not have uniform, radially symmetric lobes at all angles; at grazing angles the lobes often becoming sharper and thinner. Also, the lengths of the lobes normally vary with elevation angle.

Cabral et al. [108] realize the limitations of having a single reflection map and use an image warping approach instead. A view-dependent EM such as a sphere map can be computed precisely, using the exact BRDF to find the contribution of the illumination for a given eye and reflection direction, so including such factors as the Fresnel term. In their scheme, 20 reflection sphere maps are generated for orthographic views located at the vertices of an icosahedron imposed on the scene. For any given view, the three sphere maps that are closest to the view direction (essentially, the three views at the vertices of the icosahedron face that the view is on) are warped and blended using barycentric coordinates. The resulting sphere map is then used for that view. This method can result in some grazing angle errors, but for the most part, gives high-quality results, at the cost of warping and blending three sphere maps for every view direction change.

Kautz and McCool address the problem by approximating the BRDF with one or more lobes, resulting in one or more reflection maps added together [406]. Kautz et al. present an overview and classification of these and other filtering schemes, and also present a technique for rapidly generating filtered paraboloid reflection maps [407].

In the Phong lighting model, light from anything that is not a light source is lumped into a single ambient term. Using environment mapping techniques, the diffuse and ambient lighting contributions to the surface can be represented quickly and accurately. A surface is lit by the combination of lights and reflected light from all objects above it, with the contributions falling off with the cosine of the angle to the surface (Lambert's Law). An environment map captures the radiance for an environment. Summing up the weighted contributions for a given direction gives the diffuse and ambient lighting for that direction. See Figure 6.14. Making a texture of these contributions and accessing it by the direction of the surface normal will then retrieve this lighting during rendering. Such a texture is called an *irradiance environment map* [641]. A sphere map and its corresponding irradiance map is shown in Plates XXIV and XXV (following page 274). Plate XXVI (after page 562) shows an example of an irradiance map in use.

There are two ways to store and access such lighting. Since sphere maps are made with respect to a given eye direction, they can be thought of as mapping the set of all reflection directions, as well as mapping the set of normals on the half of the sphere facing the eye. That is, a single sphere map can store both the specular reflection color and the diffuse color for the hemisphere above the sphere's surface at the same time [287]. Figure 5.26 on page 160 shows a point **h** on the sphere: Now instead of storing just the reflected color, also add in the color coming in from the hemisphere above the surface, centered around the surface normal **n**. That this technique works is easily proven by example: Instead of using a shiny sphere, photograph a sphere painted with flat white paint and use the image as a sphere map. Now, a reflection direction accesses the sphere map, and the color retrieved is what light reaches the surface for that normal direction.

A drawback of using a sphere map is that it truly is valid for only this eye direction. The reflection direction and normal direction point different ways, and so adding their contributions into one sphere map binds a view-dependent and view-independent contribution into one, so the eye direction cannot be changed without destroying the illusion.

The second technique for accessing diffuse lighting in this way is to store it in a separate EM. A spheremap could still be used for the irradiance map and the math adjusted accordingly to capture all normal directions, but it is usually easier and better simply to use a view-independent EM such as a cube map. See Figure 6.16. Instead of using the reflection vector, the interpolated surface normal is used to access the cube map to retrieve the diffuse and ambient contribution.

Figure 6.16. A cube map and its corresponding filtered irradiance map. *(Reprinted with permission from Microsoft Corporation.)*

Using irradiance mapping has the advantage of eliminating per vertex lighting calculations from the pipeline. Any number of lights can be used, and the diffuse and ambient contributions are more realistic and convincing. The limitations are due to the assumptions of environment mapping in general: that lights and reflected objects are distant and so do not change with location of the object viewed. This means local light sources cannot easily be used.[6] Using EM often makes it difficult for an object to move among different lighting situations, e.g., from one room to another. Cubic environment maps can be regenerated on the fly from frame to frame, so specular reflection maps are practical, but the filtering involved to create the full diffuse component is expensive.

An irradiance map can be created similarly to how a blurred reflection map is created. Instead of using reflection directions, the dot product of the surface normal on the reflection map and the input EM is used to weight the EM samples. Normally, generating an irradiance map is a costly process: Each texel generated is computed from about half the texels in the original map, i.e., all the texels visible in the hemisphere above the surface normal. Ramamoorthi and Hanrahan [641] present a fast way, based on spherical harmonics, to convert a standard environment map into an irradiance function represented by nine colors. The function

---

[6]It is possible to change the orientation of an EM over time, either to simulate lights rotating around the object or to react to the movement of the object compared to a single light in the EM.

represents the diffuse and ambient contributions for the environment map. Because irradiance varies slowly, the irradiance from the environment map can be approximated by only nine terms (and with an average error of 1%). Nearby texels on an irradiance map are affected by nearly the same hemisphere of radiance values. For this reason, irradiance maps can often be of much lower resolution than the original environment map.[7] Plate XXV, following page 274, shows how an irradiance map derived directly compares to one synthesized by the nine-term function. This function can be evaluated during rendering at each vertex normal and interpolated, or can be used to rapidly create an irradiance environment map for use at the vertex or pixel level. Such lighting is inexpensive and gives visually impressive results, such as those seen in Plate XXVI, following page 562. Simpler synthetic functions can also be used (and changed on the fly) for irradiance mapping, such as a curve representing lighting based on only the elevation angle [547].

A practical real-time solution for dynamic light sources is given by Brennan [99]. Imagine an irradiance map for a single light source. In the direction of the light the radiance is at a maximum, as the light hits the surface straight on. Radiance for a given surface normal direction (i.e., a given texel) falls off with the cosine of the angle to the light, then is zero as the surface faces away from the light. This is simply another way of computing and storing the diffuse contribution of one light. Moving the light means recomputing the diffuse term for each texel of the irradiance map. However, the accelerator can be used to rapidly compute this contribution. Instead of rendering a point light to a cube map and filtering the map, the filtered appearance of the light is represented by an object. This object can be visualized as a hemisphere centered around the observer, with the pole of the hemisphere along the light's direction. The hemisphere itself is brightest in this direction, falling off to zero at its edge. Rendering this object directly into the cube map gives an irradiance map for that light. In this way each light in a scene can add its contribution to the irradiance map by rendering its corresponding hemisphere. This process is rapid enough that it can be done every frame, so that dynamic light sources can be simulated. Plate XVII (following page 274) uses this technique.

One problem with environment mapping is that the dynamic range of the light captured is usually limited to 8 bits per color channel [162]. Directly visible light sources are usually hundreds to thousands times brighter than the indirect illumination (bounced light from walls, ceilings, and other

---

[7]This idea also applies to blurred reflection maps—more blur means less resolution is needed [50].

objects in the environment), so 8 bits is not enough to simultaneously capture the full range of incident illumination. For example, suppose a highly specular object (say a brass candlestick, reflecting 70% of the light) and a darker specular object (say an ebony statue, reflecting 5% of the light) use the same EM. If the EM contains just the lights in the room, then the statue will look good and the candlestick will not; if the EM contains all the objects in the room, the opposite is true. This is because the statue is only shiny enough to visibly reflect direct light sources and little else, while the candlestick will reflect a nearly mirror-like image of the environment. Cohen et al. give a solution based on capturing a *High Dynamic Range Image* (HDRI) and providing properly reexposed range maps as needed for real-time rendering [132].

The view-independent EM techniques assume the BRDF is isotropic. Anisotropic surfaces have BRDFs that require two input azimuth angles instead of just one relative angle. Of course, any BRDF function can be evaluated in software and a highly tessellated surface rendered with the results (this is how Figure 6.12 was generated), but this is usually too slow. The approach generally taken so far for real-time work is to use the Banks model [38] without self-shadowing. See Heidrich and Seidel [345] and Kautz et al. [407] for two approaches. Isidoro and Brennan [387] discuss implementing the Banks model with a pixel shader. The factorization technique discussed in the previous section also handles anisotropic surfaces.

6.5 Vertex Shaders

In general terms, vertex shaders provide a way to modify values associated with each polygon's vertex, such as its color, normal, texture coordinates, and position. This functionality was first introduced with DirectX 8, and is also available as OpenGL extensions. It arose in part because of the need to provide more flexibility for lighting models computed on the graphics accelerator.

The capability to perform transform and lighting of vertices on the graphics accelerator became available on commodity (i.e., games) cards in 1999. Up to this point, transform and lighting was normally done on the host CPU. Offloading this task as part of the accelerator's pipeline freed the CPU for other tasks. The drawback was that it forced the use of the basic Gouraud/Phong model for lighting. Any other variations could not be handled by the graphics hardware.

The vertex shader goes a long way to remedy this situation. When the vertex shader is enabled, the hard-wired transform and lighting model

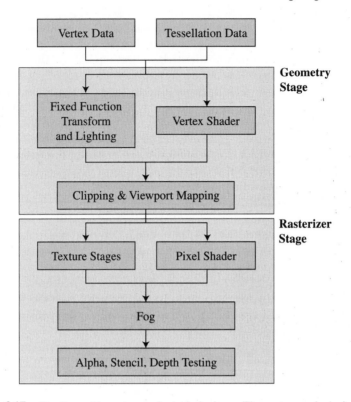

Figure 6.17. Pipeline with vertex and pixel shaders. The vertex and pixel shaders replace different parts of the traditional pipeline with programmable units.

(sometimes referred to as the *fixed function pipeline*) is no longer available. In its place, this part of the pipeline is replaced by a vertex shader unit that executes a series of commands written by the user. See Figure 6.17. Vertex shaders and the fixed function pipeline can both be used in rendering a frame, by switching between one and the other; they simply cannot be used simultaneously. The vertex shader program is stored in a form of assembly language, though macros or higher level languages can be used to aid in programming.

Vertex shaders work on all systems supporting the API, in that if the graphics accelerator does not have support for them, the vertex shaders are evaluated by the host CPU.[8] Since transform and lighting happens early on

---

[8]DirectX optimizes CPU code for the Intel SSE and AMD 3DNow! SIMD instruction sets.

in the pipeline, these operations can be done on the host or the accelerator. As with all graphics operations, hardware-assisted vertex shaders have a single advantage over software shaders: speed. They can help free the CPU to be able to perform other tasks (e.g., collision detection, physical simulation, pathfinding, and artificial intelligence). It is possible to emulate all of the functionality of the fixed function pipeline with a vertex shader, at the same speed [523]. There is a small overhead in setting up each vertex shader, as the shader program itself must be loaded when needed.

A pure vertex shader implementation of a lighting model can actually be faster than the hard-wired path. McCool et al. [530] report that on a GeForce3, they displayed 10.6 million diffuse triangles per second using the standard path, 13.3 million triangles per second with an optimized vertex shader. By knowing in advance about special conditions of the model being sent through the vertex shader, various optimizations can be made. For example, if normals are transformed by matrices consisting of only rotations and translations, then the normals do not have to be renormalized. Another technique usable with some modeling matrices is to transform the lights once into the model's space and perform lighting there. This allows just a single vertex transform (the concatenation of modeling and projection matrices) to be performed per vertex, instead of the usual series of transform/illuminate/transform [83].

Every vertex passed in is processed by the vertex shader program. The vertex shader can neither create nor destroy vertices, and results generated by one vertex cannot be passed on to another vertex. In the first version of the vertex shader specification (which is the one we will discuss unless otherwise noted), a vertex shader program has 128 steps, and the assembly language has 17 different instructions. There are no explicit flow control statements such as if, for, while, or goto. There are also no early return statements. This means that the vertex shader is executed in the same amount of time for each vertex, regardless of input data or conditions encountered. Shorter vertex shaders therefore execute faster; each program step almost always directly corresponds with a hardware clock cycle. The vertex shader may not be the bottleneck in the pipeline, so shorter shader programs do not necessarily translate into faster performance overall (see Chapter 10). This fixed execution time length and the fact that vertices cannot interact with each other means that vertex shaders can be implemented as SIMD parallel processing units, so obtaining additional speed overall [499]. For example, the Xbox has two vertex shaders that work in lockstep.

Four types of memory are available to a vertex shader (see Figure 6.18). There are per-vertex input data and output registers, a temporary register

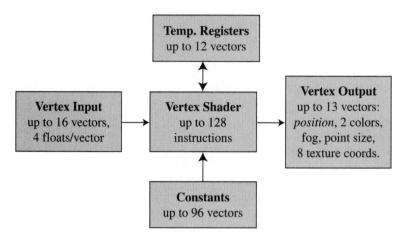

Figure 6.18. First generation vertex shader architecture and register layout, under DirectX 8.1. The constant memory can also be accessed by an address register (*not shown*). The homogeneous location (in italics) must always be output.

area, and constant memory. Each memory location stores a four-element vector, with each element being a signed 32-bit floating point number. Vectors are typically locations ($xyzw$), normals, matrix rows, colors ($rgba$), or texture coordinates ($uvwq$), but can contain any sort of data desired.

Per-vertex and constant memory is loaded by the application. The per-vertex input data consists of up to 16 vector memory locations, with one to four elements in each. These are read-only for the vertex shader. Constant memory is also read-only to the shader, and holds the same data for all vertices processed. It consists of 96 vector memory locations, and holds light attributes (position, color, etc.), transforms, vertex blending matrices, or any other data.

The temporary register area is read-write and consists of 12 vector memory locations. It is scratch space for, and only accessible by, the vertex shader. There is also an address register that is used for offsetting constant memory.

The results of vertex shader computations are written into up to 13 vector memory locations. A vertex's homogeneous clip position must always be output. Beyond this, there are many values that can be modified, including the diffuse and specular colors, eight sets of texture coordinates, the fog value, and the point sprite size.

Describing the entire programming language is beyond the scope of this book, and there are many documents that already do so [180, 210, 523, 811].

However, a few comments are in order. The 17 instructions are tailored toward graphical computation. In a single clock-tick, these can perform three- and four-element dot products, inverse square root, reciprocal, light attenuation, specular power computation, and low-precision exponentiation and logarithm calculation. Square root, division, floor, and cross product are examples of operations that take only two instructions [811]. In addition, for each instruction,the source (input) argument can specify the swizzling or replication of any vector component. In other words, a vector's elements can be reordered or duplicated in any fashion before the instruction takes place, which can make for more compact code by avoiding "move" instructions. Masking (where only the specified vector elements are used) and negation of any register are also for free.

While there are no explicit flow control statements, it is possible to do various "if-then-else" operations by using 0 and 1 values. For example, to translate:

$$\begin{array}{l} \text{if } (a \geq b) \; c = d \\ \text{else } c = e \end{array}$$

branchless pseudo-code would be:

$$\begin{array}{ll} r0 = (a \geq b)?1{:}0 & \texttt{SGE r0, a, b} \\ r1 = d - e & \texttt{ADD r1, d, } -\texttt{e} \\ c = r0 * r1 + e & \texttt{MAD c, r0, r1, e} \end{array}$$

This code maps directly onto three (pseudo-)vertex shader instructions, shown to the right [811].

While the vertex shader architecture is essentially a very simple computer available on the graphics accelerator, it marks a significant change in how this accelerator is considered. Previous graphics hardware presented a relatively fixed pipeline with a few controls. The vertex shader concept points toward making parts of the hardware pipeline itself programmable, providing more flexibility and a much wider set of options.

This section has briefly described the architecture of the DirectX 8.1 vertex shader. For a more detailed account, as well as the design decisions behind it, see Lindholm et al. [499]. In DirectX 9, the instruction count doubles to 256 instructions, and constant memory rises to 256 vectors. Vertex inputs stay the same, though a special register for displacement mapping is available. There are also new data formats, such as 11/11/10 bits for storing low-precision normals in a 32-bit field. Flow control instructions that can be controlled by constants are available, so that a vertex shader program can be modified without reloading. New instructions are added to jump forward, loop a fixed number of times, and call subroutines, which means that the number of instructions is no longer the upper limit of the execution length of the program. Vertex shaders in DirectX 10 and beyond will have predicate conditionals, a subroutine stack, and more control in general. There will also be more integration with the pixel shader.

Since DirectX attempts to span offerings from a number of hardware vendors, additional functionality is often available on specific hardware. For example, NVIDIA's high-end NV30 is has a number of capabilities available through OpenGL extensions. The most significant addition is true branching and variable looping. These new instructions break the mold of the standard accelerator pipeline model, which is to use a fixed set of operations that can be performed in lock-step, SIMD fashion. A four-level subroutine stack is available. If a program executes too many steps (e.g., it is in an infinite loop), it is automatically terminated. There are also a wide variety of new arithmetic instructions, including floor, frac, cos, sin, log2, and exp2, as well as new capabilities, such as user-defined clip planes and new forms of address offsetting.

This and other chapters discuss a number of vertex shader effects, such as shadow volume creation, vertex blending, motion blur, and silhouette rendering. See Figure 6.19. Other uses for vertex shaders include:

- Lens effects, so that the screen appears fish-eyed, underwater, or otherwise distorted.

- Object definition, by making a mesh only once and having it be deformed by the vertex shader.

- Object twist, bend, and taper operations.

- Procedural deformations, such as the movement of flags, cloth, or water [386].

- Primitive creation, by sending degenerate meshes down the pipeline and having these be given an area as needed.

- Page curls, heat haze, water ripples and other effects can be done by using the entire frame buffer's contents as a texture on a mesh.

Figure 6.19. Some vertex shader effects. In the top row, a spaceship model is shown undeformed, then just its left side is locally deformed, then the whole model is deformed, by a single time-controlled vertex shader. The bottom pair of images shows a vertex shader creating a fish-eye lens view of a normal scene. *(Images courtesy of NVIDIA Corp.)*

Vertex shaders can help increase the speed of algorithms that compute more elaborate lighting models [530]. They can calculate values that slowly change over a surface, and the hardware will then interpolate such values. However, by their nature, vertex shaders do not provide per-pixel shading. For this, we turn next to pixel shading.

6.6   Pixel Shading

Pixel shading, also called *fragment shading*, takes place on a per-pixel, per-object basis during a rendering pass. It is an evolutionary extension of the fixed-function multitexture pipeline, explained in Section 5.5. The idea is the same, that a series of instructions operate on a set of constants, interpolated values, and retrieved texture values to produce a pixel color, and optionally an alpha value. However, pixel shaders can also perform operations such as general dependent texture reads (where texture coordinates are computed and then used by the pixel shader), can modify the z-depth value, and can perform many other operations that do not fit well into the texture stage concept. Pixel shading provides a flexible way to create more realistic illumination models and many different effects.

DirectX 8 introduced the concept of pixel shading and specifies texture operations with a special assembly-like language. However, unlike vertex shading, pixel shading does not have to be specified using a programming language. For example, NVIDIA and ATI implement OpenGL pixel shaders through API calls. The advantage of using an API means that platform-specific capabilities can be exposed. In the case of NVIDIA, they enhance each texture stage with a *register combiner* [624], a unit with more flexibility, and their OpenGL API more directly maps to it. The language-based approach taken with DirectX provides a somewhat more portable and platform-neutral, and certainly less verbose, representation of a pixel shader, at the cost of somewhat less power being exposed. Since this functional model of pixel shading is more general and better for capturing complexity in the long-term, it is what is described here. In 2001 DirectX 8.1 has five versions of the pixel shader language, 1.0 through 1.4, and in 2002 DirectX 9 introduces version 2.0. Some versions are associated with specific hardware, e.g., version 1.4 reflects the capabilities of the ATI Radeon 8500. Hardware running a particular version of a DirectX pixel shader language is able to run older versions. To avoid such specifics, only the general ideas behind these languages are outlined, with a bias toward the newer language abilities.

The pixel shader is an alternate part of the pipeline that can replace the set of texture stages. See Figure 6.17 on page 214. There are three sets of inputs for pixel shaders: the interpolated diffuse and specular colors and alphas, eight constants, and four or more texture coordinates. Each of these is a vector of up to four values. A pixel shader consists of definitions of the constants, a number of texture address instructions to route various data, and a number of arithmetic instructions (previously called "texture

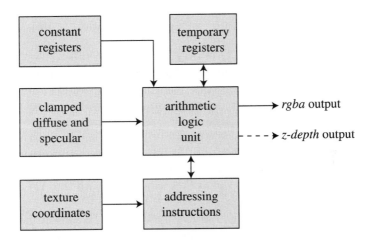

Figure 6.20. Generalized pixel shader. Variants in the pixel shader language primarily affect the way texture address instructions work, where temporary results can be stored, and whether the z-depth can be modified and output.

blending" instructions in DirectX 8.0, and equivalent to NVIDIA's register combiners) to process the data. See Figure 6.20.

The term "texture coordinates" is something of a misnomer at this point, as the data stored can represent anything. Each texture coordinate is accessed by a texture address instruction, which treats the coordinate as either a traditional lookup and filtering of a texture, or as a vector, or as part of a matrix. The intent of many of these address instructions is straightforward. For example, there are instructions to set up so environment map bump mapping or dot product bump mapping can be performed, or so that cubic environment maps can be accessed. It is also possible to wire up general dependent texture reads, so that texture coordinates that are calculated in a pixel shader can be used to read a texture. Texture projection is available, even for dependent reads. The texture coordinates themselves can be passed through and directly accessed by arithmetic instructions. It is also possible to kill a fragment on a comparison; that is, if the texture coordinate does not pass a test, then the fragment is not rendered. This can be a useful operation, such as for simulating user-defined clip planes[9] if otherwise unavailable, but can cause aliasing artifacts.

The addressing instructions do not truly perform operations; they set up the routing for the texture related data. This data is then available for use by the arithmetic instructions, along with any constants set. The

---

[9]In fact, nonplanar clipping regions can be used, e.g., spherical.

interpolated diffuse and specular colors are also available. However, for version 1.x pixel shader languages, these two vectors are normally of low precision (8-bits), and clamped to the range [0, 1], so texture coordinates are better places for more precise data. Constant data is also available, and, as operations are performed, so are intermediate results stored in temporary registers. The inputs are treated as $rgba$ data, and instructions can operate on just the rgb values, the a value, or all four. Arithmetic instructions can be paired, with one operation (e.g., addition) happening to the rgb data[10] and another operation (e.g., multiply) happening in parallel to the a data. Arithmetic operations are done at a low precision signed 9 bits per channel for versions 1.0 through 1.3. Version 1.4, associated with the ATI Radeon 8500, supports 16-bit values with a range $[-8, 8]$.

Each arithmetic instruction has five parts: input, argument modifiers, the operation itself, instruction modifiers, and output location. On input, the instruction specifies what channels are to be used, rgb and/or a. Input modifiers then can invert, negate, bias (subtract 0.5), or perform a signed scale (remap the range [0, 1] to [−1, 1]) on the inputs. A signed scale is something commonly used with normal maps, for example, as each value starts out as a [0, 1] range value. Next, a color and/or alpha operation is performed, such as addition, dot product, conditional, linear interpolation, multiply and add, etc. The results of this operation can then be further modified, multiplying or dividing the result by 2, 4, or 8. In addition, this result can then be clamped to the range [0, 1]. Finally, the data is stored in a temporary register in the desired channels. Masking can be done so that only certain channels are affected. Note that true if/then/else conditionals cannot be performed, but pixel shaders can use the same conditional technique as vertex shaders, explained starting on page 217.

After all arithmetic instructions are performed, one of two things can happen. In earlier versions of the language, the results in register r0 would then continue on down the pipeline to be fogged, and then z-depth compared and blended with the frame buffer. As of version 1.4, a second pass through the pixel manipulation hardware can be done (marked in the language as a **phase** command). At the end of this second pass, the resulting data in r0 then proceeds down the pipeline as before. This additional pass makes it possible to perform complex texturing and arithmetic operations and use the results to perform dependent texture lookups and arithmetic. If this second pass is not available (and even if it is), there is another, less

---

[10]In versions 1.4 and newer, vectors can be defined to denote xyz coordinates instead of rgb colors. This does not add any additional functionality in itself, but makes the code more readable.

efficient way to store intermediate results and perform additional passes. The idea is to render to a texture.[11] This texture can then be immediately remapped in screen space to the visible surfaces. In this way, successive rendering passes can have as an input the resulting colors from earlier passes, albeit at limited precision.

The ability to render to a texture efficiently is relatively new for mainstream graphics systems. In the past, it has been possible to perform this task by rendering to the back buffer or a *pixel buffer* (an offscreen buffer, also called a *pbuffer*), reading the results back to the host, then sending the image back to the accelerator as a texture, but this is slow and inefficient. Recent hardware and API changes make it possible to render to the frame buffer and use the resulting image as a texture without needing to move back through the CPU. Pallister [613] discusses a number of ways to perform render to texture, along with other uses for this capability. Using pixel shaders in combination with render to texture gives a powerful and fast way to evaluate arbitrarily complex illumination equations.

In some versions of the pixel shading language, it is also possible to modify the z-depth of the output fragment. This makes some image-based rendering effects (Section 8.2) possible, such as representing a sphere with a normal map and a depth map.[12] One operation done in the fixed function pipeline not done to the result of the pixel shader is the addition of the specular color (discussed on page 128). If needed, this must be made a part of the pixel shader's program.

The number of textures used can affect the fill rate performance. For example, the NVIDIA GeForce3 pixel shader pipeline runs at half the speed when using three or four textures versus using one or two. The number of arithmetic operations is limited by hardware constraints, and using more of these has a similar slowdown effect on some architectures. Again, with the GeForce3, using seven or eight arithmetic instructions gives one quarter the fill rate speed of using only one or two. ATI's Radeon 8500 has similar performance characteristics. This slowdown matters only if the fill rate is the bottleneck (see Chapter 10).

To give a flavor of the increase in functionality, and to give a sense of how rapidly things change in the industry in just a year, it is worth

---

[11]NVIDIA supports this concept of saving intermediate results directly by providing a *texture rectangle* format for texturing, which can be of arbitrary size and so fit any screen. This type of texture is meant specifically for multipass rendering, and mipmapping is not supported for it. Bilinear filtering is supported, though, as is rendering to a mipmap level.

[12]However, the depth can be difficult to set properly when viewing in perspective, since the z-depth varies nonlinearly.

comparing NVIDIA's NV30 accelerator to its GeForce3. Released in 2002, the NV30 has a number of new capabilities. Some of these are also found in other hardware vendors' DirectX 9 pixel shading language compliant offerings, while other features are unique to the NV30 and are exposed only through OpenGL extensions.

- New number representation types are available, such as 16- and 32-bit floating point channels. See the end of Section 6.7 for more information.

- There are no limits on when and how texture fetches are performed, making dependent texture reads more flexible and easier to use.

- Eight texture coordinate value sets (up from four). These can be used to access up to 16 textures; note that a coordinate set has four values, so can store two pairs of (u, v) values.

- Textures have additional parameters that can be manipulated, such as doing a projective fetch, or scaling and offsetting the screen x and y differentials for LOD bias control.

- Other new inputs include the $(x, y, z, 1/w)$ position in window space (in pixels) and fog distance. Colors are still interpolated at 8 bits per channel, but are treated as floating point values within the shader, making the design more symmetric among inputs.

- The number of constants is effectively unlimited.

- There are many new arithmetic operations, such as `floor`, `frac`, `exp2`, `log2`, `cos`, `sin`, `lit`, `lerp`, `mad`, `max`, `min`, `pow`, `recip`, and `recip sqrt`.

- Possibly most important, the maximum number of steps in a pixel shader is now 1024, making it much easier to perform many algorithms in a single pass. Executing more instructions still costs more time, but with this addition, the only reasons to use multipass methods is if some other resource runs out, such as the number of textures or temporary registers.

These additions make vertex and pixel shaders look much more similar with respect to data formats and instruction set and capabilities. The main remaining differences are that vertex shaders have flow control such as branch and jump, and also array addressing (i.e., a pixel shader cannot choose on the fly which texture to access).

So far, the pixel shader has been described on a functional level. What is of more interest here is how it can be used to evaluate more elaborate lighting models. Previous texture mapping effects such as environment mapping and the various forms of bump mapping can all be used and combined in new ways. The additional flexibility of newer hardware supporting pixel shaders allows even more complex combinations. See Plate XXII (following page 274) for an example.

One operation that can be done with a pixel shader is Phong shading. This is not to be confused with Phong highlighting, which has been used in hardware for a long time. Rather, it is the process of evaluating the lighting equation at each pixel instead of at each vertex. Gouraud shading is poor for a number of lighting situations, as discussed in Section 4.3. Specular highlights often look poor when rendered with Gouraud shading, and in animation give an even worse impression. Spotlights cannot have a sharp falloff with Gouraud shading, as the edge where the light stops is blurry when interpolated (see Figure 4.3 on page 71). Phong shading has been known to be the answer for decades, but has almost always been too expensive to put into hardware. Phong shading can now be performed by using pixel shaders.

The idea behind Phong shading is that, instead of interpolating colors across a triangle, the parameters that are used in the lighting equation are interpolated. The diffuse term is dependent on only the surface normal and light direction. To compute the diffuse term per pixel with a pixel shader, first put the normal into one texture coordinate, and the light direction into another. As discussed in Section 5.7.5, the light vector is best left unnormalized when interpolated, then normalized using a normalizing cube map. The interpolated normal vector can also be normalized in this fashion, if needed. Linearly interpolating the normal across the surface yields normals that are less than unit length. See Figure 6.21. For diffuse surfaces, this shortening means a slight dimming of the interpolated pixels, so normalization may not be critical.

With these two vectors now available as register values in the pixel shader, a dot product is taken and the result is the diffuse term. This process is somewhat like dot product bump mapping without the bumps. Instead, the interpolated normal is used. The diffuse term can be affected by other values, such as a solid color or a texture. In addition, other terms of the lighting equation could be interpolated and used per pixel, such as an attenuation factor for the light itself (e.g, due to distance or spotlight

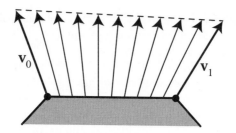

Figure 6.21. Linear interpolation of unit normals at vertices across a surface gives interpolated vectors that are less than a length of one.

effect). The main limiting factors are the cost in speed due to using more arithmetic instructions and the total number of program steps available.

Beaudoin [52] gives an implementation of Phong highlighting using a pixel shader. The Blinn half angle and the light vector are interpolated and normalized. Normalization of the interpolated half angle vector is vital here, because the dot product is raised to a power, so the effect of a slightly short normal is magnified, causing excessive dimming. The dot product is then computed and raised to a power. However, the power function is not available as an instruction in the $1.x$ pixel shader languages. Beaudoin provides various solutions to this problem, such as using a one-dimensional texture lookup or using other arithmetic operations to approximate the function. Using one of these solutions computes the specular term, thus providing per-pixel Phong shaded highlighting.

Per pixel evaluation of more complex BRDF models is an active area of research. Heidrich and Seidel use two texture maps to represent terms in the Torrance-Sparrow illumination model and Banks' model [345]. Kautz and Seidel render surfaces using anisotropic representations such as Banks' model, an anisotropic Blinn-Phong model, and Ward's model [408]. Their key idea is that BRDF models are generally a series of functions that are added or multiplied together. By treating each term separately, arbitrarily complex illumination equations can be evaluated. The functions themselves can be represented by textures if they are too computationally expensive to compute directly on the accelerator. This technique is illustrated in the following example.

EXAMPLE: VARIABLE SHININESS   The goal is to render a surface that has a diffuse color texture, a gloss map to vary the strength of the specular contribution, a normal map for bumpiness, and a shininess map to vary

Figure 6.22. The left image shows a bumpy, shiny surface. The right image shows the same surface, but with a varying shininess power; the lower left pane has a shininess of 10, the upper right a shininess of 120. *(Images courtesy of J.L. Mitchell, ATI Technologies Inc.)*

the power of the specular contribution. The effect of varying the shininess for each tile is shown in Figure 6.22. The textures used to generate this surface are shown in Figure 6.23.

For each pixel, the contribution of the specular highlight is computed as a function of the shininess and the dot product of the normal and the half angle. This example uses the functionality of version 1.4 of the shading language. In versions 1.0 through 1.4 of the language there is no power function, so other means are needed to compute it. Instead of using Beaudoin's arithmetic methods for computing the power function [52], the function is represented as a precomputed texture, which will be referred to as a function texture. See Figure 6.24.

Specifically, we would like to evaluate the following expression:

$$\mathbf{c} = (\mathbf{n} \cdot \mathbf{l} + a)\mathbf{d} + (\mathbf{n} \cdot \mathbf{h})^{m_{shi}}\mathbf{g} \qquad (6.19)$$

where $\mathbf{c}$ is the resulting color, $\mathbf{n}$ is the normal read from the bump map, $\mathbf{l}$ is the light vector in the bump map's tangent space, $\mathbf{d}$ denotes the diffuse texture map, a is an ambient constant, $\mathbf{h}$ is the half-angle vector, m_{shi} is the specular exponent, and, finally, $\mathbf{g}$ is the gloss map. One texture holds the diffuse and the gloss maps; another holds the normal map and shininess data. With these two textures and the function texture in place, the pixel shader program is [556]:

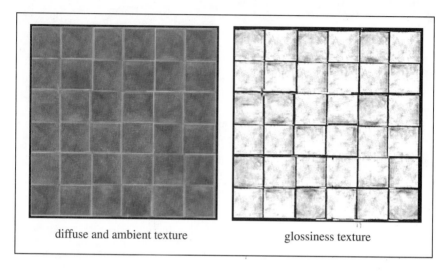

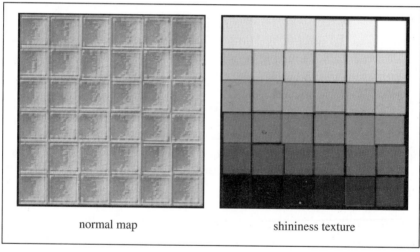

Figure 6.23. Two surface definition textures. The upper texture has a diffuse color texture in the color channels, and a gloss map in the alpha channel. The lower texture has a normal map (colors not shown) in the color channels, and a shininess power map in the alpha channel, ranging from 10 to 120. *(Images courtesy of J.L. Mitchell, ATI Technologies Inc.)*

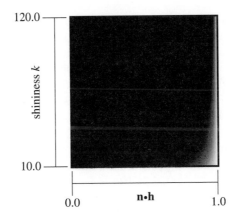

Figure 6.24. Specular power function as a texture. Much of the texture is black—the version 1.4 pixel shader language does not allow scaling and biasing the map in the pixel shader to make better use of the resolution. *(Image courtesy of J.L. Mitchell, ATI Technologies Inc.)*

```
ps.1.4
texld    r1, t0                    ; normal N, in bump map
texld    r2, t1                    ; normalize tangent space
                                   ; light vector L
texcrd   r3.rgb, t2                ; tangent space
                                   ; half angle vector H
dp3_sat  r5.xyz, r1_bx2, r2_bx2    ; N.L
dp3_sat  r2.xyz, r1_bx2, r3        ; N.H
mov      r2.y, r1.a                ; K = specular exponent
phase                              ;   Start second pass
texld    r0, t0                    ; diffuse & gloss texture
texld    r3, r2                    ; dep. read (N.H) by K map
add      r4.rgb, r5, c7            ; add in constant ambient
mul      r0.rgb, r0, r4            ; diffuse X (ambient + N.L)
+mul_x2  r0.a, r0.a, r3.a          ; gloss map X specular
add      r0.rgb, r0, r0.a          ; add the two values above
```

This program does not show other operations needed, such as setting up the texture locations, etc. We will not focus on the exact meaning of every bit of syntax, but rather on the general intent.

Before this program begins a few inputs and mappings are set up. The diffuse/gloss texture is set to be associated with register r0, the bump normal map with r1, a normalizing map with r2 (more on that later), and the function texture with r3. This is a fair bit different than typical assembly language functionality. What it means is that a specific register must be used to receive the results of sampling a specific texture, though any set of texture coordinates can be used to access the texture. The texture coordinates of the location on the surface are associated with texture coordinate vector t0, the unnormalized light vector with t1, and the half-angle with t2.

Coming into the program, the light and half angle vectors have been transformed into tangent space (typically with a vertex shader). The first texld addressing instruction uses the texture coordinates of the surface location to retrieve the bump map's normal and make it available in register r1. The next texld takes the unnormalized light vector and uses it to access a normalizing cube map. As discussed on page 172, this cube map returns a normalized version of any vector used to access it. The net effect is to normalize the previously unnormalized light vector. The texcrd addressing instruction does not access a texture, rather it takes the t2 texture coordinates and puts them into register r3. Now the normal, light vector, and half angle are available for computations.

The first dp3_sat arithmetic instruction computes the dot product of the normal and the lighting vector. The _bx2 suffix transforms each register's value from its input $[0, 1]$ range to $[-1, 1]$, so each is then treated as a signed unit vector. The dot product is performed and the _sat suffix means to clamp the result to the range $[0, 1]$. This clamping is done so that if the light is below the horizon its contribution will be zero, i.e., so that it will not subtract light from the surface.

The next dp3_sat computes the dot product of the normal and half angle, which is put into register r2 (which is being reused, as the light vector that was there is no longer needed). The mov instruction copies the shininess power (which is in the alpha channel of the bump map texture) into the second location of register r2. At this point, register r2 has the data needed for a dependent read of the function texture. This ends the first phase of the pixel shader.

The diffuse and gloss texture is now retrieved to register r0 by the first texld after the phase, using the same surface coordinates as used for accessing the normal bump map. Register r2 is then used to perform a dependent texture read of the function texture, which is retrieved to register r3. The retrieved value is the brightness of the specular contribution due to the light and view directions and shininess. At this point r0 is the surface color and gloss texture, all values in r3 hold the specular contribution, and r5 holds the diffuse contribution. Now all that remains is to combine various computed values, as shown in the comments in the code. The arithmetic instruction with a "+" sign in front of it is paired with the instruction above it. These happen in parallel, since one instruction accesses just the color channels, the other just the alpha channel. The final instruction adds the alpha channel (the final specular intensity) to the color channel (the ambient and diffuse color) to give the result, in r0.

This example is from a presentation by Jason L. Mitchell, who provides many other interesting vertex and pixel shader examples [556]. Other resources for example pixel shaders are vendor websites such as NVIDIA's and ATI's [34, 590], books such as *ShaderX* [210], and event presentations online such as the Meltdown conference [547]. □

In the example, a computationally expensive function is rapidly evaluated by using a two-dimensional lookup table in the form of a texture. It is also perfectly reasonable to use one or three-dimensional textures to represent functions with these numbers of inputs. High-end hardware without pixel shaders, but supporting OpenGL 1.2 image processing extensions, can modify images with one-dimensional lookups [344]. There are also many techniques to approximate functions. Schlick [686] gives an approximation of Fresnel reflectance accurate to within 1%:

$$F = f_\lambda + (1 - f_\lambda)(1 - \mathbf{v} \cdot \mathbf{h})^5 \tag{6.20}$$

The value f_λ is the Fresnel reflectance of the material at normal incidence, $\mathbf{v}$ points to the eye, and $\mathbf{h}$ is the half-angle. For dielectrics, another less accurate, but more hardware-friendly approximation is:

$$F = (1 - \mathbf{v} \cdot \mathbf{h})^4 \tag{6.21}$$

which is relatively simple to implement directly with a pixel shader and without the need for a function texture [547]. Just squaring this term, or even not raising it to a power at all, can give acceptable results [772]. Jensen and Golias [394] found that for water a closely fitting approximation is:

$$F = \frac{1}{(1 + \mathbf{v} \cdot \mathbf{h})^7} \tag{6.22}$$

though, in practice, they use a power of 8 to simplify computation.[13]

The concept of factoring a complex formula works for many other rendering techniques. See Plate XXIII following page 274 for another example. The challenge to the programmer is in breaking down the algorithm into

---

[13]For lighting from reflection maps, $\mathbf{n}$ is substituted for $\mathbf{h}$ in these three equations.

pieces that can be computed on the host, by the vertex shader, or by the
pixel shader. There are limitations on the number and type of program
instructions, varying precision of mathematical computations, texture size
and type constraints, and pipeline bottleneck concerns. With these additional concerns, the puzzle of balancing efficiency and quality as complexity
rises becomes ever more difficult to solve each time from scratch.

6.7   Shading Languages

Creating assembly language programs for vertex and pixel shaders, rather
than defining complex multitexturing pipeline setups, means that editing
and reading code is easier. Tools such as macros and shader previewers
can help ease the burden of debugging. Nonetheless, individual shaders for
particular hardware are tedious to write, often have portability problems,
and can quickly become obsolete or inefficient without active maintenance
to move them to newer architectures.

Given an assembly language, the next natural step is to create a higher
level language. For shaders, this is an old idea, dating back to Cook's *shade
trees* back in 1984 [140]. The idea is that, instead of manipulating a fixed
lighting equation, a shader is organized in the form of a tree. The internal
nodes of the tree are operations such as add, multiply, and blend, and the
child nodes are inputs such as the surface normal. A simple shader is shown
in Figure 6.25. Shade trees can be defined not only for surfaces, but also for
light sources (e.g., to describe the radiance coming from a light in a given
direction) and for atmospheric effects. Each tree is represented in a language. The RenderMan specification [22, 761] uses this shade tree concept
for its surface description language. RenderMan's shaders use a declara-
tive or functional language, in contrast to vertex or pixel shaders, which
use imperative languages. In other words, RenderMan stresses defining
expressions to evaluate over specifying commands to execute.

In the field of real-time rendering, programmable shading was first done
on the experimental PixelFlow system [473, 595]. This SIMD multiprocessor system used a language based on RenderMan. Each processor could
be given a program to execute, with texturing performed by using procedurally generated textures. This parallel system used techniques such as
deferred shading, in which no shading is done until the visible surface is determined. PixelFlow is impressive as a proof-of-concept, but current graphics architectures are considerably different. However, the idea of deferred
shading can be used indirectly to increase efficiency. By performing an
initial rendering of the scene into only the Z-buffer, succeeding passes that

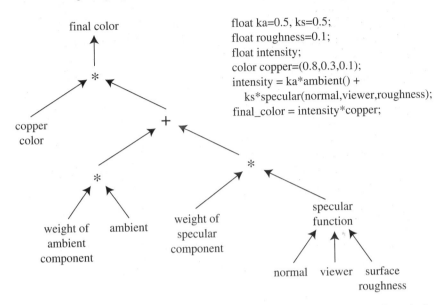

float ka=0.5, ks=0.5;
float roughness=0.1;
float intensity;
color copper=(0.8,0.3,0.1);
intensity = ka*ambient() +
    ks*specular(normal,viewer,roughness);
final_color = intensity*copper;

Figure 6.25. Shade tree for a simple copper shader, and its corresponding shader language program. *(After Cook [140].)*

use complex pixel shaders will waste no fill rate on unseen surfaces [309]. See page 423 for more details.

The "Quake III: Arena" scripting language is the first widespread commercial real-time shading language. It provides multipass and multitexturing support, texture coordinate creation and transformation, and other abilities [391]. This approach has been picked up by other game engines.

The graphics system as a whole can be thought of as a parallel SIMD machine [173, 731]. Peercy et al. [619] use this idea to perform arbitrarily complex shading. They also use RenderMan as a basis for a shading language. The multitexture pipeline is used as a simple computer, with each pass performing the equivalent of a SIMD instruction on all pixels on the screen. The frame buffer can act as an accumulator for a pass of this computer. Additional memory is available by offscreen rendering, and can be accessed rapidly with the capability of rendering to a texture. Mathematical functions can be evaluated by using look-up tables to convert frame buffer values. Flow control is available by using alpha testing and the stencil buffer.

Peercy et al. found they needed two hardware extensions to make their system be able to render a huge variety of RenderMan shaders. One extension is what SGI calls pixel textures, i.e., dependent texture reads, a feature now commonly available. The other feature they needed is extended range and precision of data types. The problem with multipass rendering methods as implemented on fixed-function pipelines and first-generation pixel shaders is that intermediate results are stored as 8-bit values. These values are clamped to $[0, 1]$ and lack precision, so care is needed to make sure everything is in the most accurate space for the computations to be performed. Even then, after a very few passes, the precision errors become serious, leading to artifacts. Ideally, the pipeline would use 32-bit floating point numbers throughout, but this is expensive. Peercy et al. experimented with alternate representations, such as a 16-bit floating point (a sign bit, 5 bits of exponent, and 10 bits of mantissa). They found this 16-bit float to be sufficient for most shaders, except for computing derivatives and other calculations involving taking the difference between two similar-sized values.

With the introduction of vertex and pixel shaders, the idea of a pass as a SIMD instruction breaks down. A programmable pipeline yields an incredibly huge number of possibilities in a single pass. Computing power is increasing faster than bandwidth, so it is important to minimize the number of rendering passes. Proudfoot et al. [624] break operations in shaders down into four classes of computational frequency. There is data that is constant for the scene (e.g., lighting is usually in this class). The second class is data that is constant for a group of primitives (e.g., material properties for a mesh). Third, there is data that can vary per vertex. Finally, there is fragment data, which can vary per pixel. Vertex data is used when the data is varying slowly enough that few artifacts are caused by using it. Per-pixel operations are needed to accurately capture rapidly varying changes.

These four stages are represented in their shading language. Based on RenderMan, it is tailored toward hardware implementation. The user can decide on the specific frequency of various operations, or can let the shading compiler infer a frequency by using a set of rules. The compiler itself is based on well-established technology. Because the first-generation vertex and pixel shaders have no branching or looping operators, optimization of a given shader is very good, close to levels achieved by hand-coding. This procedural shading system provides the advantages of ease-of-use and portability. Different architectures are represented by different modules, so a single shader program can create the necessary code for different platforms. See Figure 6.26 and Plate XXVII for an example of a shader.

It is worth noting that the specification for OpenGL 2.0 includes a high-level shading language [36]. This language is also built on RenderMan, the work by Proudfoot et al., and others. DirectX is likely to follow with a high-level language as well.

Figure 6.26. A shader language program performed as a series of texture applications. The series shown here displays some (not all) intermediate steps. In practice, multiple stages are typically rendered in a single pass. In the leftmost image, the base texture is applied; the next figure shows the result after three decal textures are each applied, then the marks are shown, then the diffuse lighting, and finally specular highlighting. *(Images courtesy of Kekoa Proudfoot, Computer Graphics Laboratory, Stanford University.)*

Proudfoot et al. also note the problem of low precision passes on current pixel shader hardware, as well as the problem of having to deal with different precisions at different places in the pipeline. The idiosyncrasies and limitations of the first-generation shader hardware implementations make it difficult to compile code for them. These problems will fade as succeeding generations of accelerators provide more flexibility and capabilities.

For example, NVIDIA's NV30 solves the precision problem by providing "fat pixels," 16- and 32-bit floating point numbers[14] for each channel, so providing up to 128 bits per pixel. The idea is that textures and pixel shaders can use this higher precision for storing information during processing and so remove the last major impediment to computing elaborate shading models. In this design, there are 16 32-bit vectors of 4 floating point numbers, or 32 16-bit vectors, used for temporary results. These are called *first class temporaries*. The results of a pixel shader can also be rendered to a "deep" frame buffer with this extended storage and then be accessed as a texture on succeeding passes. The final result is still stored as an 8 bit per channel color.

---

[14]The 16-bit floating point representation is 1-bit for the sign, 5 bits exponent, and 10 bits mantissa.

NV30 pixel shader arithmetic operations and precision are similar to those of the vertex shader. The combination of nearly unlimited instructions being available in a single pass along with no branch instructions means that writing an optimizing compiler for shaders is a relatively simple task.

6.8   Motion Blur

In a movie, motion blur comes from the movement of an object across the screen during a frame. For example, if an object moves from left to right, it would be more realistic for it to be represented by an object blurred horizontally on the screen. If the camera is tracking an object, the object does not blur—the background does. Sometimes motion blur is added to computer graphics images for the same reason lens flares are added: to give a psychological cue to the user. The blur itself may be overemphasized to add to the feeling of motion. See Plate XXVIII (following page 562) for an example.

There are a number of approaches to producing motion blur in computer rendering. One straightforward, but limited, method is to model and render the blur itself. In fact, this is the rationale for drawing lines to represent particles (see Section 8.5). This concept can be extended. Imagine a sword slicing through the air. Before and behind the blade, two polygons are added along its edge. These polygons use an alpha opacity per vertex, so that where a polygon meets the sword, it is fully opaque, and at the outer edge of the polygon, the alpha is fully transparent. This is a simplification, but the idea is that the model has transparency to it in the direction of movement, simulating blur.

One way to create blur is to average a series of images using the accumulation buffer [300]. The object is moved to some set of the positions it occupies during the frame and is rendered into the accumulation buffer. The final result gives a blurred image. However, for real-time rendering such a process is normally counterproductive (unless there is a good deal of extra processing power available), because it lowers the frame rate. If what is desired is the suggestion of movement instead of pure realism, the accumulation buffer can be used in a clever way that is not as costly. Imagine that eight frames of a model in motion have been generated and stored in the accumulation buffer, then displayed. On the ninth frame, the model is rendered again and accumulated, but also at this time the first frame is rendered again and subtracted from the accumulation buffer. The buffer now has 8 frames of a blurred model, frames 2 through 9. On the next frame, we subtract frame 2 and add in frame 10, giving the 8 frames 3 through 10. In this way, only two renderings per frame are needed to continue to obtain the blur effect [536].

Averaging the current and previous frame gives a more realistic blur. It also helps avoid pixel-popping artifacts and other temporal aliasing problems. However, a slow frame rate will show ghost images, so a high rate is essential for this sort of technique [558].

Another method to perform motion blur can be done in two passes with vertex shaders [810, 812]. In the first pass, the object is rendered normally. In the second pass, a vertex shader applies the previous frame's and the current frame's transform to each vertex. The difference between these locations gives a motion vector per vertex. If the dot product of this motion vector and the vertex's normal is negative, then the vertex is facing away from the direction of motion. When this is detected, the vertex's previous position is output from the vertex shader; else, the vertex's current position is used. This has the effect of stretching the model out between the set of polygons facing forward and those facing backward. The length of the motion vector is used to modulate the alpha component of the backward-facing vertices to give a motion-line effect.

6.9   Depth of Field

Within the field of photography there is a range where objects are in focus. Objects outside of this range are blurry, the further outside the blurrier. To simulate this effect, the accumulation buffer can be used [300]. See Figure 6.27. By varying the view and keeping the point of focus fixed, objects will be rendered blurrier relative to their distance from this focal point.

For layer-based rendering systems, depth-of-field effects can be created by blurring a particular layer using image processing techniques [724]. Vertex and pixel shaders can perform this type of technique by rendering the scene to a texture and storing the amount to blur each object (based on its distance) in the alpha channel. The texture is then rerendered using filtering techniques to blur it (see Section 8.11), and blur it again, resulting in three textures. Then a pixel shader is used to access the alpha channel blur factor and interpolate among the three textures for each pixel [812] and Plate XXIX following page 562.

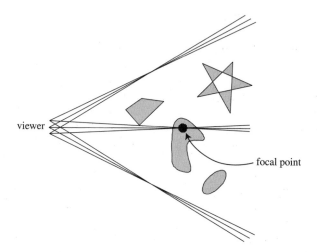

Figure 6.27. Depth of field. The viewer's location is moved a small amount, keeping the view direction pointing at the focal point, and the images are accumulated.

6.10 Reflections

Reflection, refraction, and shadowing are all examples of *global illumination* effects, in which one object in a scene affects the rendering of another. Effects such as reflections and shadows contribute greatly to increasing the realism in a rendered image, but they perform another important task as well. They are used by the viewer as cues to determine spatial relationships, as shown in Figure 6.28.

Figure 6.28. The left image was rendered without shadow and reflections, and so it is hard to see where the object is truly located. The right image was rendered with both shadow and reflections, and the spatial relationships are easier to estimate. *(Car model is reused courtesy of Nya Perspektiv Design AB.)*

Environment mapping techniques for providing reflections of objects at a distance have been covered in Section 5.7.4 and 6.4.2, with reflected rays computed using Equation 4.5 on page 76. The limitation of such techniques is that they work on the assumption that the reflected objects are located far from the reflector, so that the same texture can be used by all reflection rays. Generating planar reflections of nearby objects will be presented in this section, along with methods for rendering frosted glass and handling curved reflectors.

6.10.1 Planar Reflections

Planar reflection, by which we mean reflection off a flat surface such as a mirror, is a special case of reflection off arbitrary surfaces. As often occurs with special cases, planar reflections are easier to implement and execute more rapidly than general reflections.

An ideal reflector follows the *law of reflection*, which states that the angle of incidence is equal to the angle of reflection. That is, the angle between the incident ray and the normal is equal to the angle between the reflected ray and the normal. This is depicted in Figure 6.29, which illustrates a simple object that is reflected in a plane. The figure also shows an "image" of the reflected object. Due to the law of reflection, the reflected image of the object is simply the object itself physically reflected

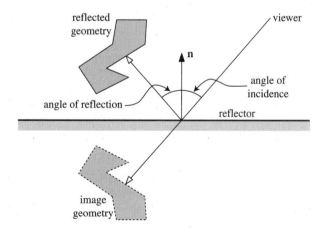

Figure 6.29. Reflection in a plane, showing angle of incidence and reflection, the reflected geometry, and the reflector.

through the plane. That is, instead of following the reflected ray, we could follow the incident ray through the reflector and hit the same point, but on the reflected object. The conclusion that can be drawn from this principle is that a reflection can be rendered by creating a copy of the object, transforming it into the reflected position, and rendering it from there. To achieve correct lighting, light sources have to be reflected in the plane as well [562, 593], with respect to both position and direction.

If for a moment we assume that the reflecting plane has a normal, $\mathbf{n} = (0, 1, 0)$, and that it goes through the origin, then the matrix that reflects in this plane is simply this mirror scaling matrix: $\mathbf{S}(1, -1, 1)$. For the general case, we derive the reflection matrix $\mathbf{M}$ given the normal of the reflector $\mathbf{n}$ and some point $\mathbf{p}$ on the reflector plane. Since we know how to reflect in the plane $y = 0$, the idea is to transform the plane into $y = 0$, then perform the simple scaling, and finally transform back. The concatenation of these matrices yields $\mathbf{M}$.

First, we have to translate the plane so that it passes through the origin, which is done with a translation matrix: $\mathbf{T}(-\mathbf{p})$. Then the normal of the reflector plane, $\mathbf{n}$, is rotated so that it becomes parallel to the y-axis: $(0, 1, 0)$. This can be done with a rotation from $\mathbf{n}$ to $(0, 1, 0)$ using $\mathbf{R}(\mathbf{n}, (0, 1, 0))$ (see Section 3.3.2). The concatenation of these operations is called $\mathbf{F}$:

$$\mathbf{F} = \mathbf{R}(\mathbf{n}, (0, 1, 0))\mathbf{T}(-\mathbf{p}). \tag{6.23}$$

After that, the reflector plane has become aligned with the plane $y = 0$, and then scaling, $\mathbf{S}(1, -1, 1)$, is performed; finally, we transform back with $\mathbf{F}^{-1}$. Thus, $\mathbf{M}$ is constructed as in Equation 6.24.

$$\mathbf{M} = \mathbf{F}^{-1} \, \mathbf{S}(1, -1, 1)^T \, \mathbf{F} \tag{6.24}$$

Note that this matrix has to be recomputed if the position or orientation of the reflector surface changes.

The scene is rendered by first drawing the objects to be reflected (transformed by $\mathbf{M}$), followed by drawing the rest of the scene with the reflector included. An example of this process is shown in Figure 6.30, and the results appear in Plate XXXII (following page 562). The reflector has to be partially transparent if the reflection is to be visible. As such, the transparency acts like a kind of reflectivity factor; the reflector appears more reflective with increasing transparency, and less reflective with decreasing transparency.

However, sometimes the reflections can be rendered incorrectly, as in the left part of Figure 6.31. This happens because the reflected geometry

Figure 6.30. The floor reflection for Plate XXXII (following page 562) is created by rendering much of the model again mirrored beneath the castle's floor. The floor is later rendered semitransparently (blended) so that both it and the reflection are seen. *(Image courtesy of Agata and Andrzej Wojaczek [agand@clo.com], Advanced Graphics Applications Inc.)*

can appear at places where there is no reflector geometry. In other words, the viewer will figure out the trick, seeing that the reflected objects are actually real. The correct image can be generated with the use of the *stencil buffer* (see page 22).

To solve the problem, the reflector is rendered into the stencil buffer, with the stencil parameters set so that we can write to the screen only where the reflector is present. Then the reflected geometry is rendered with stenciling turned on. In this way, the reflected geometry is rendered only where the stencil buffer is set. Drawing one image atop another, when both occupy the same space, is called decaling.

Another problem that occurs with planar reflections is due to face culling (see Section 9.3). If backface culling is turned on and we scale an object with a reflection matrix, then backface culling will appear to be turned off and frontface culling will appear to be turned on. Two solutions are to turn off face culling (with the likelihood of slower rendering) or switch from backface to frontface culling.

Figure 6.31. The left image shows an incorrectly rendered reflection against three mirrored squares. The right image was rendered with the use of the stencil buffer to mask out the part where there is visible reflector geometry, which yields a correct reflection.

Objects that are on the far side of (i.e., behind) the reflector plane should not be reflected. This problem can be solved by using the reflector's plane equation. Put each triangle's vertices into this plane equation in turn; if the value is negative, the vertex is beyond the reflector plane. Discard all triangles that are on the opposite side from the viewpoint. However, triangles that intersect the plane then need to be clipped, which generates new polygons. One way to avoid having to add code for this clipping procedure is to use a user-defined clipping plane, if one is available. All graphics APIs clip against the view frustum, of course. Many APIs, including OpenGL and DirectX, allow the user to define additional planes that clip primitives sent against them.

Place the clipping plane so that it coincides with the plane of the reflector [317]. Using such a clipping plane when rendering the reflected objects will clip away all reflected geometry that is on the same side as the viewpoint, i.e., all objects that were originally behind the mirror.

If clipping planes are available, a simple and faster form of planar reflection can be used. Instead of using a mirror reflection transform on all the objects being reflected, simply reflect the viewer's position and orientation through the mirror to the opposite side of the reflector. Use the clipping plane to remove all objects behind the mirror and render the scene. What appears is the reflection image. Then, use the original view to blend in the reflector and render the normal scene, as before. The advantage of moving the viewer is that none of the geometry has to be manipulated in any way before being sent down to form the reflection [317, 536, 593].

Other algorithms can be combined with the planar reflection technique. For example, the reflection image can be created separately and treated as a texture, which can then be applied to the reflecting surface. This image can be used with environment mapped bump mapping (Section 5.7.5) to reflect local and dynamic objects. See Plate XXX (following page 562) for an example. Another way such effects can be performed is by applying the texture to a regular grid of polygons on the reflector. Instead of using a uniformly spaced set of (u, v) parameter-space values, these values are modified slightly (e.g., by adding in a noise function) [536]. This distorts the reflected image and thereby creates the illusion of the reflector's waviness. Using render to texture, such two-dimensional warping techniques could be applied to the entire scene's image, allowing for underwater effects or other distortions. The scene is rendered, and the generated image is then used as a texture on a warping grid filling the screen.

Recursive curved (using environment mapping) and planar reflections can be combined in one framework as presented by Nielsen [586]. Reflections are rendered into textures in order to approximate glossy reflections by low-pass filtering reflection images. To save render-to-texture memory, a depth-first traversal of the reflection tree is used. To speed up the rendering of recursive reflections, the technique from page 163 is also used, i.e., environment maps are reused from previous frames. Combined with shadows, this gives a convincing effect, as shown in Plate XXXIII (following page 562).

Planar reflections for real-time rendering have also been treated by Diefenbach and Badler [173], and in the SIGGRAPH course on advanced OpenGL [536].

6.10.2 Glossy Effects

A number of significant global illumination effects and lighting models are presented by Diefenbach and Badler [173]. We will discuss two here, glossy reflection and refraction. The previous section presented methods that produce sharp reflections. A simple way to enhance the illusion that the reflector is truly a mirror is to fog the reflected objects seen in it. An example is shown in Plate XIII (following page 274). This effect is created by having the object fade to black as the distance from the reflector increases. Something to note about the plate's image is that each reflected

Figure 6.32. In the left image, reflections are absent, while in the middle image, a hard reflection is rendered in the plane. To the right, a fuzzy reflection has been rendered using shears and accumulating the images. A nice property of fuzzy reflections is that they are not mistaken for a real object. They tend to make the viewer focus on the object and not the reflection.

object has been given its own rate of extinction. The eraser is made to fade away quickly relative to its distance from the reflector, while the pear can fade more slowly since it is relatively tall. This technique does not use hardware fogging here. Rather, the distance from the reflector must be computed in the application stage (or by a vertex shader) and used to diminish the object's color with distance.

The accumulation and stencil buffers can be used together to produce the effects of fuzzy reflection and frosted glass. The stencil buffer creates the window into the effect, and the accumulation buffer captures the effect from jittering the position of the object. Fogging to black is used for the reflection, fogging to white for the refraction. Examples of these techniques are shown in Plate XXXIV (following page 562). A comparison of using no reflections, hard reflections, and fuzzy reflections is shown in Figure 6.32. Here, the fuzzy reflection was also created using the accumulation buffer. The reflected object was jittered by shearing in a direction parallel to the viewing plane, with the amount of shearing determined by the distance to the reflecting plane.

Bastos et al. [50] use image-based techniques combined with signal processing to create glossy reflections. They also use a more elaborate BRDF model of how a surface reflects, as well as radiosity for the diffuse lighting. While their method is more complex, it avoids having to perform multiple accumulation buffer passes.

6.10.3 Reflections from Curved Reflectors

Ray tracing is the traditional solution for producing reflections. See Section 6.13.2 for details. A reflection ray starts from the viewed location and picks up and adds in the color in the reflection direction. Ofek and Rappoport [593] present a technique for sharp, true reflections from convex and concave reflectors that can be considerably faster. Their observation is that in a convex reflector (e.g., a sphere), the reflected object is distorted by the surface, but otherwise unchanged. That is, each reflected vertex is reflected by only one point on the reflector (unlike what can happen with a concave reflector). The curved reflector can be treated like a window into a mirror world, in a similar manner to the planar reflector. The full description of this method is fairly involved, and the interested reader should see the original paper [593].

6.11 Refractions

There are a few physical effects that come into play in simulating refraction. One has already been described, the Fresnel term. For transparent objects, this term is essentially a blend factor of reflection and refraction. That is, if the Fresnel term is, say, 0.7, then reflected light is attenuated to 70% and refracted light coming through the surface to 30%. Plate XXXV (following page 562) shows this effect; objects underwater are visible when looking directly into the water, but looking at a grazing angle mostly hides what is beneath the waves.

Another important factor is Snell's Law, which states the relationship between the incoming and outgoing vectors when moving from one medium (such as air) to another (such as water):

$$n_1 \sin(\theta_1) = n_2 \sin(\theta_2) \tag{6.25}$$

where n_i is the index of refraction of each medium and θ_i the angle compared to the surface normal. See Figure 6.33. Water has an index of refraction of 1.33, glass typically around 1.5, and air essentially 1.0. When travelling from a higher index of refraction to a lower one (e.g., looking out from under water to the sky), total internal reflection will start to occur at some critical angle. At this angle, all light is reflected and none refracted through the surface.

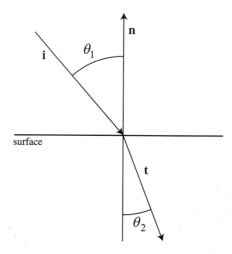

Figure 6.33. Snell's Law. Light travelling from one medium to another refracts depending on each medium's index of refraction. The angle of incidence for the incoming ray is greater than or equal to the angle of refraction when travelling from a lower to higher index of refraction.

Defining **i** as the incoming vector and **n** as the surface normal, both normalized, an efficient method of computing the refraction vector from Bec [53] is:

$$\mathbf{t} = r\mathbf{i} + (w - k)\mathbf{n} \qquad (6.26)$$

where **t** is the resulting normalized refraction vector, $r = n_1/n_2$ is the relative index of refraction, and:

$$w = -(\mathbf{i} \cdot \mathbf{n})\mathbf{n},$$
$$k = \sqrt{1 + (w - r)(w + r)}. \qquad (6.27)$$

This evaluation can be expensive. Oliveira [597] notes that because the contribution of refraction drops off near the horizon, an approximation for small incoming angles is:

$$\mathbf{t} = -c\mathbf{n} + \mathbf{i} \qquad (6.28)$$

where c is somewhere around 1.0 for simulating water. Note that the resulting vector **t** needs to be normalized when using this formula.

The techniques for simulating refraction are somewhat comparable to those of reflection. However, for refraction through a planar surface, it is not as straightforward as just moving the viewpoint. Diefenbach [172] discusses this problem in depth, noting that a homogeneous transform matrix is needed to properly warp an image generated from a refracted viewpoint. Warped refraction images can be combined with environment map bump mapping (EMBM) to make the refracting surface appear to be irregular. See Plate XXX (following page 562) for an example. Such techniques are not physically correct, but are often fine for fooling the eye. Vlachos [775] presents the shears necessary to render the refraction effect of a fish tank.

Another way to give an impression of refraction is to generate a cubic environment map generated from the eye's position that does not include objects between the viewer and the refracting object. This culling could be done by using a clip plane perpendicular to the view and near the refracting object, as the only part of the EM accessed will be beyond the refractor. The refracting object is then rendered, accessing this EM by using the refraction direction. This method will overstate the refraction effect, as the refractor's view of the surroundings is different than the eye's. Better (but more involved) is to create a correction vector using a pixel shader [98]. Plate XVII (following page 274) shows the final effect. Refraction can also be used in a skybox setting (see Section 8.9), as shown in Plate XXXVI (after page 562).

These techniques give the impression of refraction, but usually bear little resemblance to physical reality. The refraction ray gets redirected when it enters the transparent solid, but the ray never gets bent the second time when it is supposed to leave this object; this backface never comes into play. This flaw often does not matter, because the eye is forgiving for what the right appearance should be.

For rippled water surfaces, Oliveira [597] details the use of a single texture representing the water's container. This method can look unrealistic for a moving viewer, giving the impression of a dish-shaped container. To counter this, Vlachos and Mitchell [772] generate the refraction ray and use simple ray tracing on the fly to find which actual wall of the water's container is hit. The point found is transformed to a point on a texture representing the walls and floor. See Figure 6.34. The distance to the container wall can also be used to attenuate the light by the water's color. *Caustics*, i.e., light focused by the curves of the waves, can be simulated by animating textures. Trendall and Stewart [754] use six passes to compute caustics. Brennan et al. [386] simulate ocean waves using vertex and pixel shaders. The vertex shader animates the ocean surface, while two normal maps give reflective detail texture bumps. A one-dimensional map is accessed to compute the Fresnel effect for the water. Jensen and Golias [394] create realistic ocean water effects in real time by using a variety

Figure 6.34. A pool of water. The walls of the pool appear warped due to refraction through the water. *(Image courtesy of Alex Vlachos, ATI Technologies Inc.)*

of techniques, including the Fresnel term, environment mapping to vary the water color dependent on viewing angle, bump mapping for the water's surface, caustics from projecting the surface of the water to the ocean bottom, simplified volume rendering for godrays, textured foam, and spray using a particle system.

6.12   Shadows

Shadows are important elements in creating realistic images and in providing the user with visual cues about object placement. A review of many different shadow algorithms is found in the survey published by Woo et al. [819] and in Watt and Watt's book [793]. Here we will present the most important real-time algorithms for dynamic shadows. These techniques can be mixed as desired in order to maintain quality while still being efficient.

The terminology used throughout this section is illustrated in Figure 6.35, where *occluders* are objects that cast shadows onto *receivers*. Point light sources generate only fully shadowed regions, sometimes called *hard shadows*. If area or volume light sources are used, then soft shadows are produced. Each shadow can then have a fully shadowed region, called the *umbra*, and a partially shadowed region, called the *penumbra*. Soft shadows are recognized by their soft shadows edges. However, it is important to note that they usually cannot be rendered correctly by just blurring the edges of a hard shadow with a low-pass filter. As can be seen

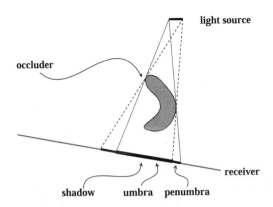

Figure 6.35. Shadow terminology: light source, occluder, receiver, shadow, umbra, and penumbra.

in Figure 6.36, a correct soft shadow is sharper the closer the shadow casting geometry is to the receiver. The umbra region of a soft shadow is not equivalent to a hard shadow generated by a point light source. Instead, the umbra region of a soft shadow is decreasing in size the larger the light source, and in fact, it might even disappear given a big enough light source. Soft shadows are generally preferable, if they are possible, because the soft edges let the viewer know that the shadow is indeed a shadow. Hard-edged

Figure 6.36. The left image was rendered with hard shadows, while the right was rendered with soft shadows. The soft shadow has a smaller umbra region (i.e., fully in shadow), and the softness increases with the distance from the receiving point (floor) to the shadow generating point (chair).

shadows usually look less realistic and can sometimes be misinterpreted as actual geometric features, such as a crease in a surface.

More important than having a penumbra is having any shadow at all. Without some shadow as a visual cue, scenes are often unconvincing and more difficult to perceive. As Wanger shows [790], it is usually better to have an inaccurate shadow than none at all, as the eye is fairly forgiving about the shape of the shadow. For example, a blurred black circle applied as a texture on the floor can anchor a person to the ground. A simple black rectangular shape fading off around the edges, perhaps a total of 10 triangles, is often all that is needed for a car's soft shadow.

In the following sections, we will go beyond these simple modeled shadows and present methods that compute shadows automatically in real time from the occluders in a scene. The first section handles the special case of shadows cast on planar surfaces, and the second section covers more general shadow algorithms, i.e., casting shadows onto arbitrary surfaces. Both hard and soft shadows will be covered. Finally, in Section 6.12.5, some optimization techniques are presented that apply to various shadow algorithms.

The algorithms that follow normally discuss interactions between discrete objects. Special cases such as terrain rendering allow many simplifying assumptions. For example, Hoffman and Mitchell [362] store for each point on a heightfield the altitudes at which the sun is barely and fully visible at sunrise and sunset. A soft shadow edge from the sun can then be generated, as each point can determine whether it is partially or fully in shadow.

6.12.1   Planar Shadows

A simple case of shadowing occurs when objects cast shadows on planar surfaces. Two kinds of algorithms for planar shadows are presented in this section.

Projection Shadows

In this scheme, the three-dimensional object is rendered a second time in order to create a shadow. A matrix can be derived that projects the vertices of an object onto a plane [72, 748]. Consider the situation in Figure 6.37, where the light source is located at l, the vertex to be projected is at v, and the projected vertex is at p. We will derive the projection matrix for the special case where the shadowed plane is $y = 0$, then this result will be generalized to work with any plane.

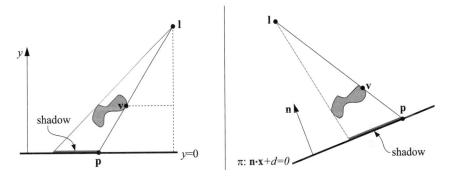

Figure 6.37. Left: A light source, located at **l**, casts a shadow onto the plane $y = 0$. The vertex **v** is projected onto the plane. The projected point is called **p**. The similar triangles are used for the derivation of the projection matrix. Right: The notation of the left part of this figure is used here. The shadow is being cast onto a plane, $\pi : \mathbf{n} \cdot \mathbf{x} + d = 0$.

We start by deriving the projection for the x-coordinate. From the similar triangles in the left part of Figure 6.37, the following equation is obtained.

$$\frac{p_x - l_x}{v_x - l_x} = \frac{l_y}{l_y - v_y}$$

$$\Longleftrightarrow \tag{6.29}$$

$$p_x = \frac{l_y v_x - l_x v_y}{l_y - v_y}$$

The z-coordinate is obtained in the same way: $p_z = (l_y v_z - l_z v_y)/(l_y - v_y)$, while the y-coordinate is zero. Now these equations can be converted into the projection matrix **M** below.

$$\mathbf{M} = \begin{pmatrix} l_y & -l_x & 0 & 0 \\ 0 & 0 & 0 & 0 \\ 0 & -l_z & l_y & 0 \\ 0 & -1 & 0 & l_y \end{pmatrix} \tag{6.30}$$

It is easy to verify that $\mathbf{Mv} = \mathbf{p}$, which means that **M** is indeed the projection matrix.

In the general case, the plane onto which the shadows should be cast is not the plane $y = 0$, but instead $\pi : \mathbf{n} \cdot \mathbf{x} + d = 0$. This case is depicted in the right part of Figure 6.37. The goal is again to find a matrix that projects $\mathbf{v}$ down to $\mathbf{p}$. To this end, the ray emanating at $\mathbf{l}$, which goes through $\mathbf{v}$, is intersected by the plane π. This yields the projected point $\mathbf{p}$:

$$\mathbf{p} = \mathbf{l} - \frac{d + \mathbf{n} \cdot \mathbf{l}}{\mathbf{n} \cdot (\mathbf{v} - \mathbf{l})}(\mathbf{v} - \mathbf{l}). \tag{6.31}$$

This equation can also be converted into a projection matrix, shown in Equation 6.32, which satisfies $\mathbf{Mv} = \mathbf{p}$.

$$\mathbf{M} = \begin{pmatrix} \mathbf{n} \cdot \mathbf{l} + d - l_x n_x & -l_x n_y & -l_x n_z & -l_x d \\ -l_y n_x & \mathbf{n} \cdot \mathbf{l} + d - l_y n_y & -l_y n_z & -l_y d \\ -l_z n_x & -l_z n_y & \mathbf{n} \cdot \mathbf{l} + d - l_z n_z & -l_z d \\ -n_x & -n_y & -n_z & \mathbf{n} \cdot \mathbf{l} \end{pmatrix} \tag{6.32}$$

As expected, this matrix turns into the matrix in Equation 6.30 if the plane is $y = 0$ (that is, $\mathbf{n} = (0 \ 1 \ 0)^T$ and $d = 0$).

To render the shadow, simply apply this matrix to the objects that should cast shadows on the plane π, and render this projected object with a dark color and no illumination. In practice, you have to take measures to avoid allowing the projected polygons to be rendered beneath the surface receiving them. One method is to add some bias to the plane we project upon so that the shadow polygons are always rendered in front of the surface. Getting this bias just right is often tricky: Too much and the shadows start to cover the objects and so break the illusion; too little and the ground plane pokes through the shadows due to precision error. As the angle of the surface normal away from the viewer increases, the bias must also increase. This functionality is provided in OpenGL by `glPolygonOffset`, for example. It takes a constant offset argument, but also biases the polygon based on its plane orientation. In this way, the bias increases along with the polygon's angle.

A safer method is to draw the ground plane first, then draw the projected polygons with the Z-buffer off, then render the rest of the geometry as usual. The projected polygons are then always drawn on top of the ground plane, as no depth comparisons are made.

A flaw with projection shadows is one we ran into with reflections: The projected shadows can fall outside of our plane. To solve this problem, we can use a stencil buffer. First, draw the receiver to the screen and to the stencil buffer. Then, with the Z-buffer off, draw the projected polygons only where the receiver was drawn, then render the rest of the scene normally.

Projecting the polygons this way works if the shadows are opaque. For semitransparent shadows, where the underlying surface color or texture can be seen, more care is usually needed. A convex object's shadow is guaranteed to have exactly two (or, by culling backfaces, exactly one) projected polygons covering each shadowed pixel on the plane. Objects with concavities do not have this property, so simply rendering each projected polygon as semi-transparent will give poor results. The stencil buffer can be used to ensure that each pixel is covered at most once. Do this by incrementing the stencil buffer's count by each polygon drawn, allowing only the first projected polygon covering each pixel to be rendered. Alternately, the ground plane could be drawn, Z-buffer cleared, and then each successive shadow polygon is drawn increasingly offset (e.g., using `glPolygonOffset`) so that it is further away than the previous polygon. In this way, each shadowed pixel is drawn only once [429]. This works, but the ground plane may need to be redrawn into the Z-buffer (only) to reestablish the correct z-depths, if needed.

A disadvantage of the projection method, in addition to its limitation to planar surfaces, is that the shadow has to be rendered for each frame, even though the shadow may not change. Since shadows are view-independent (their shapes do not change with different viewpoints), an idea that works well in practice is to render the shadow into a texture that is then rendered as a textured rectangle. The shadow texture would be recomputed only when the shadow changes, that is, when the light source or any shadow-casting or -receiving object moves. This idea is discussed further in Sections 6.12.1 and 6.12.2.

The matrices in Equations 6.30 and 6.32 do not always generate the desired results. For example, if the light source is below the topmost point on the object, then an *antishadow* [72] is generated, since each vertex is projected through the point of the light source. Correct shadows and antishadows are shown in Figure 6.38.

A similar rendering error as that found with planar reflections can occur for this kind of shadow generation. For reflections, errors occur when objects located on the opposite side of the reflector plane are not dealt with properly. In the case of shadow generation, errors occur when we use a shadow-casting object that is on the far side of the receiving plane. This is because an object beyond the shadow receiver does not cast a shadow on to it. Shadows generated in this manner are called *false shadows*. To avoid this error the receiving plane must be used to clip and cull the shadowing objects before they create their projected shadow polygons. Because the clip must happen before projection, this process must be done by the application. Another method to avoid antishadows and false shadows takes

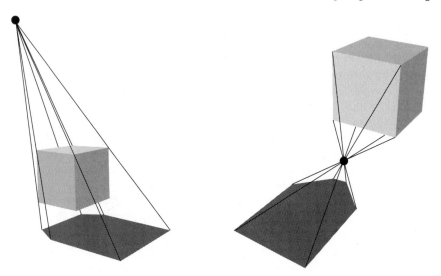

Figure 6.38. At the left, a correct shadow is shown, while in the figure on the right, an antishadow appears, since the light source is below the topmost vertex of the object.

advantage of the accelerator. It uses a projection matrix with clipping, and is presented next.

Soft Shadows

Projective shadows can also be made soft, by using a variety of techniques. Here, we describe an algorithm from Heckbert and Herf [335, 355] that produces soft shadows. The algorithm's goal is to generate a texture on a ground plane that shows a soft shadow.[15] We then describe less accurate, but faster methods.

Soft shadows appear whenever a light source has an area. One way to approximate the effect of an area light is to sample it by using a number of point lights placed on its surface. For each of these point light sources, an image is rendered and added to the accumulation buffer. The average of these images is then an image with soft shadows. Note that, in theory, any algorithm that generates hard shadows can be used along with this accumulation technique to produce penumbrae. In practice, doing so may be difficult because of memory constraints or other factors.

Heckbert and Herf use a frustum-based method to produce their shadows. For each point light source, the occluders inside the pyramid formed

---

[15]Basic hard shadows can also be generated using this technique.

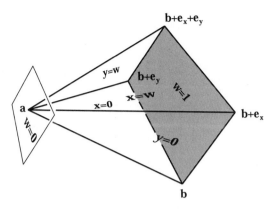

Figure 6.39. A pyramid is formed by a point, **a**, on the light source, and a parallelogram, i.e., the shadow receiver, which has one vertex at **b**, and the edge vectors $\mathbf{e}_x$ and $\mathbf{e}_y$. *(Illustration after Heckbert and Herf [335].)*

by the point light source and the receiver parallelogram are transformed into a parallelepiped with the matrix, **M**, below. The parallelepiped lies in unit-screen space, which means from $(x, y) = (0, 0)$ to $(1, 1)$, and with $z = 1$ at the receiver, and $z = \infty$ at the light source. Essentially, the light is viewing the receiver, and a perspective projection is performed. Following the notation from Heckbert and Herf, the point light source is located at **a**, and the receiver parallelogram has one vertex at **b**, and the edge vectors $\mathbf{e}_x$ and $\mathbf{e}_y$. This is illustrated in Figure 6.39.

$$
\mathbf{M} = \begin{pmatrix}
q_u n_{ux} & q_u n_{uy} & q_u n_{uz} & -q_u \mathbf{n}_u \cdot \mathbf{b} \\
q_v n_{vx} & q_v n_{vy} & q_v n_{vz} & -q_v \mathbf{n}_v \cdot \mathbf{b} \\
0 & 0 & 0 & 1 \\
q_w n_{wx} & q_w n_{wy} & q_w n_{wz} & -q_w \mathbf{n}_w \cdot \mathbf{a}
\end{pmatrix}
\tag{6.33}
$$

$$
\begin{aligned}
\mathbf{e}_w &= \mathbf{b} - \mathbf{a} \\
\mathbf{n}_u &= \mathbf{e}_w \times \mathbf{e}_y & q_u &= 1/\mathbf{n}_u \cdot \mathbf{e}_x \\
\mathbf{n}_v &= \mathbf{e}_x \times \mathbf{e}_w & q_v &= 1/\mathbf{n}_v \cdot \mathbf{e}_y \\
\mathbf{n}_w &= \mathbf{e}_y \times \mathbf{e}_x & q_w &= 1/\mathbf{n}_w \cdot \mathbf{e}_w
\end{aligned}
\tag{6.34}
$$

The matrix **M** of Equation 6.33 is not a projection matrix as were the matrices used in the previous section on planar projection shadows. Here, the transformation is from three dimensions to three dimensions (versus from three to two). What is ingenious about this transformation is that by using the third dimension for clipping (using the near and far planes),

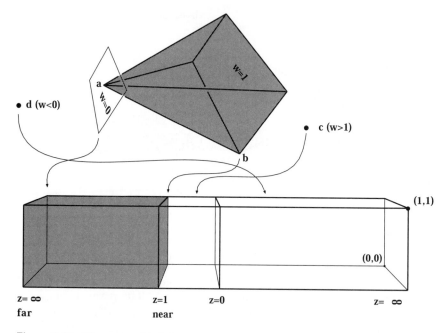

Figure 6.40. The pyramid is being mapped, using **M**, into a parallelepiped, with near and far planes as shown.

we can avoid both antishadows and incorrectly generated shadows due to objects behind the receiver (false shadows).

The pyramid in Figure 6.39 is transformed by **M** into a parallelepiped. To simplify implementation, we should use either a perspective or an orthographic projection call from a graphics API so that clipping, etc., is done correctly. Since the matrix **M** transforms the pyramid to a parallelepiped, we can use an orthographic matrix after using **M**. So the final projection matrix, **P**, that should be used is $\mathbf{P} = \mathbf{P}_o\mathbf{M}$, where $\mathbf{P}_o$ is an orthographic projection matrix. To get the correct three-dimensional clip, the clipping planes in $\mathbf{P}_o$ should be set to $n = 1$ (near) and $f = \infty$ (far). See Section 3.5.1 for the effect on $\mathbf{P}_o$ of the near and far values. If **P** is used as the projection matrix in the rendering pipeline, then every polygon outside the pyramid will be culled away, and thus, only the correct occluders will generate shadows on the receiver.

Let us examine what happens to points that are located behind the light source **a**, or behind the receiver. Such points should not contribute to the shadows. The mapping from the pyramid into the parallelepiped is shown in Figure 6.40. The occluders that produce shadows must be

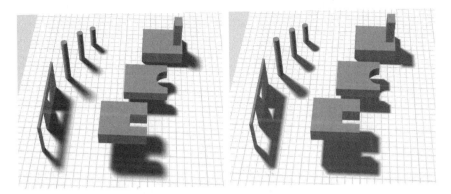

Figure 6.41. On the left, a rendering using Heckbert and Herf's method, using 256 passes. On the right, Haines' method in one pass. The umbrae are too large with Haines' method, which is particularly noticeable around the doorway and window.

located in the gray volume, and a point **d** located behind the light source (that is, $w < 0$), will be transformed into a negative z-value, and thus not contribute to the shadow. Likewise, a point **c**, located behind the receiver ($w > 1$), will be mapped into $0 < z < 1$, and will also not contribute to any shadow. As promised, the three-dimensional clip avoids antishadows and false shadows.

A shadow texture for the receiver is generated in the following way. For each sample on the light source, the receiver is first rendered by using this sample as a point light source. Then the projection matrix is used to render all objects inside the pyramid. Since these objects should generate shadows, they are drawn in black (and so Z-buffering, texturing, and lighting can be turned off). All of these images are averaged into the accumulation buffer to produce a shadow texture. See the left side of Figure 6.41.

The shadow is rendered as a textured parallelogram, which can be done very efficiently. The shadow texture has to be recomputed each time the objects or the light source move. If the shadow texture must be recomputed, then the bottleneck is the downloading of the texture into texture memory [335]. If the hardware supports some form of render to texture [613], this cost can be avoided.

A problem with the sampled area light method is that it tends to look like what it is: a number of overlapping shadows from point light sources. Instead of varying the location of samples on the light's surface, Gooch et al. [279] move the receiving plane's location up and down and the projections cast upon it are averaged. See Figure 6.42.

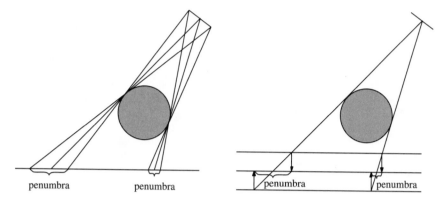

Figure 6.42. On the left, Heckbert and Herf's method: A number of point samples are distributed over the surface of the light, with the hard shadow silhouette lines drawn. On the right, Gooch's method: A stack of planes capture a penumbra.

This method has the advantage that the shadows created are nested, which generally looks better and so requires fewer samples. Also, we can eliminate the need to project and render the occluder multiple times. A single shadow projection can be used to generate a texture of the shadow. This texture could be copied into texture memory and then remapped correctly to accumulate the other samples. Figure 6.43 shows the result.

A problem with this method is that if the object touches the receiver then the shadow will not be modeled correctly. Darkness will appear to leak out from under the object. This problem can be overcome by rendering

Figure 6.43. A non-photorealistic car with a hard projected shadow and with a soft shadow formed using the concentric projection method from Gooch et al. *(Images courtesy of Bruce Gooch, University of Utah.)*

and averaging only the lower planes. The resulting shadow is less realistic, but does not have the disturbing shadow creep effect. In fact, all texture shadow methods can suffer from a different form of shadow creep, in which the resolution of the texture is low compared to the screen it covers. Under these conditions, shadows can creep from under objects due to bilinear filtering pulling the darkness out from under objects touching the receiver. This same sort of problem can happen in meshed radiosity solutions (see Section 6.13.1) when the meshing or generated texture is not fine enough.

Another problem with both of these methods are that the shadows are quantized between a limited number of grayscale shades. For n shadow passes, only $n+1$ distinct shades can be generated. One answer is to apply a texture to the receiver, as the texture will have a masking effect and hide this quantization [230]. Another approach is to use convolution. Soler and Sillion [725] create soft shadows by rendering the hard shadow to a texture and then softening (convolving) it by using a filter in the shape of the area light source. They vary the amount of blurring of the shadow dependent on the occluder silhouette's distance from the receiver, blending between blurred shadow images. The filtering could be performed using traditional algorithms on the CPU [691]. A potentially faster way is to take the created hard-edged shadow texture and render it a number of times to a second texture, jittering the location each time, to get a soft shadow fringe. A filtered soft shadow example is shown in Plate XXXI (following page 562). Pixel shaders can also be used to blur the texture (see Section 8.11).

This technique gives smooth, soft shadows for objects at a constant distance from the shadow receiver. Objects touching the ground can cause problems, as the shadow is sharp where it touches and becomes softer as the distance increases. Haines [312] presents a method that creates soft shadows in a single pass for circular area lights. The idea is to start with a normal projected hard shadow and then paint the silhouette edges with gradients that go from dark in the center to white on the edges to create penumbrae. These gradient areas have a width proportional to the height of the silhouette edge casting the shadow. Each silhouette edge casts a quadrilateral gradient area, and each edge endpoint casts a circular gradient area. By using the Z-buffer and painting these penumbrae objects using three-dimensional primitives such as planes and cones, the rendered gradient areas are made to properly overlap (see Figure 6.44). The method is rapid and relatively easy to implement, but one problem is that if the area light is too large then concave corners along the shadow edge look unrealistic.

The methods of Gooch et al. and Haines both share another problem. They create umbra regions that are too large, since the projected shadow

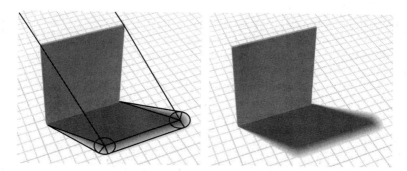

Figure 6.44. On the left, a visualization of Haines' method of soft shadowing on a plane. The object casts a hard shadow, and then gradient areas are drawn to simulate the penumbra. On the right is the result.

will always be larger than the object. In reality, if an area light is larger than the width of an occluder, the occluder will cast a smaller or nonexistent umbra region. See Figure 6.41 on page 257 for a comparison.

6.12.2   Shadows on Curved Surfaces

One way to extend the idea of planar shadows to curved surfaces is to use a generated shadow image as a projective texture [536, 579, 588, 694]. Think of shadows from the light's point of view (literally). Whatever the light sees is illuminated; what it does not see is in shadow. Say the occluder is rendered in black from the light's viewpoint into an otherwise white texture. This texture can then be projected onto the surfaces that are to receive the shadow. Effectively, each vertex on the receivers has a (u, v) texture coordinate computed for it and has the texture applied to it. These texture coordinates can be computed explicitly by the application or implicitly using the projective texturing functionality of the graphics hardware. We call this the *shadow texture* technique. It is also sometimes known as the *shadow map* method in the game developer community, as it is analogous to light mapping, but for shadows. Because a different technique, covered in Section 6.12.4, has been called shadow mapping by researchers for more than a decade, we use the term "shadow map" to mean this other algorithm.

When rendered, the shadow texture modulates the receiver surfaces. This idea is an extension of the light map concept, discussed in Section 5.7.2. One example is shown in Figure 6.45. This technique works particularly well for circumstances where the silhouette of the shadowing

Figure 6.45. Shadow projection. On the left is the scene from the light's view. In the middle is the occluding object rendered as a shadow texture. On the right, the texture coordinates have been determined for the stairs and the shadow texture has been applied. *(Images courtesy of Hubert Nguyen.)*

object does not change shape, so that the texture generated can be reused. Bloom [86] gives a wide range of optimizations that can be performed to minimize the cost of this technique.

A drawback of this method is that the designer must identify which objects are occluders and which are their receivers. Also, occluding objects cannot shadow themselves. The next two sections present algorithms that generate correct shadows without the need for such intervention.

6.12.3 Shadow Volumes

Presented by Heidmann in 1991 [341], a method based on Crow's *shadow volumes* [150] can cast shadows onto arbitrary objects by clever use of the stencil buffer. This technique is also sometimes called *volumetric shadows*.

To begin, imagine a point and a triangle. Extending the lines from a point through the vertices of a triangle to infinity yields an infinite pyramid. The part under the triangle, i.e., the part that does not include the point, is a truncated infinite pyramid, and the upper part is simply a pyramid. This is illustrated in Figure 6.46. Now imagine that the point is actually a point light source. Then, any part of an object that is inside the volume of the truncated pyramid (under the triangle) is in shadow. This volume is called a shadow volume.

Say we view some scene and follow a ray through a pixel until the ray hits the object to be displayed on screen. While the ray is on its way to this object, we increment a counter each time it crosses a face of the shadow volume that is frontfacing (i.e., facing toward the viewer). Thus,

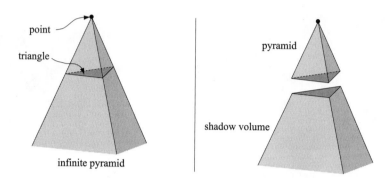

Figure 6.46. Left: The lines from a point light are extended through the vertices of a triangle to form an infinite pyramid. Right: The upper part is a pyramid, and the lower part is an infinite truncated pyramid, also called the shadow volume. All geometry that is inside the shadow volume is in shadow.

the counter is incremented each time the ray goes into shadow. In the same manner, we decrement the same counter each time the ray crosses a backfacing face of the truncated pyramid. The ray is then going out of a shadow. The ray hits the object that is to be displayed at that pixel. If the counter is greater than zero, then that pixel is in shadow; otherwise it is not. This principle also works when there is more than one polygon that casts shadows. See Figure 6.47.

Doing this geometrically is tedious and time-consuming. But there is a much smarter solution [341]: The stencil buffer can do the counting for us. First, the stencil buffer is cleared. Second, the whole scene is drawn into the frame buffer with only ambient and emission components used, in order to get these lighting components in the color buffer and the depth information into the Z-buffer. Third, Z-buffer updates and writing to the color buffer are turned off (though Z-buffer testing is still done), and then the front-facing polygons of the shadow volumes are drawn. During this process, the stencil operation is set to increment the values in the stencil buffer wherever a polygon is drawn. Fourth, another pass is done with the stencil buffer, this time drawing only the backfacing polygons of the shadow volumes. For this pass, the values in the stencil buffer are decremented when the polygons are drawn. Incrementing and decrementing are done only when the pixels of the rendered shadow-volume face are visible (i.e., not hidden by any real geometry). Finally, the whole scene is rendered again, this time with only the diffuse and the specular components of the materials active, and displayed only where the value in the stencil buffer is 0. A 0 value

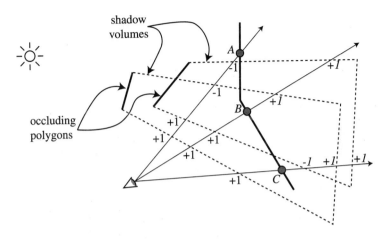

Figure 6.47. A two-dimensional view of counting shadow volume crossings using two different counting methods. In z-pass volume counting, the count is incremented as a ray passes through a front facing polygon of a shadow volume and decremented on leaving through a backfacing polygon. So at point A, the ray enters two shadow volumes for +2, then leaves two volumes, leaving a net count of zero, so the point is in light. In z-fail volume counting, the count starts beyond the surface (these counts are shown in italics). For the ray at point B, the z-pass method gives a +2 count by passing through two front facing polygons, and the z-fail gives the same count by passing through two backfacing polygons. Point C shows the importance of capping. The ray starting from point C first hits a frontfacing polygon, giving −1. It then exits two shadow volumes (through their endcaps, necessary for this method to work properly), giving a net count of +1. The count is not zero, so the point is in shadow. Both methods always give the same count results for all points on the viewed surfaces.

indicates that the ray has gone out of shadow as many times as it has gone into a shadow volume—i.e., this location is illuminated by the light.

The stencil buffer is not required for this method. Roettger et al. [655] discuss a number of strategies for using the color and alpha buffers to take the place of the stencil buffer, and they obtain comparable performance. Sim Dietrich and Alex Clarke [247] note that on the Xbox it is possible to do a signed addition to the frame buffer, so the individual frontfacing and backfacing passes can be performed in a single pass. Two-sided lighting is used to determine whether a polygon adds or subtracts from the count; one facing gets lit with a positive one, the other with a negative one.[16] This said, for this hardware the stencil buffer approach was found to be faster due to bandwidth issues.

---

[16]The NV30 can use this two-sided, single-pass method with an extended stencil buffer [218].

The separate front and backface passes can be combined into one pass if shadow volumes are guaranteed to not overlap. In this case, the stencil buffer is toggled on and off for all shadow volume faces rendered. In the final pass, if the stencil bit is on, then the surface is in shadow.

The general algorithm has to be adjusted if the viewer is inside a shadow volume. In this case, a value of 0 does not mean a point is in the light. For this condition, the stencil buffer should be cleared to the number of shadow volumes the viewer starts inside (instead of 0). Another more serious problem is that the near plane of the viewer's viewing frustum might intersect one or more shadow volume planes. The traditional method to solve this problem is to perform some form of *capping* at the near plane [58, 424, 536]. Capping is where additional polygons are drawn so as to make the object appear solid. However, such methods are generally not robust and general.

Bilodeau and Songy [62] were the first to present an alternate approach to avoid this near plane clipping problem; Carmack also independently discovered this technique [424]. Nonintuitive as it sounds, the idea is to render the shadow volumes that are obscured by visible surfaces. The first stencil buffer pass becomes: Render the backfacing shadow volume polygons and increment the stencil count when the polygon is equal to *or farther than* the stored z-depth. In the next stencil pass, render the frontfacing shadow volume polygons and decrement the count when the polygon is, again, equal to or farther than the stored z-depth. Because the shadow volumes are drawn only when the Z-buffer test has failed, they are sometimes called *z-fail shadow volumes*, versus *z-pass*. The other passes are done as before. In the original algorithm, a point is in shadow because the number of frontfacing polygons crossed was larger than the number of backfacing polygons; in this version, the object is in shadow if the number of backfacing polygons not seen is larger than the number of frontfacing polygons not seen, something of a logical equivalent. The difference is that now all shadow volume polygons in front of surfaces, including those which could encompass the viewer, are not rendered, so avoiding most viewer location problems. See Figure 6.47.

For the z-pass algorithm, the original polygons generating the quadrilaterals do not actually need to be rendered to the stencil buffer. These polygons are always made invisible by the first pass, which will set z-depths such that these polygons will match and so not be rendered. This is not the case for the z-fail algorithm. To properly maintain the count, these originating polygons must be rendered. In addition, the shadow volumes must be closed up at their far ends, and these far endcaps must be inside the far plane. The z-fail algorithm has the inverse of the problem that the z-pass

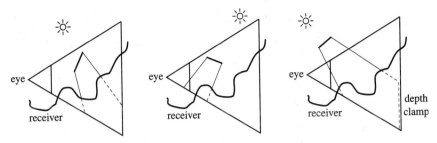

Figure 6.48. The z-pass and z-fail shadow volume methods; z-pass is shown as solid lines emanating from the occluder, z-fail as dashed lines beyond the receiver. On the left, if the z-fail method was used for the case shown, the shadow volume would need to be capped before reaching the far plane. In the middle, z-pass would give an incorrect count, as it penetrates the near plane. On the right, neither method can work without some way to avoid the clip by either the near or far plane; depth clamping's effect is shown on z-fail.

has. In z-pass, it is possible for shadow volumes to penetrate the view frustum's near plane; in z-fail, shadow volumes can potentially penetrate the far plane and cause serious shadowing errors. See Figure 6.48.

Everitt and Kilgard [218] present two simple, robust solutions to this problem, one implemented in hardware and the other in software. In hardware, the solution is called *depth clamping*. Beginning with the GeForce3, NVIDIA has added the NV_depth_clamp extension. What this does is to no longer clip objects to the far view plane, but rather force all objects that would normally be clipped away by the far plane to instead be drawn on the far plane with a maximum z-depth. This extension was introduced specifically to solve the z-fail shadow volume capping problem automatically. The edge and capping polygons can be projected out an arbitrarily far distance and will be properly handled by hardware. With this addition, z-fail shadow volumes become a simple and robust way to generate hard shadows. The only drawback (besides hardware dependence) is that in some cases, z-pass will fill less pixels overall, so always using z-fail with depth clamping may be slower.

Their software solution elegantly uses some of the lesser-known properties of homogeneous coordinates. Normally, positions are represented as $\mathbf{p} = (p_x, p_y, p_z, 1)$ in homogeneous coordinates. When the fourth component, w, is 0, the resulting coordinate $(p_x, p_y, p_z, 0)$ is normally thought of as a vector. See Section A.4. However, $w = 0$ can also be thought of as a point "at infinity" in a given direction. It is perfectly valid to think of points at infinity in this way, and is, in fact, used as a matter of course in environment mapping. The assumption in EM is that the environment is far enough away to access with just a vector, and for this to work perfectly, the environment should be infinitely far away.

When a shadow is cast by an object, the shadow volume planes extend toward infinity. In practice, they are extended some large, finite distance, but this is not necessary. Given a shadow volume edge formed by $\mathbf{v}_0$ and $\mathbf{v}_1$ and a light at $\mathbf{l}$, the direction vectors $\mathbf{v}_0 - \mathbf{l}$ and $\mathbf{v}_1 - \mathbf{l}$ can be treated as the two other points (that is, with $w = 0$) forming a quadrilateral side of the shadow volume. The accelerator works with such points just fine, transforming and clipping the object to the view frustum. Similarly, the far cap of the shadow volume for z-fail can be generated by projecting the triangle out to infinity.

Doing this procedure does not solve anything in and of itself, as the far plane still will clip the shadow volume, and the z-fail method will not work. The other, key part of the software solution is that the far plane itself is set to infinity. In Section 3.5.2, the near and far planes are finite, positive numbers. As the far plane goes to infinity, Equation 3.68 on page 64 for the projection matrix becomes:

$$
\mathbf{P}_p = \begin{pmatrix} \dfrac{2n}{r-l} & 0 & -\dfrac{r+l}{r-l} & 0 \\ 0 & \dfrac{2n}{t-b} & -\dfrac{t+b}{t-b} & 0 \\ 0 & 0 & 1 & -2n \\ 0 & 0 & 1 & 0 \end{pmatrix}. \tag{6.35}
$$

Setting the far plane number to infinity loses surprisingly little precision normally. Say the near plane is 1 meter away and the far plane is 20, and these map to $[-1, 1]$ in z-depth. Moving the far plane to infinity would map the 1 to 20 meter range to $[-1, 0.9]$, with the z-depth values from 20 meters to infinity mapped to $[0.9, 1]$. The amount of numerical range lost between the near plane, n, and the original far plane, f, turns out to be only n/f. In other words, when the distance to the far plane is significantly greater than the near plane (which is often the case), moving the far plane to infinity has little overall effect on precision.

The z-fail method will work with the far plane at infinity. The triangle closing the shadow volume at infinity will be properly rendered, and nothing will be clipped against the far plane. In truth, the occluder's edges could just be projected some large distance outwards and the far plane set further out. For example, the length of the diagonal of a box containing the scene could be used for both of these distances. However, projecting to infinity is faster to compute. For directional lights (i.e., those also "at infinity") the

Figure 6.49. Shadow volumes. On the left, a square with cutouts casts a shadow on various objects. On the right, the various faces of the shadow volume are shown. Note that the teapot does not have a shadow volume, and so casts no shadows. *(Images courtesy of Mark Kilgard, NVIDIA Corp.)*

two quadrilateral points at infinity are even easier to compute: They are always equal to the direction from the light. This has the interesting effect that all the points at infinity from directional lights are the same point. For this case, the quadrilaterals actually become triangles, and no cap at infinity is necessary.

An example of the shadows that the shadow volume algorithm generates is shown in Figure 6.49. Though the teapot shown in the figure does not cast a shadow, in practice, this particular shadow could be generated rapidly. Since the teapot casts a shadow onto a plane, a projective shadow could be used instead of a shadow volume. Different shadow techniques can be used as appropriate, thereby saving time overall.

There are some limitations to the shadow volume technique. Semitransparent objects cannot receive shadows properly, because the stencil buffer stores only one object's shadow state per pixel. It is also difficult to use translucent occluders, e.g., stained glass or other objects that attenuate or change the color of the light. Another area of concern is the explosion in the number of polygons rendered. Each triangle and each light create three additional quadrilaterals that must be properly extended and rendered into the stencil buffer. For solid occluders, only the set of polygons facing toward (or the set facing away from) the light needs to be used to create shadow volumes. To further cut down on the number of polygons, the silhouette edges of the object could (and should) be found. For this technique to work, the object must be manifold (see Section 11.3). A silhouette edge is an edge of the object where one polygon faces toward the light and the other faces away from it. So, with the basic shadow volume method, only the silhouette edges need to generate shadow volume quadrilaterals—a considerable savings. The simplest brute-force algorithm for finding the silhouettes just tests every edge in the mesh—if one of the adjacent polygons is frontfacing, and the other backfacing, then that edge belongs to the silhouette. Edge detection is discussed in detail in Section 7.2.4.

The vertex shader also offers the ability to create shadow volumes on the fly. For example, the game *Neverwinter Nights* accelerates shadow volumes by first finding the silhouette edges on the CPU. Then the centroid of the object is used to generate a tristrip of four triangles, using six vertices, for each silhouette edge: one from the centroid to the edge, two degenerate triangles of no area that use repeats of the edge's vertices, and a last triangle back to the centroid. The vertex shader then projects the last three vertices in this strip to the proper distance away from the object, so that the two middle triangles form the projected quadrilateral and the last triangle the cap. These tristrips are used with z-fail testing to produce shadows.

Another vertex shader technique from ATI [100, 323] is to send every edge of the object down the pipeline as a degenerate quadrilateral, similar to the previous approach. In addition, the geometric normals of the two triangles that share the edge are sent with it. Specifically, the two vertices of one edge of the degenerate quadrilateral gets one face's surface normal; the other edge's vertices gets the second face's normal. See Figure 6.50. The vertex shader then checks these normals against the view direction. If the vertex's stored normal faces toward the light, the vertex is passed through unperturbed. If it faces away from the light, the vertex shader

Figure 6.50. Forming a shadow volume using the vertex shader. This process is done twice, once for each of the two stencil buffer passes. The occluder is shown in the left figure. In the middle figure, all its edges are sent down as degenerate quadrilaterals, shown schematically here as thin quadrilaterals. On the right, those edges found by the vertex shader to be silhouette edges have two of their vertices projected away from the light, so forming quadrilaterals that define the shadow volume sides. Edges that are not silhouettes render as degenerate (no area) polygons and so cover no pixels.

projects the vertex far away along the vector formed by the light's position to the vertex. The effect of these two rules is to form shadow volumes automatically. For edge quadrilaterals that have both triangle neighbors face the light, the quadrilateral is not moved and so stays degenerate, i.e., never gets displayed. For edge quadrilaterals with both normals facing away, the entire degenerate quadrilateral is moved far away from the light, but stays degenerate and so is never seen. Only for silhouette edges is one edge projected outwards and the other remains in place. One advantage of this method is that the vertex shader can also be used at the same time to deform the object (for example, using vertex blending, described in Section 3.4). Another advantage is that, for static objects, the edge quadrilaterals can be formed once into a vertex buffer and stored on the accelerator [98].

The shadow volume algorithm algorithm has some advantages. First, it can be used on general-purpose graphics hardware. The only requirement is a stencil buffer, preferably with eight bits (which is standard on modern graphics hardware). Second, since it is not image-based (unlike the shadow map algorithm described in Section 6.12.4), it avoids sampling problems, and thus produces correct sharp shadows everywhere. This can sometimes be a disadvantage. For example, a character's clothing may have folds that give thin, sharp shadows that alias badly.

A major performance problem is that this algorithm burns fill rate, as shadow volume polygons often cover many pixels, and so the rasterizer becomes a bottleneck. For example, if a tree's leaves cast shadows, a large number of overlapping shadow volumes, each covering a large number of pixels, would have to be rendered. Like most hard-edged shadow algorithms, multiple shadow volumes can be blended to create soft shadows [104], but this technique can be expensive because of the potentially huge amount of fill bandwidth required. Another problem is that curved surfaces that are created by the hardware, such as N-patches, cannot also generate shadow volumes. The next method presented avoids the fill rate problem and can cast shadows from any hardware generated surface.

6.12.4 Shadow Map

In 1978, Williams [801] proposed that a common Z-buffer-based renderer could be used to generate shadows quickly on arbitrary objects. The idea is to render the scene, using the Z-buffer algorithm, from the position of the light source that is to cast shadows. For each pixel in the Z-buffer, the z-depth now contains the distance to the object closest to the light source.

We call the entire contents of the Z-buffer the *shadow map*, also sometimes known as the *shadow depth map* or *shadow buffer*. To use the shadow map, the scene is rendered a second time, but this time with respect to the viewer. Now, as each drawing primitive is being rendered, its location is compared to the shadow map; if a rendered point is farther away from the light source than the value in the shadow map, then that point is in shadow; otherwise it is not. See Figure 6.51.

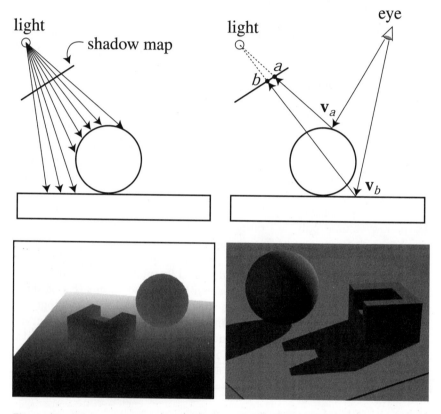

Figure 6.51. Shadow mapping. On the top left, a shadow map is formed by storing the depths to the surfaces in view. On the top right, the eye is shown looking at two locations. The sphere is hit at point $\mathbf{v}_a$, and this point is found to be located at texel a on the shadow map. The depth stored there is not (much) less than point $\mathbf{v}_a$ is from the light, so the point is illuminated. The rectangle hit at point $\mathbf{v}_b$ is (much) farther away than the depth stored at texel b, so is is shadow. On the bottom left is the view of a scene from the light's perspective, with white being further away. On the bottom right is the scene rendered with this shadow map.

This technique can be implemented by exploiting texture mapping hardware [344, 425, 694]. The shadow map is generated as described above. Then the scene is rendered from the viewer using only ambient lighting, in order to resolve visibility. A shadow testing step is then performed, which compares the z-value in the Z-buffer with the z-value (which is transformed from the coordinate system of the light source into the coordinate system of the viewer) in the shadow map. An additional value, α, for each pixel, p, in the frame buffer is set according to the outcome of this comparison. If the two z-values are (almost) equal, then $\alpha = 1$, indicating that the pixel is not in shadow. Otherwise, $\alpha = 0$, which indicates that the pixel is in shadow. Finally, the whole scene is rendered using the whole lighting equation. The final color of each pixel is the color from the ambient pass plus the color from the full rendering pass multiplied by α. This means that when $\alpha = 0$, the pixel color is taken from the ambient rendering pass, and when $\alpha = 1$, then the pixel color is that of a normal rendering pass.

Note that, when the shadow map is generated, only Z-buffering is required; that is, lighting, texturing, and the writing of color values into the color buffer can be turned off. Also, the shadow map can be used in several frames as long as neither the light source nor the objects move. The viewer is allowed to move, since shadows are view-independent.

Advantages of this method are that general-purpose graphics hardware can be used to render arbitrary shadows, and that the cost of building the shadow map is linear in the number of rendered primitives and access time is constant. One disadvantage is that the quality of the shadows depends on the resolution (in pixels) of the shadow map, and also on the numerical precision of the Z-buffer. While general purpose hardware can perform this method, the Z-buffer has to be stored as a color channel, giving only 8 bits of precision, which is usually not enough. It is possible to boost this on some hardware to 16 bits by dual texture accesses [423]. The trend is that hardware dedicated to supporting shadow mapping is becoming more prevalent. For example, the Xbox and GeForce3 have it, as do the SGI RealityEngine and InfiniteReality.

Since the shadow map is sampled during the comparison, the algorithm is susceptible to aliasing problems, especially close to shadow edges. A common problem is *self-shadow aliasing*, in which a polygon is incorrectly considered to shadow itself because of the imprecision inherent in this point sampling method. That is, samples generated for the light are generally not exactly at the same locations as the screen samples. When the light's stored depth value is compared to the viewed surface's depth, the light's value may be slightly lower than the surface's, resulting in this error. Such errors are shown in Figure 6.52.

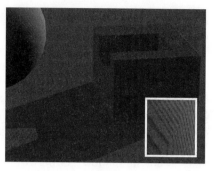

Figure 6.52. Shadow mapping problems. On the left, the bias is set too high, so the shadow creeps out from under the block object. The shadow map resolution is also too low, so the texels of the map appear in the shadow, giving it a blocky appearance. On the right there is no bias, so the surface erroneously shadows itself, in this case producing a Moiré pattern. The inset shows a zoom of part of the sphere's surface.

One method to help renderers avoid (but not always eliminate) these problems is to introduce a bias factor [649, 820]. Another helpful method is to make sure the light frustum's near plane is as far away from the light as possible and the far plane is as close as possible. Doing so increases the effective precision of the Z-buffer.

An extension of the shadow map technique using bilinear interpolation can provide pseudo-soft shadows. This extension can also help ameliorate resolution problems that cause shadows to look blocky when a single light sample cell covers many screen pixels. The solution is similar to texture magnification (see Section 5.2.1). Instead of a single sample being taken off the shadow map, a set of four samples is taken [649]. The four texel depth values closest to the sample's location on the light map are used. The technique, a form of *percentage closer filtering*, does not blend depths themselves, but rather the results of their comparisons with the surface's depth. That is, the surface's depth is compared to the four texel depths, and the point is then determined to be in light or shadow for each shadow map sample. These results are then bilinearly interpolated to calculate how much the light actually contributes to the surface location. This filtering results in an artificially soft shadow. Such shadows all have more or less the same-sized penumbrae, and these penumbrae change depending on the shadow map's resolution and other factors. Still, a little penumbra and smoothing, regardless how nonphysical it is, is better than none at all. See Everitt et al. [217] and Kilgard's presentation [425] for discussion of this technique and many other technical details, as well as implementation guidelines. In related work, Keating [414] discusses how to use A-buffer techniques to antialias shadow edges. Zhang [837] presents an approach of using image warping to reverse the normal shadow map algorithm, which also makes shadow edge antialiasing easier.

While percentage-close filtering only blurs the edges of a hard shadow, Heidrich et al. [346] extend shadow mapping to produce soft shadows rapidly for linear light sources. Agrawala et al. [4] use layered depth images to produce soft shadows at interactive rates. Lokovic and Veach [502] present the concept of deep shadow maps, in which the depth buffer is multilayered and stores a function of how light drops off through space. This is useful for rendering objects such as hair and clouds, where self-shadowing is critical for realism. The technique is currently not usable at interactive rates, but points to the potential power of the shadow map in the future.

Another problem with shadow maps is that a single map texel can cover many screen texels, giving shadow edges a stair-stepped look. It is important to limit the light's view frustum to tightly bound any shadow casting objects (shadow receivers outside the frustum are always in light). However, if the viewer can move arbitrarily close to a shadow edge, then stair-stepping is always possible. Fernando et al. [229] have researched a hierarchical caching scheme combining hardware and software to provide arbitrarily high resolution shadow maps.

Woo [820] proposes a method of avoiding many biasing problems by creating an intermediate surface. This method is a part of the original Talisman architecture [752]. Instead of keeping just the closest depth value, the two closest values are tracked in separate buffers. When the tracking is complete, these two buffers are averaged into one, which is then used as the shadow map. For a solid object, this technique usually creates a shadowing surface that passes through the middle of the object. For example, a sphere would create a circle passing through its center and facing the light. However, this technique can also have problems. See Figure 6.53. In practice, the problems seen at $\mathbf{j}$ and $\mathbf{k}$ are relatively rare and not that noticeable, especially when using bilinear interpolation. By creating an intermediate surface we can eliminate most biasing and self-shadowing problems. Unfortunately, some current hardware cannot easily determine the two closest surfaces. Everitt's depth peeling technique is one way to generate these [216].

Hourcade [372] introduced a different form of shadow mapping that also solves the biasing problem and lends itself to hardware implementation. Called the *priority buffer*, this method stores IDs instead of depths. Each object or each polygon is given a different ID (think of it as a different solid color) and is rendered into a color buffer from the light's point of

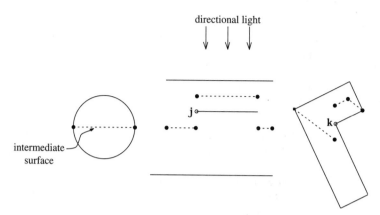

Figure 6.53. Woo's shadow mapping method. A directional light comes from directly above. The depths from each of the two surfaces closest to the light are combined to give an intermediate surface that is stored in the shadow map. This surface is shown as a dashed line. The two sets of surfaces on the right have problems due to sampling limitations. At location **j**, the point may be found to be in light if the closest shadow texel sampled is to the left of it, since this intermediate surface is farther from the light. Similarly, point **k** may be considered to be in light because the intermediate surface to its left is below it.

view. The Z-buffer is used to resolve ordering differences. The objects can be rendered in any order, since only the closest ID is saved. The color buffer is then accessed similarly to a shadow map. Instead of comparing z-depths, IDs are compared. If the IDs match, the light sees the object at this pixel and so is illuminated. An image rendered using this technique is shown in Plate XIII (following page 274). Unfortunately, no commercial real-time hardware currently supports this method, though ATI has researched providing it. What can be done instead is to use the alpha channel to store IDs and use an alpha test to compare the current ID to see if it is higher than the stored ID. However, this implementation is much weaker, as it requires that objects be rendered in a strict sorted order [176, 776].

This method has the advantage that no bias at all is necessary; only IDs are stored, not depths. However, shadowing due to resolution limits of the shadow map can occur where polygon edges are shared. That is, a location near an edge may access the shadow map and find an ID of an adjoining polygon, resulting in a shadow near the edge. One solution is to assign IDs to entire objects instead of individual polygons. Doing so has the additional advantage that the set of IDs will then usually take 8 bits per pixel or less to store. Using an ID per object helps avoid edge problems, but it also means that an object with a single ID cannot cast

Plate I. Doctor Sid from the film *Final Fantasy*. This image was generated in real-time on NVIDIA hardware, at about 10 frames per second. Vertex shaders are used to make the clothing realistic and dynamic. Normal maps capture fine details such as wrinkles. The cyan vectors that seem to appear on the forehead are actually the backfaces of the hair at the nape of the neck. *(Images © 2002 Final Fantasy Film Partners, Inc. All rights reserved.)*

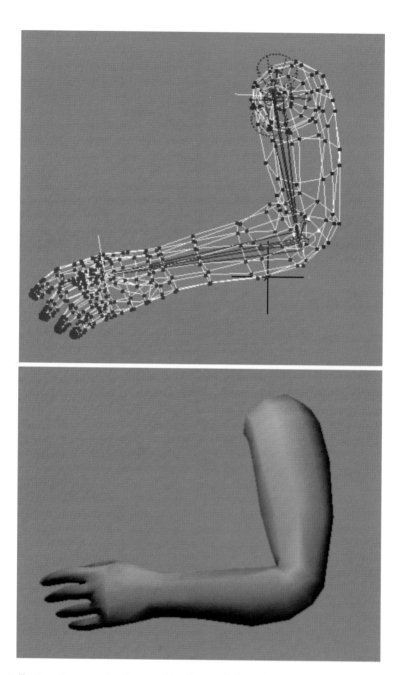

Plate II. Top: An example of vertex blending and the underlying vertices. Each vertex is marked with a color showing the bone to which it is attached. Bottom: Gouraud shaded mesh in a slightly different position. *(Images courtesy of Jeff Lander.)*

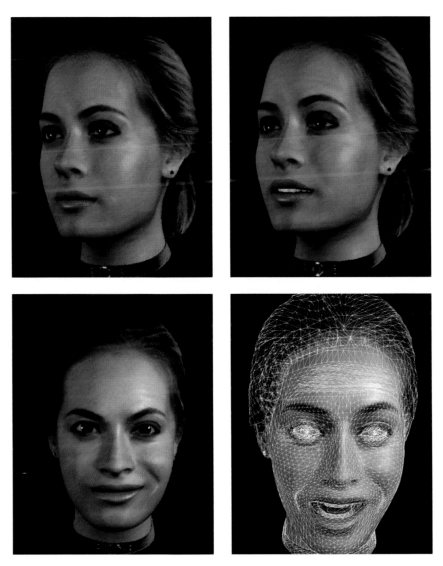

Plate III. The Rachel character's facial expressions and movements are controlled by skinning and other interpolation methods, which are accelerated by using graphics hardware support. *(Images by Alex Vlachos, John Isidoro, Dave Gosselin, and Eli Turner; courtesy of ATI Technologies Inc. and LifeFX.)*

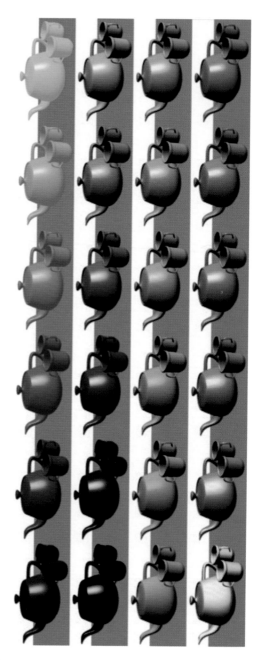

Plate IV. Tea for two. Holding the book sideways, the first row varies the ambient contribution, the second varies diffuse, the third varies specular, and the fourth varies shininess. *(Tea cup model courtesy of Joachim Helenklaken.)*

Plate V. On the left, the teapot's diffuse and specular shading contributions are stored in one color triplet and modulated by the checker texture. Note how any specular highlight disappears where the texture is black. On the right, these contributions are stored and interpolated separately and only the diffuse contribution is modulated by the texture. *(Images courtesy of NVIDIA Corp.)*

Plate VI. Specular highlighting. Per vertex specular is shown on the left, environment mapping of just the lights in the middle, and environment mapping of the entire surrounding scene on the right. *(Images courtesy of J.L. Mitchell, M. Tatro, and I. Bullard.)*

Plate VII. Factorization of a BRDF for gold, using the Cook-Torrance surface model [138]. The two textures are accessed with the incoming light and outgoing view directions, and are multiplied together at each pixel to generate the teapot's illumination. *(Images from a program by Chris Wynn, NVIDIA Corp.)*

Plate VIII. Materials rendered using factorization, where the BRDF is approximated by pairs of two-dimensional textures. From top to bottom, the materials are a blue krylon latex enamel, satin, and a textured velvet body with garnet red paint on the knot shape. The paints are from measured BRDF data, the satin computed using the analytic Poulin-Fournier anisotropic reflectance model [622]. *(Images generated by the "brdfview" program by McCool, Ang, and Ahmad.)*

Plate IX. High resolution terrain mapping accessing a huge image database. Rendered with clipmapping to reduce the amount of data needed at one time. *(Image courtesy of Aechelon Technology, Inc., 1999. C-Nova/C-Radiant Image Generator by Aechelon Technology Inc. based on SGI hardware.)*

Plate X. On the left, a transparent helicopter is rendered by turning off *z*-writing. The shading order is arbitrary and so causes blending artifacts. The right image is generated with a multi-pass "depth-peeling" technique. This automatically gives a correctly ordered rendering without the need for sorting. *(Images courtesy of Ashutosh Rege, NVIDIA Corp.)*

Plate XI. High resolution light maps yield sharp, detailed illumination effects. *(Image courtesy of Brian Yen, Any Channel Inc.)*

Plate XII. A still from the Xbox game, *Project Gotham Racing*. Glare effects from the headlights make it clear it is nighttime. A cube map of the environment from the car's location is created each frame to provide dynamic reflections off the car. *(Image courtesy of Bizarre Creations and Microsoft Corp.)*

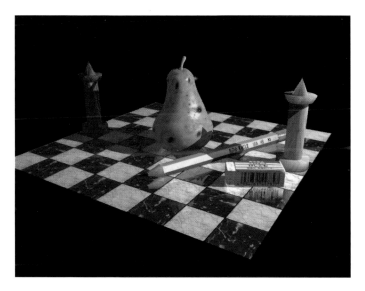

Plate XIII. Gloss mapping, shadows, and fogged reflections. Shadows are added using Hourcade's algorithm, and the reflections are diminished using fog as their distance from the plane increases. *(Image courtesy of J.L. Mitchell and E. Hart, ATI Technologies Inc.)*

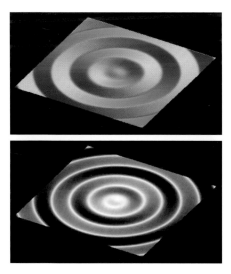

Plate XIV. Bump mapping with a normal map. At the top is the surface normal map. Each color channel is actually a surface normal coordinate. The red channel is the x coordinate, with the x axis going from upper left to right across the surface. Green is y, and blue is z, with the plane facing up along the $+z$ axis. Each color [0,255] maps to a normal coordinate [−1,1]. At the bottom is the image produced using the normal map. *(Example pictures generated by software. Images courtesy of NVIDIA Corp.)*

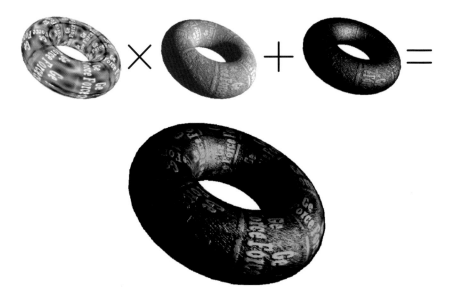

Plate XV. Diffuse and specular bump mapping. The color texture is modulated by the diffuse contribution computed using a normal bump map. The specular contribution is computed with a normalized version of the normal map and added in. *(Images courtesy of NVIDIA Corp.)*

Plate XVI. Examples of normal mapping combined with cubic environment mapping, giving a shiny, bumpy surface that reflects the environment. *(Left image courtesy of NVIDIA Corp. Right image courtesy of ATI Technologies Inc.)*

Plate XVII. Bump map, environment map, irradiance map, and refraction effects. Diffuse bump mapping with light attenuation is done with 4 colored lights in one pass (14 pixel shader instructions + 6 texture fetches). One of the lights' locations is visible in the scene as an orange sprite in the upper left of the image. The chest bumps the environment map for a shiny effect. An irradiance cube map capturing the diffuse lighting and an environment cube map are rendered every frame. The stained glass window uses a bump map combined with the base map and irradiance map for diffuse lighting, and also with the environment map and transparency map for refraction, in one pass. *(Image courtesy of ATI Technologies Inc.)*

Plate XVIII. From left to right, a tessellated sphere rendered without modification, with bump mapping, and with displacement mapping. Note how the silhouette of the bump mapped sphere does not change, since bump mapping modifies the surface normal but not the geometry. *(Images courtesy of Juan Guardado, Matrox Graphics Inc.)*

Plate XIX. Environment mapped bump mapping is used to make the water reflect the sky. In the foreground, a sprite flies by and generates alpha-blended billboard sprites. *(Image courtesy of Digital Illusions and Matrox Graphics Inc.)*

Plate XX. Light mapping. The wall texture on the left is multiplied by the light map in the middle to yield the texture on the right. *(Images courtesy of J.L. Mitchell, M. Tatro, and I. Bullard.)*

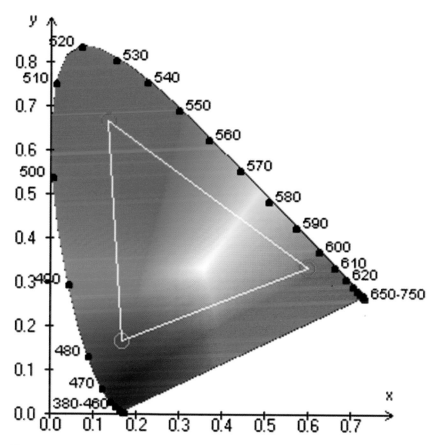

Plate XXI. The chromaticity diagram. The curve is labeled with the corresponding pure wavelength colors, and a typical gamut is shown with the triangle. *(Image generated by a Java applet from the Computer Science Department, Rochester Institute of Technology.)*

Plate XXII. The body of the squid is rendered with an iridescent pixel shader, with the specular color changed based on the view vector and surface normal. Vertex shaders are used to perform a variety of animated effects such as skinning and procedural displacements. *(Image courtesy of NVIDIA Corp.)*

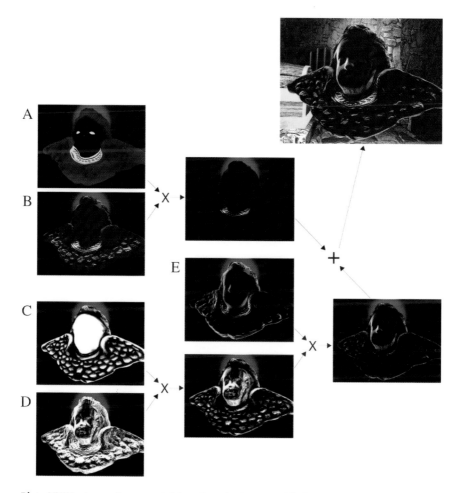

Plate XXIII. A complex material done in a single pass with the 1.4 pixel shader language. The diffuse component is a base color texture (A) modulated by a lit normal map $\mathbf{n} \cdot \mathbf{l}$ (B). The specular component is computed by using a gloss map (C) to modulate an environment map (D), then modulating by Fresnel reflectance (E), which was generated by computing $(1 - \mathbf{n} \cdot \mathbf{v})^2$ using a pixel shader. *(Images courtesy of Chris Brennan, ATI Technologies Inc.)*

Plate XXIV. A light probe image used for sphere mapping, formed by photographing a reflective sphere. This image is of the interior of Grace Cathedral, San Francisco. *(Image courtesy of Paul Debevec, www.debevec.org.)*

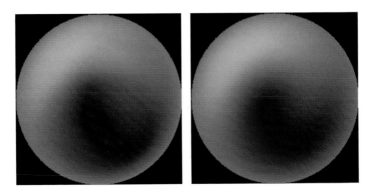

Plate XXV. Irradiance maps formed from the Grace Cathedral sphere map. The left figure is formed by summing the weighted colors in the hemisphere above each pixel. The right figure is formed by deriving a 9-term function approximating the sphere map, then evaluating this function for each pixel. *(Images courtesy of Ravi Ramamoorthi, Computer Graphics Laboratory, Stanford University.)*

a shadow on itself, since the occluding part will have the same ID as the receiver. Vlachos et al. [776] solve this problem by splitting objects into a few roughly convex pieces. Sharing IDs also fails to solve the problem of improper shadowing where separate objects touch. Another solution is to check for a surface's location the four closest texels in the priority buffer. If any of these matches the ID, the surface is considered illuminated. This technique needs four texture fetches; an improvement is to pre jitter the single-channel texture in advance, making a four-channel texture with the pixel offset built in [176]. However, if a polygon is so small that it covers no pixels in the priority buffer, it can never be found to be illuminated. A hybrid approach is to first check the priority buffer, falling back on using a shadow map if no match is found.

A limitation of all of these shadow map methods is that the light is assumed to view the scene from somewhere outside of it, something like a spotlight. This is because the light looks at the scene through a single frustum. Positional lights inside a scene can be represented by a six-view cube, similar to cubic environment mapping. However, getting the shadows to join properly along the seams of the cube is problematic, because factors such as bias can sometimes be different along such edges than they are on the rest of the surface. Using the same near and far plane distances for each cube face view helps.

6.12.5 Shadow Optimizations

It has already been noted that shadows add to the level of realism of a rendered image, and that shadows can be used as visual cues to determine spatial relationships. However, shadows may also incur a great cost both in terms of performance and in memory usage. Some optimization strategies for faster shadow generation are presented here. Often these trade quality for speed.

Since it is fairly difficult to perceive whether a shadow is correct, some shortcuts can be taken. These simplifications can cause inaccuracies in the shadows, but given a high enough frame rate, these are often difficult to notice [86]. One technique is to use a low level of detail model to actually cast the shadow. Whether this method helps performance is dependent on the algorithm and the location of the bottleneck (see Chapter 10). Using a simpler occluder lessens the load on the bus and geometry stage of the pipeline, as fewer vertices are processed. However, the shadow volume algorithm is often fill-limited, so using a model with fewer silhouette edges will be of little help there. At best, if silhouette edges are being found by the CPU, then a small bit of CPU time will be saved by using this method.

Another optimization technique is to update the relevant shadow information only every other frame (or even more seldom). So, for projective shadow textures, this would involve creating the shadow textures only every other frame. In addition, these shadow textures can be created and stored in a single, larger texture, to avoid having to switch textures. For shadow volumes, the silhouettes may be reused from the previous frame, every other frame. The update frequency could also decrease with the distance to the viewer [86]. Also, shadows can be made to fade out to nothing in the distance, and so then not be rendered.

You yourself are currently in the shadows of billions of light sources around the world. Light reaches you from only a few of these. In real-time rendering, large scenes with multiple lights can become swamped with computation if all lights are active at all times. Various culling strategies can also work for lights. For example, the portal culling technique in Section 9.5 can find which lights affect which cells. Another strategy is to use lights that drop off with distance and that are made inactive when beyond some given distance. Alternately, as the distance from a set of lights increases beyond some value, the lights can be coalesced into a single light source.

The idea of culling polygons facing away from the light source can be used with most shadow algorithms; alternately, the polygons facing toward the light can be culled instead. If a light source is inside the view frustum, then no object outside the frustum can cast a shadow that is in the view. Thus, objects outside the view frustum need not be processed. Note that this is not true in general. Lights outside the view frustum can have shadows cast by objects outside the frustum and so affect the image. Another frustum (or more simply, a bounding volume) can be formed by using the light's position and the area of affect, and this can be used to avoid unnecessary shadow generation and rendering by frustum and occlusion culling (see Section 9.2) [86].

6.13   Global Illumination

In real-time rendering, using a local lighting model is the norm. That is, only the surface data at the visible point is needed to compute the lighting. This is a strength of the hardware pipeline, that primitives can be generated, processed, and then be discarded. Transparency, reflections, and shadows are examples of global illumination algorithms, in that they use information from other objects than the one being illuminated. One way to think of the problem of illumination is the paths the photons take. In the local lighting model, photons travel from the light to a surface (ignoring intervening objects), then to the eye. With reflection, the photon goes from the light to some object, bounces off and travels to a shiny object, then reflects off it and travels to the eye. There are many possible paths light can take. The *rendering equation*, presented by Kajiya in 1986 [401], expresses this idea of summing up all possible paths to find the radiance for a given direction. A higher level of realism can be obtained by accounting for more of these sets of paths. Global illumination research focuses on methods for efficiently computing the effect of various sets of paths. Two basic algorithms, radiosity and ray tracing, are described here.

6.13.1 Radiosity

The fixed-function pipeline allows point lights to have a constant illumination or fall off with distance or distance-squared. Often local light sources are not set to drop off with the square of the distance, as they would in the real world. One reason is that such lights are difficult to control. As discussed in Section 4.7, such lights appear to drop off too quickly due to a lack of gamma correction. Another factor is that tone reproduction is difficult to perform in real time [192]. But an important reason that distance-squared lights look unrealistic is because most real-time systems do not properly account for indirect illumination. In reality, a significant amount of light in a scene comes from light reflecting from surfaces. At night, go into a room and close the blinds and drapes and turn a light on. The reason you can see anything not in line of sight of the light source is because the light bounces off objects in the room. This additional light is so significant that using distance-squared point lights without accounting for indirect illumination often means making errors in the opposite direction, with the overall lighting falling off too rapidly. Qualitatively, direct lighting from point sources gives a harsh look that indirect illumination will soften.

There are many different global illumination techniques for determining the amount of light reaching a surface and then travelling to the eye. Jensen's recent book [392] begins with a good technical overview of the subject. While many of these techniques are not currently interactive, research shows a trend towards using the power of graphics accelerators to make them so. The hemicube method of creating form factors for radiosity algorithms naturally lends itself to hardware acceleration [133, 711]. Stürzlinger and Bastos [736] render photon-mapped[17] surfaces by using textured sprites as splats. Stamminger et al. [729] use projective textures to blend ray tracing samples to hardware accelerated renderings. Another example is Hakura and Snyder's work [315], where they use a combination of minimal ray tracing for local objects and layered environment maps to produce reflections and refractions that closely match fully ray traced solutions. Atmospheric effects such as clouds are another area of research. For example, Harris and Lastra [322] use an anisotropic multiple scattering approximation to generate cloud images, which are then displayed using impostors.

One technique that has found use within the real-time arena is *radiosity*, specifically meshed radiosity. There have been whole books written on this algorithm [30, 133, 711], but the basic idea is relatively simple. Light bounces around an environment; you turn a light on and the illumination quickly reaches a stable state. In this stable state, each surface can be considered as a light source in its own right. When light hits a surface, it can be absorbed, diffusely reflected, or reflected in some other fashion (specularly, anisotropically, etc). Basic radiosity algorithms first make the simplifying assumption that all indirect light is from diffuse surfaces. This assumption fails for places with polished marble floors or large mirrors on the walls, but for most architectural settings, this is a reasonable approximation. The BRDF of a diffuse surface is a simple, uniform hemisphere, so the surface's radiance from any direction is proportional purely to the amount of incoming irradiance multiplied by the reflectance of the surface. The outgoing radiance is then:

$$L_{surf} = \frac{rE}{\pi} \tag{6.36}$$

where E is the irradiance and r is the reflectance of the surface. Note that, though the hemisphere covers 2π steradians, the integration of the cosine term for surface irradiance brings this divisor down to π.

To begin the process, each surface is represented by a number of patches (i.e., polygons). The patches do not have to match one-for-one with the underlying polygons of the rendered surface. There can be fewer patches, as for a mildly curving spline surface, or more patches can be generated during processing, in order to capture features such as shadow edges.

To create a radiosity solution, the basic idea is to form a matrix of *form factors* among all the patches in a scene. Given some point or area on the

---

[17]In photon mapping, photons are shot from the lights, tracked through the environment, and deposited on surfaces.

surface (such as at a vertex or the patch itself), imagine a hemisphere above it. Similar to environment mapping, the entire scene can be projected onto this hemisphere. The form factor is a purely geometric value denoting the proportion of how much light travels directly from one patch to the surface. A significant part of the radiosity algorithm is accurately determining the form factors between the receiving patch and each other patch in the scene. The area, distance, and orientations of both patches affect this value. The basic form of a differential form factor, f_{ij}, between a point with differential area, da_i, to another point with da_j, is:

$$df_{ij} = \frac{\cos\theta_i \cos\theta_j}{\pi d^2} h_{ij} da_j. \tag{6.37}$$

The angles between the normals at the two points, and the vector between the points, are denoted θ_i and θ_j. Furthermore, h_{ij} is a visibility factor, which is either 0 (not visible) or 1 (visible), which describes whether the two points can "see" each other, and d is the distance between the two points. This formula is not practical since the form factor cannot be computed between all points in a scene. Instead, larger areas are used, and so Equation 6.37 has to be integrated. Cohen and Wallace [133], and Sillion and Puech [711], cover a wide range of such formulae. As can be seen in Equation 6.37, if the receiving patch faces away from the viewed patch, or vice versa, the form factor is 0, since no light can travel from one to the other. As the viewed patch nears the horizon of the receiving patch's hemisphere its effect lessens, just the same as how a light's effect on a diffuse surface lessens under the same circumstances.

Another important factor is visibility between patches. If something else partially or fully blocks the tested patch from being seen by the receiver, the form factor is correspondingly reduced. Thinking back on the hemisphere, there is essentially only one surface visible in any given direction. Calculating the form factor of a patch for a receiving point is equivalent to finding the area of the patch visible on the hemisphere and then projecting the hemisphere onto the ground plane. The proportion of the circle on the ground plane beneath the hemisphere that the patch covers is the patch's form factor. See Figure 6.54. Called the *Nusselt analog*, this projection effectively folds in the cosine term that affects the importance of the viewed patch to the receiving point.

Given the geometric relations among the various patches, some patches are designated as being emitters (i.e., lights). Energy travels through the system, reaching equilibrium. One way used to compute this equilibrium

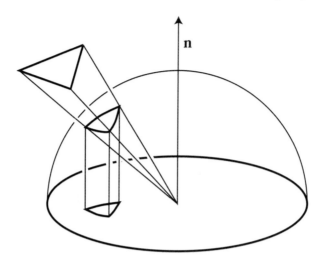

Figure 6.54. For a given receiving point, a patch is projected onto the hemisphere, then onto the ground plane to compute the form factor between the two.

(in fact, the first way discovered, using heat transfer methods) is to form a square matrix, with each row consisting of the form factors for a given patch times that patch's reflectivity. The *radiosity equation* is then:

$$
\begin{pmatrix} e_1 \\ e_2 \\ \vdots \\ e_n \end{pmatrix} = \begin{pmatrix} 1 - r_1 f_{11} & -r_1 f_{12} & \cdots & -r_1 f_{1n} \\ r_2 f_{21} & 1 - r_2 f_{22} & \cdots & -r_2 f_{2n} \\ \vdots & \vdots & \ddots & \vdots \\ r_n f_{n1} & -r_n f_{n2} & \cdots & 1 - r_n f_{nn} \end{pmatrix} \begin{pmatrix} b_1 \\ b_2 \\ \vdots \\ b_n \end{pmatrix}
\tag{6.38}
$$

where r_i is the reflectance of patch i, f_{ij} the form factor between two patches (i and j), e_i the initial radiant exitance (i.e., nonzero only for light sources), and b_i the radiosities to be discovered. Performing Gaussian elimination on this matrix gives the radiant exitance (radiosity) of each patch, so providing the radiance of the surface, since the radiance is constant (i.e., independent of view angle) for a diffuse material.

It is worth mentioning that the radiosity solutions for independent lights can be solved for individually and combined later. For example, given a few light sources in a scene, a set of light maps capturing the radiosity solution for each light could be created. As lights are turned off and on, the various sets of light maps can be added together as needed.

A significant amount of research has focused on simplifying the solution of this matrix. For example, in progressive radiosity, the idea is to shoot the light out from the light sources and collect it at each patch. The patch receiving the most light is then treated like an emitter, bouncing light back into the environment. The next brightest patch then shoots its light out, possibly starting to refill the first shot patch with new energy to shoot. This process continues until some level of diminishing returns is reached. This algorithm takes no less time to fully converge on a solution to the matrix, but has a number of advantages. Form factors are created for only one column of the radiosity equation for each patch shoot, an $O(n)$ process. After any given shoot step, a preliminary radiosity solution can be output. This means a usable solution can be rapidly generated and displayed in seconds or less, with the ability to refine the solution over time with unused cycles.

A recent improvement on the progressive algorithm is eigenvector radiosity, proposed by Ashdown [31], which is three orders of magnitude faster for moderately complex environments. The approach has reasonable memory requirements, and is good for simulating static environments under changing illumination conditions. Ashdown reports computing converged radiosity results in under a tenth of a second for 1000 element environments.

Typically, however, the radiosity process itself is usually performed off-line. The resulting computed illumination is applied to the surfaces by either storing the amount of light reaching each vertex and interpolating, or by storing a light map for the surface. See Plate XXXVII (following page 562) for an example of a radiosity solution and page 474 for its underlying mesh. Plate XXXII shows a model that uses a mixture of light maps and per vertex light colors for the indirect illumination.

Radiosity is an approach that gives a visual richness to an environment, while also precomputing all diffuse components, thereby allowing faster redisplay than computing these on the fly. There are a few drawbacks to the technique beyond the time cost of the algorithm itself and any visual artifacts caused by it. First, the solution is fixed in place for a given set of lights and object positions. Turning on and off a light is only a state change, so could be captured by storing two solution sets. However, as with any global illumination algorithm, moving an object will invalidate the rendering for other objects. Movement modifies some of the form factors, e.g., the object's angle and position to the lighting will change, the shadows cast by the object will change, and the light reflected by the object itself will change.

Specular highlights have to be handled carefully in a radiosity environment, as the visibility of each light affects whether a highlight exists or not. Ignoring this detail means that objects in shadow will still shine. Also, if light reflects from a patch onto an object, this source of light will not cause a specular highlight to appear. Walter et al. [789] address this problem by creating a more elaborate radiosity solution that also stores the directional specular component, fit point lights to best represent these highlights, then use these lights in conjunction with a displayed diffuse solution.

Radiosity theory has been used for terrain rendering in games. As mentioned at the beginning of Section 6.12, Hoffman and Mitchell [362] determine how much each vertex is directly illuminated by the sun by storing critical angles. They also compute the lighting effect of the sky and surrounding terrain by using horizon mapping. In horizon mapping, for each point on the terrain, the altitude angle of the horizon is determined for some set of azimuth directions (e.g., eight: north, northeast, east, southeast, etc.). By using this information and making some simplifying assumptions, they are able to get a reasonable approximation of the effect of surrounding terrain and the sky. Specifically, they use Stewart and Langer's result that for a scene under diffuse lighting conditions, the points near a given point have the same radiance [730]. The result is the creation of a light map that is multiplied by the sky's color during run time.

6.13.2   Ray Tracing

Ray tracing is a rendering method in which rays are used to determine the visibility of various elements. The basic mechanism is very simple, and in fact, functional ray tracers have been written that fit on the back of a business card [334]. In classical ray tracing, rays are shot from the eye through the pixel grid into the scene. For each ray, the closest object is found. This intersection point then can be determined to be in light or shadow by shooting a ray from it to each light and finding if anything blocks or attenuates the light.

Other rays can be spawned from an intersection point. If the surface is shiny, a ray is generated in the reflection direction. This ray picks up the color from any object in this direction by recursively repeating the process of checking for shadows and reflecting rays, until a diffuse surface is hit or some maximum depth is reached. Environment mapping can be thought about as a very simplified version of ray traced reflections; the ray reflects and the light coming from the reflection direction is retrieved. The difference is that, in ray tracing, nearby objects can be intersected by the reflection rays. Note that if these nearby objects are all missed, an environment map can be used to represent the rest of the environment.

Rays can also be generated in the direction of refraction for transparent solid objects, again recursively evaluated. When the maximum number of

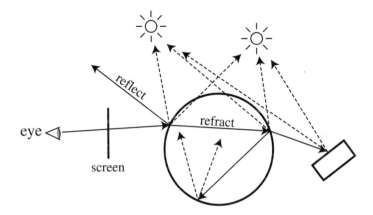

Figure 6.55. A single ray traces from the eye through the screen into a scene. It hits a glass sphere and generates four rays; two to the two lights and one reflection and one refraction ray. These rays continue on, possibly spawning yet more rays, until the maximum tree depth (artificially low for this example) is reached.

reflections and refractions is reached, a ray tree has been built up. This tree is then evaluated from the deepest reflection and refraction rays on back to the root, so yielding a color for the sample. See Figure 6.55. Ray tracing provides sharp reflection, refraction, and shadow effects. Because each sample on the image plane is essentially independent, any point sampling and filtering scheme desired can be used for antialiasing. Another advantage of ray tracing is that true curved surfaces and other untessellated objects can be intersected directly by rays.

The main problem with ray tracing is simply speed. One reason graphics hardware is so fast is that it uses coherence efficiently. Each triangle is sent through the pipeline and covers some number of pixels, and all these related computations can be shared when rendering a single triangle. Other sharing occurs at higher levels, such as when a vertex is used to form more than one triangle or a shader configuration is used for rendering more than one primitive. In ray tracing, the ray performs a search to find the closest object. Some caching and sharing of results can be done, but each ray potentially can hit a different object. Much research has been done on making the process of tracing rays as efficient as possible [260].

There are a number of ways ray tracing can be used in a real-time context. One is for precomputing high-quality synthetic images to use for making environment maps, impostors, skyboxes, or other image-based parts of the scene (see Section 8.2). Ray tracing can also be used to generate and store other information, such as depths, normals, or transparency at each pixel of some distant object. By directly accessing this stored data in a pixel shader, it becomes possible to rapidly rerender the object when, say, lighting conditions change (see Section 8.10). Another use is that, during rendering itself, reflection or shadow rays can be generated for small parts of the scene. The resulting samples are blended into the Z-buffer image, and the process can be relatively inexpensive, though CPU intensive. Another way to integrate ray tracing is to fold it into the per vertex lighting computations. Tracing rays from only the vertices can significantly reduce the amount of computation, but suffers from typical Gouraud-shading artifacts. Sharp reflections will usually not be captured, though this could be considered an advantage, as the reflections will look blurry. Lindholm et al. [499] give an example of a vertex shader performing ray tracing to reflect a nearby sphere in a curved surface.

In classical ray tracing, rays are spawned in the most significant directions: toward the lights and for mirror reflections and refractions. *Monte Carlo path tracing* takes the approach of having a single ray reflect or refract through the scene, with each surface's BRDF influencing the direction that the ray next travels. By shooting many rays for each pixel, a fuller sampling of each surface's incoming irradiance is formed. This technique is very expensive, with thousands or millions or more rays needed per pixel to converge to a precise solution. It fully solves Kajiya's rendering equation [401], given enough time. See Shirley's recent book [705] for more on the theory and practice of classical and Monte Carlo ray tracing.

Shooting rays through the entire scene and distributing them with respect to the BRDF in real time is well beyond even the fastest machines. However, the idea of sampling the hemisphere with ray casting is a feasible preprocess. The idea is that vertices in cracks and crevices will tend to get less illumination. To approximate this effect of self-shadowing, shoot a set of rays outwards in a hemisphere from each vertex in a model. Weight the distribution by the cosine of the angle to the normal. Sum up the proportion of rays that do not intersect the model itself. This value is stored for each vertex and used during rendering to dim its illumination level. The effect is to make objects have more definition and look more realistic [547, 839]. See Figure 6.56 and Plate XL (following page 562).

Another way to use hemisphere sampling is to precompute soft shadow textures for characters. An old technique is to put a fuzzy gray circle texture beneath a character. By using hemisphere ray casting at each texel's location and checking for intersection with the character, a more realistic all-purpose drop shadow texture can be created.

Interactive ray tracing has been possible on a limited basis for some time. For example, the *demo scene* [680] has made real-time programs

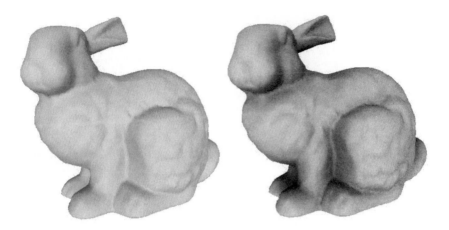

Figure 6.56. On the left, the Stanford bunny is rendered with traditional diffuse lighting. On the right, the geometric self-occlusion of each vertex is precomputed with ray casting, so that indentations and crevices are darker. *(Reprinted with permission from Microsoft Corporation.)*

for years that have used ray tracing for some or all of the rendering. Because each ray is, by its nature, evaluated independently from the rest, ray tracing is "embarrassingly parallel," with more processors being thrown at the problem usually giving a nearly linear speedup. Ray tracing also has another interesting feature, that the time for finding the closest (or for shadows, any) intersection for a ray is typically order $O(\log n)$ for n objects, when an efficiency structure is used. For example, bounding volume hierarchies (see Section 9.1 for information on these and other spatial data structures) typically have $O(\log n)$ search behavior. This compares well with the typical $O(n)$ performance of the basic Z-buffer, in which all polygons have to be sent down the pipeline. Techniques discussed in Chapter 9 and in Section 15.3.5 can be used to speed up the Z-buffer to give it a more $O(\log n)$ response, but with ray tracing, this performance comes with minimal user intervention.

One advantage of the Z-buffer is its use of coherence, sharing results to generate a set of fragments from a single triangle. As scene complexity rises, this factor loses importance. As Wald et al. have shown [783, 785], by carefully paying attention to the cache and other architectural features of the CPU, as well as taking advantage of CPU SIMD instructions, interactive and near-interactive rates can be achieved. See Figure 6.57. While the results are impressive (160 million polygons per second for the left image), Z-buffer graphics accelerators will be the mainstay for most real-time

Figure 6.57. A power plant model of 12.5 million triangles rendered by a cluster of 7 dual-Pentium III's (800–866 MHz) at 640 × 480. The image on the left is rendered at about 13 frames per second. On the right, shadows and reflections have been enabled, and the frame rate is about 4 fps. *(Images courtesy of Ingo Wald, Computer Graphik Universität des Saarlandes.)*

rendering work. Ray tracing also has its own limitations to work around. For example, the efficiency structure that reduces the number of ray/object tests needed is critical to performance. When an object moves, this structure needs to be updated rapidly to keep efficiency at a maximum, a task that can be difficult to do well. There are other issues as well, such as the cache-incoherent nature of reflection rays. See Wald and Slusallek's report [784] for an excellent summary of the state of the art in interactive ray tracing. Since then, Purcell et al. [638] have described how to use a graphics accelerator to accelerate ray tracing directly.

Further Reading and Resources

A valuable reference for information on BRDFs, global illumination methods, color space conversions, and much else is Dutré's free online *Global Illumination Compendium* [194]. Glassner's *Principles of Digital Image Synthesis* [264, 265] discusses the physical aspects of the interaction of light and matter. *Advanced Global Illumination* by Dutré et al. [195] provides a strong foundation in radiometry and on (primarily offline) methods of solving Kajiya's rendering equation. Diefenbach's thesis [172] discusses and contrasts reflection, refraction, and shadow volume techniques in depth, as well as transparency, light volume filtering, and other techniques. Despite its age, it provides much interesting food for thought.

Information about vertex and pixel shaders alone can easily fill a book. Our best advice: Get the *ShaderX* book [210] and later books in the *Game Programming Gems* series [169, 170], and visit the ATI [34] and NVIDIA [590] developer web sites for the latest techniques. The research papers cited sometimes also have demonstrations programs and source code associated with them, notably the latest factorization work by McCool et al. [530]. Events such as the Game Developers Conference and Meltdown have online archives of articles and presentations. See this book's website (http://www.realtimerendering.com/) for many related links.

Since shaders draw so heavily on RenderMan, the two books about this scene description language are useful for ideas and inspiration [22, 761]. Proudfoot provides a detailed description of a real-time shading language [623]. McCool presents an API called SMASH targeting programmable graphics hardware [529]. The book *Real-Time Shading* by Olano et al. [596] discusses hardware implementation of these and other shading languages and BRDFs in detail, with a focus on underlying principles. Lake presents a practical tutorial on creating a vertex shader compiler, including code [455].

Implementing radiosity algorithms is not for the faint-of-heart. A good practical introduction is Ashdown's book [30], sadly now out of print. Shirley's recent book on ray tracing [705] gives a good step-by-step approach for writing a ray tracer (classical or Monte Carlo), and the book by Glassner et al. [260] provides further material. The online publication *The Ray Tracing News* [304] discusses many different techniques related to the topic.

Chapter 7
Non-Photorealistic Rendering

"Using a term like 'nonlinear science' is like referring to the bulk of zoology as 'the study of nonelephant animals.' "
–Stanislaw Ulam

Photorealistic rendering attempts to make an image indistinguishable from a photograph. *Non-photorealistic Rendering* (NPR), also called stylistic rendering, has a wide range of goals. One objective of some forms of NPR is to create images similar to technical illustrations. Only those details relevant to the goal of the particular application are the ones that should be displayed. For example, a photograph of a shiny Ferrari engine may be useful in selling the car to a customer, but to repair the engine, a simplified line drawing with the relevant parts highlighted may be more meaningful (as well as cheaper to print).

Another area of NPR is in the simulation of painterly styles and natural media, e.g., pen and ink, charcoal, watercolor, etc. This is a huge field that lends itself to an equally huge variety of algorithms that attempt to capture the feel of various media. Two examples are shown in Figure 7.1. Gooch and Gooch give thorough coverage to technical and painterly NPR algorithms in their book on the subject [280]. Our goal here is to give a

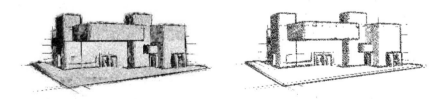

Figure 7.1. Two non-photorealistic rendering styles. *(Generated using Viewpoint LiveStyles.)*

289

flavor of some algorithms used for NPR in real time. This chapter opens with a detailed discussion of ways to implement a cartoon rendering style, then discusses other themes within the field of NPR. The chapter ends with fast and accurate line rendering techniques.

7.1 Toon Shading

Just as varying the font gives a different feel to the text, different styles of rendering have their own mood, meaning, and vocabulary. There has been a large amount of attention given to one particular form of NPR, *cel* or *toon rendering*. Since this style is identified with cartoons, it has strong connotations of fantasy and (in the West, at least) childhood. At its simplest, objects are drawn with solid lines separating areas of different solid colors. One reason this style is popular is what McCloud, in his classic book *Understanding Comics* [528], calls "amplification through simplification." By simplifying and stripping out clutter, one can amplify the effect of information relevant to the presentation. For cartoon characters, a wider audience will identify with those drawn in a simple style.

The toon rendering style has been used in computer graphics for over a decade to integrate three-dimensional models with two-dimensional cel animation. It lends itself well to automatic generation by computer because it is easily defined, compared to other NPR styles. In recent years, games such as *Jet Grind Radio* and *Cel Damage* have used it to good effect. See Figure 7.2 and Plate XLI.

There are a number of different approaches to toon rendering. For models with textures and no lighting, a solid-fill cartoon style can be approximated by quantizing the textures [462]. For shading, the two most common methods are to fill the polygonal areas with solid (unlit) color or to use a two-tone approach, representing lit and shadowed areas. Solid shading is trivial, and the two-tone approach, sometimes called *hard shading*, can be performed by remapping traditional lighting equation elements to different color palettes. This approach is related to the lighting model work by Gooch et al. [112, 278, 279] for NPR technical illustration. Also, silhouettes are often rendered explicitly in a black color, which amplifies the cartoon look. Silhouette finding and rendering is dealt with in the next section.

Lake et al. [453, 454] and Lander [463] both use the idea of computing the diffuse shading dot product $\mathbf{n} \cdot \mathbf{l}$ for each vertex and using this value as a texture coordinate to access a one-dimensional texture map. This can be

Figure 7.2. An example of real-time toon-style rendering from the game "Cel Damage." *(Image courtesy of Pseudo Interactive Inc.)*

done on the CPU or implemented as a simple vertex shader [454, 467]. The texture map itself contains only the two shades, light and dark. So, as the surface faces toward the light, the lighter shade in the texture is accessed. The standard use of the diffuse term is that $n \cdot l < 0$ means the surface is facing away from the light and so is in shadow. However, this term can be used and remapped to any other values as desired. For example, in Figure 7.3, the two-tone rendering uses a threshold value of 0.5. Similarly, simple one-dimensional textures can be used to remap the effect of specular highlights. Card and Mitchell [112] describe how to perform this shading algorithm efficiently with vertex and pixel shaders.

7.2 Silhouette Edge Rendering

Algorithms used for cel edge rendering reflect some of the major themes and techniques of NPR. Methods used can be roughly categorized as based on surface angle, procedural geometry, image processing, vector edge detection, or a hybrid of these.

Figure 7.3. On the left, a Gouraud-shaded duck. The rest of the ducks have silhouettes rendered, with solid shading, diffuse two-tone shading, and specular/diffuse three-tone shading. *(Reprinted by permission of Adam Lake and Carl Marshall, Intel Corporation, copyright Intel Corporation 2002.)*

There are a number of different types of edges that can be used in toon rendering:

- A *boundary* or *border edge* is one not shared by two polygons, e.g., the edge of a sheet of paper. A solid object typically has no boundary edges.

- A *crease* or *hard edge* is one that is shared by two polygons, and the angle between the two polygons (called the *dihedral angle*) is greater than some predefined value. A good default crease angle is 60 degrees [469]. Alternately, a crease edge is one in which the vertex normals differ between the two neighboring polygons. For example, a cube has crease edges. Crease edges can be further subcategorized into *ridge* and *valley* edges.

- A *material edge* appears when the two triangles sharing it differ in material, or otherwise cause a change in shading. It also can be an edge that the artist wishes to always have displayed, e.g., forehead lines or a line to separate the same colored pants and shirt.

- A *silhouette edge* is one in which the two neighboring triangles face in different directions compared to some direction vector.

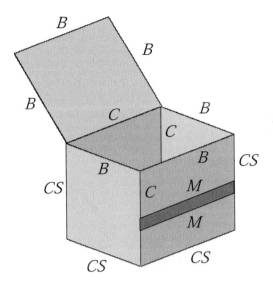

Figure 7.4. A box open on the top, with a stripe on the front. The boundary (B), crease (C), material (M), and silhouette (S) edges are shown.

See Figure 7.4. This categorization is based on common usage within the literature, but there are some variations, e.g., what we call crease and material edges are sometimes called boundary edges elsewhere.

For toon rendering, the direction used to define silhouette edges is the vector from the eye to some point on the edge. In other words, silhouette edges are those for which one neighboring triangle is frontfacing and the other is backfacing. The definition of silhouette edges can include boundary edges, which can be thought of as joining the front and back faces of the same triangle (and so in a sense are always silhouette edges). We define silhouette edges here specifically to not include boundary edges. Section 11.3 discusses processing polygon data to create connected meshes with a consistent facing and determining the boundary, crease, and material edges.

7.2.1 Surface Angle Silhouetting

In a similar fashion to the surface shader in Section 7.1, the dot product between the direction to the viewpoint and the surface normal can be used to give a silhouette edge [279]. If this value is near zero, then the surface is nearly edge-on to the eye and so is likely to be near a silhouette edge. The technique is equivalent to shading the surface using a spherical Environment Map (EM) with a black ring around the edge. See Figure 7.5. In practice, a one-dimensional texture can be used in place of the environment map. Marshall [521] performs this silhouetting method by using a vertex shader. Instead of computing the reflection direction to access the EM, he uses the dot product of the view ray and vertex normal to access

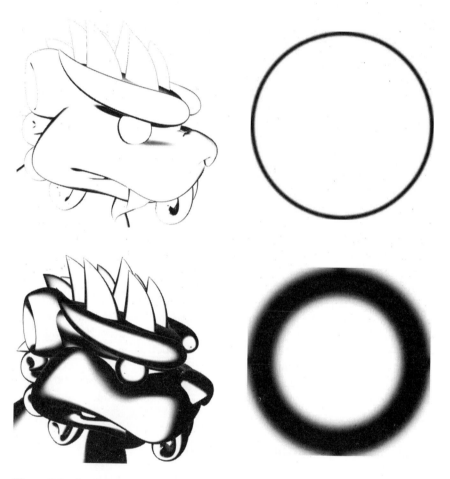

Figure 7.5. Silhouettes rendered by using a spheremap. By widening the circle along the edge of the spheremap, a thicker silhouette edge is displayed. *(Images courtesy of Kenny Hoff.)*

the one-dimensional texture. Everitt [215] uses the mipmap pyramid to perform the process, coloring the topmost layers with black. As a surface becomes edge-on, it accesses these top layers and so is shaded black. Since no vertex interpolation is done, the edge is sharper. These methods are extremely fast, since the accelerator does all the work in a single pass, and the texture filtering can help antialias the edges.

This type of technique can work for some models, in which the assumption that there is a relationship between the surface normal and the silhouette edge holds true. For a model such as a cube, this method fails, as the silhouette edges will usually not be caught. However, by explicitly drawing the crease edges, such sharp features will be rendered properly, though with a different style than the silhouette edges. A feature or drawback of this method is that silhouette lines are drawn with variable width, depending on the curvature of the surface. Large, flat polygons will turn entirely black when nearly edge-on, which is usually not the effect desired. In experiments, Wu found that for the game *Cel Damage* this technique gave excellent results for one quarter of the models, but failed on the rest [826].

7.2.2 Procedural Geometry Silhouetting

One of the first techniques for real-time silhouette rendering was presented by Rossignac and van Emmerik [661], and later refined by Raskar and Cohen [643]. The basic idea is to render the frontfaces normally, then render the backfaces in a way as to make their silhouette edges visible. There are a number of methods of rendering these backfaces, each with its own strengths and weaknesses. Each method has as its first step that the frontfaces are drawn. Then frontface culling is turned on and backface culling turned off, so that only backfaces are displayed.

One method to render the silhouette edges is to draw only the edges (not the faces) of the backfaces. Using biasing or other techniques (see Section 7.4) ensures that these lines are drawn just in front of the frontfaces. In this way, all lines except the silhouette edges are hidden [661, 462]. This technique works well for single-pixel wide lines. If the lines are wider than this (which is possible in OpenGL, but not DirectX 8), there is often nothing joining the separate line segments together, resulting in noticeable gaps.

One way to make wider lines is to render the backfaces themselves in black. Without any bias, these backfaces would remain invisible. So, what is done is to move the backfaces forward in screen Z by biasing them. In this way, only the edges of the backfacing triangles are visible. Raskar and

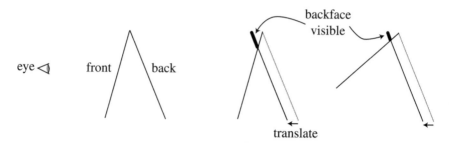

Figure 7.6. The z-bias method of silhouetting, done by translating the backface forward. If the front face is at a different angle, as shown on the right, a different amount of the backface is visible. *(Illustration after Raskar and Cohen [643].)*

Cohen give a number of biasing methods, such as translating by a fixed amount, or by an amount that compensates for the nonlinear nature of the z-depths, or using a call such as `glPolygonOffset`. A problem with all these methods is that they do not create lines with a uniform width. To do so, the amount to move forward depends not only on the backface, but also on the neighboring frontface(s). See Figure 7.6. The slope of the backface can be used to bias the polygon forward, but the thickness of the line will also depend on the angle of the front face.

Raskar and Cohen [643] solve this neighbor dependency problem by instead fattening each backface triangle out along its edges by the amount needed to see a consistently thick line. That is, the slope of the triangle and the distance from the viewer determine how much the triangle is expanded. One method is to expand the three vertices of each triangle outwards along its plane. A safer method of rendering the triangle is to move each edge of the triangle outwards and connect the edges. Doing so avoids having the vertices stick far away from the original triangle. See Figure 7.7. Note that

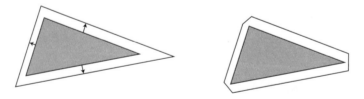

Figure 7.7. Triangle fattening. On the left, a backface triangle is expanded along its plane. Each edge moves a different amount in world space to make the resulting edge the same thickness in screen space. For thin triangles, this technique falls apart, as one corner becomes elongated. On the right, the triangle edges are expanded and joined to form mitered corners to avoid this problem.

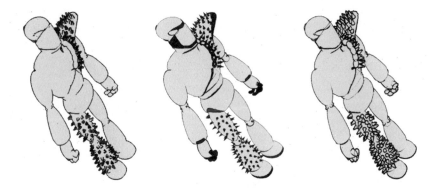

Figure 7.8. Silhouettes rendered with backfacing edge drawing with thick lines, z-bias, and fattened triangle algorithms. The backface edge technique gives poor joins between lines and nonuniform lines due to biasing problems on small features. The z-bias technique gives nonuniform edge width because of the dependence on the angles of the front faces. *(Images courtesy of Raskar and Cohen [643].)*

no biasing is needed with this method, as the backfaces expand beyond the edges of the front faces. See Figure 7.8 for results from the three methods. An improved way of computing the edge expansion factors is presented in a later paper by Raskar [644].

In the method just given, the backface triangles are expanded along their original planes. Another method is to move the backfaces outwards by shifting their vertices along the shared vertex normals, by an amount proportional to their z-distance from the eye [323]. This is referred to as the shell or halo method, as the shifted backfaces form a shell around the original object. Imagine a sphere. Render the sphere normally, then expand the sphere by a radius that is 5 pixels wide with respect to the sphere's center. That is, if moving the sphere's center one pixel is equivalent to moving it in world space by 3 millimeters, then increase the radius of the sphere by 15 millimeters. Render only this expanded version's backfaces in black.[1] The silhouette edge will be 5 pixels wide. See Figure 7.9. This method has some advantages when used with modern graphics hardware. Moving vertices outwards along their normals is a perfect task for a vertex shader, so the accelerator can create silhouettes without any help from the CPU. Vertex information is shared and so entire meshes can be rendered, instead of individual polygons. The method is simple to implement, effi-

---

[1] A forcefield or halo effect can be made by expanding further and shading these backfaces dependent on their angle.

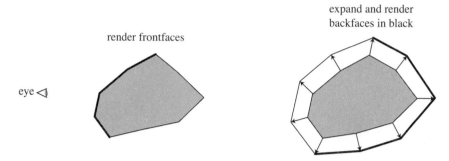

render frontfaces

expand and render
backfaces in black

eye ◁

Figure 7.9. The triangle shell technique creates a second surface by shifting the surface along its vertex normals.

cient, robust, and gives steady performance. It is the technique used by the game *Cel Damage* [826] for example. See Figure 7.2 on page 291.

The shell technique has a number of potential pitfalls. Imagine looking head-on at a cube so that only one face is visible. Each of the four backfaces forming the silhouette edge will move in the direction of its corresponding cube face, so leaving gaps at the corners. This occurs because while there is a single vertex at each corner, each face has a different vertex normal. The problem is that the expanded cube does not truly form a shell, because each corner vertex is expanding in a different direction. One solution is to force vertices in the same location to share a single, new, average vertex normal. Another technique is to create degenerate geometry at the creases that then gets expanded into polygons with area [826].

Shell and fattening techniques waste some fill: Many pixels are touched, but only a few are actually rendered. This is not a real problem for most modern accelerators. Fattening techniques cannot currently be performed on curved surfaces generated by the accelerator. Shell techniques can work with curved surfaces, as long as the surface representation can be displaced outwards along the surface normals. The z-bias technique works with all curved surfaces, since the only modification is a shift in z-depth. Other limitations of all of these techniques is that there is limited control over the edge appearance, semitransparent surfaces are difficult to render with silhouettes, and without some form of antialiasing the edges look fairly poor [826].

One worthwhile feature of this entire class of geometric techniques is that no connectivity information or edge lists are needed. Each polygon is processed independently from the rest, so such techniques lend themselves to hardware implementation [644]. However, as with all the methods discussed here, each mesh should be preprocessed so that the faces are consistent (see Section 11.3).

This class of algorithms renders only the silhouette edges. Other edges (boundary, crease, and material) have to be rendered in some other fashion. These can be drawn using one of the line drawing techniques in Section 7.4. For deformable objects, the crease lines can change over time. Raskar [644] gives a clever solution for drawing ridge lines without having to create and access an edge connectivity data structure. The idea is to generate an additional polygon along each edge of the triangle being rendered. These edge polygons are bent away from the triangle's plane by the user-defined critical dihedral angle that determines when a crease should be visible. Now if two adjoining triangles are at greater than this crease angle, the edge polygons will be visible, else they will be hidden by the triangles. For valley edges, this technique can be performed by using the stencil buffer and up to three passes.

7.2.3   Silhouetting by Image Processing

The algorithms in the previous section are sometimes classified as image-based, as the screen resolution determines how they are performed. Another type of algorithm is more directly image-based, in that it operates entirely on data stored in buffers and does not modify (or even know about) the geometry in the scene.

Saito and Takahashi [668] first introduced this concept, and Decaudin [163] refined it to perform toon rendering. The basic idea is simple: NPR can be done by performing image processing techniques on various buffers of information. By looking for discontinuities in neighboring Z-buffer values, most silhouette edge locations can be found. Discontinuities in neighboring surface normal values signal the location of boundary (and often silhouette) edges. Rendering the scene in ambient colors can also be used to detect edges that the other two techniques may miss.

Card and Mitchell [112] perform these image processing operations in real time by first using vertex shaders to render the world space normals and z-depths of a scene to a texture. The normals are written as a normal map to the color channels and the most significant byte of z-depths as the alpha channel.

Once this image is created, the next step is to find the silhouette, boundary, and crease edges. The idea is to render a screen-filling quadrilateral with the normal map and again with the z-depth map (in the alpha channel) and detect edge discontinuities. Mitchell [557] describes how to im-

Figure 7.10. Edges found by processing a normal map of the scene, and a z-depth map of the scene. The image on the right is the thickened composite. Note that in this case, the normal map was sufficient to detect all edges. *(Images courtesy of Drew Card and Jason L. Mitchell, ATI Technologies Inc.)*

plement edge detection filters using version 1.4 pixel shaders, making such techniques feasible in real time. The idea is to sample the same texture six times in a single pass and implement a Sobel edge detection filter [277]. The texture is sampled six times by sending six pairs of texture coordinates down with the quadrilateral. This filter is actually applied twice to the texture, once along each axis, and the two resulting images are composited. One other feature is that the thickness of the edges generated can be expanded or eroded by using further image processing techniques [112]. See Figure 7.10 and Plate XLII (following page 562) for some results.

This algorithm has a number of advantages. The method handles all primitives, even curved surfaces, unlike most other techniques. Meshes do not have to be connected or even consistent, since the method is image-based. From a performance standpoint, the CPU is not involved in creating and traversing edge lists.

There are relatively few flaws with the technique, other than the obvious limitation of needing sufficiently powerful pixel shader hardware. For nearly edge-on surfaces, the z-depth comparison filter can falsely detect a silhouette edge pixel across the surface. Another problem with z-depth comparison is that if the differences are minimal, then the silhouette edge can be missed. For example, a sheet of paper on a desk will usually have its edges missed. Similarly, the normal map filter will miss the edges of this piece of paper, since the normals are identical. One way to detect this case is to add a filter on an ambient or object ID color rendering of the scene [163]. This is still not foolproof; for example, a piece of paper folded onto itself will create undetectable edges where the paper overlaps [357].

With the z-depth information being only the most significant byte, thicker features than a sheet of paper can also be missed, especially in large scenes where the z-depth range is spread. This could be alleviated by rendering the scene in layers [112]. In time, higher precision depth information will be able to be stored and processed by pixel shaders.

7.2.4 Silhouette Edge Detection

Most of the techniques described so far have the disadvantage of needing two passes to render the silhouette. For procedural geometry methods, the second, backfacing pass typically tests many more pixels than it actually shades. Also, various problems arise with thicker edges, and there is little control of the style in which these are rendered. Image methods have similar problems with creating thick lines. Another approach is to detect the silhouette edges and render them directly. This form of silhouette edge rendering allows more fine control of how the lines are rendered. Another advantage is that, since the edges are independent of the model, it is possible to create effects such as having the silhouette jump in surprise while the mesh is frozen in shock [826].

A silhouette edge is one in which one of the two neighboring triangles faces toward the viewer and the other faces away. The test is:

$$(\mathbf{n}_0 \cdot \mathbf{v} > 0) \neq (\mathbf{n}_1 \cdot \mathbf{v} > 0) \tag{7.1}$$

where $\mathbf{n}_0$ and $\mathbf{n}_1$ are the two triangle normals and $\mathbf{v}$ is the view direction from the eye to the edge (i.e., to either endpoint). For this test to work correctly, the surface must be consistently oriented (see Section 11.3).

The standard method for finding the silhouette edges in a model is to loop through the list of edges and perform this test [521]. Lander [469] notes that a worthwhile speedup is to cull out edges that are inside planar polygons. That is, given a connected triangle mesh, if the two neighboring triangles for an edge lie in the same plane, do not add this edge to the list of edges to test for being a silhouette edge. Implementing this test on a simple clock model dropped the edge count from 444 edges to 256.

Buchanan and Sousa [105] present an efficient method for determining which edges are on the silhouette. It avoids the need for doing separate dot product tests for each edge by reusing the dot product test for each individual face. When a face is tested for backfacing culling, the result of the test is used to flip the sense of a corresponding front or back bit for the attached edges. After all faces have been processed, any edge with both bits set is a silhouette edge. Alternately, if the model has no boundary edges, use only one bit per edge. This is set to zero before processing starts. Test each face and XOR in 0 for frontfacing and 1 for backfacing. Afterwards, an edge is on the silhouette if the edge bit is 1. The method can be extended to determine which crease and material edges are also visible and should be processed. This is done simply by adding one more bit that is turned on (and not flipped off) when a polygon touching the edge is frontfacing.

A randomized search algorithm for rapidly finding silhouettes is given by Markosian et al. [517]. This algorithm relies on first finding one silhouette edge in each silhouette. A silhouette always consists of a single closed curve, though there can be more than one silhouette curve on a surface. Similarly, a silhouette edge can belong to only one curve. This does not necessarily mean that each vertex on the silhouette curve has only two incoming silhouette edges. For example, a curve shaped like a figure eight has one vertex with four incoming edges. Once an edge has been found in each silhouette, this edge's neighbors are tested to see whether they are silhouette edges as well. This is done repeatedly until the entire silhouette is traced out. If the camera view and the objects move little from frame to frame, it is reasonable to assume that the silhouette edges from previous frames might still be valid silhouette edges. Therefore, a fraction of these can be tested to find starting silhouette edges for the next frame. Also, the silhouette edges can be ordered by decreasing dihedral angle. If the angle is smaller, then the probability is higher that it is still a silhouette in the next frame, and so therefore testing occurs in this sort order. The advantage of this method, compared to many others, is that it does not require a special data structure (often expensive to set up) to find the edges. Therefore, it can be used for animated (in any way) meshes. A disadvantage is that one may miss a silhouette using this technique. This has to do with how many edges are tested before one assumes that there are no more silhouettes in a mesh. Such a value should be adapted to the circumstances, which involves the actual meshes used, how fast they are animated, and what kind of accuracy is needed. Compared to the brute-force algorithm, Markosian et al. reported about a five times speedup.

A disadvantage of explicit edge detection is that it is CPU intensive. The major bottleneck is the potentially nonsequential memory access. It is difficult, if not impossible, to order faces, edges, and vertices simultaneously in a manner that is cache friendly [826]. To address this problem, Card and Mitchell [112] use the vertex shader to detect and render silhouette edges. The idea is to send every edge of the model down the pipeline as a degenerate quadrilateral, with the two adjoining triangle normals attached to each vertex. When an edge is found to be part of the silhouette, the quadrilateral's points are moved so that it is no longer degenerate (i.e., is made visible). This results in a thin quadrilateral "fin," representing the edge, being drawn. This technique is based on the same idea as the vertex shader for shadow volume creation, described on page 268. Boundary edges, which have only one neighboring triangle, can also be handled by passing in a second normal that is the negation of this triangle's normal. In this way, the boundary edge will always be flagged as one to be rendered. The main drawbacks to this technique are a large increase in the number of polygons sent to through the pipeline, and that it does not perform well if the mesh undergoes nonlinear transforms [826].

Once the silhouettes are found, the lines are drawn. An advantage of explicitly finding the edges is that they can be rendered with line drawing, textured impostors (see Section 8.3.4), or any other method desired. Biasing of some sort is needed to ensure that the lines are properly drawn in front of the surfaces. If thick edges are drawn, these can also be properly capped and joined without gaps. This can be done by drawing a screen-aligned circle at each silhouette vertex [279].

One flaw of silhouette edge drawing is that it accentuates the polygonal nature of the models. That is, it becomes more noticeable that the model's silhouette is made of straight lines. Lake et al. [453] give a technique for drawing curved silhouette edges. The idea is to use different textured strokes depending on the nature of the silhouette edge. This technique works only when the objects themselves are given a color identical to the background; otherwise the strokes may form a mismatch with the filled areas. A related flaw of silhouette edge detection is that it does not work for vertex blended, N-patch, or other accelerator-generated surfaces, since the polygons are not available on the CPU.

Other silhouette finding methods exist. Gooch et al. [278] use Gauss maps for determining silhouette edges. In the last part of Section 9.3, hierarchical methods for quickly categorizing sets of polygons as front or back facing are discussed. See Hertzman's article [357] or the Goochs' book [280] for more on this subject.

7.2.5 Hybrid Silhouetting

Northrup and Markosian [589] use a silhouette rendering approach that has both image and geometric elements. Their method first finds a list of silhouette edges. They then render all the object's triangles and silhouette edges, assigning each a different ID number (i.e., giving each a unique color). This ID buffer is read back and the visible silhouette edges are determined from it. These visible segments are then checked for overlaps

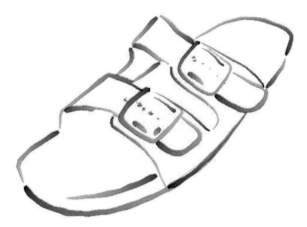

Figure 7.11. An image produced using Northrup and Markosian's hybrid technique, whereby silhouette edges are found, built into chains, and rendered as strokes. *(Image courtesy of Lee Markosian.)*

and linked together to form smooth stroke paths. Stylized strokes are then rendered along these reconstructed paths. The strokes themselves can be stylized in many different ways, including effects of taper, flare, wiggle, and fading, as well as depth and distance cues. An example is shown in Figure 7.11.

7.3   Other Styles

While toon rendering is a popular style to attempt to simulate, there is an infinite variety of other styles. NPR effects can range from modifying realistic textures [432, 462, 470] to having the algorithm procedurally generate geometric ornamentation from frame to frame [402, 518]. In this section, we briefly survey techniques relevant to real-time rendering. With the advent of vertex and pixel shaders, some of the noninteractive techniques of NPR will undoubtedly move into the real-time realm.

In addition to toon rendering, Lake et al. [453] discuss using the diffuse shading term to select which texture is used on a surface. As the diffuse term gets darker, a texture with a darker impression is used. The texture is applied with screen space coordinates to give a hand-drawn look. A paper

Figure 7.12. An image generated by using a palette of textures, a paper texture, and silhouette edge rendering. *(Reprinted by permission of Adam Lake and Carl Marshall, Intel Corporation, copyright Intel Corporation 2002.)*

texture is also applied in screen space to all surfaces to further enhance the sketched look. As objects are animated, they "swim" through the texture, since the texture is applied in screen space. It could be applied in world space for a different effect. See Figure 7.12.

One limitation of Lake et al.'s original approach is that polygons that need to have two textures applied need to be split into two separate polygons. Lander [464] avoids such geometric operations by using multitexturing. Say a palette of two textures is to be used on a surface. Apply the first texture everywhere; say this is the darker one. To apply the second, lighter, texture in a given region, e.g., where $\mathbf{n} \cdot \mathbf{l} > 0.5$, a variant of the one-dimensional texture method described in Section 7.1 is used. The dot product is used to access a one-dimensional texture, but this time, the texture stores only alpha values. The texture is set so that alpha is zero where the texture should not be applied and is one where it should. This texture is applied to the surface, so chopping away all areas where the surface is dark. This leaves the lighter pixels on the surface, which are filled with the lighter texture. This technique uses more fill rate as the number of textures in the palette increases.

For grayscale textures, Praun et al. [633] store each different texture in the palette in a separate color channel. For example, six palette textures

Figure 7.13. *Tonal Art Maps* (TAMs). Strokes are drawn into the mipmap levels. Each mipmap level contains all the strokes from the textures to the left and above it. In this way, interpolation between mip levels and adjoining textures is smooth. *(Images courtesy of Emil Praun, Princeton University.)*

can be stored in two textures. Using this method, a multitexture pipeline or pixel shader can then access the two textures and select the proper channel to display. With color textures, an access of each palette texture normally would be needed, a somewhat expensive proposition. However, as discussed in Section 6.6, dependent texture reads allow texture coordinates to be computed at each pixel, then used to access a single texture. By putting the palette of textures into a single larger image, a pixel shader can then offset to access the correct texture, with no wasted fill.

The hard shading look provided by switching between textures is a mix between strokes and toon shading. Praun et al. [633] present a real-time method of generating stroke textured mipmaps and applying these to surfaces in a smooth fashion. The first step is to form the textures to be used, called *Tonal Art Maps* (TAMs). The idea is to draw strokes into the mipmap levels.[2] See Figure 7.13. Care must be taken to avoid having strokes clump together. With these textures in place, the model is rendered by interpolating between the tones needed at each vertex. Praun et al. give a number of ways to implement this scheme on the accelerator. Applying this technique to surfaces with a lapped texture parameterization [632] results in images with a hand-drawn feel. See Figure 7.14. Card and Mitchell [112] give an efficient implementation of this technique by using pixel shaders. Instead of interpolating the vertex weights, they compute the diffuse term and interpolate this per pixel. This is then used as a texture coordinate into two one-dimensional maps, which yields per pixel TAM weights. This gives better results when shading large polygons.

---

[2]Klein et al. [432] use a related idea in their "art maps" to maintain stroke size for NPR textures.

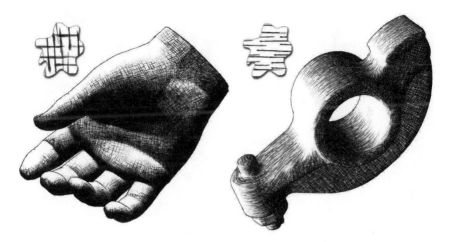

Figure 7.14. Two models rendered using *Tonal Art Maps* (TAMs). The swatches show the lapped texture pattern used to render each. *(Images courtesy of Emil Praun, Princeton University.)*

With regards to strokes, many other operations are possible than those already discussed. To give a sketched effect, edges can be jittered [156, 469] or extended beyond their original locations, as seen in the left image in Figure 7.1 on page 289.

Girshick et al. [259] discuss rendering strokes along the principal curve direction lines on a surface. That is, from any given point on a surface, there is a *first principal direction* tangent vector that points in the direction of maximum curvature. The *second principal direction* is the tangent vector perpendicular to this first vector, and gives the direction in which the surface is least curved. These direction lines are important in the perception of a curved surface. They also have the advantage of needing to be generated once for static models, since such strokes are independent of lighting and shading.

Mohr and Gleicher [559] intercept OpenGL calls and perform NPR effects upon the low level primitives, creating a variety of drawing styles. By making the system that replaces OpenGL, existing applications can instantly be given a different look.

The idea of graftals [402, 518] is that geometry or decal textures can be added as needed to a surface to produce a particular effect. They can be controlled by the level of detail needed, by the surface's orientation to the eye, or by other factors. These can also be used to simulate pen or brush strokes. An example is shown in Figure 7.15. Geometric graftals

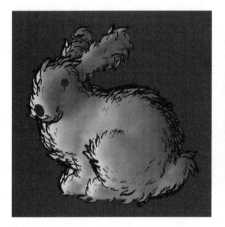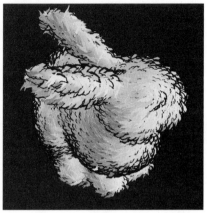

Figure 7.15. Two different graftal styles render the Stanford bunny. See page 285 for a Gouraud shaded version of the bunny for comparison. *(Images courtesy of Bruce Gooch and Matt Kaplan, University of Utah.)*

are a form of procedural modeling [201]. This type of modeling has use in photorealistic rendering, too. For example, Lengyel [487, 488] uses the idea of procedural geometry to create fur at the silhouette edges by using the angle to the eye. The fur is represented by textures on "fins" that are faded out at the tips. See Plates XXXVIII and XLIX. One way in which such techniques can be implemented is by sending down degenerate geometry to the vertex shader, similar to the method used on page 268 to create shadow volume sides. The vertex shader can use information passed with the vertex to decide if it should be shifted in space, so making the triangle no longer degenerate (i.e., visible) [323].

7.4 Lines

Rendering of simple lines is often considered relatively uninteresting. However, they are important in fields such as CAD for seeing the underlying model facets and discerning the object's shape. They are also useful in highlighting a selected object and in areas such as technical illustration. In addition, some of the techniques involved are applicable to other problems. We cover a few useful techniques here; more are covered by McReynolds et al. [536]. Antialiased lines are briefly discussed in Section 4.4.2.

7.4.1   Edge Highlighting

Edge highlighting is a fixed-view technique useful for rapid interaction with large models (see Section 8.10). To highlight an object, we draw its edges in a different color, without having to redraw the surface itself. This is an extremely fast form of highlighting, since no polygons are rendered. For example, imagine a blue polygon with gray edges. As the cursor passes over the polygon, we highlight it by drawing the edges in red, then drawing gray edges again when the cursor leaves. Since the view is not moving, the blue polygon never has to be redrawn; only the red highlight edges are drawn on top of the existing image. The idea is that the original gray edges were drawn properly, so that when a red edge is drawn using the same geometric description, it should perfectly replace the gray edge. This technique works well for highlighting objects in a two-dimensional drawing or when only edges are being drawn.

7.4.2   Polygon Edge Rendering

Correctly rendering edges on top of filled polygons is more difficult than it first appears. If a line is at exactly the same location as a polygon, how do we ensure that the line is always rendered in front? One simple solution is to render all lines with a bias [356, 536]. That is, each line is rendered slightly closer than it should truly be, so that it will be above the surface. This works most of the time, but there are exceptions. For example, the right side of Figure 6.30 on page 241 demonstrates some flaws of this method. As polygons become edge-on to the view, they tend to obscure some of the drawn edges due to imprecision. Also, if the bias is too large, parts of edges that should be hidden appear, spoiling the effect. Calls like the `glPolygonOffset` routine in OpenGL can solve this problem by pushing the polygons back by the proper bias, but for a precise rendering, it is preferable to avoid biasing altogether.

One method [356] for producing high-quality edges that avoids biasing goes as follows:

1. Render the filled polygon, with Z-buffer depth comparison on, Z-buffer replacement off, and the color buffer on.

2. Render the polygon edges normally (everything on).

3. Render the filled polygon again, with the Z-buffer fully on, but the color buffer off.

The first step properly draws the filled polygon on the screen but does not modify the Z-buffer values. This allows the edges to draw on top of the filled polygon, since there are filled-area z-depths that could cover the edges. The final step then fills in the depths for the filled area so that the Z-buffer is in synch again with what is displayed.

This technique usually looks good, but does not work well with the edge highlighting technique (unlike the bias method, which works fine with it). When the three-step algorithm is used to draw the original image, each edge is properly drawn on top of the filled region. But the edge's z-depth values are sometimes overwritten by the filled polygon's z-depth values during the third step. In other words, the edge's color may be drawn properly, but the depth values where the edge is drawn might actually be those of the filled polygon. In this case, when a highlight edge is drawn to replace the original edge, it will not appear wherever the filled polygon was in front of the original edge. In our example, the highlights will be displayed in a broken-up manner, with the edge partially the original gray and partially red.

To solve this, Herrell et al. [356] present a scheme that uses a modified one-bit stencil buffer. The steps are:

1. Render the filled polygon normally, also marking its location in the stencil buffer.

2. Render the polygon edges. If a pixel is not marked in the stencil buffer, perform a normal depth compare and replace. If a pixel is marked, do not compare; instead, always replace the stored z-depth with the edge's value.

3. Clear the stencil buffer for the next pass (possibly by redrawing the filled polygon).

The method works by forcing the edge's depth values into the Z-buffer. Now when an edge is redrawn as a highlight, it will have exactly the same depth values as those that are stored and so will be drawn correctly. Step 2 of this algorithm can be performed as two separate passes using a standard stencil buffer [356, 536].

7.4.3   Hidden-Line Rendering

In normal wireframe drawing, all edges of a model are visible. Hidden-line rendering treats the model as solid and so draws only the visible lines.

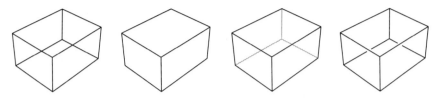

Figure 7.16. Four line rendering styles. From left to right: wireframe, hidden-line, obscured-line, and haloed line.

The straightforward way to perform this operation is simply to render the polygons with a solid fill color the same as the background's and also render the edges, using a technique from the previous section. Thus the polygons are painted over the hidden lines. A potentially faster method is to draw all the filled polygons to the Z-buffer, but not the color buffer, then draw the edges [536]. This second method avoids unnecessary color fills.

Lines can also be drawn as partially obscured instead of fully hidden. For example, hidden lines could appear in light gray instead of not being drawn at all. To do this, first draw all the edges in the obscured style desired. Now draw the filled polygons to the Z-buffer only. In this way, the Z-buffer protects the hidden lines from being drawn upon. Finally, draw the edges again in the style desired for visible lines.

The method just described has the property that the obscured lines are rendered overlapping in the right order, since the Z-buffer is first used to render them. If this feature is not necessary, there are other ways to perform the task that are normally more efficient. One technique is to first draw the surfaces to the Z-buffer. Next, draw the lines in the visible style. Now reverse the sense of the Z-buffer, so that only lines that are *beyond* the current pixel z-depth are drawn. Also turn off Z-buffer modification, so that these lines drawn do not change any depth values. Draw the lines again in the backfacing style. This method performs fewer pixel operations, as visible lines are not drawn twice, and obscured lines do not modify the Z-buffer.

Figure 7.16 shows results for some of the different line rendering methods discussed here.

7.4.4 Haloing

When two lines cross, a common convention is to erase a part of the more distant line, making the ordering obvious. In computer graphics, this can be accomplished relatively easily by drawing each line twice, once with a halo. This method erases the overlap by drawing over it in the background color. Assume the lines are black and the background white. For each line, first draw a thick version in the background color, then draw the line itself normally. A bias or other method will have to be used to ensure that the thin black line lies atop the thick white background line.

As with hidden-line rendering, this technique can be made more efficient by first drawing all the white halo lines only to the Z-buffer, then drawing the black lines normally [536].

A potential problem with haloing is that lines near each other can get obscured unnecessarily by one line's halo. For example, in Figure 7.16, if the haloing lines extend all the way to the corners, then near the corners, the closer lines may halo the lines further away. One solution is to shorten the lines creating the halos. Because haloing is a technical illustration convention and not a physical phenomenon, it is difficult to automate perfectly.

Further Reading and Resources

For inspiration about non-photorealistic rendering and toon rendering, read Scott McCloud's *Understanding Comics* [528]. Lander's series of articles [462, 463, 464, 467, 469, 470] focuses on implementing real-time NPR techniques. The book by the Goochs [280] is an excellent guide to NPR algorithms in general. Newer research can be found in the proceedings of the *International Symposium on Non-Photorealistic Animation and Rendering (NPAR)*, held every other year. This book's website at http://www.realtimerendering.com/ has pointers to a number of worthwhile tutorials, demonstration programs, and code related to NPR. In particular, Craig Reynolds' non-photorealistic rendering techniques survey page [651] is an excellent resource.

Chapter 8
Image-Based Rendering

"Landscape painting is really just a box of air with little marks in it telling you how far back in that air things are."
–Lennart Anderson

Image-based Rendering (IBR) has become a paradigm of its own during the last decade. As its name proclaims, images are the primary data used for rendering. A great advantage of representing an object with an image is that rendering is proportional to the number of pixels rendered, and not to, say, the number of vertices in a geometrical model. So, one use of image-based rendering is as a more efficient way to render models. IBR techniques have a wider use than this. Many objects, such as clouds and fur, are difficult to impossible to represent with polygons. Clever use of layered semitransparent images can be used to display such complex surfaces. In addition, photos or photorealistic images can be used to enhance the level of realism.

In this chapter, image-based rendering is first compared and contrasted with traditional polygon rendering, and an overview of algorithms presented. Commonly used techniques such as sprites, billboards, and impostors are then described, along with more experimental methods. Applications are discussed, such as lens flares and particle systems. Full-screen and environmental image-based methods are then covered, followed by how image processing can be performed by pixel shaders. The chapter ends with a brief description of a related rendering technique, volume rendering.

8.1   The Rendering Spectrum

Up to this point in the book, we have focused on showing three-dimensional objects on the screen by representing them with polygons. This is not

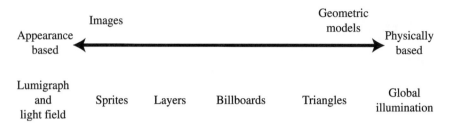

Figure 8.1. The rendering spectrum. *(After Lengyel [486].)*

the only way to get an object to the screen, nor is it always the most appropriate one. The goal of rendering is to portray an object on the screen; how we attain that goal is our choice. There is no correct way to render a scene. Each rendering method is an approximation of reality, at least if photorealism is the goal.

Polygons have the advantage of representing the object in a reasonable fashion from any view. As the camera moves, the representation of the object does not have to change. However, to improve quality, we may wish to substitute a more highly detailed model as the viewer gets closer to the object. Conversely, we may wish to use a simplified form of the model if it is off in the distance. These are called level of detail techniques (see Section 9.8). Their main purpose is to make the scene display faster.

However, other techniques can come into play as an object recedes from the viewer. Speed can be gained by using images instead of polygons to represent the object. It is less expensive to represent an object with a single image that can be sent quickly to the screen. One way to represent the continuum of rendering techniques comes from Lengyel [486] and is shown in Figure 8.1.

An important principle of real-time work is to precompute whenever possible. For example, global illumination techniques such as radiosity can be used to calculate lighting effects offline, with the results displayable at interactive rates. Image-based rendering for object representation draws on the idea of reusing a computed image over a series of frames.

8.2   Overview of Algorithms

One of the simplest image-based rendering primitives is the sprite [253]. A sprite is an image that moves around on the screen. A mouse cursor is a sprite, for example. The sprite does not have to have a rectangular shape, since various pixels can be rendered as transparent. For simple sprites, there is a one-to-one mapping with pixels on the screen. Each pixel stored in the sprite will be put in a pixel on the screen. Various acceleration schemes exist for sprites, such as precompiling them into a list of individual spans of pixels and so eliminating the need to test for transparency at each pixel [129].

Animation can be generated by displaying a succession of different sprites. Another use for a set of sprites is interactive object representation. As the viewer sees an object from different angles, different sprites can be used to represent it. The illusion is fairly weak, however, because of the jump when switching from one sprite to another.

A sprite can also be treated as an image texture on a polygon, with the image's alpha channel providing full or partial transparency. With the use of texturing acceleration hardware, such techniques incur little more cost than direct copying of pixels. Images applied to polygons can be kept facing the viewer using various billboard strategies (see Section 8.3). Even traditional two-dimensional applications such as fixed view games have begun to use three-dimensional sprites as a way to easily perform alpha blending and sprite scaling, while also offloading work from the CPU to the accelerator [253, 534].

One way to think of a scene is as a series of layers, as is commonly done for two-dimensional cel animation. For example, in Plate XXXIX, the tailgate is in front of the chicken, which is in front of the truck's cab, which is in front of the road and trees. This layering holds true for a large set of viewpoints. Each sprite layer has a depth associated with it. By rendering in a back-to-front order, we can build up the scene without need for a Z-buffer, thereby saving time and resources. Camera zooms simply make the object larger, which is simple to handle with the same sprite. Moving the camera in or out actually changes the relative coverage of foreground and background, which can be handled by changing each sprite layer's coverage independently. As the viewer moves perpendicularly to the direction of view, the layers can be moved relative to their depths.

However, as the view changes, the appearance of the object changes. For example, viewing a cube straight-on results in a square. As the view moves, the square appears as a warped quadrilateral. In the same way, a sprite representing an object can also be warped as its relation to the view changes. Note that as the view changes, however, new faces of the cube become visible, invalidating the sprite. At such times, the sprite layer is regenerated. Determining when to warp and when to regenerate is one of the more difficult aspects of image-based rendering. In addition to surface features appearing and disappearing, the effect of specular highlights and shadows adds to the challenge.

This layer and image warping process is the basis of the experimental Talisman architecture [46, 752]. Objects are rendered into sprite layers, which are then composited on the screen. The idea is that each sprite layer can be formed and then reused for a number of frames. Warping and redisplaying an image is considerably simpler than resending an object's whole set of polygons for each frame. Each layer is managed independently. For example, in Plate XXXIX (following page 562), the chicken may be regenerated frequently because it moves or the view changes. The cab of the truck needs less frequent regeneration, because its angle to the camera is not changing as much in this scene. Performing warping and determining when to regenerate a layer's image is discussed in depth by Lengyel and Snyder [485].

Interpenetrating objects such as the wing and the tailgate are treated as one sprite. This is done because the wing has feathers both in front of and behind the tailgate. This means that each time the wing moves, the entire layer has to be regenerated. One way of avoiding this full regeneration is to split the wing into one component that is fully in front of the tailgate and one that is fully behind it. Another method was introduced by Snyder and Lengyel [724]; this method resolves some occlusion cycles (where object A partially covers B, which partially covers C, which in turn partially covers A) by using layers and compositing operations.

Pure image-layer rendering depends on fast, high-quality image warping, filtering, and compositing. Image-based techniques can also be combined with polygon-based rendering. Section 8.3.4 and 8.6 deal extensively with impostors, depth sprites, and other ways of using images to take the place of polygonal content.

At the far end of the image-based rendering spectrum are image-based techniques such as QuickTime VR and the Lumigraph. In the Quicktime VR system [121], a 360-degree panoramic image, normally of a real scene, surrounds the viewer as a cylindrical image. As the camera's orientation changes, the proper part of the image is retrieved, warped, and displayed. Though limited to a single location, this technique has an immersive quality compared to a static scene, because the viewer's head can turn and tilt. Such scenes can serve as backdrops, and polygonal objects can be rendered in front of them. This technology is practical today using just software rendering, and is particularly good for capturing a sense of the space in a building, on a street, or in another location, be it real or synthetic. See Figure 8.2. A related technique is skyboxing, in which a scene is put on six faces of a cube (see Section 8.9).

Figure 8.2. A panorama of the Mission Dolores, used by QuickTime VR to display a wide range of views, with three views below generated from it. Note how the views themselves are undistorted. *(Images courtesy of Ken Turkowski.)*

The Lumigraph [282] and light-field rendering [490] techniques are related to QuickTime VR. However, instead of viewing much of an environment from a single location, a single object is viewed from a set of viewpoints. Given a new viewpoint, these techniques perform an interpolation process between stored views in order to create the new view. This is a more complex problem, with a much higher data requirement (tens of megabytes for even small image sets). The concept is akin to holography, where a two-dimensional array of views captures the object. A tantalizing aspect of the Lumigraph and light-field rendering is the ability to capture a real object and be able to redisplay it from any angle. Any real object, regardless of surface and lighting complexity, can be displayed at a nearly constant rate [714]. As with the global illumination end of the rendering spectrum, these techniques currently have limited use in real-time rendering, but they demarcate what is possible in the field of computer graphics as a whole.

To return to the realm of the mundane, what follow are detailed explanations of a number of image-based techniques commonly used in real-time rendering.

8.3   Billboarding

Many "special effects," such as lens flares (Section 8.4), render an image onto a polygon facing the viewer. Orienting the polygon based on the view direction is called *billboarding*, and the polygon is called a *billboard* [536]. As the view changes, the orientation of the polygon changes. Billboarding, combined with alpha texturing and animation, can be used to represent many phenomena that do not have solid surfaces. Smoke, fire, fog, explosions, energy shields, vapor trails, and clouds are just a few of the objects that can be represented by these techniques [180, 536]—see Plates XIX, XXXI, XXXV, and XLIII (following page 274 and page 562).

A few popular forms of billboards are described in this section. In each, a surface normal and an up direction are found for orienting the polygon, usually a quadrilateral. These two vectors are sufficient to create an orthonormal basis for the surface. In other words, these two vectors describe the rotation matrix needed to rotate the quadrilateral to its final orientation (see Section 3.2.4). An *anchor location* on the quadrilateral (e.g., its center) is then used to establish its position in space.

Often the desired surface normal n and up vector u are not perpendicular. In all billboarding techniques, one of these two vectors is established as being a fixed vector that must be maintained in the given direction. The process is always the same to make the other vector perpendicular to this fixed vector. First, create a "right" vector r, a vector pointing toward the right edge of the quadrilateral. This is done by taking the cross product of u and n. Normalize this vector r, as it will be used as an axis of the orthonormal basis for the rotation matrix. If vector r is of zero length, then u and n must be parallel and the technique [377] described in Section 3.2.4 can be used.

The vector that is to be adjusted (i.e., is not fixed), either n or u, is modified by taking the cross product of the fixed vector and r, which

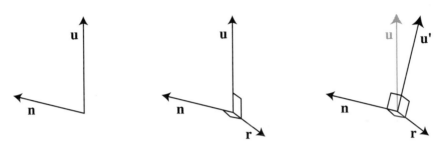

Figure 8.3. Given a desired surface normal direction **n** and an approximate up vector direction **u**, we wish to establish a set of three mutually perpendicular vectors to orient the billboard. In the middle figure, the "right" vector **r** is found by taking the cross product of **u** and **n**, and so is perpendicular to both of them. In the right figure, the fixed vector **n** is crossed with **r** to give a mutually perpendicular up vector **u′**.

creates a vector perpendicular to both. Specifically, if the normal **n** is fixed (as is true for most billboarding techniques), then the new up vector **u′** is:

$$\mathbf{u}' = \mathbf{n} \times \mathbf{r}. \tag{8.1}$$

This process is shown in Figure 8.3. If instead the up direction is fixed (true for axially aligned billboards such as trees on landscape), then the new normal vector **n′** is:

$$\mathbf{n}' = \mathbf{r} \times \mathbf{u}. \tag{8.2}$$

The new vector is then normalized and the three vectors are used to form a rotation matrix. For example, for a fixed normal **n** and adjusted up vector **u′** the matrix is:

$$\mathbf{M} = \left(\, \mathbf{r},\ \mathbf{u}',\ \mathbf{n} \,\right). \tag{8.3}$$

This matrix transforms a quadrilateral in the xy plane with $+y$ as pointing toward its top edge, and centered about its anchor position, to the proper orientation. A translation matrix is then applied to move the quadrilateral's anchor point to the desired location.

With these preliminaries in place, the main task that remains is deciding what surface normal and up vector is used to define the billboard's orientation. The various methods of establishing these vectors are described in the following sections.

8.3.1   Screen-Aligned Billboard

The simplest form of billboarding is a *screen-aligned billboard*. This form
is similar to a two-dimensional sprite, in that the image is always parallel
to the screen and has a constant up vector. For this type of billboard the
desired surface normal is the negation of the view plane's normal. This
view direction is a constant vector $\mathbf{v}_n$ that the camera looks along, in
world space. The up vector $\mathbf{u}$ is from the camera itself, i.e., it is a vector in
the view plane that defines the camera's up direction. These two vectors
are already perpendicular, so all that is needed is the "right" direction
vector $\mathbf{r}$ to form the rotation matrix for the billboard. Since $\mathbf{n}$ and $\mathbf{u}$ are
constants for the camera, this rotation matrix is the same for all billboards
of this type.

Screen-aligned billboards are useful for information such as annotation
text, as the text will always be aligned with the screen itself (hence the
name "billboard").

8.3.2   World-Oriented Billboard

The previous billboarding technique can be used for circular sprites such as
particles, as the up vector direction actually is irrelevant for these. If the
camera rolls, i.e., rotates along its view direction axis, due to symmetry, the
appearance of the sprites does not change. For other sprites, the screen's
up vector is normally not appropriate. If the sprite represents a physical
object, it is often oriented with respect to the world's up direction, not the
camera's. For such sprites, one way to render these is by using this world
up vector to derive the rotation matrix. In this case, the normal is still the
negation of the view plane normal, which is the fixed vector, and a new
perpendicular up vector is derived from the world's up vector, as explained
previously. As with screen-aligned billboards, this matrix can be reused for
all sprites, since these vectors do not change within the rendered scene.

Using the same rotation matrix for all sprites carries a risk. The problem arises because of the nature of the perspective projection. This projection warps objects that are away from the view direction axis. See the
bottom two spheres in Figure 8.4. The spheres become elliptical due to
projection onto a plane. This phenomenon is not an error, and looks fine
if a real viewer's eyes are the proper distance and location from the screen.
That is, if the virtual camera's field of view matches the eye's actual field
of view, then these spheres look unwarped. We usually notice this warping

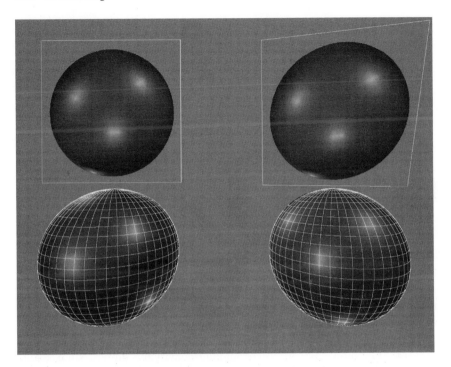

Figure 8.4. A view of four spheres, with a wide field of view. The upper left is a billboard texture of a sphere, using view plane alignment. The upper right billboard is viewpoint oriented. The lower row shows two real spheres.

because the real viewing conditions are rarely exactly those portrayed in the two-dimensional image.[1] For example, the field of view is often made wider than expected viewing conditions so that more of the surrounding scene is presented to the user (see Section 3.5.2).

When the field of view and the sprites are small, this warping effect can often be ignored and a single orientation aligned to the view plane used. Otherwise, the desired normal needs to equal the vector from the center of the billboard to the viewer's position. This we call a *viewpoint oriented* billboard. See Figure 8.5. The effect of using different alignments is shown in Figure 8.4. As can be seen, view plane alignment has the effect of making the billboard have no distortion, regardless of where it is on the

---

[1] For centuries, artists have realized this problem and compensated as necessary. Objects expected to be round, such as the moon, were painted as circular regardless of their positions on the canvas [302].

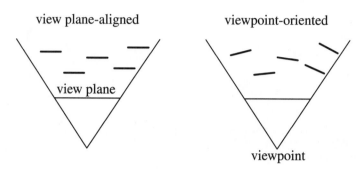

Figure 8.5. A top view of the two billboard alignment techniques. The five billboards face differently depending on the method.

screen. Viewpoint orientation distorts the sphere image in the same way in which real spheres are distorted by projecting the scene onto the plane. For impostors, discussed in Section 8.3.4, viewpoint orientation is normally more appropriate. Impostors are meant to simulate geometry in a scene, so the simulation should distort in the same way as real geometry does.

This form of billboarding is useful for rendering many different phenomena. Guymon [298] discusses making convincing flames, smoke, and explosions by clustering and overlapping animated sprites in a random and chaotic fashion. Doing so helps hide the looping pattern of the animated sequences, while also avoiding making each fire or explosion look the same.

Dobashi et al. [182] simulate clouds and render them with billboards, and create shafts of light by rendering concentric semitransparent shells. Harris and Lastra [322] also use impostors to simulate clouds. See Figure 8.6 and Plate XLIV (following page 562). They treat the clouds as three-dimensional objects, in that if a plane is seen flying into a cloud, the impostor is split into two pieces, one behind the plane and one in front. It is worth noting that the world up vector is just one choice for defining an impostor's orientation. For example, Harris and Lastra use the up vector of the view used to create the impostor originally. Consistency is maintained as long as the same up vector is used frame to frame to orient the impostor.

Billboards are not the only cloud rendering technique possible, of course. For example, Elinas and Stuerzlinger [209] generate clouds using Gardner's method of rendering sets of nested ellipsoids that become more transparent around the viewing silhouettes. Pallister [615] discusses procedurally generating cloud images and animating these across an overhead sky mesh.

Figure 8.6. Clouds created by a set of world-oriented impostors. *(Images courtesy of Mark Harris, UNC-Chapel Hill.)*

8.3.3 Axial Billboard

The last common type is called *axial billboarding*. In this scheme the textured object does not normally face straight-on toward the viewer. Instead, it is allowed to rotate around some fixed world space axis and align itself so as to face the viewer as much as possible within this range. This billboarding technique is commonly used for displaying trees. Instead of representing a tree with a solid surface, or even with a pair of tree outlines as described in Section 5.7.1, a single tree billboard is used. The world's up vector is set as an axis along the trunk of the tree. The tree faces the viewer as the viewer moves, as shown in Figure 8.7.[2] For this form of billboarding, the world up vector is fixed and the viewpoint direction is used as the second, adjustable vector. Once this rotation matrix is formed, the tree is translated to its position.

A problem with the axial billboarding technique is that if the viewer flies over the trees and looks straight down, the illusion is ruined, as the trees will look like the cutouts they are. If necessary, adding a circular, horizontal, cross section texture of the tree (which needs no billboarding) can help ameliorate the problem. Another technique is to use level of detail techniques to change from an impostor to a three-dimensional model. Meyer et al. [545] give an overview of other real-time tree rendering techniques.

Just as screen-aligned billboards are good for representing symmetric spherical objects, axial billboards are useful for representing objects with cylindrical symmetry. For example, laser beam effects can be rendered with axial billboards, since their appearance looks the same from any angle around the axis. See Figure 8.8 for an example of this and other billboards.

Figure 8.7. As the viewer moves around the scene, the tree billboard rotates to face forward.

---

[2]More elaborate tree simulation techniques can be found in Section 8.7.

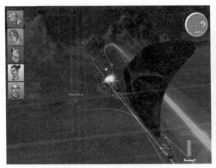 

Figure 8.8. Billboard examples. The *Heads-up Display* (HUD) graphics and star-like projectiles are screen-aligned billboards. The large teardrop explosion in the right image is a viewpoint-oriented billboard. The curved beams are axial billboards made of a number of quadrilaterals. To create a continuous beam, these quadrilaterals are joined at their corners, and so are no longer rectangular. *(Images courtesy of Maxim Garber, Mark Harris, Vincent Scheib, Stephan Sherman, and Andrew Zaferakis, from "BHX: Beamrunner Hypercross",* www.cs.unc.edu/~andrewz/twa.*)*

8.3.4 Impostors

An impostor[3] is a billboard that is created on the fly by rendering a complex object from the current viewpoint into an image texture, which is mapped onto the billboard. The rendering is therefore proportional to the number of pixels the impostor covers on the screen, instead of the number of vertices or the depth complexity of the object. The impostor can be used for a few instances of the object or a few frames so that a speedup is obtained. In this section different strategies for updating impostors will be presented.

This image is opaque where the object is present; everywhere else it is totally transparent. Sometimes, impostors are called sprites. One of the best uses for impostors is for collections of small static objects [237]. The use of an impostor is visualized in Figure 8.9. Impostors are also useful for rendering distant objects rapidly. A different approach is to use a very low level of detail model (see Section 9.8). However, such simplified model often lose shape and color information. Impostors do not necessarily have this disadvantage, since a higher quality impostor can be created [17, 806]. Another advantage is that the texture image can be lowpass filtered to create an out-of-focus image for a depth-of-field effect.

---

[3]Maciel and Shirley [508] identify several different types of impostors in 1995, including the one used in this chapter. Since that time, the definition of an impostor has narrowed to the one we use here [237].

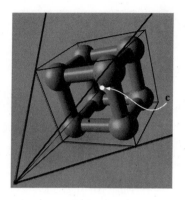 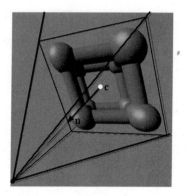

Figure 8.9. At the left, an impostor is created of the object in the bounding box. The view direction is toward the center, **c**, of the bounding box, and an image is rendered and used as an impostor texture. This is shown on the right, where the texture is applied to a quadrilateral. The center of the impostor is equal to the center of the bounding box, and the normal (emanating from the center) points directly toward the viewpoint.

In practice, an impostor should be faster to draw than the object it represents, and it should closely resemble the object. Also of importance is that an impostor should be reused for several viewpoints located close together, and therefore efficiently exploits frame-to-frame coherence. This is usually the case because the movement of the projected image of an object diminishes with an increased distance from the viewer. This means that slowly moving objects that are located far from the viewer are candidates for this method. Another situation in which impostors can be used is for objects located close to the viewer that tend to expose the same side to the viewer as they move [674].

An impostor of an object is created by initializing the alpha channel of an offscreen buffer to $\alpha = 0.0$ (i.e., fully transparent). The object is then drawn into an offscreen image, with the alpha channel set to opaque ($\alpha = 1.0$) where the object is present. The pixels that are not written retain their transparency. Before rendering the object to create the impostor image, the viewer is set to view the center of the bounding box of the object, and the impostor polygon is chosen so as to point directly toward the viewpoint (at the left in Figure 8.9). The size of the impostor's quadrilateral is the smallest rectangle containing the projected bounding box of the object. The impostor image is then used as a texture on the polygon. Newer graphics accelerators provide the capability to render directly to a texture, thus saving time [613]. Note that the impostor texture is of the format $RGB\alpha$. Once created, the rendering of the impostor starts with placing the impostor polygon at the center of the bounding box, and orienting the polygon so its normal points directly to the viewer (see the image on the right in Figure 8.9). This is therefore a viewpoint oriented billboard. Just mapping the texture onto a polygon facing the viewer does not always give a convincing effect. Forsyth suggests projecting the texture along the view direction onto the bounding box of the object instead [237]. The main advantage of this is that the box is a three-dimensional world space object, instead of just a view-oriented two-dimensional one. This avoids some of the problems shown in Figure 8.15. Other shapes can also be used to project the impostor texture on, as long as the shape is convex and the object fully contained in the shape [237].

The resolution of the texture need not exceed the screen resolution and so can be computed by Equation 8.4 [674].

$$texres = screenres \frac{objsize}{2 \cdot distance \cdot \tan(fov/2)} \qquad (8.4)$$

There are many ways in which an impostor may give a bad approximation of the underlying geometry. This happens when the error incurred becomes larger than some threshold, and the impostor is then said to be invalid. One limit to the usefulness of an impostor is its resolution. If a distant impostor comes closer, the individual pixels of the texture may become obvious, and so the illusion breaks down. The angles β_{scr}, which represents the angle of a pixel, and β_{tex}, which represents the angle of a texel of the impostor, can be used to determine when the lifetime of an impostor has expired. This is illustrated in Figure 8.10. When $\beta_{tex} > \beta_{scr}$, there is a possibility that the texels will be clearly visible, and so the impostor has to be regenerated from the current position of both the viewer and the object. In this way, the impostor texture adapts to the screen resolution.

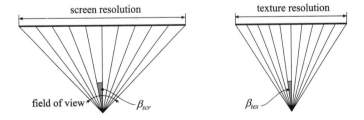

Figure 8.10. The angle of a screen pixel is computed as $\beta_{scr} = fov/screenres$, and the angle for the texture is computed similarly. Note that these are both approximations as neither of the angles are constant for all pixels/texels.

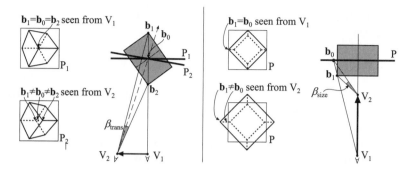

Figure 8.11. The left part illustrates the overestimate of the error angle β_{trans}, and the right part shows the overestimate of β_{size}. When any of these angles becomes greater than β_{scr}, the impostor needs to be regenerated. *(Illustration after Schaufler [674].)*

We must also test whether the impostors are valid from the current point of view. Here we present Schaufler's method [674, 675]. The first observation is that when only the view direction changes, the impostors need not be updated. The reason is that even though the projection plane changes as the viewer rotates, the projection itself does not. Rather, it is the sampling of the object that may change. The set of rays from the viewer that hit the object is the same no matter what plane we project to. This is why we can assume that the impostor will still be a good approximation under rotations of the view direction.

So we need to consider regenerating an impostor only in cases where the viewer moves. Here, we will look at the two extreme cases, which are shown in Figure 8.11. The left case in this figure shows how to compute an error angle called β_{trans} that increases as the viewer moves sideways (parallel to the plane of the impostor). The apparent displacement of the object from two such viewpoints is called the *parallax*. The error angle is computed by considering how the extreme points on a bounding box create an angle when the viewer moves. When the viewer has moved sufficiently far, the impostor will need to be updated because $\beta_{trans} > \beta_{scr}$.

The right case in Figure 8.11 shows the extreme case when the viewer moves toward the impostor. This angle is computed by considering how extreme points on the bounding box project onto the impostor plane when the viewer moves toward the impostor. Both angles β_{trans} and β_{size} can be computed with, for example, the law of cosines (see Section B.2). This is a different test than that for β_{tex}, as it measures the amount of change in perspective effect. In conclusion, an impostor needs to be regenerated every time β_{tex}, β_{trans}, or β_{size} is greater than β_{scr}.

Forsyth [237] gives many practical techniques for using impostors in games. He suggests that some heuristic is used to update the texture coordinates (on more complex shapes containing the object) to reduce parallax errors. Also, when impostors are used for dynamic objects, he suggests a preprocessing technique that determines the largest distance, d, any vertex moves during the entire animation. This distance is divided by the number of time steps in the animation, so that $\Delta = d/\text{frames}$. If an impostor has been used for n frames without updating, then $\Delta * n$ is projected onto the image plane. If this distance is larger than a threshold set by the user, the impostor is updated. Other ideas include updating the objects close to the near plane or the mouse cursor more often. For efficient updating of impostors, he suggests rendering a number of them to subregions of a large texture.

Forsyth also uses prediction in an interesting way. Normally, an impostor is created for a certain frame, and it is only correct for that frame. A number of frames later, the impostor is updated again. If some prediction of camera and animation parameters can be done for the frame in between these generation times, then the average quality of the impostor can be improved. However, using impostors for dynamic objects, especially unpredictable ones such as players, is hard. Often it is best to just render the geometry when an object moves, and switch to impostors when the object is static [237].

8.4 Lens Flare and Bloom

Lens flare is a phenomenon that is caused by the lens of the eye or camera when directed at bright light. It consists of a halo and a ciliary corona. The halo appears because the lens material refracts light of different wavelengths by different amounts, as a prism does. The halo looks like a ring around the light, with its outside edge tinged with red, and its inside with violet. The ciliary corona comes from density fluctuations in the lens, and appears as rays radiating from a point, which may extend beyond the halo [726]. Camera lenses can also create secondary effects when parts of the lens reflect or refract light internally. For example, hexagonal patterns can appear due to the camera's diaphragm blades. Bloom is caused by scattering in the lens and other parts of the eye, creating a glow around the light and dimming contrast elsewhere in the scene. In video production, the video camera captures an image by converting photons to charge using a *Charge-coupled Device* (CCD). Bloom occurs in a video camera when a charge site in the CCD gets saturated and overflows into neighboring sites. As a class, halos, coronae, and bloom are called glare effects.

In practice, what this means is that we associate these effects with brightness. Once thought of as relatively rare image artifacts, they are now routinely added digitally to real photos to enhance their effect. There are limits to the light intensity produced by the computer monitor, so to give the impression of increased brightness in a scene, these glare effects are explicitly rendered. The lens flare effect is now something of a cliché due to its common use. Nonetheless, when skillfully employed, it can give strong visual cues to the viewer; see Plate XII (following page 274).

Figure 8.12 shows a typical lens flare. It is produced by using a set of textures for the glare effects. Each texture is applied to a square that is made to face the viewer, so forming a billboard. The texture is treated as an alpha map that determines how much of the square to blend into the scene. Because it is the square itself that is being displayed, the square can be given a color (typically a pure red, green, or blue) for prismatic effects for the ciliary corona. Where they overlap, these sprites are blended using an additive effect to get other colors. Furthermore, by animating the ciliary corona, we create a sparkle effect [419].

To provide a convincing effect, the lens flare should change with the position of the light source. King [428] creates a set of squares with different textures to represent the lens flare. These are then oriented on a line going from the light source position on screen through the screen's center. When

Figure 8.12. A lens flare and its constituent textures. On the right, a halo and a bloom are shown above, and two sparkle textures below. *(Images from a Microsoft DirectX SDK program.)*

the light is far from the center of the screen, the sprites are small and more transparent, becoming larger and more opaque as the light moves inwards. Maughan [524] varies the brightness of a lens flare by using only accelerator hardware to compute the occlusion of an on-screen area light source.

8.5   Particle Systems

A particle system is a set of separate small objects that are set into motion using some algorithm. Applications include simulating fire, smoke, explosions, water flows, trees, whirling galaxies, and other phenomena. Particle systems are not a form of rendering, but rather a method of animation. The idea is that there are controls for creating, moving, changing, and deleting particles during their lifetimes. Plate XXXV (following page 562) shows an example of particles in action.

There are many articles on the subject of generating and controlling particle systems [459, 536, 647, 648, 766, 793, 794]. What is relevant here is the way the particles are represented. Representations even simpler than billboards are common—namely, points and lines. Each particle can be a single point rendered on the screen. Particles can also be represented by billboards. As mentioned in Section 8.3.2, if the particle is round, then the up vector is irrelevant to its display. In other words, all that is needed is the particle's position to orient it. DirectX supports this by providing a point sprite primitive, thereby eliminating the need to send down an entire quadrilateral for each point. LeGrand [483] discusses implementing particle systems with vertex shaders. Figure 8.13 shows a typical particle system, a firework display.

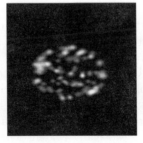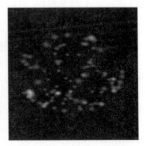

Figure 8.13. Firework using a single screen-aligned, alpha-textured billboard for each particle, varied in size and shade over time *(from a DirectX demonstration program, Microsoft)*.

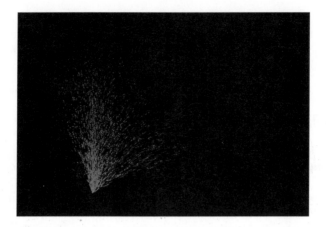

Figure 8.14. Particle system. Each of the 4000 particles in this system is a short line segment that changes intensity over time. *(Images courtesy of Jeff Lander.)*

Another simple technique is to represent a particle by a line segment drawn from the particle's previous location to its current location. An example is shown in Figure 8.14. Axial billboards can be used to display thicker lines.

In addition to animating explosions, waterfalls, froth, and other phenomena, particle systems can also be used for rendering. For example, some trees can be modeled by using particle systems to represent the geometry, with more particles generated and displayed as the viewer comes closer to the model.

8.6 Depth Sprites

If the texture of an impostor is augmented with a depth component, we get a related rendering primitive called a *depth sprite* or a *nailboard* [677]. The texture image is thus an RGB image augmented with a Δ parameter for each pixel, forming an RGBΔ texture. The Δ stores the depth deviation from the depth sprite polygon to the correct depth of the geometry that the depth sprite represents. Because depth sprites contain localized depth information, they are superior to impostors because they can help avoid visibility problems. This is especially evident when the depth sprite polygon penetrates nearby geometry. Such a case is shown in Figure 8.15. If impostors are used, closely located objects must be grouped together and treated as one [677].

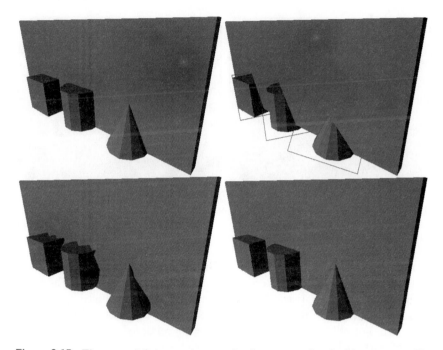

Figure 8.15. The upper left image shows a simple scene rendered with geometry. The upper right image shows what happens if impostors are created and used for the cube, the cylinder, and the cone. The bottom image shows the result when depth sprites are used. The depth sprite in the left image uses two bits for depth deviation, while the one on the right uses eight bits. *(Images courtesy of Gernot Schaufler.)*

When a depth sprite is rendered, the depth of the depth sprite polygon is used as an offset for the Δ-values. For impostors, a single-bit α-value was used at each pixel for transparency. Depth sprites do not need to have a separate alpha value, since one of the Δ-values can be used to represent full transparency. Since depth-difference values are stored in the Δ-components, a small number of bits can be used to store these. Typically, 8 to 16 bits suffice. Schaufler also derives a method for transforming between different spaces and so obtains correct depths in the depth buffer [677]. The nailboard algorithm is primarily a pure software rendering method. Hardware pixel shaders are able to perform this algorithm by varying the z-depth per pixel. Dynamic lighting can also be computed using pixel shaders. See Figure 8.16 for an example. This hardware rendering method is mostly limited to orthographic or near-orthographic views, as the z-depths need to vary uniformly and the sprites must be aligned

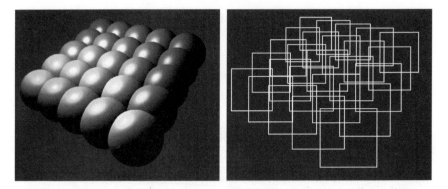

Figure 8.16. Each sphere to the left is rendered as one textured quadrilateral with depth. To the right, the wire frame of the scene is shown. *(Images from a program by NVIDIA Corp.)*

with the view plane (see Section 8.3). Graphics hardware architectures are currently not streamlined for creating and reusing nailboards on the fly.

Related to depth sprites is relief texture mapping introduced by Oliveira et al. [598]. The relief texture is an image with an orthogonal displacement per texel. For efficient rendering, this map is rendered as a standard texture for extremely distant objects, and for closer viewing a prewarp of the image is done before texturing the polygon. For really close views, the micropolygons can be generated. As a preprocess, the map is prewarped, and during rendering, two one-dimensional warps are done. After that follows standard texture mapping. The advantage of this method is that it produces correct parallax effects and real displacements. It is possible that this algorithm will be implemented in hardware in the future.

Shade et al. [697] also describe a depth sprite primitive, where they use warping to account for new viewpoints. They also describe another primitive called a *layered depth image*, which has several depths per pixel. The reason for multiple depths is to avoid the gaps that are created due to deocclusion (i.e., where hidden areas become visible) during the warping. Related techniques are also presented by Schaufler [678] and Meyer and Neyret [544]. To control the sampling rate, a hierarchical representation called the LDI tree was presented by Chang et al. [119].

8.7 Hierarchical Image Caching

Hierarchical image caching is an algorithm that uses impostors arranged in a hierarchy for better performance. This technique was invented independently by Schaufler and Stürzlinger [675] and Shade et al. [696]. The basic idea is to partition the scene into a hierarchy of boxes and create an impostor for each box, and also to hierarchically create impostors for the parents in the partitioning. The impostors are then updated hierarchically. We describe these algorithms briefly in this section.

The scene is partitioned by a BSP tree (see Section 9.1.2) where the dividing planes are parallel to the main axes in order to form axis-aligned boxes. The algorithms are not restricted to the use of axis-aligned boxes—that choice merely simplifies the processing. The algorithms try to construct a partitioning that generates nearly cubic boxes. It is also important when forming the tree to make it balanced, which means that we want approximately the same number of primitives in each pair of boxes. Another goal is to minimize the number of dividing-plane/object intersections [696]. See Section 9.1.2 for information on how to use an axis-aligned BSP tree. There is a threshold that limits the recursion, and in this case, recursion must end before the number of primitives in a box becomes too small. If this number is too small, then the relative overhead to generate the impostor becomes large and the method inefficient. Shade et al. [696] describe a greedy algorithm for making the subdivision. Both algorithms may generate cracks because one single object may be represented by more than one impostor. Cracks can occur when rendering the two images beside each other, because of numerical precision issues at various places. One solution is to make each box in the BSP tree a little larger. [675, 696]. Note that the scene partition tree can also be used for view frustum culling (see Section 9.4).

For each box, an impostor is generated for a certain point of view using the method in Section 8.3.4. User-defined clipping planes can be used to clip the primitives against the faces of the box. This generation starts at the leaves, and the impostors propagate upward in the hierarchy toward the root of the scene partition in order to generate impostors for the parents of the leaves, and so forth on up. The impostor of a parent box is generally created by rendering the impostors of its children. Rerendering an impostor is done only when one or more of its children's impostors need to be updated due to movement—either the texels become magnified, which makes the impostor look unconvincing, or the viewer moves to a location where the error of the approximation becomes too large. So, for small movements of the viewer, a large impostor can, in some cases, be used to render a large portion of the scene, and a considerable speedup may be achieved. Also, when one must rerender an impostor for a parent node, performance may still be improved if only some of its children have to be rerendered and the old impostors for the rest can be reused.

Figure 8.17. On the left, true geometry is used to render the scene, while on the right, hierarchical image caching has been used with a maximum allowed error of 8 pixels. Even with this large amount, it is hard to detect any differences. *(Images courtesy of J. Shade, D. Lischinski, D. Salesin, T. DeRose, and J. Snyder.)*

The rendering of a scene using hierarchical image caching is divided into two steps. First, the objects outside the view frustum are culled using view frustum culling (and their allocated texture memory is released for others to use), and the impostors that have become invalid are rendered and propagated toward the root of the hierarchy. The second step is to render the impostors of the hierarchy that are inside the view frustum. This is done by traversing the tree from back to front in order to avoid transparency problems.

For an extremely large outdoor scene, Shade et al. [696] report a speed-up factor of about 12. The speed-up could be increased by allowing a larger error in the impostor approximation. See Figure 8.17 for an example. The first frame in their rendering, which then included the creation of impostors for all boxes in the scene, took twice as much time as rendering only the geometry.

Normally, the hierarchical image cache only works for static objects, since the subdivision of the scene takes significant time. However, if a depth sprite primitive is available, then dynamic objects can be rendered with depth sprites in order to avoid visibility and penetration problems.

8.7.1   Related Work

Sillion et al. [712] describe a more sophisticated impostor technique suited for urban scenery. Distant geometry is replaced with a texture that is mapped onto a mesh that coarsely follows the geometry it approximates. Decoret et al. [164] present a taxonomy of rendering errors that may occur when impostors are used, and they also introduce a new impostor, called the *Multimesh Impostor* (MMI). The MMI addresses the different errors by using several meshes per impostor, and by using both pregenerated and dynamically updated impostor images. Schaufler [676] also describes a constant-frame-rate algorithm for impostors, which is similar to Funkhouser and Séquin's work [245] presented in Section 9.8.3. Rafferty et al. [640] present a technique that replaces the geometry seen through a portal with an impostor. They also use image warping to give longer lifetimes to the impostors, as does Schaufler [678]. Aliaga and Lastra [17] develop a constant-frame-rate algorithm, where an automatic preprocessing technique creates layered depth images that are used to replace distant geometry during rendering. Wimmer et al. [806] develop new sampling techniques in order to accurately create a new type of primitive called point-based impostors.

Meyer et al. [545] use a hierarchy of *Bidirectional Texture Functions* (BTF) to render trees realistically. A BTF is an impostor of a shaded tree for a given view and light direction. Several such BTFs, evenly located on a sphere, are thus used in a hierarchy to represent the tree. Nine BTFs are combined to reconstruct the tree for a particular view and light direction. At rendering time, they also use a hierarchy of cube maps to compute shadows on the trees.

8.8 Full-Screen Billboarding

A screen-aligned billboard that covers the entire view can be used for a few different effects. One effect is changing the look of an environment by placing the billboard in front of everything else in the scene. For example, to give the feel (if not the real effect) of viewing a scene through night goggles, alpha-blend a green billboard on top of the entire scene [363]. This is expensive in that the entire screen must be filled, but from a programming standpoint it is simpler than modifying the materials of all the objects in the scene. A flash effect can be created by making this foreground billboard increase in brightness and having its opacity value increase over time, then decrease. See Plate XLIII (following page 562). Note that Z-buffering can be disabled in order to accelerate processing during the rendering of a full-screen billboard. A related concept is using the stencil buffer to perform screen dissolves and other video-like effects [443].

Billboards can also be placed behind everything in a scene, to simulate an environment. If the viewer changes direction, the texture on this billboard should be moved accordingly. For example, imagine a sky background for a driving simulator. As the driver turns left, the billboard continues to fill the background. However, if there are clouds in this sky background, they will not move, making the experience unconvincing. By setting the texture to repeat and uniformly modifying the u coordinates at the corners (i.e., adding the same value to each u coordinate), we can make the sky appear to rotate along with the view change. This is a form of texture animation (see Section 5.6).

8.9   Skyboxes

An important principle, introduced in Section 6.1, is that for a given viewpoint and direction there is an incoming radiance. It does not matter how this radiance is computed or at what distance from the eye it is generated; the eye does not detect distance, only color. As discussed in Section 8.2, the QuickTime VR technique immerses the viewer in an environment by sampling and warping an image of the surroundings. This same type of immersion can be performed in hardware using a *skybox*. An environment map represents the incoming radiance for a local area of space. While such maps are typically used for simulating reflections, they can also be used directly to represent the surrounding environment. Spherical and paraboloid environment maps represent curved surfaces and so would be complex to render as surroundings, but cubic maps are ideal for this purpose. An example is shown in Plate XXXVI, following page 562.

Simply put, the surrounding environment is put on the faces of a cube and the cube is rendered centered around the viewpoint. The cube is made to be large enough to enclose all other objects in the scene. It can change size if needed, since the net effect is always the same. This technique is typically used for representing far away objects (such as starfields or the sky) that will not change as the viewer moves. If the application often has the viewer stay in a single location and only change view direction and orientation, it can be profitable to render the entire scene to the six cube faces and simply redisplay these.

For skyboxes to be convincing, the resolution has to be sufficient, i.e., a texel per screen pixel [698]. The formula for the necessary resolution is approximately:

$$textureresolution = \frac{screenresolution}{\tan(fov/2)} \qquad (8.5)$$

where fov is the field of view. This formula can be derived from the fact that the texture of one face of the cube map must cover a field-of-view (horizontally and vertically) of 90 degrees. The seams where the cube faces join should also be as well-hidden as possible. At these edges, the samples from adjoining faces need to affect each other. If cube map data is used, then proper edge clamping is important (and the seams may still be noticeable). One technique to avoid seam problems is to form the cube from six slightly larger squares that overlap and poke through each other at the edges. In this way, the samples from neighboring faces can be copied into each square face's texture and so be properly interpolated. The disadvantage of this technique is that these textures cannot be cleanly reused as a cubic environment map, because of the additional pixel row around the edge.

8.10   Fixed-View Effects

The viewer is not always moving. For example, for some applications, the view is fixed to one location and orientation, and the environment does not move. This is common in some computer games, and also useful for training software and other situations where the user is meant to be limited to certain options. In such situations, the scene itself can be photographed, drawn, or computed in advance. To make this static part of the world more convincing, one can use a depth map associated with it. For example, a still image of a set of fences might be generated using ray tracing, with a z-depth stored per pixel. As a horse (polygonal or image-based) moves through this environment, its depth will be compared to the depth of the stored image. If it passes behind a fence, the fence will appear in front of the horse. The color rectangle and z-depths from the fence image must be sent to the screen as the horse moves through each frame. However, note that only the rectangle where the horse was needs to be repaired, since the rest of the static scene is exactly the same for every frame. Such screen repair techniques are also commonly used in modeling programs and other applications where the user is working from a fixed location for some time.

Such a static scene can be panned, as the scene itself can be made larger than the visible screen. Zooming is also possible, though one difficulty is aliasing problems, as z-depths cannot be filtered. Similarly, each texel in a skybox or QuickTime VR image could also have a depth value associated with it, which would allow it to occlude objects as they move through the environment. Capturing such depth information from a real scene is currently an expensive operation, though straightforward to save for a synthetic rendering. Varying the depth of a polygon fragment in screen space is feasible with a pixel shader. Using stored depths allows the user to rotate the view of an arbitrarily complex static scene that can include dynamic objects.

For complex scenes and shading models, it can be expensive to rerender the entire scene at interactive rates. Guenter et al. [296] describe a system that allows editing local lighting model parameters. It automatically optimizes computations for the current parameter, giving an increase in rendering speed of as much as 95 times. Such techniques are used in modeling and film editing packages to allow real-time manipulation of highly detailed scenes, and in rendering packages such as Piranesi to interactively create non-photorealistic images. Fixed-view techniques for editing global lighting in elaborate scenes are also possible with help from the accelerator. For example, Gershbein et al. [254] implement a system for interactive lighting design that includes BRDF storage and shadow occlusion.

A concept related to the static scene is *golden thread*, or *adaptive refinement* rendering [57]. The idea is that while the viewer and scene is not moving, the computer can produce a better and better image as time goes on. Objects in the scene can be made to look more realistic. Such higher-quality renderings can either be swapped in abruptly or blended in over a series of frames. This technique is particularly useful in CAD and visualization applications. There are many different types of refinement that could be done. One possibility is to use an accumulation buffer to do antialiasing (see Section 4.4.2) and show various accumulated images along the way [564]. Another possibility is to perform slower per-pixel shading (e.g., ray tracing) off screen and then fade-in this improved image.

8.11   Image Processing

Pixel shaders are truly revolutionary, as they provide functionality that was extremely slow or unavailable on previous accelerators. Unlike vertex shaders, such functionality cannot be executed quickly on the CPU. Combined with render to texture, pixel shaders open up a huge world of possibilities. One of the more interesting capabilities that comes from these two features is that a number of image processing operations can be done extremely rapidly. Prior to their introduction, some high-end workstations had implemented the OpenGL 1.2 image processing extensions, but these API calls were not added to consumer level graphics hardware. Now pixel shaders on such hardware can be used to sample a texture and blur it, remap its colors to grayscale or heat signatures, perform edge detection, and many other image-related operations [390, 556, 557]. See Figure 8.18 and Plate XLV (following page 562). Sections 6.9 and 7.2.3 describe how some of these techniques can be used.

Image processing can be performed on a scene first rendered to a texture, or to any image, for that matter. To do so, map the image to a

Figure 8.18. Image processing using pixel shaders. In the upper left, the original image. In the upper right, a blurred image by averaging 16 samples. In the lower left, edge detection by differencing diagonals. In the lower right, the edges are multiplied with a 7-bit version of the original image for an interesting non-photorealistic rendering effect. *(Images courtesy of NVIDIA Corp.)*

screen-aligned quadrilateral, sized so that the image will render onto the screen at a pixel per texel.[4] Now, instead of simply rendering the image as is, use a pixel shader to sample it more than once and combine the samples. For example, say the goal is to take the average of the nine texels forming a 3×3 grid around a given texel and display this blurred result. This could be done by sending nine texture coordinate pairs down with the quadrilateral. Each pair would be offset by one texel in screen x or y as needed. These nine texture samples would then be weighted and summed together by the pixel shader, which would then output the blurred result to the pixel. Nine samples is unnecessary, however. By using bilinear filtering of a texture, a single texture access can retrieve the weighted sum of up to four neighboring texels, so the 3×3 grid could be sampled with just four texture accesses.

James [390] shows how a variety of animated effects can be done by modifying textures from frame to frame. That is, a texture image can be modified by a pixel shader and the result rendered on a surface. Then in the next frame, the result is modified again by the same pixel shader and rendered. Using one- and two-dimensional cellular automata rules, effects such as fire, smoke, and interactive rippling water can be created on a surface. James is even able to run Conway's game of *Life* as a series of pixel shader passes.

8.12   Volume Rendering

Volume rendering is concerned with rendering data that is represented by voxels. "Voxel" is short for "volumetric pixel," and each voxel represents a regular volume of space. For example, creating clinical diagnostic images (such as CT or MRI) of a person's head may create a data set of $256 \times 256 \times 256$ voxels, each location holding one or more values. This can be seen as a three-dimensional image, and so volume rendering is a type of IBR. Voxel rendering can be used to show a solid model, or to make various materials (e.g., the skin and skull) partially or fully transparent. Cutting planes can be used to show only parts of the model. In addition to its use for visualization in such diverse fields as medicine and oil prospecting, volume rendering can also produce photorealistic imagery. For example, Fedkiw et al. [228] simulate the appearance and movement of smoke by using volume rendering techniques.

---

[4]Duttweiler [196] notes that care must be taken to have this work properly under DirectX.

There are a wide variety of voxel rendering techniques. Lacroute and Levoy [450] present a method of treating the voxel data as a set of two-dimensional image slices, then shearing and warping these and compositing the resulting images. A method that renders a surface or volume in a significantly different fashion is that of *splatting* [475, 800]. Each voxel is treated as a volume of space that is represented by an alpha-blended circular object, called a *splat*, that drops off in opacity at its fringe. The idea is that a surface or volume can be represented by screen-aligned geometry or sprites which, when rendered together, form a surface. Implicit surface techniques are another way in which voxel samples can form polygonal surfaces [89]. See Section 12.4.

Another method for volume rendering makes direct use of the texturing and compositing capabilities of graphics hardware by rendering volume slices directly as textured quadrilaterals [536]. OpenGL Volumizer [603] is an API that uses this technique for fast volume rendering. See Figure 8.19. A related concept is *volumetric textures*, which are volume descriptions that are represented by layers of two-dimensional, semitrans-

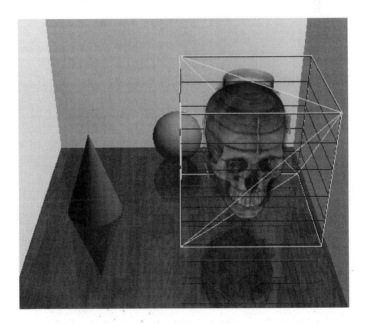

Figure 8.19. Volume visualization mixed with traditional three-dimensional techniques, done with OpenGL Volumizer. Note the reflection of the voxel-based skull in the floor. *(Image courtesy of Robert Grzeszczuk, SGI.)*

parent textures [544]. Like two-dimensional textures, volumetric textures can be made to flow along the surface. They are good for complex surfaces, such as landscape details, organic tissues, and fuzzy or hairy objects [487]. See Plates XXXVIII and XLIX following page 562. Related work includes Kautz and Seidel's image-based approach for rendering displacement maps [411].

Further Reading and Resources

For an overview of early image-based rendering research, see Lengyel's article [486], also available on the web. The SIGGRAPH Advanced OpenGL course notes [536] provide more details on the use of sprites and billboards. The Virtual Terrain Project [771] has solid summaries of research and resources for modeling and rendering many types of natural objects and phenomena, including clouds and trees.

Chapter 9
Acceleration Algorithms

"Now here, you see, it takes all the running you can do to keep in the same place. If you want to get somewhere else, you must run at least twice as fast as that!"
–Lewis Carroll

One of the great myths concerning computers is that one day we will have enough processing power. Even in a relatively simple application like word processing, we find that additional power can be applied to all sorts of things, such as on-the-fly spell and grammar checking, antialiased text display, automated voice recognition and dictation, etc.

In real-time rendering, we have at least three performance goals: more frames per second, higher resolution, and more (and more realistic) objects in the scene. A speed of 60–85 frames per second is generally considered enough, and perhaps 1600×1200 is enough resolution for a while, but there is no real upper limit on scene complexity. The rendering of a Boeing-777 would include $132,500$ unique parts and over $3,000,000$ fasteners, which would yield a polygonal model with over $500,000,000$ polygons [149]. Our conclusion: Acceleration algorithms will always be needed.

It should also be emphasized that a high enough frame rate, and a steady (unvarying) frame rate, are both important. Smooth and continuous motion is preferable, and too low a frame rate is experienced as jerky motion. As an example, 24 frames per second is used in movie theaters, and this is normally not considered as jerky. However, this depends on several factors, including that theaters are dark and the temporal response of the eye is less sensitive to flicker in the dark. Also, movie projectors change the image at 24 fps but reduce flickering by redisplaying each image 2–4 times before displaying the next image. Investigations [353] show that if the frame rate is lower than the update frequency of the monitor (e.g., 85 Hz), then the displayed images appear with unnatural motion. Also, if frame rate drops from 85 Hz to, say, 30 Hz, then this is also experienced as jerky. Therefore, the ideal situation is to render images at the same frame rate as the monitor frequency, and that the rate should never vary [807].

In this chapter, a smörgåsbord of algorithms for accelerating computer graphics rendering will be presented and explained. The core of many such algorithms is based on *spatial data structures*, which are described in the next section. Based on that knowledge, we then continue with *culling techniques*. These are algorithms that try to find out which objects are at all visible and need to be treated further. *Level of detail* techniques reduce the complexity of rendering the remaining objects. Finally, systems for rendering very large models and point rendering are briefly discussed.

9.1   Spatial Data Structures

A spatial data structure is one that organizes geometry in some n-dimensional space. Only two- and three-dimensional structures are used in this book, but the concepts can often easily be extended to higher dimensions. These data structures can be used to accelerate queries about whether geometric entities overlap. Such queries are used in a wide variety of operations such as culling algorithms, during intersection testing and ray tracing, and for collision detection.

The organization of spatial data structures is usually hierarchical. This means, loosely speaking, that the topmost level encloses the level below it, which encloses the level below that level, and so on. Thus, the structure is nested and of recursive nature. The main reason for using a hierarchy is that different types of queries get significantly faster, typically an improvement from $O(n)$ to $O(\log n)$. It should also be noted that the construction of most spatial data structures is expensive, and is usually done as a preprocess. Incremental updates are possible in real time, though.

Some different types of spatial data structures are *Bounding Volume Hierarchies* (BVHs), variants of BSP trees, and octrees. BSP trees and octrees are data structures based on *space subdivision*. This means that the entire space of the scene is subdivided and encoded in the data structure. For example, the union of the space of all the leaf nodes is equal to the entire space of the scene (and the leaf nodes do not overlap, with the exception of loose octrees). Both variants of BSP trees are *irregular*, which loosely means that the space can be subdivided more arbitrarily. The octree is *regular*, meaning that space is split in a uniform fashion. Though more restrictive, this uniformity can often be a source of efficiency.

A bounding volume hierarchy, on the other hand, is not a space subdivision structure. Rather, it encloses the regions of the space surrounding geometrical objects, and thus the BVH need not enclose all space. In addition to improving efficiency of queries, BVHs are also commonly used to describe model relationships and for controlling hierarchical animation.

BVHs, BSP trees, and octrees are all described in the following sections, together with the scene graph, which is a higher level data structure.

9.1.1 Bounding Volume Hierarchies

A *Bounding Volume* (BV) is a volume that encloses a set of objects. The point of a BV is that it should be a much simpler geometrical shape than the contained objects, so that doing tests using a BV can be done much faster than using the objects themselves. Examples of BVs are spheres, *Axis-aligned Bounding Boxes* (AABBs), *Oriented Bounding Boxes* (OBBs), and k-DOPs (see Section 13.2 for definitions). A BV does not contribute visually to the rendered image. Instead, it is commonly used to speed up rendering and different computations and queries.

For real-time rendering of three-dimensional scenes, the bounding volume hierarchy (BVH) is probably the most common spatial data structure. For example, the BVH is often used for hierarchical view frustum culling (see Section 9.4). The scene is organized in a hierarchical tree structure, consisting of a root, internal nodes, and leaves. The topmost node is the *root*, which has no parents. A *leaf node* holds actual geometry to be rendered, and it does not have any children. In contrast, an *internal node* has pointers to its children. The root is thus an internal node, unless it is the only node in the tree. Each node, including leaf nodes, in the tree has a bounding volume that encloses the geometry in its entire subtree—thus the name *bounding volume hierarchy*. This means that the root has a BV that contains the entire scene. An example of a BVH is shown in Figure 9.1.

The underlying structure of a BVH is a tree, and in the field of computer science, the literature on tree data structures is vast. Here, only a few important results will be mentioned. For more information, see, for example, the book *Introduction to Algorithms* by Cormen et al. [145].

Consider a k-ary tree, that is, a tree where each internal node has k children. A tree with only one node (the root) is said to be of height 0. A leaf node of the root is at height 1, and so on. A balanced tree is a tree in which all leaf nodes either are at height h or $h - 1$. In general, the height, h, of a balanced tree is $\lfloor \log_k n \rfloor$, where n is the total number of nodes (internal and leaves) in the tree.

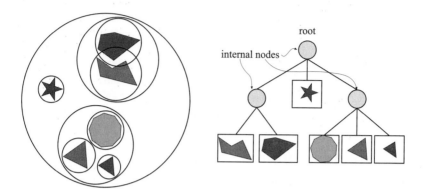

Figure 9.1. The left part shows a simple scene with six objects, each enclosed by a bounding sphere. The bounding spheres are then grouped together into larger bounding spheres until all objects are enclosed by the largest sphere. The right part shows the bounding volume hierarchy (tree) that is used to represent the object hierarchy on the left. The BV of the root encloses all objects in the scene.

A full tree is one where all leaf nodes are at the same height, h. Some properties of (only) full trees follow. The total number of nodes can be computed as a geometric sum :

$$n = k^0 + k^1 + \ldots k^{h-1} + k^h = \frac{k^{h+1} - 1}{k - 1}. \tag{9.1}$$

Thus, the number of leaf nodes, l, is $l = k^h$, and the number of internal nodes, i, is $i = n - l = \frac{k^h - 1}{k - 1}$. Assuming only the number of leaf nodes, l, is known, then the total number of nodes is $n = i + l = \frac{kl - 1}{k - 1}$. For a binary tree, where $k = 2$, this gives $n = 2l - 1$. Note that a higher k gives a tree with a lower height, which means that it takes fewer steps to traverse the tree, but it also requires more work at each node. The binary tree is often the simplest choice, and one that gives good performance. However, there is evidence that a higher k (e.g., $k = 4$ or $k = 8$) gives slightly better performance for some applications [472]. Using $k = 2$, $k = 4$, or $k = 8$ makes it simple to construct trees; just subdivide along the longest axis for $k = 2$, and for the two longest axes for $k = 4$, and for all axes for $k = 8$. It is much more difficult to form trees for other values of k.

BVHs are also excellent for performing various queries. For example, assume that a ray should be intersected with a scene, and the first intersection found should be returned. To use a BVH for this, testing starts at the root. If the ray misses its BV, then the ray misses all geometry contained in the BVH. Otherwise, testing continues recursively, that is, the BVs of the children of the root are tested. As soon as a BV is missed by the ray, testing can terminate on that subtree of the BVH. If the ray hits a leaf node's BV, then the ray is tested against the geometry at this node. The performance gains come partly from the fact that testing the ray with the BV is fast. This is why simple objects such as spheres and boxes are used as BVs. The other reason is the nesting of BVs, which allows us to avoid testing large regions of space due to early termination in the tree.

Often the closest intersection, not the first found, is what is desired. Note that unlike finding the first intersection, testing cannot stop once an intersection is discovered. The only additional data needed is the distance and identity of the closest object found while traversing the tree. The current closest distance is also used to cull the tree during traversal. If a BV is intersected, but its distance is beyond the closest distance found so far, then the BV can be discarded.

BVHs can be used for dynamic scenes as well [645]. When an object contained in a BV has moved, simply check whether it is still contained in its parent's BV. If it is, then the BVH is still valid. Otherwise, the object node is removed and the parent's BV recomputed. The node is then recursively inserted back into the tree from the root. Another method is to grow the parent's BV to hold the child recursively up the tree as needed. With either method, the tree can become unbalanced and inefficient as more and more edits are performed.

To create a BVH, one must first be able to compute a tight BV around a set of objects. This topic is treated in Section 13.3 on page 564. Then, the actual hierarchy of BVs must be created. Strategies for this are treated in Section 14.3.1 on page 14.3.1.

9.1.2 BSP Trees

Binary Space Partitioning trees, or BSP trees for short, exist as two noticeably different variants in computer graphics, which we call *axis-aligned* and *polygon-aligned*. The trees are created by using a plane to divide the space in two, and then sorting the geometry into these two spaces. This division is done recursively. One interesting property that these trees have is that if the trees are traversed in a certain way, then the geometrical contents of the tree can be sorted from any point of view (approximately for axis-aligned and exactly for polygon-aligned). This is in contrast to BVHs, which do not include any type of sorting.

Axis-Aligned BSP Trees

An axis-aligned BSP tree[1] is created as follows. First, the whole scene is
enclosed in an *Axis-aligned Bounding Box* (AABB). The idea is then to
recursively subdivide that box into smaller boxes. Now, consider a box at
any recursion level. One axis of the box is chosen, and a perpendicular
plane is generated that divides the space into two boxes. Some schemes
fix this partitioning plane so that it divides the box exactly in half; others
allow the plane to vary in position. An object intersecting the plane either
is stored at this level, becoming a member of both subsets, or is truly split
by the plane into two separate objects. Each subset is now in a smaller
box, and this plane-splitting procedure is repeated, subdividing each AABB
recursively until some criterion is fulfilled to halt the process. This criterion
is often that a user-defined maximum depth of the tree is reached or when
the number of primitives in a box is below a user-defined threshold. See
Figure 9.2 for an example of an axis-aligned BSP tree.

One strategy for splitting a box is to cycle through the axes. That is, at
the root, the box is always split along the x axis, its children are split along
the y, the grandchildren along z, then the cycle repeats. BSP trees using

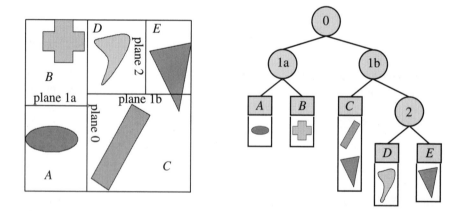

Figure 9.2. Axis-aligned BSP tree. In this example, the space partitions are allowed to
be anywhere along the axis, not just at its midpoint. The spatial volumes formed are
labeled A through E. The tree on the right shows the underlying BSP data structure.
Each leaf node represents an area, with that area's contents shown beneath it. Note
that the triangle is in the object list for two areas, C and E, because it overlaps both.

---

[1]A BSP tree that is not polygon-aligned may split the space in any way it wishes.
However, we focus on axis-aligned BSP trees here because this is the most commonly
used variant, and the most practical.

this strategy are sometimes called k-d trees [670]. Another strategy is to find the largest side of the box, and split the box along this direction. For example, say the box is largest in the y-direction, then splitting occurs at some plane, $y = d$, where d is a scalar constant. To get a balanced tree, d should be set so that there are equally many primitives on both side of the plane. This is a costly computation, though, so instead, one often chooses a value at the average or median center point of the primitives.

Rough front-to-back sorting is an example of how axis-aligned BSP trees can be used. This is useful for occlusion culling algorithms (see Section 9.7 and 15.3.5). Assume that a node called N is currently traversed. N is the root at the start of traversal. The plane of N is examined, and tree traversal continues recursively on the side of the plane where the viewer is located. Thus, it is only when the entire half of the tree has been traversed that we can start to traverse the other side. Traversal of the closer part of the tree can end when a box of a node is entirely behind the viewer (more precisely: behind the near plane). This does not give exact front-to-back sorting since the contents of the leaf nodes are not sorted and because objects may be in many nodes of the tree. However, it gives a rough sorting, which often is useful. By starting traversal on the other side of a node's plane as compared to where the viewer is, rough back-to-front sorting can be obtained. This is useful for transparency sorting (see Section 4.5). This traversal can also be used to test a ray against the scene geometry. The viewer's location is simply exchanged for the ray's origin. Another use is in view frustum culling (Section 9.4).

Polygon-Aligned BSP Trees

The other type of BSP tree is the polygon-aligned form [2, 242, 243, 281]. In this scheme, a polygon is chosen as the divider, splitting space into two halves. That is, at the root, a polygon is selected. The plane in which the polygon lies is used to divide the rest of the polygons in the scene into two sets. Any polygon that is intersected by the dividing plane is broken into two separate pieces along the intersection line. Now in each half-space of the dividing plane another polygon is chosen as a divider, which divides only the polygons in its half-space. This is done recursively until all polygons are in the BSP tree. Creating an efficient polygon-aligned BSP tree is a time-consuming process, and such trees are normally computed once and stored for reuse. This type of BSP tree is shown in Figure 9.3.

It is generally best to form a balanced tree, i.e., one where the depth of each leaf node is the same or at most off by one. A totally unbalanced tree is inefficient. An example would be a tree where each selected splitting polygon divides the space into one empty space, and the other with the

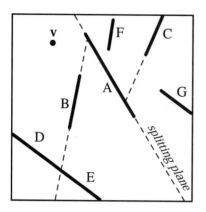
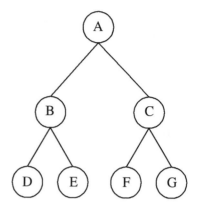

Figure 9.3. Polygon-aligned BSP tree. Polygons A through G are shown from above. Space is first split by polygon A, then each half-space is split separately by B and C. The splitting plane formed by polygon B intersects the polygon in the lower left corner, splitting it into separate polygons D and E. The BSP tree formed is shown on the right.

rest of the polygons. There are many different strategies for finding a polygon used for splitting that gives a good tree. One simple strategy is the *least-crossed criterion* [242]. First, a number of candidate polygons are randomly selected. The polygon whose plane is crossed the least number of times by other polygons is used. For a test scene of 1,000 polygons, James provides empirical evidence that only five polygons need to be tested per split operation in order to get a good tree [389]. Testing more than five polygons did not improve the results. This is also what Fuchs et al. [242] originally used. However, this number should probably be increased with the number of polygons in the scene. James gives a review of a wide range of other strategies as well as providing a new one of his own.

This second type of BSP tree has some useful properties. One is that, for a given view, the structure can be traversed strictly from back to front (or front to back). Determine on which side of the root plane the camera is located (a simple point/plane comparison). The polygon set on the far side of this plane is then beyond the near side's set. Now with the far side's set, take the next level's dividing plane and determine which side the camera is on. The subset where the camera is located is again beyond the nearer subset, and the subset on the far side is the subset farthest away from the camera. By continuing recursively, this process establishes a strict back-to-front order, and a *painter's algorithm* can be used to render the scene. The painter's algorithm does not need a Z-buffer; if all objects are drawn in a back-to-front order, each closer object is drawn in front of whatever is behind it, and so no z-depth comparisons are required.

For example, consider what is seen by a viewer **v** in Figure 9.3. Regardless of the viewing direction and frustum, **v** is to the left of the splitting plane formed by A. So C, F, and G are behind B, D, and E. Comparing **v** to the splitting plane of C, we find G to be on the opposite side of this plane, so it is displayed first. A test of B's plane determines that E should be displayed before D. The back-to-front order is then G, C, F, A, E, B, D. Note that this order does not guarantee that one object is closer than another, rather it provides a strict occlusion order, a subtle difference. For example, polygon F is closer to **v** than polygon E, even though it is further back in occlusion order.

Other uses for polygon-aligned BSP trees are intersection testing (see Chapter 13), and collision detection (see Section 14.2).

9.1.3   Octrees

The octree is similar to the axis-aligned BSP tree. A box is split simultaneously along all three axes, and the split point must be the center of the box. This creates eight new boxes—hence the name octree. This makes the structure regular, and some queries may become more efficient because of this.

An octree is constructed by enclosing the entire scene in a minimal axis-aligned box. The rest of the procedure is recursive in nature, and stops recursion when a stopping criterion is fulfilled. These criteria can include that a maximum number of recursion level has been reached, or that there is fewer than a threshold number of primitives in a box [669, 670]. If recursion is stopped, the algorithm binds the primitives to the box and terminates the recursion. Otherwise, it subdivides the box along its main axes using three planes, thereby forming eight equal-sized boxes. Each new box is tested and possibly subdivided again into $2 \times 2 \times 2$ smaller boxes. This is illustrated in two dimensions, where the data structure is called a *quadtree*, in Figure 9.4. Octrees can be used in the same manner as axis-aligned BSP trees, and thus, handle the same type of queries. They are also used in occlusion culling algorithms (see Section 9.7.5).

In the above description, objects are always stored in leaf nodes; therefore, certain objects have to be stored in more than one leaf node. Another option is to place the object in the box that is the smallest that contains the entire object. For example, the star-shaped object in the figure should be placed in the upper right box in the second illustration from the left.

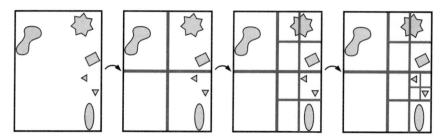

Figure 9.4. The construction of a quadtree (which is the two-dimensional version of an octree). The construction starts from the left by enclosing all objects in a bounding box. Then the boxes are recursively divided into four equal-sized boxes until each box (in this case) is empty or contains one object.

This has a significant disadvantage in that a (small) object that, for example, is located at the center of the octree will be placed in the topmost (largest) node. This is not efficient, since a tiny object may be bounded by a box that encloses the entire scene. One solution is to split the objects, but that introduces more primitives. Another is to put a pointer to the object in each leaf box it is in, losing efficiency and making octree editing more difficult. Ulrich presents a third solution, *loose octrees* [760].

The basic idea of loose octrees is the same as for ordinary octrees, but the choice of the size of each box is relaxed. If the side length of an ordinary box is l, then kl is used instead, where $k > 1$. This is illustrated for $k = 1.5$, and compared to an ordinary octree in Figure 9.5. Note that the boxes'

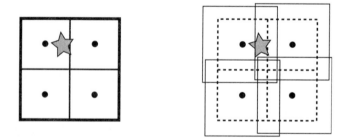

Figure 9.5. An ordinary octree compared to a loose octree. The black circles indicate the center points of the boxes (in the first subdivision). To the left, the star pierces through one splitting plane of the ordinary octree. Thus, one choice is to put the star in the largest box (that of the root). To the right, a loose octree with $k = 1.5$ (that is, boxes are 50% larger) is shown. The boxes are slightly displaced so that they can be discerned. The star can now be placed fully in the upper left box.

center points are the same. By using larger boxes, the number of objects that cross a splitting plane is reduced, so that the object can be placed deeper down in the octree. An object is always inserted into only one octree node, so deletion from the octree is trivial. Some advantages accrue by using $k = 2$. First, insertion and deletion of objects is $O(1)$. Knowing the object's size means immediately knowing the level of the octree it can successfully be inserted in, fully fitting into one loose box.[2] The object's centroid determines which loose octree box to put it in. Because of these properties, this structure lends itself well to bounding dynamic objects, at the expense of some efficiency and the loss of a strong sort order when traversing the structure. Also, often an object moves only slightly from frame to frame, so that the previous box still is valid the next frame. Therefore, only a fraction of the objects in the octrees need updating each frame.

9.1.4 Scene Graphs

BVHs, BSP trees, and octrees all use some sort of tree as its basic data structure; it is in how they partition the space and store the geometry that they differ. They also store geometrical objects, and nothing else, in a hierarchical fashion. However, rendering a three-dimensional scene is so much more than just geometry. The *scene graph* is a higher level tree structure that is augmented with textures, transforms, levels-of-detail, render states (material properties, for example), light sources, and whatever else is found suitable. It is represented by a tree, and this tree is traversed in depth-first order to render the scene. For example, a light source can be put at an internal node, which affects only the contents of its subtree. Another example is when a texture is encountered in the tree. The texture can similarly be applied to all the geometry in that node's subtree. See also Figure 9.32 on page 396 on how different levels of detail can be supported in a scene graph. In a sense, every graphics application has some form of a scene graph, even if the graph is just a root node with a set of children to display.

A node in the scene graph often has a *Bounding Volume* (BV), and is thus quite similar to a BVH. A leaf in the scene graph stores geometry. However, one often allows this geometry to be encoded in any spatial data structure that is desired. So, a leaf may hold an entire BSP tree that stores the geometry of, say, a car.

---

[2]In practice it is sometimes possible to push the object to a deeper box in the octree. Also, if $k < 2$, the object may have to be pushed up the tree if it does not fit.

Without motion, real-time graphics is pretty meaningless. One way of animating objects is to put transforms in internal nodes in the tree. Scene graph implementations then transform the entire contents of that node's subtree with that transform. Since a transform can be put in any internal node, hierarchical animation can be done. For example, the wheels of a car can spin, and the steering wheel can be used to turn the spinning wheels, and the car itself can move forward.

When several nodes may point to the same child node, the tree structure is called a *Directed Acyclic Graph* (DAG) [145]. The term *acyclic* means that it must not contain any loops or cycles. By *directed*, we mean that as two nodes are connected by an edge, they are also connected in a certain order, e.g., from parent to child. Scene graphs are often DAGs because they allow for instantiation, i.e., when we want to make several copies (instances) of an object without replicating its geometry. An example is shown in Figure 9.6, where two internal nodes have different transforms applied to their subtrees. It is often only the leaf nodes, where most object data is located, that are shared. This simplifies handling of the scene graph, and the expense of an additional set of internal nodes is minimal.

When objects are to move in the scene, the scene graph has to be updated. This can be done with a recursive call on the tree structure. Transforms are updated on the way from the root toward the leaves. The matrices are multiplied in this traversal and stored in relevant nodes. However, when transforms have been updated, the BVs are obsolete. There-

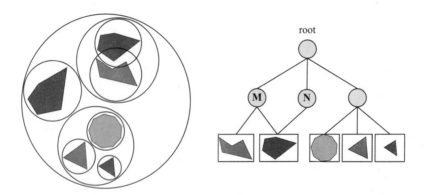

Figure 9.6. A scene graph with different transforms **M** and **N** applied to internal nodes, and their respective subtrees. Note that these two internal nodes also point to the same object, but since they have different transforms, two different objects appear (one is rotated and scaled).

fore, the BVs are updated on the way back from the leaves toward the root. A too-relaxed tree structure complicate these tasks enormously, and so DAGs are often avoided, or a limited form of DAGs are used, where only the leaf nodes are shared. See Eberly's book [199] for more information on this topic.

It should also be noted that more than one scene graph can be used for the same scene. This is the idea of *spatialization*, in which the user's scene graph is augmented with a separate scene graph created for a different task, e.g., faster culling and picking. The leaf nodes, where most models are located, are shared, so the expense of an additional set of internal nodes is minimal.

9.2 Culling Techniques

To *cull* means to "remove from a flock," and in the context of computer graphics, this is exactly what *culling techniques* do. The flock is the whole scene that we want to render, and the removal is limited to those portions of the scene that are not considered to contribute to the final image. The rest of the scene is sent through the rendering pipeline. Thus, the term *visibility culling* is also often used in the context of rendering. However, culling can also be done for other parts of a program. Examples include collision detection (by doing less accurate computations for invisible objects), physics computations, and AI. Here, only culling techniques related to rendering will be presented. Examples of such techniques are backface culling, view frustum culling, and occlusion culling. These are illustrated in Figure 9.7. Backface culling eliminates polygons facing away from the viewer. This is a simple technique that operates on only a single polygon at a time. View frustum culling eliminates groups of polygons outside the view frustum. As such, it is a little more complex. Occlusion culling eliminates objects hidden by groups of other objects. It is the most complex culling technique, as it requires an object or group of objects to gather and use information about other objects' locations.

The actual culling can theoretically take place at any stage of the rendering pipeline, and for some occlusion culling algorithms, it can even be precomputed. For culling algorithms that are implemented in hardware, we can sometimes only enable/disable or set some parameters for the culling function. For full control, the programmer can implement the algorithm in the application stage (on the CPU). Assuming the bottleneck is not on the

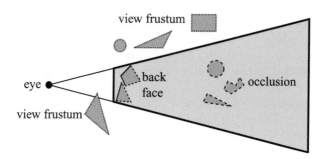

Figure 9.7. Different culling techniques. Culled geometry is dashed. *(Illustration after Cohen-Or et al. [135].)*

CPU, the fastest polygon to render is the one never sent down the accelerator's pipeline. Culling is often achieved by using geometric calculations but is in no way limited to these. For example, an algorithm may also use the contents of the frame buffer.

The ideal culling algorithm would send only the *Exact Visible Set* (EVS) of primitives through the pipeline. In this book, the EVS is defined as all primitives that are partially or fully visible. One such data structure, that allows for ideal culling, is the *aspect graph*, from which the EVS can be extracted given any point of view [256]. Creating such data structures is possible in theory, but not really in practice, since worst-time complexity can be as bad as $O(n^9)$ [135]. Instead, practical algorithms attempt to find a set, called the *Potentially Visible Set* (PVS), that is a prediction of the EVS. If the PVS fully includes the EVS, so that only invisible geometry is discarded, the PVS is said to be *conservative*. A PVS may also be *approximate*, in which the EVS is not fully included. This type of PVS may therefore generate incorrect images. The goal is to make these errors as small as possible. Since a conservative PVS always generates correct images, it is considered more useful. By overestimating or approximating the EVS, the idea is that the PVS can be computed much faster. The difficulty lies in how these estimations should be done to gain overall performance. For example, an algorithm may treat geometry at different granularities, i.e., polygons, whole objects, or groups of objects. When a PVS has been found, it is rendered using the Z-buffer, which resolves the final visibility [135].

In the following sections, we treat backface and clustered backface culling, hierarchical view frustum culling, portal culling, detail culling, and occlusion culling.

9.3 Backface and Clustered Backface Culling

Imagine that you are looking at an opaque sphere in a scene. Approximately half of the sphere will not be visible.[3] The obvious conclusion from this observation is that what is invisible need not be rendered since it does not contribute to the image. Therefore, the back side of the sphere need not be processed, and that is the idea of backface culling. Backface culling can also be done for whole groups at a time. This is then called clustered backface culling.

9.3.1 Backface Culling

All backfacing polygons that are part of an opaque object can be culled away from further processing. A consistently oriented polygon (see Section 11.3) is backfacing if the projected polygon is oriented in, say, a counterclockwise fashion in screen space. This test can be implemented by computing the normal of the projected polygon in two-dimensional screen space: $\mathbf{n} = (\mathbf{v}_1 - \mathbf{v}_0) \times (\mathbf{v}_2 - \mathbf{v}_0)$. This normal will either be $(0,0,a)$ or $(0,0,-a)$, where $a > 0$. If the negative z-axis is pointing into the screen, the first result indicates a frontfacing polygon. This test can also be formulated as a computation of the signed area of the polygon (see Section A.5.4). Either culling test can be implemented immediately after the screen-mapping procedure has taken place (in the geometry stage). Backface culling decreases the load on the rasterizer since we do not have to scan convert the backfacing polygons. But the load on the geometry stage might increase because the backface computations are done there.

Another way to determine whether a polygon is backfacing is to create a vector from an arbitrary point on the plane in which the polygon lies (one of the vertices is the simplest choice) to the viewer's position.[4] Compute the dot product of this vector and the polygon's normal. A negative dot product means that the angle between the two vectors is greater than $\pi/2$ radians, so the polygon is not facing the viewer. This test is equivalent to computing the signed distance from the viewer's position to the plane of the polygon (see Section A.5.2). If the sign is positive, the polygon is frontfacing. Note that the distance is obtained only if the normal is

---

[3]For orthographic viewing, about 50 percent is not visible. For perspective viewing, the percentage of backfaces increases to more than 50 percent as the viewer moves closer to the object.

[4]For orthographic projections, the vector to the eye position is replaced with the negative view direction, which is constant for the scene.

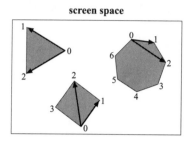 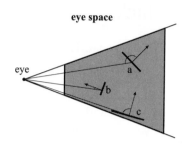

Figure 9.8. Two different tests for determining whether a polygon is backfacing. The left figure shows how the test is done in screen space. The triangle and the quadrilateral are frontfacing, while the seven-sided polygon is backfacing and can be omitted from rasterization. The right figure shows how the backface test is done in eye space. Polygon A is backfacing, while B and C are frontfacing.

normalized, but this is unimportant here, as only the sign is of interest. This test can be performed after the model transform (into world space) or after the model and view transforms (into eye space), which is a bit earlier in the geometry stage than with the screen-space method. These culling techniques are illustrated in Figure 9.8.

In the article "Backface Culling Snags" [76], Blinn points out that these two tests are geometrically the same. Both compute the dot product between the normal and the vector from a point on the polygon to the eye. In the test that is done in screen space, the eye has been transformed to $(0, 0, \infty)$, and the dot product is thus only the z-component of the polygon vector in screen-space. In theory, what differentiates these tests is the space where the tests are computed—nothing else. In practice, the screen space test is often safer, because edge-on polygons that appear to face slightly backward in eye space can become slightly forward in screen space. This happens because the eye-space coordinates get rounded off to screen-space integer pixel or subpixel coordinates.

Using an API such as OpenGL or DirectX, backface culling is normally controlled with a few functions that either enable backface or frontface culling or disable all culling. Note also that the objects need not be closed (solid) in order to take advantage of backface culling. It suffices to know that only one side of a polygon will be seen. This is often the case for buildings, where wall polygons are visible only from one side. Also, be aware that a mirroring transform (i.e., a negative scaling operation) turns backfacing polygons into frontfacing ones and vice versa [76] (see Section 3.1.3).

9.3.2 Clustered Backface Culling

While backface culling is a simple technique for avoiding the rasterizing of many polygons without due cause, it would be even faster if the CPU could decide with a single test if a whole set of polygons should be sent through the entire pipeline or not. Such techniques are called *clustered backface culling* algorithms. The basic concept that many such algorithms use is the *normal cone* [706]. Processing is made faster by dealing with a set of primitives. This can, for example, be a triangle mesh or region of a parametric surface. For each such set, a truncated cone is created that contains all the normal directions of the set, and all the points of the set. See Figure 9.9 for an example. As can be seen, a cone is defined by a normal, $\mathbf{n}$, and half-angle, α, and an anchor point, $\mathbf{a}$, and some offset distances along the normal that truncates the cone. In the right part of Figure 9.9, a cross section of a normal cone is shown. Shirman and Abi-Ezzi [706] prove that if the viewer is located in the frontfacing cone, then all faces in the cone are frontfacing, and similarly for the backfacing cone. Assuming the location of the viewer is $\mathbf{e}$, then $\mathbf{e}$ is in the frontfacing region if:

$$\mathbf{n} \cdot \left(\frac{\mathbf{e} - \mathbf{f}}{||\mathbf{e} - \mathbf{f}||} \right) \geq \cos(\pi/2 - \alpha) = \sin(\alpha). \tag{9.2}$$

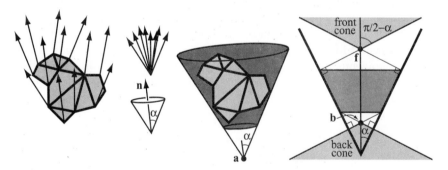

Figure 9.9. Left: A set of polygons and their normals. Middle-left: The normals are collected (top), and a minimal cone (bottom), defined by one normal $\mathbf{n}$, and a half-angle, α, is constructed. Middle-right: The cone is anchored at a point $\mathbf{a}$, and truncated so that it also contains all points on the polygons. Right: A cross section of a truncated cone. The light gray region on the top is the frontfacing cone, and the light gray region at the bottom is the backfacing cone. The points $\mathbf{f}$ and $\mathbf{b}$ are respectively the apexes of the front and backfacing cones.

This means that if the test above is true, then all polygons in the cone are frontfacing. Similarly, the entire set of polygons in the cone are backfacing with respect to the viewer if:

$$-\mathbf{n} \cdot \left(\frac{\mathbf{e} - \mathbf{b}}{||\mathbf{e} - \mathbf{b}||} \right) \geq \cos(\pi/2 - \alpha) = \sin(\alpha). \qquad (9.3)$$

Uses of normal cones include clustered backface culling, and silhouette extraction [706]. Note that backface culling can be used to avoid lighting computations on surfaces facing away from a light source.

Zhang and Hoff [834] present a simpler method in which the space of the normals of an object is divided into small frustums that are called clusters. The frustums emanate from the center of a cube and extend to uniformly subdivided squares on the sides of the cube. In a preprocessing stage, each polygon is put into the cluster where its normal lies. Thus, each cluster holds a set of polygons with similar normals. When a frame is rendered, the clusters that are backfacing for a certain object are first determined. The remaining clusters are then rendered. For parallel projection, we can cull a cluster if all four rays through the cluster's frustum corners are backfacing with respect to the view direction. For perspective projection, the field of view is used to trim back the number of normals considered backfacing, since positional information matters. Figure 9.10 illustrates how this is done. Since the clusters do not include any positional information (as did the normal cones), this test makes a conservative estimate of how much can be culled. This means that we sometimes determine a cluster to be frontfacing, when in fact, some of its contents may be backfacing. The opposite is not true, so no decisions are made that result in incorrect images.

Kumar and Manocha [448] take another approach whereby they partition the polygons into a set of clusters, and then hierarchically reorganize each cluster into a tree of subclusters. Each cluster is then divided into a

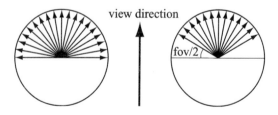

Figure 9.10. The left part illustrates the normals that can be culled for parallel projection. The right side shows the same for perspective projection with a certain field of view (fov). *(Illustration after Zhang and Hoff [834].)*

FrontRegion, a BackRegion, and a MixedRegion. The FrontRegion and Back-Region are defined by the intersection of the halfplanes of the polygons in these regions. If the viewer is in the FrontRegion (BackRegion) of a cluster, then all polygons in that cluster (that is, all the polygons in the subtree of that cluster) are frontfacing (backfacing). Otherwise, the polygons may be facing either way. At run time, the tree is traversed for each cluster, and the traversal may be pruned when all polygons in a (sub)cluster can be determined to be either frontfacing or backfacing, or when a leaf has been reached. This scheme also exploits frame-to-frame coherency in order to track the region where the viewer lies.

An extension of the normal cone technique for parametric surfaces is presented by Kumar and Manocha [447]. A different approach to clustered culling is taken by Johannsen and Carter [396]. Sander et al. [672] present yet another data structure for hierarchical clustered backface culling.

9.4 Hierarchical View Frustum Culling

As seen in Section 2.3.4, only primitives that are totally or partially inside the view frustum need to be rendered. One way to speed up the rendering process is to compare the bounding volume (BV) of each object to the view frustum. If the BV is outside the frustum, then the geometry it encloses can be omitted from rendering. Since these computations are done within the CPU, this means that the geometry inside the BV does not need to go through the geometry and the rasterizer stages in the pipeline. If instead the BV is inside or intersecting the frustum, then the contents of that BV may be visible and must be sent through the rendering pipeline. See Section 13.13 for methods of testing for intersection between various bounding volumes and the view frustum.

By using a spatial data structure, this kind of culling can be applied hierarchically [126]. For a bounding volume hierarchy (BVH), a preorder traversal [145] from the root does the job. Each node with a BV is tested against the frustum. If the BV of any type of node is outside the frustum, then that node is not processed further. The tree is pruned, since the BV's subtree is outside the view.

If the BV intersects the frustum, then the traversal continues and its children are tested. When a leaf node is found to intersect, its contents (i.e., its geometry) is sent through the pipeline. The primitives of the leaf are not guaranteed to be inside the view frustum. Clipping (see Section 2.3.4)

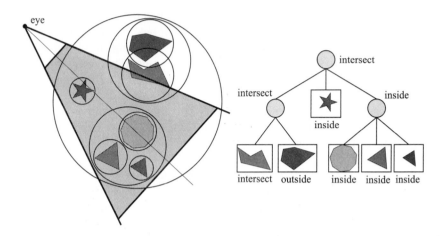

Figure 9.11. A set of geometry and its bounding volumes (spheres) are shown on the left. This scene is rendered with view frustum culling from the point of the eye. The BVH is shown on the right. The BV of the root intersects the frustum, and the traversal continues with testing its children's BVs. The BV of the left subtree intersects, and one of that subtree's children intersects (and thus is rendered), and the BV of the other child is outside and therefore is not sent through the pipeline. The BV of the middle subtree of the root is totally inside and is rendered immediately. The BV of the right subtree of the root is also fully inside, and the entire subtree can therefore be rendered without further tests.

takes care of ensuring that only primitives inside the view frustum are being rendered. If the BV is fully inside the frustum, its contents must all be inside the frustum. Traversal continues, but no further frustum testing is needed for the rest of such a subtree. An example of view frustum culling is shown in Figure 9.11.

View frustum culling operates in the application stage (CPU), which means that both the geometry and the rasterizer stages can benefit enormously. For large scenes or certain camera views, only a fraction of the scene might be visible, and it is only this fraction that needs to be sent through the rendering pipeline. In such cases a large gain in speed can be expected. View frustum culling techniques exploit the spatial coherence in a scene, since objects that are located near each other can be enclosed in a BV, and nearby BVs may be clustered hierarchically.

Other spatial data structures than the BVH can also be used for view frustum culling. This includes octrees and *Binary Space Partitioning* (BSP) trees [670]. These methods are usually not flexible enough when it comes to rendering dynamic scenes. That is, it takes too long to update the corresponding data structures when an object stored in the structure moves (an exception is loose octrees). But for static scenes, these methods can perform better than BVHs.

Polygon-aligned BSP trees are simple to use for view frustum culling. If the box containing the scene is visible, then the root node's splitting plane is tested. If the plane intersects the frustum (i.e., if two corners on the frustum are found to be on opposite sides of the plane [see Section 13.9]), then both branches of the BSP tree are traversed. If instead, the view frustum is fully on one side of the plane, then whatever is on the other side of the plane is culled. Axis-aligned BSP trees and octrees are also simple to use. Traverse the tree from the root, and test each box in the tree during traversal. If a box is outside the frustum, traversal for that branch is terminated.

For view frustum culling, there is a simple technique for exploiting frame-to-frame coherency.[5] If a BV is found to be outside a certain plane of the frustum in one frame, then (assuming that the viewer does not move too quickly) it will probably be outside that plane in the next frame too. So if a BV was outside a certain plane, then an index to this plane is stored (cached) with the BV. In the next frame in which this BV is encountered during traversal, the cached plane is tested first, and on average a speed-up can be expected [33].

If the viewer is constrained to only translation or rotation around one axis at a time from frame to frame, then this can also be exploited for faster frustum culling. When a BV is found to be outside a plane of the frustum, then the distance from that plane to the BV is stored with the BV. Now, if the BV only, say, translates, then the distance to the BV can be updated quickly by knowing how much the viewer has translated. This can provide a generous speed-up in comparison to a naive view frustum culler [33].

9.5 Portal Culling

For architectural models, there is a set of algorithms that goes under the name of *portal culling*. The first of these were introduced by Airey [6, 7] in 1990. Later, Teller and Séquin [745, 746] and Teller and Hanrahan [747] constructed more efficient and more complex algorithms for portal culling. The rationale for all portal-culling algorithms is that walls often act as large occluders in indoor scenes. The idea is therefore to do view frustum culling

---

[5]This is also called temporal coherency.

through each portal (e.g., door or window). When traversing a portal, the frustum is diminished to fit closely around the portal. Therefore, this algorithm can be seen as an extension of view frustum culling. Portals that are outside the view frustum are discarded. Portal culling is a kind of occlusion culling algorithm, but is treated separately because of its importance.

Portal-culling methods preprocess the scene in some way, either automatically or by hand. The scene is divided into *cells* that usually correspond to rooms and hallways in a building. The doors and windows that connect adjacent rooms are called *portals*. Every object in a cell and the walls of the cell are stored in a data structure that is associated with the cell. We also store information on adjacent cells and the portals that connect them in an adjacency graph. Teller presents algorithms for computing this graph [746]. A commonly used alternative is to manually create it.

Luebke and Georges [505] use a simple method that requires only a small amount of preprocessing. The only information that is needed is the data structure associated with each cell, as described above. Rendering such a scene is accomplished through the following steps:

1. Locate the cell V where the viewer (eye) is positioned.

2. Initialize a two-dimensional bounding box P to the rectangle of the screen.

3. Render the geometry of the cell V using view frustum culling for the frustum that emanates from the viewer and goes through the rectangle P (initially the whole screen).

4. Recurse on portals of the cells neighboring V. For each portal of the current cell, project the portal onto the screen and find the two-dimensional axis-aligned *Bounding Box* (BB) of that projection. Compute the logical intersection of P and the BB of the portal (which is done with a few comparisons).

5. For each intersection: If it is empty, then the cell that is connected via that portal is invisible from the current point of view, and that cell can be omitted from further processing. If the intersection is not empty, then the contents of that neighbor cell can be culled against the frustum that emanates from the viewer and goes though the (rectangular) intersection.

6. If the intersection was not empty, then the neighboring cells of that neighbor may be visible, and so we recurse to Step 3 with P being

the intersection BB. Each object may be tagged when it has been rendered in order to avoid rendering objects more than once.

An optimization that can well be worth implementing is to use the stencil buffer for more accurate culling. Since the portals are overestimated with an AABB, the real portal will most likely be smaller. The stencil buffer can be used to mask away rasterization (e.g., texturing and depth test) outside that real portal.

The portal culling algorithm is illustrated in Figure 9.12 with an example. The viewer or eye is located in cell E and therefore rendered together with its contents. The neighboring cells are C, D, and F. The original frustum cannot see the portal to cell D and is therefore omitted from further processing. Cell F is visible, and the view frustum is therefore diminished so that it goes through the portal that connects to F. The contents of F are then rendered with that diminished frustum. Then, the neighboring cells of F are examined—G is not visible from the diminished frustum and so is omitted, while H is visible. Again, the frustum is diminished with the portal of H, and thereafter the contents of H are rendered. H does not have any neighbors that have not been visited, so traversal ends there. Now, recursion falls back to the portal into cell C. The frustum is diminished to fit the portal of C, and then rendering of the objects in C follows, with frustum culling. No more portals are visible, so rendering is complete.

See Plate XLVI (following page 562) for another view of the use of portals. This form of portal culling can also be used to trim content for

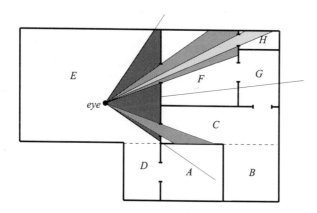

Figure 9.12. Portal culling: Cells are enumerated from A to H, and portals are openings that connect the cells. Only geometry seen through the portals is rendered.

planar reflections (see Section 6.10). The left image of the plate shows a building viewed from the top; the white lines indicate the way in which the frustum is diminished with each portal. The red lines are created by reflecting the frustum at a mirror. The actual view is shown in the image on the right side of the same plate, where the white rectangles are the portals and the mirror is red. Note that it is only the objects inside any of the frustums that are rendered.

There are many other uses for portals. Mirror reflections can be created by transforming the viewer when the contents of a cell seen through a portal are about to be rendered. That is, if the viewer looks at a portal, then the viewer's position and direction can be reflected in the plane of that portal (see Section 6.10.1). Other transformations can be used to create other effects, such as simple refractions. Portals can also be "one-way." For example, assume that you walk from cell A to cell B through a portal. If the portal is one-way, then we cannot go back from B to A—instead we may turn around and see another cell C. This is perfectly suited for creating a difficult maze.

9.6   Detail Culling

Detail culling is a technique that sacrifices quality for speed. The rationale for detail culling is that small details in the scene contribute little or nothing to the rendered images when the viewer is in motion. When the viewer stops, detail culling is usually disabled. Consider an object with a bounding volume, and project this BV onto the projection plane. The area of the projection is then estimated in pixels, and if the number of pixels is below a user-defined threshold, the object is omitted from further processing. For this reason, detail culling is sometimes called *screen-size culling*. Detail culling can also be done hierarchically on a scene graph. The geometry and rasterizer stages both gain from this algorithm. Note that this could be implemented as a simplified LOD technique (see Section 9.8), where one LOD is the entire model, and the other LOD is an empty object.

9.7   Occlusion Culling

As we have seen, visibility may be solved via a hardware construction called the Z-buffer (see Section 2.4). Even though it may solve visibility correctly, the Z-buffer is not a very smart mechanism in all respects. For

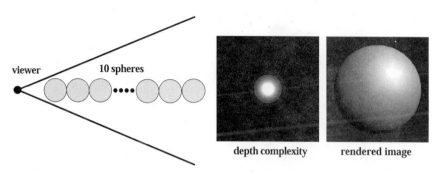

Figure 9.13. An illustration of how occlusion culling can be useful. Ten spheres are placed in a line, and the viewer is looking along this line (left). The depth complexity image in the middle shows that some pixels are written to several times, even though the final image (on the right) only shows one sphere.

example, imagine that the viewer is looking along a line where 10 spheres are placed. This is illustrated in Figure 9.13. An image rendered from this viewpoint will show but one sphere, even though all 10 spheres will be scan-converted and compared to the Z-buffer, and then potentially written to the color buffer and Z-buffer. The middle part of Figure 9.13 shows the depth complexity for this scene from the given viewpoint. Depth complexity refers to how many times each pixel is overwritten. In the case of the 10 spheres, the depth complexity is 10 for the pixel in the middle as 10 spheres are rendered there (assuming backface culling was on), and this means that 9 writes to the pixel are unnecessary. This uninteresting scene is not likely to be found in reality, but it describes (from the given viewpoint) a densely populated model. These sorts of configurations are found in real scenes such as those of a rain forest, an engine, a city, and the inside of a skyscraper. An example of a Manhattan-style city is shown in Figure 9.14.

Given the examples in the previous paragraph, it seems plausible that an algorithmic approach to avoid this kind of inefficiency may pay off in terms of speed. Such approaches go under the name of *occlusion culling algorithms*, since they try to cull away (avoid drawing) objects that are occluded, that is, hidden by other objects in the scene. The optimal occlusion culling algorithm would select only the objects that are visible. In a sense, the Z-buffer selects and renders only those objects that are visible, but not without having to send all objects through most of the pipeline. The idea behind efficient occlusion culling algorithms is to perform some simple tests early on and so avoid sending data through much of the pipeline.

There are two major forms of occlusion culling algorithms, namely point-based and cell-based. These are illustrated in Figure 9.15. Point-

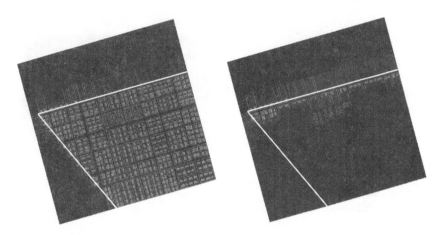

Figure 9.14. A bird's eye view of a city. The left image shows view frustum culling, while the right shows occlusion culling and view frustum culling.

based visibility is just what is normally used in rendering, that is, what is seen from a single viewing location. Cell-based visibility, on the other hand, is done for a cell, which is a region of the space, normally a box or a sphere. An invisible object in cell-based visibility must be invisible from all points within the cell. The advantage of cell-based visibility is that once it is computed for a cell, it can usually be used for a few frames, as long as

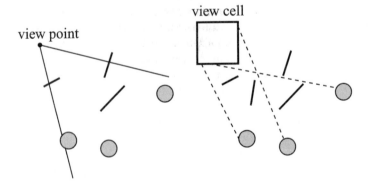

Figure 9.15. The left figure shows point-based visibility, while the right shows cell-based visibility, where the cell is a box. As can be seen, the circles are occluded to the left from the viewpoint. To the right, however, the circles are visible, since rays can be drawn from somewhere within the cell to the circles without intersecting any occluder.

the viewer is inside the cell. However, it is usually more time consuming to compute than point-based visibility. Therefore, it is often done as a preprocessing step, and this is, in fact, the major reason this type of algorithm was developed. Note that point-based and cell-based visibility often are compared to point and area light sources. For an object to be invisible, it has to be in the umbra region, i.e., fully occluded.

One can also categorize occlusion culling algorithms into those that operate in *image space*, *object space*, or *ray space*. Image space algorithms do visibility testing in two dimensions after some projection, while object space algorithms use the original three-dimensional objects. Ray space [66, 67, 441] methods performs their tests in a dual space. Each point (often two-dimensional) of interest is converted to a ray in this dual space. The idea is that testing is simpler, more exact, or more efficient in this space. Such algorithms are treated only briefly here.

Pseudocode for one type of occlusion culling algorithm is shown in Figure 9.16, where the function isOccluded, often called the *visibility test*, checks whether an object is occluded. G is the set of geometrical objects to be rendered, O_R is the occlusion representation, and P is a set of potential occluders that can be merged with O_R. Depending on the particular

```
1:   OcclusionCullingAlgorithm(G)
2:   O_R =empty
3:   P =empty
4:   for each object g ∈ G
5:      if(isOccluded(g,O_R))
6:         Skip(g)
7:      else
8:         Render(g)
9:         Add(g, P)
10:        if(LargeEnough(P))
11:           Update(O_R, P)
12:           P =empty
13:        end
14:     end
15:  end
```

Figure 9.16. Pseudocode for a general occlusion culling algorithm. G contains all the objects in the scene, and O_R is the occlusion representation. P is a set of potential occluders, that are merged into O_R when it contains sufficiently many objects. *(After Zhang [836].)*

algorithm, O_R represents some kind of occlusion information. O_R is set to be empty at the beginning. After that, all objects (that pass the view frustum culling test) are processed.

Consider a particular object. First, we test whether the object is occluded with respect to the occlusion representation O_R. If it is occluded, then it is not processed further, since we then know that it will not contribute to the image. If the object is determined not to be occluded, then that object has to be rendered, since it probably contributes to the image (at that point in the rendering). Then the object is added to P, and if the number of objects in P is large enough, then we can afford to merge the *occluding power* of these objects into O_R. Each object in P can thus be used as an *occluder*. Depending on the algorithm, the merging can be done at different frequencies. Also, all algorithms cannot afford to merge all objects in P. Therefore, one often estimates how good an occluder is and only merges the good ones. Some measures for this are presented in Section 9.8.2. This last operation in the pseudocode is very important as it provides a mechanism to *fuse* occluders [835]. This means that several occluders together can occlude more than each occluder considered as a single entity. Occluder fusion is essential to get good cull rates. However, not all algorithms can fuse occluders.

Occluder fusion is even more important for cell-based than for point-based algorithms, as the occluded space for cell-based algorithms is smaller. For conservative visibility algorithms, the visibility test needs to overestimate the object to be tested for occlusion. This is often done with a bounding volume around the object. However, if the object is to be used as an occluder (inserted into the O_R), the occluding power of the object needs to be underestimated.

For some algorithms, it is expensive to update the occlusion representation, so this is only done once (before the actual rendering starts) with the objects that are believed to be good occluders. This set is then updated from frame to frame.

Note that for the majority of occlusion culling algorithms, the performance is dependent on the order in which objects are drawn. As an example, consider a car with a motor inside it. If the hood of the car is drawn first, then the motor will (probably) be culled away. On the other hand, if the motor is drawn first, then the hood of the car will not be culled. Therefore, performance can be improved by techniques such as rough front-to-back sorting of the objects by their approximate distance from the viewer and rendering in this order. Also, it is worth noting that small objects potentially can be excellent occluders, since the distance to the occluder decides how much it can occlude [5]. As an example, a matchbox can occlude the Golden Gate Bridge if the viewer is sufficiently close to the matchbox.

A number of occlusion algorithms will be presented in this section. A hardware implementation of occlusion culling is discussed in Section 15.3.5.

9.7.1 Occlusion Horizons

In this section, an occlusion culling algorithm based on horizons in image space will be presented. It is a simple, point-based algorithm that can fuse occluders, and so is useful in demonstrating this important concept. Wonka and Schmalstieg [814] developed such an algorithm first[6] and implemented it using graphics hardware to fuse occluders. It was then independently developed and implemented by Downs et al. [185] using geometrical computations. We will follow the latter presentation here. This type of algorithm focuses on speeding up rendering of urban environments, that is, cities and villages. The observation that is exploited in these scenes is that the major occluders are the buildings, that buildings are connected to the ground, and an observer cannot see through or below these. Therefore, the occluding objects in the scene plus the ground are treated as a heightfield. Such a scene is called $2\frac{1}{2}$D, meaning that the depth complexity is never greater than one along some axis. However, it should be noted that other three-dimensional objects can be inserted and used in the scene. The algorithm is point-based, so occlusion culling has to be done each frame.

In a preprocessing step, a quadtree in the xy-plane of the scene is built. Alternatively, a loose quadtree (see page 354) can be used for dynamic scenes. Each object is stored in the node as deep down in the tree as possible and such that the node size is larger than the object size. The main idea is then to sweep a plane (parallel to the near plane) away from the viewer. During this sweep, an occlusion horizon is created on the fly. This horizon accumulates the occluding power of occluders, and is also used to cull objects conservatively. Objects to be culled are overestimated with a bounding box, and occluders are underestimated with a set of *Convex Vertical Prisms* (CVPs): See Figure 9.17. The union of the ground mesh and the CVPs form a heightfield, which is a conservative estimate of the occluding power of the scene. By traversing the scene's quadtree in a rough front-to-back order, an occlusion horizon can be built in the image plane.

The occlusion horizon is a piecewise constant function of the x-coordinate on the image. At all x-values, it describes roughly the highest of the

---

[6]Note that horizons have been used in algorithms such as the floating horizon, which dates back to 1972 [656], and also more recently by Wimmer et al. [805].

Figure 9.17. The occluding power of a simple house (left) is approximated with three *Convex Vertical Prisms* (CVPs), shown in the middle. In this case, boxes have been used. To the right, a few other examples of CVPs are shown.

projected points within a distance from the viewer. Therefore, at any time during a frame, the horizon describes the occluding power of the processed objects so far. At the start of a frame, the horizon is initialized to a horizontal line at the bottom of the screen, that is, $y = 0$, for all $x \in [0, width - 1]$. To be able to describe more detailed occlusion and thus, get better performance, the horizon is represented by a binary tree. Each node in this tree has a minimum and maximum x-value, x_{min} and x_{max}. Every leaf node stores the height, y, which is constant for its range $[x_{min}, x_{max}]$. Internal nodes store both the minimum and maximum heights, y_{min} and y_{max}, that are represented in its range. This tree is constructed on the fly in this algorithm. An example is shown in Figure 9.18. Two important operations to be performed on this tree are how an object is tested for occlusion against it, and how the occluding power of an object is added to the horizon. Both of these operate on a sorted event queue, Q, implemented as a priority queue. This is to ensure that events are processed sorted on the distance (along the view direction) to the viewpoint.

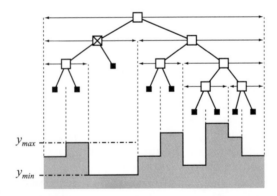

Figure 9.18. A binary tree representing an occlusion horizon. The horizon is at the bottom, and the tree is above. Horizontal arrows represent an internal node's x-range. The heights, y_{min} and y_{max}, are shown for the internal node marked with a cross.

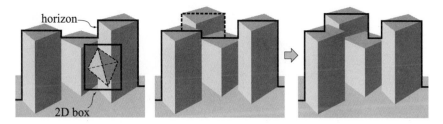

Figure 9.19. The left image tests the box of a tetrahedron against the horizon. Note that testing always occurs in front-to-back order, so that the tetrahedron is actually behind the objects in the occlusion horizon. The box is below the horizon, and so can be culled. The two rightmost figures show a visible object, and how its occluding power is added to the horizon.

During the rough front-to-back traversal, each encountered potentially visible object is added to Q. The actual event takes place at the object's bounding box smallest z-value (z is the viewing direction). When such an event is popped from the queue, Q, the object's bounding box is projected onto the screen, then bounded with a two-dimensional, axis-aligned box, B. Then B is tested against the occlusion horizon represented by the binary tree. This is done with a recursive routine, which terminates recursion as soon as B is found to be under the horizon. If the entire box is under the horizon, the object can be safely culled. This is shown to the left in Figure 9.19.

For an object that is not occluded, its occluding power is added to the occlusion horizon. Care must be taken when adding its occluding power so that it is not added too early, as doing so could result in visibility errors. The simplest choice for the event's order would be the point on the occluder with the farthest z-value. When such an event is popped from the event queue, it is guaranteed that we have processed all objects before that point. However, this location can be improved upon, as will be seen. The occluding power must be underestimated in order to achieve conservative occlusion culling. This process is illustrated in Figure 9.20. The two lines with minimum x and maximum x are found. The smallest in height (y) of these determine the height of the two-dimensional box to be added to the horizon. The farthest of the two points is used to trigger this event, because it is at this point that the entire occluding power of the object has been reached. The event, shown in Figure 9.20, is pushed onto the queue, Q, so that events are processed in sorted order. When such an event is reached, its occluding power is added to the horizon. This is done in the right part of Figure 9.19. An important property of this algorithm is that

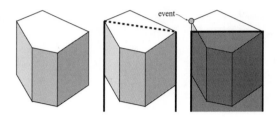

Figure 9.20. Underestimation of the occluding power of a convex vertical prism (CVP).

it can fuse occluders into the horizon, and thus use the occluding power of several objects together. The adding of the occluding power to the horizon is also done using a short recursive routine. After all objects have been rendered, the entire horizon is again initialized to $y = 0$, and creation of the horizon starts from scratch. An example of a horizon at the end of the rendering of an image is shown in Figure 9.21.

Objects to be tested for occlusion and occluders whose occluding power is added to the horizon can move when using this algorithm. The key is that the (loose) quadtree has to be updated to compensate for such moves. *Level of Detail* (LOD) rendering (see Section 9.8) can also be supported [185]. To select an appropriate level of detail, the estimated visible area with respect to the horizon is computed. This is the dashed area in the middle of Figure 9.19. The larger the area, the higher the level of detail needed. In some situations it might be better to combine the visible area with the distance. For example, if an object is very close to the viewer

Figure 9.21. The black piecewise constant function is the horizon, used in occlusion culling.

and only a small visible area is estimated, then a LOD with low detail is chosen. However, since we are so close, we should be able to see a lot of detail. Another extension of this algorithm would be to cull the object to be rendered against horizon as well. If the object is described using several small parts, and arranged in, say, a bounding volume hierarchy, then this should yield a further speedup. Andújar et al. [19] also combine LODs with occlusion culling by estimating the level of visibility to choose the LOD.

9.7.2 Occluder Shrinking and Frustum Growing

The occlusion horizon algorithm presented in Section 9.7.1 is point-based. Cell-based visibility is sometimes preferable, but is in general much more complex to compute than point-based visibility. *Occluder shrinking* is a technique developed by Wonka et al. [815] that can use a point-based occlusion algorithm to generate cell-based visibility. The idea is to extend the validity of point visibility by *shrinking* all occluders in the scene by a given distance, d. They also present *frustum growing* [816], which is often used in conjunction with occluder shrinking. Given that the viewer can move and change orientation at certain speeds, a grown frustum is created that is a frustum that includes all possible changes in view position and orientation. Consult Wonka's Ph.D. thesis [817] for all the details on these algorithms.

Assume that point-based visibility can be computed from a point $\mathbf{v}$. Use this point-based visibility algorithm to compute visibility with occluders that are shrunk by an amount, d. It can be shown that this is a conservative approximation of cell-based visibility within a view-cell centered around $\mathbf{v}$ with a radius of d [815]. See Figure 9.22 for an illustration of occluder shrinking. The algorithm works with *volumetric* occluders. The operation of shrinking the occluder corresponds to "eroding" the occluder by a sphere with radius d. Shrinking can be calculated using polyhedral set operations on generic three-dimensional objects, but simpler shrinking operations can be obtained when regular volumetric data structures (octree, grid) are used to store the occluders.

If cell-based visibility is to be useful, then the view cell has to be large enough that it can be used for at least a few frames. Using a large d value will shrink the occluders so that they occlude little or nothing. Therefore, Wonka et al. [815] suggest using occluder shrinking for several point samples on the view cell. The occluders are shrunk only once, at startup of the algorithm, and stored in a database. To calculate visibility for a particular view cell, proceed as follows:

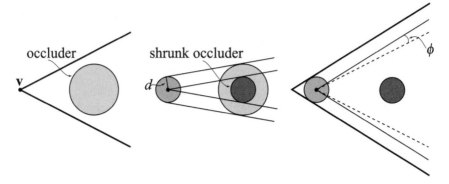

Figure 9.22. Left: A view frustum and an occluder. Middle: The occluder is shrunk with an amount of d. Right: Frustum growing.

1. Choose a number of points so that the union of the spheres with radius d of the points cover the boundary of the view cell.

2. For each point, calculate a PVS with a point-visibility algorithm using the shrunk occluders.

3. The cell-based visibility solution is given by the union of those PVSs and can be stored with the view cell.

The choice of d depends on the overall type of the scene. It should be chosen in a way such that the spheres with radius d are small compared to the size of an average occluder. This is important because for any given viewpoint, the visibility solution using the shrunk occluders should still be similar to the solution using regular occluders. However, as d gets smaller, more spheres are needed to cover the view cell boundary, and visibility calculation become slower. The choice of d is therefore a tradeoff between culling speed and efficiency.

The technique can also be useful for on-the-fly visibility processing. However, the original frustum (to the left in Figure 9.22) must be grown to accommodate changes in viewer orientation and position [816]. This is shown to the right in Figure 9.22. The speed, v, of the viewer has to be restricted by the application. Then the cell-based visibility will be valid for $t = d/v$ seconds. This time-span will usually be several frames, so that visibility calculations do not need to be done for every frame. Thus, temporal coherence is exploited. Also, the turning speed has to be, at most, ω radians per second. Now, the frustum's field of view must first be enlarged. This is done with an increase $\phi = \omega t$. Then that enlarged frustum is moved back, so that it encloses the entire sphere.

An algorithm called "instant visibility" uses occluder shrinking and frustum growing to compute visibility on-the-fly, simultaneous to rendering done on another machine [816]. The basic idea is to calculate visibility in parallel to the rendering pipeline on a visibility server, possibly a distinct computer communicating with the display host over a local network. In the resulting system, the display host continues rendering new frames while the visibility server calculates visibility for future frames. Therefore, a visibility solution is always ready at the start of each frame, and no additional latency is introduced to the rendering pipeline. Allotting more than one rendering frame to visibility calculations allows for improved visibility solutions. The instant visibility system combines the advantages of online visibility processing and cell-based visibility by decoupling visibility calculations and rendering. Another algorithm for cell-based visibility is presented by Koltun et al. [440], where they notice that the fusion of several occluders can be replaced by a much simpler occluder that covers almost as much. Such a replacement is called a virtual occluder.

9.7.3 Shaft Occlusion Culling

In this section, an algorithm by Schaufler et al. that uses shafts for occlusion culling will be presented [679]. Like occluder shrinking, it is designed to be cell-based, and uses interesting techniques to fuse occluders and it operates in object-space. This algorithm is one of the first cell-based occlusion culling algorithms that can deal with three-dimensional scenes. It has been used for visibility preprocessing for walkthroughs, and for accelerating ray tracing with area light sources. This algorithm will be presented for the two-dimensional case first, and then extended.

The view cells in this algorithm are axis-aligned bounding boxes (AABBs). A quadtree is used to describe the occluding power of the scene. A leaf node in the quadtree is categorized as *opaque, boundary,* or *empty.* This means that there must be a way to say whether a leaf node (that corresponds to an AABB) is fully inside of a building or other object, for example. A boundary leaf node contains geometry not fully inside any objects. Schaufler et al. [679] use a seed-filling algorithm to categorize leaf nodes, but any method will do (even manually, if feasible).

To find visible geometry from a view cell, the quadtree is traversed recursively until an opaque leaf node is found. This traversal is done outwards from the view cell in order to maximize occlusion. This occluder is then

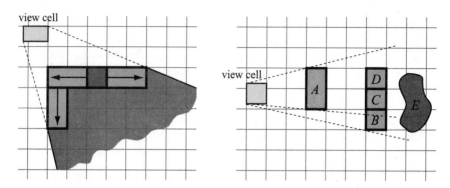

Figure 9.23. Left: The first occluder that is found is the darkest gray. Then it is extended in the x-direction as much as possible. Finally, it is also extended in the y-direction. Right: A is opaque and it is also the occluder gathered so far. B is then encountered during traversal, and since C and D are hidden by A, B can be extended into C and D. At this point, BCD are used as occluders. As can be seen, neither A nor B can alone occlude E, but BCD can. *(Illustrations after Schaufler et al. [679].)*

extended along the coordinate axis that gives the largest angle from the view cell's center to the occluder. That occluder can thus grow in two opposite directions if its neighbors also are opaque. It may even be L-shaped as shown in Figure 9.23. However, at some point, the occluder cannot be extended further because there are not any neighboring opaque leaf nodes. Leaf nodes that are occluded, i.e., in hidden space, can be considered opaque independent of their real category. Therefore, occluders can be extended into hidden space, which generally allows much larger occluders to be built using occluder fusion. This is shown to the right in Figure 9.23. The algorithm restricts the fused occluder to be only an AABB. This is because a semi-infinite shaft (see Section 13.14) is constructed from the view cell to the occluder. All objects inside this shaft are occluded, and so can be culled. This is done by traversing the quadtree and culling nodes' boxes against the shaft.

In three dimensions, occluder extension must be done along one more dimension. Figure 9.24 shows how this is done. Schaufler et al. reported good results with this technique and point out that extending occluders into hidden space was the crucial part in getting good occlusion [679]. When using this algorithm in three dimensions, the shafts are also three-dimensional, and the quadtree is replaced by an octree.

Schaufler et al. [679] show how their algorithm can be extended to handle $2\frac{1}{2}$D scenes as well.

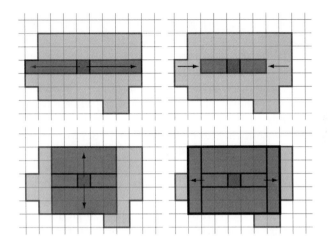

Figure 9.24. Top left: The dark gray square is the box that extension starts from. First, the occluder is extended horizontally. Top right: The extension is halved. Bottom left: Extension vertically. Bottom right: Extension horizontally again. *(Illustrations after Schaufler et al. [679].)*

9.7.4 Hardware Occlusion Queries

Hewlett-Packard has implemented a type of occlusion culling, which we call *occlusion queries*, in the VISUALIZE fx graphics hardware [692].[7] Simply put, the user can query the hardware to find out whether a set of polygons is visible when compared to the current contents of the Z-buffer. Those polygons are most often the bounding volume (for example, a box or k-DOP) of a more complex object. If none of those polygons are visible, then the object can be culled. The implementation in hardware scan-converts the polygons of the query, and compares their depths to the Z-buffer. If all depths are hidden, all polygons are occluded. Therefore, the occlusion queries also operate in image space. Similar queries are used by the hierarchical Z-buffer algorithm (Section 9.7.5).

If a complex object is obscured, then instead of drawing the whole object, only a bounding volume is scan-converted (but not drawn into the frame buffer). In this case, we gain performance by avoiding sending the complex object through the rendering pipeline. Otherwise, the bounding volume is scan-converted and the object is drawn, and we actually lose a bit of performance.

---

[7]It appears that this was first implemented on a computer called Kubota Pacific Titan 3000 with Denali GB graphics hardware [288].

With such techniques, performance has been reported to be between 25 and 100 percent faster than rendering that does not use any occlusion culling [692]. With newer hardware (fx5 and fx10), several queries can be executed in parallel. HP's OpenGL implementation also attempts to use this technology automatically. For sufficiently long display lists, bounding boxes are created automatically and queried [154]. The latency of a query is often a relatively long time; often hundreds or thousands of polygons can be displayed within this time (see Section 15.3.4 for more on latency). Hence, this hardware-based occlusion culling method is worthwhile when the bounding boxes contain a large number of objects and a relatively large amount of occlusion is occurring. Therefore, it has been shown that using tighter bounding volumes can speed up rendering. Bartz et al. [48] achieved a 50 percent increase in frame rate using k-DOPs (26-DOPs) for mechanical CAD models (where the interiors of the objects often are complex).

NVIDIA supports an extension for an alternative occlusion query, here called the NV query. It overcomes two limitations of the previous query. First, instead of returning a boolean, the number of pixels, n, that pass the depth test is returned. Thus, if $n = 0$, then the entire bounding volume is completely occluded, and the contained objects can safely be discarded. If $n > 0$ then a fraction of the pixels failed the test. If n is smaller than a threshold number of pixels, then some applications may want to skip rendering the contained object anyway. In this way, speed can be traded for quality. Another use would be to let n determine the LOD (see Section 9.8) of an object. If n is small, then a smaller fraction of the object is (potentially) visible, and so a less detailed LOD can be used. The NV query can also be used in techniques such as depth peeling. The previous query can be used to determine when all layers have been peeled. However, for better performance, some approximations might be acceptable, and the NV query can be used to determine when a sufficient amount has been peeled off. The second improvement is that the NV query allows for testing whether the result is back yet. If it is not back, then execution is returned to the application. This was not the case for the previous query, which stalled execution on the CPU until the result was back. This also allows several queries to be tested in parallel. One potential disadvantage of the NV query is that it has to test all pixels against the Z-buffer before the result can be returned. The previous query could return as soon as one pixel was found to be visible. However, the latency of the test is so long that this probably does not matter.

Meißner et al. [538] use occlusion queries in a hierarchical setting. The scene is represented in a hierarchical data structure, such as a BVH or octree. First, view frustum culling is used to find nodes not fully outside the view frustum. These are sorted, based on a node's center point (for example, the center of a bounding box), in front-to-back order. The nearest leaf node is rendered without occlusion testing to the frame buffer. Using the occlusion query, the BVs of subsequent objects are tested. If a BV is visible, then its contents is tested recursively, or rendered. Klosowski and Silva have developed a constant-frame-rate algorithm using an occlusion culling algorithm, called the *prioritized-layered projection* algorithm [435]. However, at first this was not a conservative algorithm, i.e., it sacrificed image quality in order to keep constant frame rate. Later, they developed a conservative version of the algorithm using occlusion queries [436].

9.7.5   Hierarchical Z-Buffering

Hierarchical Z-buffering (HZB), an algorithm developed by Greene et al., [288, 291] has had a significant influence on occlusion culling research. At this point, it is not implemented in hardware, and thus for the most part it is impractical for real-time rendering. However, the algorithm may very well be implemented in hardware someday, and the concepts are important for occlusion culling. The algorithm maintains the scene model in an octree, and a frame's Z-buffer as an image pyramid, which we call a Z-pyramid—the algorithm thus operates in image space. The octree enables hierarchical culling of occluded regions of the scene, and the Z-pyramid enables hierarchical Z-buffering of individual primitives and bounding volumes. The Z-pyramid is thus the occlusion representation of this algorithm. Examples of these data structures are shown in Figure 9.25. Any method can be employed for organizing scene primitives in an octree, although Greene et al. [288] recommend a specific algorithm that avoids assigning small primitives to large octree nodes.

Now we will describe how the Z-pyramid is maintained and how it is used to accelerate culling. The finest (highest-resolution) level of the Z-pyramid is simply a standard Z-buffer. At all other levels, each z-value is the farthest z in the corresponding 2×2 window of the adjacent finer level. Therefore, each z-value represents the farthest z for a square region of the screen. To maintain a Z-pyramid, whenever a z-value is overwritten in the Z-buffer, it is propagated through the coarser levels of the Z-pyramid. This is done recursively until the top of the image pyramid is reached, where only one z-value remains. Pyramid formation is illustrated in Figure 9.26.

Next, we describe how hierarchical culling of octree nodes is done. Traverse the octree nodes in a rough front-to-back order. A bounding box of the octree is tested against the Z-pyramid using an extended occlusion

Figure 9.25. Example of occlusion culling with the HZB algorithm [288, 291], showing a complex scene (lower right) with the corresponding Z-pyramid (on the left), and octree subdivision (upper right). By traversing the octree from front to back and culling occluded octree nodes as they are encountered, this algorithm visits only visible octree nodes and their children (the nodes portrayed at the upper right) and renders only the polygons in visible boxes. In this example, culling of occluded octree nodes reduces the depth complexity from 84 to 2.5. *(Image courtesy of Ned Greene/Apple Computer.)*

query (Section 9.7.4). We begin testing at the coarsest Z-pyramid cell that encloses the face's screen projection. The face's nearest depth within the cell (z_{near}) is then compared to the Z-pyramid value, and if z_{near} is farther, the face is known to be occluded. This testing continues recursively down the Z-pyramid until the box is found to be occluded, or until the bottom level of the Z-pyramid is reached, at which point the box is visible.

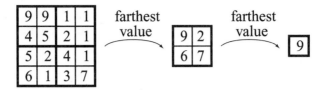

Figure 9.26. On the left, a 4 × 4 piece of the Z-buffer is shown. The numerical values are the actual z-values. This is downsampled to a 2 × 2 region where each value is the farthest (largest) of the four 2 × 2 regions on the left. Finally, the farthest value of the remaining four z-values is computed. These three maps compose an image pyramid that is called the hierarchical Z-buffer.

For visible octree boxes, testing continues recursively down in the octree, and finally potentially visible geometry is rendered into the hierarchical Z-buffer. This is done so that subsequent tests can use the occluding power of previously rendered objects.

To enable real-time rendering, Greene et al. [288] suggest modifying the hardware Z-buffer pipeline to support HZB, which requires substituting a Z-pyramid for the Z-buffer, and including a fast feedback path to report visibility of bounding volumes. It is likely that these modifications would extend the domain of real-time rendering to much more complex scenes, such as the scene in Figure 9.25. More recently, Greene has suggested an even more streamlined hardware implementation [293]. One nice feature of this system is that the tip of the pyramid can be read out from the hardware to the application, so that culling can be done at the start of the rendering pipeline. The suggested algorithm also handles dynamic scenes, given that a bounding volume hierarchy can be rebuilt efficiently. Greene [292] has also developed another extension to the HZB algorithm, where a BSP tree is used for strict front-to-back traversal in order to avoid doing tests against a hierarchical Z-buffer. Instead, coverage masks are kept in a pyramid, and the masks indicates whether a pixel has been written (and thus occludes everything rendered subsequently, due to the strict front-to-back traversal). Meißner et al. [539] give a hardware implementation of another tile-based occlusion culling algorithm.

In the absence of this kind of hardware support, the HZB algorithm can be accelerated on systems having conventional Z-buffer hardware by exploiting frame-to-frame coherency [288]. The idea is that octree nodes that were visible in one frame tend to be visible in the next. With this variation, the first frame of an animation sequence is generated with the standard HZB algorithm, except that after completing the frame, a list of octree nodes that were visible in that frame (the visible node list) is created by testing nodes for visibility against the Z-pyramid. Subsequent frames are generated with the following two-pass algorithm. In the first rendering pass, primitives associated with nodes on the visible node list are rendered by Z-buffer hardware. Then, the Z-buffer of the partially rendered scene is read back from the hardware, and a Z-pyramid is built from this Z-buffer. In the second rendering pass, the standard HZB algorithm is run in software, traversing the octree from front-to-back, but skipping nodes that have already been rendered. This second pass fills in any missing parts of the scene. The final step in processing a frame is to update the visible node list. Typically, this variation of the HZB algorithm runs considerably faster than the all-software version, because only the visible and a small subset of invisible polygons are rendered with Z-buffer hardware.

9.7.6   The HOM algorithm

The *Hierarchical Occlusion Map* (HOM) algorithm [835] is another way of enabling hierarchical image space culling (such as the HZB algorithm on page 383). It takes advantage of graphics hardware and can also handle dynamic scenes. The HOM algorithm is described in detail in Zhang's Ph.D. thesis [836].

We start by describing how the function isOccluded works. This function, used in the pseudocode in Figure 9.16, is a key part of the algorithm. The test is divided into two parts: a one-dimensional *depth test* in the z-direction and a two-dimensional *overlap test* in the xy plane, i.e., in image space. The overlap test supports approximate visibility culling, where objects that "shine through" small holes in the occluders can be culled away using an opacity threshold parameter.

For both tests, a set of potentially good occluders is identified before the scene is rendered, and the occlusion representation is built from these. To speed up this part, simplified versions of the occluders can be used. This works as long as the simplified occluder fits inside the original occluder [476, 836]. After finding this set of occluders, the occluder set is rendered, without performing an occlusion test on this set itself. Then the rest of the scene is processed by having each object tested against the occlusion representation. If the object is occluded by the occluder representation, it is not rendered.

For the two-dimensional overlap test, the occluders are first rendered into the color buffer with a white color on a black background. Therefore, texturing, lighting, and Z-buffering can be turned off. As with the HZB algorithm, an advantage of this operation is that a number of small occlud-

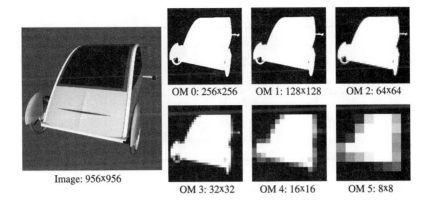

Figure 9.27. On the left is an image of 956 × 956 pixels. Since this object covers many pixels on the screen and is rather close to the viewer, it is a good candidate for an occluder. Its HOM is created by rendering this object in white against a black background in 256 × 256 pixels, an image that is called occlusion map 0. This image is subsampled into 128 × 128 pixels by averaging over 2 × 2 pixels. This is done recursively down to 8 × 8 pixels. *(Model reused courtesy of Nya Perspektiv Design AB.)*

ers can be combined into a large occluder. The rendered image is called an *occlusion map*, which is assumed to be $2^n \times 2^n$ pixels for simplicity. An HOM, i.e., an image pyramid of occlusion maps, is created by averaging over 2×2-pixel blocks to form an image of $2^{n-1} \times 2^{n-1}$ pixels. The grayscale values in the HOM are said to be the *opacity* of the pixels. A high opacity value (near white) for a pixel in any level means that most of the pixels it represents are occluded by the HOM. An example of a HOM is shown in Figure 9.27.

The overlap test (in image space) is done in a similar way as the test for the HZB algorithm described in the previous section. If all pixels for such an occlusion query are opaque (which means fully white for nonapproximate culling), then the box is occluded in the xy plane and the object is said to pass the test. On the other hand, if a pixel is not opaque, then the test for that pixel continues recursively toward the bottom of the pyramid.

For approximate visibility culling, the pixels in the HOM are not compared to full opacity, i.e., white, but rather against an opacity threshold value, a grayscale value. The lower the threshold value, the more approximate the culling. The advantage here is that if a pixel is not fully opaque (white), but still higher than the threshold, then the overlap test can terminate earlier. The penalty is that some object may be omitted from rendering even though it is (partially) visible. The opacity values are not

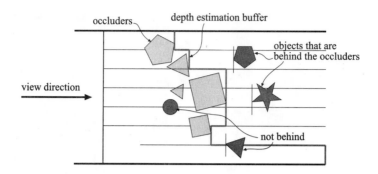

Figure 9.28. Illustration of the depth estimation buffer. *(Illustration after Zhang [836].)*

constant from one level to another in the HOM. See the paper by Zhang et al. or Zhang's Ph.D. thesis [835, 836] for more details on this.

For the one-dimensional z-depth test, we must be able to determine whether an object is behind the selected occluders. Zhang [836] describes a number of methods, and we choose to describe the *depth estimation buffer*, which provides reasonable estimation and does not require a Z-buffer. It is implemented as a software Z-buffer that divides the screen into a number of rectangular regions that are rather large in relation to the pixel size. The selected occluders are inserted into this buffer. For each region the farthest z-value is stored. This is in contrast to a normal Z-buffer, which stores the nearest z-value at each pixel. The z-value of the farthest vertex of the bounding box is used to estimate the farthest z-value of an occluder. An example of a depth estimation buffer is shown in Figure 9.28. The depth estimation buffer is used for testing in the z-direction, just as with a standard Z-buffer. A resolution of 64×64 regions in the depth estimation buffer was used by Zhang et al. [835].

For an object to be occluded, it must pass both the overlap test and the depth test. That is, the rectangle of the projected bounding volume of the object must pass the HOM test. Then it must pass the depth test, i.e., it must be behind the occluders. If an object passes both tests, the object is occluded and is not rendered.

Aila and Miettinen [5] suggest and implement what they call *Incremental Occlusion Maps* (IOM) by combining several different existing algorithms with new techniques. Their implementation can handle dynamic scenes at impressive rates. However, it is a complex system to implement. As of 2002, this system is considered state-of-the-art in occlusion culling. Durand et al. [193] propose *extended projections*, which can be seen as an extension of image space visibility (such as hierarchical occlusion maps) to region visibility. The overall algorithm is similar to hierarchical occlusion maps, but the projection of occluders and occludees (objects tested for visibility, typically bounding boxes) onto the occlusion map is modified. They define the extended projection of occluders onto a plane to be the intersection of all views in the view cell, and the extended projection of an occludee as the union of all views in the view cell. To assign depth values to the projection, they define the extended depth, which is the maximum depth of the occluders (or the minimum depth for the occludees). Sudarsky and Gotsman also deal with dynamic scenes [737]. To avoid updating the hierarchical data structure each frame, they use a temporal BV (TBV). A TBV is made larger so that it is valid over several frames. This can be done if the motion of an object is known or constrained.

9.7.7 Ray Space Occlusion Culling

Bittner et al. [66] introduce a powerful $2\frac{1}{2}$D ray space occlusion culling algorithm to analytically calculate a conservative PVS for a view cell. The idea of the algorithm is to calculate visibility information in a dual space, the ray space. Each two-dimensional occluder polygon in primary space corresponds to another two-dimensional polygon in ray space. The algorithm maintains a subdivision of ray space into areas of "similar" visibility and is essentially two-dimensional. To calculate the combined effect of multiple occluders, Bittner et al. merge the occluder polygons in line space using BSP trees. The algorithm is exact in two dimensions and conservative in $2\frac{1}{2}$D, using additional subdivisions based on the height structure of occluders. A similar ray space algorithm was introduced by Koltun et al. [441], where they use shafts and graphics hardware to accelerate culling.

9.8 Level of Detail

The basic idea of *Levels of Detail* (LODs) is to use simpler versions of an object as it makes less and less of a contribution to the rendered image. For example, consider a detailed car that may consist of 10, 000 triangles. This representation can be used when the viewer is close to the car. When the object is farther away, say covering only 10×5 pixels, we do not need all 10, 000 triangles. Instead, we can use a simplified model that has only, say, 100 triangles. Due to the distance, the simplified version looks approximately the same as the more detailed version. In this way, a significant speedup can be expected. Note also that fog, described in Section 4.6, is often used together with LODs. This allows us to completely skip the rendering of an object as it enters opaque fog. Also, the fogging mechanism can be used to implement time-critical rendering (see Section 9.8.3). By moving the far plane closer to the viewer, objects can be culled earlier and more rapid rendering achieved to keep the frame rate up.

Some objects, such as spheres, Bézier surfaces, and subdivision surfaces have levels of detail as part of their geometrical description. The underlying geometry is curved, and a separate LOD control determines how it is tessellated into displayable polygons. Here, we describe some common methods for using LODs. See Section 12.3.2 and 12.6.8 for algorithms that adapt the quality of tessellations for parametric surfaces and subdivision surfaces.

In general, LOD algorithms consist of three major parts, namely, *generation*, *selection*, and *switching*. LOD generation is the part where different representations of a model are generated with different detail. The simplification methods discussed in Section 11.5 can be used to generate the desired number of LODs. Another approach is to make models with different levels of detail by hand. The selection mechanism chooses a level of detail model based on some criteria, such as estimated area on the screen. Finally, we need to change from one level of detail to another, and this process is termed LOD switching. Different LOD switching and selection mechanisms are presented in this section.

9.8.1   LOD Switching

When switching from one LOD to another, an abrupt model substitution is often noticeable and distracting. This difference is called *popping*. Several different ways to perform this switching will be described here, and they all have different popping traits.

Discrete Geometry LODs

In the simplest type of LOD algorithm, the different representations are models of the same object containing different numbers of primitives. This algorithm is well-suited for modern graphics hardware [507], because the LODs can be turned into indexed triangle strips and pulled directly from DMA memory (see Section 15.3.3 and Section 11.4.5). A more detailed LOD has a higher number of primitives. An example of three LODs of an object is shown in Figure 9.29. This figure also shows the different LODs at different distances from the viewer.   The switching from one LOD to

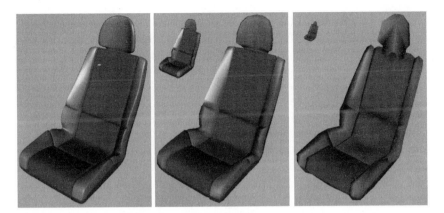

Figure 9.29. Here we show three different levels of detail for a car chair. The two pictures in the upper left corner of the middle and right images show the two chairs farther away from the viewer; still, these simplified models seem to approximate the chair fairly well from these distances. Note also how the shading degenerates as fewer triangles are used. *(Model reused courtesy of Nya Perspektiv Design AB.)*

another just happens, that is, on the current frame a certain LOD is used. Then on the next frame, the selection mechanism selects another LOD, and immediately uses that for rendering. Popping is typically the worst for this type of LOD method. Better alternatives are described next.

Blend LODs

Conceptually, a pretty obvious way to switch from one LOD to another is possible. Just do a linear blend between the two LODs over a short period of time. This is definitely going to make for a smoother switch. However, it is expensive to make such blends. Rendering two LODs for one object is naturally more expensive that just rendering one LOD, so this somewhat defeats the purpose of LODs. However, LOD switching takes place during only a short amount of time, and often not for all objects in a scene at the same time, so this may very well be profitable.

Since the results of a blending operation depend on the current contents of the frame buffer, care has to be taken to draw the models in an order that does not lead to additional artifacts due to the blend. Giegl and Wimmer [255] propose a method that works well in practice.[8] Assume a

---

[8] Another approach using flexible multisampling hardware on the InfiniteReality is possible. Say the multisample mask has eight samples. Then the first LOD is rendered to four of these, and the second LOD is rendered to the remaining samples. Even though this usually looks much better and greatly reduces the popping effect, during the transition, two LODs have to be rendered and blended, which costs time. Also, this kind of flexible multisampling is not available in most accelerators.

transition between two LODs—say LOD1 and LOD2—is desired, and that LOD1 is the current LOD being rendered. Now instead of drawing both LODs transparently, first draw LOD1 opaquely to the frame buffer (both color and Z). Then fade in LOD2 by increasing its alpha value from 0 to 1 and using the "over" blend mode, described in Section 4.5. When LOD2 has faded so it is completely opaque, it is turned into the current LOD, and LOD1 will start to fade out. The LOD that is being faded (in or out) should be rendered with the z-test enabled and z-writes disabled. Note that in the middle of the transition, both LODs are rendered opaquely, one on top of the other.

The advantage of the method is that it works on current graphics hardware and is simple to implement. It also avoids the problems usually associated with alpha blending by always drawing one of the LODs opaquely. Sometimes the silhouettes of the different LODs might not match very well. In such cases, it is advisable to draw all opaque LODs first, and the LODs currently being faded afterwards. This makes sure a correct Z-buffer is established before transparent objects are drawn. The technique works best if the transition intervals are kept short, which also helps keeping the rendering overhead small.

Alpha LODs

A simple method that avoids popping altogether is to use what we call alpha LODs. These do not use a number of differently detailed instances of the same object, but rather only one instance per object. As the metric used for LOD selection (e.g., distance to the object) increases the overall transparency of the object is increased (α is decreased), and the object finally disappears when it reaches full transparency ($\alpha = 0.0$). This happens when the metric value is larger than a user-defined invisibility threshold. There is also another threshold that determines when an object shall start to become transparent. When the invisibility threshold has been reached, the object need not be sent through the rendering pipeline at all as long as the metric value remains above the threshold. When an object has been invisible and its metric falls below the invisibility threshold, then it decreases its transparency and starts to be visible again.

The advantage of this technique is that it is experienced as much more continuous than the discrete geometry LOD method, and so avoids popping. Also, since the object finally disappears altogether and need not be rendered, a significant speed-up can be expected. The disadvantage is that the object entirely disappears, and it is only at this point that speedup is obtained. Figure 9.30 shows an example of alpha LODs.

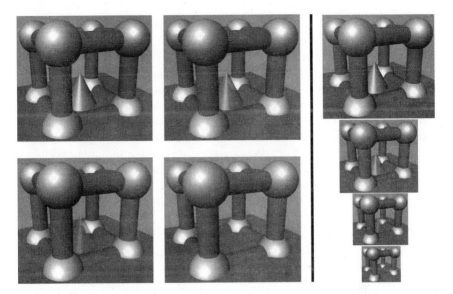

Figure 9.30. The cone in the middle is rendered using an alpha LOD. The transparency of the cone is increased when the distance to it increases, and it finally disappears. The images on the left are shown from the same distance for viewing purposes, while the images to the right of the line are shown at different sizes.

CLODs and Geomorph LODs

The process of mesh simplification can be used to create various LOD models from a single complex object. Algorithms for performing this simplification are discussed in Section 11.5.1. One approach is to create a set of discrete LODs and use these as discussed previously. However, edge collapse methods have an interesting property that allows other ways of making a transition between LODs.

A model has two fewer polygons after each edge collapse operation is performed. What happens in an edge collapse is that an edge is shrunk until its two endpoints meet and it disappears. If this process is animated, a smooth transition occurs between the original model and its slightly simplified version. For each edge collapse, a single vertex is joined with another. Over a series of edge collapses, a set of vertices move to join other vertices. By storing the series of edge collapses, this process can be reversed, so that a simplified model can be made more complex over time. The reversal of an edge collapse is called a *vertex split*. So one way to change the level of detail of an object is to precisely base the number of polygons visible on the LOD selection value. At 100 meters away, the model might consist of 1000 polygons, and moving to 101 meters, it might drop to 998 polygons.

Such a scheme is called a *Continuous Level of Detail* (CLOD) technique. There is not, then, a discrete set of models, but rather a huge set of models available for display, each one with two less polygons than its more complex neighbor. While appealing, using such a scheme in practice has some drawbacks. Not all models in the CLOD stream look good. Triangle strips, which can be displayed more quickly than single triangles, are more difficult to use with CLOD techniques than with static models. If there are a number of the same objects in the scene, then each CLOD object needs to specify its own specific set of triangles, since it does not match any others. Bloom [85] and Forsyth [236] discuss solutions to these and other problems.

In a vertex split, one vertex becomes two. What this means is that every vertex on a complex model comes from some vertex on a simpler version. *Geomorph LODs* [365] are a set of discrete models created by simplification, with the connectivity between vertices maintained. When switching from a complex model to a simple one, the complex model's vertices are interpolated between their original positions and those of the simpler version. When the transition is complete, the simpler level of detail model is used to represent the object. See Figure 9.31 for an example of a transition. There are a number of advantages to geomorphs. The individual static models can be selected in advance to be of high quality, and easily can be turned into triangle strips. Like CLOD, popping is also avoided by smooth transitions. The main drawback is that each vertex needs to be interpolated; CLOD techniques usually do not use interpolation, so the set of vertex positions themselves never changes. Another drawback is that the objects always appear to be changing, which may be distracting. This is especially true for textured objects.

Figure 9.31. The left and right images show a low detail model and a higher detail model. The image in the middle shows a geomorph model interpolated approximately halfway between the left and right models. Note that the cow in the middle has equally many vertices and triangles as the model to the right. *(Images generated using Melax's simplification demo [540].)*

A related idea called fractional tessellation has been finding its way onto hardware. In such schemes, the tessellation factor for a curved surface can be set to any floating point number, and so a popping can be avoided. Fractional tessellation has been used for Bézier patches, and displacement mapping primitives. See Section 12.3.3 for more on these techniques.

9.8.2 LOD Selection

Given that different levels of detail of an object exist, a choice must be made for which one of them to render, or which ones to blend. This is the task of LOD selection, and a few different techniques for this will be presented here. These techniques can also be used to select good occluders for occlusion culling algorithms.

In general, a metric, also called the benefit function, is evaluated for the current viewpoint and the location of the object, and the value of this metric picks an appropriate LOD. This metric may be based on, for example, the distance from the viewpoint to the object, or the projected area of the bounding volume (BV) of the object. The value of the benefit function is denoted r here. See also Section 12.3.2 on how to rapidly estimate the projection of a line onto the screen.

Range-Based

A common way of selecting a LOD is to associate the different LODs of an object with different ranges. The most detailed LOD has a range from zero to some user-defined value r_1, which means that this LOD is visible when the distance to the object is less than r_1. The next LOD has a range from r_1 to r_2 where $r_2 > r_1$. If the distance to the object is greater than or equal to r_1 and less than r_2, then this LOD is used, and so on. Examples of four different LODs with their ranges, and their corresponding LOD node used in a scene graph are illustrated in Figure 9.32.

Projected Area-Based

Another common metric for LOD selection is the projected area of the bounding volume (or an estimation of it). Here, we will show how the number of pixels of that area, called the *screen space coverage*, can be estimated for spheres and boxes with perspective viewing, and then present how the solid angle of a polygon can be efficiently approximated.

Starting with spheres, the estimation is based on the fact that the size of the projection of an object diminishes with the distance from the viewer along the view direction. This is shown in Figure 9.33, which illustrates

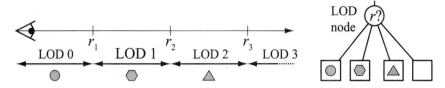

Figure 9.32. The left part of this illustration shows how range-based LODs work. Note that the fourth LOD is an empty object, so when the object is farther away than r_3, nothing is drawn, because the object is not contributing enough to the image to be worth the effort. The right part shows a LOD node in a scene graph. Only one of the children of a LOD node is descended based on r.

how the size of the projection is halved if the distance from the viewer is doubled. We define a sphere by its center point $\mathbf{c}$ and a radius r. The viewer is located at $\mathbf{v}$ looking along the normalized direction vector $\mathbf{d}$. The distance from the view direction is simply the projection of the sphere's center onto the view vector: $\mathbf{d} \cdot (\mathbf{c} - \mathbf{v})$. We also assume that the distance from the viewer to the near plane of the view frustum is n. The near plane is used in the estimation so that an object that is located on the near plane returns its original size. The estimation of the radius of the projected sphere is then:

$$p = \frac{nr}{\mathbf{d} \cdot (\mathbf{c} - \mathbf{v})}. \tag{9.4}$$

The area of the projection is thus πp^2. A higher value selects a more detailed LOD.

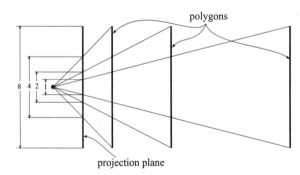

Figure 9.33. This illustration shows how the size of the projection of objects is halved when the distance is doubled.

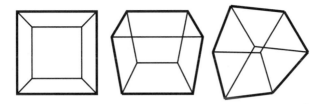

Figure 9.34. Three cases of projection of a cube, showing one, two, and three frontfaces. *(Illustration after Schmalstieg and Tobler [687].)*

Schmalstieg and Tobler have developed a rapid routine for calculating the projected area of a box [687]. The idea is to classify the viewpoint of the camera with respect to the box, and use this classification to determine which projected vertices are included in the silhouette of the projected box. This is done via a *Look-up Table* (LUT). Using these vertices, the area can be computed using the technique presented on page 737. The classification is categorized into three major cases, shown in Figure 9.34. Practically, this classification is done by determining on which side of the planes of the bounding box the viewpoint is located. For efficiency, the viewpoint is transformed into the coordinate system of the box, so that only comparisons are needed for classification. The result of the comparisons are put into a bitmask, which is used as an index into a LUT. This LUT determines how many vertices there are in the silhouette as seen from the viewpoint. Then, another lookup is used to actually find the silhouette vertices. After they have been projected to the screen, the area is computed. Source code is available on the web.

To select a good occluder, Coorg and Teller [143] estimate the solid angle that a polygon subtends. This can also be used for LOD selection. Their approximation is:

$$r = -\frac{a(\mathbf{n} \cdot \mathbf{v})}{\mathbf{d} \cdot \mathbf{d}}. \tag{9.5}$$

Here, a is the area of the polygon, $\mathbf{n}$ is the normal of the polygon, $\mathbf{v}$ is the view direction vector, and $\mathbf{d}$ is the vector from the viewpoint to the center of the polygon. Both $\mathbf{v}$ and $\mathbf{n}$ are assumed to be normalized. The geometry involved is shown in Figure 9.35. The higher the value of r, the higher benefit. The solid angle approximation estimates the benefit because the larger the area, the larger the value, and the value is inversely proportional to the distance to the polygon. Also, the maximum value is reached when the viewer looks at a polygon "head-on," and the value decreases with an increasing angle between the polygon normal and the view direction [143].

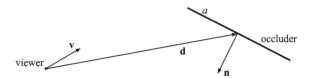

Figure 9.35. The geometry involved in the estimation of the solid angle.

However, this property is mostly useful for occluder selection and not for LOD selection.

Hysteresis

Unnecessary popping can occur if the metric used to determine which LOD to use varies from frame to frame around some value, r_i. A rapid cycling back and forth between levels can occur. This can be solved by introducing some hysteresis around the r_i value [427, 659]. This is illustrated in Figure 9.36 for a range-based LOD, but applies to any type. Here, the upper row of LOD ranges are used only when r is increasing. When r is decreasing, the bottom row of ranges is used.

Other

Range-based and projected area-based LOD selection are typically the most common metrics used. However, many other are possible, and some will be mentioned here. Besides projected area, Funkhouser and Séquin [245] also suggest using the importance of an object (e.g., walls are more important than a clock on the wall), motion, hysteresis (when switching LOD the benefit is lowered), and focus. The viewer's focus of attention can be an

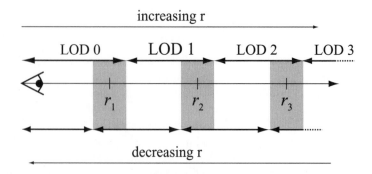

Figure 9.36. The gray areas illustrate the hysteresis regions for the LOD technique.

important factor. For example, in a sports game, the figure controlling the ball is where the user will be paying the most attention, so the other characters can have relatively lower levels of detail [427]. Other, more global metrics are possible, such as limiting the overall number of highly detailed LODs used in order to stay within a given polygon budget [427]. See the next section for more on this topic. Other factors are visibility, colors, and textures. Perceptual metrics can also be used to choose a LOD [646].

9.8.3 Time-Critical LOD Rendering

It is often a desirable feature of a rendering system to have a constant frame rate. In fact, this is what often is referred to as "hard real time" or time-critical. Such a system is given a specific amount of time, say 30 ms, and must complete its task (e.g., render the image) within that time. When time is up, the system has to stop processing. A hard real-time rendering algorithm can be achieved if the objects in a scene are represented by, for example, LODs.

Funkhouser and Séquin [245] have presented a heuristic algorithm that adapts the selection of the level of detail for all visible objects in a scene to meet the requirement of constant frame rate. This algorithm is *predictive* in the sense that it selects the LOD of the visible objects based on desired frame rate and on which objects are visible. Such an algorithm contrasts with a *reactive* algorithm, which bases its selection on the time it took to render the previous frame.

An object is called O and is rendered at a level of detail called L, which gives (O, L) for each LOD of an object. Two heuristics are then defined. One heuristic estimates the cost of rendering an object at a certain level of detail: $Cost(O, L)$. Another estimates the benefit of an object rendered at a certain level of detail: $Benefit(O, L)$. The benefit function estimates the contribution to the image of an object at a certain LOD.

Assume the objects inside or intersecting the view frustum are called S. The main idea behind the algorithm is then to optimize the selection of the LODs for the objects S using the heuristically chosen functions. Specifically, we want to maximize

$$\sum_S Benefit(O, L) \tag{9.6}$$

under the constraint

$$\sum_S Cost(O, L) \leq TargetFrameTime. \qquad (9.7)$$

In other words, we want to select the level of detail for the objects that gives us "the best image" within the desired frame rate. Next we describe how the cost and benefit functions can be estimated, and then we present an optimization algorithm for the above equations.

Both the cost function and the benefit function are hard to define so that they work under all circumstances. The cost function can be estimated by timing the rendering of a LOD several times with different viewing parameters. See Section 9.8.2 for different benefit functions. In practice, the projected area of the BV of the object often suffices as a benefit function.

Finally, we will discuss how to choose the level of detail for the objects in a scene. First, we note the following: For some viewpoints, a scene may be too complex to be able to keep up with the desired frame rate. To solve this, we can define a LOD for each object at its lowest detail level, which is simply an object with no primitives—i.e., we avoid rendering the object [245]. Using this trick, we render only the most important objects and skip the unimportant ones.

To select the "best" LODs for a scene, Equation 9.6 has to be optimized under the constraint shown in Equation 9.7. This is an NP-complete problem, which means that to solve it correctly, the only thing to do is to test *all* different combinations and select the best. This is clearly infeasible for any kind of algorithm. A simpler, more feasible approach is to use a greedy algorithm that tries to maximize the $Value = Benefit(O, L)/Cost(O, L)$ for each object. This algorithm treats all the objects inside the view frustum and chooses to render the objects in descending order, i.e., the one with the highest value first. If an object has the same value for more than one LOD, then the LOD with the highest benefit is selected and rendered. This approach gives the most "bang for the buck." For n objects inside the view frustum, the algorithm runs in $O(n \log n)$ time, and it produces a solution that is at least half as good as the best [245, 246]. Funkhouser and Séquin also exploit frame-to-frame coherence for speeding up the sorting of the values.

More information about LOD management and the combination of LOD management and portal culling can be found in Funkhouser's Ph.D. thesis [246]. Maciel and Shirley [508] combine LODs with impostors and present an approximately constant-time algorithm for rendering outdoor scenes. The general idea is that a hierarchy of different representations (some LODs, hierarchical impostors, etc.) of an object is used. Then the tree is traversed in some fashion to give the best image given a certain amount of time. Mason and Blake [522] present an incremental hierarchical LOD selection algorithm. Again, the different representations of an object can be arbitrary. Eriksson et al. [211] present hierarchical level of details (HLODs). Using these, a scene can be rendered with constant frame rate as well, or rendered such that the rendering error is bounded. Wimmer and Schmalstieg present analytical formulae for selecting balanced choices of the polygon count for continuous levels of detail [804]. They use Lagrange multipliers to solve the same problem Funkhouser and Séquin solved for managing static LODs [245].

9.9 Large Model Rendering

So far it has been implied that the model that is rendered fits into the main memory of the computer. This may not always be the case. One example is to render a model of the earth. This is a complex topic, and so we only point to some relevant literature. Very briefly, several nested data structures are used. Often a quadtree-like data structure is used to cover the surface of the earth [160, 222]. Inside each leaf node different data structures can be used depending on its contents. Also, in order to maintain a reasonable frame rate, areas that are about to come into view are paged in from disk just before they are needed. The quadtree is used for that as well. The combination of different acceleration algorithms is nontrivial. Aliaga et al. [14, 15, 16] have combined several algorithms for extremely large scenes. Section 5.3 discusses clip-mapping, a related technique for managing large textures. The SIGGRAPH course notes on large model rendering are a good resource for the interested reader [18].

9.10 Point Rendering

In 1985, Levoy and Whitted wrote a pioneering technical report [489] where they suggested the use of points as a new primitive used to render everything. The general idea is to represent a surface using a large set of points and render these. In a subsequent pass, Gaussian filtering is performed in order to fill in gaps between rendered points. The radius of the Gaussian filter depends on the density of points on the surface, and the projected density on the screen. Levoy and Whitted implemented this system on a VAX-11/780. However, it was not until about 15 years later that point-based rendering again became of interest. Two reasons for this resurgence are that computing power reached a level where point-based rendering truly made sense, and that extremely large models obtained from laser range scanners became available [491]. Such models are initially represented as unconnected three-dimensional points. Rusinkiewicz and Levoy present a system called *QSplat* [665], which uses a hierarchy of spheres to represent the model. This hierarchy is used for hierarchical backface and view frustum culling, and level of detail rendering. The nodes in this tree are compressed in order to be able to render scenes consisting of several hundred million points. A point is rendered as a shape with a radius, called a splat. Different splat shapes that can be used are squares, opaque circles, and fuzzy circles. See Figure 9.37 for an example. Rendering may stop at any level in the tree. The nodes at that level are rendered as splats with the same radius as the node's sphere. Therefore, the bounding sphere hierarchy is constructed so that no holes are visible at all levels. Since traversal of the tree can stop at any level, interactive frame rates can be obtained by stopping the traversal at an appropriate level. When the user stops moving around, the quality of the rendering can be refined repeatedly until the leaves of the hierarchy are reached. Pfister et al. [620] present the *surfel*— a surface element. A surfel is also a point-based primitive. An octree is used to store the sampled surfels (position, normal, filtered texels). During

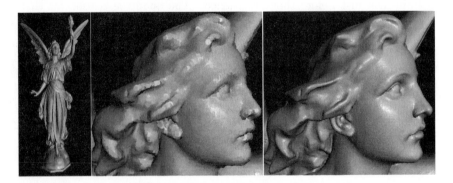

Figure 9.37. These models were rendered with point-based rendering, using circular splats. The left image shows the full model of an angel named Lucy, with 10 million vertices. However, only about 3 million splats were used in the rendering. The middle and right images zoom in on the head. The middle image used about 40,000 splats during rendering. When the viewer stopped moving, the result converged to the image shown to the right, with 600,000 splats. *(Images generated by the QSPlat program by Szymon Rusinkiewicz. The model of Lucy was created by the Stanford Graphics Laboratory.)*

rendering, the surfels are projected onto the screen, and subsequently, a visibility splatting algorithm is used to fill in any holes created.

Further Reading and Resources

The Inventor Mentor [799] discusses the way scene graphs operate. For an in-depth treatment of a wide range of tree structures and their precise definitions, see Samet's books [669, 670]. Abrash's book [2] offers a thorough treatment of the use of polygon-based BSP trees and their application in games such as *Doom* and *Quake*. A thorough treatment of BSP trees and their history is also given by James [389]. A number of different view frustum culling optimizations (and their combinations) are presented by Assarsson and Möller [33].

There is a wealth of literature about occlusion culling. Three good starting places are the visibility surveys by Cohen-Or et al. [135], Durand [191], and the Umbra Reference Manual [5], which contains an entire thesis. The first two surveys are included in the SIGGRAPH course notes on visibility [134].

Greene and Kass [290] have developed an extension to hierarchical Z-buffering that renders antialiased scenes with error bounds. Another interesting algorithm for occlusion culling is the visibility skeleton developed by Durand et al. [189, 190]. The best resource for information on levels of detail is the SIGGRAPH course by Luebke et al. [507].

Chapter 10
Pipeline Optimization

"We should forget about small efficiencies, say about 97% of the time: premature optimization is the root of all evil."
–Donald Knuth

As we saw in Chapter 2, the process of rendering an image is based on a pipelined architecture with three conceptual stages: *application, geometry,* and *rasterizer.* Due to this architecture, one of these stages, or the communication path between them, will *always* be the bottleneck—the slowest stage in the pipeline. This implies that the bottleneck stage sets the limit for the throughput, i.e., the total rendering performance, and so is a prime candidate for *optimization.*

Optimizing the performance of the rendering pipeline resembles the process of optimizing a pipelined processor (CPU) [354] in that it consists mainly of two steps. First, the bottleneck of the pipeline is located. Second, that stage is optimized in some way; and after that, step one is repeated if the performance goals have not been met. Note that the bottleneck may or may not be located at the same place after the optimization step. It is a good idea to put only enough effort into optimizing the bottleneck stage so that the bottleneck moves to another stage. Several other stages may have to be optimized before this stage becomes the bottleneck again. This is why effort should not be wasted on over-optimizing a stage.

The location of the bottleneck may change within a frame. At one moment the geometry stage may be the bottleneck because many tiny triangles are rendered. Later in the frame the rasterizer could be the bottleneck because triangles covering large parts of the screen are rendered. So, when we talk about, say, the rasterizer stage being the bottleneck, we mean it is the bottleneck most of the time during that frame.

Another way to capitalize on the pipelined construction is to recognize that when the slowest stage cannot be optimized further, the other stages can be made to work just as much as the slowest stage. This will not change performance, since the speed of the slowest stage will not be altered. For example, say that the bottleneck is in the application stage, which takes 50 milliseconds (ms), while the others each take 25 ms. This means that without changing the speed of the rendering pipeline (50 ms equals 20 frames per second), the geometry and the rasterizer stages could also do their work in 50 ms. For example, we could use a more sophisticated lighting model or increase the level of realism with shadows and reflections (assuming that this does not increase the workload on the application stage).

The division of the pipeline into the three stages—application, geometry, and rasterizing—is a conceptual division. Depending on the architecture, the true pipeline stages may look different. For example, the application and geometry stages are sometimes both performed by a single CPU, and so should be treated as one stage when optimizing.

Pipeline optimization is a process in which we first maximize the rendering speed, then allow the stages that are not bottlenecks to consume as much time as the bottleneck. When reading this chapter, the dictum

KNOW YOUR ARCHITECTURE

should constantly be in the back of your mind, since optimization techniques vary greatly for different architectures. A related dictum is, simply, "Measure." The sections that follow give you methods to determine where the slowdowns are and what to do about them.

10.1   Locating the Bottleneck

The process of optimization can be very time consuming, and so it is often infeasible to optimize every stage in the graphics pipeline. If every stage is optimized, then a boost in performance is guaranteed, but with a cost of the programmer's time and possibly with a potentially unnecessary trade-off in rendering quality. Another drawback of optimizing everything is that we will not learn which stages in the pipeline are not bottleneck stages. These stages can be exploited to create higher-quality rendering without affecting overall performance.

The first step in optimizing a pipeline is to locate the bottleneck. At any given time there is always one bottleneck, and this bottleneck sets the limit of the speed of the application. The goal is then to track it down and then eliminate it. Finding the bottleneck is not easily done simply by timing the process, since if you clock the time from the start of rendering until the image has been rendered, you will be looking at the time it takes for the data to pass through the *entire* pipeline. It is more reasonable to check the time at one location in the code (for example, after a screen clear), and stop timing the next time that location is executed. This way, however, you will only obtain information on how long the bottleneck stage takes to execute, not on where the bottleneck is located. Recall that the total time of rendering an image is the time of the bottleneck stage, which may be any one of the application, geometry, and rasterizer stages, or the communication between the stages (e.g., the bus between CPU and accelerator can definitely be a bottleneck [509]). Another approach would be to clock the individual stages, but that is often difficult since the rasterizer stage, and often the geometry stage, are implemented in dedicated graphics hardware.

We have to take other approaches to locate the bottleneck. One way of doing this is to set up a number of tests, where each test only affects one stage at a time. If the total rendering time is affected, i.e., lowered, then the bottleneck has been found. A related way of testing a stage is to reduce the workload on the other stages without reducing the workload on the stage being tested. If performance does not change, then the bottleneck is the stage where the workload was not altered. What follows is a set of tests that use these methods to find the bottleneck.

10.1.1 Testing the Application Stage

If the platform being used is supplied with a utility for measuring the workload on the processor(s), then that utility can be used to see if your program uses 100 percent (or near that) of the CPU processing power. For Unix systems, there are usually programs called `top` or `osview` that show the process workload on the CPU(s). For Windows NT there is the Task Manager. If the CPU is in constant use, then your program is *CPU-limited*. This is not always foolproof, since you may be waiting for the hardware to complete a frame, and this wait operation is sometimes implemented as a busy-wait. Using a code profiler to determine where the time is spent is better. If the geometry stage is done on the CPU as well, then we cannot discern between the geometry stage and the application stage when using this technique. AMD has a tool called *CodeAnalyst* [128] for analyzing and optimizing the code run on their line of CPUs, and Intel has a similar tool called *VTune Analyzer* [782] that can analyze where the time is spent in the application or in a driver (geometry processing).

Another smarter way to test for CPU limits is to send down data that causes the other stages to do little or no work. For some APIs this can be accomplished by simply using a null driver (a driver that accepts calls but does nothing) instead of a real driver. This effectively sets an upper limit on how fast you can get the entire program to run, because we do not use the graphics hardware, and thus, the CPU is the bottleneck. Also, by doing this test, you get an idea on how much room for improvement there is for the stages not run in the application stage. That said, be aware that using a null driver can also hide any bottleneck due to communication between stages.

Another method of doing less work that is successful for some architectures is to substitute API calls. In OpenGL this can be done by replacing all `glVertex3fv` and `glNormal3fv` calls with `glColor3fv` calls [417]. This does not change the workload on the CPU at all—it sends as much data as it did before, but the workload on both the geometry and the rasterizer stages is greatly reduced. The geometry stage has no lighting to compute, no clipping to perform, no screen mapping to do, nor any vertices or normals to transform. The rasterizer stage does not receive any vertices from the geometry stage, so it does not get any primitives to render. How should this test be interpreted? If performance does not improve, then the program is definitely CPU-limited, since the geometry and rasterizer stages do not have any tasks to perform.

10.1.2   Testing the Geometry Stage

The geometry stage is the most difficult stage to test. This is because if the workload on this stage is changed, then the workload on one or both of the other stages is often changed as well. One parameter that only affects the workload on the geometry stage is the type and number of light sources. If all light sources in the scene are disabled or removed and the performance goes up, then the bottleneck is located in the geometry stage, and the program is said to be *transform-limited* or *transform-bound*. Similarly, lighting, texture coordinate generation, and fog could be disabled, as these operations also are done in the geometry stage. Another test is to increase the number of light sources (add one or two more), or to set the light source type to the most expensive one, i.e., spotlights. If the performance remains intact with these changes, then the bottleneck is *not* located in the geometry stage.

If programmable vertex shaders (see Section 6.5) are available in hardware, you can simply use a vertex program that just transforms each vertex and does no lighting calculations, which would decrease the load on the geometry stage. Again, if performance goes up, this stage is the bottleneck.

Another strategy is to test both the application and rasterizer stages for the bottleneck, and if neither of these is the bottleneck, then the geometry stage must be.

10.1.3 Testing the Rasterizer Stage

The rasterizer stage is the easiest and fastest to test: Simply decrease the resolution of the viewport where the images are being rendered. This does not affect the application stage or the geometry stage, but does affect the workload on the rasterizer stage, since the result is that it has to *fill* fewer pixels. Should the total rendering performance increase with a decrease of the rendering resolution, then the graphics pipeline is said to be *fill-limited* or *fill-bound*, and the bottleneck is in the rasterizer stage.

Other tests are to turn off blending and depth buffering, as these features affect only the rasterizer stage. Again, if the total rendering time decreases, then the rasterizer stage is the bottleneck. However, if the occlusion techniques in Section 15.3.5 are in hardware, they can have the effect that using depth buffering is actually faster than painting each polygon.

10.2 Performance Measurements

Before delving into different ways of optimizing the performance of the graphics pipeline, a brief presentation of performance measurements will be given. One way to express the performance of the geometry stage is in terms of *vertices per second*. As a historical note, the commodity graphics hardware of 2001 could handle several tens of millions of triangles per second. As in the geometry stage, one way to express the fill rate of the rasterizer stage is in terms of *pixels per second* (or sometimes *texels per second*). As of 2001, commodity graphics hardware can handle several hundreds of millions of pixels per second.

Note that graphics hardware manufacturers often present peak rates, which are impossible or, at best, hard to reach. Also, since we are dealing with a pipelined system, it is not as simple as to just give these kinds of numbers. This is because the location of the bottleneck may move from one time to another, and the different pipeline stages interact in different ways during execution. When it comes to measuring performance for CPUs, the trend has been to avoid IPS (*Instructions Per Second*), FLOPS (*Floating*

Point Operations Per Second), gigahertz, and simple short benchmarks. Instead, the method of preference is to use clock cycle counters [2], or to measure wall clock times for a range of different, real programs [354], and then compare the running times for these. Following this trend, most independent benchmarks instead measure the actual frame rate for a number of given scenes, and for a number of different screen resolutions. Find out what the peak rates represent, and try to duplicate: Usually you will find the bus getting in the way, but the exercise is guaranteed to generate insights into the architecture like nothing else can.

10.3 Optimization

Once a bottleneck has been located, we want to optimize that stage to boost the performance. Optimizing techniques for the application, geometry, and rasterizer stages are presented next. Some of these optimizations trade off quality for speed, and some are just clever tricks for making the execution of a certain stage faster.

One thing to think about during optimization is that you may already run at the full speed of the system. So, if your performance comes close to what the hardware manufacturer claims to be the performance of the graphics hardware, then you definitely do not need to optimize the parts of the pipeline that are hardware-accelerated [136]. For better performance, you have to turn to different acceleration techniques, which is the topic of Chapter 9.

10.3.1 Application Stage

The application stage is optimized by making the code faster and the memory accesses of the program faster or fewer. Detailed code optimization is out of the scope of this book, and optimization techniques usually differ from one CPU manufacturer to another. The best approach is to consult the CPU manual of the computer that is used. However, here we will give some general optimization techniques that apply to most CPUs.

First, turn on the optimization flags for the compiler. There are usually a number of different flags, and you will have to check which of these apply to your code. Make few assumptions about what optimization options to use. For example, setting the compiler to "minimize code size" instead of "optimizing for speed" may result in faster code because caching performance is improved. Also, if possible, try different compilers as these are optimized in different ways.

Compiler options may help quite a bit in some cases, but fast code cannot be created entirely by the compiler—for that, human optimization is needed, together with knowledge about the CPU architecture. For code optimization it is crucial to locate the place in the code where most of the time is spent. A good code profiler is key in finding these code hot spots. Optimization efforts should be made in these places.

The basic rule of optimization is to try a variety of tactics: Reexamine algorithms, assumptions, and code syntax, trying as many variants as possible. CPU architecture and compiler performance often limit the user's ability to form an intuition about how to write the fastest code, so question your assumptions and keep an open mind. For example, Booth [97] shows a piece of code in which a seemingly useless array access actually feeds the cache and speeds the overall routine by 25 percent.[1] Another such example shows how making sure all vertices are rewritten when part of a mesh is updated actually makes for faster AGP bus transfers [509].

Below we present tricks and methods for writing fast code, and then we address memory issues. These considerations apply to most pipelined CPUs with a memory hierarchy and a cache at the topmost level(s). The rules are constantly changing, though, so it helps to know your target architecture well (and to keep in mind that it will change someday, so some optimizations made now may eventually become useless or counterproductive). For example, float-to-long conversion is slow on Pentiums due to compliance with the C ANSI standard. A custom assembly language routine can save significant time (while sacrificing ANSI compliance) [39].

Code Issues

The list that follows gives some tricks for writing fast code.

- Single Instruction Multiple Data (SIMD) instruction sets, such as Intel's SSE and SSE2, AMD's 3DNow!, and Motorola's AltiVec, could be used in many situations with great performance gains. Typically, 2–4 elements can be computed in parallel, which thus is perfect for vector operations.

---

[1] A cache is a small fast-memory area that exists because there is usually much coherence in a program, which the cache can exploit. That is, nearby locations in memory tend to be accessed one after another (spatial coherency), and code is often accessed sequentially. Also, memory locations tend to be accessed repeatedly (temporal coherency), which the cache also exploits.

- Avoid using division as much as possible. Such instructions usually take 4 to 39 times longer to execute than most of the other instructions. For example, take normalizing a three-dimensional vector. Conceptually, this is done by dividing all elements in the vector by the length of the vector. Instead of dividing three times, it is faster to compute $1/l$, where l is the length of the vector, and then multiply all elements by this factor. Modern CPUs also have special instructions that rapidly compute low precision reciprocal $(1/x)$ and reciprocal square roots $(1/\sqrt{x})$.

- Conditional branches are often expensive, though most processors have branch prediction, which means as long as the branches can be consistently predicted, the cost can be low. However, a mispredicted branch is often very expensive on some architectures, especially those with deep pipelines.

- Another way to make conditional branches faster is to actually remove them. This can be done with "conditional move" instructions such as CMOVxx and FCMOVxx on Pentium Pros and up. These instructions can compute lines like res = a>b ? choice1 : choice2; without any conditionals, and thus without any branches. This eliminates branch misprediction.

- Unroll small loops in order to get rid of the loop overhead. However, this makes the code bigger and thus may degrade cache performance. Also, branch prediction usually works very well on loops. The compiler can do the loop unrolling for you.

- On PCs, aligning frequently used data structures to multiples of exactly 32 bytes can noticeably improve overall performance by using cache lines optimally [693]. Check the cache line size on your computer; on Pentium IVs, the L1 (level 1) cache line size is 64 bytes, and the L2 (level 2) cache line size is 128 bytes, so for these, it is better to align to either 64 or 128 bytes. On an AMD Athlon the cache line size is 64 bytes for both L1 and L2. Compiler options can help, but it helps to design your data structures with alignment, called *padding*, in mind. Tools such as *cacheprof* for Linux can help identify caching bottlenecks [109].

- Math functions such as sin, cos, tan, exp, arcsin, etc., are expensive and should be used with care. If lower precision is acceptable, develop or use approximate routines (possibly using SIMD instructions) where only the first few terms in the MacLaurin or Taylor series (see Equation B.2) are used. Since memory accesses can be expensive on modern CPUs, this is usually preferred over using lookup tables.

- Use inline code for small functions that are frequently called.

- Lessen floating-point precision when reasonable. For example, on an Intel Pentium, floating-point division normally takes 39 cycles at 80 bits of precision, but only 19 cycles at 32 bits (however, at any precision, division by a power of 2 takes around 8 cycles) [97]. When choosing `float` instead of `double`, remember to attach an `f` at the end of constants. Otherwise, they and whole expressions may be cast to `double`. So `float x=2.42f;` may be faster than `float x=2.42;`.

- Lower precision is also better, because less data is then sent down the graphics pipeline.

- Try different ways of coding the same algorithm. Predecrementing (`--cnt`) instead of postdecrementing (`cnt--`) can generate less code on some compilers, as can using indexing and avoiding pointer increments, e.g., doing `p[n] = q[n];` instead of `*p++ = *q++;` [97].

- Use `restrict` (in C, to avoid pointer aliasing) and `const` whenever possible, as the compiler may use it as a hint for optimization.

- Virtual methods, dynamic casting, (inherited) constructors, and passing structs by value have some efficiency penalties. In one case reported to us, 40% of the time spent in a frame was used on the virtual inheritance hierarchy that managed models. Blinn [80] presents techniques for avoiding overhead for evaluating vector expressions in C++.

Memory Issues

Dealing with writing fast code with respect to the memory hierarchy is becoming more and more important on the various CPU architectures. Below is a list of pointers that should be kept in consideration when programming.

- Assume nothing when it comes to the system memory routines (or anything else, for that matter). For example, if you know the direction of a copy, or that no overlap of source and destination occurs, then an assembly loop using the largest registers available is the quickest way to do a copy. This is not necessarily what the system's memory routines provide.

- Memory that is accessed sequentially in the code should also be stored sequentially in the memory. For example, when rendering a triangle mesh, store texture coordinate #0, normal #0, color #0, vertex #0, texture coordinate #1, normal #1, etc., sequentially in memory if they are accessed in that order.

- Try different organizations of data structures. For example, Hecker [336] shows how a surprisingly large amount of time was saved by testing a variety of matrix structures for a simple matrix multiplier. An array of structures,

```
struct Vertex {float x,y,z;}
Vertex myvertices[1000];
```

or a structure of arrays,

```
struct VertexChunk {float x[1000],y[1000],z[1000];}
VertexChunk myvertices;
```

may work better for a given architecture. This second structure is better for using SIMD commands, but as the number of vertices goes up, the chance of a cache miss increases. As the array size increases, a hybrid scheme,

```
struct Vertex4 {float x[4],y[4],z[4];}
Vertex4 myvertices[250];
```

may be the best choice that works well with existing code.

- Try to exploit the cache(s) of the architecture. A bad access pattern in the memory may ruin the entire performance of the code.

- Cache prefetching [23]: For good code performance, it is vital that the code that is going to be executed and the memory that is going to be accessed next is in the cache. The penalty for not having these blocks in the cache when needed can degrade performance enormously. Some architectures have a special *prefetch* instruction that fetches a block of memory into the cache before it is being accessed. For example, on SPARC processors, there is `prefetch`; for the PowerPC it is called `dcbt` (data cache block touch; for AMD Athlons they are called `PREFETCH` and `PREFETCHW`; and for Pentium III and Pentium 4 they are called `PrefetchNTA` and `PrefetchTx`, where x= $0, 1, 2$. There are also compilers that automatically generate these instructions. For those that do not have such a compiler or architecture, *garbage instructions* [97] can be used to feed a sequence of the memory into the cache. The Pentium IV has special logic that recognizes repeated memory accesses and prefetches accordingly. That said, it is very difficult to prefetch successfully by hand, so make sure to put cycle-accurate counters [2] around the code and measure.

- Avoid pointer indirection, jumps, and function calls, as these may eliminate the advantages of having a cache on the CPU. These problems can easily decrease the performance of the cache. You get pointer indirection when you follow a pointer to another pointer and so on (typical for linked lists and tree structures; use arrays instead as possible). McVoy and Staelin [537] show a code example that follows a linked list through pointers. This causes cache misses for instructions both before and after, and their example stalls the CPU more than 100 times longer than it takes to follow the pointer (if the cache could provide the address of the pointer). Note also that a large program implies a small probability that the function that is about to be called is in the cache and thus stalls the processing.

- The functions `malloc()` and `free()` may be slow on some systems, so it is often better to allocate a big pool of memory at start-up, and then use your own allocation and free routines for handling the memory of that pool. The normal `malloc()` and `free()` can then be used only when necessary [358]. Better yet, try to avoid allocate or free altogether within the rendering loop, e.g., allocate scratch space once, and have stacks, arrays, and other structures only grow (using a variable or flags to note which elements should be treated as deleted). For multiprocessor systems memory management is even more important, since a call to these functions may end up in a mutual exclusion lock.

Another way to make the application stage run faster is to change to a machine with more processors, and then parallelize the code. Since the penalties for cache misses are greater for a multiprocessor system, it is important to adapt the code to the memory system for such architectures.

10.3.2 Geometry Stage

The geometry stage is responsible for transforms, lighting, clipping, projection, and screen mapping. Transforms and lighting are processes that can be optimized relatively easily; the rest are difficult or impossible to optimize.

Connected and Compressed Primitives

Indexed vertex buffers (in OpenGL, vertex arrays) are the fastest way to provide the accelerator with data. These are discussed in detail in Section 11.4.5. Use of AGP memory, DMA pull, and storage of the data in video memory are some of the factors that affect performance. Transform, lighting, projection, clipping, and screen-mapping operations can also all gain from compact data storage.

Indexed vertex buffers are efficient, but some are more efficient than others. The overarching rule of "know your hardware" certainly applies here, as some vertex buffer schemes are fastest for a particular machine. There are variations in how memory is allocated and maintained (e.g., write-only buffers are faster), optimal vertex record sizes, how data copying can be avoided using fences, etc. Some general principles apply. Index buffers forming triangle strips will usually be more compact that lists of unconnected triangles, assuming reasonable length strips can be discovered. Even for sets of unconnected triangles, triangle order matters. Most graphics hardware has vertex caches that may be automatically used when indexed primitives are sent to the pipeline. The cache stores the transformed and lit vertices, and for cache-hits, all geometry processing is avoided. Current cache sizes are about 10–30 vertices. Optimizing triangle strips for a particular vertex cache can be dangerous, especially if the application should work well on many different graphics architectures. For example, if the vertex cache size is 12 and the strip size is 13, then strips exist that never would get any hits in the cache. One better approach is the universal algorithm described in Section 11.4.4.

Another way to decrease overall bus traffic, while also reducing application-side memory use, is to store the vertex data in a compressed form. For example, full floating point precision is unnecessary for surface normal components, as these are used for shading computations that are represented by byte values. Deering [166] discusses such techniques in depth. With the introduction of the vertex shader, such techniques become practical on commodity PCs. Calver [110] presents a variety of schemes that use the vertex shader for decompression.

Lighting

Lighting computations can be optimized in several ways. First, the types of light sources being used should be considered. Is lighting needed for all polygons? Sometimes a model only requires texturing, or texturing with colors at the vertices, or simply colors at the vertices. For example, a large background polygon might look bad when lit by positional light sources, because its vertices are far away from the lights. It might be better simply not to light the background polygon at all. If light sources must be used, then directional light sources are faster than point lights, which are, in turn, faster than spotlights. Directional lights are faster because the pipeline does not need to compute and normalize the vector from the vertex to the light source position. Instead, the light direction is used. Spotlights are more expensive than point lights because with spotlights the pipeline needs to test whether vertices are inside the light cone and also to compute the exponential fall-off from the center of the light cone. The number of light sources also influences the performance of the geometry stage. Some graphics accelerators are optimized for lighting calculations with only one light source. More light sources mean less speed. Also, two-sided lighting may be more expensive than one-sided lighting. When using distance attenuation on the light sources, it may be useful, and hardly noticeable, to turn off/on light sources on a per-object basis, depending on the distance from the object to the light sources. When the distance is great enough, turn off the light source. Another way to remove work from the geometry stage is to disable lighting and instead use an environment map (see Section 5.7.4).

Second, in some APIs, a *nonlocal viewer* can be used. This feature does not affect the view itself; it is a simplification that affects only the specular highlight computations and environment mapping calculations (only DirectX). The idea is to treat the camera as if it were at infinity, but only for these lighting computations. Normally, the vector from the eye to the vertex being illuminated is computed and normalized—a costly per-vertex computation. With a nonlocal viewer, this vector is approximated with the constant vector along the Z-axis in eye-coordinates. When used with directional lights, it means that such values as $\mathbf{h}$ (see Section 4.3.2) can be computed just once for each scene. Using this feature causes a slight shift in the locations of specular highlights, but such shifts are not usually detectable. That said, this feature is worth avoiding when previewing a scene which will be sent to a high-quality renderer, as the shift will often be noticeable between images. Another situation in which the shift is noticeable is when a flat surface is shiny and receives a bright highlight (i.e., when the light reflects toward the eye). In this case, a disturbing "flash" (sudden brightness) appears as the surface passes through this orientation, since all reflection vectors are the same. Direct3D offers a variation on the nonlocal viewer concept, using *parallel-point lights*. The idea is that the point light establishes a single direction vector from it to the center of a vertex mesh. This direction is then used for all vertices of the mesh, and the light is therefore parallel. This simplifies lighting computations.

Third, the normals of a model must be normalized when calculating the lighting. For a model that will *not* be scaled in any way during rendering, those normals should be normalized as a preprocess (with all scalings accounted for). This could be done in two ways. The model may be transformed as before, and the normals may be scaled (as a preprocess) in such a way that they are normalized after all transforms have been applied to the model. Or, this optimization could be thought of as part of the flattening: Simply flatten the transforms for the model, and after that has been done, normalize the normals. The graphics API needs to be told that the normals are already normalized so that the graphics engine does not waste time normalizing them. For uniform scaling, some implementations avoid scaling the normals. Normalization costs differ among different architectures.

Fourth, if lighting is computed for both sides of a polygon and is not needed, then turn this feature off.

Fifth, if materials or lights have a specular component set to $(0, 0, 0)$, then the rather expensive highlight calculations in the lighting equation (see Section 4.20) can be avoided. This is especially useful if the lighting computations are done with the CPU or in a vertex shader.

Finally, if light sources are static with respect to geometry, and the polygonal data is attached to a material without specular parameters, then the diffuse and ambient lighting can be precomputed and stored as colors at the vertices (though doing so means more data being sent over the bus).[2] For greater realism, simple shadows can be captured by direct visibility tests between lights and vertices, and then combined with the ambient and diffuse lighting (the diffuse lighting is set to zero if the object is in shadow). The result is that lighting computations can be turned off for those objects, and so they are often called *preshaded*, *prelit*, or *baked*. A more elaborate form of prelighting is to use radiosity methods to precompute the diffuse global illumination in a scene (see Section 6.13.1). Such illumination can be stored as colors at the vertices or as light maps (see Section 5.7.2). Specular (view-dependent) contributions can be added in, though care must be taken to avoid having highlights appear in areas that are in shadow. Simple state-changes (such as turning a light off) or animations (such as flickering torches) can be performed by creating sets of vertex colors and switching among them [642]. If the model has a limited range of motion compared to the lights, lighting could be precomputed for a number of orientations and the vertex colors for the frame determined by interpolation [239].

---

[2]Doing so is often referred to as "baking" on the lighting.

Vertex Shader Optimization

Section 6.5 dealt with programmable vertex shaders. A vertex shader is a small program that is sent down to a unit in the geometry stage, which then executes the program on each vertex sent down the pipeline. The most obvious way to optimize such programs is to keep them short, that is, to use as few instructions as possible. The average execution time is proportional to the number of instructions in the program. We say "on average" because sometimes two instructions may be issued simultaneously, and sometimes the pipeline is stalled. This tends to average to one instruction per cycle. Thus, doubling the number of instructions doubles the execution time in the geometry stage. There is also a cost in changing the actual vertex program, so try to group objects by their vertex shader.

Hardware today can have several vertex shader unit running in parallel to boost performance. For example, the Xbox has two vertex shader units that run in parallel (see Section 15.3.6). As the basic vertex shader is a dedicated SIMD CPU that cannot execute branches, we can expect that future units will follow the development of modern pipelined CPUs. In the future, it may be possible that many (more than two) instructions can be issued per cycle, that out-of-order execution will be done, and that by-passing of dependent values will be in the vertex shader units. Consult Hennessy and Patterson's book [354] on computer architecture for information on what kind of performance boosting features may be used in future hardware implementations of vertex shader units.

10.3.3 Rasterizer Stage

The rasterizer stage can be optimized in a variety of ways. For closed (solid) objects and for objects that will never show their backfaces (for example, the back side of a wall in a room), backface culling should be turned on (see Section 9.3). For a closed object this reduces the number of triangles to be rasterized by approximately 50 percent. Remember that even though backface culling may help eliminate the unnecessary processing of primitives, it comes with a cost of computing whether the primitive is facing away from the viewer. For example, if all polygons are front-facing, then the backface culling calculations may actually slow down the geometry stage.

Another technique that does not degrade the rendering quality is to turn off Z-buffering at certain times. For example, after the frame buffer has been cleared, any background image can be drawn without the need for depth testing. Algorithms such as polygon-aligned BSP trees (see Section 9.1.2) have the advantage of never needing to use the Z-buffer. Local

BSP trees can also be used, which are then merged in real time during rendering [582].

If every pixel on the screen is guaranteed to be covered by some object (e.g., the scene is indoors, or a background sky image is in use), then the color buffer does not need to be cleared. The Z-buffer clear can also be avoided by sacrificing one bit of depth accuracy. Clear the Z-buffer properly on the first frame and render into only the front half of the buffer, i.e., the depth normalized device coordinates are rescaled to the range -1.0 to 0.0. On the second frame, instead of clearing the Z-buffer, flip the view direction and the sense of the depth test (i.e., so that the larger z-depth value wins), and set the depth range from 1.0 at the near plane to 0.0 at the far. On the third frame the range -1.0 to 0.0 is again used, and each frame thereafter flips between these two ranges. This has the effect that the previous frame's z-depth values will always be covered by any objects being rendered this frame, and so act as z-depth clear values [61]. That said, technologies such as *HyperZ* (Section 15.3.5) save Z-buffer clear time in hardware, in which case using this software trick is actually detrimental.

Remember to use native texture and pixel formats, i.e., use the formats that the graphics hardware use internally to avoid a possible expensive transform from one format to another [136]. Also, use `glTexSubImage2D` instead of `glTexImage2D` when you are updating textures, as on some hardware, this avoids memory allocation and deallocation. Another technique to try is texture compression. Such textures are faster to send to texture memory if they are compressed before they are sent to the graphics hardware. As an example, such compression could improve the loading time of a level in a game. If possible, compressing once off-line is best. Doing so also allows the quality of the textures to be checked in advance. Use the calls `glCompressedTexImage` and `glCompressedTexSubImage` for compressed textures in OpenGL. Another advantage of compressed textures is that they improve cache usage since they use less memory. This gives better performance. See also Section 5.3.

Decreasing the resolution of the window where the images are rendered is a common method of improving performance at the cost of quality. On the InfiniteReality graphics system [106, 568], *dynamic video resizing* can be used to lower the load on the rasterizer subsystem. This works by decreasing the actual image being rendered. When the generated image is to be displayed, the smaller image is enlarged to the desired size using a linear interpolation filter. This could be implemented on a system with a fast render-to-texture. First, render the scene to a texture smaller than the target window, and then use a bilinear texture filter to magnify the texture to cover the entire window.

On some hardware, such as the InfiniteReality, there is also hardware support (called pipeline instrumentation) for measuring the workload on different stages in the pipeline. As an example, the size of the rendering window can be dynamically changed as the workload on the different stages of the pipeline changes. The pipeline instrumentation features are of great help in generating accurate timings and simplifying the task of optimization.

Never forget to question assumptions. For example, if we use OpenGL's `glDrawPixels()`, it draws a given image directly to the screen, one screen pixel per image pixel. However, on many architectures it is faster to draw such an image by making it a texture on a screen aligned rectangle.

To understand the behavior of a program, and especially the load on the rasterizer, it is useful to visualize the depth complexity, which is the number of times a pixel is touched. One simple method of generating a depth complexity image is to use a call like OpenGL's `glBlendFunc(GL_ONE,GL_ONE)`, with Z-buffering disabled. First, the image is cleared to black. All objects in the scene are then rendered with the color $(0, 0, 1)$. The effect of the blend function setting is that for each primitive rendered, the values of the written pixels will increase by $(0, 0, 1)$. The image at the right in Figure 10.1 was rendered with this technique. A pixel with a depth complexity of 0 is then black and a pixel of depth complexity 255 is full blue $(0, 0, 255)$.

A two-pass approach can be used to count the number of pixels that pass or fail the Z-buffer depth tests. In the first pass, enable Z-buffering and use the method above to count the pixels that have passed the depth test.

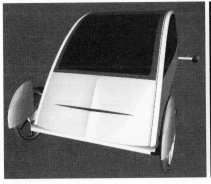 

Figure 10.1. The image on the left shows a model of a three wheeler, and its depth complexity is visualized on the right—the brighter the pixel, the more times the pixel has been overwritten. *(The three wheeler model reused courtesy of Nya Perspektiv Design AB.)*

To count the number of pixels that fail the depth test, increment the stencil buffer upon depth buffer failure. Alternately, render with Z-buffering off to obtain the depth complexity, and then subtract the first-pass results.

These methods can serve to determine the average, minimum, and maximum depth complexity in a scene; the number of pixels per primitive (assuming that the number of primitives that have made it to the scene is known); and the number of pixels that pass versus fail the depth tests. These numbers are useful for understanding the behavior of a real-time graphics application and determining where further optimization may be worthwhile.

Depth complexity tells how many surfaces cover each pixel. The amount of *pixel overdraw* is related to how many surfaces actually were rendered. Say two polygons cover a pixel, so the depth complexity is two. If the farther polygon is drawn first, the nearer polygon overdraws it, and the amount of overdraw is one. If the nearer is drawn first, the farther polygon fails the depth test and is not drawn, so there is no overdraw. For a random set of opaque polygons covering a pixel, the average number of draws is the *harmonic series* [147]:

$$H(n) = 1 + \frac{1}{2} + \frac{1}{3} + ... + \frac{1}{n}. \tag{10.1}$$

The logic behind this is that the first polygon rendered is one draw; the second polygon has a one in two chance of being in front of the first; the third has a one in three chance of being in front of the other two, etc. As n goes to infinity:

$$\lim_{n \to \infty} H(n) = \ln(n) + \gamma, \tag{10.2}$$

where $\gamma = 0.57721...$ is the Euler-Mascheroni constant. Overdraw rises rapidly when depth complexity is low, but quickly tapers off. For example, a depth complexity of 4 gives an average of 2.08 draws, 11 gives 3.02 draws, but it takes a depth complexity of $12,367$ to reach an average of 10.00 draws.

There is a performance gain in drawing the scene in front-to-back order (near to far). This is because the occluded objects that are drawn later will not write to the color or Z-buffers (i.e., overdraw is reduced). Also, more complex fill operations such as blending and texturing are also avoided for these occluded objects [203]. On some hardware, there is a simple form of occlusion culling (see Section 9.7) implemented in the rasterizer stage, and so a rough sort can help even more. The Z-occlusion culling hardware enhancement (Section 15.3.5) also further benefits from front-to-back sorting [570]. On such hardware, the performance gain may be very high. On a GeForce3, one test suite was 50–60 percent faster sorted versus random order [120].

If sorting is difficult, another technique is useful for surfaces with complex pixel shaders. On the first pass through the scene, render these surfaces into only the Z-buffer. After the whole scene is rendered and established in the Z-buffer, then render these surfaces with pixel shading. Large amounts of fill rate are saved for pixels not visible, as the pixel fragment can be rejected by occlusion culling hardware before reaching the pixel shader (see Section 15.3.5). Note that if the pixel shader changes the z-depth, this early rejection cannot occur.

If none of these methods helps, a trade-off between speed and quality can be made. All features that have a speed penalty can be turned off. Depending on the platform, examples of such features might include expensive texture filtering (bilinear versus mipmapping, and point versus trilinear for mipmapping), fog, blending, line drawing, depth testing, stencil buffer operations, and multisampling (antialiasing). Again, knowing your architecture is key. For example, if the Z-buffer is being used, on some systems it costs no additional time to also access the stencil buffer. This is because the 8-bit stencil buffer value is stored in the same word as the 24-bit z-depth value [421]. That said, if the stencil buffer is being used along with the Z-buffer, then both should be cleared at the same time as possible; clearing just the Z-buffer in this case results in slower performance. Another example is that, when minifying textures, using mipmapping may be faster than using only the original texture. This is because the memory accesses used for mipmapping may be much more cache-coherent than samples taken from the original texture.

10.3.4 Overall Optimization

Here we list some tricks and methods for increasing overall performance.

- Reduce the total number of drawing primitives that have to pass through the (entire) pipeline. This can be done by simplifying the models (see Section 11.5) or by using culling techniques (Section 9.2).

- Choose as low a precision as is possible (without rendering artifacts) on vertices, normals, colors, and texture coordinates. There is sometimes a choice between short, single, and double floating-point precision. Lower precision implies less memory, which means that the data can move more quickly through the pipeline. Note also, that some formats may be faster than others because of what is used internally in the hardware—use a native format.

- Preprocess the models for rendering in your particular context. As an example, some hardware renders only points, lines, triangles, and quadrilaterals, and some renders only triangles. If self-intersecting and concave polygons are not usually rendered correctly, it is up to the user to see to it that the system can render the data (see Section 11.2).

- Turn off features not in use. Features that are enabled but not in use, i.e., those that have no visible effect on the rendered images, may degrade performance. For example, depth buffering, blending, fog, and texturing can be turned off if a background (nontextured, nontransparent) quadrilateral is the first primitive to be drawn after a frame buffer clear.

- Minimize the number of API calls [136].

- Minimize state changes by grouping objects with a similar rendering state (vertex and pixel shader, texture, material, lighting, transparency, etc.). When changing the state, there is sometimes a need to wholly or partially flush the pipeline. Changes in material parameters, especially shininess, can be very expensive [536]. For k-ary trees (scene graphs), where $k > 2$, leaf nodes with a shared material could be grouped for better performance. However, there are exceptions to this rule of thumb—for some graphics hardware a state change costs less than rendering a triangle [148]. Rendering polygons with a shared texture minimizes texture cache thrashing [554, 825]. A way to minimize texture binding changes is to put several texture images into one large texture and recompute the texture coordinates for the objects involved (see Section 5.3). A disadvantage here is that textures tend to bleed into each other when mipmapping is used.

- A *fast path* is a highly optimized path through the graphics hardware. Find out which these are, and use them. Set up primitives in group sizes that are optimized for your architecture. For example, the RealityEngine [11, 417] has an optimized path through the pipeline if the primitives consist of a multiple of three vertices, and the best performance is achieved for 12 vertices (which equals 10 triangles in a triangle strip). For other architectures, like SIMD (Single Instruction Multiple Data), it is more beneficial to send many vertices at a time, since the SIMD may have significant set-up and tear-down overhead.

- Make sure (if possible) that all textures reside in the texture memory so that swapping is avoided.

- Separate two-dimensional from three-dimensional operations, as switching between these may have a significant overhead.

- Call glGet() during the set-up phase and avoid it during runtime.

- Make sure to take advantage of the fact that some graphics hardware is optimized for clearing the depth and color buffers simultaneously.

- When vertex blending with many bones, it may be better to precompute blended matrices and send these through the pipeline. To save memory, one can use discretized weights, e.g., $w_i = 0.1 * k$, where $k = 0 \ldots 10$.

- Multiple passes are expensive in general: Try avoiding extra passes by instead using multitexturing (Section 5.5) or pixel shaders (Section 6.6).

- Frame buffer reads are often expensive and are best avoided.

- Use *Display Lists* (DLs) if your architecture gains from it. A DL [600] stores a series of graphics API calls, typically for objects that have an unchanging shape and material. A DL is rendered by being invoked during scene traversal. The contents of the DL are stored in a chunk of consecutive memory, making for better access patterns. A DL acts as a kind of compiled command sequence that may be optimized at runtime for the current hardware configuration. Sometimes a cache for DLs is available, which may eliminate the need to send data through some parts of the pipeline. If a display list is made too small, the overhead involved makes it inefficient to use. The main drawback of DLs is data expansion [536]: In addition to all the original data, information for each command and for each list must also be stored.

A piece of general advice is that *less is more*, meaning that the less data that goes from the application to the graphics accelerator, the faster it will run.

10.4 Balancing the Graphics Pipeline

To be able to see the potential effects of pipeline optimization, it is important to measure the total rendering time per frame with double buffering disabled, i.e., in single-buffer mode. This is because with double buffering turned on, swapping of the buffers occurs only in synchronization with the frequency of the monitor. As an example, consider a monitor with an update frequency of 72 Hz. This means that it takes $t = 1/72 = 0.01389$ s $= 13.89$ ms for the electron beam of the monitor to scan and display the entire screen. Using double buffering means that the update rate of the rendered images must be a multiple of t. If your rendering takes 20 ms (50 Hz) in single-buffer mode, then that rate will be reduced to $20 < 2 * 13.89$ (36 Hz) in double-buffer mode. This means that the graphics pipeline in this example is idle for $2 * 13.89 - 20 = 7.78$ ms for each frame. This sounds bad, but it can actually be exploited to your advantage, which is the purpose of balancing the pipeline. The idle time can be used for higher-quality rendering.

First of all, additional work can be done by the bottleneck stage as long as we do not cross over into the next multiple of the monitor update time t (e.g., in our previous example, we do not go from 36 Hz to 24 Hz). In the previous example, features could be added until the rendering of a frame takes slightly less than $2 * 13.89$ ms. This will not alter the performance (in double-buffer mode), but if it is exploited correctly, the quality of the rendered image will improve.

Second, at this point of the optimization process, we have maximized the use of the bottleneck stage, but the other stages use less time to complete their tasks. In the same spirit as above, the stages that are *not* bottleneck stages can be made to work harder with no degradation of performance (as long as this extra work does not negatively affect the performance of the bottleneck stage). This is illustrated in Figure 10.2. Take this advice with a grain of salt, however. While the "average bottleneck" over a frame has been found, the location of the bottleneck can change from moment to moment during the frame. So, it is not always so simple in practice to fully use the pipeline.

Here are some ideas for using the idle time of both the bottleneck and the nonbottleneck stages:

- Increase the number of triangles (affects all stages).

- If the application stage is idle, compute more realistic animations; implement more accurate collision detection; use more sophisticated

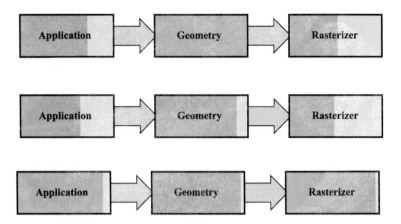

Figure 10.2. Balancing the graphics pipeline. The usage of a stage is illustrated by the dark gray rectangle—the more dark gray area there is, the less idle time a stage has. In the topmost illustration we show a system that uses only single buffering. One stage, in this case the geometry stage, uses 100% of its processing power. The application stage uses approximately 75%, and the rasterizer uses about 50% of the available time. The middle row shows a situation with double buffering enabled. This means that the rendering has to be synchronized with the update rate of the monitor, and so the idle time for all stages increases (if the rendering time is not perfectly synchronized with the update rate). The bottom row shows the pipeline after balancing. Here, the idle time at all the stages has been exploited, with no effect on frame rate.

acceleration algorithms (see Chapter 9); and perform other similar tasks.

- If the geometry stage is idle, use more lights and more expensive light source types. More expensive vertex shader programs can also be used.

- If the rasterizer stage is idle, use more expensive texture filtering, fog, blending, pixel shaders, etc.

- Immediately after a screen clear, do *not* fill the graphics pipeline with more graphics commands. Since the graphics hardware is already busy with clearing the frame buffer (which can take a significant amount of time), it is better to do application (CPU)-related work after sending a clear. This is not true for accelerators with the technique for fast clears implemented (see Section 15.3.5). Also, note

Figure 10.3. A large square is subdivided into a large number of triangles on the left, and into two triangles on the right. A transform-limited application can decrease the number of triangles without decreasing the number of filled pixels, in order to reduce the workload on the geometry stage. On the other hand, a fill-limited application can increase the number of triangles (which would result in better shading, as seen in Figure 4.5 on page 72) without degrading performance, as long as the number of filled pixels remains approximately constant.

that if all pixels are drawn at least once, then the color buffer clear can be avoided.

- As long as the number of filled pixels does not change, a fill-limited application can easily increase the number of polygons without affecting the performance of the rasterizer stage. In other words, the same object can be represented by more triangles. On the other hand, for a transform-limited application, the number of triangles can be decreased without affecting the number of pixels to be filled, in order to speed up the geometry stage. This is illustrated in Figure 10.3.

- If the rendering is not fill-limited, then the window where the images are drawn can be enlarged.

Most (if not all) pipelines have FIFO (First-in, First-out) queues [9, 11]. See Figure 10.4 for an example. The idea is that FIFOs can be queued up with jobs for the geometry and rasterizer stages. That is, one stage can continue to do its work even if a stage further down the pipeline is not ready for its results; instead, the results are saved so that the next stage can process them when it is ready. Such buffering helps to smooth out the balancing of the pipeline and make small bottlenecks invisible [127].

However, stages may be *starved* or *blocked*. A stage gets starved when, for example, the application stage is performing some computations (such as collision detection) that take a significant amount of time and the FIFOs before the geometry and the rasterizer stages are empty. In this case, both

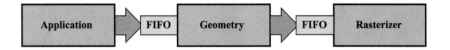

Figure 10.4. An example of a rendering pipeline with two FIFO queues. Some architectures are constructed like this, some do not have the first FIFO, some do not have any FIFOs at all, and some have many more FIFOs. The FIFOs are used to queue jobs for the subsequent stage.

the geometry and the rasterizer stages are starved because they do not have anything to do.

Stage blocking takes place, for example, when the rasterizer is filling a huge polygon. At the same time, the geometry stage can fill the FIFO to the rasterizer with tasks. At this point, the geometry stage is blocked, since it can no longer fill the FIFO.

The location of the bottleneck almost always varies over time within a single frame. This fact should definitely be considered during optimization. As an example, consider a geometrically detailed human drawn against a large polygon acting as the sky. If the human is drawn first, then the pipeline becomes transform-limited, and the rasterizer will be idle. If the drawing order is reversed, the polygon goes through the pipeline to occupy the rasterizer, and then the geometry stage can process the human. The latter order is preferable, since both the geometry stage and the rasterizer stage are not idle. Blocking may occur, and there is some unnecessary overdraw, but there will be more time when both stages are active.

Another element to consider in load balancing the pipeline is that the load may vary over time between frames. The time it takes to render a frame can be measured. If the measured time is less than a user-defined minimum threshold, then the workload (i.e., scene contents and realism) can be increased. If it goes beyond a user-defined maximum threshold, then the workload should be diminished. These maximum and minimum thresholds should be chosen with some slack, so that the workload is changed before the frame rate is affected. This technique helps to guarantee a user-defined frame rate. Another method that can help is triple buffering (see Section 15.1.4).

10.5 Multiprocessing

Multiprocessor computers can be broadly classified into *message-passing* architectures and *shared memory multiprocessors*. In message-passing de-

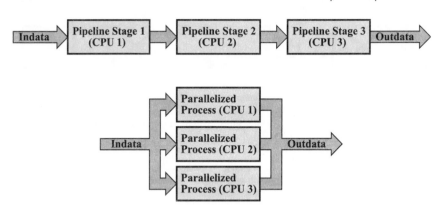

Figure 10.5. Two different ways of utilizing multiple processors. At the top we show how three processors (CPUs) are used in a *multiprocessor pipeline*, and at the bottom we show *parallel* execution on three CPUs. One of the differences between these two implementations is that lower latency can be achieved if the configuration at the bottom is used. On the other hand, it may be easier to use a multiprocessor pipeline. The ideal speed-up for both of these configurations is linear, i.e., using n CPUs would give a speed-up of n times.

signs, each processor has its own memory area, and messages are sent between the processors to communicate results. Shared memory multiprocessors are just as they sound; all processors share a logical address space of memory among themselves.

Here, we will present two methods for utilizing multiple processors for real-time graphics. The first method—*multiprocessor pipelining*, also called temporal parallelism—will be covered in more detail than the second—*parallel processing*, also called spatial parallelism. These two methods are illustrated in Figure 10.5. Multiprocessor pipelining and parallel processing can also be combined, but little research has been done in this area. For this discussion, we assume that a multiprocessor computer is available, but do not go into details about different types of multiprocessors.

10.5.1 Multiprocessor Pipelining

As we have seen, pipelining is a method for speeding up execution by dividing a job into certain pipeline stages that are executed in parallel. The result from one pipeline stage is passed on to the next. The ideal speed-up is n times for n pipeline stages, and the slowest stage (the bottleneck) determines the actual speed-up. Up to this point, we have seen pipelining used to run the application, geometry processing, and rasterization in parallel for a single-CPU system. This technique can also be used when multiple processors are available on the host, and in these cases, it is called *multiprocess pipelining* or *software pipelining*.

Since the rasterizer is always implemented in hardware, this stage cannot be pipelined further with the use of additional processors on the host.[3] The application stage can always use extra processors, while the geometry stage can use them if that stage is not implemented in hardware. For simplicity, it is assumed that the geometry stage is implemented in hardware. However, multiprocessing is not limited in any way to such an architecture—geometry processing could be done in a pipelined fashion on the host CPUs too.

So this leaves the application stage to be pipelined. Therefore, the application stage is divided into three stages [659]: APP, CULL, and DRAW. This is very coarse-grained pipelining, which means that each stage is relatively long. The APP stage is the first stage in the pipeline and therefore controls the others. It is in this stage that the application programmer can put in additional code that does, for example, collision detection. This stage also updates the viewpoint. The CULL stage can perform:

- Traversal and hierarchical view frustum culling on a scene graph (see Section 9.4).

- Level of detail selection (see Section 9.8).

- State sorting—geometry with similar state is sorted into bins in order to minimize state changes. For example, all transparent objects are sorted into one bin, and these objects are also sorted in a rough back-to-front order for correct rendering.

- Finally (and always performed), generation of a simple list of all objects that should be rendered.

The DRAW stage takes the list from the CULL stage and issues all graphics calls in this list. This means that it does not traverse anything, instead it only feeds the geometry stage, which in turn feeds the rasterizer stage. Figure 10.6 shows some examples of how this pipeline can be used. If one processor is available, then all three stages are run on that CPU. If two CPUs are available, then APP and CULL can be executed on one CPU and DRAW on the other. Another configuration would be to execute

---

[3]However, if there are multiple rasterizer units, then each CPU could feed its own rasterizer.

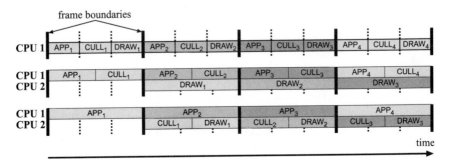

Figure 10.6. Different configurations for a multiprocessor pipeline. The thick lines represent synchronization between the stages, and the subscripts represent the frame number. At the top, a single CPU pipeline is shown. In the middle and at the bottom are shown two different pipeline subdivisions using two CPUs. The middle has one pipeline stage for APP and CULL and one pipeline stage for DRAW. This is a suitable subdivision if DRAW has much more work to do than the others. At the bottom, APP has one pipeline stage and the other two have another. This is suitable if APP has much more work than the others. Note that the bottom two configurations have more time for the APP, CULL, and DRAW stages.

APP on one processor and CULL and DRAW on the other. Which is the best depends on the workloads for the different stages. Finally, if the host has three CPUs, then each stage can be executed on a separate CPU. This possibility is shown in Figure 10.7.

The advantage of this technique is that the throughput, i.e., the rendering speed, increases. The downside is that, compared to parallel processing, the latency is greater. Latency is the time it takes from the polling of the user's actions to the final image. This should not be confused with frame rate, which is the number of frames displayed per second. For example, say the user is using a head-mounted display. The determination of the head's position may take 50 milliseconds to reach the CPU, then it takes 15 milliseconds to render the frame. The latency is then 65 milliseconds from initial input to display. Even though the frame rate is 66.7 Hz (1/0.015 seconds), interactivity will feel sluggish because of the delay in sending the position changes to the CPU. Ignoring any delay due to user interaction (which is a constant under both systems), multiprocessing has more latency because it uses a pipeline. As is discussed in detail in the next section, parallel processing breaks up the frame's work into pieces that are run concurrently.

In comparison to using a single CPU on the host, multiprocessor pipelining gives a higher frame rate and the latency is about the same or a little

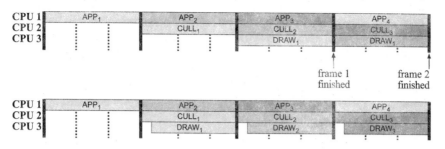

Figure 10.7. At the top, a three-stage pipeline is shown. In comparison to the configurations in Figure 10.6, this configuration has more time for each pipeline stage. The bottom illustration shows a way to reduce the latency: The CULL and the DRAW are overlapped with FIFO buffering in between.

greater due to the cost of synchronization. Note that the latency increases with the number of stages in the pipeline and that for a well-balanced application the speed-up is n times for n CPUs.

One technique for reducing the latency is to update the viewpoint and other latency-critical parameters at the end of the APP stage [659]. This reduces the latency by (approximately) one frame. Another way to reduce latency is to execute CULL and DRAW overlapped. This means that the result from CULL is sent over to DRAW as soon as anything is ready for rendering. For this to work, there has to be some buffering, typically a FIFO, between those stages. The stages are stalled on empty and full conditions; i.e., when the buffer is full, then CULL has to stall, and when the buffer is empty, DRAW has to stall. The disadvantage is that techniques such as state sorting cannot be used to the same extent, since primitives have to be rendered as soon as they have been processed by CULL. This latency reduction technique is visualized in Figure 10.7.

The pipeline in this figure uses a maximum of three CPUs, and the stages have certain tasks. However, this technique is in no way limited to this configuration—rather, you can use any number of CPUs and divide the work in any way you want. The key is to make a smart division of the entire job to be done so that the pipeline tends to be balanced. For example, multiprocessor pipelining has been used to speed up the occlusion culling algorithm in Section 9.7 using a different pipeline stage division than the one presented here [836]. Multiprocessor pipelining has also been used by Funkhouser [246] to speed up LOD management (see Section 9.8.3) and portal culling (Section 9.5).

The multiprocessor pipelining technique requires a minimum of synchronization in that it needs to synchronize only when switching frames.

In all kinds of multiprocessing systems, there are many factors to consider when it comes to data sharing, data exclusion, multibuffering, and more. Details on these topics can be found in Rohlf and Helman's paper [659].

10.5.2 Parallel Processing

The most apparent disadvantage of using a multiprocessor pipeline technique is that the latency tends to get longer. For some applications, such as flight simulators, fast games, etc., this is not acceptable. When moving the viewpoint, you usually want instant (next-frame) response, but when the latency is long this will not happen, which gives the application an unresponsive feel.

If multiple processors are available, one can try to parallelize the code instead, which may result in shorter latency. To do this, the program must possess the characteristics of *parallelism*. This means that, for a program with no or a small amount of parallelism, there is no gain in parallelizing the program—a parallel version may even become slower due to the overhead involved in extra synchronization, etc. However, many programs and algorithms do have a large amount of parallelism and can therefore benefit.

There are several different methods for parallelizing an algorithm. Assume that n processors are available. Using static assignment [153], the total work package is divided into n work packages. Each processor then takes care of a work package, and all processors execute their work packages in parallel. When all processors have completed their work packages, it may be necessary to merge the results from the processors. For this to work, the workload must be highly predictable. When that is not the case, dynamic assignment algorithms that adapt to different workloads may be used [153]. These use one or more work pools. When jobs are generated, they are put into the work pools. CPUs can then fetch one or more jobs from the queue when they have finished their current job. Care must be taken so that only one CPU can fetch a particular job, and so that the overhead in maintaining the queue does not damage performance. Larger jobs mean that the overhead for maintaining the queue becomes less of a problem, but, on the other hand, if the jobs are too big, then performance may degrade due to imbalance in the system—i.e., one or more CPUs may starve.

As for the multiprocessor pipeline, the ideal speed-up for a parallel program running on n processors would be n times. This is called *linear speed-up*. Even though linear speed-up rarely happens, actual results can sometimes be very close to it.

In Figure 10.5 on page 430, both a multiprocessor pipeline and a parallel processing system with three CPUs are shown. Temporarily assume that these should do the same amount of work for each frame and that both configurations achieve linear speed-up. This means that the execution will run three times faster in comparison to serial execution (i.e., on a single CPU). Furthermore, we assume that the total amount of work per frame takes 30 ms, which would mean that the maximum frame rate on a single CPU would be $1/0.03 \approx 33$ frames per second.

The multiprocessor pipeline would (ideally) divide the work into three equal-sized work packages and let each of the CPUs be responsible for one work packages. Each work package should then take 10 ms to complete. If we follow the work flow through the pipeline, we will see that the first CPU in the pipeline does work for 10 ms (i.e., one-third of the job) and then sends it on to the next CPU. The first CPU then starts working on the first part of the next frame. When a frame is finally finished, it has taken 30 ms for it to complete, but since the work has been done in parallel in the pipeline, one frame will be finished every 10 ms. So the latency is 30 ms, and the speed-up is a factor of three (30/10), resulting in 100 frames per second.

Now, a parallel version of the same program would also divide the jobs into three work packages, but these three packages will execute at the same time on the three CPUs. This means that the latency will be 10 ms, and the work for one frame will also take 10 ms. The conclusion is that the latency is much shorter when using parallel processing than when using a multiprocessor pipeline.

Parallel processing is a huge topic in itself. See the *Further Reading and Resources* section that follows for references to work on parallel processing.

Further Reading and Resources

The *Game Programming Gems* series [168, 169, 170] has many articles about efficient use of graphics hardware and best practices for programming itself. The *Graphics Gems* series [29, 261, 333, 431, 610] includes a number of optimized algorithms for various graphics operations. See this book's website for links to many other performance tuning tricks and procedures at: http://www.realtimerendering.com/.

Kempf and Hartman's manual [417] deals with OpenGL for a set of SGI systems and discusses ways to optimize code for their architectures.

The program *VTune Analyzer* [129, 782] facilitates much of the work of determining how various PC assembly language instructions interact. The same is true for the program called *CodeAnalyst* when optimizing code on AMD's CPUs [128].

For more information on compiler optimization techniques, consult the books by Muchnick [574] and Appel [23]. Issues that arise in the design of a parallel graphics API are treated by Igehy et al. [380].

See the book *Parallel Computer Architecture: A Hardware/Software Approach* [153] for more information on parallel programming.

Chapter 11
Polygonal Techniques

"It is indeed wonderful that so simple a figure as the triangle is so inexhaustible."
–Leopold Crelle

Up to this point, we have assumed that the model we rendered is available in exactly the format we need and with just the right amount of detail. In reality we are rarely so lucky. Modelers and data capture devices have their own particular quirks and limitations, giving rise to ambiguities and errors within the data set and so within renderings. This chapter discusses a variety of problems that are encountered within polygonal data sets, along with some of the fixes and workarounds for these problems. In addition, techniques to efficiently render polygonal models are presented.

The overarching goals for polygonal representation (or any other representation, for that matter) in computer graphics are visual accuracy and speed. "Accuracy" is a term that depends upon the context: For a machine part, it may mean that the model displayed falls within some tolerance range; for an aircraft simulation game, what is important is the overall impression. Note that the way a model is used is a key differentiator. An engineer wants to control and position a part in real time and wants every bevel and chamfer on the machine part visible at every moment. Compare this to a game where, if the frame rate is high enough, minor errors or inaccuracies in a given frame are allowable, since they may not occur where attention is focused or may disappear in the next frame. In real-time graphics work, it is important to know what the boundaries are to the problem being solved, since these determine what sorts of techniques can be applied.

The main topics covered in this chapter are *tessellation, consolidation, stripification,* and *simplification.* Polygons can arrive in many different forms, and may have to be split into more tractable primitives, such as triangles or quadrilaterals; this process is called triangulation or, more generally, tessellation.[1] Consolidation is our term for the process that encompasses merging and linking polygonal data as well as deriving new data such as normals for surface shading. Stripification is the process of turning triangle meshes into sets of triangle strips. Simplification is taking such linked data and attempting to remove unnecessary or insignificant features within it.

Triangulation ensures that data is displayable and displayed correctly. Consolidation further improves data display and often increases speed by allowing computations to be shared. Stripification can increase speed still further. Simplification can provide even more speed by removing unneeded polygons.

11.1   Sources of Three-Dimensional Data

There are a number of ways models can be created. Objects can be generated in a wide variety of ways:

- Directly typing in the geometric description.

- Transforming data found in other forms into surfaces or volumes, e.g., taking protein data and converting it into spheres, cylinders, etc.

- Writing programs that create such data, (this is called *procedural modeling*).

- Using modeling programs.

- Sampling a real model at various points using a three-dimensional digitizer,

- Reconstruction from one or more photographs of the same object (called *photogrammetry*; using a pair of photos is called *stereophotogrammetry*).

- Using three-dimensional scanners, which gather depth information.

- Using some combination of these techniques.

Our focus will be on polygonal data generated by these methods. One common thread of almost all of these techniques is that they can represent their models in polygonal form. Knowing what data sources will be used

---

[1] "Tessellation" is also the most frequently misspelled word in computer graphics.

in an application is important in determining what sort of data can be expected, and so in knowing what techniques need to be applied to it.

In the modeling world, there are two main types of modelers, solid-based and surface-based. Solid-based modelers are usually seen in the area of *Computer Aided Design* (CAD), and often emphasize modeling tools that correspond to actual machining processes, such as cutting, drilling, etc. Internally, they will have a computational engine that rigorously manipulates the underlying topological boundaries of the objects. What concerns us is that for display and analysis purposes, such modelers have *faceters*. A faceter is software that turns the internal model representation into polygons that can then be displayed. For example, a model that appears as a sphere internally may be represented by a center point and a radius, and the faceter could turn it into any number of triangles or quadrilaterals in order to represent it. Sometimes the best rendering speed-up is the simplest: Turning down the visual accuracy required when the faceter is employed can increase speed and save storage space by generating fewer polygons.

An important consideration within CAD work is whether the faceter being used is designed for graphical rendering. For example, there are faceters for *Finite Element analysis* (FEM), which aim to split the surface into nearly equal-area triangles; such tessellations are strong candidates for consolidation and simplification, as they contain much graphically useless data, while also providing no vertex normals. Similarly, some faceters produce sets of triangles that are ideal for creating actual sample objects using stereolithography, but which lack vertex normals and are often ill-suited for fast graphical display.

Surface-based modelers do not have a built-in concept of solidity; instead, all objects are thought of in terms of their surfaces. Like solid modelers, they may use internal representations and faceters to display objects such as spline surfaces. They may also allow direct manipulation of surfaces, such as adding or deleting polygons or vertices. This sort of tool can be important in keeping the polygon count low.

There are other types of modelers, such as implicit surface (including "blobby") creation systems [89], which work with concepts such as blends, weights, and fields. These modelers can create impressive organic effects by generating surfaces that are defined by the solution to some function $f(x, y, z) = 0$. Polygonalization techniques are then used to create sets of polygons for display. See Section 12.4.

Data can also be generated from satellite imagery, by various medical scanning devices (in which image slices are generated and recombined), by three-dimensional scanners (in which a quadrilateral mesh of surface data points and sometimes their associated colors are captured), and by image registration techniques (in which two or more photos of an object are compared and depth information is derived). Such data sets are strong candidates for simplification techniques, as the data is often sampled at regular intervals, and many samples have a negligible effect on the visual perception of the data.

There are many other ways in which polygonal data is generated for surface representation. The key is to understand how that data was created and for what purpose. Often the data is not generated specifically for graphical display, or even if it is, various assumptions made by the designers about the renderer may no longer hold. There are many different three-dimensional data file formats in existence [577, 662], and translating between any two is usually not a lossless operation. Understanding what sorts of limitations and problems may be encountered is a major theme of the rest of this chapter.

11.2   Tessellation and Triangulation

Tessellation is the process of splitting a surface into a set of polygons. Here, we focus on tessellating polygonal surfaces; curved surface tessellation is discussed in Section 12.3. Polygonal tessellation can be undertaken for a variety of reasons. The most common is that many graphics APIs and hardware are optimized for triangles. Triangles are almost like atoms, in that any surface can be made out of them and rendered. Converting a complex polygon into triangles is called triangulation. There are other reasons to tessellate polygons: The renderer may handle only convex polygons (such tessellation is called convex partitioning), or the surface may need to be subdivided (meshed) in order to catch shadows and reflected light using radiosity techniques [133, 711]. Figure 11.1 shows examples of these

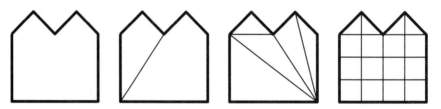

Figure 11.1. Various types of tessellation. The leftmost polygon is not tessellated, the next is partitioned into convex regions, the next is triangulated, and the rightmost is uniformly meshed.

different types of tessellation. Nongraphical reasons for tessellation include requirements such as having no polygon be larger than some given area, or for triangles to have angles at their vertices larger than some minimum angle. While angle restrictions are normally a part of nongraphical applications such as finite element analysis, these can also serve to improve the appearance of a surface. Long, thin triangles are worth avoiding, if possible, as different shades amongst the vertices will be interpolated over a long distance.

One of the first processes a surface tessellator normally needs to perform is to determine how best to project a three-dimensional polygon into two dimensions. This is done to simplify the problem and so simplify the algorithms needed. One method is to determine which one of the xyz coordinates to discard in order to leave just two; this is equivalent to projecting the polygon onto one of three planes, the xy, the yz, or the xz. The best plane is usually the one in which the polygon has the largest projected area (this same technique is used in Section 13.8 for point-in-polygon testing). This plane can be determined by computing the area directly or by simply throwing away the coordinates corresponding to the coordinate of greatest magnitude in the polygon's normal. For example, given the polygon normal $(-5, 2, 4)$, we would throw away the x coordinates because -5 has the greatest magnitude.

The area and polygon normal test are not always equivalent, depending on the way in which the normal is computed and whether the polygon is flat. Some modelers create polygon facets that can be badly warped. A common case of this problem is the warped quadrilateral that is viewed nearly edge-on; this may form what is referred to as an *hourglass* or a *bowtie* quadrilateral. Figure 11.2 shows a bowtie quadrilateral. While this figure can be triangulated simply by creating a diagonal edge, more complex warped polygons cannot be so easily managed. Casting these onto the xy, xz, or yz plane that gives the largest projected area will eliminate most, but not all, self-intersection problems. If using this plane leads to self-intersection (in which a polygon's edge crosses itself), we may consider casting upon the average plane of the polygon itself. The average plane is

Figure 11.2. Warped quadrilateral viewed edge-on, forming an ill-defined bowtie or hourglass figure, along with the two possible triangulations.

computed by taking the three projected areas and using these to form the normal [657]. That is, the area on the yz plane forms the x component, xz the y, and xy the z. This method of computing an average normal is called *Newell's formula*. If self-intersection is a possibility, then a laborious comparison among the polygon's edges is called for. If the polygon has a large number of edges, then a *plane sweep* can be used so as to limit the amount of edge/edge testing that is done [56]. See Section 13.15 for efficient methods for performing the intersection test itself.

Schneider & Eberly [688], Held [352], O'Rourke [605], and de Berg et al. [56] each give an overview of a variety of triangulation methods. The most basic triangulation algorithm is to examine each line segment between any two given points on a polygon and see if it intersects or overlaps any edge of the polygon. If it does, the line segment cannot be used to split the polygon, so examine the next possible pair of points; else split the polygon into two parts by this segment and triangulate these new polygons by the same method. This method is extremely inefficient at $O(n^3)$. A more efficient method is *ear clipping*, which is $O(n^2)$ when done as two processes. First, a pass is made over the polygon to find the ears, that is, to look at all triangles with vertex indices $i, (i+1), (i+2)$ (modulo n) and check if the line segment $i, (i+2)$ does not intersect any polygon edges. If so, then triangle $(i+1)$ forms an ear. See Figure 11.3. Each ear available is removed from the polygon in turn, and the triangles at vertices i and $(i+2)$ are reexamined to see if they are ears or not. Eventually all ears are removed and the polygon is triangulated. Other, more complex methods are $O(n \log n)$ and some are effectively $O(n)$ for typical cases. Pseudocode for ear clipping and other, faster triangulation methods is given by Schneider & Eberly [688].

Partitioning a polygon into convex regions can be more efficient in terms of storage and rendering time than triangulating it. This is because convex polygons can easily be represented by fans or strips of triangles, as discussed

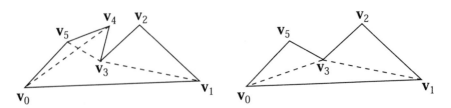

Figure 11.3. Ear clipping. A polygon with potential ears at v_2, v_4, and v_5 shown. On the right, the ear at v_4 is removed. The neighboring vertices v_3 and v_5 are reexamined to see if they now form ears; v_5 does.

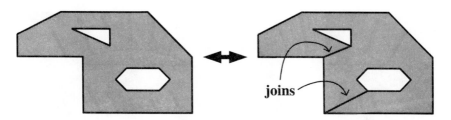

Figure 11.4. A polygon with three outlines converted to a single-outline polygon.

in Section 11.4. Code for a robust convexity test is given by Schorn and Fisher [689]. Some concave polygons can be treated as fans (such polygons are called star-shaped), but detecting these requires more work [605, 634]. Schneider and Eberly [688] give two convex partitioning methods, a quick and dirty method and an optimal one.

Polygons are not always made of a single outline. Figure 11.4 shows a polygon made of three outlines (also called loops or contours). Such descriptions can always be converted to a single-outline polygon by carefully generating join edges (also called keyholed or bridge edges) between loops. This conversion process can also be reversed in order to retrieve the separate loops.

Tessellation and triangulation algorithms are an area of computational geometry that has been well explored and documented [56, 581, 605, 688]. That said, writing a robust and general tessellator is a difficult undertaking. Various subtle bugs, pathological cases, and precision problems make fool-proof code surprisingly tricky to create. We give some pointers to existing code in the Further Reading and Resources section at the end of this chapter.

11.2.1 Shading Problems

Often data will arrive as quadrilateral meshes and must be converted into triangles for display, both to avoid bowtie problems and to provide proper input to the renderer. Once in a great while, a quadrilateral will be concave, in which case there is only one way to triangulate it (without adding new vertices); otherwise, we may choose either of the two diagonals to split it. Spending a little time picking the better diagonal can sometimes give significantly better visual results.

There are a few different ways to determine how to split a quadrilateral. The basic idea is to minimize differences. For a flat quadrilateral with no

Figure 11.5. The left figure is rendered as a quadrilateral; the middle is two triangles with upper-right and lower-left corners connected; the right shows what happens when the other diagonal is used. The middle figure is better visually than the right one.

additional data at the vertices, it is often best to choose the shortest diagonal. For radiosity solutions or prelit quadrilaterals (see Section 10.3.2) that have a diffuse color per vertex, choose the diagonal which has the smaller difference between the colors [6]. An example of this technique is shown in Figure 11.5. For terrain heightfields, there are a number of possibilities, depending on the effect desired: Use the diagonal that gives the largest angle between the two triangle normals [536]; connect the diagonal that gives triangles closest in size; connect the two vertices closest in height; or even connect the two most different in height. Any of these is normally preferable to simple consistent diagonal connections; see Figure 11.6. A

Figure 11.6. On the left is a heightfield mesh with each quadrilateral split along the same diagonal (the view looks along these diagonals—note how visible these are). On the right, the split is made using the diagonal whose corners are closer in height, and so breaks up the pattern formed.

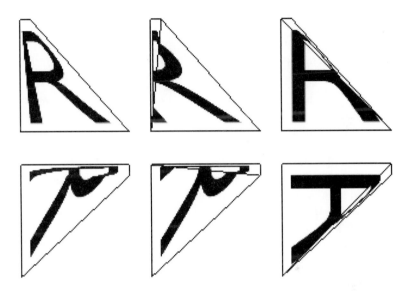

Figure 11.7. The top left shows the intent of the designer, a distorted quadrilateral with a square texture map of an "R." The two images on the right show the two triangulations and how they differ. The bottom row rotates all of the polygons; the Gouraud-interpolated quadrilateral changes its appearance.

drawback of such schemes is that they will destroy the regular nature of the data, making it difficult to form triangle strips.

There are cases where triangles cannot properly capture the intent of the designer. If a texture is applied to a warped quadrilateral, neither triangulation preserves the intent; that said, neither does pure Gouraud shading using the untessellated quadrilateral (i.e., interpolating from the left to the right edge of the quadrilateral itself). Figure 11.7 shows the problem. This problem arises because the image being applied to the surface is to be warped when displayed. A triangle has only three texture coordinates, so it can establish an affine transformation, but not a warp. At most, a basic (u, v) texture on a triangle can be sheared, not warped. Woo et al. [821] discuss this problem further. A number of solutions are possible:

- Warp the texture in advance and reapply this new image.

- Tessellate the surface to a finer mesh; this only lessens the problem.

- Use projective texturing to warp the texture on the fly [330]; this has the undesirable effect of nonuniform spacing of the texture on the surface.

- Use a bilinear mapping scheme [330]; this is normally not feasible in hardware, though may be possible with pixel shaders.

While texture distortion sounds like a pathological case, it actually happens with a common primitive: the cone. When a texture is applied to the cone and the cone is triangulated, this sort of distortion is encountered near the tip of the cone [310].

Figure 11.7 also shows why rendering using only triangles is usually better than Gouraud interpolation across the original polygon: The quadrilateral's rendering is not rotation-invariant. Such shading will shift around when animated; triangles' shading and textures at least do not move. Gouraud interpolation on a triangle is, in fact, equivalent to interpolating across the surface using a triangle's barycentric coordinates (see Section 13.7).

11.2.2   Edge Cracking and T-Vertices

A problem encountered with tessellated objects is *edge cracking*. Curved surfaces, discussed in detail in Chapter 12, are usually tessellated into meshes for rendering. This tessellation is done by stepping along the spline curves defining the surface and so computing vertex locations and normals.

When we use a simple stepping method, problems can occur where spline surfaces meet. At the shared edge, the points for both surfaces need to coincide. Sometimes this may happen, due to the nature of the model, but often the points generated for one spline curve will not match those generated by its neighbor. This effect is called edge cracking, and it can lead to disturbing visual artifacts as the viewer peeks through the surface. Even if the viewer cannot see through the cracks, the seam is often visible because of differences in the way the shading is interpolated.

The process of fixing these cracks is called *edge stitching*. The goal is to make sure that all vertices along the shared edge are shared by both spline surfaces so that no cracks appear. See Figure 11.8.

A related problem encountered when joining flat surfaces is that of T-vertices. This sort of problem can appear whenever two models' edges meet, but do not share all vertices along them. Even though the edges should theoretically meet perfectly, if the renderer does not have enough precision in representing vertex locations on the screen, then cracks can appear. One way to ameliorate this problem is to use graphics hardware

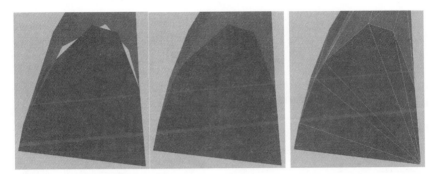

Figure 11.8. The left figure shows cracking where the two surfaces meet. The middle shows the cracking fixed by matching up edge points. The right shows the corrected mesh.

with subpixel addressing [474]. However, this solution does not avoid shading artifacts that can appear [51]. Figure 11.9 shows the problem, which can be fixed by finding such edges (sometimes a difficult procedure) and making sure to share common vertices with bordering faces. Cignoni et al. [125] describe a way to avoid creating degenerate (zero-area) triangles when triangulating convex polygons with T-vertices. For example, in the figure, if the quadrilateral **abcd** had been triangulated into triangles **abc** and **acd**, the T-vertex problem would not be solved.

11.3 Consolidation

Once polygons have passed through any tessellation algorithms needed, we are left with a set of polygons to render. We may have opportunities for greater efficiency and problems with the quality of the data. To address these concerns, it is useful to find and adjust the connectivity among polygons; we call this phase *consolidation.*

One source of efficiency comes from forming triangle strips, fans, and meshes from sets of separate polygons. These are discussed in depth in Section 11.4.

Another opportunity for improved efficiency is in the area of backface culling. This topic is discussed in depth in Section 9.2; what is important here is that a model has to be found to be solid, also known as *manifold*[2]

---

[2]More technically correct is that a solid is a manifold without boundary edges. A manifold surface is one without any topological inconsistencies, such as having three or more polygons sharing an edge or two or more corners sharing a vertex.

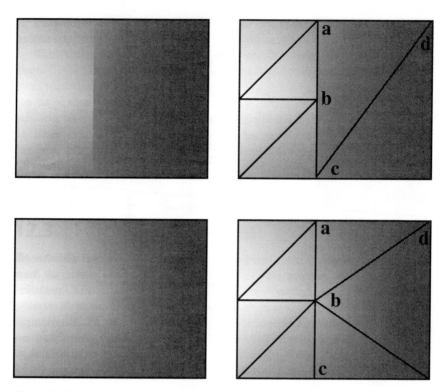

Figure 11.9. In the top row, the underlying mesh of a surface shows a shading discontinuity. Vertex **b** is a T-vertex, as it belongs to the polygons to the left of it but is not
a part of the triangle **acd**. One solution is to add this T-vertex to this triangle and
create triangles **abd** and **bcd** (not shown). Long and thin triangles are more likely to
cause other shading problems, so retriangulating is often a better solution, shown in the
bottom row.

or *closed.* Solid, in this context, means that none of the backfaces should
ever be visible from the outside. If this is the case, then backface culling
is possible. Solidity is also important in stereolithography, the process of
taking a computer-generated model and using lasers to solidify a polymer
mixture with which to make an actual prototype; models without solidity
can cause errors.

One quality-related problem with model data is face orientation. Some
model data comes in oriented properly, with surface normals either explicitly or implicitly pointing in the correct directions. For example, in CAD
work, the standard is that the vertices in the polygon outline proceed in
a counterclockwise direction when the frontface is viewed. This is called a

Figure 11.10. The object on the left does not have normals per vertex; the one on the right does.

handed viewing or modeling orientation used): Think of the fingers of your right hand wrapping around the polygon's vertices in counterclockwise order. Your thumb then points in the direction of the polygon's normal.

Other model data has no orientation or surface normals provided with it. In this case, steps must be taken to ensure that the polygon orientations are consistent and pointing outwards. This consistency is important for backface culling (we need to know which are the backfaces) and for performing vertex normal smoothing. Some polygon meshes form curved surfaces, but the polygon vertices do not have normal vectors, so they cannot be rendered with the illusion of curvature. See Figure 11.10.

Finally, many model formats do not provide surface edge information. See Section 7.2 for the various types of edges. These edges are important for a number of reasons. They can be used to highlight a single area of the model made of a set of polygons or for a nonphotorealistic rendering. Because they are often important visual cues, such edges are often favored to avoid being simplified by progressive mesh algorithms (see Section 11.5). Figure 11.10 shows surfaces with crease edges displayed. Reasonable crease edges and vertex normals can often be derived with some success from a connected mesh.

These are the problems; now to the solution. What follows is an algorithm that takes a set of arbitrary polygons with no known orientation and no stored normals and forms polygonal meshes with properly oriented polygons with vertex normals as desired. It also determines the solidity of the various meshes formed. Here is the overall approach:

1. Form edge-face structures for all polygons and sort these.

2. Find groups of polygons that touch each other; determine solidity and find boundary edges.

3. For each group, flip faces to gain consistency.

4. Determine what the inside of the mesh is, and flip all faces if needed.

5. Find smoothing groups and compute vertex normals.

6. Find crease edges.

7. Create polygonal meshes.

Not all of these steps have to be performed for all data; some can be skipped if the data is already present or the result is not needed. A detailed explanation of each step follows.

The first step is to form a list of all edges of all the polygons, with each edge referring back to the face (polygon) with which it is associated. Store each edge with its first vertex stored before the second vertex, using sorting order. One vertex comes before another in sorting order if its x-coordinate value is smaller. If the x-coordinates are equal, then the y-value is used; if these match, then z is used. For example, vertex $(-3, 5, 2)$ comes before vertex $(-3, 6, -8)$; the -3's match, but $5 < 6$.

If the coordinates are identical, then the edge has no length and could be discarded if the rest of the vertex data is the same. In practice, data sometimes comes in with vertices extremely close, but not identical. See Glassner's article [263] for one method of merging these vertices.

Once this edge list is formed, the goal is to find which edges are identical. By finding such matching edges, each polygon can quickly identify its neighbor along each edge. Since each edge is stored such that the first vertex is less than the second, comparing edges is simply a matter of comparing first to first and second to second vertices; no permutations such as one edge's first vertex to another's second vertex is needed. A hash table can be used to find matching edges [263]; alternately, system routines such as `qsort` are fairly efficient and can be comparable in speed to hashing in many cases.

Once matching edges are found, connections among neighboring polygons can be found. Also, boundary edges can be determined: Any edge that does not have two neighboring polygons is a boundary edge. Groups of polygons that touch each other form a continuous group. Note that a single data set can have a number of continuous groups. For example, a teapot can have two groups, the pot and the lid.

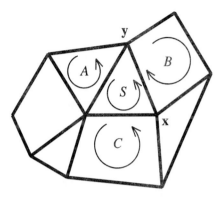

Figure 11.11. A starting polygon S is chosen and its neighbors are checked. Because the vertices in the edge shared by S and B are traversed in the same order (from **x** to **y**), the outline for B needs to be reversed.

The next step is to give the mesh orientation consistency, e.g., we may want all polygons to have counterclockwise outlines. For each continuous group of polygons, choose an arbitrary starting polygon. Check each of its neighboring polygons and determine whether the orientation is consistent. Orientation checking is simple: If the direction of traversal for the edge is the same for both polygons, then the neighboring polygon must be flipped. See Figure 11.11. Recursively check the neighbors of these neighbors, until all polygons in a continuous group are tested once. Checking once is important because pathological forms such as Möbius strips can create internally inconsistent results.

A group can be determined to be a solid (manifold) by testing whether all its edges are shared by two polygons. A group may actually form separate objects if any edges share four or more polygons—e.g., if two cubes touch at one edge, that edge is part of four polygons. Such cases can be difficult to differentiate: Is the surface formed one or two objects? Another problem case is when there are T-vertices, so a seemingly solid object is not properly sealed, since the matching edges are not found.

Although all the faces are properly oriented at this point, they could all be oriented inward. In most cases we want them outward. The test for whether all surface normals should be flipped is to take the signed volume of the group and check the sign; if it is negative, reverse all the loops and normals.

The way to get the signed volume is as follows. First, get the center point of the group's bounding box. Then compute the signed volume of each volume formed by joining the center point to each polygon (e.g., for a triangle polygon and a point, a tetrahedron is formed). The volume is equal to one-third the distance of the center point from the polygon's plane times the polygon's area. The 1/3 term can be dropped, since we need only the sign of the volume. The calculation of the area of a triangle is given in Appendix A.

This method is not fool-proof. If the object is not solid, but simply a surface description, it is certainly possible for the orientation still to be incorrect. Human intervention is needed in such cases. Even solids can be oriented incorrectly in special cases. For example, if the object is a room, the user wants its normals to face inward toward the camera.

Once the orientation is consistent, vertex normals can be generated by *smoothing techniques*. Smoothing information is something that the model's format may provide by specifying smoothing groups for the polygons, or by providing a crease angle. Smoothing group values are used to explicitly define which polygons in a group belong together to make up a curved surface. A crease angle is used when there is no smoothing group information. In this case, if two polygons' dihedral angle is found to be within the specified angle, then these two polygons are made to share vertex normals along their common edge. If the dihedral angle between the polygons is greater than the crease angle, then the edge between the polygons is a crease edge. This technique is sometimes called *edge preservation*.

Once a smoothing group is found, vertex normals can be computed. The standard textbook solution for finding the vertex normal is to average the surface normals of the polygons sharing the vertex [262, 263]. However, this method can lead to inconsistent and poorly weighted results. Thürmer and Wüthrich [750] present an alternate method, in which each polygon normal's contribution is weighted by the angle it forms at the vertex. This method has the desirable property of giving the same result whether a polygon sharing a vertex is triangulated or not. If the tessellated polygon turned into, say, two triangles sharing the vertex, the equal weight method would then give twice the weight to the two triangles as it would to the original polygon. See Figure 11.12.

Max [525] gives a different weighting method, based on the assumption that long edges form polygons that should affect the normal less. This type of smoothing may be superior when using simplification techniques, as larger polygons formed will be less likely to follow the surface's curvature. The algorithm is

$$\mathbf{n} = \sum_{i=0}^{n-1} \frac{\mathbf{e}_i \times \mathbf{e}_{i+1}}{||\mathbf{e}_i||^2 ||\mathbf{e}_{i+1}||^2} \tag{11.1}$$

for n counter-clockwise oriented polygons sharing a vertex. The $\mathbf{e}_i$ vectors

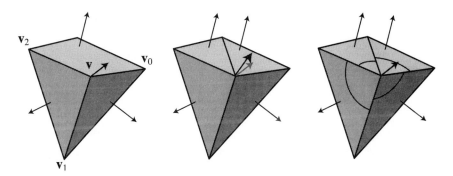

Figure 11.12. On the left, the surface normals of a rectangle and two triangles are averaged to give a vertex normal. In the middle, the square has been triangulated. This results in the average normal shifting, since each polygon's normal is weighted equally. On the right, Thürmer and Wüthrich's method weights each normal's contribution by its angle between the pair of edges forming it, so triangulation does not shift the normal.

are formed by the edges from the center vertex location $\mathbf{v}$, e.g., $\mathbf{e}_2$ is equal to $\mathbf{v}_2 - \mathbf{v}$. Modulo arithmetic is used for the edge vertices, i.e., if $i+1$ equals n, use 0. The numerator computes the normal for each pair of edges, and the squared length terms in the denominator make this normal's effect less for larger polygons. The resulting normal $\mathbf{n}$ is then normalized.

Using a smoothing angle can sometimes give an improper amount of smoothing, rounding edges that should be creased or vice versa. However, even smoothing groups can have their own problems. Imagine the curved surface of a cone made of polygons. All the polygons are in the same smoothing group. But at the tip of the cone, there should actually be many normals at a single vertex. Simply smoothing gives the peculiar result that the tip has one normal pointing directly out along the cone's axis. The cone tip is a singularity; either the faceter has to provide the vertex normals or the modeler sometimes cuts off the very tip, thereby providing separate vertices to receive these normals properly.

Once smoothing is done, boundaries for highlighting or for a vector representation of the surface can be found. This is done by identifying all edges that have polygons in different smoothing groups, or that have an odd number of neighboring polygons. These are then the boundaries of each curved surface.

The polygons are now properly oriented, smoothed, etc. The next step is to form the meshes themselves, which are typically stored as lists of shared vertices and outlines indexing them. Eliminating duplicate vertices can be done by hashing or sorting in a fashion similar to that used with edges and so finding matches.

One question is whether to merge separate surfaces into one polygon mesh. Each separate surface (almost always) has the property that a vertex has one and only one vertex normal and set of texture coordinates. For example, the corner of a cube is a single vertex, but this vertex is usually treated as three separate vertices with three separate vertex normals for the three separate squares. Hoppe [367] discusses memory-efficient ways to share vertex-face information while retaining surface-surface connectivity.

An additional step that could be performed at this time is triangulation. None of the previous steps depends on having triangles, so triangulation, if needed, could be delayed until the end.

11.4   Triangle Strips, Fans, and Meshes

An extremely common way to increase graphics performance is to send fewer than three vertices per triangle to the graphics pipeline. The benefits of this are quite obvious: Fewer points and normals need to be transformed, fewer line clips need to be performed, less lighting needs to be computed, etc. However, if the bottleneck of an application is the fill rate (i.e., the number of pixels that can be filled per second), little or no performance gain is to be expected from such savings. A variety of methods that use less data, namely triangle strips, fans, and meshes, will be described below, along with methods for converting a triangle mesh into triangle strips.

11.4.1   Strips

How is it possible to describe a triangle with less than three vertices? The secret is not to describe one triangle at a time, but instead to give a sequence of connected triangles. Consider Figure 11.13, in which connected triangles are shown. If these are treated as a triangle strip, then a more compact way of sending them to the rendering pipeline is possible. For the first triangle (denoted T_0), all three vertices (denoted $\mathbf{v}_0$, $\mathbf{v}_1$, and $\mathbf{v}_2$) are sent in that order. For subsequent triangles in this strip, only one vertex has to be sent, since the other two have already been sent with the previous triangle. For example, after sending triangle T_0, only vertex $\mathbf{v}_3$ is sent, and the vertices $\mathbf{v}_1$ and $\mathbf{v}_2$ from triangle T_0 are used to form triangle T_1. For triangle T_2, only vertex $\mathbf{v}_4$ is sent, and so on through the rest of the strip.

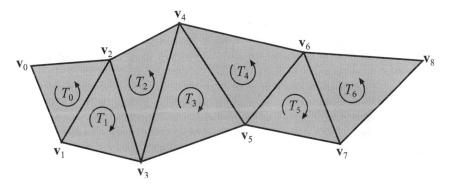

Figure 11.13. A sequence of triangles that can be represented as one triangle strip. Note that the orientation changes from triangle to triangle in the strip, and that the first triangle in the strip sets the orientation of all triangles. Internally, counter-clockwise order is kept consistent by traversing vertices 0-1-2, 1-3-2, 2-3-4, 3-5-4, and so on.

A sequential triangle strip of n vertices is defined as an ordered vertex list

$$\{\mathbf{v}_0, \mathbf{v}_1, \ldots, \mathbf{v}_{n-1}\}, \tag{11.2}$$

with a structure imposed upon it indicating that triangle i is

$$\triangle \mathbf{v}_i \mathbf{v}_{i+1} \mathbf{v}_{i+2}, \tag{11.3}$$

where $0 \leq i < n - 2$. This sort of strip is called *sequential* because the vertices are sent in the above mentioned sequence. The definition implies that a sequential triangle strip of n vertices has $n - 2$ triangles; we call it a triangle strip of length $n - 2$.

If a sequential triangle strip consists of m triangles, then three vertices are sent for the first one, followed by one more for each of the remaining $m - 1$ triangles. This means that the average number of vertices, v_a, sent for a sequential triangle strip of length m can be expressed as:

$$v_a = \frac{3 + (m-1)}{m} = 1 + \frac{2}{m}. \tag{11.4}$$

As can easily be seen, $v_a \to 1$ as $m \to \infty$. This might not seem to have much relevance for real-world cases, but consider a more reasonable value. If $m = 10$, then $v_a = 1.2$, which means that, on average, only 1.2 vertices are sent per triangle. The attractiveness of triangle strips stems from this fact. Depending on where the bottleneck is located in the rendering pipeline, there is a potential for saving two-thirds of the time spent rendering without sequential triangle strips.[3] The speed-up is due to avoiding redundant operations, such as sending the data to the graphics hardware, performing lighting calculations, clipping, matrix transformations, etc.

By not imposing a strict sequence on the triangles, as was done for the sequential triangle strips, one can create longer, and thus more efficient, strips. These are called *generalized triangle strips* [165]. To be able to use such strips, there must be some kind of vertex cache[4] on the graphics card that holds transformed and lit vertices. The vertices in this buffer can be accessed and replaced by sending short bit codes [165]. So the triangle strip creator has full control over the contents in the buffer. However, sometimes those buffers are of the *First-in, First-out* (FIFO) type [369], making them more transparent in that the user does not need to control them. When a vertex ends up in the buffer, other triangles can reuse these with little or no cost. Bar-Yehuda and Gotsman prove that a controllable buffer (non-FIFO) of size $O(\sqrt{n})$ is sufficient to send each vertex only once, which is the optimum [49].

A trick to "generalize" sequential triangle strips is to introduce a *swap* operation, which swaps the order of the two latest vertices In Iris GL [385], there is an actual command for doing a swap, but in OpenGL [600] and Direct3D, a swap command must be implemented by resending a vertex, and thus there is a penalty of one vertex per swap. This implementation of a swap results in a triangle with no area. Since starting a new triangle strip costs two vertices, accepting the penalty imposed by a swap is still better than restarting. Also, the actual API call to send a strip includes some cost, so fewer API calls may also increase performance too. A triangle strip wanting to send the vertices $(\mathbf{v}_0, \mathbf{v}_1, \mathbf{v}_2, \mathbf{v}_3, swap, \mathbf{v}_4, \mathbf{v}_5, \mathbf{v}_6)$ could be implemented as $(\mathbf{v}_0, \mathbf{v}_1, \mathbf{v}_2, \mathbf{v}_3, \mathbf{v}_2, \mathbf{v}_4, \mathbf{v}_5, \mathbf{v}_6)$, where the swap has been implemented by resending vertex $\mathbf{v}_2$. This is shown in Figure 11.14.

Before we examine how to decompose an arbitrary triangle mesh into triangle strips, we will take a glance at a similar concept—namely, triangle fans.

11.4.2   Fans

Take a look at Figure 11.15, which shows a triangle fan, another kind of set of connected triangles. If we wish to render these triangles, we are in ex-

---

[3]This also holds for triangle fans. In practice, some manufacturers such as NVIDIA recommend using strips over fans whenever possible, due to driver optimizations.

[4]Vertex caches are also sometimes called *vertex buffers* in the literature. We avoid this term here, as vertex buffer is used in DirectX to mean a primitive consisting of a set of vertices.

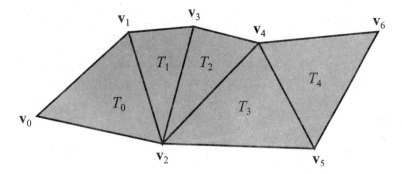

Figure 11.14. We would have to send $(\mathbf{v}_0, \mathbf{v}_1, \mathbf{v}_2, \mathbf{v}_3, \mathbf{v}_2, \mathbf{v}_4, \mathbf{v}_5, \mathbf{v}_6)$ to the graphics pipeline, to use these triangles as a strip. As can be seen, a swap has been implemented by including $\mathbf{v}_2$ twice in the list.

actly the same beneficial situation as we were for triangle strips, because of the triangle-fan construction primitive supported by most low-level graphics APIs. Notice that a general convex polygon[5] is easily converted into one triangle fan, though can also be converted to a simple triangle strip. The vertex shared by all triangles is called the *center vertex* and is vertex 0 in the figure. For the starting triangle 0, send vertices 0, 1, and 2 (in

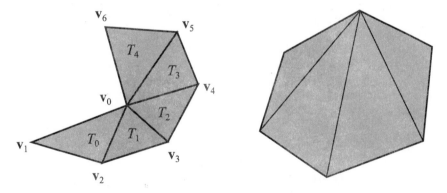

Figure 11.15. The left figure illustrates the concept of a triangle fan. Triangle T_0 sends vertices $\mathbf{v}_0$ (the center vertex), $\mathbf{v}_1$, and $\mathbf{v}_2$. The subsequent triangles, T_i $(i > 0)$, send only vertex $\mathbf{v}_{i+2}$. The right figure shows a convex polygon, which can always be turned into one triangle fan.

---

[5]Convexity testing is discussed and code is given by Schorn and Fisher [689].

that order), which is a similar start-up phase as that used for triangle strips. For subsequent triangles, the center vertex (number 0) is always used together with the previously sent vertex and the vertex currently being sent. Triangle 1 is therefore easily formed merely by sending vertex 3, thereby forming a triangle defined by vertices 0 (always included), 2 (the previously sent vertex), and 3 (the newly sent vertex, which is sent to create triangle 1). Further on, triangle 2 is constructed by sending vertex 4. Subsequent triangles are formed in the same manner.

A triangle fan of n vertices is defined as an ordered vertex list

$$\{\mathbf{v}_0, \mathbf{v}_1, \ldots, \mathbf{v}_{n-1}\} \tag{11.5}$$

(where $\mathbf{v}_0$ is called the center vertex), with a structure imposed upon the list indicating that triangle i is

$$\triangle\mathbf{v}_0\mathbf{v}_{i+1}\mathbf{v}_{i+2}, \tag{11.6}$$

where $0 \le i < n - 2$.

The analysis of the average number of vertices for a triangle fan of length m (i.e., consisting of m triangles), also denoted v_a, is the same as for triangle strips (see Equation 11.4), since they have the same start-up phase and then send only one vertex per new triangle. Similarly, when $m \to \infty$, v_a for triangle fans naturally also tends toward one vertex per triangle. For $m = 5$ (it is harder to find fans than strips, and so we use a smaller value of m than we might for strips), $v_a = 1.4$, which is still much better than 3. As for triangle strips, the start-up cost for the first triangle (always costing three vertices) is amortized over the subsequent triangles.

Any triangle fan can be converted into a triangle strip (which will contain many swaps), but not vice versa.

11.4.3   Creating Strips

Given an arbitrary triangle mesh, it is useful to decompose it efficiently into triangle strips. There is much free software for performing this task, but it is important to know how this software works. A visualization of the triangle strips of a model is shown in Figure 11.16.

Obtaining optimal triangle strips has been shown to be an NP-complete problem [25], and therefore, we have to be satisfied with heuristic methods that come close to the lower bound on the number of strips. This section will present one greedy method for constructing sequential triangles strips.

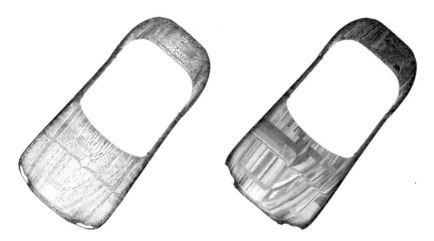

Figure 11.16. The left image shows some surfaces of a car in wireframe mode. The right image shows the same model, but here, each triangle strip has been randomly colored. *(Model reused courtesy of Nya Perspektiv Design AB.)*

Dual graph algorithms for stripping is also briefly discussed. First, some background information is in order.

Every triangle strip creation algorithm starts by creating an adjacency data structure for the polygon set; i.e., for each edge belonging to a polygon, a reference to its neighbor polygon is stored. See Section 11.3 for an algorithm for creating this data structure. The number of neighbors of a polygon is called its *degree* and is an integer between zero and the number of vertices of the polygon.

Euler's Theorem for *connected planar graphs* [56], which is shown in Equation 11.7, helps in determining the average number of vertices that have to be sent to the pipeline:

$$v - e + f = 2. \tag{11.7}$$

Here v is the number of vertices, e is the number of edges, and f is the number of faces in the graph. Since every edge has two faces (in a connected graph), and every face has at least three edges (exactly three for triangles), $2e \geq 3f$ holds. Inserting this fact into Euler's theorem and simplifying yields $f \leq 2v - 4$. If all faces are triangles, then $2e = 3f \Rightarrow f = 2v - 4$. All in all, this means that the number of triangles is less than or equal to twice the number of vertices in a triangulation. Since the average number of vertices per triangle in a strip approaches one, every vertex has to be sent at least twice (on average) using sequential triangle strips. Furthermore, at least twice (on average) using sequential triangle strips. Furthermore, this implies that generalized triangle meshes (Section 11.4.4) can be, at most, twice as efficient as sequential triangle strips.

Improved SGI Stripping Algorithm

This algorithm works for only fully triangulated models, meaning that if a model contains polygons with more than three vertices, then these polygons have to be triangulated before being fed into the triangle strip creation code.

Greedy algorithms are optimization methods that make choices that are locally optimal (they choose what looks best at the moment) [145]. The SGI algorithm [10] is greedy, in the sense that the beginning triangle it chooses always has the lowest degree (lowest number of neighbors). With some improvements [123], the SGI algorithm works like this:

1. Choose a starting triangle.

2. Build three different triangle strips; one for each edge of the triangle.

3. Extend these triangle strips in the opposite direction.

4. Choose the longest of these three strips; discard the others.

5. Repeat Step 1 until all triangles are included in a strip.

In Step 1, the original SGI algorithm picks any triangle of lowest degree (greater than zero). If there is a tie—that is, if there is more than one triangle with the (same) lowest degree—then the algorithm looks at the neighbors' neighbors (degrees). If again there is no unambiguous way to make a selection, a triangle is arbitrarily selected. Finally, the strip is extended as much as possible in both its start and end directions, making each strip potentially longer. The idea behind this method is that isolated triangles will not make any strip at all, and this is exactly what the SGI algorithm tends to minimize. A linear time algorithm can be implemented by using hash tables to store the adjacency data structure and a priority queue for finding the starting triangle of each new strip [10]. However, Chow reports that choosing any arbitrary triangle works almost as well [123]. Gumhold and Straßer report the same for their related geometry compression algorithm [297]. So, the effort of choosing a good starting triangle may not be worth it. Steps 2 through 4 guarantee that the longest strip in the current mesh containing the starting triangle is found.

A practical aspect here is that the orientation of triangles should be preserved in order to get correct shading and backface culling. Recall that

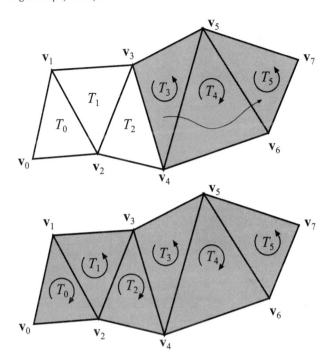

Figure 11.17. Strip extension. In the top figure, T_3 (oriented counter-clockwise) is chosen as the starting triangle, and the strip is grown to the right, including T_4 and T_5. At the bottom, the strip is extended to the left to make it longer. The triangle $T_0 \mathbf{v}_0 \mathbf{v}_1 \mathbf{v}_2$ is chosen as the first triangle in the resulting strip. However, this changes orientation of the entire strip to clockwise, since T_0 is oriented that way. To avoid this problem, the first vertex could be duplicated in the strip, creating a zero-area triangle.

the first triangle in a triangle strip determines the orientation of the triangles in a strip, and that the order appears to be reversed between adjacent triangles (see Figure 11.13). An example of what can happen to the orientation during the extension in the reverse direction is shown in Figure 11.17. Assume that the triangle $T_3 : \Delta \mathbf{v}_3 \mathbf{v}_4 \mathbf{v}_5$ (oriented counterclockwise) is chosen as the starting triangle, and that the triangle strip first is grown to the right. After that, the strip includes triangles T_3, T_4, and T_5. Then an attempt is made at extending the strip to the left of the starting triangle. Now the strip includes all triangles in the mesh and T_3 is no longer used as the starting triangle of the strip. Instead, T_0 is chosen as the starting triangle. However, T_0 is oriented clockwise, so this makes all triangles clockwise, which will render incorrectly. This is because there was an odd

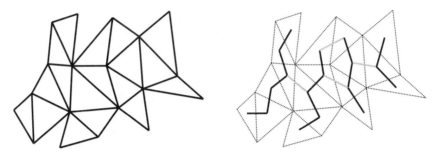

Figure 11.18. Left: A triangle mesh. Right: The dual graph (gray and black bold lines) of the mesh to the left. Connected bold black lines indicate the four different triangle strips in this example.

number of triangles that were added to the left. In such cases the starting vertex could simply be replicated in order to correct the orientation. Thus, the strip would be $v_0 v_0 v_1 v_2 v_3 v_4 v_5 v_6 v_7$. Alternately, if the triangle at the right end of the strip is oriented clockwise (not true in this example), then the whole strip could be reversed, which would then need no replication.

Dual Graph Stripping Algorithms

Another strategy for creating triangle strips is to create the dual graph of the triangle mesh [743]. This is shown in Figure 11.18, where edges in the dual graph are created between the centers of the faces of adjacent triangles. This graph of edges is called a *spanning tree*, which subsequently is used in search for good triangle strips. Xiang et al. [831] presents search algorithms of the dual graph, using dynamic programming. Stewart [731] discusses joining strips in the dual graph, which can be used for updating strips on the fly for progressive meshes.

Cache-Friendly Stripping

Assume that triangle strips have been created for a triangle mesh. Since many graphics cards have vertex caches, the order in which the strips are sent through the pipeline will give different vertex cache performance. Different accelerators have different cache sizes. See Section 10.3.2. A simple preprocess to improve the order is to start with some triangle strip and push its vertices onto a software simulation of the vertex cache (FIFO). Next, the remaining triangle strips are examined to find the one that best exploits the contents of the cache. This procedure is repeated until all triangle strips has been processed. NVIDIA's NVTriStrip software works exactly like this. NVTriStrip is partially built on work by Hoppe [369].

11.4.4 Triangle Meshes

Triangle fans and strips are popular acceleration primitives, but there is support for polygon meshes within both Direct3D and OpenGL. The trend is for graphics accelerators to take advantage of meshes as much as possible. Essentially, it is more efficient to transform a vertex only once. Strips and fans allow some data sharing, but meshes allow full sharing.

Triangle meshes consist of a list of vertices and a set of outlines. Each vertex contains a position and other additional data, such as diffuse and specular colors, shading normal, texture coordinates, etc. Each triangle outline has a list of integer indices. Each index is a number from 0 to $n - 1$, where n is the number of vertices, and so points to a vertex in the list. Forming such lists and outlines from a set of unconnected triangles is discussed in depth in Section 11.3.

Creating Universal Rendering Sequences

Given that indexed triangle meshes are efficient rendering primitives on graphics hardware with vertex caches (with FIFO queues) in the geometry stage, there is still the matter of sending the indices to the hardware in a good order. On top of that, different hardware has different sized vertex caches. One solution is to generate unique index orders for each vertex cache size. This is obviously not an attractive solution. To solve this problem for all cache sizes, Bogomjakov and Gotsman [95] suggest an algorithm that creates *universal* index sequences for the triangle mesh. By universal, they mean an index order that works well for every possible vertex cache size.

Before describing their algorithm, some background information on space-filling curves is needed. A space-filling curve is a single, continuous curve that, without intersecting itself, fills a square or rectangle containing a uniform grid by visiting every grid cell once. One example is the Hilbert curve, which is shown in Figure 11.19. A good space-filling curve has good spatial coherence, which means that when walking along the curve, you stay close to the previously visited points (at all scales). The Hilbert curve is an example of a curve with good spatial coherency. See Sagan's book [667] or Voorhies' article [780] for more information on this topic.

If a space-filling curve is used to visit the triangles on a triangle mesh, then one could expect a high hit ratio in the vertex cache. Inspired by this, Bogomjakov and Gotsman [95] proposed a recursive algorithm for generating good index sequences for triangle meshes. The idea is to split the mesh into two approximately equally sized submeshes. Then the first submesh is rendered, followed by rendering the second submesh. This

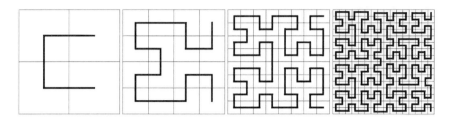

Figure 11.19. An illustration of four generations of Hilbert curves. The thin lines represent the grid, and the bold lines the Hilbert curve. As can be seen, the curve visits every grid cell, and it is self-similar at all scales. A nice property is that the Hilbert curve visits every grid cells within 2×2 cells, then within 4×4 cells, then within 8×8 cells, and so on.

is repeated recursively, that is, the first submesh is split again into two pieces and rendered, etc. The mesh splitting is done as a preprocess, and is implemented by using a *balanced edge-cut* algorithm using the MeTiS software package [404], which minimizes the number of edge cuts. The complexity of this algorithm is linear in the number of triangles in the mesh.

More precisely, the algorithm works like this. First, we construct the dual graph of the triangle mesh (see page 462). Then the balanced edge-cut algorithm removes a minimal set of edges in the dual graph in order to split the mesh into two disjoint meshes of approximately the same size. To get good cache performance in the vertex cache, it is advantageous to try to see to it that the last triangle in the first submesh is close to the first triangle in the second submesh. This is done by letting the last triangle in the first submesh and the first triangle in the second submesh share an edge in the dual graph that has been cut off. After this has been repeated recursively, the index sequence of the vertices can be generated. The rendering order is determined by the recursion process; the first submesh is traversed recursively first, and finally the second submesh is traversed recursively. This gives the index order.

For cache sizes from about ten[6] and up, this algorithm consistently outperforms Xiang's triangle strip algorithm [831].

11.4.5   Vertex and Index Buffers/Arrays

The best way to provide a modern graphics accelerator with model data is by using what OpenGL calls vertex arrays and DirectX calls vertex buffers. The idea of a vertex buffer is to store model data in a contiguous chunk of memory. The largest savings in time from using vertex buffers is sim-

---

[6]The GeForce2 has ten entries in its vertex cache.

ply that the data does not have to be copied from the application to the driver. The application puts the data into the relevant buffers, then passes the pointers to the driver, which then accesses the data directly (e.g., over the AGP bus). Copying memory is expensive in and of itself, and it also pollutes the CPU memory cache. There are other savings that come from using vertex buffers. Each transfer of data to the accelerator has an overhead cost and causes system bus traffic. These costs are minimized by sending a large amount of data at one time in a vertex buffer. A vertex buffer or array also needs fewer API calls, but the savings from this on modern accelerators is negligible.

In DirectX 8 a vertex buffer is a collection of vertex data of a single format. The *Flexible Vertex Format* (FVF) specifies the format. It is a set of flags that specifies whether a vertex contains a normal, diffuse or specular colors, texture coordinates, etc. Data can also include view-space location coordinates, i.e., the coordinates that result after view matrix transformation.

Vertex buffers are used in two different ways: for static and for dynamic data. Static data usually means models that are rigid and do not change in shape throughout the lifetime of the scene.[7] For this type of data, a write-only vertex buffer can be created, locked, loaded with the data, unlocked, and then optimized by the graphics system. Such optimization can significantly help the performance of systems without hardware transform and lighting support [374, 520]. Dynamic data for display works similarly, but with no optimization step performed, as this process can be costly.

How the vertex buffer is accessed is up to the device's `DrawPrimitive` method. The data can be treated as:

1. A list of individual points.

2. A list of unconnected line segments, i.e., pairs of vertices.

3. A single polyline.

4. A triangle list, where each group of three vertices form a triangle, e.g., vertices $[0, 1, 2]$ form one, $[3, 4, 5]$ form the next, etc.

5. Triangle fans, where the first vertex forms a triangle with each successive pair of vertices, e.g., $[0, 1, 2]$, $[0, 2, 3]$, $[0, 3, 4]$.

6. Triangle strips, where every group of three contiguous vertices for a triangle, e.g., $[0, 1, 2]$, $[1, 2, 3]$, $[2, 3, 4]$.

---

[7]This does not necessarily have to be the case. Vertex shaders could be used to deform the data.

See Figure 11.20 for examples of some of these. Triangle strips are normally the most efficient representation for model data. It is important to avoid switching between vertex buffers, as this is an expensive operation, so putting all triangles of the same vertex format in a single buffer is recommended [180]. Obviously, no single triangle strip is normally this long, so to connect two strips, what is done is to double the last vertex of one strip and the first vertex of the next strip. Doing so has the effect of creating four degenerate triangles that are never seen (except in wireframe). See Figure 11.21. Hardware is efficient at detecting and deleting these degenerate triangles [236]. Triangle fan vertex buffers cannot be connected like triangle strips and so are inefficient in practice. Convex polygons can be triangulated into fans or strips, so strips can be used in place of most fans.

A faster way to access vertex buffer data is to use indexed lists or indexed strips.[8] DirectX calls these *index buffers*, and they are analogous to vertex buffers in functionality. As discussed in Section 11.4.4, a set of vertices can form a mesh (or even a set of meshes). Each triangle is described by three indices, giving the locations in the vertex array of the three vertices. Similarly, a vertex buffer can have an associated index buffer. That is, the index buffer consists of sets of three indices to form single triangles, or it defines one long triangle strip, with indices repeated to join separate triangle strips. In this case the vertex buffer data can be in any order, since it is not accessed directly. That said, techniques to maintain data locality will improve performance. See Section 11.4.4. In any case, indexed vertex buffers are usually the most efficient way to render models, as vertex sharing is maximized and so overall data sent on the bus minimized.

Vertex and index buffers can be categorized by whether they reside in system memory or not, by whether they are write-only, and by their vertex format. System memory vertex buffers are used when the graphics accelerator does not offer hardware transform and lighting, or when the data needs to be read by the CPU for other processing. Similarly, vertex buffers cannot be marked write-only if the CPU needs to later access the data in them. Vertex and index buffers are most efficient if they can be declared as being write-only and as not being in system memory [374]. Such buffers are then placed by the graphics system into AGP or video memory for faster access. Video memory is usually preferable, as then the data is sent across the bus only once and reused by the accelerator each frame. See Section 15.3.2.

---

[8] As of January 2002, index buffers are not necessarily faster. However, NVIDIA, for example, encourages their use because they expect index buffers to be more efficient on their hardware at some point in the future.

Three triangles, made of vertex positions
$\mathbf{p}_0$ through $\mathbf{p}_3$, and normals $\mathbf{n}_0$ through $\mathbf{n}_3$

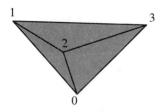

The triangles could be rendered through a series of individual calls: begin, $\mathbf{p}_0$, $\mathbf{n}_0$, $\mathbf{p}_1$, $\mathbf{n}_1$, $\mathbf{p}_2$, $\mathbf{n}_2$, end, begin, $\mathbf{p}_1$, $\mathbf{n}_1$, $\mathbf{p}_3$, $\mathbf{n}_3$, $\mathbf{p}_2$, $\mathbf{n}_2$, end, begin, $\mathbf{p}_2$, $\mathbf{n}_2$, $\mathbf{p}_3$, $\mathbf{n}_3$, $\mathbf{p}_0$, $\mathbf{n}_0$, end.

The positions and normals could be put into two separate lists. These two arrays get treated as a list of triangles, so that each separate trio in the array is a triangle:

| $\mathbf{p}_0$ | $\mathbf{p}_1$ | $\mathbf{p}_2$ | $\mathbf{p}_1$ | $\mathbf{p}_3$ | $\mathbf{p}_2$ | $\mathbf{p}_2$ | $\mathbf{p}_3$ | $\mathbf{p}_0$ | array of positions

| $\mathbf{n}_0$ | $\mathbf{n}_1$ | $\mathbf{n}_2$ | $\mathbf{n}_1$ | $\mathbf{n}_3$ | $\mathbf{n}_2$ | $\mathbf{n}_2$ | $\mathbf{n}_3$ | $\mathbf{n}_0$ | array of normals

The positions and normals could be put in arrays and every trio define a triangle:

| $\mathbf{p}_0$ | $\mathbf{p}_1$ | $\mathbf{p}_2$ | $\mathbf{p}_3$ | $\mathbf{p}_0$ | array of positions

| $\mathbf{n}_0$ | $\mathbf{n}_1$ | $\mathbf{n}_2$ | $\mathbf{n}_3$ | $\mathbf{n}_0$ | array of normals

Each vertex could be put in a single interleaved array, with each separate trio or every trio (i.e., a tristrip) making a triangle. Here is the array for the tristrip:

| $\mathbf{p}_0\,\mathbf{n}_0$ | $\mathbf{p}_1\,\mathbf{n}_1$ | $\mathbf{p}_2\,\mathbf{n}_2$ | $\mathbf{p}_3\,\mathbf{n}_3$ | $\mathbf{p}_0\,\mathbf{n}_0$ | array of vertices

Each vertex could be in a single array, with an index list giving separate triangles:

| $\mathbf{p}_0\,\mathbf{n}_0$ | $\mathbf{p}_1\,\mathbf{n}_1$ | $\mathbf{p}_2\,\mathbf{n}_2$ | $\mathbf{p}_3\,\mathbf{n}_3$ | array of vertices

| 0 1 2   1 3 2   2 3 0 | index array

Each vertex could be in a single array, with an index list defining the triangle strip:

| $\mathbf{p}_0\,\mathbf{n}_0$ | $\mathbf{p}_1\,\mathbf{n}_1$ | $\mathbf{p}_2\,\mathbf{n}_2$ | $\mathbf{p}_3\,\mathbf{n}_3$ | array of vertices

| 0 1 2 3 0 | index array

Figure 11.20. Different ways of defining primitives: separate triangles, or as a vertex triangle list or triangle strip, or an indexed vertex list or strip.

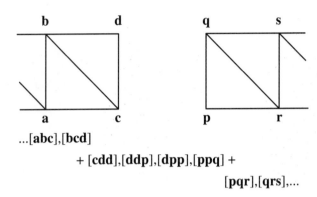

...[abc],[bcd]

+ [cdd],[ddp],[dpp],[ppq] +

[pqr],[qrs],...

Figure 11.21. Two triangle strips are joined by replicating the end vertex **d** and beginning vertex **p**, forming four degenerate triangles. *(Illustration after Huddy [374].)*

Vertex data can be grouped by vertex or by data type. For example, say the vertex format consists of a position, **p**, and a normal, **n**. A single vertex buffer has data in the order $p_0n_0p_1n_1 \ldots$. Alternately, a set of *vertex streams* are created, and one holds an array of positions $p_0p_1p_2 \ldots$ and another a separate array of normals $n_0n_1n_2 \ldots$. Each vertex stream can actually hold more than one piece of vertex data, e.g., one stream could hold the position and normal in one vertex buffer, and color and texture coordinates in another vertex buffer. Use of the streamed format can help on systems without accelerator transform and lighting capabilities. For accelerators with a hardware geometry stage, there is typically no performance advantage of one organization over the other.

OpenGL has similar mechanisms for vertex arrays [520]. The terminology is a bit different. A basic vertex array is similar to a vertex stream holding one type of data. An *interleaved array* has data stored by vertex. The length in bytes of the vertex record is called the *stride*. Optimized data is referred to as *compiled vertex arrays*. Hardware vendors offer extensions to OpenGL to avoid copying the input vertex arrays and to be able to use DMA pull (see Section 15.3.2). These extensions let the user specially allocate memory similar to DirectX. For example, NVIDIA has NV_vertex_array_range (VAR) for this type of fast vertex array.

11.5 Simplification

Research into simplification and alternate model descriptions is an active and wide-ranging field. One area of interest is algorithms to convert surface features into bump maps [131, 673]. Sander et al. [672] use bump maps and a coarse mesh for the model, but create a higher precision silhouette. Impostors [508], described in Section 8.3.4, are another form of alternate rendering of the same model. Kajiya [400] presents a hierarchy of scale showing how surface lighting models overlap texture mapping methods, which in turn overlap geometric details. Work such as Cook's [140] in shading languages blurs the distinction and unifies these different scales. Sprites and layered depth images can replace geometry in scenes (see Sections 8.2 and 8.3.4). A particularly impressive example of the range of techniques that can be used to represent an object is from Lengyel et al. [487, 488]. In this research, fur is represented by geometry when extremely close up, alpha blended polylines when further away, then a blend with volume texture "shells," finally becoming a texture map when far away. See Plate XLIX following page 562. Knowing when and how best to switch from one

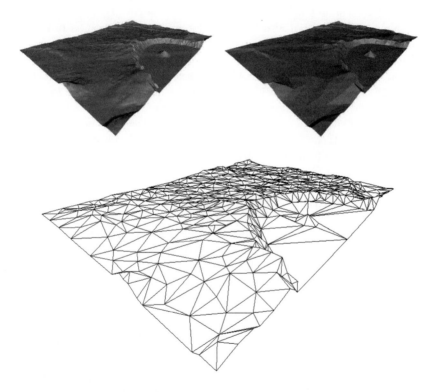

Figure 11.22. On the left is a heightfield of Crater Lake rendered with 200,000 triangles. The right figure shows this model simplified down to 1000 triangles. The underlying simplified mesh is shown below. *(Images courtesy of Michael Garland.)*

set of modeling and rendering techniques to another in order to maximize frame rate and quality is still an art and an open area for exploration.

Mesh simplification, also known as *data reduction* or *decimation*, is the process of taking a detailed model and reducing its polygon count while attempting to preserve its appearance. For real-time work normally this process is done to reduce the number of vertices stored and sent down the pipeline. This can be important in making the application scalable, as older machines may need to display lower numbers of polygons [614]. Model data may also be received with more tessellation than is necessary for a reasonable representation. Figure 11.22 gives a sense of how the number of stored triangles can be reduced by data reduction techniques.

Luebke [507] identifies three types of polygonal simplification: static, dynamic, and view-dependent. Static simplification is the idea of creating separate level of detail (LOD) models before rendering begins, and the renderer chooses among these. This form is covered in Section 9.8. Batch simplification can also be useful for other tasks, such as providing coarse meshes for subdivision surfaces to refine [479, 480]. Dynamic simplification gives a continuous spectrum of LOD models instead of a few discrete models, and so such methods are referred to as *continuous level of detail* (CLOD) algorithms. View-dependent techniques are meant for models where the level of detail varies within the model. Specifically, terrain rendering is a case in which the nearby areas in view need detailed representation while those in the distance are at a lower level of detail. These two types of simplification are discussed in this section.

11.5.1   Dynamic Simplification

One method of reducing the polygon count is to use an *edge collapse* operation. In this operation, an edge is removed by moving its two vertices to one spot. See Figure 11.23 for an example of this operation in action. For a solid model, an edge collapse removes a total of two triangles, three edges, and one vertex. So a closed model with 3000 triangles would have 1500 edge collapses applied to it to reduce it to zero faces. A rule of thumb is that a triangulated polygon mesh with v vertices has about $2v$ faces and $3v$ edges. This rule can be derived using Euler's theorem that $f - e + v = 2$ for a solid's surface. See Section 11.4.3.

The edge collapse process is reversible. By storing the edge collapses in order, we can start with the simplified model and reconstruct the complex model from it. This characteristic is useful for network transmission of models, in that the edge-collapsed version of the database can be sent in

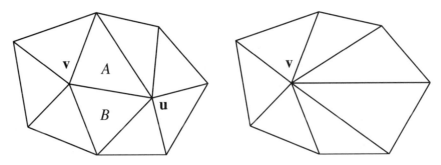

Figure 11.23. On the left is the figure before the **uv** edge collapse occurs; the right figure shows point **u** collapsed into point **v**, thereby removing triangles A and B and edge **uv**.

an efficiently compressed form and progressively built up and displayed as the model is received [365, 744]. Because of this feature, this simplification process is often referred to as *View-independent Progressive Meshing* (VIPM).

In Figure 11.23, **u** was collapsed into the location of **v**, but **v** could have been collapsed into **u**. A simplification system limited to just these two possibilities is using a *subset placement* strategy. An advantage of this strategy is that, if we limit the possibilities, we may implicitly encode the choice actually made [251, 365]. This strategy is faster because fewer possibilities need to be examined, but it also can yield lower-quality approximations because a smaller solution space is examined. The DirectX 8 utility library uses this strategy [236], as do other systems, such as Melax's [540].

By using an *optimal placement* strategy, we examine a wider range of possibilities. Instead of collapsing one vertex into another, both vertices for an edge are contracted to a new location. Hoppe [365] examines the case in which **u** and **v** both move to some location on the edge; he notes that in order to improve compression of the final data representation the search can be limited to checking the midpoint. Garland and Heckbert [251] solve a quadratic equation to find an optimal position (which may be located off of the edge). Another strategy is to limit the new placement point to anywhere on the edge. The advantage of optimal placement strategies is that they tend to give higher-quality meshes. The disadvantages are extra processing, code, and memory for recording this wider range of possible placements.

To determine the best point placement, we perform an analysis on the local neighborhood. This locality is an important and useful feature for a number of reasons. If the cost of an edge collapse depends on just a few local variables (e.g., edge length and face normals near the edge), the cost function is easy to compute, and each collapse affects only a few of its neighbors. For example, say a model has 3000 possible edge collapses that are computed at the start. The edge collapse with the lowest cost-function value is performed. Because it affects only a few nearby triangles and their edges, only those edge collapse possibilities whose cost functions are affected by these changes need to be recomputed (say 10 instead of 3000), and the list requires only a minor bit of resorting. Because an edge-collapse affects only a few other edge-collapse cost values, a good choice for maintaining this list of cost values is a heap or other priority queue [713].

The collapse operation itself is an edit of the model's database. Data structures for storing these collapses are well-documented [84, 236, 367, 540, 740]. Each edge collapse is analyzed with a cost function, and the one with the smallest cost value is performed next. An open research problem is finding the best cost function under various conditions [507]. Depending on the problem being solved, the cost function may make trade-offs among speed, quality, robustness, and simplicity. It may also be tailored to maintain surface boundaries, material locations, lighting effect, texture placement, volume, or other constraints.

Garland and Heckbert [250] introduced the idea that any pair of vertices, not just edge vertices, can form a pair and be contracted into one vertex. To limit the numbers of pairs to test, only those vertices within some distance t of each other can form a pair. This concept of pair contraction is useful in joining together separate surfaces that may be close to each other, but are not precisely joined.

Some contractions must be avoided regardless of cost; see the example in Figure 11.24. These can be detected by checking whether a neighboring polygon flips its normal direction due to a collapse.

We will present Garland and Heckbert's basic cost function [250, 251] in order to give a sense of how such functions work. Because of its efficiency and reasonable results, it is the cost function used in the DirectX utility library and a number of other simplification libraries. For a given vertex there is a set of triangles that share it, and each triangle has a plane equation associated with it. The cost function for moving a vertex is the sum of the squared distances between each of these planes and the new location. More formally:

$$c(\mathbf{v}) = \sum_{i=1}^{m} (\mathbf{n}_i \cdot \mathbf{v} + d_i)^2$$

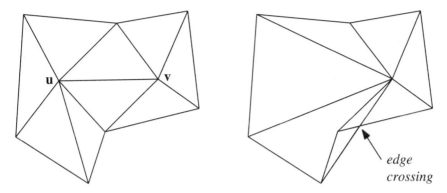

Figure 11.24. Example of a bad collapse. On the left is a mesh before collapsing vertex *u* into *v*. On the right is the mesh after the collapse, showing how edges now cross.

is the cost function for new location **v** and *m* planes, where **n** is the plane's normal and *d* its offset from the origin.

An example of two possible contractions for the same edge is shown in Figure 11.25. Say the cube is two units long. The cost function for collapsing **e** into **c** (**e** → **c**) will be 0, because the point **e** does not move off of the planes it shares when it goes to **e**. The cost function for **c** → **e** will be 1, because **c** moves away from the plane of the right face of the cube by a squared distance of 1. Because it has a lower cost, the **e** → **c** collapse would be done before **c** → **e**.

This cost function can be modified in various ways. Imagine two triangles that share an edge that form a very sharp edge, e.g., they are part of a fish's fin or turbine blade. The cost function for collapsing a vertex on this

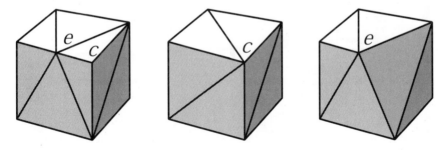

Figure 11.25. The left figure shows a cube with an extra point along one edge. The middle figure shows what happens if this point **e** is collapsed to corner **c**. The right figure shows **c** collapsed to **e**.

edge is low, because a point sliding along one triangle does not move far
from the other triangle's plane. The basic function's cost value is related
to the volume change of removing the feature, but is not a good indicator
of its visual importance. One way to maintain an edge with a sharp crease
is to add an extra plane that includes the edge and has a normal that is
the average of the two triangle normals. Now vertices that move far from
this edge will have a higher cost function [252]. A variation is to weight
the cost function by the change in the areas of the triangles [84].

Another type of extension is to use a cost function based on maintaining
other surface features. For example, the crease and boundary edges of a
model are important in portraying it, so these should be made less likely to
be modified (see Plate XLVII, following page 562). Other surface features
worth preserving are locations where there are material changes, texture
map edges, and color-per-vertex changes [370]. Radiosity solutions use
color per vertex to record the illumination on a meshed surface and so are
excellent candidates for reduction techniques [365]. See Plate XXXVII for
an example. The underlying mesh is shown in Figure 11.26.

The best edge to collapse is the one that makes the least perceptible
change in the resulting image. Lindstrom and Turk [501] use this idea to
produce an image-driven collapse function. Images of the original model
are created from a set of different view directions, say 20 in all. Then all
potential edge collapses are tried for a model and for each one a set of

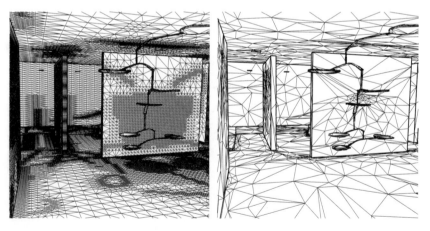

Figure 11.26. Simplification of radiosity solution. Left is the original mesh (150,983
faces); right is simplified mesh (10,000 faces). *(Images courtesy of Hugues Hoppe, Microsoft Research.)*

images is generated and compared to the original. The edge with the least visual difference is collapsed. This cost function is expensive to compute, and is certainly not a technique that can be done on the fly. However, simplification is a process that can be precomputed for later use. The advantage of the scheme is that it directly evaluates the visual effect of each collapse, versus the approximation provided by simpler functions.

One serious problem that occurs with most simplification algorithms is that textures often deviate in a noticeable way from their original appearance [507]. As edges are collapsed, the underlying mapping of the texture to the surface can become distorted. A related concept is the idea of turning a surface's original geometry into a normal map for bump mapping. Sander et al. [673] discuss previous work in this area and provide a solution. Their idea is to split the mesh into reasonable submeshes, each of which is to give a local texture parameterization. The goal is to treat the surface position separately from the color and bump information.

Edge-collapse simplification can produce a large number of *Level of Detail* (LOD) models (see Section 9.8) from a single complex model. A problem found in using LOD models is that the transition can sometimes be seen if one model instantly replaces another between one frame and the next [245]. This problem is called "popping." One solution is to use *geomorphs* [365] to increase or decrease the level of detail. Since we know how the vertices in the more complex model map to the simple model, it is possible to create a smooth transition. See Section 9.8.1 for more details.

One advantage of using VIPM is that a single vertex buffer can be created once and shared among copies of the same model at different levels of detail [740]. However, under the basic scheme, a separate index buffer needs to be made for each copy. Another problem is efficiency. Static LOD models can undergo stripification to improve their display speeds. For dynamic models, basic VIPM does not take into account the underlying accelerator hardware. Because the order of collapses determines the triangle display order, vertex cache coherency is poor. Bloom [85] and Forsyth [236] discuss a number of practical solutions to improve efficiency when forming and sharing index buffers.

Polygon reduction techniques can be useful, but they are not a panacea. A talented model maker can create low-polygon-count objects that are better in quality than those generated by automated procedures. One reason for this is that most reduction techniques know nothing about visually important elements or symmetry. For example, the eyes and mouth are the most important part of the face [540]. A naive algorithm will smooth these away as inconsequential. The problem of maintaining symmetry is shown in Figure 11.27.

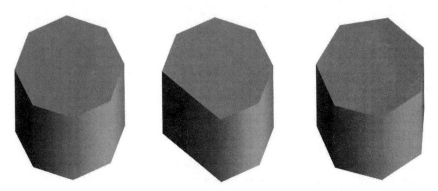

Figure 11.27. Symmetry problem. The cylinder on the left has 10 flat faces (including top and bottom). The middle cylinder has 9 flat faces after 1 face is eliminated by automatic reduction. The right cylinder has 9 flat faces after being regenerated by the modeler's faceter.

11.5.2   View-Dependent Simplification

One type of model with unique properties is terrain. The data typically is represented by uniform heightfield grids. View-independent methods of simplification can be used on this data, as seen in Figure 11.22 on page 469. The model is simplified until some limiting criteria is met [249]. Small surface details can be captured by color or normal bump map textures. The resulting static mesh, often called a *Triangulated Irregular Network* (TIN), is a useful representation when the terrain area is small and relatively flat in various areas [771].

For other outdoor scenes, continuous level of detail techniques are often used to minimize the number of vertices that must be processed. The idea is that terrain that is in view and close to the viewer should be shown with a greater level of detail. One type of algorithm is to use edge collapses and geomorphing, as described in the previous section, but with a cost function based on the view [366, 368]. The entire terrain is not represented as a single mesh, but rather as smaller tiles. This allows techniques such as frustum culling and potential visible sets to be used to quickly remove tiles from further consideration. Such culling techniques are applicable to most terrain rendering algorithms.

Another class of algorithms is based on using the underlying structure of the heightfield grid itself. The method by Lindstrom et al. [500], and the ROAM scheme by Duchaineau et al. scheme [186, 758] are the two seminal papers in this area. The idea is to impose a hierarchical struc-

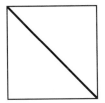 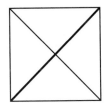 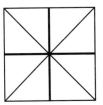 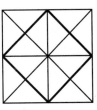

Figure 11.28. The triangle bintree. On the left, the heightfield is represented by two triangles at the topmost level. At each successive level, every triangle is split into two, with splits shown by the thick lines.

ture on the data, then evaluate this hierarchy and render only the level of complexity needed to sufficiently represent the terrain. A commonly used hierarchical structure introduced in ROAM is the triangle binary tree (bintree). Starting with a large right triangle, with vertices at the corners of the heightfield tile, this triangle can be subdivided by connecting its centerpoint along the diagonal to the opposite corner. This splitting process can be done on down to the limit of the heightfield data. See Figure 11.28. In the ROAM algorithm, an error bound is created for each triangle. This error bound represents the maximum amount that the associated terrain heightfield varies from the plane formed by the triangle. In other words, three points on the heightfield define a triangle, and all the heightfield samples covered by this triangle are compared to the triangle's plane and the absolute value of the maximum difference is the error bound. The vertical error bound and the triangle together define a pie-shaped wedge of space that contains all the terrain associated with that triangle.

During run-time, these error bounds are projected on to the view plane and evaluated for their effect on the rendering. For example, looking edge-on through a wedge means that the silhouette of the terrain is visible through that wedge, so a highly tessellated version of the terrain is needed. Looking down through the triangular part of the wedge means the geometry itself is not critical. Due to projection, a distant wedge will have a smaller projected error, and so will be tessellated less. Blow [91] discusses improved error metrics for ROAM.

Once the subdivision level of each visible triangle is computed, tessellation can occur. Crack avoidance and repair is a major part of any terrain rendering algorithm. That is, if one triangle is highly subdivided and its neighbors are not, cracks or T-vertices can develop between the levels. The bintree structure lends itself to avoiding such splits. See Figure 11.29. Bloom [84] gives a number of general techniques of welding splits between terrain tiles.

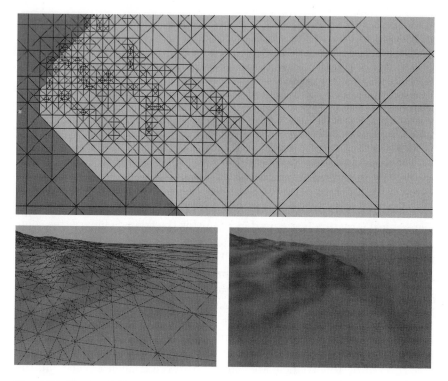

Figure 11.29. A ROAM view-dependent subdivision of the terrain. *(Images courtesy of Mark Duchaineau, LLNL.)*

There are some useful advantages to the ROAM algorithm. The effect of each triangle wedge can be used to prioritize which triangles to split first. This allows a limit to the number of triangles rendered to be set. If the view is slowly and smoothly changing, the previous frame's tessellation can be used as a starting point to create the current frame, thereby saving traversal time. Because priority queues are used and the maximum number of triangles can be specified, the frame rate can be guaranteed. See Section 9.8.3 for more on the concept of a guaranteed frame rate.

For all of these view-dependent techniques, it is best to either precompute and store the effect of lighting in the surface's texture map, or use a separate normal bump map for the heightfield's surface normals. Otherwise, as the terrain's level of detail shifts, the lighting and interpolation changes will be extremely noticeable.

Many improvements to terrain rendering algorithms have been made. Triangles can be given a cone of normals describing the underlying terrain's surface details, and this cone can be used for culling. See Section 9.3.2. However, given modern accelerators and the cost in memory, such culling may actually slow down the system [81]. Snook [722] discusses clustering the triangles in the lower levels of the bintree so that vertex buffers can be used. Ulrich [759] uses quadtrees to avoid needing to load all the data in huge heightfields. Bloom [84] uses VIPM techniques with tiles.

Further Reading and Resources

Schneider & Eberly [688] present a wide variety of algorithms concerning polygons and triangles, along with pseudocode. Narkhede and Manocha [581] have code available for their triangulator. The OpenGL Utility Library [600] includes a robust triangulator; this standalone utility library can be used even if you do not use OpenGL itself.

For translating three-dimensional file formats, the best book is Rule's *3D Graphics File Formats: A Programmer's Reference* [662], which includes a file translator with source code. Murray and VanRyper's *Encyclopedia of Graphics File Formats* [577] includes some information on three-dimensional file format layout.

For more on determining polygon properties such as convexity and area, see Farin and Hansford's *The Geometry Toolbox* [225]. Schorn and Fisher's convexity test code [689] is robust and fast, and available on the web.

Tools such as NVIDIA's NVTriStrip can help in forming efficient vertex buffers. There are a number of other free stripifiers available on the web; see this book's web site at: http://www.realtimerendering.com/ for current links.

Eberly's *3D Game Engine Design* book [199] provides detailed information on his implementation of view-independent progressive meshing and terrain rendering algorithms. Svarovsky [740] also presents a nuts and bolts guide to implementing a VIPM system. Garland distributes source code for his simplification algorithm [251]. Forsyth [236] discusses using VIPM techniques efficiently with index buffers. Luebke [506] gives a good overview of the entire field of polygonal simplification, with the exception of terrain rendering algorithms. For those, the web site for the Virtual Terrain Project [771] has a summary of research and pointers to many related resources. Zhao et al. [838] give a more in-depth overview of some of the research in this field.

Chapter 12
Curves and Curved Surfaces

"Where there is matter, there is geometry."
–Johannes Kepler

The triangle is a basic atomic rendering primitive. It is what graphics hardware is tuned to rapidly turn into lit and textured fragments and put into the Z-buffer. However, objects and animation paths that are created in modeling systems can have many different underlying geometric descriptions. Curves and curved surfaces can be described precisely by equations. These equations are evaluated and sets of triangles are then created and sent down the pipeline to be rendered.

The beauty of using curves and curved surfaces is at least fourfold: (1) they have a more compact representation than a set of polygons, (2) they provide scalable geometric primitives, (3) they provide smoother and more continuous primitives than straight lines and planar polygons, and (4) animation and collision detection may become simpler and faster.

There are a number of advantages of a compact curve representation for real-time rendering. First, there is a savings in memory for model storage (and so some gain in memory cache efficiency). This is especially useful for game consoles, which typically have little memory compared to a PC. Transforming curved surfaces generally involves fewer matrix multiplications than transforming a mesh representing the surface. If the graphics hardware can accept such curved surface descriptions directly, the amount of data the host CPU has to send to the graphics hardware is usually much less than sending a polygon mesh.

Curved model descriptions such as N-patches and subdivision surfaces have the interesting property that a model with few polygons can be made more convincing and realistic. The individual polygons are treated as curved surfaces, so creating more vertices on the surface. The result of a higher vertex density is better lighting of the surface and more realistic silhouette edges.

Another major advantage of curved surfaces is that they are scalable. A curved surface description could be turned into 2 triangles or 2000. Curved surfaces are a natural form of on-the-fly level of detail modeling: When the curved object is close, generate more triangles from its equations. Also, if an application is found to have a bottleneck in the rasterizer, then turning up the level of detail will increase quality while not hurting performance. Alternately, if the transform and lighting stage is the bottleneck, the tessellation rate can be turned down to increase the frame rate.

In terms of animation, curved surfaces have the advantage that a much smaller number of points needs to be animated. These points can then be used to form a curved surface and a smooth surface can be generated. Also, collision detection can potentially be more efficient and more accurate [445, 446].

The topic of curves and curved surfaces has been the subject of entire books [224, 371, 573, 654, 792]. Our goal here is to cover curves and surfaces that are finding common use in real-time rendering. In particular, a number of surface types are likely to become or have become a part of graphics APIs and have direct accelerator support.

Curves and surfaces have the potential for making real-time computer graphics applications faster, simpler to code, and last longer (i.e., survive a number of generations of graphics hardware). Graphics accelerators are just beginning to include support for curved surfaces as basic primitives. A problem with these early implementations is a lack of generality. An example is that the shadow volume method (Section 6.12.3) needs to use the silhouette edge of a model in order to generate projected quadrilaterals. Computing such silhouette edges from the curved surfaces currently has to be done on the software side. Even with such limitations, the potential quality and speed improvements offered by curved surface descriptions makes them useful today, and future graphics hardware promises to be more powerful and flexible.

12.1   Parametric Curves

In this section, we will introduce parametric curves. These are used in many different contexts and are implemented using a great many different methods. For real-time graphics, parametric curves are often used to move the viewer or some object along a predefined path. This may involve changing both the position and the orientation; however, in this chapter, we consider only positional paths. See Section 3.3.2 on page 3.3.2 for information on orientation interpolation.

Say you want to move the camera from one point to another in a certain amount of time, independent of the performance of the underlying hardware. As an example, assume that the camera should move between these points in one second, and that the rendering of one frame takes 50 ms. This means that we will be able to render 20 frames along the way during that second. On a faster computer, one frame might take only 25 ms, which would be equal to 40 frames per second, and so we would want to move the camera to 40 different locations. This is possible to do with parametric curves.

A parametric curve describes points using some formula as a function of a parameter t. Mathematically, we write this as $\mathbf{p}(t)$, which means that this function delivers a point for each value of t. The parameter t may belong to some interval, called the *domain*, e.g., $t \in [a, b]$. The generated points are continuous, that is, as $\epsilon \to 0$ then $\mathbf{p}(t + \epsilon) \to \mathbf{p}(t)$. Loosely speaking, this means that if ϵ is a very small number, then $\mathbf{p}(t)$ and $\mathbf{p}(t + \epsilon)$ are two points very close to each other.

In the next section, we will start with an intuitive and geometrical description of Bézier curves, a common form of parametric curves, and then put this into a mathematical setting. Then we discuss how to use piecewise Bézier curves and introduce the concept of continuity for curves. In Section 12.1.3 and 12.1.4, we will present two other useful curves, namely cubic hermites and Kochanek-Bartels splines.

12.1.1 Bézier Curves

Linear interpolation traces out a path, which is a straight line, between two points, $\mathbf{p}_0$ and $\mathbf{p}_1$. This is as simple as it gets. See the left illustration in Figure 12.1. Given these points, the following function describes a linearly interpolated point $\mathbf{p}(t)$, where t is the curve parameter, and $t \in [0, 1]$.

$$\mathbf{p}(t) = \mathbf{p}_0 + t(\mathbf{p}_1 - \mathbf{p}_0) = (1 - t)\mathbf{p}_0 + t\mathbf{p}_1 \tag{12.1}$$

The parameter t controls where on the line the point $\mathbf{p}(t)$ will land; $\mathbf{p}(0) = \mathbf{p}_0$, $\mathbf{p}(1) = \mathbf{p}_1$, and $0 < t < 1$ gives us a point on the straight line between $\mathbf{p}_0$ and $\mathbf{p}_1$. So if we would like to move the camera from $\mathbf{p}_0$ to $\mathbf{p}_1$ linearly in 20 steps during 1 second, then we would use $t_i = i/(20 - 1)$, where i is the frame number (starting from 0).

When you are interpolating between only two points, linear interpolation may suffice, but for more points, it often does not. For example, when

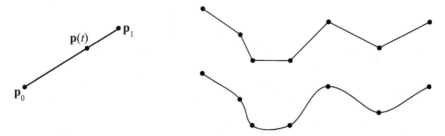

Figure 12.1. Linear interpolation between two points is the path on a straight line (left). For seven points, linear interpolation is shown at the upper right, and some sort of smoother interpolation is shown at the lower right. What is most objectionable about using linear interpolation are the discontinuous changes (sudden jerks) at the joints between the linear segments.

several points are interpolated, the sudden changes at the points (also called joints) that connect two segments become unacceptable. This is shown at the right of Figure 12.1.

To solve this, we take the approach of linear interpolation one step further, and linearly interpolate repeatedly. By doing this, we arrive at the geometrical construction of the Bézier curve.[1] First, to be able to repeat the interpolation, we have to add more points. For example, three points, **a**, **b**, and **c**, called the *control points*, could be used. Say we want to find $\mathbf{p}(1/3)$, that is, the point on the curve for $t = 1/3$. We compute two new points **d** and **e** by linear interpolation from **a** & **b** and **b** & **c** using $t = 1/3$. See Figure 12.2. Finally, we compute **f** by linear interpolation from **d** and **e** again using $t = 1/3$. We define $\mathbf{p}(t) = \mathbf{f}$. Using this technique, we get the following relationship:

$$
\begin{aligned}
\mathbf{p}(t) &= (1-t)\mathbf{d} + t\mathbf{e} \\
&= (1-t)[(1-t)\mathbf{a} + t\mathbf{b}] + t[(1-t)\mathbf{b} + t\mathbf{c}] \\
&= (1-t)^2\mathbf{a} + 2(1-t)t\mathbf{b} + t^2\mathbf{c},
\end{aligned}
\tag{12.2}
$$

which is a parabola since the maximum degree of t is two (quadratic). In fact, given $n + 1$ control points, it turns out that the degree of the curve is n. This means that more control points gives more degrees of freedom for the curve. A second degree curve is also called a *quadratic*, a third degree curve is called a *cubic*, a fourth degree curve is called a *quartic*, and so on.

---

[1]As a historical note, the Bézier curves were developed independently by Paul de Casteljau and Pierre Bézier for use in the French car industry. They are called *Bézier* curves because Bézier was able to make his research publicly available before de Casteljau, even though de Casteljau wrote his technical report before Bézier [224].

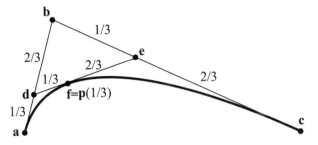

Figure 12.2. Repeated linear interpolation gives a Bézier curve. This curve is defined by three control points, **a**, **b**, and **c**. Assuming we want to find the point on the curve for the parameter $t = 1/3$, we first linearly interpolate between **a** and **b** to get **d**. Next, **e** is interpolated from **b** and **c**. The final point, $\mathbf{p}(1/3) = \mathbf{f}$ is found by interpolating between **d** and **e**.

This kind of repeated or recursive linear interpolation is often referred to as the *de Casteljau algorithm* [224, 371]. An example of what this looks like when using five control points is shown in Figure 12.3. To generalize, instead of using points **a–f**, as in this example, the following notation is used. The control points are denoted $\mathbf{p}_i$, so in the example, $\mathbf{p}_0 = \mathbf{a}$, $\mathbf{p}_1 = \mathbf{b}$, and $\mathbf{p}_2 = \mathbf{c}$. Then, after linear interpolation has been applied k times, intermediate control points $\mathbf{p}_i^k$ are obtained. In our example, we have $\mathbf{p}_0^1 = \mathbf{d}$, $\mathbf{p}_1^1 = \mathbf{e}$, and $\mathbf{p}_0^2 = \mathbf{f}$. The Bézier curve for $n+1$ control points can be described with the recursion formula shown below, where $\mathbf{p}_i^0 = \mathbf{p}_i$ are the initial control points.

$$\mathbf{p}_i^k(t) = (1-t)\mathbf{p}_i^{k-1}(t) + t\mathbf{p}_{i+1}^{k-1}(t), \quad \begin{cases} k = 1 \ldots n \\ i = 0 \ldots n-k \end{cases} \quad (12.3)$$

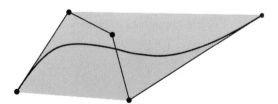

Figure 12.3. Repeated linear interpolation from five points gives a fourth degree (quartic) Bézier curve. The curve is inside the convex hull (gray region), of the control points, marked by black dots. Also, at the first point, the curve is tangent to the line between the first and second point. The same also holds for the other end of the curve.

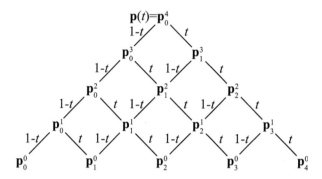

Figure 12.4. An illustration of how repeated linear interpolation works for Bézier curves. In this example, the interpolation of a quartic curve is shown. This means there are five control points, $\mathbf{p}_i^0$, $i = 0, 1, 2, 3, 4$, shown at the bottom. The diagram should be read from the bottom up, that is, $\mathbf{p}_0^1$ is formed from weighting $\mathbf{p}_0^0$ with weight $1 - t$ and adding that with $\mathbf{p}_1^0$ weighted by t. This goes on until the point of the curve $\mathbf{p}(t)$ is obtained at the top. *(Illustration after Goldman [269].)*

Note that a point on the curve is described by $\mathbf{p}(t) = \mathbf{p}_0^n(t)$. This is not as complicated as it looks. Consider again what happens when we construct a Bézier curve from three points; $\mathbf{p}_0$, $\mathbf{p}_1$, and $\mathbf{p}_2$, which are equivalent to $\mathbf{p}_0^0$, $\mathbf{p}_1^0$, and $\mathbf{p}_2^0$. Three controls points means that $n = 2$. To shorten the formulae, sometimes "(t)" is dropped from the $\mathbf{p}$'s. In the first step $k = 1$, which gives $\mathbf{p}_0^1 = (1 - t)\mathbf{p}_0 + t\mathbf{p}_1$, and $\mathbf{p}_1^1 = (1 - t)\mathbf{p}_1 + t\mathbf{p}_2$. Finally, for $k = 2$, we get $\mathbf{p}_0^2 = (1 - t)\mathbf{p}_0^1 + t\mathbf{p}_1^1$, which is the same as sought for $\mathbf{p}(t)$. An illustration of how this works in general is shown in Figure 12.4. Now that we have the basics in place on how Bézier curves work, we can take a look at a more mathematical description of the same curves.

Bézier Curves Using Bernstein Polynomials

As seen in Equation 12.2, the quadratic Bézier curve could be described using an algebraic formula. It turns out that every Bézier curve can be described with such an algebraic formula, which means that you do not need to do the repeated interpolation. This is shown below in Equation 12.4, which yields the same curve as described by Equation 12.3. This description of the Bézier curve is called the *Bernstein form*.

$$\mathbf{p}(t) = \sum_{i=0}^{n} B_i^n(t)\mathbf{p}_i \qquad (12.4)$$

This function contains the Bernstein polynomials[2]:

$$B_i^n(t) = \binom{n}{i} t^i (1-t)^{n-i} = \frac{n!}{i!(n-i)!} t^i (1-t)^{n-i}. \qquad (12.5)$$

The first term, the binomial coefficient, in the equation above is defined in Equation 1.4 in Chapter 1. Two basic properties of the Bernstein polynomial are the following:

$$B_i^n(t) \in [0,1], \text{ when } t \in [0,1],$$

$$\sum_{i=0}^{n} B_i^n(t) = 1. \qquad (12.6)$$

The first formula means that the Bernstein polynomials are in the interval between from 0 to 1 when t also is from 0 to 1. The second formula means that all the Bernstein polynomial terms in Equation 12.4 sum to one for all different degrees of the curve (this can be seen in Figure 12.5). Loosely speaking, this means that the curve will stay "close" to the control points, $\mathbf{p}_i$. In fact, the entire Bézier curve will be located in the convex hull (see Section A.5.3) of the control points, which follows from Equation 12.4 and 12.6. This is a useful property when computing a bounding area or volume for the curve. See Figure 12.3 for an example.

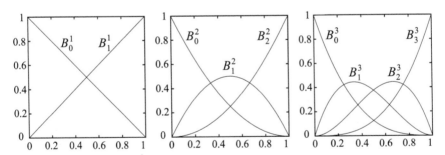

Figure 12.5. Bernstein polynomials for $n = 1$, $n = 2$, and $n = 3$ (left to right). The left figure shows linear interpolation, the middle quadratic interpolation, and the right cubic interpolation. These are the blending functions used in the Bernstein form of Bézier curves. So, to evaluate a quadratic curve (middle diagram) at a certain t-value, just find the t-value on the x-axis, and then go vertically until the three curves are encountered, which gives the weights for the three control points. Note that $B_i^n(t) \geq 0$, when $t \in [0,1]$, and the symmetry of these blending functions: $B_i^n(t) = B_{n-i}^n(1-t)$.

---

[2]The Bernstein polynomials are sometimes called Bézier basis functions.

In Figure 12.5, the Bernstein polynomials, for $n = 1$, $n = 2$, and $n = 3$ are shown. These are also called *blending functions*. The case when $n = 1$ (linear interpolation) is illustrative in the sense that it shows the curves $y = 1 - t$ and $y = t$. This implies that when $t = 0$, then $\mathbf{p}(0) = \mathbf{p}_0$, and when t increases, the blending weight for $\mathbf{p}_0$ decreases, while the blending weight for $\mathbf{p}_1$ increases by the same amount, keeping the sum of the weights equal to 1. Finally, when $t = 1$, $\mathbf{p}(1) = \mathbf{p}_1$. In general, it holds for all Bézier curves that $\mathbf{p}(0) = \mathbf{p}_0$ and $\mathbf{p}(1) = \mathbf{p}_n$, that is, the endpoints are interpolated (i.e., are on the curve). It is also true that the curve is tangent to $\mathbf{p}_1 - \mathbf{p}_0$ at $t = 0$, and to $\mathbf{p}_n - \mathbf{p}_{n-1}$ at $t = 1$. Another interesting property is that instead of computing points on a Bézier curve, and then rotating the curve, the control points can first be rotated, and then the points on the curve can be computed. This is a nice property that most curves and surfaces have, and it means that a program can rotate the control points (which are few) and then generate the points on the rotated curve. This is much faster than doing the opposite.

As an example on how the Bernstein version of the Bézier curve works, assume that $n = 2$, i.e., a quadratic curve. Equation 12.4 is then

$$
\begin{aligned}
\mathbf{p}(t) &= B_0^2 \mathbf{p}_0 + B_1^2 \mathbf{p}_1 + B_2^2 \mathbf{p}_2 \\
&= \binom{2}{0} t^0 (1-t)^2 \mathbf{p}_0 + \binom{2}{1} t^1 (1-t)^1 \mathbf{p}_1 + \binom{2}{2} t^2 (1-t)^0 \mathbf{p}_2 \quad (12.7) \\
&= (1-t)^2 \mathbf{p}_0 + 2t(1-t)\mathbf{p}_1 + t^2 \mathbf{p}_2,
\end{aligned}
$$

which is the same as Equation 12.2. Note that the blending functions above, $(1-t)^2$, $2t(1-t)$, and t^2, are the functions displayed in the middle of Figure 12.5. In the same manner, a cubic curve is simplified into the formula below.

$$
\mathbf{p}(t) = (1-t)^3 \mathbf{p}_0 + 3t(1-t)^2 \mathbf{p}_1 + 3t^2(1-t)\mathbf{p}_2 + t^3 \mathbf{p}_3 \quad\quad (12.8)
$$

By collecting terms of the form t^k in Equation 12.4, it can be seen that every Bézier curve can be written in the following form, where the $\mathbf{c}_i$ are points that fall out by collecting terms.

$$
\mathbf{p}(t) = \sum_{i=0}^{n} t^i \mathbf{c}_i \quad\quad (12.9)
$$

This form may be useful when implementing rapid curve generation (see Section 12.3.1).

It is straightforward to differentiate Equation 12.4, in order to get the derivative of the Bézier curve. The result, after reorganizing and collecting terms, is shown below [224].

$$\frac{d}{dt}\mathbf{p}(t) = n \sum_{i=0}^{n-1} B_i^{n-1}(t)(\mathbf{p}_{i+1} - \mathbf{p}_i) \qquad (12.10)$$

The derivative is, in fact, also a Bézier curve, but with one degree lower than $\mathbf{p}(t)$.

One downside of Bézier curves is that they do not pass through all the control points (except the end points). Another problem is that the degree increases with the number of control points, making evaluation more and more expensive. A solution to this is to use a simple, low-degree curve between each pair of subsequent control points, and see to it that this kind of piecewise interpolation has a high enough degree of continuity. This is the topic of Section 12.1.2–12.1.4.

Rational Bézier Curves

While Bézier curves can be used for many things, they do not have that many degrees of freedom—only the position of the control points can be chosen freely. Also, not every curve can be described by Bézier curves. For example, the circle is normally considered a very simple shape, but it cannot be described by one or a collection of Bézier curves. One alternative is the *rational Bézier curve*. This type of curve is described by the formula shown in Equation 12.11.

$$\mathbf{p}(t) = \frac{\sum_{i=0}^{n} w_i B_i^n(t)\mathbf{p}_i}{\sum_{i=0}^{n} w_i B_i^n(t)} \qquad (12.11)$$

The denominator is a weighted sum of the Bernstein polynomials, while the numerator is a weighted version of the standard Bézier curve (Equation 12.4). For this type of curve, the user has the weights, w_i, as additional degrees of freedom. More about these curves can be found in Hoschek and Lasser's [371] and in Farin's book [224]. Farin also describes how a circle can be described by three rational Bézier curves.

12.1.2 Continuity and Piecewise Bézier Curves

Assume that we have two Bézier curves that are cubic, that is, defined by four control points each. The first curve is defined by $\mathbf{q}_i$, and the second by $\mathbf{r}_i$, $i = 0, 1, 2, 3$. To join the curves, we could set $\mathbf{q}_3 = \mathbf{r}_0$. This point

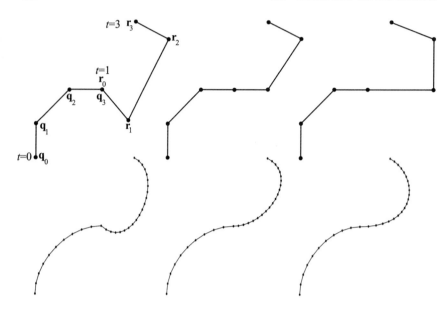

Figure 12.6. This figure shows from left to right C^0, G^1, and C^1 continuity between two cubic Bézier curves (four control points each). The top row shows the control points, and the bottom row the curves, with 10 sample points for the left curve, and 20 for the right. The following time-point pairs are used for this example: $(0.0, \mathbf{q}_0)$, $(1.0, \mathbf{q}_3)$, and $(3.0, \mathbf{r}_3)$. With C^0 continuity, there is a sudden jerk at the join (where $\mathbf{q}^3 = \mathbf{r}^0$). This is improved with G^1 by making the tangents at the join parallel (and equal in length). Though, since $3.0 - 1.0 \neq 1.0 - 0.0$, this does not give C^1 continuity. This can be seen at the join where there is a sudden acceleration of the sample points. To achieve C^1, the right tangent at the join has to be twice as long as the left tangent.

is called a *joint*. However, as shown in Figure 12.6, the joint will not be smooth using this simple technique. The composite curve formed from several curve pieces (in this case two) is called a *piecewise Bézier curve*, and is denoted $\mathbf{p}(t)$ here. Further, assume we want $\mathbf{p}(0) = \mathbf{q}_0$, $\mathbf{p}(1) = \mathbf{q}_3 = \mathbf{r}_0$, and $\mathbf{p}(3) = \mathbf{r}_3$. Thus, the times for when we reach $\mathbf{q}_0$, $\mathbf{q}_3 = \mathbf{r}_0$, and $\mathbf{r}_3$, are $t_0 = 0.0$, $t_1 = 1.0$, and $t_2 = 3.0$. See Figure 12.6 for notation. From the previous section we know that a Bézier curve is defined for $t \in [0, 1]$, so this works out fine for the first curve segment defined by the $\mathbf{q}_i$'s, since the time at $\mathbf{q}_0$ is 0.0, and the time at $\mathbf{q}_3$ is 1.0. But what happens when $1.0 < t \leq 3.0$? The answer is simple: We must use the second curve segment, and then translate and scale the parameter interval from $[t_1, t_2]$ to $[0, 1]$. This is done using the formula below:

$$t' = \frac{t - t_1}{t_2 - t_1}. \tag{12.12}$$

Hence, it is the t' that is fed into the Bézier curve segment defined by the r_i's. This is simple to generalize to stitching several Bézier curves together.

A better way to join the curves is to use the fact that at the first control point of a Bézier curve, the tangent is parallel to $q_1 - q_0$ (see Section 12.1.1). Similarly, at the last control point, the cubic curve is tangent to $q_3 - q_2$. This behavior can be seen in Figure 12.3. So, to make the two curves join tangentially at the joint, the tangent for the first and the second curve should be parallel there. Put more formally, the following should hold:

$$(q_3 - q_2) = c(r_1 - r_0) \quad \text{for } c > 0. \tag{12.13}$$

This simply means that the incoming tangent, $q_3 - q_2$, at the joint should be parallel to and have the same direction as the outgoing tangent, $r_1 - r_0$.

It is possible to achieve even better continuity than that, using in Equation 12.13 the c defined by Equation 12.14 [224]:

$$c = \frac{t_2 - t_1}{t_1 - t_0}. \tag{12.14}$$

This is also shown in Figure 12.6. If we instead set $t_2 = 2.0$, then $c = 1.0$, so when the time intervals on each curve segment are equal, then the incoming and outgoing tangent vectors should be identical. However, this does not work when $t_2 = 3.0$. The curves will look identical, but the speed at which $p(t)$ moves on the composite curve will not be smooth. This is what the constant c in Equation 12.14 takes care of.

Some advantages of using piecewise curves are that lower degree curves can be used, and that the resulting curves will go through a set of points. In the example above, a degree of three, i.e., a cubic, was used for each of the two curve segments. Cubic curves are often used for this, as those are the lowest-degree curves that can describe an *S-shaped* curve, called an *inflection*. The resulting curve $p(t)$ interpolates, i.e., goes through, the points q_0, $q_3 = r_0$, and r_3.

At this point, two important continuity measures have been introduced by example. A slightly more mathematical presentation of the continuity concept for curves follows. For curves in general, we use the C^n notation to differentiate between different kinds of continuity at the joints. This means that all the n:th first derivatives should be continuous and nonzero all over the curve. Continuity of C^0 means that the segment should join at the same point, so linear interpolation fulfills this condition. This was the case for the first example in this section. Continuity of C^1 means that if we derive once at any point on the curve (including joints), the result should also be continuous. This was the case for the third example in this section, where Equation 12.14 was used.

There is also a measure that is denoted G^n. Let us look at G^1 (geometrical) continuity as an example. For this, the tangent vectors from the curve segments that meet at a joint should be parallel, but nothing about the lengths is assumed. In other words, G^1 is a weaker continuity than C^1, and a curve that is C^1 is always G^1. The concept of geometrical continuity can be extended to higher dimensions. The second example in the beginning of this section was G^1.

12.1.3   Cubic Hermite Interpolation

Bézier curves are very useful in describing the theory behind the construction of smooth curves, but their use is not always intuitive. In this section, we will present cubic Hermite interpolation, and these curves tend to be simpler to control. The reason is that instead of giving four control points to describe a cubic Bézier curve, the cubic Hermite curve is defined by starting and ending points, $\mathbf{p}_0$ and $\mathbf{p}_1$, and starting and ending tangents, $\mathbf{m}_0$ and $\mathbf{m}_1$. The Hermite interpolant, $\mathbf{p}(t)$, where $t \in [0, 1]$, is:

$$\mathbf{p}(t) = (2t^3 - 3t^2 + 1)\mathbf{p}_0 + (t^3 - 2t^2 + t)\mathbf{m}_0 + (t^3 - t^2)\mathbf{m}_1 + (-2t^3 + 3t^2)\mathbf{p}_1. \tag{12.15}$$

We also call $\mathbf{p}(t)$ a Hermite curve segment or a cubic spline segment. This is a cubic interpolant, since t^3 is the highest exponent in the blending functions in the above formula. The following holds for this curve:

$$\mathbf{p}(0) = \mathbf{p}_0, \quad \mathbf{p}(1) = \mathbf{p}_1, \quad \frac{\partial \mathbf{p}}{\partial t}(0) = \mathbf{m}_0, \quad \frac{\partial \mathbf{p}}{\partial t}(1) = \mathbf{m}_1. \tag{12.16}$$

This means that the Hermite curve interpolates $\mathbf{p}_0$ and $\mathbf{p}_1$, and the tangents at these points are $\mathbf{m}_0$ and $\mathbf{m}_1$. The blending functions in Equation 12.15 are shown in Figure 12.7, and they can be derived from Equations 12.4 and 12.16. Some examples of cubic Hermite interpolation can be seen in Figure 12.8. All these examples interpolate the same points, but have different tangents. Note also that different lengths of the tangents give different results; longer tangents have a greater impact on the overall shape.

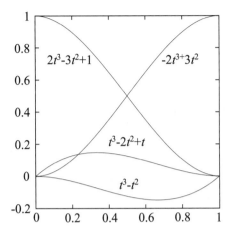

Figure 12.7. Blending functions for Hermite cubic interpolation. Note the asymmetry of the blending functions for the tangents. Negating the blending function $t^3 - t^2$ and m_1 would give a symmetrical look.

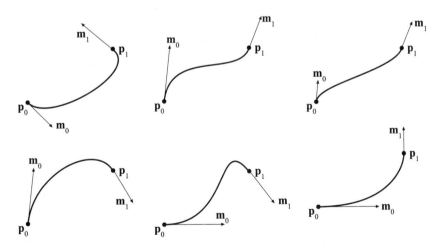

Figure 12.8. Hermite interpolation. A curve is defined by two points, p_0 and p_1, and a tangent, m_0 and m_1, at each point.

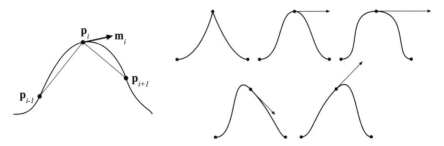

Figure 12.9. One method of computing the tangents is to use a combination of the chords (left). The upper row at the right shows three curves with different tension parameters (a). The left curve has $a \approx 1$, which means high tension; the middle curve has $a \approx 0$, which is default tension; and the right curve has $a \approx -1$, which is low tension. The bottom row of two curves at the right shows different bias parameters. The curve on the left has a negative bias, and the right curve has a positive bias.

12.1.4 Kochanek-Bartels Curves

When interpolating between more than two points using Hermite curves, a way is needed to control the shared tangents. Here, we will present one way to compute such tangents, called Kochanek-Bartels curves. Assume that we have n points, $\mathbf{p}_0, \ldots, \mathbf{p}_{n-1}$, which should be interpolated with $n-1$ Hermite curve segments. We assume that there is only one tangent at each point, and we start to look at the "inner" tangents, $\mathbf{m}_1, \ldots, \mathbf{m}_{n-2}$. A tangent at $\mathbf{p}_i$ can be computed as a combination of the two chords [439]: $\mathbf{p}_i - \mathbf{p}_{i-1}$, and $\mathbf{p}_{i+1} - \mathbf{p}_i$, as shown at the left in Figure 12.9.

First, a tension parameter, a, is introduced that modifies the length of the tangent vector. This controls how sharp the curve is going to be at the joint. The tangent is computed as:

$$\mathbf{m}_i = \frac{1-a}{2}((\mathbf{p}_i - \mathbf{p}_{i-1}) + (\mathbf{p}_{i+1} - \mathbf{p}_i)). \tag{12.17}$$

The top row at the right in Figure 12.9 shows different tension parameters. The default value is $a = 0$; higher values give sharper bends (if $a > 1$, there will be a loop at the joint), and negative values give less taut curves near the joints. Second, a bias parameter, b, is introduced that influences the direction of the tangent (and also, indirectly, the length of the tangent). If we ignore the tension ($a = 0$) for a while, then the tangent is computed as below:

$$\mathbf{m}_i = \frac{1+b}{2}(\mathbf{p}_i - \mathbf{p}_{i-1}) + \frac{1-b}{2}(\mathbf{p}_{i+1} - \mathbf{p}_i). \tag{12.18}$$

The default value is $b = 0$. A positive bias gives a bend that is more directed toward the chord $\mathbf{p}_i - \mathbf{p}_{i-1}$, and a negative bias gives a bend that is more directed toward the other chord: $\mathbf{p}_{i+1} - \mathbf{p}_i$. This is shown in the bottom row on the right in Figure 12.9. Combining the tension and the bias gives:

$$\mathbf{m}_i = \frac{(1-a)(1+b)}{2}(\mathbf{p}_i - \mathbf{p}_{i-1}) + \frac{(1-a)(1-b)}{2}(\mathbf{p}_{i+1} - \mathbf{p}_i). \quad (12.19)$$

The user can either set the tension and bias parameters or let them have their default values, which gives a Catmull-Rom spline [114]. The tangents at the first and the last points can also be computed with these formulae; one of the chords is simply set to a length of zero.

Yet another parameter that controls the behavior at the joints can be incorporated into the tangent equation [235, 439]. However, this requires the introduction of two tangents at each joint, one incoming, denoted $\mathbf{s}_i$ (for source) and one outgoing, denoted $\mathbf{d}_i$ (for destination). See Figure 12.10. Note that the curve segment between $\mathbf{p}_i$ and $\mathbf{p}_{i+1}$ uses the tangents $\mathbf{d}_i$ and $\mathbf{s}_{i+1}$. The tangents are computed as below, where c is the *continuity* parameter:

$$\begin{aligned}
\mathbf{s}_i &= \frac{1-c}{2}(\mathbf{p}_i - \mathbf{p}_{i-1}) + \frac{1+c}{2}(\mathbf{p}_{i+1} - \mathbf{p}_i), \\
\mathbf{d}_i &= \frac{1+c}{2}(\mathbf{p}_i - \mathbf{p}_{i-1}) + \frac{1-c}{2}(\mathbf{p}_{i+1} - \mathbf{p}_i).
\end{aligned} \quad (12.20)$$

Again, $c = 0$ is the default value, which makes $\mathbf{s}_i = \mathbf{d}_i$. Setting $c = -1$, gives $\mathbf{s}_i = \mathbf{p}_i - \mathbf{p}_{i-1}$, and $\mathbf{d}_i = \mathbf{p}_{i+1} - \mathbf{p}_i$, producing a sharp corner at the joint, which is only C^0. Increasing the value of c makes $\mathbf{s}_i$ and $\mathbf{d}_i$ more and more alike. For $c = 0$, then $\mathbf{s}_i = \mathbf{d}_i$. When $c = 1$ is reached, we get $\mathbf{s}_i = \mathbf{p}_{i+1} - \mathbf{p}_i$, and $\mathbf{d}_i = \mathbf{p}_i - \mathbf{p}_{i-1}$. Thus, the continuity parameter c is another way to give even more control to the user, and it makes it possible to get sharp corners at the joints, if desired.

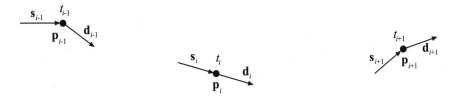

Figure 12.10. Incoming and outgoing tangents for Kochanek-Bartels curves. At each control point $\mathbf{p}_i$, its time t_i is also shown, where $t_i > t_{i-1}$, for all i.

The combination of tension, bias, and continuity, where the default parameter values are $a = b = c = 0$, is:

$$\mathbf{s}_i = \frac{(1-a)(1+b)(1-c)}{2}(\mathbf{p}_i - \mathbf{p}_{i-1}) + \frac{(1-a)(1-b)(1+c)}{2}(\mathbf{p}_{i+1} - \mathbf{p}_i),$$

$$\mathbf{d}_i = \frac{(1-a)(1+b)(1+c)}{2}(\mathbf{p}_i - \mathbf{p}_{i-1}) + \frac{(1-a)(1-b)(1-c)}{2}(\mathbf{p}_{i+1} - \mathbf{p}_i).$$

$$(12.21)$$

Both Equations 12.19 and 12.21 work only when all curve segments are using the same time interval length. To account for different time length of the curve segments, the tangents have to be adjusted, similar to what was done in Section 12.1.2. The adjusted tangents, denoted $\mathbf{s}_i'$ and $\mathbf{d}_i'$, are shown below:

$$\mathbf{s}_i' = \mathbf{s}_i \frac{2\Delta_i}{\Delta_{i-1} + \Delta_i},$$

$$(12.22)$$

$$\mathbf{d}_i' = \mathbf{d}_i \frac{2\Delta_{i-1}}{\Delta_{i-1} + \Delta_i},$$

where $\Delta_i = t_{i+1} - t_i$. This concludes the presentation of Kochanek-Bartels splines, which gives the user three intuitive parameters, bias, tension, and continuity, with which to design curves.

12.2 Parametric Curved Surfaces

A natural extension of parametric curves (Section 12.1) is parametric surfaces. An analogy is that a triangle or polygon is an extension of a line segment, in which we go from one to two dimensions. Parametric surfaces can be used to model objects with curved surfaces. A parametric surface is defined by a small number of control points. Tessellation of a parametric surface is the process of evaluating the surface representation at a number of positions, and connect these to form triangles that approximate the true surface. This is done since graphics hardware can efficiently render triangles. At runtime, the surface can then be tessellated into as many triangles as desired. Thus, they are perfect for making a tradeoff between quality and speed; more triangles take more time to render, but give better shading and silhouettes. Another advantage of parametric surfaces is that the control points can be animated and then the surface can be tessellated. This is in contrast to animating a large triangle mesh directly, which can be more expensive.

This section starts by introducing *Bézier patches*, which are curved surfaces with rectangular domains. These are also often called *tensor-product Bézier surfaces*. Then *Bézier triangles* are presented, which have triangular domains. An *N-patch* is a triangular Bézier surface, which can replace each triangle in a triangle mesh. The goal of these is to improve the silhouette and shading of a coarse mesh. They are presented in Section 12.2.3. Finally, the topic of continuity is briefly treated in Section 12.2.5.

12.2.1 Bézier Patches

The concept of Bézier curves, introduced in Section 12.1.1, can be extended from using one parameter to using two parameters, thus forming surfaces instead of curves. Let us start with extending linear interpolation to *bilinear interpolation*. Now, instead of just using two points, we use four points, called **a**, **b**, **c**, and **d**, as shown in Figure 12.11. Instead of using one parameter called t, we now use two parameters (u, v). Using u to linearly interpolate **a** & **b** and **c** & **d** gives **e** and **f**:

$$\begin{aligned} \mathbf{e} &= (1 - u)\mathbf{a} + u\mathbf{b}, \\ \mathbf{f} &= (1 - u)\mathbf{c} + u\mathbf{d}. \end{aligned} \tag{12.23}$$

Next, the linearly interpolated points, **e** and **f**, are linearly interpolated in the other direction, using v. This yields bilinear interpolation:

$$\begin{aligned} \mathbf{p}(u, v) &= (1 - v)\mathbf{e} + v\mathbf{f} \\ &= (1 - u)(1 - v)\mathbf{a} + u(1 - v)\mathbf{b} + (1 - u)v\mathbf{c} + uv\mathbf{d}. \end{aligned} \tag{12.24}$$

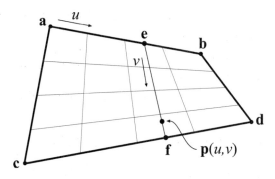

Figure 12.11. Bilinear interpolation using four points.

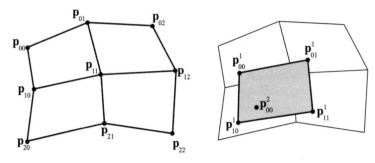

Figure 12.12. Left: A biquadratic Bézier surface, defined by nine control points, $\mathbf{p}_{ij}$. Right: To generate a point on the Bézier surface, four points $\mathbf{p}_{ij}^1$ are first created using bilinear interpolation from the nearest control points. Finally, the point surface $\mathbf{p}(u, v) = \mathbf{p}_{00}^2$ is bilinearly interpolated from these created points.

Equation 12.24 describes the simplest nonplanar parametric surface, where different points on the surface are generated using different values of (u, v). The domain, i.e., the set of valid values, is $(u, v) \in [0, 1] \times [0, 1]$, which means that both u and v should belong to $[0, 1]$. When the domain is rectangular, the resulting surface is often called a *patch*.

To extend a Bézier curve from linear interpolation, more points were added and the interpolation repeated. The same strategy can be used for patches. Assume nine points, arranged in a 3×3 grid, are used. This is shown in Figure 12.12, where the notation is shown as well. To form a biquadratic Bézier patch from these points, we first need to bilinearly interpolate four times to create four intermediate points, also shown in Figure 12.12. Next, the final point on the surface is bilinearly interpolated from the previously created points.

The repeated bilinear interpolation described above is the extension of de Casteljau's algorithm to patches. At this point we need to define some notation. The degree of the surface is n. The control points are $\mathbf{p}_{i,j}$, where i and j belong to $[0 \ldots n]$. Thus, $(n + 1)^2$ control points are used for a patch of degree n. Note that the control points should be superscripted with a zero, i.e., $\mathbf{p}_{i,j}^0$, but this is often omitted, and sometimes we use the subscript $_{ij}$ instead of $_{i,j}$ when there can be no confusion. The Bézier patch using de Casteljau's algorithm is described in the equation below.

de Casteljau [patches]:

$$\mathbf{p}_{i,j}^k(u, v) = (1-u)(1-v)\mathbf{p}_{i,j}^{k-1} + u(1-v)\mathbf{p}_{i,j+1}^{k-1} + (1-u)v\mathbf{p}_{i+1,j}^{k-1} + uv\mathbf{p}_{i+1,j+1}^{k-1}$$
$$k = 1 \ldots n, \quad i = 0 \ldots n - k, \quad j = 0 \ldots n - k$$

$$(12.25)$$

Similar to the Bézier curve, the point at (u, v) on the Bézier patch is $\mathbf{p}_{0,0}^{n}(u, v)$.

The Bézier patch can also be described in Bernstein form using Bernstein polynomials, as shown in Equation 12.26.

Bernstein [patches]:

$$
\begin{aligned}
\mathbf{p}(u, v) &= \sum_{i=0}^{m} B_i^m(u) \sum_{j=0}^{n} B_j^n(v) \mathbf{p}_{i,j} = \sum_{i=0}^{m} \sum_{j=0}^{n} B_i^m(u) B_j^n(v) \mathbf{p}_{i,j} \\
&= \sum_{i=0}^{m} \sum_{j=0}^{n} \binom{m}{i} \binom{n}{j} u^i (1-u)^{m-i} v^j (1-v)^{n-j} \mathbf{p}_{i,j}
\end{aligned}
\tag{12.26}
$$

Note that in Equation 12.26, there are two parameters, m and n, for the degree of the surface. The "compound" degree is sometimes denoted $m \times n$. Most often $m = n$, which simplifies the implementation a bit. The consequence of, say, $m > n$ is to first bilinearly interpolate n times, and then linearly interpolate $m - n$ times. This is shown in Figure 12.13. An interesting interpretation of Equation 12.26 is found by rewriting it as:

$$
\begin{aligned}
\mathbf{p}(u, v) &= \sum_{i=0}^{m} B_i^m(u) \sum_{j=0}^{n} B_j^n(v) \mathbf{p}_{i,j} \\
&= \sum_{i=0}^{m} B_i^m(u) \mathbf{q}_i(v).
\end{aligned}
\tag{12.27}
$$

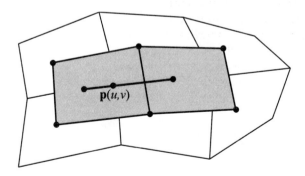

Figure 12.13. Different degrees in different directions.

Here, $\mathbf{q}_i(v) = \sum_{j=0}^{n} B_j^n(v)\mathbf{p}_{i,j}$ for $i = 0 \ldots m$. As can be seen in the bottom row in Equation 12.27, this is just a Bézier curve when we fix a v-value. Assuming $v = 0.35$, the points $\mathbf{q}_i(0.35)$ can be computed from a Bézier curve, and then Equation 12.27 describes a Bézier curve on the Bézier surface, for $v = 0.35$.

Next, some useful properties of Bézier patches will be presented. By setting $(u, v) = (0, 0)$, $(u, v) = (0, 1)$, $(u, v) = (1, 0)$, and $(u, v) = (1, 1)$ in Equation 12.26, it is simple to prove that a Bézier patch interpolates, that is, goes through, the corner control points, $\mathbf{p}_{0,0}$, $\mathbf{p}_{0,n}$, $\mathbf{p}_{n,0}$, and $\mathbf{p}_{n,n}$. Also, each boundary of the patch is described by a Bézier curve of degree n formed by the control points on the boundary. Therefore, the tangents at the corner control points are defined by these boundary Bézier curves. Each corner control point has two tangents, one in each of the u and v directions. As was the case for Bézier curves, the patch also lies within the convex hull of its control points, and

$$\sum_{i=0}^{m}\sum_{j=0}^{n} B_i^m(u)B_j^n(v) = 1$$

for $(u, v) \in [0, 1] \times [0, 1]$. Finally, rotating the control points and then generating points on the patch is the same as generating points on the patch, and then rotating these. Partially differentiating Equation 12.26 gives [224] the equations below.

Derivatives [patches]:

$$\frac{\partial \mathbf{p}(u, v)}{\partial u} = m \sum_{j=0}^{n}\sum_{i=0}^{m-1} B_i^{m-1}(u)B_j^n(v)[\mathbf{p}_{i+1,j} - \mathbf{p}_{i,j}]$$

$$\frac{\partial \mathbf{p}(u, v)}{\partial v} = n \sum_{i=0}^{m}\sum_{j=0}^{n-1} B_i^m(u)B_j^{n-1}(v)[\mathbf{p}_{i,j+1} - \mathbf{p}_{i,j}]$$

(12.28)

As can be seen, the degree of the patch is reduced by one in the direction that is differentiated. The unnormalized normal vector is then formed as

$$\mathbf{n}(u, v) = \frac{\partial \mathbf{p}(u, v)}{\partial u} \times \frac{\partial \mathbf{p}(u, v)}{\partial v}.$$

In Figure 12.14, the control mesh together with the actual Bézier patch is shown. The effect of moving a control point is shown in Figure 12.15.

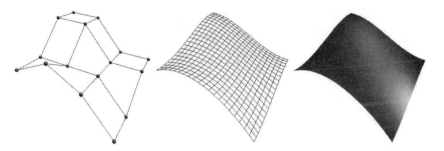

Figure 12.14. Left: Control mesh of a 4 × 4 degree Bézier patch. Middle: The actual quadrilaterals that were generated on the surface. Right: Shaded Bézier patch.

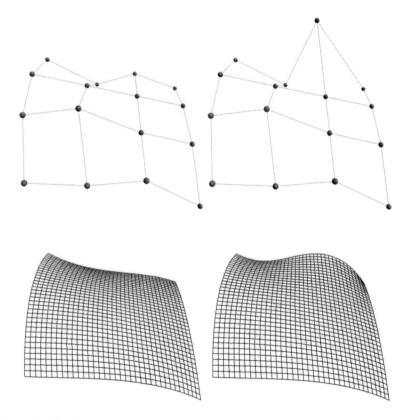

Figure 12.15. This set of images shows what happens to a Bézier patch when one vertex is moved. Most of the change is near the moved control point.

Rational Bézier Patches

Just as the Bézier curve could be extended into a rational Bézier curve (Section 12.1.1), and thus introduce more degrees of freedom, so can the Bézier patch be extended into a rational Bézier patch:

$$\mathbf{p}(u,v) = \frac{\sum_{i=0}^{m}\sum_{j=0}^{n} w_{i,j} B_i^m(u) B_j^n(v) \mathbf{p}_{i,j}}{\sum_{i=0}^{m}\sum_{j=0}^{n} w_{i,j} B_i^m(u) B_j^n(v)}. \tag{12.29}$$

Consult Farin's book [224] and Hochek and Lasser's book [371] for information about this type of patch. Similarly, the rational Bézier triangle is an extension of the Bézier triangle, treated next.

12.2.2 Bézier Triangles

Even though the triangle often is considered a simpler geometric primitive than the rectangle, this is not the case when it comes to Bézier surfaces: Bézier triangles are not as straightforward as Bézier patches. However, since the triangle is the base primitive for graphics hardware, and because they are used in Section 12.2.3, Bézier triangles are worth presenting.

The control points are located in a triangular grid, as shown in Figure 12.16. The degree of the Bézier triangle is n, and this implies that there are $n+1$ control points per side. These control points are denoted $\mathbf{p}_{i,j,k}^0$ and sometimes abbreviated to $\mathbf{p}_{ijk}$. Note that $i+j+k=n$, and $i, j, k \geq 0$ for all control points. Thus, the total number of control points is

$$\sum_{x=1}^{n+1} x = \frac{(n+1)(n+2)}{2}.$$

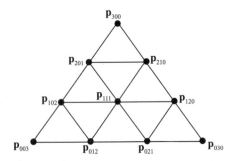

Figure 12.16. The control points of a Bézier triangle with degree three (cubic).

It should come as no surprise that Bézier triangles also are based on repeated interpolation. However, due to the triangular shape of the domain, barycentric coordinates (see Section 13.7) must be used for the interpolation. Recall that a point within a triangle $\Delta\mathbf{p}_0\mathbf{p}_1\mathbf{p}_2$, can be described as $\mathbf{p}(u, v) = \mathbf{p}_0 + u(\mathbf{p}_1 - \mathbf{p}_0) + v(\mathbf{p}_2 - \mathbf{p}_0) = (1 - u - v)\mathbf{p}_0 + u\mathbf{p}_1 + v\mathbf{p}_2$, where (u, v) are the barycentric coordinates. For points inside the triangle the following must hold: $u \geq 0$, $v \geq 0$, and $1 - u + v \geq 0 \Leftrightarrow u + v \leq 1$. Based on this, the de Casteljau algorithm for Bézier triangles is:

de Casteljau [triangles]:

$$\mathbf{p}_{i,j,k}^l(u, v) = u\mathbf{p}_{i+1,j,k}^{l-1} + v\mathbf{p}_{i,j+1,k}^{l-1} + (1 - u - v)\mathbf{p}_{i,j,k+1}^{l-1},$$
$$l = 1 \ldots n, \quad i + j + k = n - l. \tag{12.30}$$

The final point on the Bézier triangle at (u, v) is $\mathbf{p}_{000}^n(u, v)$. The Bézier triangle in Bernstein form is:

Bernstein [triangles]:

$$\mathbf{p}(u, v) = \sum_{i+j+k=n} B_{ijk}^n(u, v)\mathbf{p}_{ijk}. \tag{12.31}$$

The Bernstein polynomials now depend on both u and v, and are therefore computed differently, as shown below:

$$B_{ijk}^n(u, v) = \frac{n!}{i!j!k!}u^i v^j (1 - u - v)^k, \quad i + j + k = n. \tag{12.32}$$

When any of the following is true: $i, j, k < 0$ and $i, j, k > n$, the Bernstein polynomial is set to zero; $B_{ijk}^n(u, v) = 0$. The partial derivatives are [224]:

Derivatives [triangles]:

$$\frac{\partial\mathbf{p}(u, v)}{\partial u} = \sum_{i+j+k=n-1} B_{ijk}^{n-1}(u, v)\mathbf{p}_{i+1,j,k},$$
$$\frac{\partial\mathbf{p}(u, v)}{\partial v} = \sum_{i+j+k=n-1} B_{ijk}^{n-1}(u, v)\mathbf{p}_{i,j+1,k}. \tag{12.33}$$

Some unsurprising properties of Bézier triangles are that they interpolate (pass through) the three corner control points, and that each boundary is a Bézier curve described by the control points on that boundary. Also, the surfaces lies in the convex hull of the control points. Finally, rotating

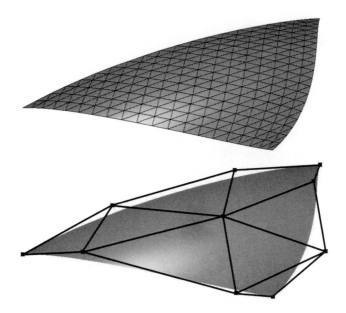

Figure 12.17. Top: wireframe of a Bézier triangle. Bottom: Shaded surface together with control points.

the control points and then generating points on the Bézier triangle is the same as generating points on the Bézier triangle and then rotating these. A Bézier triangle is shown in Figure 12.17.

Next, we will discuss a direct application of Bézier triangles.

12.2.3 N-Patches

Given an input triangle mesh with normals at each vertex, the goal of the *N-patches* scheme by Vlachos et al. [773] is to construct a better looking surface on a triangle basis. The term "N-patches" is short for "Normal-Patches," and these patches are also called *PN triangles*. This scheme attempts to improve the triangle mesh's shading and silhouette by creating a curved surface to replace each triangle. Hardware is able to make each surface on the fly because the tessellation is generated from each triangle's points and normals, with no neighbor information needed. API changes are minimal; all that is needed is a flag telling whether to generate N-patches,

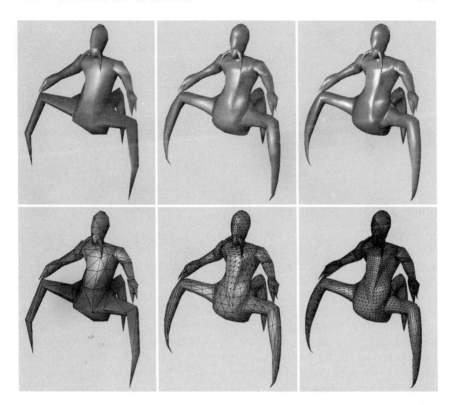

Figure 12.18. The columns show different levels of detail of the same model. The original triangle data, consisting of 414 triangles, is shown on the left. The middle model has 3,726 triangles, while the right has 20,286 triangles, all generated with the presented algorithm. Note how the silhouette and the shading improves. The bottom rows show the models in wireframe, which reveals that each original triangle generates the same amount of subtriangles. *(Model courtesy of id Software. Image from ATI Technologies Inc. demo.)*

and a level of tessellation. See Figure 12.18 for an example. The algorithm presented here builds upon work by van Overveld and Wyvill [768].

Assume we have a triangle with vertices $\mathbf{p}_{300}$, $\mathbf{p}_{030}$, and $\mathbf{p}_{003}$ with normals $\mathbf{n}_{200}$, $\mathbf{n}_{020}$, and $\mathbf{n}_{002}$. The basic idea is to use this information to create a cubic Bézier triangle for each original triangle, and generate as many triangles as we wish from the Bézier triangle.

To shorten notation, $w = 1 - u - v$ will be used. A cubic Bézier triangle (see Figure 12.16) is given by:

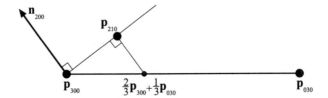

Figure 12.19. How the Bézier point $\mathbf{p}_{210}$ is computed using the normal $\mathbf{n}_{200}$ at $\mathbf{p}_{300}$, and the two corner points $\mathbf{p}_{300}$ and $\mathbf{p}_{030}$.

$$
\mathbf{p}(u, v) = \sum_{i+j+k=3} B^3_{ijk}(u, v)\mathbf{p}_{ijk}
$$
$$
= u^3\mathbf{p}_{300} + v^3\mathbf{p}_{030} + w^3\mathbf{p}_{003} + 3u^2v\mathbf{p}_{210} + 3u^2w\mathbf{p}_{201}
$$
$$
+ 3uv^2\mathbf{p}_{120} + 3v^2w\mathbf{p}_{021} + 3vw^2\mathbf{p}_{012} + 3uw^2\mathbf{p}_{102} + 6uvw\mathbf{p}_{111}.
$$
$$
(12.34)
$$

To ensure C^0 continuity at the borders between two N-patch triangles, the control points on the edge can be determined from the corner control points and the normals at the respective control point (assuming that normals are shared between adjacent triangles). Also, to get reasonable behavior of the surface at the control points, the normals there should be normals of the surface in Equation 12.34. Therefore, the following strategy is adopted to compute the six different control points for the borders. Say that we want to compute $\mathbf{p}_{210}$ using the control points $\mathbf{p}_{300}$, $\mathbf{p}_{030}$, and the normal $\mathbf{n}_{200}$ at $\mathbf{p}_{300}$. Simply take the point $\frac{2}{3}\mathbf{p}_{300} + \frac{1}{3}\mathbf{p}_{030}$ and project it in the direction of the normal, $\mathbf{p}_{200}$, onto the tangent plane defined by $\mathbf{p}_{300}$ and $\mathbf{n}_{200}$ [223, 224, 773]. See Figure 12.19. Assuming normalized normals, the point $\mathbf{p}_{210}$ is computed as:

$$
\mathbf{p}_{210} = \frac{1}{3}\left(2\mathbf{p}_{300} + \mathbf{p}_{030} - (\mathbf{n}_{200} \cdot (\mathbf{p}_{030} - \mathbf{p}_{300}))\mathbf{n}_{200}\right). \qquad (12.35)
$$

The other border control points can be computed similarly, so it only remains to compute the interior control point, $\mathbf{p}_{111}$. This is done as shown in Equation 12.36, and this choice follows a quadratic polynomial [223, 224].

$$
\mathbf{p}_{111} = \frac{1}{4}(\mathbf{p}_{210}+\mathbf{p}_{120}+\mathbf{p}_{102}+\mathbf{p}_{201}+\mathbf{p}_{021}+\mathbf{p}_{012}) - \frac{1}{6}(\mathbf{p}_{300}+\mathbf{p}_{030}+\mathbf{p}_{003}) \quad (12.36)
$$

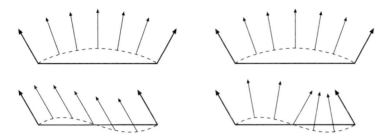

Figure 12.20. This figure illustrates why quadratic interpolation of normals is needed, and why linear interpolation is not sufficient. The left column shows what happens when linear interpolation of normals are used. This works fine when the normals describe a convex surface (top), but breaks down when the surface has an inflection (bottom). The right column illustrates quadratic interpolation. *(Illustration after van Overveld and Wyvill [767].)*

Instead of using Equation 12.33 to compute the two tangents on the surface, and subsequently the normal, Vlachos et al. [773] choose to interpolate the normal using a quadratic scheme as shown below:

$$
\mathbf{n}(u, v) = \sum_{i+j+k=2} B_{ijk}^2(u, v)\mathbf{n}_{ijk}
$$
$$
= u^2\mathbf{n}_{200} + v^2\mathbf{n}_{020} + w^2\mathbf{n}_{002} + uv\mathbf{n}_{110} + uw\mathbf{n}_{101} + vw\mathbf{n}_{011}.
$$
$$(12.37)$$

This can be thought of as a Bézier triangle of degree two, where the control points are six different normals. In Equation 12.37, the choice of the degree, i.e., quadratic, is quite natural since the derivatives are of one degree lower than the actual Bézier triangle, and because linear interpolation of the normals cannot describe an inflection. See Figure 12.20.

To be able to use Equation 12.37, the normal control points $\mathbf{n}_{110}$, $\mathbf{n}_{101}$, and $\mathbf{n}_{011}$, need to be computed. One intuitive, but flawed, solution is to use the average of $\mathbf{n}_{200}$ and $\mathbf{n}_{020}$ (normals at the vertices of the original triangle) to compute $\mathbf{n}_{110}$. However, when $\mathbf{n}_{200} = \mathbf{n}_{020}$, then the problem shown at the lower left in Figure 12.20 will once again be encountered. Instead, $\mathbf{n}_{110}$ is constructed by taking the average of $\mathbf{n}_{200}$ and $\mathbf{n}_{020}$. Then this normal is reflected in the plane π, which is shown in Figure 12.21. This plane has a normal parallel to the difference between the endpoints; $\mathbf{p}_{300}$ and $\mathbf{p}_{030}$. The plane π is passing through the origin since direction vectors are reflected, and these are independent on the position on the

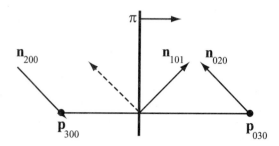

Figure 12.21. Construction of n_{010} for N-patches. The dashed normal is the average of n_{200} and n_{020}, and n_{010} is this normal reflected in the plane π. The plane π has a normal that is parallel to $p_{030} - p_{300}$.

plane. Also, note that each normal should be normalized. Mathematically, the unnormalized version of n_{110} is expressed as [773]:

$$n'_{110} = n_{300} + n_{030} - 2\frac{(p_{030} - p_{300}) \cdot (n_{300} + n_{030})}{(p_{030} - p_{300}) \cdot (p_{030} - p_{300})}(p_{030} - p_{300}). \quad (12.38)$$

van Overveld and Wyvill originally used a factor $3/2$ instead of the 2 in the equation above. Which value is best is hard to judge from looking at images, but using 2 gives the nice interpretation of a true reflection in the plane. Lee and Jen analyze artifacts involved in normal interpolation, and suggest solutions [481].

At this point, all Bézier points of the cubic Bézier triangle and all the normal vectors for quadratic interpolation have been computed. It only remains to create triangles on the Bézier triangle so these can be rendered. Advantages of this approach are that the surface gets a better silhouette and shape relatively cheaply, and that only minor modifications must be made to existing code to make this work. All that is needed is that tessellation should be done (instead of rendering as usual), down to some *Level of Detail (LOD)*. A hardware implementation is pretty straightforward.

One way to specify LODs is the following. The original triangle data is LOD 0. Then the LOD number increases with the number of newly introduced vertices on a triangle edge. So LOD 1 introduces one new vertex per edge, and so creates four subtriangles on the Bézier triangle, and LOD 2 introduces two new vertices per edge, generating nine triangles. In general, LOD n generates $(n+1)^2$ triangles. To prevent cracking between Bézier triangles, each triangle in the mesh must be tessellated with the same LOD. This is a big disadvantage since a tiny triangle will be tessellated as much as a large triangle. Adaptive tessellation (Section 12.3.2) and fractional tessellation (Section 12.3.3) are possible, but not yet supported. Creases are hard to control, and often one needs to insert extra triangles near the desired crease. The continuity between Bézier triangles is only C^0, but still it looks acceptable in many cases. This is mainly because the normals are continuous across triangles, so that a set of N-patches mimic a G^1 surface. Note that to get good looking texturing, C^1 continuity is required across borders between triangles (or patches). Also worth knowing is that cracks will appear if two adjacent triangles do not share the same normals.

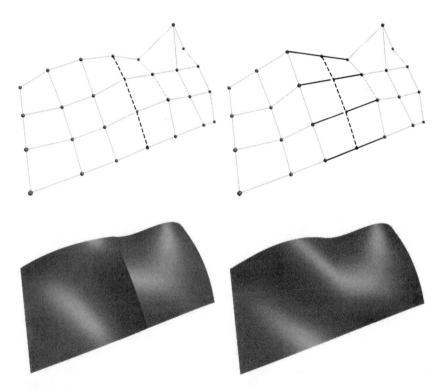

Figure 12.22. The left column shows two Bézier patches joined with only C^0 continuity. Clearly, there is a shading discontinuity between the patches. The right column shows similar patches joined with C^1 continuity, which looks better. In the top row, the dashed lines indicate the border between the two joined patches. To the upper right, the black lines show the collinearity of the control points of the joining patches.

12.2.4   API and Hardware Support

The OpenGL API has support for Bézier patches and rational Bézier patches. However, this does not mean that all hardware supports tessellation in hardware. NVIDIA's GeForce3 has OpenGL extensions for their own evaluators for Bézier patches and triangles, both rational and nonrational. They also handle B-splines (not treated in this book). NVIDIA also supports fractional tessellation as described in Section 12.3.3.

N-patches are supported by the DirectX 8 API and through extensions in OpenGL. Version 8.0 of DirectX has support for the interpolation of normals, but only with linear interpolation. Version 8.1 also allows quadratic interpolation of normals. There is a performance cost in normal interpolation; quadratic interpolation is more expensive than linear. Besides the standard N-patch interpolation (cubic Bézier triangles), version 8.1 also allows linear interpolation of vertex positions. This means that a triangle is tessellated with many smaller coplanar triangles with interpolated normals across each. ATI accelerates N-patches in hardware, which they call TRUFORM, beginning with their 8000 series of chips. N-patches are also used in the displacement mapping primitive proposed by Matrox (see Section 5.7.5).

12.2.5   Continuity

When constructing an interesting object from Bézier surfaces, one often wants to stitch together several different Bézier surfaces to form one composite surface. To get a good looking result, care must be taken to ensure that reasonable continuity is obtained across the surfaces. This is in the same spirit as for curves, in Section 12.1.2.

Assume two bicubic Bézier patches should be pieced together. These have 4×4 control points each. This is illustrated in Figure 12.23, where the left patch has control points, $\mathbf{a}_{ij}$, and the right has control points, $\mathbf{b}_{ij}$, for $0 \leq i, j \leq 3$. To ensure C^0 continuity, the patches must share the same control points at the border, that is, $\mathbf{a}_{3j} = \mathbf{b}_{0j}$. However, this is not sufficient to get a nice looking composite surface. Instead, a simple technique will be presented that gives C^1 continuity [224]. To achieve this, we must constrain the position of the two rows of control points closest to the shared control points. These rows are $\mathbf{a}_{2j}$ and $\mathbf{b}_{1j}$. For each j, the points $\mathbf{a}_{2j}$, $\mathbf{b}_{0j}$, and $\mathbf{b}_{1j}$ must be collinear, that is, they must lie on a line. Moreover, they must have the same ratio, which means that $||\mathbf{a}_{2j} - \mathbf{b}_{0j}|| = k||\mathbf{b}_{0j} - \mathbf{b}_{1j}||$. Here, k is a constant, and it must be the same for all j.

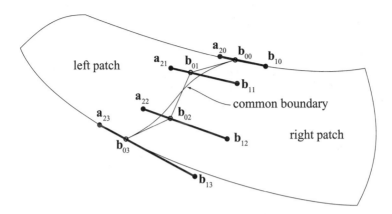

Figure 12.23. How to stitch together two Bézier patches with C^1 continuity. All control points on bold lines must be collinear, and they must have the same ratio between the two segment lengths. Note that $\mathbf{a}_{3j} = \mathbf{b}_{0j}$ to get a shared boundary between patches. This can also be seen to the right in Figure 12.22.

This sort of construction uses up many degrees of freedom of setting the control points. This can be seen even more clearly when stitching together four patches, sharing one common corner. The construction is visualized in Figure 12.24. The result is shown to the right in this figure, where the locations of the eight control points around the shared control point are shown. These nine point must all lie in the same plane, and they must form a bilinear patch, as shown in Figure 12.11. If one is satisfied with

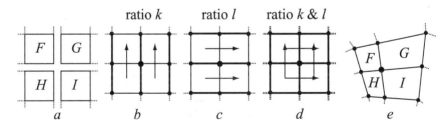

Figure 12.24. *a*) Four patches, F, G, H, and I, are to be stitched together, where all patches share one corner. *b*) In the vertical direction, the three sets of three points (on each bold line) must use the same ratio, k. This relationship is not shown here; see the rightmost figure. A similar process is done for *c*), where, in the horizontal direction, both patches must use the same ratio, l. *d*) When stitched together, all four patches must use ratio k vertically, and l horizontally. *e*) The result is shown, in which the ratios are correctly computed for the nine control points closest to (and including) the shared control point.

G^1 continuity at the corners (and only there), it suffices to make the nine points coplanar. This uses fewer degrees of freedom.

Continuity for Bézier triangles is generally more complex, as well as the G^1 conditions for both Bézier patches and triangles [224, 371]. When constructing a complex object of many Bézier surfaces, it is often hard to see to it that reasonable continuity is obtained across all borders. One solution to this is to turn to subdivision surfaces, treated in Section 12.6.

Note that C^1 continuity is required for good looking texturing across borders. For reflections and shading, a reasonable result is obtained with G^1 continuity. C^1 or higher gives even better results. An example is shown in Figure 12.22.

12.3   Efficient Tessellation

To actually use parametric surfaces in a real-time rendering context, we need to create triangles on the surface. This process is known as *tessellation*. The simplest form of tessellation is called *uniform tessellation*. Assume that we have a parametric Bézier patch, $\mathbf{p}(u,v)$, as described in Equation 12.26. We want to tessellate this patch by computing 11 points per patch side, resulting in $10 \times 10 \times 2 = 200$ triangles. The simplest way to do this is to sample the uv-space *uniformly*. Thus, we evaluate $\mathbf{p}(u,v)$ for all $(u_k, v_l) = (0.1k, 0.1l)$, where both k and l can be any integer from 0 to 10. This can be done with a two nested `for`-loops. Two triangles can be created for the four surface points $\mathbf{p}(u_k, v_l)$, $\mathbf{p}(u_{k+1}, v_l)$, $\mathbf{p}(u_{k+1}, v_{l+1})$, and $\mathbf{p}(u_k, v_{l+1})$.

While this certainly is straightforward, there are faster ways to do it. The next subsection presents *differencing* schemes, which reduce the amount of computation when creating triangles uniformly (in the uv-space) over a surface. In Section 12.3.2, methods will be presented that adapt the size of triangles in the tessellation to the shape of the surface, i.e., more triangles where the surface bends more. This is done to avoid wasting triangles where not needed. Finally, Section 12.3.3 presents a technique for using independent fractional tessellation factors on the sides of a parametric surface. This is to allow smoother level of detail of these surfaces.

12.3.1   Differencing Schemes

In this section, two schemes, called forward differencing and central differencing will be presented. Both aim at reducing the cost of evaluating polynomials.

Forward Differencing

As seen in Equation 12.9, a Bézier curve could be rewritten as:

$$\mathbf{p}(t) = \sum_{i=0}^{n} t^i \mathbf{c}_i. \tag{12.39}$$

In fact, every polynomial curve can be written in this form. Note that Equation 12.39 can be seen as three independent polynomials (one for each x, y, and z). Therefore, our discussion focuses only on a scalar polynomial:

$$f(t) = \sum_{i=0}^{n} t^i c_i = c_0 + t c_1 + t^2 c_2 + \cdots + t^n c_n. \tag{12.40}$$

Forward differencing is a technique to rapidly evaluate such polynomials at uniformly spaced t-values, e.g., $t = 0.1k$, where k is a nonnegative integer. To generalize, assume we want to evaluate the curve at $t = sk$, where s is a real positive number, and again k is a nonnegative integer. This means, that we want to evaluate the polynomial at $t = 0$, $t = s$, $t = 2s$, $t = 3s$, and so on. To simplify the presentation, we introduce $f_k = f(sk)$, and the forward differences as:

$$\begin{aligned}
\delta_k^1 &= f_{k+1} - f_k && \text{(1st forward difference)}, \\
\delta_k^2 &= \delta_{k+1}^1 - \delta_k^1 && \text{(2nd forward difference)}, \\
\delta_k^3 &= \delta_{k+1}^2 - \delta_k^2 && \text{(3rd forward difference)}, \\
&\cdots \\
\delta_k^n &= \delta_{k+1}^{n-1} - \delta_k^{n-1} && \text{(nth forward difference)}.
\end{aligned} \tag{12.41}$$

For a polynomial of degree n, it can be shown that all the forward differences δ^{n+1} are zero. Before actually evaluating the polynomial, the forward differencing scheme computes some startup information that consists of: $f_0, \delta_0^1, \delta_0^2, \delta_0^3, \ldots, \delta_0^n$. The algorithm to evaluate the curve at $t = sk$ is shown in the pseudocode below, where the subscripts have been dropped:

```
1 :   compute f, δ¹, δ², δ³, ..., δⁿ
2 :   for i = 1 to l
3 :       f = f + δ¹
4 :       δ¹ = δ¹ + δ²
5 :       δ² = δ² + δ³
6 :       ...
7 :       δⁿ⁻¹ = δⁿ⁻¹ + δⁿ
8 :   end
```

In the pseudocode above, $l + 1$ evaluations of f are computed; every loop iteration produces a new f-value. It is worth noting that after the startup information has been computed, only additions are used. After startup, each new point on the curve is evaluated at a cost of $O(n)$, where n is the degree of the polynomial. Since the de Casteljau and Bernstein evaluation of Bézier curves costs $O(n^2)$ per point, forward differencing is, in general, much faster.

Note that due to the inherent accumulation in this technique, roundoff errors can occur for large loops [788]. Also interesting is that forward differencing can easily be used for evaluating a parametric polynomial patch, such as a Bézier patch. Equation 12.27 shows how a Bézier curve on the Bézier surface is obtained when keeping a v-value fixed. This is used by Moreton [572] to tessellate parametric polynomial surfaces. The driver computes the control points of Bézier curves (on the Bézier surface), which are sent to the graphics hardware. The accelerator evaluates the Bézier curve and connects it to a previously evaluated curve to form triangles.

EXAMPLE: FORWARD DIFFERENCING Assume the following polynomial is to be evaluated at $t = 0.1k$, $k = 0, \ldots, 10$:

$$f(t) = 2 + 5t + t^2. \tag{12.42}$$

To set up the forward difference scheme, the startup information is computed:

$$
\begin{aligned}
f_0 &= 2 & f_1 &= 2.51 & f_2 &= 3.04 \\
\delta_0^1 &= f_1 - f_0 = 0.51 & \delta_1^1 &= f_2 - f_1 = 0.53 \\
\delta_0^2 &= \delta_1^1 - \delta_0^1 = 0.02
\end{aligned}
\tag{12.43}
$$

Now, enter the loop with $f = 2$, $\delta^1 = 0.51$, and $\delta^2 = 0.02$ in the pseudocode above. In the first iteration, the following is obtained: $f = 2 + 0.51 = 2.51$, and $\delta^1 = 0.51 + 0.02 = 0.53$; and in the second iteration: $f = 2.51 + 0.53 = 3.04$ and $\delta^1 = 0.53 + 0.02 = 0.55$. As can be seen, both of these f-values have already been computed as part of the startup phase, so they need not really be computed again. However, it shows that the scheme works. In the third iteration, we obtain: $f = 3.04 + 0.55 = 3.59$, and $\delta^1 = 0.55 + 0.02 = 0.57$, and so on.   □

A tutorial on forward differencing is given by Wallis [788]. The step length in forward differencing can be adapted during rendering to get better accuracy where needed [494].

Central Differencing

In this section, an efficient way of evaluating curves and surfaces, called *central differencing* [115], will be presented.

A scalar function, $f(x)$, can be expanded as a Taylor series:

$$f(x + \Delta) = \sum_{k=0}^{\infty} \frac{\Delta^k}{k!} f^{(k)}(x). \tag{12.44}$$

In the equation above, $f^{(k)}$ is the k:th derivative of f. Thus, this formula means that if all derivatives can be evaluated in a certain point x, then the function at $f(x + \Delta)$ can also be efficiently evaluated. Since a curve is described as $\mathbf{p}(t) = (x(t), y(t), z(t))$, the above formula can be used three times for a curve. Now, assume we have a cubic Bézier curve:

$$\begin{aligned}
\mathbf{p}(t) &= B_0^3 \mathbf{p}_0 + B_1^3 \mathbf{p}_1 + B_2^3 \mathbf{p}_2 + B_3^3 \mathbf{p}_3 \\
&= (1-t)^3 \mathbf{p}_0 + 3t(1-t)^2 \mathbf{p}_1 + 3t^2(1-t)\mathbf{p}_2 + t^3 \mathbf{p}_3 \\
&= t^3 \mathbf{u} + t^2 \mathbf{v} + t\mathbf{w} + \mathbf{x}.
\end{aligned} \tag{12.45}$$

Here, the vectors $\mathbf{u}$, $\mathbf{v}$, $\mathbf{w}$, and $\mathbf{x}$ are found by collecting terms for the t^i, $i = 0 \ldots 3$. Deriving the curve function repeatedly gives:

$$\begin{aligned}
\mathbf{p}'(t) &= 3t^2 \mathbf{u} + 2t\mathbf{v} + \mathbf{w}, \\
\mathbf{p}''(t) &= 6t\mathbf{u} + 2\mathbf{v}, \\
\mathbf{p}^{(3)}(t) &= 6\mathbf{u}, \\
\mathbf{p}^{(k)}(t) &= 0, \quad k \geq 4.
\end{aligned} \tag{12.46}$$

Since these terms become zero after just four derivations, it is clear that Equation 12.44 can be evaluated quite efficiently. Adding $\mathbf{p}(t + \Delta)$ and $\mathbf{p}(t - \Delta)$ can be simplified considerably because of the altering signs on odd terms:

$$\begin{aligned}
\mathbf{p}(t - \Delta) + \mathbf{p}(t + \Delta) &= 2\mathbf{p}(t) + \Delta^2 \mathbf{p}''(t) \\
&\Longleftrightarrow \\
\mathbf{p}(t) &= \frac{\mathbf{p}(t - \Delta) + \mathbf{p}(t + \Delta) - \Delta^2 \mathbf{p}''(t)}{2}.
\end{aligned} \tag{12.47}$$

The application for this formula is the subdivision of the Bézier curve. Assume we have $\mathbf{p}(0)$ and $\mathbf{p}(1)$, and that we wish to compute $\mathbf{p}(0.5)$. Equation 12.47 can be used for this operation by setting $t = 0.5$ and $\Delta = 0.5$.

However, the term $\mathbf{p}''(t)$ still need to be computed. By applying the same technique as used for $\mathbf{p}(t)$, the following formula is obtained:

$$\mathbf{p}''(t) = \frac{\mathbf{p}''(t - \Delta) + \mathbf{p}''(t + \Delta)}{2}. \tag{12.48}$$

Now, to be able to start using these formulae, $\mathbf{p}(0)$, $\mathbf{p}(1)$, $\mathbf{p}''(0)$, and $\mathbf{p}''(1)$ need to be evaluated. This can be done using Equations 12.45 and 12.46. After that, $\mathbf{p}(0.5)$ and $\mathbf{p}''(0.5)$ can be efficiently computed using Equations 12.47 and 12.48. This is then done repeatedly for $\mathbf{p}(0.25)$, $\mathbf{p}(0.75)$, and so on.

This technique can be expanded to work for rectangular and triangular surface patches as well. DeLoura [167] shows how to do this for bicubic Bézier patches. To evaluate 9×9 points on such a surface using direct evaluation of the Bernstein-Bézier formula described in Equation 12.26 uses about 12,500 operations. In contrast, central differencing uses only about 3,000 operations [167].

12.3.2 Adaptive Tessellation

Uniform tessellation gives good results if the sampling rate is high enough. However, in some regions on a surface there may not be as great a need for high tessellation as in other regions. This may be because the surfaces bend more rapidly in some area and therefore may need higher tessellation there, while other parts of the surface are almost flat, and only a few triangles are needed to approximate them. A solution to the problem of generating unnecessary triangles is *adaptive tessellation*, which refers to algorithms that adapt the tessellation rate depending on some measure (for example curvature, triangle edge length, or some screen size measure). Care must be taken to avoid cracks that can appear between different tessellated regions. See Figure 12.25. What follows is a simple adaptive tessellation algorithm for parametric surfaces that avoids cracks [124].

For parametric surfaces with a rectangular domain (e.g., a Bézier patch), points are first created at the corner of the domain. This means that four points are created for the uv-values of $(0,0)$, $(0,1)$, $(1,0)$, and $(1,1)$. Then, two triangles are created from these four points. These two triangles, represented by their points and their respective uv-values, are fed to a recursive tessellator algorithm. Surfaces with other than rectangular domains can also be used to start the algorithm. For example, for a triangular parametric surface, the three points at the corners of the domain are used.

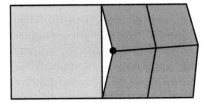 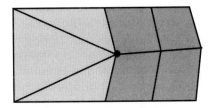

Figure 12.25. To the left, a crack is visible between the two regions. This is because the right has a higher tessellation rate than the left. The problem lies in that the right region has evaluated the surface where there is a circle, and the left region has not. The standard solution is shown to the right.

When a triangle, $\triangle pqr$ (here we assume that a point $\mathbf{p}$ consists of both its position in the three-dimensional space and its uv-coordinates), reaches the tessellator algorithm, a user-supplied routine, `curveTessEnough(a, b)`, is called for each of the three edges, where $\mathbf{a}$ and $\mathbf{b}$ are edge vertices. The task of this routine is to determine whether the edge between two points is tessellated enough so that the line segments approximate the true curve sufficiently. If it is, then that edge need not be tessellated any further. If all edges are tessellated enough, then another routine, `triTessEnough(a, b, c)`, is called for the entire triangle. Even though the edges are sufficiently tessellated, something may be happening in the interior of the triangle. If the triangle as a whole is tessellated enough, then nothing further needs to be done. How `curveTessEnough` and `triTessEnough` are constructed will be described later in this section.

If one or more of the edges or the triangle's interior is not tessellated enough, then further tessellation is needed. The four different cases that can occur are shown in Figure 12.26. When an edge is not tessellated enough, a point is created halfway between the edge points' uv-values.

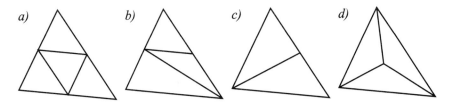

Figure 12.26. Four cases of further tessellation. *a)* Neither of the three edges are tessellated enough, so the triangle is split into four new triangles. *b)* Only two edges need to be subdivided. *c)* Only one edge is subdivided. *d)* All edges are tessellated enough, but the interior of the triangle needs more.

Then new triangles are created and the tessellator is once again called with the new triangles as input data. Note that in case *b* in the figure there is another choice of creating the two bottom triangles. Chung and Field choose the split that minimizes the length of the new edges [124]. Since only the edges themselves determine whether they should be further tessellated, each edge will always be tessellated in the same way (each edge can be tested for tessellation twice, one time for each triangle that uses that edge). The triangle itself is tested to see if it is sufficiently tessellated, but no new vertices are created for the edges, so avoiding cracking.

The algorithm is summarized in the pseudocode below, where all points are assumed to be two-dimensional uv-coordinates, e.g., $\mathbf{p} = (p_u, p_v)$. The actual points on the surface at those uv-coordinates could also be sent, but are omitted for a cleaner presentation. For simplicity, only one permutation of case *b* (Lines 9–12), and one permutation of case *c* (Lines 13–15) has been included.

```
      AdaptiveTessellate(p, q, r)
 1 :  tessPQ = not curveTessEnough(p, q);
 2 :  tessQR = not curveTessEnough(q, r);
 3 :  tessRP = not curveTessEnough(r, p);
 4 :  if(tessPQ and tessQR and tessRP)
 5 :     AdaptiveTessellate(p, (p + q)/2, (p + r)/2);
 6 :     AdaptiveTessellate(q, (q + r)/2, (q + p)/2);
 7 :     AdaptiveTessellate(r, (r + p)/2, (r + q)/2);
 8 :     AdaptiveTessellate((p + q)/2, (q + r)/2, (r + p)/2);
 9 :  else if(tessPQ and tessQR)
10 :     AdaptiveTessellate(p, (p + q)/2, r);
11 :     AdaptiveTessellate((p + q)/2, (q + r)/2, r);
12 :     AdaptiveTessellate((p + q)/2, q, (q + r)/2);
13 :  else if(tessPQ)
14 :     AdaptiveTessellate(p, (p + q)/2, r);
15 :     AdaptiveTessellate(q, r, (p + q)/2);
16 :  else if(not triTessEnough(p, q, r))
17 :     AdaptiveTessellate((p + q + r)/3, p, q);
18 :     AdaptiveTessellate((p + q + r)/3, q, r);
19 :     AdaptiveTessellate((p + q + r)/3, r, p);
20 :  end;
```

Infinite recursion can occur for badly constructed `curveTessEnough` and `triTessEnough` routines (for example, when they always return `false`). To avoid this, a *degeneracy* measure, d, is used [124]:

$$d = \frac{||(\mathbf{p} - \mathbf{q}) \times (\mathbf{p} - \mathbf{r})||}{||\mathbf{p} - \mathbf{r}||^2 + ||\mathbf{p} - \mathbf{q}||^2 + ||\mathbf{q} - \mathbf{r}||^2}. \tag{12.49}$$

In the formula above, $\mathbf{p}$, $\mathbf{q}$, and $\mathbf{r}$ are the two-dimensional uv-coordinates of a triangle. The formula computes the ratio of twice the surface area to the sum of the squared edge lengths (in parametric space). This ratio is scale invariant. The maximum value of this function is $\sqrt{(3)}/6$, for an equilateral triangle. If d is close to zero then the triangle is close to degenerate, and infinite recursion may occur. The user of this algorithm supplies a threshold value, and when d is below this value, tessellation terminates in the following way. First, each edge of the triangle is tessellated until all parts of it are tessellated so that they approximate the original shapes sufficiently. Then, a point in the middle of the triangle is generated, and a fan of triangles (see Section 11.4) is created from this middle point to the points on the edges. Chung and Field reports that a good threshold value is between 0.005 and 0.05, but it may have to be adapted to the particular surface being tessellated.

The major advantage of this method is its simplicity; it does not need nor maintain a complex data structure (such as a restricted quadtree [779]). You also do not need to store the triangles. Instead, you can render them on the fly as they are created. However, for efficiency, it is usually desirable to render groups of triangles, in which case all triangle can be stored in a list and triangle strips created after tessellation. The major disadvantage of the algorithm is that `curveTessEnough` is called twice for each edge, that is, there is no sharing of computations between neighbors. One solution to this would be to store the generated tests in a hash table. As soon as an entry is found in this hash table, the entry can be deleted (since it has been used twice at that time).

The routines `curveTessEnough` and `triTessEnough` can be implemented in a number of ways. A good implementation of `curveTessEnough(p, q)` is to compute the points, $\mathbf{a}$ and $\mathbf{b}$, in three-dimensional space using the parameters $\mathbf{p}$ and $\mathbf{q}$. This is shown in Figure 12.27. Then the midpoint, $\mathbf{m}$, in parametric space between $\mathbf{p}$ and $\mathbf{q}$ is found and its three-dimensional counterpart, $\mathbf{c}$, is computed. Finally, the length, l, between $\mathbf{c}$ and its projection, $\mathbf{d}$, onto the line between $\mathbf{a}$ and $\mathbf{b}$ is computed. This length, l, is used to determine whether the curve segment on that edge if flat enough. If l is small enough, then it is considered flat. Note that this method may falsely consider an S-shaped curve segment to be flat. A solution to this is to randomly perturb the parametric sample point [231] or even use multiple randomly perturbed sample points [770]. An alternative to using just l is to use the ratio $l/||\mathbf{a} - \mathbf{b}||$ [199]. To be certain that the algorithm

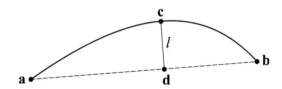

Figure 12.27. The points **a** and **b** have already been generated on this surface. The question is: Should more points, that is **c**, be generated on the surface? The average of the parametric coordinates of **a** and **b** is computed, and a point, **c**, for that parametric coordinate is generated. By projecting it on the edge, between **a** and **b**, the length, l, can be found. If l is large enough, **c** is added to the tessellation.

terminates, it is common to set some upper limit on how many subdivisions can be made. When that limit is reached, the subdivision ends. This test can easily be extended to implement `triTessEnough`—just compute the surface point in the middle of the triangle and use the distance from that point to the triangle's plane.

So far, we have discussed only how to determine the tessellation rate from the shape of the surface. Other factors, that typically are used for on-the-fly tessellation, include whether the local neighborhood of a vertex is [366, 830]:

1. Inside the view frustum,

2. Front facing,

3. Occupying a large area in screen-space,

4. Close to the silhouette of the object, and

5. Illuminated by a significant amount of specular lighting.

These factors will be discussed in turn here. For view frustum culling, one can place a sphere to enclose the edge. This sphere is then tested against the view frustum. If it is outside, then `curveTessEnough` returns true, and we do not subdivide that edge further.

For face culling, the normals at **a**, **b**, and possibly **c** can be computed from the surface description. These normals together with **a**, **b**, and **c** define three planes. If all are backfacing, then it is likely that no further subdivision is needed for that edge.

There are many different ways to implement screen space coverage (see also Section 9.8.2). All methods project some simple object onto the screen and estimate the length or area in screen space. A large area or length

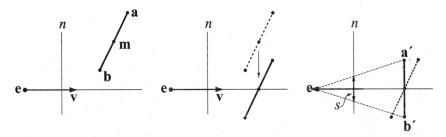

Figure 12.28. Estimation of the screen space projection, s, of the line segment.

implies that tessellation should proceed. A fast estimation of the screen-space projection of a line segment from **a** to **b** is shown in Figure 12.28. First, the line segment is translated so that its midpoint is on the view ray. Then, the line segment is assumed to be parallel to the near plane, n, and the screen space projection, s, is computed from this line segment. Using the points of the line segment $\mathbf{a}'$ and $\mathbf{b}'$ to the right in the illustration, the screen space projection is then

$$s = \frac{n\sqrt{(\mathbf{a}' - \mathbf{b}') \cdot (\mathbf{a}' - \mathbf{b}')}}{\mathbf{v} \cdot (\mathbf{a}' - \mathbf{e})}. \tag{12.50}$$

The numerator is the near plane distance, n, multiplied by the length of the line segment. This is divided by the distance from the eye, $\mathbf{e}$, to the line segment's midpoint. The computed screen space projection, s, is then compared to a threshold, t, representing the maximum edge length in screen space. Rewriting the previous equation to avoid computing the square root, if the following condition is true, then the tessellation should continue:

$$s > t \quad \Longleftrightarrow \quad (\mathbf{a}' - \mathbf{b}') \cdot (\mathbf{a}' - \mathbf{b}') > \frac{t^2}{n^2}(\mathbf{v} \cdot (\mathbf{a}' - \mathbf{e})). \tag{12.51}$$

Note that t^2/n^2 is a constant and so can be precomputed.

Increasing the tessellation rate for the silhouettes is important since they play an important role for the perceived quality of the object. Finding if a triangle is near the silhouette edge can be done by testing whether the dot product between the normal at **a** and the vector from the eye to **a** is close to zero. If this is true for any of **a**, **b**, or **c**, then further tessellation should be done.

Specular illumination changes rapidly on a surface, and so shading artifacts appear most frequently with it (see Figure 4.5 on page 72). Therefore, it makes sense to increase the tessellation in regions where the specular highlight appears. Test if the dot product between the light vector reflected around the normal at a point and the vector from the point to the eye is close to one. If so, then the specular highlight is strong at that point and the tessellation should continue there. This could again be done for points **a**, **b**, and **c**.

It is hard to say what methods will work in all applications. The best advice is to test several of the presented heuristics and combinations of them.

Another more common method for adaptive tessellation is to do it on a quad basis. Assume a rectangular patch is used. Then start a recursive routine with the entire parametric domain, i.e., the square from $(0, 0)$ to $(1, 1)$. Using the subdivision criteria just described, test whether the surface is tessellated enough. If it is, then terminate tessellation. Otherwise, split this domain into four different equally large squares and call the routine recursively for each of the four subsquares. Continue recursively until the surface is tessellated enough or a predefined recursion level is reached. The nature of this algorithm implies that a quadtree is recursively created during tessellation. However, this will give cracks if adjacent subsquares are tessellated to different levels. The standard solution is to see to it that two adjacent subsquares only differ in one level at most. This is called a *restricted quadtree*. Then the technique shown to the right in Figure 12.25 is used to fill in the cracks. The disadvantage with this method is that the bookkeeping is more involved.

Lindstrom et al. [500] and Sharp [699] present different variations of algorithms for avoiding cracks. Bookkeeping in these algorithms is more involved. Also, Lindstrom [500] presents a geometric screen space flatness test for heightfields, which Hoppe [366] generalizes to arbitrary geometry. Both these tests are designed for mesh simplification. Eberly describes many different flatness tests both for curves and surfaces [199]. Chhugani and Kumar [122] present an algorithm for adaptive tessellation of spline surfaces, where tessellation is view-dependent. Note that adaptive tessellation can be used for subdivision surfaces as well. See Section 12.6.8.

12.3.3 Fractional Tessellation

To obtain smoother level of detail for parametric surfaces, Moreton introduced fractional tessellation factors [572]. Also, a limited form of adaptive tessellation is provided by allowing different tessellation factors on different

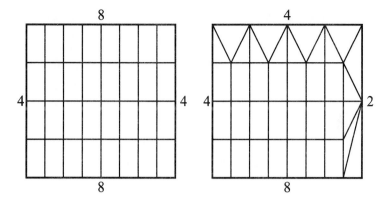

Figure 12.29. Left: normal tessellation—one factor is used for the rows, and another for the columns. Right: independent tessellation factors on all four edges. *(Illustration after Moreton [572].)*

sides of the parametric surface. Here, an overview of what can be achieved using these techniques will be presented.

In Figure 12.29, constant tessellation factors for rows and columns are shown to the left, and independent tessellation factors for all four edges to the right. Note that the tessellation factor of an edge is the number of points generated on that edge minus one. In the patch on the right, the greater of the top and bottom factors is used for both of these edges, and similarly the greater of left and right factors is used for those. Thus, the basic tessellation rate is 4×8. For the sides with smaller factors, triangles are filled in along the edges. Moreton [572] describes this process in more detail.

The concept of fractional tessellation factors is shown for an edge in Figure 12.30. For an integer tessellation factor of n, $n + 1$ points are generated at k/n, where $k = 0, \ldots, n$. For a fractional tessellation factor, r, $\lceil r \rceil$ points are generated at k/r, where $k = 0, \ldots, \lfloor r \rfloor$. Then, the rightmost point is just "snapped" to the rightmost endpoint. As can be seen in the middle illustration in Figure 12.30, this pattern in not symmetric. This leads to problems, since an adjacent patch may generate the points in the other direction, and so give cracks between the surfaces.

Moreton solves this by splitting each patch into four subpatches, and applying the pattern shown in the middle of Figure 12.30 to each subpatch so that a symmetric pattern is formed (shown at the bottom in Figure 12.30). See Figure 12.31 for an example. Fractional tessellation and

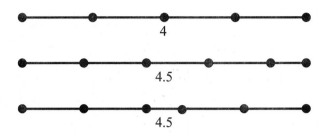

Figure 12.30. Top: integer tessellation. Middle: fractional tessellation, with fraction to the right. Bottom: fractional tessellation with fraction in middle. This configuration avoids cracks between adjacent patches.

independent tessellation factors are available through OpenGL extensions, and is supported by NVIDIA's GeForce3.

Guardado at Matrox has invented a fractional tessellation scheme for triangles, which is used in their displacement mapping hardware. See page 176 and Section 12.6.6 for more on displacement mapping. Tessellation is divided into four phases, which can be seen in Figure 12.32. Phase I creates a new vertex that coincides with one of the original triangle vertices. This new vertex is then moved to the center of the triangle, which ends phase I. Phase II creates three new vertices; one per triangle vertex.

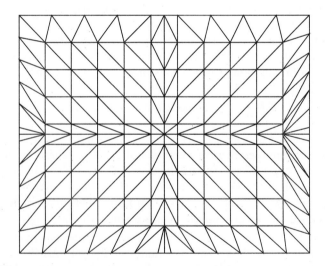

Figure 12.31. A patch with the rectangular domain fractionally tessellated. *(Illustration after Moreton [572].)*

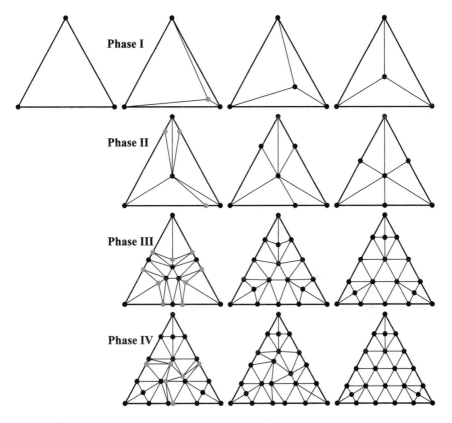

Figure 12.32. Fractional tessellation for triangles. Each gray dot indicates a newly created vertex.

These are moved along the triangle edge, and they reach their final position at the center of the edge. We call these vertices middle-edge vertices. Phase III creates two new vertices for each middle-edge vertex, and the middle vertex of the triangle turns into three vertices as shown in the figure. After phase III, an almost uniform interior is obtained. In the last figure of phase III, the middle vertices on the original triangle edges are replicated into two vertices in phase IV. After phase IV has ended, those two vertices can be replicated again, and phase IV applied once more. Thus, phase IV can be applied any number of times. A nice property is that the general structure of the mesh is maintained after applying phase IV repeatedly; the uniform interior is kept, and it is only at the corners of the original triangle where nonuniformity occurs. By using degenerate triangles, adaptive tessellation is also possible.

12.4   Implicit Surfaces

To this point, only parametric curves and surfaces have been discussed. However, another interesting and useful class of surfaces are *implicit surfaces*. Instead of using some parameters, say u and v, to explicitly describe a point on the surface, the following form, called the implicit function, is used:

$$f(x, y, z) = f(\mathbf{p}) = 0. \tag{12.52}$$

This is interpreted as follows: A point $\mathbf{p}$ is on the implicit surface if the result is zero when the point is inserted into the implicit function f. Implicit surfaces are often used in intersection testing with rays (see Sections 13.5–13.8), as they can be simpler to intersect than the corresponding (if any) parametric surface. Another advantage of implicit surfaces is that *constructive solid geometry* algorithms can be applied easily to them, that is, objects can be subtracted from each other, logically and:ed or or:ed with each other. Also, objects can be easily blended and deformed.

A simple example is the unit sphere, which has $f(x, y, z) = x^2 + y^2 + z^2 - 1$ as its implicit function. Sometimes it is also useful to use *isosurfaces* of an implicit function. An isosurface is $f(x, y, z) = c$, where c is a scalar function. So, for the unit sphere, $f(x, y, z) = 3$ describes an isosurface that is a sphere centered around the origin with a radius of two.

The normal of an implicit surface is described by the partial derivatives, called the gradient and denoted ∇f:

$$\nabla f(x, y, z) = \left(\frac{\partial f}{\partial x}, \frac{\partial f}{\partial y}, \frac{\partial f}{\partial z} \right). \tag{12.53}$$

To be able to evaluate it, Equation 12.53 must be differentiable, and thus also continuous.

Blending of implicit surfaces is a nice feature that can be used in what is often referred to as blobby modeling [71], soft objects, or meta-balls [89]. See Figure 12.33 for a simple example. The basic idea is to use several simple primitives, such as spheres or ellipsoids, and blend these smoothly. Each sphere can be seen as an atom, and after blending the molecule of the atoms is obtained. More mathematically, the blended surface is described by:

$$f(\mathbf{p}) = \sum_{i=0}^{n-1} h(r_i). \tag{12.54}$$

Figure 12.33. The two spheres on the left are blended together into the shape on the right.

In Equation 12.54, we assume that there are n primitive objects (atoms), and for each atom a distance r_i is computed. The r_i is often the distance from $\mathbf{p}$ to the center of the sphere, or some other distance. Finally, the blending function h describes the region of influence of the atom i. Therefore, $h(0) = 1$, and $h(r) = 0$ for $r \geq R$, where R defines where the region of influence ends. As an example, the following blending function by Wyvill [89] gives second-order continuity:

$$h(r) = \left(1 - \frac{r^2}{R^2}\right)^3, \quad h(r) = 0, \ r \geq R. \tag{12.55}$$

Wyvill also recommends using $c = 1/2$, that is, use the implicit surface defined by $f(\mathbf{p}) = 1/2$.

Every implicit surface can also be turned into a surface consisting of triangles. There are a number of algorithms available for performing this operation [87, 89, 403, 769]. One well-known example is the *marching cubes* algorithm [504], which is patented. This algorithm places a three-dimensional grid over the entire surface, and samples the implicit function at each grid point. Each point is either inside or outside the implicit surface. Because a cube has 8 grid points for corners, there are 256 different combinations. Each combination then generates from zero to four triangles inside the cube to represent the implicit surface.

See Karkanis and Stewart's article for a review of past work on triangulation of implicit surfaces [403]. Code for performing polygonalization using algorithms by Wyvill and Bloomenthal is available on the web [88].

12.5 Subdivision Curves

Subdivision techniques are a relatively new way for creating curves and surfaces. One reason why they are interesting is that they bridge the gap

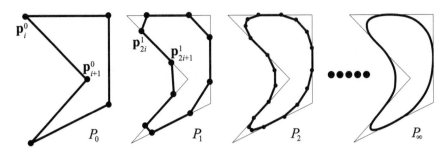

Figure 12.34. Chaikin's subdivision scheme in action. The initial polygon P_0 is subdivided once into P_1, and then again into P_2. As can be seen, the corners of each polygon, P_i, are cut off during subdivision. After infinitely many subdivisions, the limit curve P_∞ is obtained. This is an approximating scheme as the curve does not go through the initial points.

between discrete surfaces (triangle meshes) and continuous surfaces (e.g., a collection of Bézier patches). Here, we will first describe how subdivision curves work, and then discuss the more interesting subdivision surface schemes.

Subdivision curves are best explained by an example that uses *corner cutting*. See Figure 12.34. The corners of the leftmost polygon are cut off, creating a new polygon with twice as many vertices. Then the corners of this new polygon are cut off, and so on to infinity (or more practically: until we cannot see any difference). The resulting curve, called the *limit curve*, is smooth since all corners are cut off.[3] This is often written as $P_0 \rightarrow P_1 \rightarrow P_2 \cdots \rightarrow P_\infty$, where P_0 is the starting polygon, and P_∞ is the limit curve.

This subdivision process can be done in many different ways, and each is characterized by a subdivision scheme. The one shown in Figure 12.34 is called Chaikin's scheme [118] and works as follows. Assume the n vertices of a polygon are $P_0 = \{\mathbf{p}_0^0, \ldots, \mathbf{p}_{n-1}^0\}$, where the superscript denotes the level of subdivision. Chaikin's scheme creates two new vertices between each subsequent pair of vertices, say $\mathbf{p}_i^k$ and $\mathbf{p}_{i+1}^k$, of the original polygon as:

$$\mathbf{p}_{2i}^{k+1} = \frac{3}{4}\mathbf{p}_i^k + \frac{1}{4}\mathbf{p}_{i+1}^k,$$

$$\mathbf{p}_{2i+1}^{k+1} = \frac{1}{4}\mathbf{p}_i^k + \frac{3}{4}\mathbf{p}_{i+1}^k. \tag{12.56}$$

---

[3]This process can also be thought of as a lowpass filter since all sharp corners (high frequency) are removed.

As can be seen, the superscript changes from k to $k+1$, which means that we go from one subdivision level to the next, i.e., $P_k \rightarrow P_{k+1}$. After such a subdivision step is performed, the original vertices are discarded and the new points are reconnected. This kind of behavior can be seen in Figure 12.34, where new points are created $1/4$ away from the original vertices toward neighboring vertices. The beauty of subdivision schemes comes from the simplicity of rapidly generating smooth curves. However, you do not immediately have a parametric form of the curve as in Section 12.1, though it can be shown that Chaikin's algorithm generates a quadratic B-spline [47, 224, 371, 792].[4] So far, the presented scheme works for (closed) polygons, but most schemes can be extended to work for open polylines as well. In the case of Chaikin, the only difference is that the two endpoints of the polyline are kept in each subdivision step (instead of being discarded). This makes the curve go through the endpoints.

In general, there are two different types of subdivision schemes, namely *approximating* and *interpolating*. Chaikin's scheme is approximating, as the limit curve, in general, does not lie on the vertices of the initial polygon. This is because the vertices are discarded (or updated, for some schemes). In contrast, an interpolating scheme keeps all the points from the previous subdivision step, and so the limit curve P_∞ goes through all the points of P_0, P_1, P_2, and so on. This means that the scheme interpolates the initial polygon. An example, using the same polygon as in Figure 12.34, is shown in Figure 12.35. This scheme uses the four nearest points to create a new point [197]:

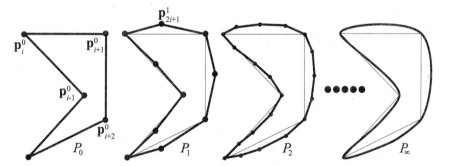

Figure 12.35. The 4-point subdivision scheme in action. This is an interpolating scheme as the curve goes through the initial points, and in general curve P_{i+1} goes through the points of P_i. Note that the same control polygon is used in Figure 12.34.

---

[4]A type of curve that we do not cover in this book.

$$\mathbf{p}_{2i}^{k+1} = \mathbf{p}_i^k,$$

$$\mathbf{p}_{2i+1}^{k+1} = (\frac{1}{2} + w)(\mathbf{p}_i^k + \mathbf{p}_{i+1}^k) - w(\mathbf{p}_{i-1}^k + \mathbf{p}_{i+2}^k). \tag{12.57}$$

The first line in Equation 12.57 simply means that we keep the points from the previous step without changing them (i.e., interpolating), and the second line is for creating a new point in between $\mathbf{p}_i^k$ and $\mathbf{p}_{i+1}^k$. The weight w is called a *tension parameter*. When $w = 0$, linear interpolation is the result, but when $w = 1/16$, we get the kind of behavior shown in Figure 12.35. It can be shown [197] that the resulting curve is C^1 when $0 < w < 1/8$. For open polylines, we run into problems at the endpoints because we need two points on both sides of the new point, and we only have one. This can be solved if the point next to the endpoint is reflected across the endpoint. So, for the start of the polyline, $\mathbf{p}_1$ is reflected across $\mathbf{p}_0$ to obtain $\mathbf{p}_{-1}$. This point is then used in the subdivision process. The creation of $\mathbf{p}_{-1}$ is shown in Figure 12.36.

Another interesting approximating scheme uses the following subdivision rules:

$$\mathbf{p}_{2i}^{k+1} = \frac{3}{4}\mathbf{p}_i^k + \frac{1}{8}(\mathbf{p}_{i-1}^k + \mathbf{p}_{i+1}^k),$$

$$\mathbf{p}_{2i+1}^{k+1} = \frac{1}{2}(\mathbf{p}_i^k + \mathbf{p}_{i+1}^k). \tag{12.58}$$

The first line updates the existing points, and the second computes the midpoint on the line segment between two neighboring points. This scheme generates a cubic B-spline curve. Consult the SIGGRAPH course [845] on subdivision, the Killer B's book [47], Warren and Weimer's subdivision book [792], or Farin's CAGD book [224] for more about these curves.

Given a point $\mathbf{p}$ and its neighboring points, it is possible to directly "push" that point to the limit curve, i.e., determining what the coordinates of $\mathbf{p}$ would be on P_∞. This is also possible for tangents. See, for example, Joy's online introduction to this topic [398].

The topic of subdivision curves has only been touched upon, but it is sufficient for the presentation of subdivision surfaces that follows in the

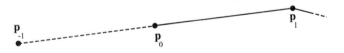

Figure 12.36. The creation of a reflection point, $\mathbf{p}_{-1}$, for open polylines. The reflection point is computed as: $\mathbf{p}_{-1} = \mathbf{p}_0 - (\mathbf{p}_1 - \mathbf{p}_0) = 2\mathbf{p}_0 - \mathbf{p}_1$.

next section. See the Further Reading and Resources section at the end of this chapter for more references and information.

12.6 Subdivision Surfaces

Subdivision surfaces are a powerful paradigm in defining smooth, continuous, crackless surfaces from meshes with arbitrary topology. As with all other surfaces in this chapter, subdivision surfaces also provide infinite level of detail. That is, you can generate as many triangles or polygons as you wish, and the original surface representation is compact. An example of a surface being subdivided is shown in Figure 12.37. Another advantage

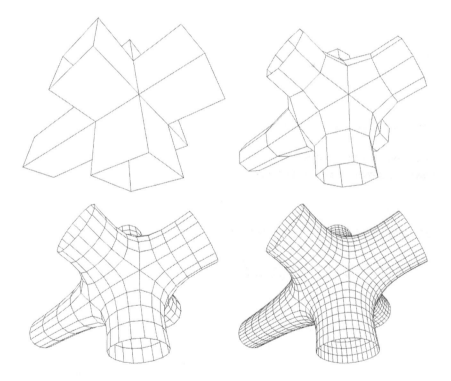

Figure 12.37. The top left image shows the control mesh, i.e., that original mesh, which is the only geometrical data that describes the resulting subdivision surface. The following images are subdivided one, two, and three times. As can be seen, more and more polygons are generated and the surface gets smoother and smoother. The scheme used here is the Catmull-Clark scheme, described in Section 12.6.4.

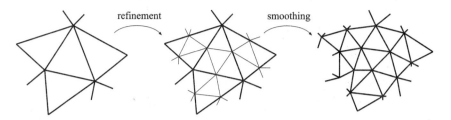

Figure 12.38. Subdivision as refinement and smoothing. The refinement phase creates new vertices and reconnects to create new triangles, and the smoothing phase computes new positions for the vertices.

is that subdivision rules are simple and easily implemented. A disadvantage is that the analysis of surface continuity often is very mathematically involved. However, this sort of analysis is often only of interest to those who wish to create new subdivision schemes, and is out of the scope of this book—consult Warren and Weimer's book [792] and the SIGGRAPH course on subdivision [845].

In general, the subdivision of surfaces (and curves) can be thought of as a two-phase process [438]. Starting with a polygonal mesh, called the *control mesh*, the first phase, called the *refinement phase*, creates new vertices and reconnects to create new, smaller triangles. The second, called the *smoothing phase*, typically computes new positions for some or all vertices in the mesh. This is illustrated in Figure 12.38. It is the details of these two phases that characterize a subdivision scheme. In the first phase, a polygon can be split in different ways, and in the second phase, the choice of subdivision rules give different characteristics such as the level of continuity, and whether the surface is approximating or interpolating.

A subdivision scheme can be characterized by whether it is *stationary*, whether it is *uniform*, and whether it is *triangle-based* or *polygon-based*. A stationary scheme uses the same subdivision rules at every subdivision step, while a nonstationary may change the rules depending on which step currently is being processed. The schemes treated below are all stationary. A uniform scheme uses the same rules for every vertex or edge, while a nonuniform scheme may use different rules for different vertices or edges. As an example, a different set of rules is often used for edges that are on the boundaries of a surface. A triangle-based scheme only operates on triangles, and thus only generates triangles, while a polygon-based scheme operates on arbitrary polygons. We will mostly present triangle-based schemes here because that is what graphics hardware is targeted for, but we will also briefly cover some well-known polygon-based schemes.

Several different subdivision schemes are presented next. Following these, two techniques are presented that extend the use of subdivision surfaces, along with methods for subdividing normals, texture coordinates, and colors. Finally, some practical algorithms for subdivision and rendering are presented.

12.6.1 Loop Subdivision

Loop's subdivision scheme [503][5] was the first subdivision scheme for triangles. It is similar to the last scheme in Section 12.5 in that it is approximating, and that it updates each existing vertex and creates a new vertex for each edge. The connectivity for this scheme is shown in Figure 12.39. As can be seen, each triangle is subdivided into four new triangles, so after n subdivision steps, a triangle has been subdivided into 4^n triangles.

First, let us focus on an existing vertex $\mathbf{p}^k$, where k is the number of subdivision steps. This means that $\mathbf{p}^0$ is the vertex of the control mesh. After one subdivision step, $\mathbf{p}^0$ turns into $\mathbf{p}^1$. In general, $\mathbf{p}^0 \to \mathbf{p}^1 \to \mathbf{p}^2 \to \cdots \to \mathbf{p}^\infty$, where $\mathbf{p}^\infty$ is the limit point. If the *valence* of $\mathbf{p}^k$ is n, then $\mathbf{p}^k$ has n neighboring vertices, $\mathbf{p}_i^k$, $i \in \{0, 1, \ldots, n-1\}$. See Figure 12.40 for the notation described above. Also, a vertex that has valence 6 is called *regular* or *ordinary*; otherwise it is called *irregular* or *extraordinary*.

Below, the subdivision rules for Loop's scheme are given, where the first formula is the rule for updating an existing vertex $\mathbf{p}^k$ into $\mathbf{p}^{k+1}$, and the second formula is for creating a new vertex, $\mathbf{p}_i^{k+1}$, between $\mathbf{p}^k$ and each of the $\mathbf{p}_i^k$. Again, n is the valence of $\mathbf{p}^k$:

$$\mathbf{p}^{k+1} = (1 - n\beta)\mathbf{p}^k + \beta(\mathbf{p}_0^k + \cdots + \mathbf{p}_{n-1}^k),$$
$$\mathbf{p}_i^{k+1} = \frac{3\mathbf{p}^k + 3\mathbf{p}_i^k + \mathbf{p}_{i-1}^k + \mathbf{p}_{i+1}^k}{8}, \quad i = 0 \ldots n-1. \tag{12.59}$$

Figure 12.39. The connectivity of two subdivision steps for schemes such as Loop's and the modified butterfly scheme (see Section 12.6.2). Each triangle generates four new triangles.

---

[5] A brief overview of Loop's subdivision scheme is also presented by Hoppe et al. [364].

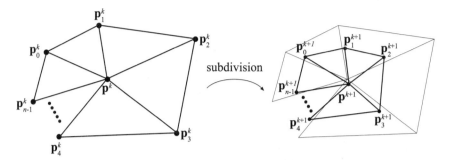

Figure 12.40. The notation used for Loop's subdivision scheme. The left neighborhood is subdivided into the neighborhood to the right. The center point $\mathbf{p}^k$ is updated and replaced by $\mathbf{p}^{k+1}$, and for each edge between $\mathbf{p}^k$ and $\mathbf{p}_i^k$, a new point is created ($\mathbf{p}_i^{k+1}$, $i \in 1, \ldots, n$).

Note that we assume that the indices are computed modulo n, so that if $i = n - 1$, then for $i + 1$, we use index 0, and likewise when $i = 0$, then for $i - 1$, we use index $n - 1$. These subdivision rules can easily be visualized as masks, also called stencils; see Figure 12.41. The major use of these is that they communicate almost an entire subdivision scheme using only a simple illustration. Note that the weights sum to one for both masks. This is a characteristic that is true for all subdivision schemes, and the rationale for this is that a new point should lie in the neighborhood of the weighted points. In Equation 12.59, the constant β is actually a function of n, and is given by:

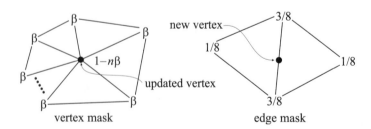

Figure 12.41. The masks for Loop's subdivision scheme (black circles indicate which vertex is updated/generated). A mask shows the weights for each involved vertex. For example, when updating an existing vertex, the weight $1 - n\beta$ is used for the existing vertex, and the weight β is used for all the neighboring vertices, called the 1-ring.

$$\beta(n) = \frac{1}{n}\left(\frac{5}{8} - \frac{(3 + 2\cos(2\pi/n))^2}{64}\right). \tag{12.60}$$

Loop's suggestion [503] for the β-function gives a surface of C^2 continuity at every regular vertex, and C^1 elsewhere [843], that is, at all irregular vertices. As only regular vertices are created during subdivision, the surface is only C^1 at the places where we had irregular vertices in the control mesh. See Figure 12.42 for an example of a mesh subdivided with Loop's scheme. A variant of Equation 12.60, which avoids trigonometric functions, is given by Warren and Weimer [792]:

$$\beta(n) = \frac{3}{n(n+2)}. \tag{12.61}$$

For regular valences, this gives a C^2 surface, and C^1 elsewhere. The resulting surface is hard to distinguish from a regular Loop surface. For a mesh that is not closed, we cannot use the presented subdivision rules. Instead, special rules have to be used for such boundaries. For Loop's scheme, the reflection rules of Equation 12.58 can be used. This is also treated in Section 12.6.5.

The surface after infinitely many subdivision steps is called the limit surface. Limit surface points and limit tangents can be computed using closed form expressions. The limit position of a vertex is computed [364,

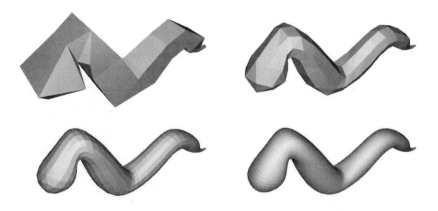

Figure 12.42. A worm subdivided three times with Loop's subdivision scheme.

845] using the formula on the first row in Equation 12.59, by replacing $\beta(n)$ with:

$$\gamma(n) = \frac{1}{n + \frac{3}{8\beta(n)}}. \tag{12.62}$$

Two limits tangents for a vertex $\mathbf{p}^k$ can be computed by weighting the immediate neighboring vertices, called the *1-ring* or *1-neighborhood*, as shown below [364, 503]:

$$\mathbf{t}_u = \sum_{i=0}^{n-1} \cos(2\pi i/n)\mathbf{p}_i^k, \quad \mathbf{t}_v = \sum_{i=0}^{n-1} \sin(2\pi i/n)\mathbf{p}_i^k. \tag{12.63}$$

The normal is then $\mathbf{n} = \mathbf{t}_u \times \mathbf{t}_v$. Note that this often is less expensive [845] than the methods described in Section 11.3, which need to compute the normals of the neighboring triangles. More importantly, this gives the exact normal at the point.

A major advantage of approximating subdivision schemes is that the resulting surface tends to get very fair. *Fairness* is, loosely speaking, related to how smoothly a curve or surface bends [571]. A higher degree of fairness implies a smoother curve or surface. Another advantage is that approximating schemes converge faster than interpolating schemes. However, this comes at the cost of the shape being kind of low-pass filtered, which in turn means that the shapes often shrink. This is most notable for small meshes, such as the tetrahedron shown in Figure 12.43. One way to decrease this effect is to use more vertices in the control mesh. i.e., care

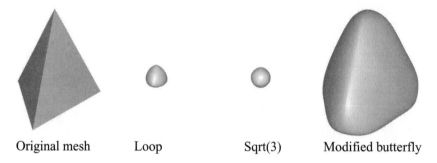

Original mesh   Loop   Sqrt(3)   Modified butterfly

Figure 12.43. A tetrahedron is subdivided five times with Loop's, the $\sqrt{3}$, and the *Modified Butterfly* (MB) scheme. Loop's and the $\sqrt{3}$-scheme are both approximating, while MB is interpolating. Approximating schemes are acting as lowpass filters, which means that shrinking occurs.

must be taken while modeling the control mesh. Maillot and Stam present a framework for combining subdivision schemes so that the shrinking can be controlled [512]. A characteristic that can be used to great advantage at times is that a Loop surface is contained inside the convex hull of the original control points [843].

The Loop subdivision scheme generates a generalized three-directional quartic box spline.[6] So, for a mesh consisting only of regular vertices, we could actually describe the surface as a type of spline surface. However, this description is not possible for irregular settings. Being able to generate smooth surfaces from any mesh of vertices is one of the great strengths of subdivision schemes. See also Sections 12.6.5 and 12.6.6 for different extensions to subdivision surfaces that use Loop's scheme.

12.6.2 Modified Butterfly Subdivision

Here we will present the subdivision scheme by Zorin et al. [840, 843], which is a modification of the butterfly scheme by Dyn et al. [198], and therefore often referred to as the *Modified Butterfly* (MB) scheme. This scheme is nonuniform, both because it uses different rules at the boundaries, and because different rules are used depending on the valence of the vertices. The main difference from Loop subdivision, however, is that it is interpolating, rather than approximating. An interpolating scheme means that once a vertex exists in the mesh, its location cannot change. Therefore, this scheme never modifies, but only generates new vertices for the edges. See Figure 12.44 for an example between interpolating and approximating schemes. The connectivity is the same as for Loop's scheme, shown in Figure 12.39.

The MB scheme uses four different subdivision rules for creating new vertices between two existing vertices. These are all described below, and the corresponding masks are shown in Figure 12.45.

1. Regular setting: Assume that we want to generate a new vertex between two existing vertices, **v** and **w**, that each has valence 6. These vertices are called regular or ordinary, and we call the situation a *regular setting*. The mask for this situation is shown to the left in Figure 12.45.

2. Semiregular setting: A *semiregular* setting occurs when one vertex is regular ($n = 6$), and another is irregular ($n \neq 6$), also called extraordinary, and we want to generate a new vertex between these vertices. The following

---

[6]These spline surfaces are out of the scope of this book. Consult Warren's book [792], the SIGGRAPH course [845], or Loop's thesis [503].

Figure 12.44. To the left is a simple three-dimensional star mesh. The middle image shows the resulting surface using Loop's subdivision scheme, which is approximating. The right image shows the result using the modified butterfly scheme, which is interpolating. An advantage of using interpolating schemes is that they often resemble the control mesh more than approximating schemes do. However, for detailed meshes the difference is not as distinct as shown here.

formula computes the new vertex, where n is the valence of the irregular vertex:

$$n = 3 : \quad w_0 = 5/12, \quad w_1 = -1/12, \quad w_2 = -1/12,$$
$$n = 4 : \quad w_0 = 3/8, \quad w_1 = 0, \quad w_2 = -1/8, \quad w_3 = 0,$$
$$n \geq 5 : \quad w_j = \frac{0.25 + \cos(2\pi j/n) + 0.5\cos(4\pi j/n)}{n}. \tag{12.64}$$

Note that we used only the immediate neighborhood of the irregular vertex to compute the new vertex, as shown in the mask in Figure 12.45.

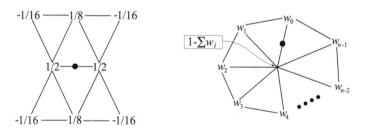

Figure 12.45. The mask to the left is the "butterfly" mask, which is used when generating a new vertex between two regular vertices (those with weights $1/2$). The mask to the right shows the weights when one vertex is irregular (the one with weight $1-\sum w_i$), and one vertex is regular (with weight w_0). Note that black circles indicate which vertex is generated. *(Illustration after Zorin et al. [845].)*

3. Irregular setting: When an edge connects two vertices, where both vertices are irregular ($n \neq 6$), we temporarily compute a new vertex for each of these two vertices using the formula for the semiregular setting (2). The average of these two vertices is used as the new vertex. This can happen at only the first subdivision step, because after that there will be only regular and semiregular settings in the mesh. Therefore the continuity of this choice does not affect the limit surface. Zorin et al. [840] note that this rule generates shapes with better fairness.

4. Boundaries: At boundaries, where an edge in the triangle mesh has only one triangle connected to it, the interpolating scheme [197] with $w = 1/16$, described in Section 12.5, is used. This means that the weights, whose masks are shown in Figure 12.45, are:

$$w_{-1} = -1/16, \quad w_0 = 9/16, \quad w_1 = 9/16, \quad w_2 = -1/16. \tag{12.65}$$

More types of boundary cases exist—consult the SIGGRAPH course for more about this [845]. Implementation details are discussed by Sharp [701]. Since this scheme is interpolating, limit positions of the vertices are the vertices themselves. Limit tangents are more complex to compute. For extraordinary vertices ($n \neq 6$), the tangents can be calculated using Equation 12.63, that is, the same formulae as for Loop [843]. For ordinary vertices ($n = 6$), the *2-ring* (also called the *2-neighborhood*) is used. The 1-ring and the 2-ring of an ordinary vertex, $\mathbf{p}$, is shown in Figure 12.46. The tangents vectors, $\mathbf{t}_u$ and $\mathbf{t}_v$, are then computed as:

$$\begin{aligned}
\mathbf{t}_u &= \mathbf{u} \cdot \mathbf{r}, \\
\mathbf{t}_v &= \mathbf{v} \cdot \mathbf{r},
\end{aligned} \tag{12.66}$$

where $\mathbf{r}$ is a vector of the difference vectors $\mathbf{p}_i - \mathbf{p}$ of the entire 2-ring, and $\mathbf{u}$ and $\mathbf{v}$ are vectors of scalars:

$$\begin{aligned}
\mathbf{r} &= (\mathbf{p}_0 - \mathbf{p}, \mathbf{p}_1 - \mathbf{p}, \mathbf{p}_2 - \mathbf{p}, \dots, \mathbf{p}_{16} - \mathbf{p}, \mathbf{p}_{17} - \mathbf{p}), \\
\mathbf{u} &= (16, -8, -8, 16, -8, -8, -\frac{8}{\sqrt{3}}, \frac{4}{\sqrt{3}}, \frac{4}{\sqrt{3}}, -\frac{8}{\sqrt{3}}, \frac{4}{\sqrt{3}}, \frac{4}{\sqrt{3}}, \\
&\quad\; 1, -\frac{1}{2}, -\frac{1}{2}, 1, -\frac{1}{2}, -\frac{1}{2}), \\
\mathbf{v} &= (0, 8, -8, 0, 8, -8, 0, -\frac{4}{\sqrt{3}}, \frac{4}{\sqrt{3}}, 0, -\frac{4}{\sqrt{3}}, \frac{4}{\sqrt{3}}, \\
&\quad\; 0, \frac{1}{2}, -\frac{1}{2}, 0, \frac{1}{2}, -\frac{1}{2}).
\end{aligned} \tag{12.67}$$

This means that, for example, $\mathbf{t}_u$ is computed as:

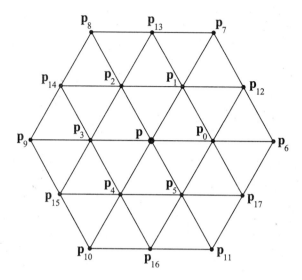

Figure 12.46. An ordinary vertex, $\mathbf{p}$, with its 1-ring $(\mathbf{p}_0, \ldots, \mathbf{p}_5)$, and its 2-ring $(\mathbf{p}_6, \ldots, \mathbf{p}_{17})$.

$$\mathbf{t}_u = 16(\mathbf{p}_0 - \mathbf{p}) - 8(\mathbf{p}_1 - \mathbf{p}) - \cdots - 0.5(\mathbf{p}_{17} - \mathbf{p}). \qquad (12.68)$$

After computing both t_u and $\mathbf{t}_v$, the normal is $\mathbf{n} = \mathbf{t}_u \times \mathbf{t}_v$.

When an interpolating scheme is desired, the MB scheme is a good choice. For example, say you have modeled a human, and decide that you want to subdivide it to get better shading. An interpolating scheme will generate a surface that is more like the control mesh. This is most notable when using meshes with few triangles. For larger meshes, the differences disappear. However, the interpolating characteristics come at the cost that the scheme may generate weird shapes with "unnatural" undulations, and thus, less fairness. This is common for all interpolating schemes. See Figure 12.47 for a nasty example. Another disadvantage is that the masks are bigger than those used for Loop's scheme and the $\sqrt{3}$-scheme presented in Section 12.6.3, and thus it is more expensive to evaluate.

Despite these disadvantages, interpolating schemes such as MB can be well-suited for real-time rendering work. Meshes for real-time work are normally not finely tessellated, so an interpolated surface is usually more intuitive, as it more closely matches the location of the control mesh. The tradeoff is that fairness problems can occur, but in many cases, minor adjustments to the underlying mesh can smooth out rippling [700]. The MB

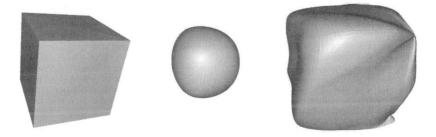

Figure 12.47. The cube on the left is subdivided using Loop's scheme (middle), and the modified butterfly scheme (right). Each face on the cube consists of two triangles. Note the "unnatural" undulations on the right surface. This is because it is much harder to interpolate a given set of vertices.

scheme is C^1-continuous all over the surface, even at irregular vertices [843]. See Figure 12.43 on page 536, and Figure 12.48 for two examples. More about this scheme can be found in Zorin's Ph.D. thesis [843] and in Sharp's articles [700, 701].

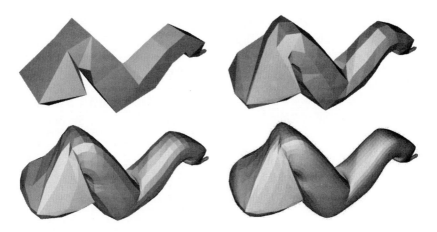

Figure 12.48. A worm is subdivided three times with the modified butterfly scheme. Notice that the vertices are interpolated at each subdivision step.

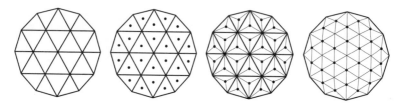

Figure 12.49. Illustration of the $\sqrt{3}$-subdivision scheme. A 1-to-3 split is performed instead of a 1-to-4 split as for Loop's and the modified butterfly schemes. First, a new vertex is generated at the center of each triangle. Then, this vertex is connected to the triangle's three vertices. Finally, the old edges are flipped. *(Illustration after Kobbelt [438].)*

12.6.3 $\sqrt{3}$-Subdivision

Both Loop's and the MB schemes split each triangle into four new ones, and so create triangles at a rate of $4^n m$, where m is the number of triangles in the control mesh, and n is the number of subdivision steps. A feature of Kobbelt's $\sqrt{3}$-scheme [438] is that it creates only three new triangles per subdivision step.[7] The trick is to create a new vertex (here called *mid-vertex*) in the middle of each triangle, instead of one new vertex per edge. This is shown in Figure 12.49. To get more uniformly shaped triangles, each old edge is flipped so that it connects two neighboring midvertices. In the subsequent subdivision step (and in every second subdivision step thereafter), the shapes of the triangles more resemble the initial triangle configuration due to this edge flip.

The subdivision rules are shown in Equation 12.69, where $\mathbf{p}_m$ denotes the midvertex, computed as the average of the triangle vertices: $\mathbf{p}_a$, $\mathbf{p}_b$, and $\mathbf{p}_c$. Each of the old vertices, $\mathbf{p}^k$, are updated using the formula in the second line, where $\mathbf{p}_i^k$ ($i = 0 \ldots n - 1$) denotes the immediate neighbors of $\mathbf{p}^k$, and n is the valence of $\mathbf{p}^k$. The subdivision step is denoted by k as before.

$$\mathbf{p}_m^{k+1} = (\mathbf{p}_a^k + \mathbf{p}_b^k + \mathbf{p}_c^k)/3$$

$$\mathbf{p}^{k+1} = (1 - n\beta)\mathbf{p}^k + \beta \sum_{i=0}^{n-1} \mathbf{p}_i^k \tag{12.69}$$

---

[7]The name stems from the fact that while Loop's and the MB schemes divide each edge into two new edges per subdivision step, Kobbelt's scheme creates three new edges per two subdivision steps. Thus the name $\sqrt{3}$-subdivision.

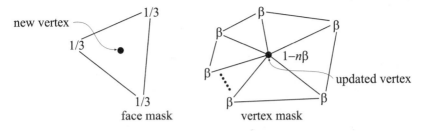

Figure 12.50. The masks for the $\sqrt{3}$-subdivision scheme. As can be seen, the face mask gives minimal support, since it uses only the three vertices of the triangle. The vertex mask uses all the vertices in the ring, called the 1-ring, around the vertex.

Again, β is a function of the valence n, and the following choice of $\beta(n)$ generates a surface that is C^2 continuous everywhere except at irregular vertices $(n \neq 6)$, where the continuity is at least C^1 [438].

$$\beta(n) = \frac{4 - 2\cos(2\pi/n)}{9n} \tag{12.70}$$

The masks, which are of minimum size, for the $\sqrt{3}$-scheme are shown in Figure 12.50.

The major advantage of this scheme is that it supports adaptive subdivision in a more natural way. See Kobbelt's paper [438] for details. Some other advantages of this scheme are smaller masks, and slower triangle growth rate than Loop's and the MB scheme.

The continuity of this scheme is the same as Loop's. Disadvantages include that the edge flip introduces a little complexity, and that the first subdivision step sometimes generates unintuitive shapes due to the flip. In Figure 12.51, a worm is subdivided with the $\sqrt{3}$-scheme, and in Figure 12.43 on page 536, a tetrahedron is subdivided.

12.6.4 Catmull-Clark Subdivision

The two most famous subdivision schemes that can handle polygonal meshes (rather than just triangles) are Catmull-Clark [117] and Doo-Sabin [183].[8] Here, we will only briefly present the former. Catmull-Clark surfaces have been used in Pixar's short film *Geri's Game* [171] and in *Toy Story 2*. As pointed out by DeRose et al. [171], Catmull-Clark surfaces tend to gener-

---

[8] Incidentally, both were presented in the same issue of the same journal.

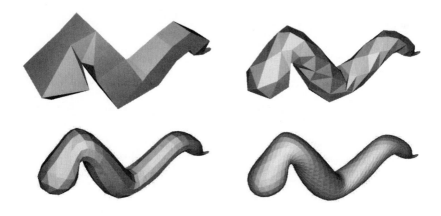

Figure 12.51. A worm is subdivided three times with the $\sqrt{3}$-subdivision scheme.

ate more symmetrical surfaces. For example, an oblong box results in a symmetrical ellipsoid-like surface, which agrees with intuition.

The basic idea for Catmull-Clark surfaces is shown in Figure 12.52, and an actual example of Catmull-Clark subdivision is shown in Figure 12.37 on page 531. As can be seen, this scheme only generates faces with four vertices. In fact, after the first subdivision step, only vertices of valence 4 are generated, thus such vertices are called ordinary or regular (compared to valence 6 for triangular schemes).

Following the notation from Halstead et al. [318], let us focus on a vertex $\mathbf{v}^k$ with n surrounding edge points $\mathbf{e}_i^k$, where $i = 0 \ldots n - 1$. Now, for each face, a new face point $\mathbf{f}^{k+1}$ is computed as the face centroid,

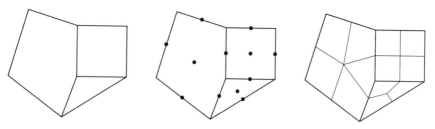

Figure 12.52. The basic idea of Catmull-Clark subdivision. Each polygon generates a new point, and each edge generates a new point. These are then connected as shown to the right. Weighting of the original points is not shown here.

i.e., the mean of the points of the face. Given this, the subdivision rules are [117, 318, 845]:

$$\mathbf{v}^{k+1} = \frac{n-2}{n}\mathbf{v}^k + \frac{1}{n^2}\sum_{j=1}^{n-1}\mathbf{e}_j^k + \frac{1}{n^2}\sum_{j=1}^{n-1}\mathbf{f}_j^{k+1},$$

$$\mathbf{e}_j^{k+1} = \frac{\mathbf{v}^k + \mathbf{e}_j^k + \mathbf{f}_{j-1}^{k+1} + \mathbf{f}_j^{k+1}}{4}.$$

(12.71)

As can be seen, new edge points are computed by the average of the considered vertex, the edge point, and the two newly created face points that have the edge as a neighbor. On the other hand, the vertex is computed as weighting of the considered vertex, the average of the edge points, and the average of the newly created face points.

The Catmull-Clark surface describes a generalized bicubic B-spline surface. So, for a mesh consisting only of regular vertices we could actually describe the surface as a B-spline surface.[9] However, this is not possible for irregular settings, and being able to do this using subdivision surfaces is one of the scheme's strengths. Limits positions and tangents are also possible to compute [318].

12.6.5 Piecewise Smooth Subdivision

In a sense, curved surfaces may be considered boring because they lack detail. Two ways to improve such surfaces are to use bump or displacement maps (Section 12.6.6). A third approach, *piecewise smooth subdivision*, is described here. The basic idea is to change the subdivision rules so that *darts, corners,* and *creases* can be used. This increases the range of different surfaces that can be modeled and represented. Hoppe et al. [364] first described this for Loop's subdivision surfaces. See Figure 12.53 for a comparison of a standard Loop subdivision surface, and one with piecewise smooth subdivision.

To actually be able to use such features on the surface, the edges that we want to be sharp are first tagged, so we know where to subdivide differently. The number of sharp edges coming in at a vertex is denoted s. Then the vertices are classified into: smooth ($s = 0$), dart ($s = 1$), crease ($s = 2$), and corner ($s > 2$). Therefore, a crease is a smooth curve on the surface, where the continuity across the curve is C^0. A dart is a nonboundary vertex where a crease ends and smoothly blends into the surface. Finally, a

---

[9]See the SIGGRAPH course notes for more on this topic [845].

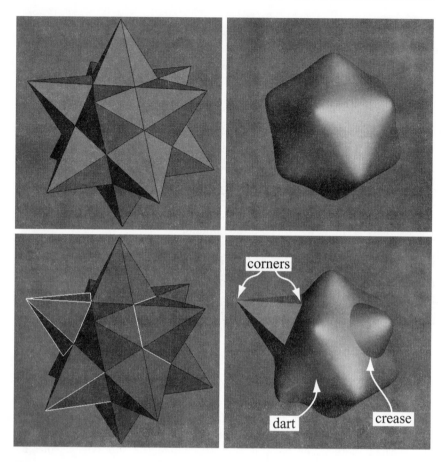

Figure 12.53. The top row shows a control mesh, and the limit surface using the standard Loop subdivision scheme. The bottom row shows piecewise smooth subdivision with Loop's scheme. The lower left image shows the control mesh with tagged edges (sharp) shown in a light gray. The resulting surface is shown to the lower right, with corners, darts, and creases marked. *(Image courtesy of Hugues Hoppe.)*

corner is a vertex where three or more creases come together. Boundaries can be used by marking each boundary edge as sharp.

After classifying the various vertex types, Hoppe et al. use a table to determine which mask to use for the various combinations. They also show how to compute limit surface points and limit tangents. Biermann et al. [60] present several improved subdivision rules. For example, when extraordinary vertices are located on a boundary, the previous rules could result in gaps. This is avoided with the new rules. Also, their rules make it possible to specify a normal at a vertex, and the resulting surface will adapt to get that normal at that point. DeRose et al. [171] present a technique for creating soft creases. Basically, they allow an edge to first be subdivided as sharp a number of times (including fractions), and after that, standard subdivision is used.

12.6.6 Displaced Subdivision

While parametric surfaces and subdivision surfaces are great for describing smooth surfaces, they are sometimes not that useful because the surfaces lack detail. One solution would be to use bump mapping (see Section 5.7.5). However, this is just an illusionary trick that changes the normal in each pixel, and thus, the shading. The silhouette of an object looks the same with or without bump mapping. The natural extension of bump mapping is *displacement mapping* [140], where the surface is displaced. This is usually done along the direction of the normal. So, if the point of the surface is $\mathbf{p}$, and its normalized normal is $\mathbf{n} = \mathbf{n}'/||\mathbf{n}'||$, then the point on the displaced surface is:

$$\mathbf{s} = \mathbf{p} + d\mathbf{n}. \qquad (12.72)$$

Here, the scalar d is the displacement at the point $\mathbf{p}$. The displacement could also be vector-valued [444]. An example of this technique used for parametric surfaces is shown in Figure 5.39 on page 177.

In this section, the *displaced subdivision surface* [479] will be presented. The general idea is to describe a displaced surface as a coarse control mesh that is subdivided into a smooth surface that is then displaced along its normal using a scalar field. In the context of displaced subdivision surfaces, $\mathbf{p}$ in Equation 12.72 is the limit point on the subdivision surface (of the coarse control mesh), and $\mathbf{n}$ is the normalized normal at $\mathbf{p}$, computed as:

$$\mathbf{n}' = \mathbf{p}_u \times \mathbf{p}_v,$$

$$\mathbf{n} = \frac{\mathbf{n}'}{||\mathbf{n}'||}. \qquad (12.73)$$

In Equation 12.73, $\mathbf{p}_u$ and $\mathbf{p}_v$ are the first-order derivative of the subdivision surface. Thus, they describe two tangents at $\mathbf{p}$. Lee et al. [479] use a Loop subdivision surface for the coarse control mesh, and its tangents can be computed using Equation 12.63. Note that the notation is slightly different here; we use $\mathbf{p}_u$ and $\mathbf{p}_v$ instead of $\mathbf{t}_u$ and $\mathbf{t}_v$. Equation 12.72

describes the displaced position of the resulting surface, but we also need a normal, $\mathbf{n}_s$, on the displaced subdivision surface in order to render it correctly. It is computed analytically as shown below [479]:

$$\mathbf{s}_u = \frac{\partial \mathbf{s}}{\partial u} = \mathbf{p}_u + d_u \mathbf{n} + d\mathbf{n}_u,$$

$$\mathbf{s}_v = \frac{\partial \mathbf{s}}{\partial v} = \mathbf{p}_v + d_v \mathbf{n} + d\mathbf{n}_v, \tag{12.74}$$

$$\mathbf{n}_s = \mathbf{s}_u \times \mathbf{s}_v.$$

To simplify computations, Blinn [70] suggests that the third term can be ignored if the displacements are small. Otherwise, the following expressions can be used to compute $\mathbf{n}_u$ (and similarly $\mathbf{n}_v$) [479]:

$$\bar{\mathbf{n}}_u = \mathbf{p}_{uu} \times \mathbf{p}_v + \mathbf{p}_u \times \mathbf{p}_{uv},$$

$$\mathbf{n}_u = \frac{\bar{\mathbf{n}}_u - (\bar{\mathbf{n}}_u \cdot \mathbf{n})\mathbf{n}}{||\mathbf{n}'||}. \tag{12.75}$$

Note that $\bar{\mathbf{n}}_u$ is not any new notation, it is merely a "temporary" variable in the computations. For an ordinary vertex (valence $n = 6$), the first and second order derivatives are particularly simple. Their masks are shown in Figure 12.54. For an extraordinary vertex (valence $n \neq 6$), the third term in rows one and two in Equation 12.74 is omitted.

The displacement map for one triangle in the coarse mesh is a scalar field, that is, a heightfield. The storage requirements for one triangle is one half of $(2^k + 1) \times (2^k + 1)$, where k is the number of subdivisions that

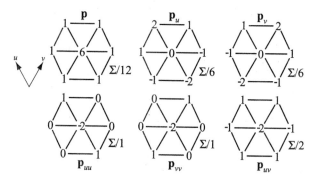

Figure 12.54. The masks for an ordinary vertex in Loop's subdivision scheme. Note that after using these masks, the resulting sum should be divided as shown. *(Illustration after Lee et al. [479].)*

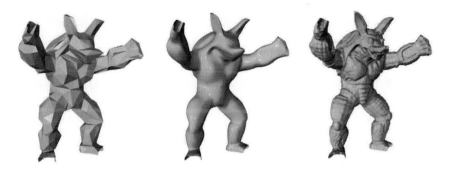

Figure 12.55. To the left is a coarse mesh. In the middle, it is subdivided using Loop's subdivision scheme. The right image shows the displaced subdivision surface. *(Image courtesy Aaron Lee, Henry Moreton, and Hugues Hoppe.)*

the displacement map should be able to handle, which depends on the desired accuracy. The displacement map uses the same parameterization as the underlying subdivision mesh. So, for example, when one triangle is subdivided, three new points are created. Displacements for these three points are retrieved from the displacement map. This is done for k subdivision levels. If subdivision continues past this maximum of k levels, the displacement map is subdivided as well, using Loop's subdivision scheme. The subdivided displacement, d, is added using Equation 12.72. When the object is farther away, the displacement map is pushed to the limit points, and a mipmap pyramid of displacements is built as a preprocess and used. The resulting displaced subdivision surface is C^1 everywhere, except at extraordinary vertices, where it is C^0. Remember that after sufficiently many subdivision steps, there is only a small fraction of vertices that are extraordinary. An example is shown in Figure 12.55.

When a displaced surface is far away from the viewer, standard bump mapping could be used to give the illusion of a displaced surface. This is especially advantageous if the rendering bottleneck is geometry processing. Some bump mapping schemes need a tangent space coordinate system at the vertex, and the following can be used for that: $(\mathbf{b}, \mathbf{t}, \mathbf{n})$, where $\mathbf{t} = \mathbf{p}_u / \|\mathbf{p}_u\|$ and $\mathbf{b} = \mathbf{n} \times \mathbf{t}$.

Lee et al. [479] also present how adaptive tessellation and backpatch culling can be used to accelerate rendering. More importantly, they present algorithms to derive the control mesh and the displacement field from a detailed polygon mesh. See page 176 for displacement mapping of a triangle mesh.

12.6.7   Normal, Texture, and Color Interpolation

In this section, we will present different strategies for dealing with normals, texture coordinates and color per vertex.

As shown for Loop's scheme in Section 12.6.1, and the MB scheme in Section 12.6.2, limit tangents, and thus, limit normals can be computed explicitly. This involves trigonometric functions that are expensive to evaluate. However, a very short look-up table can do the job efficiently. Another approach is to compute limit normals (that are exact) at the vertices of the control mesh, and then use the same subdivision scheme used for the vertices to subdivide the normals as well [399]. However, this increases the storage need during subdivision, and it is not obvious whether this is faster. Also, with this scheme, the exact normals will not be generated in the end.

Assume that each vertex in a mesh has a texture coordinate and a color. To be able to use these for subdivision surfaces, we also have to create colors and texture coordinates for each newly generated vertex, too. The most obvious way to do this is to use the same subdivision scheme as we used for subdividing the polygon mesh. For example, you can treat the colors as four dimensional vectors (RGBA), and subdivide these to create new colors for the new vertices [701]. This is a reasonable way to do it, since the color will have a continuous derivative (assuming the subdivision scheme is at least C^1), and thus abrupt changes in colors are avoided over the surface The same can certainly be done for texture coordinates [171], though some argue that linear interpolation works better for the MB scheme [701], i.e., when you create a new vertex on an edge between two existing vertices, you simply use the average of the texture coordinates of the existing vertices for the new vertex. Once you have the basic subdivision machinery in place, it is simple to try both approaches to find what is best in your application. Note also that several different textures may be used on a surface, so that the vertices may have several different sets of texture coordinates. A sophisticated scheme for texturing subdivision surfaces is given by Piponi and Borshukov [627].

12.6.8   Practical Subdivision and Rendering

In order to implement a subdivision scheme, it is clear from the formulae that the neighboring vertices of a vertex or edge are needed. This adjacency information can be obtained using the technique presented in Section 11.3. After that, subdivision of the mesh can start. Depending on the subdivision scheme, each vertex, edge, and/or face is processed, possibly generating a new or updated vertex using the subdivision rules for that scheme. Care must be taken not to overwrite old vertex information, as this may be needed to update or create other vertices. When all points have been created, it is time to update all the adjacency information to reflect the new subdivided mesh. This is not hard to do, but tedious to implement. Thus, the major parts of this technique are neighbor finding (of vertex, edges, faces), and mesh updating after subdivision. Still, this method works pretty well, and can also be adapted to deal with the Catmull-Clark and Doo-Sabin schemes too. However, in terms of performance and memory it is not always the best choice. That said, if the surface is just going to be subdivided once and then used as such, all extra allocated memory can be freed after subdivision and triangles strips can be created for efficient rendering.

Some schemes for more efficient subdivision, and an adaptive subdivision technique, are presented below.

Uniform Subdivision

For uniform subdivision, that is, where each triangle is subdivided a fixed number of times without any adaptivity, a two-dimensional array can be allocated for each top-level triangle [845]. Assume that subdivision should be done k times, where $k > 1$. For each edge in a top-level triangle,

$$n = 2 + \frac{k(k+1)}{2}$$

vertices result. Then, for that top-level triangle, $(n+1)n/2$ vertices are created. An array, A, of vertex pointers of the same size is allocated. On row r, where $0 \le r < n$, $r+1$ vertices are stored. Therefore, an array, B, of length n is allocated, and each element in that array points into the address in A, where the first vertex on that row is located. This is illustrated in Figure 12.56. So, to find a vertex on row i, simply find the pointer to the first vertex on that row as $B[i]$. Then, to find a vertex on column j on that row, simply access $B[i][j]$. As can be seen, this arrangement simplifies neighbor finding. There are six neighbors for each vertex at (i, j), and these are at $(i \pm 1, j)$, $(i, j \pm 1)$, $(i - 1, j - 1)$, and $(i + 1, j + 1)$. Care has to be taken near the boundary so that the neighbors of adjacent triangles are accessed. Neighbor finding is much simpler than the method described in the introduction of Section 12.6.8, and updating the mesh is implicit in this method.

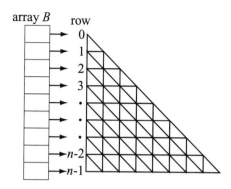

Figure 12.56. The array A is used to point into a the array of vertices. Each pointer points at the first vertex on the respective row. This arrangement makes neighbor finding simple (see text).

Rapid Subdivision by Tabulation

Here, a technique for extremely fast subdivision will be presented. It was independently developed by Bloom [82], Bolz and Schröder [96], and Brickhill [102]. Here, the presentation by Bolz and Schröder will be followed, mostly because they flesh out more details than the others and they provide an implementation online. We restrict our discussion to triangle-based schemes, even though Bolz and Schröder use Catmull-Clark subdivision surfaces (which uses quads after the first subdivision).

Each newly updated or created point during subdivision always is some linear combination of the vertices from the previous subdivision step. This implies that each vertex, whatever the level of subdivision, is a linear combination of the vertices of the control mesh. Since only the immediate neighborhood of a vertex or edge is used to update or create a vertex, only the neighboring vertices of a triangle will be used in that linear combination in order to create new points inside that triangle (this is also true for the limit points on the surface) [96]:

$$\mathbf{s}(u, v) = \sum_i B^i(u, v)\mathbf{p}_i. \tag{12.76}$$

Here, $\mathbf{s}$ is a new subdivided point at the parametric coordinates (u, v). The B^i is a basis function, and the points $\mathbf{p}_i$, are the neighboring vertices. By restricting the maximum level of subdivision (Bolz and Schröder use five), and by allowing only uniform generation of points inside a triangle, a finite-sized table, B^i, can be built that stores these constants. This is possible also because the contents of the table depend only on the connectivity in the mesh, and not on the positions of the vertices. The new evaluation formula then becomes:

$$\mathbf{s}(u_m, v_n) = \sum_i B^i(u_m, v_n)\mathbf{p}_i. \tag{12.77}$$

Here the (u_m, v_n) describes a point in the subdivision up to the maximum subdivision limit. The basis functions, $B^i(u_m, v_n)$, can be computed and stored during "normal" subdivision, using, for example, the method described in the beginning of Section 12.6.8.

Once the tables, B^i, have been created, each triangle in the control mesh is processed in turn. For each triangle, a part of the subdivision surface is generated. First, the neighboring vertices of the triangle are fetched, and then the tables are used to generate points on the surface "inside" that triangle. This is very fast since recursion and neighbor finding are avoided. By moving the vertices of the control mesh each frame, the subdivision process has to be done each frame too, in order to generate the subdivision surface. For more details, consult Bolz and Schröder [96], who implement the algorithm efficiently using Intel's SSE instructions.

Adaptive Subdivision

The limit surface is achieved only after infinitely many subdivision steps. Clearly, this is not feasible. Often, only a few (3–5) steps are done, and then the vertices are pushed to the limit surface (only needed for approximating schemes). The subdivision procedure gives exponential growth of triangles (or polygons), and thus we may waste triangles in areas where the geometry changes slowly. Therefore, *adaptive subdivision* of the meshes is useful. See also Section 12.3.2 for algorithms for adaptive tessellation. The tests presented there for determining when to tessellate further can be used with little or no change for subdivision surfaces. Note that to subdivide a point one more step, say, to level n, the neighbors that are used in computing the new point must all be subdivided to level $n - 1$. If points from, say, level $n - 2$ are used, then incorrect subdivision will occur.

Using the tabulation technique for rapid subdivision just described, adaptive subdivision is fairly simple. As pointed out by Bolz and Schröder, each top-level triangle (or quad), is tessellated independently of the others, and therefore different tessellation rates can be used for different top-level triangles. Cracks appear between two top-level triangles if they are subdivided a different number of times. A simple solution is to create triangle fans (see Section 11.4) between such top-level triangles. This is illustrated in Figure 12.57. This allows for adjacent top-level triangles to be subdi-

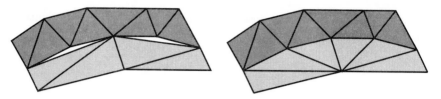

Figure 12.57. To the left, two top-level triangles (light and dark gray) have been tessellated to different levels. Thus, they do not match up, and cracks appear. To the right, this is fixed by creating a fan from the top-level triangle with lowest degree of tessellation.

vided to levels that differ by more than one level. However, the triangles in the fan may be degenerate (long and thin). The presented approach is not as flexible as the methods by Zorin et al. [842], Kobbelt [438], or Müller and Havemann [576], where tessellation may be adapted at any point in the subdivision process.

A comparison of uniform and adaptive subdivision is shown in Figure 12.58. See Plate XLVIII (following page 562) for shaded versions of these meshes. As can be seen, the shading and the silhouette look much better on the adaptively subdivided surface.

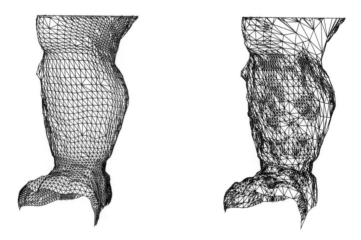

Figure 12.58. Left: uniform subdivision with 9,000 triangles. Right: adaptive subdivision using approximately the same number of triangles. *(Image courtesy of Denis Zorin.)*

Further Reading and Resources

The topic of curves and surfaces is huge, and for more information, it is best to consult the books that focus solely on this topic. Mortenson's book [573] serves as a good general introduction to geometric modeling. Books by Farin [224, 227], and by Hoschek and Lasser [371] are general and treat many aspects of *Computer Aided Geometric Design* (CAGD). For implicit surfaces, consult the excellent book by Bloomenthal et al. [89]. For much more information on subdivision surfaces, consult Warren and Heimer's book [792], and the SIGGRAPH course notes on "Subdivision for Modeling and Animation" [845] by Zorin et al.

For spline interpolation, we refer the interested reader to Watt and Watt [793], Rogers [656], and the Killer-B's book [47]. Many properties of Bernstein polynomials, both for curves and surfaces, are given by Goldman [272]. Almost everything about triangular Bézier surfaces can be found in Farin's article [223]. Another class of rational curves and surfaces are the Non-Uniform Rational B-Splines (NURBS) [226, 625, 658]

An easy-to-read article on how to implement a subdivision algorithm is given by Sharp [701], which is a follow-up article on subdivision surface theory [700]. While Kobbelt's $\sqrt{3}$-scheme is approximating, there is also an interpolating $\sqrt{3}$-scheme [449]. Proposals for implementing Loop's subdivision scheme in hardware have been presented by various researchers [637, 64]. Biermann et al. present schemes that have normal control [60], i.e., that a normal can be set at a vertex and a tangent-plane continuous surface generated. Many good presentations on continuity analysis on subdivision surfaces are available [438, 650, 792, 841, 844, 845]. See also Stam's paper [727] on how to evaluate Catmull-Clark at arbitrary parameter values using explicit formulae.

Chapter 13
Intersection Test Methods

"I'll sit and see if that small sailing cloud
Will hit or miss the moon."
–Robert Frost

Intersection testing is often used in computer graphics. We may wish to click the mouse on an object, or to determine whether two objects collide, or to make sure we maintain a constant height for our viewer as we navigate a building. All of these operations can be performed with intersection tests. Given its wide range of uses, intersection testing is an operation that will remain in the application stage of the pipeline for the foreseeable future. In this chapter, we cover the most common ray/object and object/object intersection tests.

In interactive computer graphics applications, it is often desirable to let the user select a certain object by *picking* (clicking) on it with the mouse or any other input device. Naturally, the performance of such an operation needs to be high. One picking method, supported by OpenGL, is to render all objects into a tiny pick window. All the objects that overlap the window are returned in a list, along with the minimum and maximum z-depth found for each object. This sort of system usually has the added advantage of being able to pick on lines and vertices in addition to surfaces. This pick method is always implemented entirely on the host processor and does not use the graphics accelerator. Some other picking methods do use the graphics hardware, and are covered in Section 13.1.

Intersection testing offers some benefits that OpenGL's picking method does not. Comparing a ray against a triangle is normally faster than sending the triangle through OpenGL, having it clipped against a pick window, then inquiring whether the triangle was picked. Intersection testing methods can compute the location, normal vector, texture coordinates, and other surface data. Such methods are also independent of API support (or lack thereof).

The picking problem can be solved efficiently by using a bounding volume hierarchy. First, we compute the ray from the camera's position through the pixel that the user picked. Then, we recursively test whether this ray hits a bounding volume of the scene graph. If at any time the ray misses a *Bounding Volume* (BV), then that subtree can be discarded from further tests, since the ray will not hit any of its contents. However, if the ray hits a BV, its children's BVs must be tested as well. Finally, the recursion may end in a leaf that contains geometry, in which case the ray must be tested against each primitive in the geometry node.

As we have seen in Section 9.4, view frustum culling is a means for efficiently discarding geometry that is outside the view frustum. Tests that decide whether a bounding volume is totally outside, totally inside, or partially inside a frustum are needed to use this method.

In collision detection algorithms (see Chapter 14), which are also built upon hierarchies, the system must decide whether or not two primitive objects collide. These primitive objects include triangles, spheres, *Axis-aligned Bounding Boxes* (AABBs), *Oriented Bounding Boxes* (OBBs), and *Discrete Oriented Polytopes* (k-DOPs).

In all of these cases, we have encountered a certain class of problems that require *intersection tests*. An intersection test determines whether two objects, A and B, intersect, which may mean that A is totally inside B (or vice versa), that the boundaries of A and B intersect, or that they are totally disjoint. However, sometimes more information may be needed, such as the exact intersection point(s), the distance(s) to the intersection point(s), etc. In this chapter, a set of fast intersection test methods is identified and studied thoroughly. We not only present the basic algorithms, but also give advice on how to construct new and efficient intersection test methods. Naturally, the methods presented in this chapter are also of use in offline computer graphics applications. For example, the algorithms presented in Sections 13.5 through 13.8 can be used in ray tracing and global illumination programs.

After briefly covering hardware-accelerated picking methods, this chapter continues with some useful definitions, followed by algorithms for forming bounding volumes around primitives. Rules of thumb for constructing efficient intersection test methods are presented next. Finally, the bulk of the chapter is made up of a cookbook of intersection test methods.

13.1 Hardware-Accelerated Picking

There are a few hardware-accelerated picking methods worth mentioning. One method was first presented by Hanrahan and Haeberli [320]. To support picking, the scene is rendered into the Z-buffer with lighting off and with each polygon having a unique color value that is used as an identifier. The image formed is stored off-screen and is then used for extremely rapid picking. When the user clicks on a pixel, the color identifier is looked up in this image and the polygon is immediately identified. The major disadvantage of this method is that the entire scene must be rendered in a separate pass to support this sort of picking. This method was originally presented in the context of a three-dimensional paint system. In this sort of application, the amount of picking per view is extremely high, so the cost of forming the buffer once for the view becomes inconsequential.

It is also possible to find the relative location of a point inside a triangle using the color buffer [466]. Each triangle is rendered using Gouraud interpolation, where the colors of the triangle vertices are red $(255, 0, 0)$, green $(0, 255, 0)$, and blue $(0, 0, 255)$. Say that the color of the picked pixel is $(23, 192, 40)$, This means that the red vertex contributes with a factor $23/255$, the green with $192/255$, and the red with $40/255$. This information can be used to find out the actual coordinates on the triangle, the (u, v) coordinates of the picked point, and for normal interpolation. The values are barycentric coordinates, which are discussed further in Section 13.7.1. In the same manner, the normals of the vertices can be directly encoded into RGB colors. The interval $[-1, 1]$ per normal component has to be transformed to the interval $[0, 1]$ so it can be rendered. After rendering the triangles using Gouraud interpolation, the normal at any point can be read from the color buffer.

Another method of using graphics hardware for picking is to render the identifiers into the stencil buffer. When z-buffering is used, also using the stencil buffer comes for free if the 8 bits of the stencil buffer share the same word as the 24 bits of the Z-buffer.[1] So, pick identifiers can be used at no extra cost while rendering the scene itself. The limitation is that there are only 256 identifiers available. One way to overcome this limit is to split the scene into 255 parts (with one identifier left over for the background) and use the rendering pass to identify a range of polygons picked. Then, rerender just this range to the stencil buffer, splitting it into 255 parts; repeat until done. The additional passes normally take little extra time compared with rendering the whole scene.

13.2 Definitions and Tools

This section introduces notation and definitions useful for this entire chapter.

---

[1] ATI and NVIDIA hardware do this, for example.

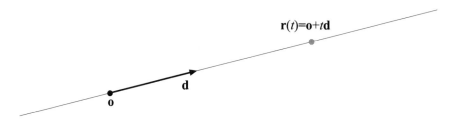

Figure 13.1. A simple ray and its parameters: **o** (the ray origin), **d** (the ray direction), and t, which generates different points on the ray, $\mathbf{r}(t) = \mathbf{o} + t\mathbf{d}$.

A ray, $\mathbf{r}(t)$, is defined by an origin point, **o**, and a direction vector, **d** (which, for convenience, is usually normalized, so $||\mathbf{d}|| = 1$). Its mathematical formula is shown in Equation 13.1, and an illustration of a ray is shown in Figure 13.1.

$$\mathbf{r}(t) = \mathbf{o} + t\mathbf{d} \qquad (13.1)$$

The scalar t is a variable that is used to generate different points on the ray, where t-values of less than zero are said to lie behind the ray origin (and so are not part of the ray), and the positive t-values lie in front of it. Also, since the ray direction is normalized, a t-value generates a point on the ray that is situated t distance units from the ray origin.

In practice, we often store a current distance l, which is the maximum distance we want to search along the ray. For example, while picking, we usually want the closest intersection along the ray; objects beyond this intersection can be safely ignored. The distance l starts at ∞. As objects are successfully intersected, l is updated with the intersection distance. In the ray/object intersection tests we will be discussing, we will normally not include l in the discussion. If you wish to use l, all you have to do is perform the ordinary ray/object test, then check l against the intersection distance computed and take the appropriate action.

When talking about surfaces, we distinguish *implicit* surfaces from *explicit* surfaces. An implicit surface is defined by Equation 13.2.

$$f(\mathbf{p}) = f(p_x, p_y, p_z) = 0 \qquad (13.2)$$

Here, **p** is any point on the surface. This means that if you have a point that lies on the surface and you plug this point into f, then the result will be 0. Otherwise, the result from f will be nonzero. An example of an implicit surface is $p_x^2 + p_y^2 + p_z^2 = r^2$, which describes a sphere located at the origin with radius r. It is easily seen that this can be rewritten as $f(\mathbf{p}) = p_x^2 + p_y^2 + p_z^2 - r^2 = 0$, which means that it is indeed implicit. Implicit surfaces are briefly covered in Section 12.4, while modeling and rendering with a wide variety of implicit surface types is well covered in Bloomenthal et al. [89].

An explicit surface, on the other hand, is defined by a vector function $\mathbf{f}$ and some parameters $(\rho, \phi)^2$, rather than a point on the surface. Those (valid) parameters yield points, $\mathbf{p}$, on the surface. Equation 13.3 below shows the general idea:

$$\mathbf{p} = \begin{pmatrix} p_x \\ p_y \\ p_z \end{pmatrix} = \mathbf{f}(\rho, \phi) = \begin{pmatrix} f_x(\rho, \phi) \\ f_y(\rho, \phi) \\ f_z(\rho, \phi) \end{pmatrix}. \tag{13.3}$$

An example of an explicit surface is again the sphere, this time expressed in spherical coordinates, where ρ is the latitude and ϕ longitude, as shown in Equation 13.4.

$$\mathbf{f}(\rho, \phi) = \begin{pmatrix} r \sin \rho \cos \phi \\ r \sin \rho \sin \phi \\ r \cos \rho \end{pmatrix} \tag{13.4}$$

As another example, a triangle, $\triangle \mathbf{v}_0 \mathbf{v}_1 \mathbf{v}_2$, can be described in explicit form like this: $\mathbf{t}(u, v) = (1 - u - v)\mathbf{v}_0 + u\mathbf{v}_1 + v\mathbf{v}_2$, where $u \geq 0$, $v \geq 0$ and $u + v \leq 1$ must hold.

Finally, we shall give definitions of three bounding volumes, namely the AABB, the OBB, and the k-DOP, used extensively in this and the next chapter.

Definition: An *Axis-aligned Bounding Box*[3] (also called *rectangular box*), AABB for short, is a box whose faces have normals that coincide with the standard basis axes. For example, an AABB called A is described by two extreme points, $\mathbf{a}^{min}$ and $\mathbf{a}^{max}$, where $\mathbf{a}_i^{min} \leq \mathbf{a}_i^{max}$, $\forall i \in \{x, y, z\}$. □

Figure 13.2 contains an illustration of a three-dimensional AABB together with notation.

Definition: An *Oriented Bounding Box*, OBB for short, is a box whose faces have normals that are all pairwise orthogonal—i.e., it is an AABB

---

[2]The number of parameters is not limited to two, but can, in theory, be any number; however, two is the most common.

[3]In fact, neither the AABB nor OBB needs to be used as a BV, but can act as a pure geometric box. However, these names are widely accepted.

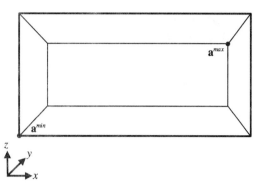

Figure 13.2. A three-dimensional AABB, called A, with its extreme points, $\mathbf{a}^{min}$ and $\mathbf{a}^{max}$, and the axes of the standard basis.

that is arbitrarily rotated. An OBB, called, for example, B, can be described by the center point of the box, $\mathbf{b}^c$, and three normalized vectors, $\mathbf{b}^u$, $\mathbf{b}^v$, and $\mathbf{b}^w$, that describe the side directions of the box. Their respective positive half-lengths are denoted h_u^B, h_v^B, and h_w^B, which is the distance from $\mathbf{b}^c$ to the center of the respective face. $\qquad\square$

A three-dimensional OBB and its notation are depicted in Figure 13.3.

Definition: A k-DOP (*Discrete Oriented Polytope*) is defined by $k/2$ (where k is even) normalized normals (orientations), $\mathbf{n}_i$, $1 \leq i \leq k/2$, and

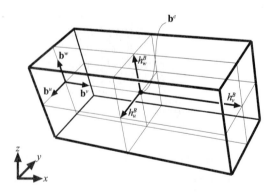

Figure 13.3. A three-dimensional OBB, called B, with its center point, $\mathbf{b}^c$, and its normalized, positively oriented side vectors, called $\mathbf{b}^u$, $\mathbf{b}^v$, and $\mathbf{b}^w$. The half-lengths of the sides, h_u^B, h_v^B, and h_w^B, are the distances from the center of the box to the center of the faces, as shown.

Plate XXVI. Character lighting performed using an irradiance map. *(Image courtesy of the game "Dead or Alive ® 3", Tecmo, Ltd. 2001.)*

Plate XXVII. A shader language program performed as a series of texture applications. The series shown here displays some (not all) intermediate steps. In practice, multiple stages are typically rendered in a single pass. In the leftmost image, the base texture is applied; the next figure shows the result after three decal textures are each applied, then the marks are shown, then the diffuse lighting, and finally specular highlighting. *(Images courtesy of Kekoa Proudfoot, Computer Graphics Laboratory, Stanford University.)*

Plate XXVIII. Motion blur done using the accumulation buffer.

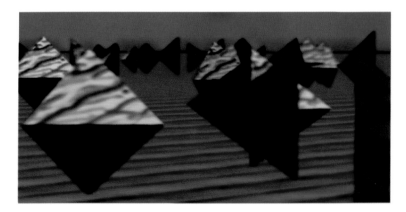

Plate XXIX. Depth of field done by rendering the scene in layers and blurring out of focus layers using pixel shaders. *(Image courtesy of NVIDIA Corp.)*

Plate XXX. The waterfall image at the bottom is generated in a number of steps. Reflections of the scene are rendered to one texture, flipping the scene along the water's surface. The geometry underneath the water is rendered to a refraction texture. The water surface is then rendered using a vertex shader with four crossing sine waves to perturb the mesh. Two additive bump maps are used to perturb the surface per pixel. These perturbations vary the access of the two rendered textures, so giving a realistic reflection and refraction effect. A Fresnel term is used to further improve the water's appearance. *(Images by Alex Vlachos, John Isidoro, Dave Gosselin, and Eli Turner; courtesy of ATI Technologies Inc.)*

Plate XXXI. An image from the Xbox game "Halo." Soft shadows are rendered by using a blurred drop shadow texture generated from the ship. Pyrotechnics are rendered using billboarding techniques. *(Image courtesy of Bungie and Microsoft Corp.)*

Plate XXXII. Castle model, viewable in real-time, 40,760 polygons. The lighting is precomputed using radiosity, with the larger surfaces' lighting contributions captured as light map textures. The water reflection is done by mirroring polygons through the water's surface and blending them with the textured water polygon. The chandelier and some other elements are replaced with sets of textured polygons. *(Image courtesy of Agata and Andrzej Wojaczek (agand@clo.com), Advanced Graphics Applications Inc.)*

Plate XXXIII. An image with "ray tracing quality" rendered with commodity graphics hardware. Shadows were generated with the shadow mapping algorithm, and the recursive reflections were rendered with environment mapping for nonplanar objects, and with a render-to-texture technique for the planes. *(Image courtesy of Kasper Høy Nielsen.)*

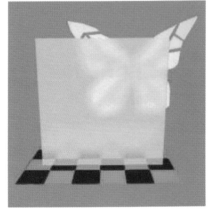

Plate XXXIV. Fuzzy reflections and refractions, done by using the accumulation and stencil buffers along with fog. Window design by Elsa Schmid. *(Images courtesy of Paul Diefenbach.)*

Plate XXXV. A still from the game "Splashdown" for the Playstation 2. The water is properly affected by the Fresnel effect, in which transparency decreases and reflection increases as the viewing angle comes close to grazing. The froth is rendered with a combination of an additional water rendering pass of tiled textured froth, along with particles splashed into the air. The water detail is handled with triangles in a proprietary level of detail scheme. The trees are billboards at a distance, becoming blended with more complete three-dimensional trees as they become nearer. Using a physics simulator, the water responds to the boats, and the boats respond to the water. *(Image courtesy of Atari and Rainbow Studios.)*

Plate XXXVI. Refraction and reflection by a glass ball of a cubic environment map, with the map itself used as a skybox background. *(Image courtesy of NVIDIA Corp.)*

Plate XXXVII. Simplification of a radiosity solution. Left is a rendering of the original mesh (150,983 faces); right is the simplified mesh (10,000 faces). *(Images courtesy of Hugues Hoppe, Microsoft Research.)*

Plate XXXVIII. The skin of the wolfman uses four textures: color, a normal map for bumps, a one-dimensional map encoding the specular function, and a map for self-shadowing. The wolfman's fur is rendered using an extension of the shells and fins technique [488]. Eight concentric layers are generated, using the vertex shader to displace each layer outwards along the surface normals. Each layer has a different two-dimensional texture that represents a slice of the fur geometry. This texture stores a per texel tangent vector in the RGB channels and a fur density in alpha. The pixel shader uses this tangent vector to light the fur with an anisotropic lighting model. A separate texture is used to color the fur and also to mark areas where no fur should appear. "Fin" quadrangles are generated for each edge in the base mesh. Each fin is textured and faded out based on the surface normal's angle to the eye, giving a fuzzy look to the edges. The character uses matrix palette skinning in the vertex shader. In total the character has 61 bones, and the scene has 100K polygons per frame. It runs at 30 fps on a GeForce4. (*Image courtesy of NVIDIA Corp.*)

Plate XXXIX. A still from the animation *Chicken Crossing*, rendered using a Talisman simulator. In this scene, 80 layers of sprites are used, some of which are outlined and shown on the left. Since the chicken wing is partially in front of and behind the tailgate, both were placed in a single sprite. *(Reprinted with permission from Microsoft Corporation.)*

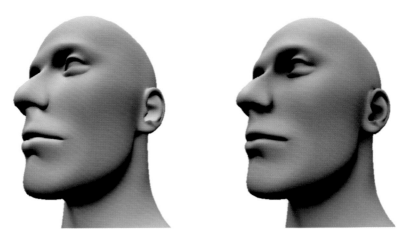

Plate XL. The original model, on the left, is preprocessed to give a more realistic shading, on the right. Ray casting from each vertex is used to precompute geometric self-shadowing. *(Reprinted with permission from Microsoft Corporation.)*

Plate XLI. A toon-style rendered image from the game "Cel Damage." The silhouette edges are rendered by expanding the mesh of the object outwards and rendering its backfaces in black. *(Image courtesy of Pseudo Interactive Inc.)*

Plate XLII. Image processing done with pixel shaders is used to render silhouette edges. On the left is an image where the surface normals are rendered as colors. On the right, a pixel shader determines where adjacent normals differ and colors such pixels black. The surface is rendered using a non-photorealistic shader in the style of Gooch et al. [278]. *(Images courtesy of Drew Card and Jason L. Mitchell, ATI Technologies Inc.)*

Plate XLIII. Special effects from "Shogo: Mobile Armored Division". Screen-aligned billboarding with alpha blended textures gives the explosion trails and smoke. The animated fire textured onto a polygon provides realism. A transparent sphere shows a shock wave effect. *(Image courtesy of Monolith Productions Inc.)*

Plate XLIV. The clouds in the scene are rendered with a set of world-oriented impostors [322]. The terrain consists of approximately 65,000 tristripped triangles. By loading this data once into video memory using NVIDIA's Vertex Array Range extension, the cost to the CPU of rendering the terrain is negligible. The clouds in the distance are rendered with a skybox. *(Image courtesy of Mark Harris, UNC-Chapel Hill.)*

Plates XLV. Neighboring pixels in a texture can be accessed by modifying texture coordinates, and pixel shaders can be used to perform image processing operations. In the upper left is the original texture, the upper right shows a Gaussian difference operation, the lower left an edge detection, and the lower right a composite of this edge detection with the original image. *(Images courtesy of Greg James, NVIDIA Corp.)*

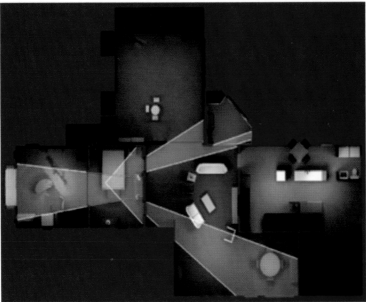

Plate XLVI. Portal culling. The left image is an overhead view of the Brooks House. The right image is a view from the master bedroom. Cull boxes for portals are in white and for mirrors are in red. *(Images courtesy of David Luebke and Chris Georges, UNC-Chapel Hill.)*

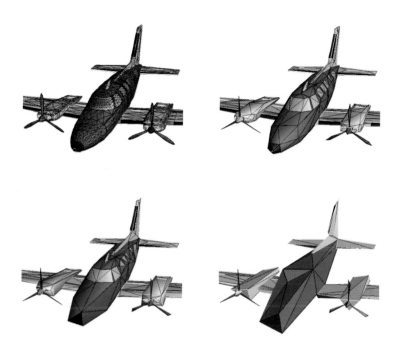

Plate XLVII. Mesh simplification. Upper left shows the original mesh of 13,546 faces, upper right is simplified to 1,000 faces, lower left to 500 faces, lower right to 150 faces. *(Images courtesy of Hugues Hoppe, Microsoft Research.)*

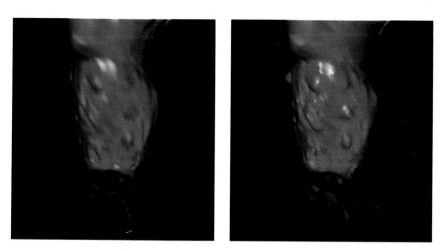

Plate XLVIII. Left: uniform subdivision with 9,000 triangles. Right: adaptive subdivision using approximately the same number of triangles. *(Images courtesy of Denis Zorin.)*

Plate XLIX. From a distance, the bunny's fur is rendered with volumetric textures. When the bunny comes closer, the hair is rendered with alpha blended polylines. When close up, the fur along the silhouette is rendered with graftal fins. *(Image courtesy of Jed Lengyel and Michael Cohen, Microsoft Research.)*

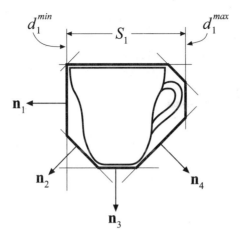

Figure 13.4. An example of a two-dimensional 8-DOP for a tea cup, with all normals, $\mathbf{n}_i$, shown along with the zero'th slab, S_1, and the "size" of the slab: d_1^{min} and d_1^{max}.

with each $\mathbf{n}_i$ two associated scalar values d_i^{min} and d_i^{max}, where $d_i^{min} < d_i^{max}$. Each triple $(\mathbf{n}_i, d_i^{min}, d_i^{max})$ describes a slab, S_i, which is the volume between the two planes, $\pi_i^{min} : \mathbf{n}_i \cdot \mathbf{x} + d_i^{min} = 0$ and $\pi_i^{max} : \mathbf{n}_i \cdot \mathbf{x} + d_i^{max} = 0$, and where the intersection of all slabs, $\bigcap_{1 \le l \le k/2} S_l$, is the actual k-DOP volume. □

Figure 13.4 depicts an 8-DOP in two dimensions.

An important general theorem on intersection testing [283, 289] follows, which holds for convex polyhedra such as AABBs, OBBs, and k-DOPs.

Separating Axis Theorem (SAT): For any two arbitrary, convex, disjoint polyhedra, A and B, there exists a separating axis where the projections of the polyhedra, which form intervals on the axis, are also disjoint. If A and B are disjoint, then they can be separated by an axis that is orthogonal (i.e., by a plane that is parallel) to either

1. A face of A,

2. A face of B, or

3. An edge from each polyhedron (e.g., cross product). □

Note that the definition of a convex polyhedra is very liberal here. A line segment and a convex polygon such as a triangle are also convex polyhedra (though degenerate, since they enclose no volume). A line segment A does not have a face, so the first test disappears. This theorem is used in deriving the box/line segment overlap test in Section 13.6.3, the triangle/box overlap test in Section 13.11, and the OBB/OBB overlap test in Section 13.12.5.

A common technique for optimizing intersection tests is to make some simple calculations early on that can determine whether the ray or object totally misses the other object. Such a test is called a *rejection test*, and if the test succeeds, the intersection is said to be *rejected*.

Another approach often used in this chapter is to project the three-dimensional objects onto the "best" orthogonal plane (xy, xz, or yz), and solve the problem in two dimensions instead.

Finally, due to numerical imprecision, we often use a very small number in the intersection tests. This number is denoted ϵ (epsilon), and its value will vary from test to test. Sometimes a reasonable value is mentioned in the text, and sometimes it can be found in online code. However, often an epsilon is chosen that works for the programmer's problem cases (what Press et al. [635] call a "convenient fiction"), as opposed to doing careful roundoff error analysis and epsilon adjustment. Such code used in another setting may well break because of differing conditions. This caveat firmly in place, we sometimes do attempt to provide epsilons that are at least reasonable starting values.

13.3   Bounding Volume Creation

Given a collection of objects, finding a tight fitting bounding volume is important to minimizing intersection costs. The chance that an arbitrary ray will hit any convex object is proportional to that object's surface area [28]. Minimizing this area increases the efficiency of any intersection algorithm, as a rejection is never slower to compute than an intersection. In contrast, it is often better to minimize the volume of BV for collision detection algorithms. This section briefly covers methods of finding optimal or near-optimal bounding volumes given a collection of polygons.

AABB and k-DOP Creation

The simplest bounding volumes to create is an AABB. Take the minimum and maximum extents of the set of polygon vertices along each axis and the AABB is formed. The k-DOP is an extension of the AABB: Project the vertices onto each normal, $\mathbf{n}_i$, of the k-DOP, and the extreme values (min,max) of these projections are stored in d^i_{min} and d^i_{max}. These two values define the tightest slab for that direction. Together, all such values define a minimal k-DOP.

Sphere Creation

Bounding sphere formation is not as clear-cut. There are a number of algorithms that perform this task, and these have speed versus quality tradeoffs. A fast, constant-time single pass algorithm is to form an AABB for the polygon set and then use the center and the diagonal of this box to form the sphere. This sometimes gives a poor fit, and the fit can often be improved by another quick pass: Starting with the center of the AABB as the center of the sphere BV, go through all vertices once again and find the one that is farthest from this center (comparing against the square of the distance so as to avoid taking the square root). This is then the new radius.

Ritter [653] presents a simple algorithm that creates a near-optimal bounding sphere. The idea is to find the vertex that is at the minimum and the vertex at the maximum along each of the x, y, and z axes. For these three pairs of vertices, find the pair with the largest distance between them. Use this pair to form a sphere with its center at the midpoint between them and a radius equal to the distance to them. Go through all the other vertices and check its distance d to the center of the sphere. If the vertex is outside the sphere's radius r, move the sphere's center toward the vertex by $(d-r)/2$, set the radius to $(d+r)/2$, and continue. This step has the effect of enclosing the vertex and the existing sphere in a new sphere. After this second time through the list, the bounding sphere is guaranteed to enclose all vertices. Code is available on the web.

Welzl [798] presents a more complex algorithm, which is implemented by Eberly [199], with code on the web. This algorithm is expected to be linear for a randomized list of vertices (randomization helps find a good sphere quickly). The idea is to find a supporting set of points defining a sphere. A sphere can be defined by a set of two, three, or four points on its surface. When a vertex is found to be outside the current sphere, its location is added to the supporting set (and possibly old support vertices removed from the set), the new sphere is computed, and the entire list is run through again. This process repeats until the sphere contains all vertices. While more complex than the previous methods, this algorithm guarantees that an optimal bounding sphere is found.

OBB Creation

OBB formation is more involved still. One method by Gottschalk [284] will be presented, followed by a brief explanation of another method by Eberly [199].

It has been shown that a tight-fitting OBB enclosing an object can be found by computing an orientation from the triangles of the convex hull [283, 284].[4] Here, we will present the formulae for computing a good-fit OBB using a statistical method. The derivation is found in Gottschalk's Ph.D. thesis [284].

First, the convex hull of an object must be computed. This can be done with, for example, the *Quickhull* algorithm [43]. This gives us, say, n triangles defined as $\triangle \mathbf{p}^k \mathbf{q}^k \mathbf{r}^k$, where $\mathbf{p}^k$, $\mathbf{q}^k$, and $\mathbf{r}^k$ are the vertices of triangle k, $0 \leq k < n$. We also denote the area of triangle k as a^k, and the total area of the convex hull as $a^H = \sum_{k=0}^{n-1} a^k$. Furthermore, the centroid of triangle i is $\mathbf{m}^i = (\mathbf{p}^i + \mathbf{q}^i + \mathbf{r}^i)/3$, that is, the mean of the vertices. The centroid of the whole convex hull, $\mathbf{m}^H$, is the weighted mean of the triangle centroids, as shown in Equation 13.5.

$$\mathbf{m}^H = \frac{1}{a^H} \sum_{k=0}^{n-1} a^k \mathbf{m}^k \tag{13.5}$$

With the use of these definitions, we will present a formula that computes a 3×3 covariance matrix, $\mathbf{C}$, whose eigenvectors (see Section A.3.1 on how to compute the eigenvectors) are the direction vectors for a good-fit box.

$$\mathbf{C} = [c_{ij}] = \left[\left(\frac{1}{a^H} \sum_{k=0}^{n-1} \frac{a^k}{12} (9m_i^k m_j^k + p_i^k p_j^k + q_i^k q_j^k + r_i^k r_j^k) \right) - m_i^H m_j^H \right],$$
$$0 \leq i, j < 3 \tag{13.6}$$

After computing $\mathbf{C}$, the eigenvectors are computed and normalized. These vectors are the direction vectors, $\mathbf{a}^u$, $\mathbf{a}^v$, and $\mathbf{a}^w$, of the OBB. We must next find the center and the half-lengths of the OBB. This is done by projecting the points of the convex hull onto the direction vectors and finding the minimum and maximum along each direction. These will determine the size and position of the box, i.e., will fully specify the OBB according to its definition (see Section 13.2).

When computing the OBB, the most demanding operation is the convex hull computation, which takes $O(n \log n)$ time, where n is the number of primitives of the object. The basis calculation takes, at most, linear time, and the eigenvector computation takes constant time, which means that computing an OBB for a set of n triangles takes $O(n \log n)$ time.

---

[4]The convex hull is used because it avoids using points in the interior of the object that should not affect the orientation of the box. Also, an integration is performed over each triangle of the convex hull. This is done since using the vertices of the convex hull can make for bad-fitting boxes, if, for example, several vertices clump in a small region.

Eberly [199] presents a method for computing a minimum-volume OBB using a minimization technique. An advantage is that the convex hull need not be computed. This is an iterative algorithm, and so the initial guess of the box determines how fast the solution converges to the minimum box. For a box with the axes $\mathbf{a}^u$, $\mathbf{a}^v$, and $\mathbf{a}^w$, the points are projection onto these axes. The min, k^u_{min}, and max, k^u_{max}, along $\mathbf{a}^u$ are found. Then k^v_{min}, k^v_{max}, k^w_{min}, and k^w_{max} are computed similarly. The center of this box is then:

$$\mathbf{a}^c = \frac{k^u_{min} + k^u_{max}}{2}\mathbf{a}^u + \frac{k^v_{min} + k^v_{max}}{2}\mathbf{a}^v + \frac{k^w_{min} + k^w_{max}}{2}\mathbf{a}^w. \qquad (13.7)$$

The half-lengths of the sides of the box are then $h_l = (k^l_{min} + k^l_{max})/2$, for $l \in \{u, v, w\}$. Eberly samples the set of possible directions of the box, and uses the axes whose box is smallest as a starting point for the numeric minimizer. Then Powell's direction set method [635] is used to find the minimum volume box. Eberly has robust code for this on the web [199].

13.4 Rules of Thumb

Before we begin studying the specific intersection methods, here are some rules of thumb that can lead to faster, more robust, and more exact intersection tests. These should be kept in mind when designing, inventing, and implementing an intersection routine:

- Perform computations and comparisons that might trivially *reject* or *accept* various types of intersections to obtain an early escape from further computations.

- If possible, exploit the results from previous tests.

- If more than one rejection or acceptance test is used, then try changing their internal order (if possible), since a more efficient test may result. Do not assume that what appears to be a minor change will have no effect.

- Postpone expensive calculations (especially trigonometric functions, square roots, and divisions) until they are truly needed (see Section 13.7 for an example of delaying an expensive division).

- The intersection problem can often be simplified considerably by *reducing the dimension* of the problem (for example, from three dimensions to two dimensions or even to one dimension). See Section 13.8 for an example.

- If a single ray or object is being compared to many other objects at a time, look for precalculations that can be done just once before the testing begins.

- Whenever an intersection test is expensive, it is often good to start with a sphere around the object to give a first level of quick rejection.

- Make it a habit always to do timing comparisons on your computer, and use real data and testing situations for the timings.

- Finally, try to make your code *robust*. This means it should work for all special cases and that it will be insensitive to as many floating point precision errors as possible. Be aware of any limitations it may have.

13.5   Ray/Sphere Intersection

Let us start with a mathematically simple intersection test—namely, that between a ray and a sphere. As we will see later, the straightforward mathematical solution can be made much faster if we begin thinking in terms of the geometry involved.

13.5.1   Mathematical Solution

A sphere can be defined by a center point, $\mathbf{c}$, and a radius, r. A more compact implicit formula (compared to the one previously introduced) for the sphere is then

$$f(\mathbf{p}) = ||\mathbf{p} - \mathbf{c}|| - r = 0, \tag{13.8}$$

where $\mathbf{p}$ is any point on the sphere's surface. To solve for the intersections between a ray and a sphere, the ray $\mathbf{r}(t)$ simply replaces $\mathbf{p}$ in Equation 13.8 to yield

$$f(\mathbf{r}(t)) = ||\mathbf{r}(t) - \mathbf{c}|| - r = 0. \tag{13.9}$$

Equation 13.9 is simplified as follows:

$$||\mathbf{r}(t) - \mathbf{c}|| - r = 0$$
$$\Longleftrightarrow$$
$$||\mathbf{o} + t\mathbf{d} - \mathbf{c}|| = r$$
$$\Longleftrightarrow$$
$$(\mathbf{o} + t\mathbf{d} - \mathbf{c}) \cdot (\mathbf{o} + t\mathbf{d} - \mathbf{c}) = r^2 \qquad (13.10)$$
$$\Longleftrightarrow$$
$$t^2(\mathbf{d} \cdot \mathbf{d}) + 2t(\mathbf{d} \cdot (\mathbf{o} - \mathbf{c})) + (\mathbf{o} - \mathbf{c}) \cdot (\mathbf{o} - \mathbf{c}) - r^2 = 0$$
$$\Longleftrightarrow$$
$$t^2 + 2t(\mathbf{d} \cdot (\mathbf{o} - \mathbf{c})) + (\mathbf{o} - \mathbf{c}) \cdot (\mathbf{o} - \mathbf{c}) - r^2 = 0.$$

The last step comes from the fact that $\mathbf{d}$ is assumed to be normalized, i.e., $\mathbf{d} \cdot \mathbf{d} = ||\mathbf{d}||^2 = 1$. Not surprisingly, the resulting equation is an equation of the second order, which means that if the ray intersects the sphere, it does so at up to two points (see Figure 13.5). If the solutions to the equation are imaginary, then the ray misses the sphere. If not, the two solutions t_1 and t_2 can be inserted into the ray equation to compute the intersection points on the sphere.

The resulting Equation 13.10 can be written as a quadratic equation:

$$t^2 + 2tb + c = 0, \qquad (13.11)$$

where $b = \mathbf{d} \cdot (\mathbf{o} - \mathbf{c})$ and $c = (\mathbf{o} - \mathbf{c}) \cdot (\mathbf{o} - \mathbf{c}) - r^2$. The solutions of the second-order equation are shown below:

$$t = -b \pm \sqrt{b^2 - c}. \qquad (13.12)$$

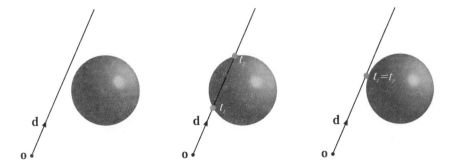

Figure 13.5. The left image shows a ray that misses a sphere and consequently $b^2 - c < 0$. The middle image shows a ray that intersects a sphere at two points ($b^2 - c > 0$) determined by the scalars t_1 and t_2. The right image illustrates the case where $b^2 - c = 0$, which means that the two intersection points coincide.

Note that if $b^2 - c < 0$, then the ray misses the sphere and the intersection can be rejected and calculations avoided (e.g., the square root and some additions). If this test is passed, both $t_0 = -b - \sqrt{b^2 - c}$ and $t_1 = -b + \sqrt{b^2 - c}$ can be computed. To find the smallest positive value of t_0 and t_1, an additional comparison needs to be executed.

If these computations are instead viewed from a geometric point of view, then better rejection tests can be discovered. The next subsection describes such a routine.

For the other quadrics, e.g., the cylinder, ellipsoid, cone, and hyperboloid, the mathematical solutions to their intersection problems are almost as straightforward as for the sphere. Sometimes, however, it is necessary to bound a surface (for example, usually you do not want a cylinder to be infinite, so caps must be added to its ends), which can add some complexity to the code.

13.5.2   Optimized Solution

For the sphere/ray intersection problem [305], we begin by observing that intersections behind the ray origin are not needed (this is normally the case in picking, etc.). Therefore, a vector $\mathbf{l} = \mathbf{c} - \mathbf{o}$, which is the vector from the ray origin to the center of the sphere, is computed. All notation that is used is depicted in Figure 13.6. Also, the squared length of this vector is computed, $l^2 = \mathbf{l} \cdot \mathbf{l}$. Now if $l^2 < r^2$, this implies that the ray origin is inside the sphere, which, in turn, means that the ray is guaranteed to hit the sphere and we can exit if we want to detect only whether or not the ray hits the sphere; otherwise, we proceed. Next, the projection of $\mathbf{l}$ onto the ray direction, $\mathbf{d}$, is computed: $s = \mathbf{l} \cdot \mathbf{d}$. Now, here comes the first rejection test: If $s < 0$ and the ray origin is outside the sphere, then the sphere is behind the ray origin and we can reject the intersection. Otherwise, the squared distance from the sphere center to the projection is computed using the Pythagorean theorem (Equation B.6): $m^2 = l^2 - s^2$. The second rejection test is even simpler than the first: If $m^2 > r^2$ the ray will definitely miss the sphere and the rest of the calculations can safely be omitted. If the sphere and ray pass this last test, then the ray is guaranteed to hit the sphere and we can exit if that was all we were interested in finding out.

To find the real intersection points, a little more work has to be done. First, the squared distance $q^2 = r^2 - m^2$ (see Figure 13.6) is calculated.[5] Since $m^2 <= r^2$, q^2 is greater than or equal to zero, and this means that

---

[5]Note that the scalar r^2 can be computed once and stored within the data structure of the sphere in order to gain further efficiency.

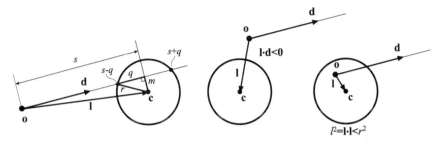

Figure 13.6. The notation for the geometry of the optimized ray/sphere intersection. In the left figure, the ray intersects the sphere in two points, where the distances are $t = s \pm q$ along the ray. The middle case demonstrates a rejection made when the sphere is behind the ray origin. Finally, at the right, the ray origin is inside the sphere, in which case the ray always hits the sphere.

$q = \sqrt{q^2}$ can be computed. Finally, the distances to the intersections are $t = s \pm q$, whose solution is quite similar to that of the second-order equation obtained in the previous mathematical solution section. If we are interested in only the first, positive intersection point, then we should use $t_1 = s - q$ for the case where the ray origin is outside the sphere and $t_2 = s + q$ when the ray origin is inside. The true intersection point(s) are found by inserting the t-value(s) into the ray equation (Equation 13.1).

Pseudocode for the optimized version is shown in the box below. The routine returns a boolean value that is REJECT if the ray misses the sphere and INTERSECT otherwise. If the ray intersects the sphere, then the distance, t, from the ray origin to the intersection point along with the intersection point, **p**, are also returned.

RaySphereIntersect$(\mathbf{o}, \mathbf{d}, \mathbf{c}, r)$
returns $(\{\text{REJECT}, \text{INTERSECT}\}, t, \mathbf{p})$
1 : $\quad \mathbf{l} = \mathbf{c} - \mathbf{o}$
2 : $\quad s = \mathbf{l} \cdot \mathbf{d}$
3 : $\quad l^2 = \mathbf{l} \cdot \mathbf{l}$
4 : $\quad$ if$(s < 0$ and $l^2 > r^2)$ return $(\text{REJECT}, 0, 0)$;
5 : $\quad m^2 = l^2 - s^2$
6 : $\quad$ if$(m^2 > r^2)$ return $(\text{REJECT}, 0, 0)$;
7 : $\quad q = \sqrt{r^2 - m^2}$
8 : $\quad$ if$(l^2 > r^2)$ $t = s - q$
9 : $\quad$ else $t = s + q$
10 : $\quad$ return $(\text{INTERSECT}, t, \mathbf{o} + t\mathbf{d})$;

Note that after line 3, we can test whether **p** is inside the sphere and, if all we want to know is whether the ray and sphere intersect, the routine can terminate if they do so. Also, after Line 6, the ray is guaranteed to hit the sphere. If we do an operation count (counting adds, multiplies, compares, etc.), we find that the geometric solution, *when followed to completion,* is approximately equivalent to the algebraic solution presented earlier. The important difference is that the rejection tests are done much earlier in the process, making the overall cost of this algorithm lower on average.

Optimized geometric algorithms exist for computing the intersection between a ray and some other quadrics and hybrid objects. For example, there are methods for the cylinder [157, 351, 702], cone [351, 703], ellipsoid, capsule (a cylinder with spherical caps), and lozenge (a box with cylindrical sides and spherical corners) [199].

13.6   Ray/Box Intersection

Three methods for determining whether a ray intersects a box are given below. The first handles both AABBs and OBBs. The second may be faster on some architectures, but can deal with only the simpler AABB. The third is based on the separating axis theorem on page 563, and handles only line segments versus AABBs. A fourth method by Schroeder is to treat the ray as a line segment and clip it against the bounding box [690]. Here, we use the definitions and notation of the BVs from Section 13.2.

13.6.1   Slabs Method

One scheme for ray/AABB intersection is presented by Haines [305]. This algorithm is based on Kay and Kajiya's slab method [413], which in turn is inspired by the Cyrus-Beck line clipping algorithm [158].

We extend this scheme to handle the more general OBB volume. It returns the closest positive t-value (i.e., the distance from the ray origin **o** to the point of intersection, if any exists). Optimizations for the AABB will be treated after we present the general case. The problem is approached by computing all t-values for the ray and all planes belonging to the faces of the OBB. The box is considered to be a set of three slabs,[6] as illustrated

---

[6] A slab is simply two parallel planes, which are grouped for faster computations.

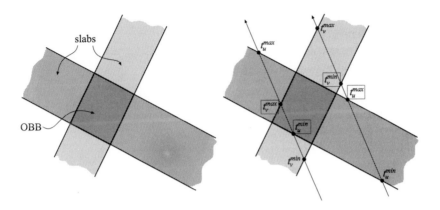

Figure 13.7. The left figure shows a two-dimensional OBB (*Oriented Bounding Box*) formed by two slabs, while the right shows two rays that are tested for intersection with the OBB. All t-values are shown, and they are subscripted with v for the light gray slab and with u for the other. The extreme t-values are marked with boxes. The left ray hits the OBB since $t^{min} < t^{max}$, and the right ray misses since $t^{max} < t^{min}$.

in two dimensions in the left part of Figure 13.7. For each slab, there is a minimum and a maximum t-value, and these are called t_i^{min} and t_i^{max}, $\forall i \in \{u, v, w\}$. The next step is to compute the variables in Equation 13.13.

$$t^{min} = \max(t_u^{min}, t_v^{min}, t_w^{min})$$
$$t^{max} = \min(t_u^{max}, t_v^{max}, t_w^{max})$$

(13.13)

Now, the clever test: If $t^{min} \leq t^{max}$, then the ray intersects the box; otherwise it misses. The reader should convince himself of this by inspecting the illustration on the right side of Figure 13.7.

Pseudocode for the ray/OBB intersection test, between an OBB (called A) and a ray (described by Equation 13.1) follows below. The code returns a boolean indicating whether or not the ray intersects the OBB (INTERSECT or REJECT), and the distance to the intersection point (if it exists). Recall that for an OBB A, the center is denoted $\mathbf{a}^c$, and $\mathbf{a}^u$, $\mathbf{a}^v$, and $\mathbf{a}^w$ are the normalized side directions of the box; h_u, h_v, and h_w are the positive half-lengths (from the center to a box face).

RayOBBIntersect$(\mathbf{o}, \mathbf{d}, A)$
returns $(\{\text{REJECT}, \text{INTERSECT}\}, t)$;
1 : $t^{min} = -\infty$
2 : $t^{max} = \infty$
3 : $\mathbf{p} = \mathbf{a}^c - \mathbf{o}$
4 : for each $i \in \{u, v, w\}$
5 : $e = \mathbf{a}^i \cdot \mathbf{p}$
6 : $f = \mathbf{a}^i \cdot \mathbf{d}$
7 : $\text{if}(|f| > \epsilon)$
8 : $t_1 = (e + h_i)/f$
9 : $t_2 = (e - h_i)/f$
10 : $\text{if}(t_1 > t_2) \ \text{swap}(t_1, t_2)$;
11 : $\text{if}(t_1 > t^{min}) \ t^{min} = t_1$
12 : $\text{if}(t_2 < t^{max}) \ t^{max} = t_2$
13 : $\text{if}(t^{min} > t^{max})$ return $(\text{REJECT}, 0)$;
14 : $\text{if}(t^{max} < 0)$ return $(\text{REJECT}, 0)$;
15 :   else $\text{if}(-e - h_i > 0 \ \text{or} \ -e + h_i < 0)$ return $(\text{REJECT}, 0)$;
16 : $\text{if}(t^{min} > 0)$ return $(\text{INTERSECT}, t^{min})$;
17 : else return $(\text{INTERSECT}, t^{max})$;

Line 7 checks whether the ray direction is not perpendicular to the normal direction of the slab currently being tested. In other words, it tests whether the ray is not parallel to the slab planes and so can intersect them. Note that ϵ is a very small number here, such as 1.0^{-20}, simply to avoid overflow when the division occurs. Lines 8 and 9 show a division by f; in practice, it is usually faster to compute $1/f$ once and multiply by this value, since division is often expensive. Line 10 ensures that the minimum of t_1 and t_2 is stored in t_1, and consequently, the maximum of these is stored in t_2. In practice, the swap does not have to be made; instead Lines 11 and 12 can be repeated for the branch, and t_1 and t_2 can change positions there. Should Line 13 return, then the ray misses the box, and similarly, if Line 14 returns, then the box is behind the ray origin. Line 15 is executed if the ray is parallel to the slab (and so cannot intersect it); it tests if the ray is outside the slab. If so, then the ray misses the box and the test terminates. For even faster code, Haines discusses a way of unwrapping the loop and thereby avoiding some code [305].

There is an additional test not shown in the pseudocode that is worth adding in actual code. As mentioned when we defined the ray, we usually want to find the closest object. So after Line 15, we could also test whether $t^{min} \geq l$, where l is the current ray length. If the new intersection is not closer, the intersection is rejected. This test could be deferred until after the entire ray/OBB test has been completed, but it is usually more efficient to try for an early rejection inside the loop.

There are other optimizations for the special case of an OBB that is an AABB. Lines 5 and 6 change to $e = p_i$ and $f = d_i$, which makes the test faster. Kay [413] and Smits [721] note that Line 7 can be avoided by allowing division by 0 and interpreting the processor's results correctly. In practice, the $\mathbf{a}^{min}$ and $\mathbf{a}^{max}$ corners of the AABB are used on Lines 8 and 9, and the addition may be avoided.

A generalization of the slabs method can be used to compute the intersection of a ray with a k-DOP, frustum, or any convex polyhedron [306]; code is available on the web.

13.6.2 Woo's Method

Woo [818] introduced some smart optimizations for finding the intersection between a ray and an AABB. Given a ray and an AABB, denoted B, the idea is to identify three candidate planes out of the six planes composing the AABB. For each pair of parallel planes, the back-facing plane can be omitted from further consideration. After finding these three planes, we compute the intersection distances (t-values) between the ray and the planes. The largest of these distances corresponds to a potential hit. This is illustrated in Figure 13.8. Finally, if a potential hit is found, the actual

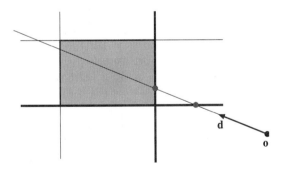

Figure 13.8. Woo's method for computing the intersection between a ray and an AABB. The candidate planes, which are front-facing and marked with fat lines, are intersected with the ray, and their intersection points are marked with gray dots. Because the left intersection point is farthest from the ray origin, it is selected as a (potential) point of intersection.

intersection point is computed, and if it is located on the corresponding face of B, then it is a real hit.

Whether the slabs method or Woo's method is faster is an open question. We believe the methods are comparable in performance, with each strongly affected by the way it is used, the processor architecture, and its implementation.

Source code for Woo's method is available on the web [818].

13.6.3 Line Segment/Box Overlap Test

In this section, it will be shown that the separating axis theorem on page 563 can be used to determine whether a line segment overlaps an AABB [294]. The line segment has finite length in contrast to a ray. Assume the line segment is defined by a center (mean of the two endpoints) $\mathbf{c}$ and a half vector $\mathbf{w}$. Furthermore, both the AABB, denoted B, and the line segment have been translated so the AABB's origin is $(0, 0, 0)$. Also, the size of the box is $(2h_x, 2h_y, 2h_z)$, i.e., $\mathbf{h}$ is the half vector of the box. This is shown in Figure 13.9.

According to the separating axis theorem, one should first test against an axis that is orthogonal to a face of both objects to be tested. Since the line segment does not have a face, it does not generate any test. The box

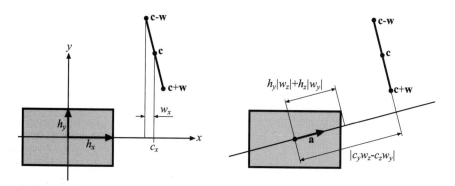

Figure 13.9. Left: The x-axis is tested for overlap between the box and the line segment. Right: The $\mathbf{a}$-axis is tested. Note that $h_y|w_z| + h_z|w_y|$ and $|c_y w_z - c_z w_y|$ are shown in this illustration as if $\mathbf{w}$ is normalized. When this is not the case, then both the shown values should be scaled with $\|\mathbf{w}\|$. See text for notation.

generates three axes to test: $(1,0,0)$, $(0,1,0)$, and $(0,0,1)$. Finally, the axes formed from the cross product between line segment direction and the box axes should be tested.

The test for the axis $(1,0,0)$ is shown below, and Figure 13.9 shows this as well. The other two axes are similar.

$$|c_x| > |w_x| + h_x \tag{13.14}$$

If this test is true then the line segment and the box do not overlap.

The cross product axis $\mathbf{a} = \mathbf{w} \times (1,0,0) = (0, w_z, -w_y)$ is tested as follows. The extent of the box projected onto $\mathbf{a}$ is $h_y|w_z| + h_z|w_y|$. Next we need to find the projected length of the line segment, and the projection of the line segment center. The projection of the line segment direction $\mathbf{w}$ onto $\mathbf{a}$ is zero, since $\mathbf{w} \cdot (\mathbf{w} \times (1,0,0)) = 0$. The projection of $\mathbf{c}$ onto $\mathbf{a}$ is $\mathbf{c} \cdot \mathbf{a} = \mathbf{c} \cdot (0, w_z, -w_y) = c_y w_z - c_z w_y$. Thus, the test becomes:

$$|c_y w_z - c_z w_y| > h_y|w_z| + h_z|w_y|. \tag{13.15}$$

Again, if this test is true, then there is no overlap. The other two cross product axes are similar.

The routine is summarized below.

RayAABBOverlap(c, w, B)
`returns ({OVERLAP, DISJOINT});`
1 : $v_x = |w_x|$
2 : $v_y = |w_y|$
3 : $v_z = |w_z|$
4 :   `if(`$|c_x| > v_x + h_x$`) return DISJOINT;`
5 :   `if(`$|c_y| > v_y + h_y$`) return DISJOINT;`
6 :   `if(`$|c_z| > v_z + h_z$`) return DISJOINT;`
7 :   `if(`$|c_y w_z - c_z w_y| > h_y v_z + h_z v_y$`) return DISJOINT;`
8 :   `if(`$|c_x w_z - c_z w_x| > h_x v_z + h_z v_x$`) return DISJOINT;`
9 :   `if(`$|c_x w_y - c_y w_x| > h_x v_y + h_y v_x$`) return DISJOINT;`
10 : `return OVERLAP;`

In terms of code, this routine is fast, but it has the disadvantage of not being able to return the intersection distance.

13.7   Ray/Triangle Intersection

In real-time graphics libraries and APIs, triangle geometry is usually stored as a set of vertices with associated normals, and each triangle is defined by three such vertices. The normal of the plane in which the triangle lies is often not stored, in which case, it must be computed if needed. There exist many different ray/triangle intersection tests, and the majority of them first compute the intersection point between the ray and the triangle's plane. Thereafter, the intersection point and the triangle vertices are projected on the axis-aligned plane (xy, yz, or xz) where the area of the triangle is maximized. By doing this, we reduce the problem to two dimensions, and we need only decide whether the (2D) point is inside the (2D) triangle. Several such methods exist, and they have been reviewed and compared by Haines [307], with code available on the web. See Section 13.8 for one popular algorithm using this technique.

Here, the focus will be on an algorithm that does not presume that normals are precomputed. For triangle meshes, this can amount to significant memory savings. This algorithm, along with optimizations, was discussed by Möller and Trumbore [560], and their presentation is used here. DirectX 8.1 uses this technique in their sample pick code.

The ray from Equation 13.1 is used to test for intersection with a triangle defined by three vertices, $\mathbf{v}_1$, $\mathbf{v}_2$, and $\mathbf{v}_3$—i.e., $\triangle\mathbf{v}_1\mathbf{v}_2\mathbf{v}_3$.

13.7.1   Intersection Algorithm

A point, $\mathbf{t}(u, v)$, on a triangle is given by the explicit formula

$$\mathbf{t}(u, v) = (1 - u - v)\mathbf{v}_0 + u\mathbf{v}_1 + v\mathbf{v}_2, \qquad (13.16)$$

where (u, v) are the *barycentric coordinates*, which must fulfill $u \geq 0$, $v \geq 0$, and $u + v \leq 1$. Note that (u, v) can be used for texture mapping, normal interpolation, color interpolation, etc. That is, u and v are the amounts by which to weight each vertex's contribution to a particular location, with $w = (1 - u - v)$ being the third weight.[7] See Figure 13.10.

Computing the intersection between the ray, $\mathbf{r}(t)$, and the triangle, $\mathbf{t}(u, v)$, is equivalent to $\mathbf{r}(t) = \mathbf{t}(u, v)$, which yields:

$$\mathbf{o} + t\mathbf{d} = (1 - u - v)\mathbf{v}_0 + u\mathbf{v}_1 + v\mathbf{v}_2. \qquad (13.17)$$

---

[7]These coordinates are often denoted α, β, and γ. We use u, v, and w here for readability and consistency of notation.

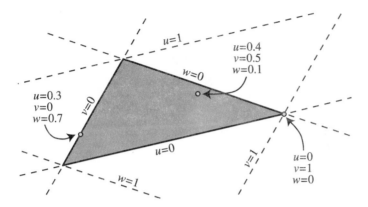

Figure 13.10. Barycentric coordinates for a triangle, along with example point values. The values u, v, and w all vary from 0 to 1 inside the triangle, and the sum of these three is always 1 over the entire plane. These values can be used as weights for how data at each of the three vertices influence any point on the triangle. Note how at each vertex, one value is 1 and the others 0, and along edges one value is always 0.

Rearranging the terms gives:

$$\left(-\mathbf{d} \quad \mathbf{v}_1 - \mathbf{v}_0 \quad \mathbf{v}_2 - \mathbf{v}_0 \right) \begin{pmatrix} t \\ u \\ v \end{pmatrix} = \mathbf{o} - \mathbf{v}_0. \tag{13.18}$$

This means the barycentric coordinates (u, v) and the distance t from the ray origin to the intersection point can be found by solving the linear system of equations above.

The above can be thought of geometrically as translating the triangle to the origin and transforming it to a unit triangle in y and z with the ray direction aligned with x. This is illustrated in Figure 13.11. If $\mathbf{M} = (-\mathbf{d} \quad \mathbf{v}_1 - \mathbf{v}_0 \quad \mathbf{v}_2 - \mathbf{v}_0)$ is the matrix in Equation 13.18, then the solution is found by multiplying Equation 13.18 with $\mathbf{M}^{-1}$.

Denoting $\mathbf{e}_1 = \mathbf{v}_1 - \mathbf{v}_0$, $\mathbf{e}_2 = \mathbf{v}_2 - \mathbf{v}_0$, and $\mathbf{s} = \mathbf{o} - \mathbf{v}_0$, the solution to Equation 13.18 is obtained by using Cramer's rule:

$$\begin{pmatrix} t \\ u \\ v \end{pmatrix} = \frac{1}{\det(-\mathbf{d}, \mathbf{e}_1, \mathbf{e}_2)} \begin{pmatrix} \det(\mathbf{s}, \mathbf{e}_1, \mathbf{e}_2) \\ \det(-\mathbf{d}, \mathbf{s}, \mathbf{e}_2) \\ \det(-\mathbf{d}, \mathbf{e}_1, \mathbf{s}) \end{pmatrix}. \tag{13.19}$$

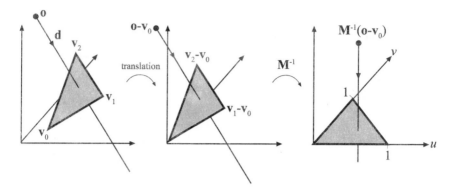

Figure 13.11. Translation and change of base of the ray origin.

From linear algebra, we know that $\det(\mathbf{a}, \mathbf{b}, \mathbf{c}) = |\mathbf{a}\ \mathbf{b}\ \mathbf{c}| = -(\mathbf{a}\times\mathbf{c})\cdot\mathbf{b} = -(\mathbf{c}\times\mathbf{b})\cdot\mathbf{a}$. Equation 13.19 can therefore be rewritten as:

$$\begin{pmatrix} t \\ u \\ v \end{pmatrix} = \frac{1}{(\mathbf{d}\times\mathbf{e}_2)\cdot\mathbf{e}_1} \begin{pmatrix} (\mathbf{s}\times\mathbf{e}_1)\cdot\mathbf{e}_2 \\ (\mathbf{d}\times\mathbf{e}_2)\cdot\mathbf{s} \\ (\mathbf{s}\times\mathbf{e}_1)\cdot\mathbf{d} \end{pmatrix} = \frac{1}{\mathbf{p}\cdot\mathbf{e}_1} \begin{pmatrix} \mathbf{q}\cdot\mathbf{e}_2 \\ \mathbf{p}\cdot\mathbf{s} \\ \mathbf{q}\cdot\mathbf{d} \end{pmatrix}, \quad (13.20)$$

where $\mathbf{p} = \mathbf{d}\times\mathbf{e}_2$ and $\mathbf{q} = \mathbf{s}\times\mathbf{e}_1$. These factors can be used to speed up the computations.

Arenberg [24] describes an algorithm that is similar to the one above. He also constructs a 3×3 matrix, but uses the normal of the triangle instead of the ray direction $\mathbf{d}$. His method requires storing the normal for each triangle or computing each normal on the fly, while the one presented here does not.

13.7.2 Implementation

The algorithm is summarized in the pseudocode below. Besides returning whether or not the ray intersects the triangle, the algorithm also returns the above described triple (u, v, t). The code does not cull backfacing triangles.

RayTriIntersect(o, d, v_0, v_1, v_2)
returns $(\{\text{REJECT}, \text{INTERSECT}\}, u, v, t)$;

```
1 :   e_1 = v_1 − v_0
2 :   e_2 = v_2 − v_0
3 :   p = d × e_2
4 :   a = e_1 · p
5 :   if(a > −ε and a < ε) return (REJECT, 0, 0, 0);
6 :   f = 1/a
7 :   s = o − v_0
8 :   u = f(s · p)
9 :   if(u < 0.0 or u > 1.0) return (REJECT, 0, 0, 0);
10 :  q = s × e_1
11 :  v = f(d · q)
12 :  if(v < 0.0 or u + v > 1.0) return (REJECT, 0, 0, 0);
13 :  t = f(e_2 · q)
14 :  return (INTERSECT, u, v, t);
```

A few lines may require some explanation. Line 4 computes a, which is the determinant of the matrix $\mathbf{M}$. This is followed by a test that avoids determinants close to zero. With a properly adjusted value of ϵ, this algorithm is extremely stable).[8] In Line 9, the value of u is compared to an edge of the triangle ($u = 0$), and also to a line parallel to that edge, but passing through the opposite vertex of the triangle ($u = 1$). See Figure 13.10. Although not actually testing an edge of the triangle, this second test efficiently rules out many intersection points without further calculation. However, on modern CPUs where conditional statements tend to be fairly expensive, this test may actually decrease performance.

C-code for this algorithm, including both culling and nonculling versions, is available on the web [560]. The C-code has two branches: One that efficiently culls all backfacing triangles, and one that performs intersection tests on two-sided triangles. All computations are delayed until they are required. For example, the value of v is not computed until the value of u is found to be within the allowable range (this can be seen in the pseudocode as well).

The one-sided intersection routine eliminates all triangles where the value of the determinant is negative. This procedure allows the routine's only division operation to be delayed until an intersection has been confirmed.

---

[8]For floating point precision, $\epsilon = 1.0^{-5}$ works fine.

The investigation by Möller and Trumbore [560] also shows that this method is the fastest ray/triangle intersection routine that does not need to store the normal of the triangle plane, and that it is comparable in speed to Badouel's method [35], which also computes barycentric coordinates (and so makes the comparison fair).

13.8   Ray/Polygon Intersection

Even though triangles are the most common rendering primitive, a routine that computes the intersection between a ray and a polygon is useful to have. A polygon of n vertices is defined by an ordered vertex list $\{\mathbf{v}_0, \mathbf{v}_1, \ldots, \mathbf{v}_{n-1}\}$, where vertex $\mathbf{v}_i$ forms an edge with $\mathbf{v}_{i+1}$ for $0 \leq i < n-1$ and the polygon is closed by the edge from $\mathbf{v}_{n-1}$ to $\mathbf{v}_0$. The plane of the polygon[9] is denoted $\pi_p : \mathbf{n}_p \cdot \mathbf{x} + d_p = 0$.

We first compute the intersection between the ray (Equation 13.1) and π_p, which is easily done by replacing $\mathbf{x}$ by the ray. The solution is presented below:

$$\mathbf{n}_p \cdot (\mathbf{o} + t\mathbf{d}) + d_p = 0$$
$$\Longleftrightarrow$$
$$t = \frac{-d_p - \mathbf{n}_p \cdot \mathbf{o}}{\mathbf{n}_p \cdot \mathbf{d}}. \tag{13.21}$$

If the denominator $|\mathbf{n}_p \cdot \mathbf{d}| < \epsilon$, where ϵ is a very small number[10], then the ray is considered parallel to the polygon plane and no intersection occurs.[11] Otherwise, the intersection point, $\mathbf{p}$, of the ray and the polygon plane is computed: $\mathbf{p} = \mathbf{o} + t\mathbf{d}$, where the t-value is that from Equation 13.21. Thereafter, the problem of deciding whether $\mathbf{p}$ is inside the polygon is reduced from three to two dimensions. This is done by projecting all vertices and $\mathbf{p}$ to one of the xy-, xz-, or yz-planes where the area of the projected polygon is maximized. In other words, the coordinate component that corresponds to $\max(|n_{p,x}|, |n_{p,y}|, |n_{p,z}|)$ can be skipped and the others kept as two-dimensional coordinates. For example, given a normal $(0.6, -0.692, 0.4)$, the y component has the largest magnitude, so all y coordinates are ignored. Note that this component information could be precomputed once and stored within the polygon for efficiency. The topology of the polygon and the intersection point is conserved during this projection (assuming the polygon is indeed flat; see Section 11.2 for more

---

[9]This plane can be computed from the vertices on the fly or stored with the polygon, whichever is most convenient. It is sometimes called the supporting plane of the polygon.

[10]An epsilon of 1.0^{-20} or smaller is fine, as the goal is to avoid overflowing when dividing.

[11]We ignore the case where the ray is in the polygon's plane.

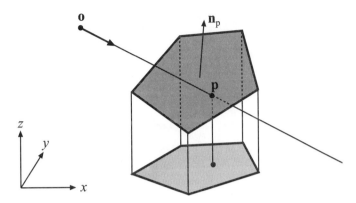

Figure 13.12. Orthographic projection of polygon vertices and intersection point **p** onto the xy-plane, where the area of the projected polygon is maximized. This is an example of using dimension reduction to obtain simpler calculations.

on this topic). The projection procedure is shown in Figure 13.12. A two-dimensional bounding box (in the above mentioned plane) for the polygon is also sometimes profitable. That is, first compute the intersection with the polygon plane and then project to two dimensions and test against the two-dimensional bounding box. If the point is outside the box, then reject and return; otherwise, continue with the full polygon test. This was found to be a better approach than using a three-dimensional bounding box for a polygon [824].

The question left is whether the two-dimensional ray/plane intersection point **p** is contained in the two-dimensional polygon. Here, we will review just one of the more useful algorithms—the "crossings" test. Haines [307] provides an extensive survey of two-dimensional, point-in-polygon strategies. More recently, Walker [786] has presented a method for rapid testing of polygons with more than 10 vertices. Also, Nishita et al. [587] discuss point inclusion testing for shapes with curved edges. A more formal treatment can be found in the computational geometry literature [56, 605, 634].

13.8.1 The Crossings Test

The crossings test is based on the *Jordan Curve Theorem*, which says that a point is inside a polygon if a ray from this point in an arbitrary direction crosses an odd number of polygon edges. This test is also known as the parity or the even-odd test. This condition does not mean that all areas enclosed by the polygon are considered inside. This is shown in Figure 13.13.

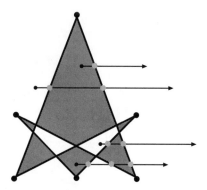

Figure 13.13. A general polygon that is self-intersecting and concave, yet all of its enclosed areas are not considered inside (only gray areas are inside). Vertices are marked with large, black dots. Three points being tested are shown, along with their test rays. According to the Jordan Curve Theorem, a point is inside if the number of crossings with the edges of the polygon is odd. Therefore, the uppermost and the bottommost points are inside (one and three crossings, respectively), while the two middle points each cross two edges and are thus considered outside the polygon.

The crossings algorithm is the fastest test that does not use preprocessing. It works by shooting a ray from the projection of the point **p** along the positive x-axis. Then the number of crossings between the polygon edges and this ray is computed. As the *Jordan Curve Theorem* proves, an odd number of crossings indicates that the point is inside the polygon.

The test point **p** can also be thought of as being at the origin, and the (translated) edges may be tested against the positive x-axis instead. This option is depicted in Figure 13.14. If the y-coordinates of a polygon edge have the same sign, then that edge cannot cross the x-axis. Otherwise, it can, and then the x-coordinates are checked. If both are positive, then the number of crossings is incremented. If they differ in sign, the x-coordinate of the intersection between the edge and the x-axis must be computed, and if it is positive, the number of crossings is again incremented.

These enclosed areas could be included as well, however; see Haines [307] for treatment.

Problems might occur when the test ray intersects a vertex, since two crossings might be detected. These problems are solved by setting the vertex infinitesimally above the ray, which, in practice, is done by interpreting the vertices with $y \geq 0$ as lying above the x-axis (the ray). The code becomes simpler and speedier, and no vertices will be intersected [305].

The pseudocode for an efficient form of the crossings test is given. It was inspired by the work of Joseph Samosky [671] and Mark Haigh-Hutchinson,

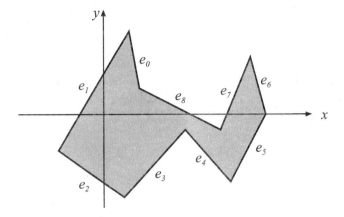

Figure 13.14. The polygon has been translated by $-\mathbf{p}$ ($\mathbf{p}$ is the point to be tested for containment in the polygon), and so the number of crossings with the positive x-axis determines whether $\mathbf{p}$ is inside the polygon. Edges e_0, e_2, e_3, and e_4 cannot cross the x-axis, since they each have both vertices on one side of the x-axis. The intersection between edge e_1 and the x-axis must be computed, but will not yield a crossing, since the intersection has a negative x-component. Edges e_7 and e_8 will each increase the number of crossings, since the vertices of these edges have positive x-components and one negative and one positive y-component. Finally, the edges e_5 and e_6 share a vertex where $y = 0$ and $x > 0$, and they will together increase the number of crossings by one.

and the code is available on the web [307]. Two-dimensional test point $\mathbf{t}$ and polygon P with vertices $\mathbf{v}_0$ through $\mathbf{v}_{n-1}$ are compared.

```
        bool PointInPolygon(t, P)
        returns ({TRUE, FALSE});
 1:     bool inside = FALSE
 2:     e₀ = vₙ₋₁
 3:     e₁ = v₀
 4:     bool y₀ = (e₀ᵧ ≥ tᵧ)
 5:     for i = 1 to n
 6:         bool y₁ = (e₁ᵧ ≥ tᵧ)
 7:         if(y₀ ≠ y₁)
 8:             if((((e₁ᵧ − tᵧ)(e₀ₓ − e₁ₓ) ≥ (e₁ₓ − tₓ)(e₀ᵧ − e₁ᵧ)) = y₁)
 9:                 inside = ¬inside
10:         y₀ = y₁
11:         e₀ = e₁
12:         e₁ = vᵢ
13:     return inside;
```

Line 4 checks whether the y-value of the last vertex in the polygon is greater than or equal to the y-value of the test point $\mathbf{t}$, and stores the result in the boolean y_0. In other words, it tests whether the first endpoint of the first edge we will test is above or below the x-axis. Line 7 tests whether the endpoints e_0 and e_1 are on different sides of the x-axis formed by the test point. If so, then Line 8 tests whether the x-intercept is positive. Actually, it is a bit trickier than that: to avoid the divide normally needed for computing the intercept, we perform a sign-cancelling operation here. By inverting *inside*, Line 9 records that a crossing took place. Lines 10 to 12 move on to the next vertex.

In the pseudocode we do not perform a test to see whether both endpoints have positive x-coordinates. Although this is how we presented the algorithm, code based on the pseudocode above often runs faster without this test. This is because we avoid the division needed to compute the x-intercept value, since all we want to know is whether the intercept is to the left or right of the test point. When you are optimizing this routine, we recommend trying both variants and seeing which is faster in practice.

The advantages of the crossings test is that it is relatively fast and robust, and requires no additional information or preprocessing for the polygon. A disadvantage of this method is that it does not yield anything beyond the indication of whether a point is inside or outside the polygon. Other methods, such as the ray/triangle test in Section 13.7.1, can also compute barycentric coordinates that can be used to interpolate additional information about the test point [307].

13.9   Plane/Box Intersection Detection

One way to determine whether a box intersects a plane, $\pi : \mathbf{n} \cdot \mathbf{x} + d = 0$, is to insert all the vertices of the box into the plane equation. If both a positive and a negative result (or a zero) is obtained, then vertices are located on both sides of (or on) the plane, and therefore, an intersection has been detected. There are smarter, faster ways to do this test, which are presented in the next two sections, one for the AABB, and one for the OBB.

The idea behind both methods is that only two points need to be inserted into the plane equation. These points are the ones that form a diagonal of the box, where the diagonal passes through the center of the box and is most aligned to the normal, $\mathbf{n}$, of the plane than are the other pairs of points that form diagonals.

13.9.1 AABB

Given an AABB, B, defined by $\mathbf{b}^{min}$ and $\mathbf{b}^{max}$, four different diagonals can be constructed. These all pass through the center of B and have endpoints at the vertices of B. For this AABB/plane intersection test, first find out which of the box diagonals is most aligned with the plane normal, $\mathbf{n}$. After the most aligned diagonal is found, the diagonal's two AABB vertices, called $\mathbf{v}^{min}$ and $\mathbf{v}^{max}$, are inserted into the plane equation π. This equation tests which side of the plane each endpoint is on. If the signs of the results differ, or at least one of them is zero, then B intersects π. This is illustrated in Figure 13.15. Note that if the AABB is in the positive half-space ($\mathbf{n} \cdot \mathbf{x} + d > 0$) of the plane, then the AABB is said to be "outside," and if it is in the negative half-space ($\mathbf{n} \cdot \mathbf{x} + d < 0$), then it is "inside." Else, it is intersecting (overlapping) the plane.

This test can be improved upon by noting that if $\mathbf{v}^{min}$ is in the positive half-space of the plane, then $\mathbf{v}^{max}$ will also be in the positive half-space [360]. In this case, the $\mathbf{v}^{max}$ point need not be tested against the plane—we already know that the AABB does not intersect the plane. The complete test is shown in the pseudocode that follows:

---

bool **PlaneAABBIntersect**(B, π)
returns($\{\texttt{OUTSIDE}, \texttt{INSIDE}, \texttt{INTERSECTING}\}$);
1 :   for each $i \in \{x, y, z\}$
2 :   if($n_i \geq 0$)
3 : $v_i^{min} = b_i^{min}$
4 : $v_i^{max} = b_i^{max}$
5 :   else
6 : $v_i^{min} = b_i^{max}$
7 : $v_i^{max} = b_i^{min}$
8 :   if($(\mathbf{n} \cdot \mathbf{v}^{min} + d) > 0$) return (OUTSIDE);
9 :   if($(\mathbf{n} \cdot \mathbf{v}^{max} + d) < 0$) return (INSIDE);
10 : return (INTERSECTING);

Note that Lines 2–7 make up the actual code that implicitly finds the diagonal most closely aligned with the plane normal $\mathbf{n}$. It is important to realize that, given a plane's orientation, the same box corners are always tested against it, regardless of the boxes' dimensions. A faster way to get $\mathbf{v}^{min}$ and $\mathbf{v}^{max}$ is to check only once which corners need to be used, instead of checking each time a box is tested [33, 308]. The sign bits of the plane

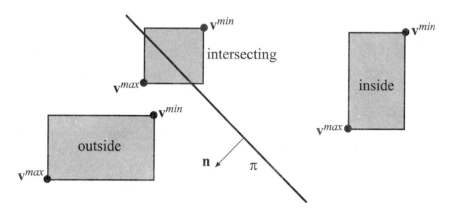

Figure 13.15. Here, the $\mathbf{v}^{min}$ and $\mathbf{v}^{max}$ vertices are shown for three AABBs (in two dimensions) for a given plane. If the pair of these vertices are on the same side of the plane, then the AABB does not intersect the plane; otherwise, it does. Note that if $\mathbf{v}^{min}$ is tested against the plane first and is found to be on the same side as the plane normal, then the AABB is "outside," i.e., in the positive half-space of the plane.

normal components are stored in a three-bit mask. For example, a normal of $(-1, 0.5, 2)$ would give a bitmask of 011; $(1.5, 1.2, -1)$ would give 110; and $(0, -1, -0.5)$ would give 100. A *Look-up Table* (LUT) with 8 sets of indices is then accessed, with each set of indices describing which coordinates to use from the bounding box to get $\mathbf{v}^{max}$ (i.e., which corner of the box to retrieve). The $\mathbf{v}^{min}$ vertex index is found by inverting the three bits in this maximum-vertex mask. For example, say the box coordinates were stored in an array $[0 \ldots 5]$ as $(b_x^{min}, b_y^{min}, b_z^{min}, b_x^{max}, b_y^{max}, b_z^{max})$. Then the LUT entry for bitmask 011 (i.e., index 3) would be $(0, 4, 5)$, meaning that the corner $(b_x^{min}, b_y^{max}, b_z^{max})$ should be retrieved from this array for $\mathbf{v}^{max}$. Inverting the bitmask gives 100 (index 4), the index needed to retrieve the opposite corner for $\mathbf{v}^{min}$ from the look-up table. Alternately, the three $\mathbf{v}^{max}$ corner array indices themselves could be stored with the plane, so avoiding the need for a look-up table [308]. So for the previous example, $(0, 4, 5)$ itself would be stored with the plane to access $\mathbf{v}^{max}$. The indices for $\mathbf{v}^{min}$ are found by adding 3 to each $\mathbf{v}^{max}$ index, modulus 6, i.e., $(3, 1, 2)$. These indices also could be stored or be computed on the fly.

13.9.2   OBB

With a small change, the test from the previous section can be used to test a plane against an OBB. The trick lies in knowing how to identify the

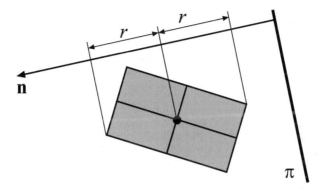

Figure 13.16. The extents of the OBB are projected onto the normal of the plane. Half the "size" of the OBB along the normal's direction is denoted r. If the distance from the center of the OBB to the plane is greater than r, then they do not intersect.

two points, $\mathbf{v}^{min}$ and $\mathbf{v}^{max}$. When that has been done, the same test as for AABBs can be used. To identify these two points, we transform the normal of the plane so that it lies in the coordinate system of the OBB. This is done as follows (see Section A.3.2 about base changing) [360]:

$$\mathbf{n}' = (\mathbf{b}^u \cdot \mathbf{n}, \quad \mathbf{b}^v \cdot \mathbf{n}, \quad \mathbf{b}^w \cdot \mathbf{n})^T. \tag{13.22}$$

So when finding the points $\mathbf{v}^{min}$ and $\mathbf{v}^{max}$, the transformed normal $\mathbf{n}'$ is used instead of $\mathbf{n}$. The rest of the test is the same as for AABBs.

Another way to test an OBB against a plane is to project the axes of the OBB onto the normal of the plane as shown in Figure 13.16. Half the length of the projection, called r, is computed by:

$$r = h_u^B |\mathbf{n} \cdot \mathbf{b}^u| + h_v^B |\mathbf{n} \cdot \mathbf{b}^v| + h_w^B |\mathbf{n} \cdot \mathbf{b}^w|. \tag{13.23}$$

If the absolute value of the distance from the center of the OBB to the plane is larger than r, then the plane and the OBB do not intersect. So if $|\mathbf{b}^c \cdot \mathbf{n} + d| > r$, then they do not intersect; otherwise, they do.

This method can also be applied to the AABB case by setting $\mathbf{b}^u = (1, 0, 0)$, $\mathbf{b}^v = (0, 1, 0)$, and $\mathbf{b}^w = (0, 0, 1)$ and simplifying.

13.10   Triangle/Triangle Intersection

Since graphics hardware uses the triangle as its most important (and optimized) drawing primitive, it is only natural to perform collision detection tests on this kind of data as well. So, the deepest levels of a collision detection algorithm typically have a routine that determines whether or not two triangles intersect. More often than not, we are concerned only about whether they intersect at all, and not interested in an exact intersection.

Two of the fastest methods for this task will be studied. These are comparable in terms of speed. We have included both because the solutions are fundamentally different, and a great deal may be learned about intersection routines and rejection tests by studying them. Note that the separating axis theorem (see page 563) can also be used to derive a triangle/triangle overlap test. The performance of such a test is comparable to the presented algorithms. However, it is not possible to get the line segment of intersection using that approach, which the other two methods can.

The problem is: Given two triangles, $T_1 = \triangle \mathbf{u}_0 \mathbf{u}_1 \mathbf{u}_2$ and $T_2 = \triangle \mathbf{v}_0 \mathbf{v}_1 \mathbf{v}_2$ (which lie in the planes π_1 and π_2, respectively), determine whether or not they intersect.

The first method of solving this problem is here called *the interval overlap method* and was introduced by Möller [561], whose presentation is followed closely here. The second, which is algorithmically simpler than the interval overlap test, comes from the ERIT package [351].

13.10.1   Interval Overlap Method

First, the plane equation $\pi_2 : \mathbf{n}_2 \cdot \mathbf{x} + d_2 = 0$ (where $\mathbf{x}$ is any point on the plane) is computed:

$$
\begin{aligned}
\mathbf{n}_2 &= (\mathbf{v}_1 - \mathbf{v}_0) \times (\mathbf{v}_2 - \mathbf{v}_0), \\
d_2 &= -\mathbf{n}_2 \cdot \mathbf{v}_0.
\end{aligned}
\tag{13.24}
$$

Then, the signed distances from the vertices of T_1 to π_2 (multiplied by a constant $\|\mathbf{n}_2\|^2$) are computed by simply inserting the vertices into the plane equation:

$$
d_{\mathbf{u}_i} = \mathbf{n}_2 \cdot \mathbf{u}_i + d_2, \quad i = 0, 1, 2.
\tag{13.25}
$$

Now, if all $d_{\mathbf{u}_i} \neq 0$, $i = 0, 1$, and 2 (that is, no point is on the plane), and all have the same sign, then T_1 lies on one side of π_2 and the overlap is

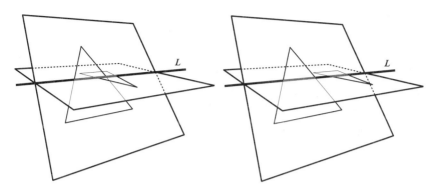

Figure 13.17. Triangles and the planes in which they lie. Intersection intervals are marked in gray in both figures. Left: The intervals along the line L overlap as well as the triangles. Right: There is no intersection; the intervals do not overlap.

rejected. The same test is done for T_2 and π_1. These two early rejection tests allow us to avoid many computations for some triangle pairs.

If all $d_{\mathbf{u}_i} = 0$ for $i = 0, 1$, and 2, then the triangles are co-planar and this case is handled separately and discussed later. If not, the intersection of π_1 and π_2 is a line, $\mathbf{l} = \mathbf{o} + t\mathbf{d}$, where $\mathbf{d} = \mathbf{n}_1 \times \mathbf{n}_2$ is the direction of the line and $\mathbf{o}$ is some point on it. Note that due to our previous calculations and rejections, both triangles are guaranteed to intersect $\mathbf{l}$. These intersections form intervals on $\mathbf{l}$, and if these intervals overlap, the triangles overlap as well. A similar interval test is used in a different context by Laidlaw et al. [452]. Two situations that can occur are depicted in Figure 13.17.

Now, assume that we want to compute a scalar interval (on $\mathbf{l}$) that represents the intersection between T_1 and $\mathbf{l}$. Furthermore, assume that, for example, the triangle vertices $\mathbf{u}_0$ and $\mathbf{u}_2$ lie on the same side of π_2 and that $\mathbf{u}_1$ lies on the other side (if not, we have already rejected it). To find scalar values that represent the intersection between the edges $\mathbf{u}_0\mathbf{u}_1$ and $\mathbf{u}_1\mathbf{u}_2$ and $\mathbf{l}$, the vertices are first projected onto $\mathbf{l}$:

$$p_{\mathbf{u}_i} = \mathbf{d} \cdot (\mathbf{u}_i - \mathbf{o}). \tag{13.26}$$

The geometrical situation is shown in Figure 13.18. Next, we want to use the intersection point, called $\mathbf{b}$, between the line $\mathbf{l} = \mathbf{o} + t\mathbf{d}$ and the edge $\mathbf{u}_0\mathbf{u}_1$. We call the t-value at the intersection point t_1. If we let $\mathbf{k}_i$ denote the projection of $\mathbf{u}_i$ onto π_2, we see that the triangles $\triangle\mathbf{u}_0\mathbf{b}\mathbf{k}_0$ and $\triangle\mathbf{u}_1\mathbf{b}\mathbf{k}_1$ are similar. This is also shown in Figure 13.18. Using the similar triangles,

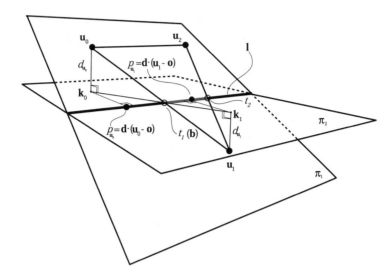

Figure 13.18. The geometrical situation. Points u_i are the vertices of T_1; π_1 and π_2 are the planes in which T_1 and T_2 lie; d_{u_i} are the signed distances from u_i to π_2; k_i are the projections of u_i onto π_2; and p_{u_i} are the projections of u_i onto l, which is the line of intersection.

t_1 can be computed as below:

$$t_1 = p_{u_0} + (p_{u_1} - p_{u_0})\frac{d_{u_0}}{d_{u_0} - d_{u_1}}. \tag{13.27}$$

Similar calculations are done to compute t_2, which represents the intersection between the line l and the edge $u_1 u_2$. Together, t_1 and t_2 represent an interval on the line l where the triangle T_1 intersects l. Using similar techniques, an interval can be computed for the other triangle, T_2, as well. If these intervals overlap, the triangles intersect.

If the triangles are co-planar, they are projected onto the axis-aligned plane where the areas of the triangles are maximized (see Section 13.8). Then, a simple two-dimensional triangle-triangle overlap test is performed. First, test all closed edges of T_1 for intersection with the closed edges of T_2. If any intersection is found, then the triangles intersect. Otherwise, we must test whether T_1 is totally contained in T_2 or vice versa. This can be done by performing a point-in-triangle test (see Section 13.7) for one vertex of T_1 against T_2 and vice versa.

Optimizations

Since the intervals can be translated without altering the result of the interval overlap test, Equation 13.26 can be simplified into:

$$p_{\mathbf{u}_i} = \mathbf{d} \cdot \mathbf{u}_i, \quad i = 0, 1, 2. \tag{13.28}$$

Therefore, $\mathbf{o}$ does not need to be computed. We can also scale the t-values in Equation 13.27 without changing the result of the overlap test, and therefore the divisions can be avoided by scaling all the t-values with appropriate factors.

Also, the result of the overlap test does not change if we project l onto the coordinate axis with which it is most closely aligned, and so Equation 13.28 can be simplified further:

$$p_{\mathbf{u}_i} = \begin{cases} u_{ix}, & \text{if } |d_x| = \max(|d_x|, |d_y|, |d_z|) \\ u_{iy}, & \text{if } |d_y| = \max(|d_x|, |d_y|, |d_z|) \\ u_{iz}, & \text{if } |d_z| = \max(|d_x|, |d_y|, |d_z|) \end{cases}, \quad i = 0, 1, 2. \tag{13.29}$$

Here, u_{0x} means the x-component of $\mathbf{u}_0$, and so on. Note that the same computations are done for the vertices of the other triangle. The same principle was used by Mirtich [552] in order to get a numerically stable simplification of an integral over a polygon's area.

Implementation

To summarize, the steps of the algorithm are as follows (complete C code is available on the web [560]):

1. Compute the plane equation of Triangle 2.

2. Trivially reject if all points of Triangle 1 are on same side.

3. Compute the plane equation of Triangle 1.

4. Trivially reject if all points of Triangle 2 are on same side.

5. Compute intersection line and project onto largest axis.

6. Compute intervals for each triangle.

7. Intersect the intervals.

Note that after Step 2, there is enough information to test immediately whether the triangles are co-planar, but because this is a rare occurrence, the test is deferred until after several more frequently hit rejection tests have been performed.

When computing the t-values in Equation 13.27, it is possible at the same time to compute the corresponding points of intersection (one of them is shown as **b** in Figure 13.18). This can be done for all four intersection points, and when intersecting the intervals, the two points that form the line segment of intersection of the two triangles can be computed. This is useful when computing accurate collision detection (Chapter 14). Source code is available for this [561].

Robustness problems may arise when the triangles are nearly co-planar or when an edge is nearly co-planar to the other triangle (especially when the edge is close to an edge of the other triangle). To handle these cases in a reasonable way, the source code provides a constant, EPSILON (ϵ), which the user defines.[12] As a result, if any $|d_{\mathbf{u}_i}| < \epsilon$, they are reset so that $d_{\mathbf{u}_i} = 0$. Geometrically, this means that if a point is "close enough" to the other triangle's plane, it is considered to be on the plane. The same is done for the points of the other triangle as well. The source code does not handle degenerate triangles (i.e., lines and points). To do so, those cases should be detected first and then handled as special cases.

13.10.2   ERIT's Method

The triangle/triangle intersection test found in ERIT [351] is outlined here.

1. Compute $\pi_2 : \mathbf{n}_2 \cdot \mathbf{x} + d_2$, the plane in which T_2 lies.

2. Trivially reject if all points of T_1 are on the same side of π_2 (also store the signed distances, $d_{\mathbf{u}_i}$, as in the previous algorithm).

3. If the triangles are coplanar, use the coplanar triangle-triangle test used in the interval overlap method.

4. Compute the intersection between π_2 and T_1, which clearly is a line segment that is coplanar with π_2. This situation is illustrated in Figure 13.19.

5. If this line segment intersects or is totally contained in T_2, then T_1 and T_2 intersect; otherwise, they do not.

Steps 1 and 2 are the same as for the interval overlap method. Step 3, on the other hand, requires computation of two points, **p** and **q**, in π_2 representing the line of intersection. Since we have the signed distances from the points of T_1 to π_2 (from Step 2), **p** and **q** can be computed by

---

[12]For floating point precision, $\epsilon = 1.0^{-6}$ works fine.

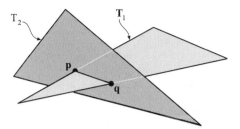

Figure 13.19. This figure depicts the way in which the ERIT method determines whether two triangles intersect. The intersection points, **p** and **q**, between triangle T_2 and triangle T_1 are computed. If the line between **p** and **q** is totally contained in T_2 or if it intersects the edges of T_2, then the triangles intersect. They are disjoint otherwise. *(Illustration after Held [351].)*

first finding points of T_1 that lie on different sides of π_2 (i.e., they have different signs on their $d_{\mathbf{u}_i}$). When such a pair, say with index i_1 and i_2, has been found, the intersection point **p** is

$$\mathbf{p} = \mathbf{u}_{i_1} + \frac{d_{\mathbf{u}_{i_1}}}{d_{\mathbf{u}_{i_1}} - d_{\mathbf{u}_{i_2}}}(\mathbf{u}_{i_2} - \mathbf{u}_{i_1}). \tag{13.30}$$

The point **q** is computed similarly, with another pair of indices found in the same manner. Step 4 is accomplished by first projecting T_2, **p**, and **q** onto the coordinate plane ($x = 0$, $y = 0$, or $z = 0$) where the area of T_2 is maximized, exactly as was done for the ray/polygon intersection methods in Section 13.8. Both points of the projected line must be tested against each *half-plane* formed by each triangle edge of T_2. The line formed by the edge of the triangle divides the plane into two sides. If both points are outside any triangle edge of T_2, the triangles do not intersect. If either endpoint is inside all three triangle edges of T_2, the triangles must intersect. It is possible that neither endpoint is inside T_2, nor both fully outside any half-plane. For this case, each edge of T_2 must be tested for intersection with the line segment **pq**, which can be done using the methods presented in Section 13.15. Finding an intersection at any time implies that the triangles intersect; otherwise, the triangles are disjoint. This last test concludes the intersection method.

13.10.3 Performance Comparison

The interval overlap method and the method from ERIT were found to be considerably faster than the brute-force method[13], which took between 1.3

---

[13] Here, each closed edge of each triangle is tested for intersection with the other triangle and if at any time an intersection occurs, then the triangles intersect.

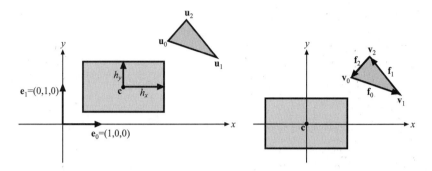

Figure 13.20. Notation used for the triangle-box overlap test. To the left the initial position of the box and the triangle is shown, while at the right, the box and the triangle has been translated so that the box center coincides with the origin.

and 1.6 times longer to execute in comparison to the two methods detailed here [561]. On a PentiumPro, ERIT's method was found to be faster, and on an Ultra-30 and on an Indigo-2, the two were comparable in speed [351].

13.11   Triangle/Box Overlap

This section presents an algorithm for determining whether a triangle intersects an axis-aligned box. Such a test can be used to build voxel-spaces, test triangles against boxes in collision detection, and test polygons against canonical view volumes (see Section 3.5), and thus potentially eliminate the need for calls to clipping and lighting routines, etc.

Green and Hatch [286] present an algorithm that can determine whether an arbitrary polygon overlaps a box. Akenine-Möller [13] developed a faster method that is based on the separating axis theorem (page 563), and which we present here.

We focus on testing an axis-aligned bounding box (AABB), defined by a center $\mathbf{c}$, and a vector of half lengths, $\mathbf{h}$, against a triangle $\Delta\mathbf{u}_0\mathbf{u}_1\mathbf{u}_2$. To simplify the tests, we first move the box and the triangle so that the box is centered around the origin, i.e., $\mathbf{v}_i = \mathbf{u}_i - \mathbf{c}$, $i \in \{0,1,2\}$. This translation and the notation used is shown in Figure 13.20. To test against an oriented box, we would first rotate the triangle vertices by the inverse box transform, then use the test here.

Based on the separating axis theorem (SAT), we test the following 13 axes:

1. [3 tests] $\mathbf{e}_0 = (1,0,0)$, $\mathbf{e}_1 = (0,1,0)$, $\mathbf{e}_2 = (0,0,1)$ (the normals of the AABB). In other words, test the AABB against the minimal AABB around the triangle.

2. [1 test] $\mathbf{n}$, the normal of $\Delta\mathbf{u}_0\mathbf{u}_1\mathbf{u}_2$. We use a fast plane/AABB overlap test (see Section 13.9.1), which tests only the two vertices of the box diagonal whose direction is most closely aligned to the normal of the triangle.

3. [9 tests] $\mathbf{a}_{ij} = \mathbf{e}_i \times \mathbf{f}_j$, $i, j \in \{0, 1, 2\}$, where $\mathbf{f}_0 = \mathbf{v}_1 - \mathbf{v}_0$, $\mathbf{f}_1 = \mathbf{v}_2 - \mathbf{v}_1$, and $\mathbf{f}_2 = \mathbf{v}_0 - \mathbf{v}_2$, i.e., edge vectors. These tests are very similar and we will only show the derivation of the case where $i = 0$ and $j = 0$ (see below).

As soon as a separating axis is found the algorithm terminates and returns "no overlap." If all tests pass, i.e., there is no separating axis, then the triangle overlaps the box.

Here we derive one of the nine tests, where $i = 0$ and $j = 0$, in Step 3 above. This means that $\mathbf{a}_{00} = \mathbf{e}_0 \times \mathbf{f}_0 = (0, -f_{0z}, f_{0y})$. So, now we need to project the triangle vertices onto $\mathbf{a}_{00}$ (hereafter called $\mathbf{a}$):

$$
\begin{aligned}
p_0 &= \mathbf{a} \cdot \mathbf{v}_0 = (0, -f_{0z}, f_{0y}) \cdot \mathbf{v}_0 = v_{0z}v_{1y} - v_{0y}v_{1z}, \\
p_1 &= \mathbf{a} \cdot \mathbf{v}_1 = (0, -f_{0z}, f_{0y}) \cdot \mathbf{v}_1 = v_{0z}v_{1y} - v_{0y}v_{1z} = p_0, \quad (13.31) \\
p_2 &= \mathbf{a} \cdot \mathbf{v}_2 = (0, -f_{0z}, f_{0y}) \cdot \mathbf{v}_2 = (v_{1y} - v_{0y})v_{2z} - (v_{1z} - v_{0z})v_{2y}.
\end{aligned}
$$

Normally, we would have had to find $\min(p_0, p_1, p_2)$ and $\max(p_0, p_1, p_2)$, but fortunately $p_0 = p_1$, which simplifies the computations. Now we only need to find $\min(p_0, p_2)$ and $\max(p_0, p_2)$, which is significantly faster because conditional statements are expensive on modern CPUs.

After the projection of the triangle onto $\mathbf{a}$, we need to project the box onto $\mathbf{a}$ as well. We compute a "radius," called r, of the box projected on $\mathbf{a}$ as

$$
r = h_x|a_x| + h_y|a_y| + h_z|a_z| = h_y|a_y| + h_z|a_z|, \quad (13.32)
$$

where the last step comes from that $a_x = 0$ for this particular axis. Then, this axis test becomes:

```
if ( min(p0, p2) > r  or  max(p0, p2) < −r) return false;    (13.33)
```

Code is available on the web [13].

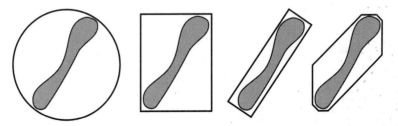

Figure 13.21. The efficiency of a bounding volume can be estimated by the "empty" volume; the more empty space, the worse the fit. A sphere (left), an AABB (middle left), an OBB (middle right), and a k-DOP (right) are shown for an object, where the OBB and the k-DOP clearly have less empty space than the others.

13.12 BV/BV Intersection Tests

A closed volume that totally contains a set of objects is (in most situations) called a *Bounding Volume* (BV) for this set. The purpose of a BV is to provide simpler intersection tests and make more efficient rejections. For example, to test whether or not two cars collide, first find their BVs and test if these overlap. If they do not, then the cars are guaranteed not to collide (which we assume is the most common case). We then have avoided testing each primitive of one car against each primitive of the other, thereby saving computation.

Bounding volume hierarchies are often part of the foundation of collision detection algorithms (see Chapter 14). Four bounding volumes that are commonly used for this purpose are the sphere, the *axis-aligned bounding box* (AABB), the *discrete oriented polytope* (k-DOP), and the *oriented bounding box* (OBB). A fundamental operation is to test whether or not two bounding volumes overlap. Methods of testing overlap for the AABB, the k-DOP, and the OBB are presented in the following sections. See Section 13.3 for algorithms that form BVs around primitives.

The reason for using more complex BVs than the sphere and the AABB is that more complex BVs often have a tighter fit. This is illustrated in Figure 13.21. Other bounding volumes are possible, of course. For example, cylinders, ellipsoids, and capsules are sometimes used as bounding volumes for objects. Also, a number of spheres can be placed to enclose a single object [373, 690].

13.12.1 Sphere/Sphere Intersection

For spheres, the intersection test is simple and quick: Compute the distance between the two spheres' centers and then reject if this distance is greater than the sum of the two spheres' radii. Otherwise, they intersect. In implementing this algorithm the squared distances of the various quantities are used, since all that is desired is the result of the comparison. In this way, computing the square root (an expensive operation) is avoided.

> bool **Sphere_intersect**$(\mathbf{c}_1, r_1, \mathbf{c}_2, r_2)$
> returns$(\{\text{OVERLAP}, \text{DISJOINT}\})$;
> 1 : $\mathbf{l} = \mathbf{c}_1 - \mathbf{c}_2$
> 2 : $l^2 = \mathbf{l} \cdot \mathbf{l}$
> 3 : if$(l^2 > (r_1 + r_2)^2)$ return (DISJOINT);
> 4 : return (OVERLAP);

13.12.2 Sphere/Box Intersection

An algorithm for testing whether a sphere and an AABB intersect was first presented by Arvo [27] and is surprisingly simple. The idea is to find the point on the AABB that is closest to the sphere's center, **c**. One-dimensional tests are used, one for each of the three axes of the AABB. The sphere's center coordinate for an axis is tested against the bounds of the AABB. If it is outside the bounds, the distance between the sphere center and the box along this axis (a subtraction) is computed and squared. After we have done this along the three axes, the sum of these squared distances is compared to the squared radius, r^2, of the sphere. If the sum is less than the squared radius, the closest point is inside the sphere, and the box overlaps.

> bool **SphereAABB_intersect**$(\mathbf{c}, r, A)$
> returns$(\{\text{OVERLAP}, \text{DISJOINT}\})$;
> 1 : $d = 0$
> 2 : for each $i \in \{x, y, z\}$
> 3 :   if$(c_i < a_i^{min})$
> 4 : $d = d + (c_i - a_i^{min})^2$;
> 5 :   else if$(c_i > a_i^{max})$
> 6 : $d = d + (c_i - a_i^{max})^2$;
> 7 : if$(d > r^2)$
> 8 :   return (DISJOINT);
> 9 : return (OVERLAP);

As Arvo shows, this algorithm can be modified to handle hollow boxes and spheres, as well as axis-aligned ellipsoids.

For sphere/OBB intersection, first transform the sphere's center into the OBB's space. That is, use the OBB's normalized axes as the basis for transforming the sphere's center. Now this center point is expressed in terms of the OBB's axes, so the OBB can be treated as an AABB. The sphere/AABB algorithm is then used to test for intersection.

13.12.3   AABB/AABB Intersection

An AABB is, as its name implies, a box whose faces are aligned with the main axis directions. Therefore, two points are sufficient to describe such a volume. Here we use the definition of the AABB presented in Section 13.2.

Due to their simplicity, AABBs are commonly employed both in collision detection algorithms and as bounding volumes for the nodes in a scene graph. The test for intersection between two AABBs, A and B, is trivial and is summarized below.

---

bool **AABB_intersect**(A, B)
returns$(\{\text{OVERLAP}, \text{DISJOINT}\})$;
1 :   for each $i \in \{x, y, z\}$
2 :   if$(a_i^{min} > b_i^{max}$ or $b_i^{min} > a_i^{max})$
3 :   return (DISJOINT);
4 :   return (OVERLAP);

Lines 1 and 2 loop over all three standard axis directions x, y, and z.

13.12.4   *k*-DOP/*k*-DOP Intersection

The bounding volume called a *discrete orientation polytope* or k-DOP was named by Klosowski et al. [433]. A k-DOP is a convex polytope[14] whose faces are determined by a small, fixed set of k normals, where the outward half-space of the normals is not considered part of the BV. Kay and Kajiya were the first to introduce this kind of BV, and they used them in the context of ray tracing. Also, they called two oppositely oriented normals a bounding *slab* and used these to keep the intersection cost down (see Section 13.6.1). This technique is used for the k-DOPs for the same reason. As a result the intersection test consists of only $k/2$ interval overlap tests.

---

[14]A (convex) polytope is the convex hull of a finite set of points (see Section A.5.3).

Klosowski et al. [433] have shown that, for moderate values of k ($k = 18$ is used in Section 14.5), the overlap test for two k-DOPs is an order of a magnitude faster than the test for two OBBs. In Figure 13.4 on page 563, a simple two-dimensional k-DOP is depicted. Note that the AABB is a special case of a 6-DOP where the normals are the positive and negative main axis directions. Also note that as k increases, the BV increasingly resembles the convex hull, which is the tightest-fitting convex BV.

The intersection test that follows is trivial and also extremely fast, as has been mentioned before. If two k-DOPs, A and B (superscripted with indices A and B), are to be tested for intersection, then test all pairs of slabs (S_i^A, S_i^B) for overlap; $s_i = S_i^A \cap S_i^B$ is a one-dimensional interval overlap test, which is solved with ease.[15] If at any time $s_i = \emptyset$ (i.e., the empty set), then the BVs are disjoint and the test is terminated. Otherwise, the slab overlap tests continues. If and only if all $s_i \neq \emptyset$, $1 \leq i \leq k/2$, then the BVs are considered to be overlapping. According to the separating axis theorem (see Section 13.2), one also needs to test an axis parallel to the cross product of one edge from each k-DOP. However, these tests are often omitted because they cost more than they give back in performance. Therefore, if the test below returns that the k-DOPs overlap, then they might actually be disjoint. Here is the pseudocode for the k-DOP/k-DOP overlap test:

$$\textbf{kDOP\_intersect}(d_1^{A,min}, \ldots, d_{k/2}^{A,min},$$
$$d_1^{A,max}, \ldots, d_{k/2}^{A,max}, d_1^{B,min}, \ldots, d_{k/2}^{B,min},$$
$$d_1^{B,max}, \ldots, d_{k/2}^{B,max})$$

$\texttt{returns}(\{\texttt{OVERLAP}, \texttt{DISJOINT}\});$

1 : $\texttt{for each } i \in \{1, \ldots, k/2\}$
2 : $\texttt{if}(d_i^{B,min} > d_i^{A,max} \texttt{ or } d_i^{A,min} > d_i^{B,max})$
3 : $\texttt{return (DISJOINT)};$
4 : $\texttt{return (OVERLAP)};$

Note that only k scalar values need to be stored with each instance of the k-DOP (the normals, $\mathbf{n}_i$, are stored once for all k-DOPs since they are static). If the k-DOPs are translated by $\mathbf{t}^A$ and $\mathbf{t}^B$, respectively, the test gets a tiny bit more complicated. Project $\mathbf{t}^A$ onto the normals, $\mathbf{n}_i$, e.g., $p_i^A = \mathbf{t}^A \cdot \mathbf{n}_i$ (note that this is independent of any k-DOP in particular and therefore needs to be computed only once for each $\mathbf{t}^A$ or $\mathbf{t}^B$) and add

---

[15]This is indeed an example of dimension reduction as the rules of thumb recommended. Here, a three-dimensional slab test is simplified into a one-dimensional interval overlap test.

p_i^A to $d_i^{A,min}$ and $d_i^{A,max}$ in the if-statement above. The same is done for $\mathbf{t}^B$. More on k-DOPs and their use can be found in Section 14.5.

13.12.5 OBB/OBB Intersection

In this section, a fast routine [283, 284] will be derived for testing whether two OBBs, A and B, overlap. The algorithm uses the separating axis theorem, and is about an order of magnitude faster than previous methods, which use closest features or linear programming. The definition of the OBB may be found in Section 13.2.

The test is done in the coordinate system formed by A's center and axes. This means that the origin is $\mathbf{a}^c = (0,0,0)$ and that the main axes in this coordinate system are $\mathbf{a}^u = (1,0,0)$, $\mathbf{a}^v = (0,1,0)$, and $\mathbf{a}^w = (0,0,1)$. Moreover, B is assumed to be located relative to A, with a translation $\mathbf{t}$ and a rotation (matrix) $\mathbf{R}$.

According to the separating axis theorem, it is sufficient to find one axis that separates A and B to be sure that they are disjoint (do not overlap). Fifteen axes have to be tested: Three from the faces of A, three from the faces of B, and $3 \cdot 3 = 9$ from combinations of edges from A and B. This is shown in two dimensions in Figure 13.22. As a consequence of the orthonormality of the matrix $\mathbf{A} = (\mathbf{a}^u \ \mathbf{a}^v \ \mathbf{a}^w)$, the potential separating axes that should be orthogonal to the faces of A are simply the axes $\mathbf{a}^u$, $\mathbf{a}^v$, and $\mathbf{a}^w$. The same holds for B. The remaining nine potential axes, formed by one edge each from both A and B, are then $\mathbf{c}^{ij} = \mathbf{a}^i \times \mathbf{b}^j$, $\forall i \in \{u,v,w\}$ and $\forall j \in \{u,v,w\}$.

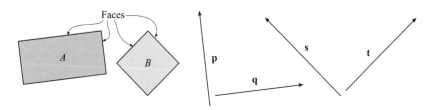

Figure 13.22. To determine whether two OBBs A and B overlap, the separating axis theorem can be used. Here, it is shown in two dimensions. The separating axes should be orthogonal to the faces of A and B. The axes $\mathbf{p}$ and $\mathbf{q}$ are orthogonal to the faces of A, and $\mathbf{s}$ and $\mathbf{t}$ are orthogonal to the faces of B. The OBBs are then projected onto the axes. If both projections overlap on all axes, then the OBBs overlap; otherwise, they do not. So it is sufficient to find one axis that separates the projections in order to know that the OBBs do not overlap. In this example, the $\mathbf{q}$ axis is the only axis that separates the projections.

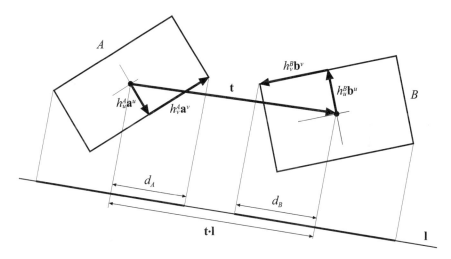

Figure 13.23. The separating axis theorem illustrated. The two OBBs, A and B, are disjoint, since the projections of their "radii" on the axis determined by $\mathbf{l}$ are not overlapping. *(Illustration after Gottschalk et al. [283].)*

Assume that a potential separating axis is denoted as $\mathbf{l}$, and adopt the notation from Figure 13.23. The "radii," d_A and d_B, of the OBBs on the axis, $\mathbf{l}$, are obtained by simple projections, as expressed in Equation 13.34. Remember that h_i^A and h_i^B are always positive, and so their absolute value does not need to be computed.

$$
\begin{aligned}
d_A &= \sum_{i\in\{u,v,w\}} h_i^A |\mathbf{a}^i \cdot \mathbf{l}| \\
d_B &= \sum_{i\in\{u,v,w\}} h_i^B |\mathbf{b}^i \cdot \mathbf{l}|
\end{aligned}
\tag{13.34}
$$

If, and only if, $\mathbf{l}$ is a separating axis, then the intervals on the axis should be disjoint. That is, the following should hold:

$$
|\mathbf{t} \cdot \mathbf{l}| > d_A + d_B.
\tag{13.35}
$$

Derivations and simplifications of Equation 13.35 for three cases follow—one for an edge of A, one for an edge of B, and one for a combination of edges from A and B.

First, let $\mathbf{l} = \mathbf{a}^u$. This gives the expression below:

$$
|\mathbf{t} \cdot \mathbf{l}| = |\mathbf{t} \cdot \mathbf{a}^u| = |t_x|.
\tag{13.36}
$$

The last step comes from the fact that we are operating in the coordinate system of A, and thus $\mathbf{a}^u = (1 \ \ 0 \ \ 0)^T$. In Equation 13.37, the expressions for d_A and d_B are simplified.

$$d_A = \sum_{i\in\{u,v,w\}} h_i^A |\mathbf{a}^i \cdot \mathbf{l}| = \sum_{i\in\{u,v,w\}} h_i^A |\mathbf{a}^i \cdot \mathbf{a}^u| = h_u^A$$

$$d_B = \sum_{i\in\{u,v,w\}} h_i^B |\mathbf{b}^i \cdot \mathbf{l}| = \sum_{i\in\{u,v,w\}} h_i^B |\mathbf{b}^i \cdot \mathbf{a}^u|$$

$$= h_u^B |b_x^u| + h_v^B |b_x^v| + h_w^B |b_x^w| = h_u^B |r_{00}| + h_v^B |r_{01}| + h_w^B |r_{02}|$$

(13.37)

The resulting equation for d_A comes from the orthonormality of $\mathbf{A}$, and in the last step in the derivation of d_B, note that

$$\mathbf{R} = \begin{pmatrix} r_{00} & r_{01} & r_{02} \\ r_{10} & r_{11} & r_{12} \\ r_{20} & r_{21} & r_{22} \end{pmatrix} = (\mathbf{b}^u \ \ \mathbf{b}^v \ \ \mathbf{b}^w), \qquad (13.38)$$

since $\mathbf{R}$ is the relative rotation matrix. The disjointedness test for the axis $\mathbf{l} = \mathbf{a}^u$ becomes

$$|t_x| > h_u^A + h_u^B |r_{00}| + h_v^B |r_{01}| + h_w^B |r_{02}|, \qquad (13.39)$$

and if this expression is true, then A and B are disjoint. Similar test expressions are derived in the same manner for $\mathbf{l} = \mathbf{a}^v$ and $\mathbf{l} = \mathbf{a}^w$.

Second, let $\mathbf{l} = \mathbf{b}^u$, for which the derivation follows:

$$|\mathbf{t} \cdot \mathbf{l}| = |\mathbf{t} \cdot \mathbf{b}^u| = |t_x b_x^u + t_y b_y^u + t_z b_z^u| = |t_x r_{00} + t_y r_{10} + t_z r_{20}|$$

$$d_A = \sum_{i\in\{u,v,w\}} h_i^A |\mathbf{a}^i \cdot \mathbf{l}| = \sum_{i\in\{u,v,w\}} h_i^A |\mathbf{a}^i \cdot \mathbf{b}^u|$$

$$= h_u^A |b_x^u| + h_v^A |b_y^u| + h_w^A |b_z^u| = h_u^A |r_{00}| + h_v^A |r_{10}| + h_w^A |r_{20}|$$

(13.40)

$$d_B = \sum_{i\in\{u,v,w\}} h_i^B |\mathbf{b}^i \cdot \mathbf{l}| = \sum_{i\in\{u,v,w\}} h_i^B |\mathbf{b}^i \cdot \mathbf{b}^u| = h_u^B.$$

This leads to the disjointedness test in Equation 13.41 for $\mathbf{l} = \mathbf{b}^u$:

$$|t_x r_{00} + t_y r_{10} + t_z r_{20}| > h_u^A |r_{00}| + h_v^A |r_{10}| + h_w^A |r_{20}| + h_u^B. \qquad (13.41)$$

Again, for the remaining axes, $\mathbf{b}^v$ and $\mathbf{b}^w$, similar tests are derived in the above manner.

Finally, the separating axis could be a combination of an edge from each OBB. As an example, the axis is chosen as $\mathbf{l} = \mathbf{a}^u \times \mathbf{b}^v$. This gives:

$$|\mathbf{t} \cdot \mathbf{l}| = |\mathbf{t} \cdot (\mathbf{a}^u \times \mathbf{b}^v)| = |\mathbf{t} \cdot (0, -b_z^v, b_y^v)|$$
$$= |t_z b_y^v - t_y b_z^v| = |t_z r_{11} - t_y r_{21}|$$

$$d_A = \sum_{i \in \{u,v,w\}} h_i^A |\mathbf{a}^i \cdot \mathbf{l}| = \sum_{i \in \{u,v,w\}} h_i^A |\mathbf{a}^i \cdot (\mathbf{a}^u \times \mathbf{b}^v)|$$
$$= \sum_{i \in \{u,v,w\}} h_i^A |\mathbf{b}^v \cdot (\mathbf{a}^u \times \mathbf{a}^i)| = h_v^A |\mathbf{b}^v \cdot \mathbf{a}^w| + h_w^A |\mathbf{b}^v \cdot \mathbf{a}^v|$$
$$= h_v^A |b_z^v| + h_w^A |b_y^v| = h_v^A |r_{21}| + h_w^A |r_{11}|$$

$$(13.42)$$

$$d_B = \sum_{i \in \{u,v,w\}} h_i^B |\mathbf{b}^i \cdot \mathbf{l}| = \sum_{i \in \{u,v,w\}} h_i^B |\mathbf{b}^i \cdot (\mathbf{a}^u \times \mathbf{b}^v)|$$
$$= \sum_{i \in \{u,v,w\}} h_i^B |\mathbf{a}^u \cdot (\mathbf{b}^i \times \mathbf{b}^v)| = h_u^B |\mathbf{a}^u \cdot \mathbf{b}^w| + h_w^B |\mathbf{a}^u \cdot \mathbf{b}^u|$$
$$= h_u^B |b_x^w| + h_w^B |b_x^u| = h_u^B |r_{02}| + h_w^B |r_{00}|.$$

The resulting test becomes:

$$|t_z r_{11} - t_y r_{21}| > h_v^A |r_{21}| + h_w^A |r_{11}| + h_u^B |r_{02}| + h_w^B |r_{00}|. \qquad (13.43)$$

Disjointedness tests for the remaining axes, formed by $\mathbf{c}^{ij} = \mathbf{a}^i \times \mathbf{b}^j$, $\forall i \in \{u, v, w\}$ and $\forall j \in \{u, v, w\}$, are derived analogously.

Once again, if any of these 15 tests is positive, the OBBs are disjoint ($A \cap B = \emptyset$). The maximum number of operations (reported to be around 180, or 240 if the transform of B into A's coordinate system is included) [284] occurs when the OBBs overlap ($A \cap B \neq \emptyset$). However, in most cases, the routine may terminate earlier because a separating axis has been found. Gottschalk et al. [283] point out that the absolute values of the elements of $\mathbf{R}$ are used four times and could therefore be computed once and reused for more rapid code.

Note that testing the axes in different orders has an impact on performance. To get a good average result for two OBBs, A and B, one should first test the three axes $\mathbf{a}^u$, $\mathbf{a}^v$, and $\mathbf{a}^w$. The main reasons for this are that they are orthogonal and thus reject the overlap faster, and that they are the simplest tests [663]. After these have been tested, the axes of B could be tested, followed by the axes formed from the axes of A and B.

Depending on the application, it may be worthwhile to add a quick rejection test before beginning the actual OBB/OBB test. The enclosing sphere for an OBB is centered at the OBB's center $\mathbf{b}^c$, and the sphere's radius is computed from the OBB's half-lengths h_u, h_v, and h_w. Then the sphere/sphere intersection test (Section 13.12.1) can be used for a possible quick rejection.

13.13   View Frustrum Intersection

As has been seen in Section 9.4, hierarchical view frustum culling is essential for rapid rendering of the scene graph. One of the few operations called during bounding-volume-hierarchy (scene-graph) cull traversal is the intersection test between the view frustum and a bounding volume. These operations are thus critical to fast execution. Ideally, they should determine whether the BV is totally inside (inclusion), totally outside (exclusion), or whether it intersects the frustum.

To review, a view frustum is a pyramid that is truncated by a near and a far plane (which are parallel), making the volume finite. In fact, it becomes a polyhedron. This is shown in Figure 13.24, where the names of the six planes, *near*, *far*, *left*, *right*, *top*, and *bottom* also are marked. The view frustum volume defines the parts of the scene that should be visible and thus rendered (in perspective for a pyramidal frustum).

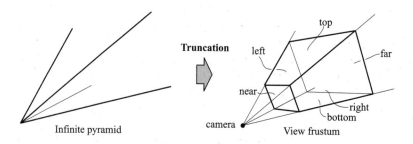

Figure 13.24. The illustration on the left is an infinite pyramid, which then is cropped by the parallel near and far planes in order to construct a view frustum. The names of the other planes are also shown, and the position of the camera is at the apex of the pyramid.

The most common bounding volumes used for internal nodes in a hierarchy (e.g., a scene graph) and for enclosing geometry are spheres, AABBs, and OBBs. Therefore frustum/sphere and frustum/AABB/OBB tests will be discussed and derived here.

To see why we need the three return results outside/inside/intersect, we will examine what happens when traversing the bounding volume hierarchy. If a BV is found to be totally outside the view frustum, then that BV's subtree will not be traversed further and none of its geometry will be rendered. On the other hand, if the BV is totally inside, then no more frustum/BV tests need to be computed for that subtree and every renderable leaf will be drawn. For a partially visible BV, i.e., one that intersects the frustum, the BV's subtree is tested recursively against the frustum. If the BV is for a leaf, then that leaf must be rendered.

The complete test is called an *exclusion/inclusion/intersection test*. Sometimes the third state, intersection, may be considered too costly to compute. In this case, the BV is classified as "probably-inside." We call such a simplified algorithm an *exclusion/inclusion test*. If a BV cannot be excluded successfully, there are two choices. One is to treat the "probably-inside" state as an inclusion, meaning that everything inside the BV is rendered. This is often inefficient, as no further culling is performed. The other choice is to test each node in the subtree in turn for exclusion. Such testing is often without benefit, as much of the subtree may indeed be inside the frustum. Because neither choice is particularly good, some attempt at quickly differentiating between intersection and inclusion is often worthwhile, even if the test is imperfect.

It is important to realize that the quick classification tests do not have to be perfect for scene-graph culling. For differentiating exclusion from inclusion, all that is required is that the test err on the side of inclusion. That is, objects which should actually be excluded can erroneously be included. Such mistakes simply cost extra time. On the other hand, objects that should be included should never be quickly classified as excluded by the tests, otherwise rendering errors will occur. With inclusion versus intersection, either type of incorrect classification is usually legal. If a fully included BV is classified as intersecting, time is wasted testing its subtree for intersection. If an intersected BV is considered fully inside, time is wasted by rendering all objects, some of which may have been culled.

Before we introduce the tests between a frustum and a sphere, AABB, or OBB, we shall describe an intersection test method between a frustum and a general object. This test is illustrated in Figure 13.25. The idea is to transform the test from a BV/frustum test to a point/volume test. Here we describe how this can be done. First, a point relative to the

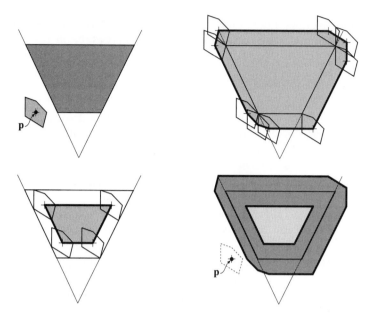

Figure 13.25. The upper left image shows a frustum (light gray) and a general bounding volume (dark gray), where a point **p** relative to the object has been selected. By tracing the point **p** where the object moves on the outside (upper right) and on the inside (lower left) of the frustum, as close as possible to the frustum, the frustum/BV can be reformulated into testing the point **p** against an outer and an inner volume. This is shown on the lower right. If the point **p** is outside the dark gray volume, then the BV is outside the frustum. The BV intersects the frustum if **p** is inside the dark gray area, and the BV is inside the frustum if **p** is inside the light gray area.

BV is selected. Then the BV is moved along the outside of the frustum, as closely as possible to it without overlapping. During this movement, the point relative to the BV is traced, and its trace forms a new volume (a polygon with thick edges in Figure 13.25). The fact that the BV was moved as close as possible to the frustum means that if the point relative to the BV (in its original position) lies inside the traced-out volume, then the BV intersects or is inside the frustum. So instead of testing the BV for intersection against a frustum, the point relative to the BV is tested against another new volume, which is traced out by the point. In the same way, the BV can be moved on the inside of the frustum and as close as possible to the frustum. This will trace out a new, smaller frustum with planes parallel to the original frustum [33]. If the point relative to the object is inside this new volume, then the BV is inside the frustum. This technique is used to derive tests in the subsequent sections. Note that the creation of the new volumes is independent of the position of the actual BV—it is dependent solely on the position of the point relative to the BV. This means that a BV with an arbitrary position can be tested against the same volumes.

Frustum/sphere intersection is presented next. Its relationship to frustum/cylinder intersection is briefly discussed, followed by an explanation of frustum/box intersection. In Section 13.13.4, the plane equations of the frustum are derived since these are needed for these sorts of tests.

13.13.1 Frustum/Sphere Intersection

A frustum for an orthographic view is a box, so the overlap test in this case becomes a sphere/OBB intersection and can be solved using the algorithm presented in Section 13.12.2. To further test whether the sphere is entirely inside the box, we treat the box as hollow when we are finding the closest point. For a full presentation of this modified algorithm, along with code, see Arvo [27].

Following the method for deriving a frustum/BV test, we select the origin of the sphere as the point **p** to trace. This is shown in Figure 13.26. If the sphere, with radius r, is moved along the inside and along the outside of the frustum and as close to the frustum as possible, then the trace of **p** gives us the volumes that are needed to reformulate the frustum/sphere test. The actual volumes are shown in the middle segment of Figure 13.26. As before, if **p** is outside the dark gray volume, then the sphere is outside

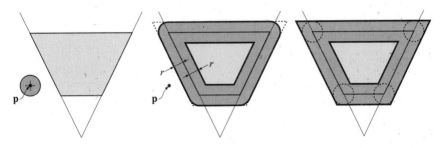

Figure 13.26. At the left, a frustum and a sphere are shown. The exact frustum/sphere test can be formulated as testing **p** against the dark and light gray volumes in the middle figure. At the right is a reasonable approximation of the volumes in the middle. If the center of the sphere is located outside a rounded corner, but inside all outer planes, then it will be incorrectly classified as intersecting even though it is outside the frustum.

the frustum. If **p** is inside the dark gray area, then the sphere is inside the frustum. In this way, the exact test can be done. However, for the sake of efficiency we use the approximation that appears on the right side of Figure 13.26. Here, the dark gray volume has been extended so as to avoid the more complicated computations that the rounded corners would require. Note that the outer volume consists of the planes of the frustum moved r distance units outwards in the direction of the frustum plane normal, and that the inner volume can be created by moving the planes of the frustum r distance units inwards in the direction of the frustum plane normals.

Assume that the plane equations of the frustum are such that the positive half-space is located outside of the frustum. Then, an actual implementation would loop over the six planes of the frustum, and for each frustum plane, compute the signed distance from the sphere's center to the plane. This is done by inserting the sphere center into the plane equation. If the distance is greater than the radius r, then the sphere is outside the frustum. If the distances to all six planes are less than $-r$, then the sphere is inside the frustum; otherwise the sphere intersects it.[16] To make the test more accurate, it is possible to add extra planes for testing if the sphere is outside. However, for the purposes of quickly culling out scenegraph nodes, occasional false hits simply cause unnecessary testing, not algorithm failure, and this additional testing will cost more time overall.

Most frustums are symmetric around the view direction, meaning that the left plane is the right plane reflected around the view direction. This also holds for the bottom and top planes. To reduce the number of planes that must be tested for a symmetric frustum, an *octant test* can be added to the previous view frustum test [33]. For this test, the frustum is divided into eight octants, much as an octree is subdivided (see Figure 13.27). When that has been done, we need to test against only the three outer planes of the octant that the sphere center is in. This means that we can actually halve the number of planes that need to be tested. While it was found that this test did not improve the performance of a frustum/sphere test, since the sphere/plane test is already so fast, it could be extended and used for arbitrary objects (see the right side of Figure 13.27). As will be seen in the next sections, this test can be used to speed up the frustum tests for AABBs and OBBs.

Bishop et al. [65] discuss the following clever optimizations for using sphere culling in a game engine. If a BV is found to be fully inside a

---

[16]More correctly, we *say* that the sphere intersects the frustum, but the sphere center may be located in the rounded corners shown in Figure 13.26. This would mean that the sphere is outside the frustum but we report it to be intersecting.

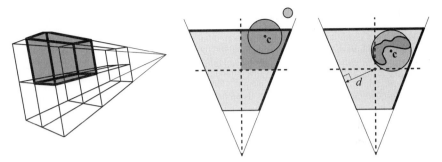

Figure 13.27. The left figure shows how a three-dimensional frustum is divided into eight octants. The other figure shows a two-dimensional example, where the sphere center **c** is in the upper right octant. The only planes that then need to be considered are the right and the far planes (thick black lines). Note that the small sphere is in the same octant as the large sphere. This technique also works for arbitrary objects, but the following condition must hold: The minimum distance, called d, from the frustum center to the frustum planes must be larger than the radius of a tight bounding sphere around the object. If that condition is fulfilled, then the bounding sphere can be used to find the octant.

certain frustum plane, then its children are also inside this plane. This means that this plane test can be omitted for all children, which can result in faster overall testing.

13.13.2 Frustum/Cylinder Intersection

Frustum/cylinder intersection is done in a similar fashion to basic frustum/sphere testing. The cylinder is treated as a line segment, and the frustum is increased in size by the sphere's radius. Instead of increasing the frustum by a uniform radius in all directions, the axis of the cylinder is used to determine how the radius affects each frustum plane.

Specifically, the absolute value of the dot product of the cylinder's (normalized) axis direction and the frustum plane's normal is multiplied by the cylinder radius. This result is how much the frustum plane is moved outward. Given the expanded frustum and the line segment representing the cylinder, it is simply a matter of intersecting the line segment with the frustum to determine whether the cylinder overlaps the frustum. As with the sphere test, this test is not exactly correct near the corners and edges of the frustum. However, this inaccuracy leads only to false hits and lost efficiency; cylinders overlapping the frustum will never be categorized as outside.

A thorough explanation and code for this algorithm is presented by Lengyel [484].

13.13.3   Frustum/Box Intersection

If the view's projection is orthographic (i.e., the frustum has a box shape), testing can be done using OBB/OBB intersection testing (see Section 13.12.5). For general frustum/box intersection testing there is a simple exclusion/inclusion test. This test is similar to the frustum/sphere test in that the OBB or AABB bounding box is checked against the six view frustum planes. If all corner points of the bounding box are outside of one such plane, the bounding box is guaranteed to be outside the frustum. However, instead of checking all corner points (in the worst case) with each plane equation, we can use the smarter test presented in Section 13.9. This algorithm states that only two bounding box corners needs to be tested against a particular plane to find out on which side of the plane the box is, or whether it is intersecting the plane.

So the algorithm tests the box against each of the six frustum planes in turn. If the box is outside one such plane, the box is outside the frustum and the test is terminated. If the box is inside all six planes, then the box is inside the frustum, else it is considered as intersecting the frustum (even though it might actually be slightly outside—see below). Pseudocode for this is shown below, where π^i, $i = 0 \ldots 5$, are the six frustum planes and B is the AABB. As can be seen, the core of this algorithm is the plane/box test from Section 13.9.

```
      bool FrustumAABBIntersect(π⁰, ..., π⁵, B)
      returns({OUTSIDE, INSIDE, INTERSECTING});
 1 :  intersecting = false;
 2 :  for k = 0 to 5
 3 :      for each i ∈ {x, y, z}
 4 :          if(nᵢᵏ ≥ 0)
 5 :              vᵢᵐⁱⁿ = bᵢᵐⁱⁿ
 6 :              vᵢᵐᵃˣ = bᵢᵐᵃˣ
 7 :          else
 8 :              vᵢᵐⁱⁿ = bᵢᵐᵃˣ
 9 :              vᵢᵐᵃˣ = bᵢᵐⁱⁿ
10 :      if((nᵏ · vᵐⁱⁿ + dᵏ) > 0) return OUTSIDE;
11 :      if((n · vᵐᵃˣ + d) >= 0) intersecting = true;
12 :  if(intersecting == true) return INTERSECTING;
13 :  else return INSIDE;
```

Similar to the frustum/sphere algorithm, this test suffers from classifying boxes as intersecting that are actually fully outside. Those kinds of

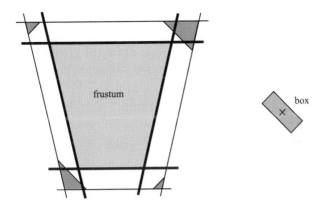

Figure 13.28. The bold black lines are the planes of the frustum. When testing the box (left) against the frustum using the presented algorithm, the box can be incorrectly classified as intersecting when it is outside. For the situation in the figure, this happens when the box's center is located in the dark gray areas.

errors are shown in Figure 13.28. An exclusion/inclusion approach that does not have this problem is to use the separating axis theorem (found in Section 13.12) to derive an intersection routine.

Since the plane/box test is more expensive than the plane/sphere test, there is often a gain in using the octant test from Section 13.13.1. This test would immediately discard three of the six frustum planes [33]. The techniques discussed in the previous section from Bishop [65] for optimizing testing and clipping of bounding spheres apply here as well.

13.13.4 Frustum Plane Extraction

In order to do view frustum culling, the plane equations for the six different sides of the frustum are needed. Here, a clever and fast way of deriving these is presented. Assume that the view matrix is V and that the projection matrix is P. The composite transform is then $M = PV$. A point s (where $s_w = 1$) is transformed into t as $t = Ms$. At this point, t may have $t_w \neq 1$ due to, for example, perspective projection. Therefore, all components in t are divided by t_w in order to obtain a point u with $u_w = 1$. For points inside the view frustum,[17] it holds that $-1 \leq u_i \leq 1$, for $i \in x, y, z$, i.e.,

---

[17]This is for the OpenGL type of projection matrices (see Section 3.5). For Direct3D, the same holds, except that $0 \leq u_z \leq 1$.

the point **u** is inside a unit cube. From this equation, the planes of the frustum can be derived, which is shown next.

Focus for a moment on the right side of the left plane of the unit-cube, for which $-1 \leq u_x$. This is expanded below:

$$-1 \leq u_x \iff -1 \leq \frac{t_x}{t_w} \iff t_x + t_w \geq 0 \iff$$

$$\iff (\mathbf{m}_0 \cdot \mathbf{s}) + (\mathbf{m}_3 \cdot \mathbf{s}) \geq 0 \iff (\mathbf{m}_0 + \mathbf{m}_3) \cdot \mathbf{s} \geq 0. \tag{13.44}$$

In the derivation above, $\mathbf{m}_i$ denotes the i:th row in **M**. The last step $(\mathbf{m}_0 + \mathbf{m}_3) \cdot \mathbf{s} \geq 0$ is, in fact, denoting a (half) plane equation of the left plane of the view frustum. This is so because the left plane in the unit-cube has been transformed back to world coordinates. Also note that $s_w = 1$, which makes the equation a plane. To make the normal of the plane point outwards from the frustum, the equation must be negated (as the original equation described the inside of the unit-cube). This gives $-(\mathbf{m}_3 + \mathbf{m}_0) \cdot (x, y, z, 1) = 0$ for the left plane of the frustum (where we use $(x, y, z, 1)$ instead to use a plane equation of the form: $ax + bx + cx + d = 0$). To summarize, all the planes are:

$$\begin{aligned}
-(\mathbf{m}_3 + \mathbf{m}_0) \cdot (x, y, z, 1) &= 0 \quad \text{[\textbf{left}]} \\
-(\mathbf{m}_3 - \mathbf{m}_0) \cdot (x, y, z, 1) &= 0 \quad \text{[\textbf{right}]} \\
-(\mathbf{m}_3 + \mathbf{m}_1) \cdot (x, y, z, 1) &= 0 \quad \text{[\textbf{bottom}]} \\
-(\mathbf{m}_3 - \mathbf{m}_1) \cdot (x, y, z, 1) &= 0 \quad \text{[\textbf{top}]} \\
-(\mathbf{m}_3 + \mathbf{m}_2) \cdot (x, y, z, 1) &= 0 \quad \text{[\textbf{near}]} \\
-(\mathbf{m}_3 - \mathbf{m}_2) \cdot (x, y, z, 1) &= 0 \quad \text{[\textbf{far}]}.
\end{aligned} \tag{13.45}$$

Code for doing this in OpenGL and DirectX is available on the web [295].

13.14 Shaft/Box and Shaft/Sphere Intersection

Sometimes it is important to find what is in between two AABBs. This operation can be useful for occlusion culling (see Section 9.7.3), for dynamic intersection testing (see Section 13.17), or for light transport algorithms such as radiosity. The volume between two AABBs, including the AABBs themselves, is called a *shaft*, and the intersection operation is called *shaft culling*. See Figure 13.29.

A shaft is actually defined by a single large AABB and set of planes. Each plane trims off some amount of volume from the AABB, and the volume inside the AABB and all the planes is the shaft. In fact, the shaft's

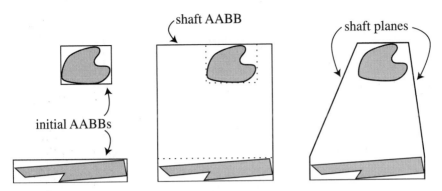

Figure 13.29. Two initial AABBs define a shaft. First, the shaft's AABB is formed to enclose these two AABBs. Then, planes are added to the shaft's definition to chop off volumes of space that are not between the initial AABBs.

AABB can be thought of as a set of six planes, thereby defining the shaft as only a set of planes. That said, it is important that six of the planes that make a shaft be axis-aligned, as this property ensures that no false hits are generated when testing against another AABB.

The shaft is defined by two initial AABBs, e.g., the bounding boxes for the two objects forming the shaft. The shaft's AABB is simply the minimal AABB surrounding these two initial AABBs. The next task is computing the set of planes connecting the two initial AABBs. Each plane is associated with, and parallel to, one of the twelve edges of the shaft's AABB. Each plane generated attaches one of the twelve edges of one of the initial AABBs to the corresponding edge of the other initial AABB.

To determine which edges form planes for the shaft, first, for each of the six faces of the shaft's AABB, find which initial AABB it touches. Now examine each edge of the shaft's AABB: if the two faces bordering this edge touch different initial AABBs, then a plane joining the corresponding edges of these initial AABBs is formed and added to the shaft definition.[18] Up to eight different planes can be added to the shaft in this way (there are twelve shaft AABB edges, but not all edges will form planes). At this point, shaft formation is done. As an example, in Figure 13.29, the upper initial AABB touches the top of the shaft's AABB, and the lower initial

---

[18]Another way to think of this process is to imagine the shaft's AABB. If the first initial AABB touches a face of the shaft's AABB, paint the shaft AABB's face red, else paint it blue (because it must be touched by the other initial AABB). Any edge touching a red and a blue face is one for which a shaft plane is formed, which will chop this edge off the shaft's AABB.

AABB touches the other sides. Planes are generated for only the upper edges, since these edges adjoin shaft AABB faces that touch different initial AABBs.

To test a shaft against another AABB or a sphere, first the shaft's AABB and then each plane in turn is tested against the primitive. If the primitive is fully outside the AABB or any plane, then testing is done and the shaft does not intersect the primitive. If the primitive is fully inside all planes, then the primitive is inside the shaft. Otherwise, the primitive overlaps the shaft. Testing against a shaft, then, is simply a series of plane/AABB (Section 13.9) or plane/sphere (Section 13.13.1) tests. While it is possible for false hits to be generated when doing shaft/sphere testing, shaft/box testing is exact.

Haines and Wallace discuss optimizations for shaft formation and culling, and code is available on the web [308, 311].

13.15　Line/Line Intersection Tests

In this section, both two- and three-dimensional line/line intersection tests will be derived and examined. Lines, rays, and line segments will be intersected, and methods that are both fast and elegant will be described.

13.15.1　Two Dimensions

First Method

From a theoretical viewpoint, this first method of computing the intersection between a pair of two-dimensional lines is truly beautiful. Consider two lines, $r_1(s) = o_1 + sd_1$ and $r_2(t) = o_2 + td_2$. Since $a \cdot a^\perp = 0$ (the perp dot product [359] from Section 1.2.1), the intersection calculations between $r_1(s)$ and $r_2(t)$ become elegant and simple. Note that all vectors are two-dimensional in this subsection.

$$1: \qquad r_1(s) = r_2(t)$$
$$\Longleftrightarrow$$
$$2: \qquad o_1 + sd_1 = o_2 + td_2$$
$$\Longleftrightarrow$$
$$3: \quad \begin{cases} sd_1 \cdot d_2^\perp = (o_2 - o_1) \cdot d_2^\perp \\ td_2 \cdot d_1^\perp = (o_1 - o_2) \cdot d_1^\perp \end{cases}$$
$$\Longleftrightarrow$$

$$4: \begin{cases} s = \dfrac{(\mathbf{o}_2 - \mathbf{o}_1) \cdot \mathbf{d}_2^{\perp}}{\mathbf{d}_1 \cdot \mathbf{d}_2^{\perp}} \\[3mm] t = \dfrac{(\mathbf{o}_1 - \mathbf{o}_2) \cdot \mathbf{d}_1^{\perp}}{\mathbf{d}_2 \cdot \mathbf{d}_1^{\perp}} \end{cases} \qquad (13.46)$$

If $\mathbf{d}_1 \cdot \mathbf{d}_2^{\perp} = 0$, then the lines are parallel and no intersection occurs. For lines of infinite length, all values of s and t are valid, but for line segments (with normalized directions), say of length l_1 and l_2 (starting at $s = 0$ and $t = 0$ and ending at $s = l_1$ and $t = l_2$), we have a valid intersection if and only if $0 \leq s \leq l_1$ and $0 \leq t \leq l_2$. Or, if you set $\mathbf{o}_1 = \mathbf{p}_1$ and $\mathbf{d}_1 = \mathbf{p}_2 - \mathbf{p}_1$ (meaning that the line segment starts at $\mathbf{p}_1$ and ends at $\mathbf{p}_2$) and do likewise for $\mathbf{r}_2$ with start and end points $\mathbf{q}_1$ and $\mathbf{q}_2$, then a valid intersection occurs if and only if $0 \leq s \leq 1$ and $0 \leq t \leq 1$. For rays with origins, the valid range is $s \geq 0$ and $t \geq 0$. The point of intersection is obtained either by plugging s into $\mathbf{r}_1$ or by plugging t into $\mathbf{r}_2$.

Second Method

Antonio [21] describes another way of deciding whether two line segments (i.e., of finite length) intersect by doing more compares and early rejections and by avoiding the expensive calculations (divisions) in the formulae above. This method is therefore very fast. The notation from above is used again, i.e., the first line segment goes from $\mathbf{p}_1$ to $\mathbf{p}_2$ and the second from $\mathbf{q}_1$ to $\mathbf{q}_2$. This means $\mathbf{r}_1(s) = \mathbf{p}_1 + s(\mathbf{p}_2 - \mathbf{p}_1)$ and $\mathbf{r}_2(t) = \mathbf{q}_1 + t(\mathbf{q}_2 - \mathbf{q}_1)$. The result from Equation 13.46 is used to obtain a solution to $\mathbf{r}_1(s) = \mathbf{r}_2(t)$:

$$\begin{cases} s = \dfrac{-\mathbf{c} \cdot \mathbf{a}^{\perp}}{\mathbf{b} \cdot \mathbf{a}^{\perp}} = \dfrac{\mathbf{c} \cdot \mathbf{a}^{\perp}}{\mathbf{a} \cdot \mathbf{b}^{\perp}} = \dfrac{d}{f} \\[3mm] t = \dfrac{\mathbf{c} \cdot \mathbf{b}^{\perp}}{\mathbf{a} \cdot \mathbf{b}^{\perp}} = \dfrac{e}{f}. \end{cases} \qquad (13.47)$$

In Equation 13.47, $\mathbf{a} = \mathbf{q}_2 - \mathbf{q}_1$, $\mathbf{b} = \mathbf{p}_2 - \mathbf{p}_1$, $\mathbf{c} = \mathbf{p}_1 - \mathbf{q}_1$, $d = \mathbf{c} \cdot \mathbf{a}^{\perp}$, $e = \mathbf{c} \cdot \mathbf{b}^{\perp}$, and $f = \mathbf{a} \cdot \mathbf{b}^{\perp}$. The simplification step for the factor s comes from the fact that $\mathbf{a}^{\perp} \cdot \mathbf{b} = -\mathbf{b}^{\perp} \cdot \mathbf{a}$ and $\mathbf{a} \cdot \mathbf{b}^{\perp} = \mathbf{b}^{\perp} \cdot \mathbf{a}$. If $\mathbf{a} \cdot \mathbf{b}^{\perp} = 0$, then the lines are collinear. Antonio [21] observes that the denominators for both s and t are the same, and that, since s and t are not needed explicitly, the division operation can be omitted. Define $s = d/f$ and $t = e/f$. To test if $0 \leq s \leq 1$ the following code is used:

```
1 : if(f > 0)
2 :     if(d < 0 or d > f) return NO_INTERSECTION;
3 : else
4 :     if(d > 0 or d < f) return NO_INTERSECTION;
```

After this test, it is guaranteed that $0 \leq s \leq 1$. The same is then done for $t = e/f$ (by replacing d by e in the code above). If the routine has not returned after this test, the line segments do intersect, since the t-value is then also valid.

Code for an integer version of this routine is available on the web [21], and is easily converted for use with floating point numbers.

13.15.2 Three Dimensions

Say we want to compute in three dimensions the intersection between two lines (defined by rays, Equation 13.1). The lines are again called $r_1(s) = o_1 + sd_1$ and $r_2(t) = o_2 + td_2$, with no limitation on the value of t. The three-dimensional counterpart of the perp dot product is, in this case, the cross product, since $a \times a = 0$, and therefore the derivation of the three-dimensional version is very similar to that of the two-dimensional version. The intersection between two lines is derived below:

$1:$
$$r_1(s) = r_2(t)$$
$$\Longleftrightarrow$$

$2:$
$$o_1 + sd_1 = o_2 + td_2$$
$$\Longleftrightarrow$$

$3:$
$$\begin{cases} sd_1 \times d_2 = (o_2 - o_1) \times d_2 \\ td_2 \times d_1 = (o_1 - o_2) \times d_1 \end{cases}$$
$$\Longleftrightarrow$$

$4:$
$$\begin{cases} s(d_1 \times d_2) \cdot (d_1 \times d_2) = ((o_2 - o_1) \times d_2) \cdot (d_1 \times d_2) \\ t(d_2 \times d_1) \cdot (d_2 \times d_1) = ((o_1 - o_2) \times d_1) \cdot (d_2 \times d_1) \end{cases} \quad (13.48)$$
$$\Longleftrightarrow$$

$5:$
$$\begin{cases} s = \dfrac{\det(o_2 - o_1, d_2, d_1 \times d_2)}{||d_1 \times d_2||^2} \\ \\ t = \dfrac{\det(o_2 - o_1, d_1, d_1 \times d_2)}{||d_1 \times d_2||^2} \end{cases}$$

Step 3 comes from subtracting o_1 (o_2) from both sides and then crossing with d_2 (d_1), and Step 4 is obtained by dotting with $d_1 \times d_2$ ($d_2 \times d_1$).

Finally, Step 5, the solution, is found by rewriting the right sides as determinants (and changing some signs in the bottom equation) and then by dividing by the term located to the right of s (t).

Goldman [267] notes that if the denominator $||\mathbf{d}_1 \times \mathbf{d}_2||^2$ equals 0, then the lines are parallel. He also observes that if the lines are skew (i.e., they do not share a common plane), then the s and t parameters represent the points of closest approach.

If the lines are to be treated like line segments, with lengths l_1 and l_2 (assuming the direction vectors $\mathbf{d}_1$ and $\mathbf{d}_2$ are normalized), then check whether $0 \leq s \leq l_1$ and $0 \leq t \leq l_2$ both hold. If not, then the intersection is rejected.

Rhodes [652] gives an in-depth solution to the problem of intersecting two lines or line segments. He gives robust solutions that deal with special cases, and he discusses optimizations and provides source code.

13.16   Intersection Between Three Planes

Given three planes, each described by a normalized normal vector, $\mathbf{n}_i$, and an arbitrary point on the plane, $\mathbf{p}_i$, $i = 1, 2$, and 3, the unique point, $\mathbf{p}$, of intersection between those planes is given by Equation 13.49 [266]. Note that the denominator, the determinant of the three plane normals, is zero if two or more planes are parallel.

$$\mathbf{p} = \frac{(\mathbf{p}_1 \cdot \mathbf{n}_1)(\mathbf{n}_2 \times \mathbf{n}_3) + (\mathbf{p}_2 \cdot \mathbf{n}_2)(\mathbf{n}_3 \times \mathbf{n}_1) + (\mathbf{p}_3 \cdot \mathbf{n}_3)(\mathbf{n}_1 \times \mathbf{n}_2)}{|\mathbf{n}_1 \; \mathbf{n}_2 \; \mathbf{n}_3|} \quad (13.49)$$

This formula can be used to compute the corners of a BV consisting of a set of planes. An example is a k-DOP, which consists of k plane equations. Equation 13.49 can calculate the corners of the polytope if it is fed with the right planes.

If, as is usual, the planes are given in implicit form, i.e., $\pi_i : \mathbf{n}_i \cdot \mathbf{x} + d_i = 0$, then we need to find the points $\mathbf{p}_i$ in order to be able to use the equation. Any arbitrary point on the plane can be chosen. We compute the point closest to the origin, since those calculations are inexpensive. Given a ray from the origin pointing along the plane's normal, intersect this with the plane to get the point closest to the origin:

$$\left.\begin{array}{l} \mathbf{r}_i(t) = t\mathbf{n}_i \\ \mathbf{n}_i \cdot \mathbf{x} + d_i = 0 \end{array}\right\} \Rightarrow$$

$$\mathbf{n}_i \cdot \mathbf{r}_i(t) + d_i = 0$$
$$\Longleftrightarrow$$
$$t\mathbf{n}_i \cdot \mathbf{n}_i + d_i = 0 \qquad\qquad (13.50)$$
$$\Longleftrightarrow$$
$$t = -d_i$$
$$\Rightarrow$$
$$\mathbf{p}_i = \mathbf{r}_i(-d_i) = -d_i\mathbf{n}_i.$$

This result should not come as a surprise, since d_i in the plane equation simply holds the perpendicular, negative distance from the origin to the plane (the normal must be of unit length if this is to be true).

13.17   Dynamic Intersection Testing

Up until now, only *static* intersection testing has been considered. This means that all objects involved are not moving during testing. However, this is not always a realistic scenario, especially since we render frames at discrete times. For example, discrete testing means that a ball that is on one side of a closed door at time t might move to the other side at $t+\Delta t$ (i.e., the next frame), without any collision being noticed by a static intersection test. This is sometimes called quantum tunneling [65].[19] One solution is to make several tests uniformly spaced between t and $t + \Delta t$. This would increase the computational load, and still the intersection could be missed. A *dynamic* intersection test is designed to cope with this problem. This section provides an introduction to the topic. More information can be found in Eberly's *3D Game Engine Design* book [199].

Methods such as shaft culling (Section 13.14) can be used to aid in intersection testing of moving AABBs. The object moving through space is represented by two AABBs at different times, and these two AABBs are joined by a shaft. However, intersection algorithms usually become simpler and faster if the moving object is contained in a bounding sphere. In fact, it is often worthwhile to use a set of a few spheres to represent the moving object [690].

---

[19]It is called quantum tunneling because it resembles the situation in quantum mechanics, where electrons tunnel through barriers that are otherwise impenetrable. However, note that it has nothing to do with quantum mechanics.

One principle that can be applied to all dynamic intersection testing situations is the fact that motion is relative. Assume object A moves with velocity $\mathbf{v}_A$ and object B with velocity $\mathbf{v}_B$, where the velocity is the amount an object has moved during the frame. To simplify calculations, we instead assume that A is moving and B is still. To compensate for B's velocity, A's velocity is then: $\mathbf{v} = \mathbf{v}_A - \mathbf{v}_B$. As such, only one object is given a velocity in the algorithms that follow.

13.17.1 Sphere/Plane

Testing a sphere dynamically against a plane is simple. Assume the sphere has its center at $\mathbf{c}$ and a radius r. In contrast to the static test, the sphere also has a velocity $\mathbf{v}$ during the entire frame time Δt. So, in the next frame, the sphere will be located at $\mathbf{e} = \mathbf{c} + \Delta t \mathbf{v}$. For simplicity, assume Δt is 1 and that this frame starts at time 0. The question is: Has the sphere collided with a plane $\pi : \mathbf{n} \cdot \mathbf{x} + d = 0$ during this time?

The signed distance, s_c, from the sphere's center to the plane is obtained by plugging the sphere center into the plane equation. Subtracting the sphere radius from this distance gives how far (along the plane normal) the sphere can move before reaching the plane. This is illustrated in Figure 13.30. A similar distance, s_e, is computed for the end point $\mathbf{e}$. Now, if the sphere centers are on the same side of the plane (tested as $s_c s_e > 0$), and if $|s_c| > r$ and $|s_e| > r$, then an intersection cannot occur, and the sphere can safely be moved to $\mathbf{e}$. Otherwise, the sphere position and the

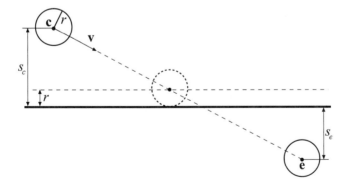

Figure 13.30. The notation used in the dynamic sphere/plane intersection test. The middle sphere shows the position of the sphere at the time when collision occurs. Note that s_c and s_e are both signed distances.

exact time when the intersection occurs is obtained as follows [275]. The time when the sphere first touches the plane is t, where t is computed as:

$$t = \frac{s_c - r}{s_c - s_e}. \tag{13.51}$$

The sphere center is then located at $\mathbf{c} + t\mathbf{v}$. A simple collision response at this point would be to reflect the velocity vector $\mathbf{v}$ around the plane normal, and move the sphere using this vector: $(1 - t)\mathbf{r}$, where $1 - t$ is the remaining time to the next frame from the collision, and $\mathbf{r}$ is the reflection vector.

13.17.2 Sphere/Sphere

Testing two moving spheres A and B for intersection turns out to be equivalent to testing a ray against a static sphere—a surprising result. This equivalency is shown by performing two steps. First, use the principle of relative motion described above to make sphere B become static. Then, a technique is borrowed from the frustum/sphere intersection test (Section 13.13.1). In that test, the sphere was moved along the surface of the frustum to create a larger frustum. By extending the frustum outwards by the radius of the sphere, the sphere itself could be shrunk to a point. Here, moving one sphere over the surface of another sphere results in a new sphere that is the sum of the radii of the two original spheres. So, the radius of sphere A is added to the radius of B to give B a new radius. Now we have the situation where sphere B is static and is larger, and sphere A is a point moving along a straight line, i.e., a ray. See Figure 13.31.

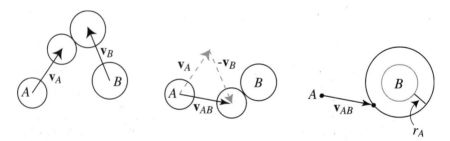

Figure 13.31. The left figure shows two spheres moving and colliding. In the center figure, sphere B has been made static by subtracting its velocity from both spheres. Note that the relative positions of the spheres at the collision point remains the same. On the right, the radius r_A of sphere A is added to B and subtracted from itself, making the moving sphere A into a ray.

As this basic intersection test was already presented in Section 13.5, we will simply present the final result:

$$(\mathbf{v}_{AB} \cdot \mathbf{v}_{AB})t^2 + 2(\mathbf{l} \cdot \mathbf{v}_{AB})t + \mathbf{l} \cdot \mathbf{l} - (r_A + r_B)^2 = 0. \qquad (13.52)$$

In the equation above, $\mathbf{v}_{AB} = \mathbf{v}_A - \mathbf{v}_B$, and $\mathbf{l} = \mathbf{c}_A - \mathbf{c}_B$, where $\mathbf{c}_A$ and $\mathbf{c}_B$ are the centers of the spheres.

This gives a, b, and c:

$$\begin{aligned}
a &= (\mathbf{v}_{AB} \cdot \mathbf{v}_{AB}) \\
b &= 2(\mathbf{l} \cdot \mathbf{v}_{AB}) \\
c &= \mathbf{l} \cdot \mathbf{l} - (r_A + r_B)^2,
\end{aligned} \qquad (13.53)$$

which are values used in the quadratic equation:

$$at^2 + bt + c = 0. \qquad (13.54)$$

The two roots are computed by first computing

$$q = -\frac{1}{2}\left(b + \text{sign}(b)\sqrt{b^2 - 4ac}\right). \qquad (13.55)$$

Here, $\text{sign}(b)$ is $+1$ when $b \geq 0$, else -1. Then the two roots are:

$$\begin{aligned}
t_0 &= \frac{q}{a}, \\
t_1 &= \frac{c}{q}.
\end{aligned} \qquad (13.56)$$

This form of solving the quadratic is not what is normally presented in textbooks, but Press et al. note that it is more numerically stable [635].

The smallest value in the range $[t_0, t_1]$ that lies within $[0, 1]$ (the time of the frame) is the time of first intersection. Plugging this t-value into:

$$\begin{aligned}
\mathbf{p}_A(t) &= \mathbf{c}_A + t\mathbf{v}_A, \\
\mathbf{p}_B(t) &= \mathbf{c}_B + t\mathbf{v}_B,
\end{aligned} \qquad (13.57)$$

yields the location of each sphere at the time of first contact. The main difference of this test and the ray/sphere test presented earlier is that the ray direction $\mathbf{v}_{AB}$ is not normalized here.

13.17.3   Sphere/Polygon

Intersecting a moving sphere with a polygon is somewhat more involved than sphere/plane intersection. Schroeder gives a detailed explanation of this algorithm, and provides code on the web [690]. We follow his presentation here, making corrections as needed.

If the sphere never overlaps the plane, then no further testing is done. The sphere/plane test presented above finds when the sphere first intersects the plane. This intersection point can then be used in performing a point in polygon test (Section 13.8). If this point is inside the polygon, the sphere first hits the polygon there and testing is done.

However, this hit point can be outside the polygon but the sphere's body can still hit a polygon edge or point while moving further along its path. If a sphere collides with the infinite line formed by the edge, the first point of contact $\mathbf{p}$ on the sphere will be radius r away from the center:

$$(\mathbf{c}_t - \mathbf{p}) \cdot (\mathbf{c}_t - \mathbf{p}) = r^2, \tag{13.58}$$

where $\mathbf{c}_t = \mathbf{c} + t\mathbf{v}$. The initial position of the sphere is $\mathbf{c}$, and its velocity is $\mathbf{v}$. Also, the vector from the sphere's center to this point will be perpendicular to the edge:

$$(\mathbf{c}_t - \mathbf{p}) \cdot (\mathbf{p}_1 - \mathbf{p}_0) = 0. \tag{13.59}$$

Here, $\mathbf{p}_0$ and $\mathbf{p}_1$ are the vertices of the polygon edge. The hit point's location $\mathbf{p}$ on the edge's line is defined by the parametric equation:

$$\mathbf{p} = \mathbf{p}_0 + d(\mathbf{p}_1 - \mathbf{p}_0), \tag{13.60}$$

where d is a relative distance from $\mathbf{p}_0$, and $d \in [0, 1]$ for points on the edge.

The variables to compute are the time t of the first intersection with the edge's line and the distance d along the edge. The valid intersection range for t is $[0, 1]$, i.e., during this frame's duration. If t is discovered to be outside this range, the collision does not occur during this frame. The valid range for d is $[0, 1]$, i.e., the hit point must be on the edge itself, not beyond the edge's endpoints. See Figure 13.32.

This set of two equations and two unknowns gives:

$$\begin{aligned}
a &= k_{ee}k_{ss} - k_{es}^2, \\
b &= 2(k_{eg}k_{es} - k_{ee}k_{gs}), \\
c &= k_{ee}(k_{gg} - r^2) - k_{eg}^2,
\end{aligned} \tag{13.61}$$

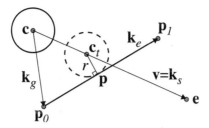

Figure 13.32. Notation for the intersection test of a moving sphere and a polygon edge. *(After Schroeder [690].)*

where:

$$\begin{aligned}
k_{ee} &= \mathbf{k}_e \cdot \mathbf{k}_e & k_{eg} &= \mathbf{k}_e \cdot \mathbf{k}_g \\
k_{es} &= \mathbf{k}_e \cdot \mathbf{k}_s & k_{gg} &= \mathbf{k}_g \cdot \mathbf{k}_g \\
k_{gs} &= \mathbf{k}_g \cdot \mathbf{k}_s & k_{ss} &= \mathbf{k}_s \cdot \mathbf{k}_s
\end{aligned} \tag{13.62}$$

and:

$$\begin{aligned}
\mathbf{k}_e &= \mathbf{p}_1 - \mathbf{p}_0 \\
\mathbf{k}_g &= \mathbf{p}_0 - \mathbf{c} \\
\mathbf{k}_s &= \mathbf{e} - \mathbf{c} = \mathbf{v}.
\end{aligned} \tag{13.63}$$

Note that $\mathbf{k}_s = \mathbf{v}$, the velocity vector for one frame, since $\mathbf{e}$ is the destination point for the sphere. This gives a, b, and c, which are the variables of the quadratic equation in Equation 13.54 on page 623, and so solved for t_0 and t_1 in the same fashion.

This test is done for each edge of the polygon, and if the range $[t_0, t_1]$ overlaps the range $[0, 1]$, then the edge's line is intersected by the sphere in this frame at the smallest value in the intersection of these ranges. The sphere's center $\mathbf{c}_t$ at first intersection time t is computed and yields a distance:

$$d = \frac{(\mathbf{c}_t - \mathbf{p}_0) \cdot \mathbf{k}_e}{k_{ee}}, \tag{13.64}$$

which needs to be in the range $[0, 1]$. If d is not in this range, the edge is considered missed.[20] Using this d in Equation 13.60 gives the point where the sphere first intersects the edge. Note that if the point of first intersection is needed, then all three edges must be tested against the sphere, as the sphere could hit more than one edge.

---

[20] In fact, the edge could be hit by the sphere, but the hit point computed here would not be where contact is actually made. The sphere will first hit one of the vertex endpoints, and this test follows next.

The sphere/edge test is computationally complex. One optimization for this test is to put an AABB around the sphere's path for the frame and test the edge as a ray against this box before doing this full test above. If the line segment does not overlap the AABB, then the edge cannot intersect the sphere [690].

If no edge is the first point of intersection for the sphere, further testing is needed. Recall that the sphere is being tested against the *first* point of contact with the polygon. A sphere may eventually hit the interior or an edge of a polygon, but the tests above check only for first intersection. The third possibility is that the first point of contact is a polygon vertex. So, each vertex in turn is tested against the sphere. Using the concept of relative motion, testing a moving sphere against a static point is exactly equivalent to testing a sphere against a moving point, i.e., a ray. Using the ray/sphere intersection routine in Section 13.5 is then all that is needed. To test the ray $c_t = c + tv$ against a sphere centered at p_0 with radius, r, results can be reused from the previous edge computations to solve t, as follows:

$$a = k_{ss},$$
$$b = -2k_{gs}, \qquad\qquad (13.65)$$
$$c = k_{gg} - r^2.$$

Using this form avoids having to normalize the ray direction for ray/sphere intersection. As before, solve the quadratic equation shown in Equation 13.54 and use the lowest valid root to compute when in the frame the sphere first intersects the vertex. The point of intersection is the vertex itself, of course.

In truth, this sphere/polygon test is equivalent to testing a ray (represented by the center of the sphere moving along a line) against a "puffy" polygon, one in which the vertices have been turned into spheres of radius r, the edges into cylinders of radius r, and the polygon itself raised and lowered by r to seal off the object. See Figure 13.33 for a visualization of this. This is the same sort of expansion as done for frustum/sphere intersection (Section 13.13.1). So the algorithm presented can be thought of as testing a ray against this puffy polygon's parts: First, the polygon facing the ray is tested, then the edge cylinders are tested against the ray, and finally, the vertex spheres are tested.

Thinking about this puffy object gives insight as to why a polygon is most efficiently tested by using the order of area, then edges, then vertices. The polygon in this puffy object that faces the sphere is not covered by the object's cylinders and spheres, so testing it first will give the closest possible

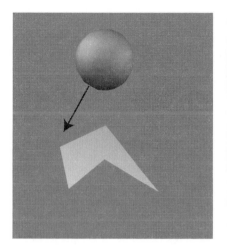
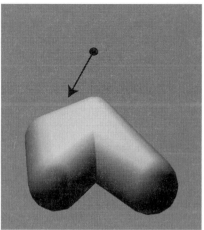

Figure 13.33. In the left figure, a sphere moves towards a polygon. In the right figure, a ray shoots at an "inflated" version of the polygon. The two intersection tests are equivalent.

intersection point without further testing. Similarly, the cylinders formed by the edges cover the spheres, but the spheres cover only the insides of the cylinders. Hitting the inside of the cylinder with a ray is equivalent to finding the point where the moving sphere last hits the corresponding edge, a point we do not care about. The closest cylinder exterior intersection (if one exists) will always be closer than the closest sphere intersection. So, finding a closest intersection with a cylinder is sufficient to end testing without needing to check the vertex spheres. It is much easier (at least for us) to think about testing order when dealing with a ray and this puffy object than the original sphere and polygon.

Another insight from this puffy object model is that, for polygons with concavities, a vertex at any concave location does not have to be tested against the moving sphere, as the sphere formed at such a vertex is not visible from the outside. Efficient dynamic sphere/object intersection tests can be derived by using relative motion and the transformation of a moving sphere into a ray.

13.17.4 Dynamic Separating Axis Method

The separating axis theorem (SAT) on page 563 is very useful in testing convex polyhedrons, e.g., boxes and triangles, against each other. This can be extended quite easily to dynamic queries as well [94, 200].

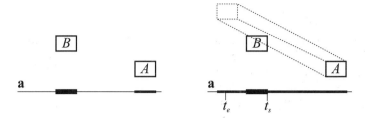

Figure 13.34. Left: The stationary SAT illustrated for an axis **a**. A and B do not overlap on this axis. Right: The dynamic SAT illustrated. A moves and the projection of its interval on **a** is tracked during the movement. Here, the two objects overlap on axis **a**.

Remember that the SAT method tests a set of axes to see whether the projections of the two objects onto these axes overlap. If all projections on all axes overlap, then the objects overlap as well. The key to solving the problem dynamically is to move the projected interval of the moving object with a speed of $(\mathbf{v} \cdot \mathbf{a})/(\mathbf{a} \cdot \mathbf{a})$ (see Equation A.17) on the axis, called **a** [94]. Again, if there is overlap on all tested axes, then the dynamic objects overlap, otherwise they do not. See Figure 13.34 for an illustration of the difference between the stationary SAT and the dynamic SAT.

Eberly [200] also computes the actual time of intersection between A and B. This is done by computing times when they just start to overlap, called t_s, and when they stop overlapping (because the intervals have moved "through" each other), called t_e. The hit between A and B occurs at the largest of all the t_ss for all the axes. Likewise, the end of overlapping occurs at the smallest of all the t_es. Optimizations include detecting when the intervals are nonoverlapping at $t = 0$ and also moving apart. Also, if at any time the largest t_s is greater than the smallest t_e, then the objects do not overlap, and so the test is terminated. This is similar to the ray/box intersection test in Section 13.6.1. Eberly has code for a wide range of tests between convex polyhedra, including box/box, triangle/box, and triangle/triangle.

Further Reading and Resources

3D Game Engine Design [199] covers a wide variety of object/object intersection tests, hierarchy traversal methods, and much else, and also includes source code. Schneider and Eberly's geometry book [688] provides many practical algorithms for two- and three-dimensional geometric intersection

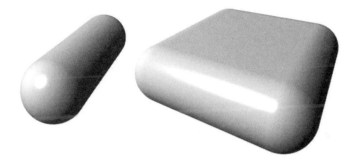

Figure 13.35. A *Line Swept Sphere* (LSS) and *Rectangle Swept Sphere* (RSS).

testing. *The Geometry Toolbox* [225] is a good source for two-dimensional intersection routines and many other geometric manipulations useful in computer graphics. The *Graphics Gems* series [29, 261, 333, 431, 610] includes many different kinds of intersection routines, and reusable code is available on the web. An overview of ray/object intersections is found in *An Introduction to Ray Tracing* [260]. The free *Maxima* [526] software is good for manipulating equations and deriving formulae. This book's website includes a page, http://www.realtimerendering.com/int/, summarizing resources available for many object/object intersection tests.

Other bounding volumes of possible interest are *Line Swept Spheres* (LSS) and *Rectangle Swept Spheres* (RSS). These are also called capsules and lozenges, respectively, and are shown in Figure 13.35. For these BVs it is a relatively quick operation to compute the minimum distance. Therefore, they are often used in tolerance verification applications, where one wants to verify that two (or more) objects are at least a certain distance apart. Eberly [199] and Larsen et al. [471] derive formulae and efficient algorithms for these types of bounding volumes.

Chapter 14
Collision Detection

"To knock a thing down, especially if it is cocked at an arrogant angle, is a deep delight to the blood."
—George Santayana

Collision Detection (CD) is a fundamental and important ingredient in many computer graphics and *Virtual Reality* (VR) applications. Areas where CD plays a vital role include virtual manufacturing, CAD/CAM, computer animation, physically based modeling, games, flight and vehicle simulators, robotics, path and motion planning (tolerance verification), assembly, and almost all VR simulations. Due to its huge number of uses, CD has been and still is a subject of extensive research.

Collision detection is part of what is often referred to as *collision handling*, which can be divided into three major parts: *collision detection*, *collision determination*, and *collision response*. The result of collision detection is a boolean saying whether two or more objects collide, while collision determination finds the actual intersections between objects; finally, collision response determines what actions should be taken in response to the collision of two objects.

In Section 14.1, we discuss simple and extremely fast collision detection techniques. The main idea is to approximate a complex object using a set of lines. These lines are then tested for intersection with the primitives of the environment. This technique is often used in games. Another approximative method is described in Section 14.2, where a BSP tree representation of the environment is used, and a capped cylinder may be used to describe a character. However, all objects cannot always be approximated with lines or cylinders, and some applications may require more accurate tests.

Imagine, for example, that we want to determine whether a three-dimensional hand collides with (grabs) a three-dimensional cup of tea, where both objects are represented by triangles. How can this be done efficiently? Certainly, each triangle of the hand can be tested for intersection with each triangle of the cup of tea using the triangle/triangle intersection tests from Section 13.10. But in the case where the two objects are far from each other, an algorithm should report this quickly, which would be impossible with such exhaustive testing. Even when the objects are close together, exhaustive testing is not efficient. There is a need for algorithms that handle these cases rapidly.

Section 14.3 deals with a general, hierarchical bounding volume collision detection algorithm. Then, two particular implementations with different design choices are presented in Sections 14.4 and 14.5. The systems that will be studied have the following features. All of these characteristics are desirable for most CD systems.

- They achieve interactive rates with models consisting of a large number of polygons, both when the models are far from each other and when they are in close proximity.

- They handle *polygon soups*, i.e., general polygon models with no restrictions such as convexity or the availability of adjacency information.

- The models can undergo rigid-body motion, i.e., rotation plus translation.

- They provide efficient *Bounding Volume* (BV) fitting, in that they try to create a small BV for a set of geometry. Small BVs improve the performance of algorithms that determine whether there are collisions between two objects. The creation of the BVs should also be fast.

Since a scenario may contain tens or hundreds of moving objects, a good CD system must be able to cope with such situations as well. If the scenario contains n moving objects and m static objects, then a naive method would perform

$$nm + \binom{n}{2} \qquad\qquad (14.1)$$

object tests for each frame. The first term corresponds to testing the number of static objects against the dynamic (moving) objects, and the last term corresponds to testing the dynamic objects against each other. The naive approach quickly becomes expensive as m and n rise. This situation calls for smarter methods, which are the subject of Section 14.6. Such a method typically uses an algorithm that first detects all potential object-to-object collisions, which are then resolved using one of the algorithms from Section 14.4 or 14.5.

After discussing hierarchical collision detection, brief subsections follow on several miscellaneous topics, such as a speed-up technique called *front tracking*, which may accelerate collision detection that uses bounding volume hierarchies. *Time-critical collision detection* is a technique for doing approximate collision detection in constant time, and is treated in Section 14.7.2. Sometimes the shortest distance between two objects is desired, and this topic is introduced in Section 14.7.3, followed by some initial research on collision detection for deformable objects. Finally, collision response is briefly covered in Section 14.7.5.

It must be pointed out that performance evaluations are extremely difficult in the case of CD, since the algorithms are sensitive to the actual collision scenarios, and there is no algorithm that performs best in all cases [283].

14.1 Collision Detection with Rays

In this section, we will present a fast technique that works very well under certain circumstances. Imagine that a car drives upward on an inclined road and that we want to use the information about the road (i.e., the primitives of which the road is built) in order to steer the car upward. This could, of course, be done by testing all primitives of all car wheels against all primitives of the road, using the techniques from Section 14.3. However, for games and some other applications, this kind of detailed collision detection is not always needed. Instead, we can approximate a moving object with a set of *rays*. In the case of the car, we can put one ray at each of the four wheels (see Figure 14.1). This approximation works well in practice, as long as we can assume that the four wheels are the only places of the car that

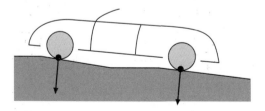

Figure 14.1. Instead of computing the collision between the entire car and the environment (the road), we place a ray at each wheel. These rays are then tested for intersection against the environment.

will be in contact with the environment (the road). Assume that the car is standing on a plane at the beginning, and that we place each ray at a wheel so that each origin lies at the place where the wheel is in contact with the environment. The rays at the wheels are then intersection-tested against the environment. If the distance from a ray origin to the environment is zero, then that wheel is exactly on the ground. If the distance is greater than zero, then that wheel has no contact with the environment, and a negative distance means that the wheel has penetrated the environment. The application can use these distances for computing a collision response— a negative distance would move the car (at that wheel) upward, while a positive distance would move the car downward (unless the car is flying though the air for a short while).

To speed up the intersection testing, we can use the same technique we most often use to speed things up in computer graphics—a *hierarchical representation*. The environment can be represented by a BSP tree (which is the same as a k-d tree). BSP trees are presented in Section 9.1.2, where they were used for view frustum culling algorithms. BSP trees can also be used to speed up intersection testing. Depending on what primitives are used in the environment, different ray-object intersection test methods are needed (see Chapter 13). A BSP tree is not the only representation that can be used to find intersection quickly—any representation (see Section 9.1) for speeding up intersection testing can be used.

Unlike standard ray tracing, where we need the closest object in front of the ray, what is actually desired is the intersection point furthest back along the ray, which can have a negative distance. To avoid having to treat the ray as searching in two directions, the test ray's origin is essentially moved back until it is outside the bounding box surrounding the environment, and is then tested against the environment. In practice, this just means that, instead of a ray starting at a distance 0, it starts at a negative distance that lets it begin outside the box.

14.2 Dynamic CD using BSP Trees

Here, the collision detection algorithm by Melax [542, 543] will be presented. It determines collisions between the geometry described by a BSP tree (see Section 9.1.2), and a collider that can be either a sphere, a cylinder, or the convex hull of an object. It also allows for dynamic collision detection. For example, if a sphere moves from a position $\mathbf{p}_0$ at frame n to $\mathbf{p}_1$ at frame $n + 1$, the algorithm can detect if a collision occurs anywhere

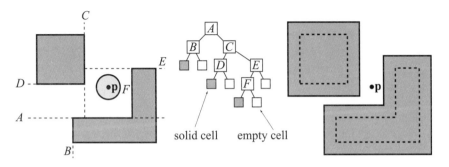

Figure 14.2. To the left is some geometry (dark gray) seen from above. Its BSP tree is shown in the middle. Now, to test this tree against a circle with origin at **p**, the BSP tree is grown outwards with the circle's radius, and then the point **p** can instead be tested against the grown BSP tree. This is shown to the right. Notice that the corners should really be rounded, so this is an approximation that this algorithm introduces.

along the straight line path from $\mathbf{p}_0$ to $\mathbf{p}_1$. The presented algorithm has been used in commercial games, where a character's geometry was approximated by a cylinder.

The standard BSP tree can be tested against a line segment very efficiently. A line segment can represent a point (particle) that moves from $\mathbf{p}_0$ to $\mathbf{p}_1$. There may be several intersections, but the first one (if any) represents the collision between the point and the geometry represented in the BSP tree. This is easily extended to handle a sphere, with radius r, that moves from $\mathbf{p}_0$ to $\mathbf{p}_1$ instead of a point. Instead of testing the line segment against the planes in the BSP tree nodes, each plane is moved a distance r along the plane normal direction (see Section 13.17 for similar ways of recasting intersection tests). This sort of plane adjustment is illustrated in Figure 14.2. This is done for every collision query on the fly, so that one BSP tree can be used for spheres of any size. Assuming a plane is $\pi : \mathbf{n} \cdot \mathbf{x} + d = 0$, the adjusted plane is $\pi' : \mathbf{n} \cdot \mathbf{x} + d \pm r = 0$, where the sign of r depends on which side of the plane you continue testing/traversing in search of a collision. Assuming that the character is supposed to be in the positive half-space of the plane, i.e., where $\mathbf{n} \cdot \mathbf{x} + d \geq 0$, we would have to subtract the radius r from d. Note then that the negative half-space is considered "solid," i.e., something that the character cannot step through.

A sphere does not approximate a character in a game very well.[1] The convex hull of the vertices of a character or a cylinder surrounding the character does a better job. In order to use these other bounding volumes,

---

[1] Schroeder notes that a few spheres can work [690].

d in the plane equation has to be adjusted differently. To test a moving convex hull of a set of vertices, S, against a BSP tree, the scalar value in Equation 14.2 below is added to the d-value of the plane equation [542]:

$$-\max_{\mathbf{v}_i \in S}(\mathbf{n} \cdot (\mathbf{v}_i - \mathbf{p}_0)). \tag{14.2}$$

The minus sign, again, assumes that characters are supposed to move in the positive half-space of the planes. The point $\mathbf{p}_0$ can be any point that is chosen as a reference point. For the sphere, the center of the sphere was implicitly chosen. For a character, a point close to the feet may be chosen, or perhaps a point at the navel. Sometimes this choice simplifies equations (as the center of a sphere does). It is this point $\mathbf{p}_0$ that is tested against the adjusted BSP tree. For a dynamic query, that is, where the character moves from one point to another during one frame, this point $\mathbf{p}_0$ is used as the starting point of the line segment. Assuming that the character is moved with a vector $\mathbf{w}$ during one frame, the end point of the line segment is $\mathbf{p}_1 = \mathbf{p}_0 + \mathbf{w}$.

The cylinder is perhaps even more useful because it is faster to test and still approximates a character in a game fairly well. However, the derivation of the value that adjusts the plane equation is more involved. What we do in general for this algorithm is that we recast the testing of a bounding volume (sphere, convex hull, and cylinder, in this case) against a BSP tree into testing a point, $\mathbf{p}_0$, against the adjusted BSP tree. Then, to extend this to a moving object, the point $\mathbf{p}_0$ is replaced by testing with a line segment from $\mathbf{p}_0$ to the destination point $\mathbf{p}_1$

We derive such a test for a cylinder, whose properties are shown to the top left in Figure 14.3, where the reference point, $\mathbf{p}_0$, is at the bottom center of the cylinder. Figure 14.3b shows what we want to solve: testing the cylinder against the plane π. In Figure 14.3c, we move the plane π so that it barely touches the cylinder. The distance, e, from $\mathbf{p}_0$ to the moved plane is computed. This distance, e, is then used in Figure 14.3d to move the plane π into its new position π'. Thus, the test has been reduced to testing $\mathbf{p}_0$ against π'. The e-value is computed on the fly for each plane each frame. In practice, a vector is first computed from $\mathbf{p}_0$ to the point $\mathbf{t}$, where the moved plane touches the cylinder. This is shown in Figure 14.3c. Next, e is computed as:

$$e = |\mathbf{n} \cdot (\mathbf{t} - \mathbf{p}_0)|. \tag{14.3}$$

Now all that remains is to compute $\mathbf{t}$. The z-component of $\mathbf{t}$ is simple; if $n_z > 0$, then $t_z = p_{0z}$, i.e., the z-component of $\mathbf{p}_0$. Else, $t_z = p_{0z} + h$. If

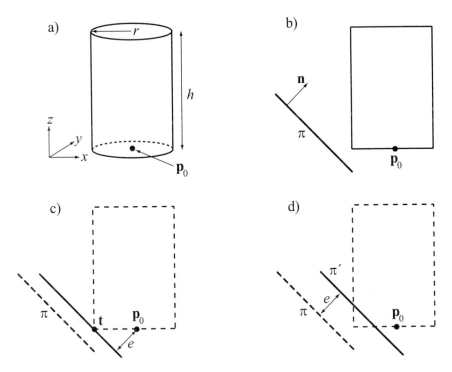

Figure 14.3. Figure a) shows a cylinder with height h, radius r, and reference point p_0. The sequence b-d then shows how testing a plane, π, against a cylinder (shown from the side) can be recast into testing a point p_0 against a new plane π'.

n_x and n_y are zero (e.g., for a floor or ceiling), then we can use any point on the caps of the cylinder. One choice is $(t_x, t_y) = (p_x, p_y)$, the center of the cylinder cap. Otherwise, the following choice gives a point on the rim of the cylinder cap:

$$t_x = \frac{rn_x}{\sqrt{n_x^2 + n_y^2}} + p_x,$$

$$t_y = \frac{rn_y}{\sqrt{n_x^2 + n_y^2}} + p_y. \tag{14.4}$$

That is, we project the plane normal onto the xy-plane, normalize it, and then scale by r to land on the rim of the cylinder.

Inaccuracies can occur using this method. One case is shown in Figure 14.4. As can be seen, this can be solved by introducing extra *bevel*

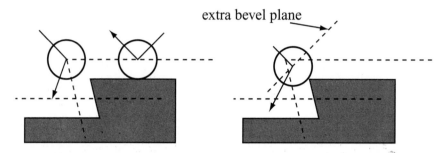

Figure 14.4. In the left illustration, the right sphere collides correctly, while the left sphere detects a collision too early. To the right, this is solved by introducing an extra bevel plane, which actually does not correspond to any real geometry. As can be seen the collision appears to be more correct using such planes. *(Illustration after Melax [542].)*

planes. In practice, the "outer" angle between two neighboring planes are computed, and an extra plane is inserted if the angle is greater than 90°. In Figure 14.5, the difference between a normal BSP tree and a BSP tree augmented with bevel planes can be seen. The beveling planes certainly improves the accuracy, but it does not remove all errors.

Pseudocode for this collision detection algorithm follows below. It is called with the root N of the BSP tree, whose children are $N.negativechild$ and $N.positivechild$, and the line segment defined by $\mathbf{p}_0$ and $\mathbf{p}_1$. Note that the point of impact (if any) is returned in a global variable called $\mathbf{p}_{impact}$.

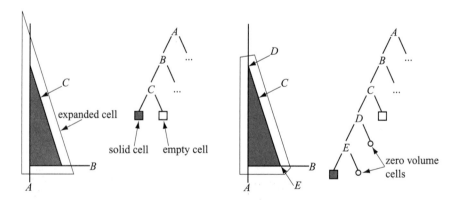

Figure 14.5. To the left, a normal cell and its BSP tree is shown. To the right, bevel planes have been added to the cell, and the changes in the BSP tree are shown. *(Illustration after Melax [542].)*

```
       HitCheckBSP(N, v₀, v₁)
       returns ({TRUE, FALSE});
1 :    if(not isSolidCell(N)) return FALSE;
2 :    else if(isSolidCell(N))
3 :       p_impact = v₀
4 :       return TRUE;
5 :    end
6 :    hit = FALSE;
7 :    if(clipLineInside(N shift out, v₀, v₁, &w₀, &w₁))
8 :       hit = HitCheckBSP(N.negativechild, w₀, w₁);
9 :       if(hit) v₁ = p_impact
10 :   end
11 :   if(clipLineOutside(N shift in, v₀, v₁, &w₀, &w₁))
12 :      hit| = HitCheckBSP(N.positivechild, w₀, w₁);
13 :   end
14 :   return hit;
```

The function isSolidCell returns TRUE if we have reached a leaf, and we are on the solid side (as opposed to the empty). See Figure 14.2 for an illustration of empty and solid cells. The function clipLineInside returns TRUE if part of the line segment (defined by v_0 and v_1) is inside the node's shifted plane, that is, in the negative half-space. It also clips the line against the node's shifted plane, and returns the resulting line segment in w_0 and w_1. The function clipLineOutside is similar. Note also that the line segments returned by clipLineInside and clipLineOutside overlap each other. The reason for this is shown in Figure 14.6, as well as how the line is clipped. Line 9 sets $v_1 = p_{impact}$, and this is simply an optimization. If a hit has been found, and thus a potential impact point, p_{impact}, then nothing beyond this point need to be tested since we want the first point of impact. On Lines 7 and 11, N is shifted "out" versus "in." These shifts refer to the adjusted plane equations derived earlier for spheres, convex hulls, and cylinders.

Melax has shown that this algorithm is between 2.5 and 3.5 times more expensive than an algorithm not using dynamically adjusted planes. This is so because there is overhead in computing the proper adjustments, and also the BSP tree gets larger due to the bevel planes. Even though this slowdown may seem serious, Melax points out that it is not so bad in the context. A frame typically takes $33,000$ μs (giving 30 fps) to compute, and his most expensive collision query takes 66 μs. The advantage of this scheme is that only a single BSP tree is needed to test all characters and

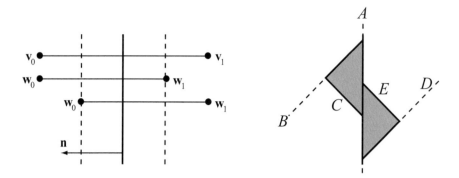

Figure 14.6. To the left, the line segment defined by $\mathbf{v}_0$ and $\mathbf{v}_1$ is clipped against a plane defined by a normal $\mathbf{n}$. The dynamic adjustments of this plane is shown as dashed lines. The functions `clipLineInside` and `clipLineOutside` returns the line segments defined by $\mathbf{w}_0$ and $\mathbf{w}_1$. Note that all three lines should have the same y-coordinates, but they are shown like this for clarity. To the right, an example is shown that explains why the lines should be clipped as shown to the left. The node A in the BSP tree belongs to both the triangle on the left and on the right. Therefore, it is necessary to move its plane in both directions.

objects. The alternative would be to store different BSP trees for each different radius and object type.

14.3   General Hierarchical Collision Detection

This section will present some general ideas and methods that are used in collision detection algorithms for detecting collisions between two given models. These algorithms have the four features listed on page 632. Common denominators of these algorithms are:

- They build a representation of each model hierarchically using bounding volumes.

- The high-level code for a collision query is similar, regardless of the kind of BV being used.[2]

- A simple cost function can be used to trim, evaluate, and compare performance.

These points are treated in the following three subsections.

---

[2]However, BV-BV overlap tests and primitive-primitive overlap tests are different depending on what BVs and primitives are used.

14.3.1   Hierarchy Building

Initially, a model is represented by a number of primitives, which in our case are polygon soups, where all polygons with more than three vertices are decomposed into triangles (see Section 11.2). Then, since each model should be represented as a hierarchy of some kind of bounding volumes, methods must be developed that build such hierarchies with the desired properties. A hierarchy that is commonly used in the case of collision detection algorithms is a data structure called a k-ary tree, where each node may at most have k children (see Section 9.1). Many algorithms have used the simplest instance of the k-ary tree, namely the binary tree, where $k = 2$. At each internal node, there is a BV that encloses all of its children in its volume, and at each leaf, there are one or more primitives (which in our case are triangles). The bounding volume of an arbitrary node (either an internal node or a leaf), A, is denoted A_{BV}, and the set of children belonging to A is denoted A_c.

There are three ways to build a hierarchy: a *bottom-up* method, an *incremental tree-insertion*, or a *top-down* approach. In order to create efficient, tight structures, typically the areas or the volumes of the BVs are minimized wherever possible [44, 273, 433, 599]. The first of these methods, bottom-up, starts by combining a number of primitives and finding a BV for them. These primitives should be located close together, which can be determined by using the distance between the primitives. Then, either new BVs can be created in the same way, or existing BVs can be grouped with one or more BVs constructed in a similar way, thus yielding a new, larger parent BV. This is repeated until only one BV exists, which then becomes the root of the hierarchy. In this way, closely located primitives are always located near each other in the bounding volume hierarchy. Barequet et al. present BOXTREE [44], a data structure for performing ray tracing and collision detection, where the tree is built from the bottom up.

The incremental tree-insertion method starts with an empty tree. Then all other primitives and their BVs are added one at a time to this tree. This is illustrated in Figure 14.7. To make an efficient tree, an insertion point in the tree must be found. This point should be selected so that the total tree volume increase is minimized. A simple method for doing this is to descend to the child that gives a smaller increase in the tree. This kind of algorithm typically takes $O(n \log n)$ time. For more sophisticated methods, see Omohundro's work [599]. Little is known about incremental tree-insertion in the context of collision detection, but it has been used with good results in ray tracing [273] and in intersection queries [599], so it probably works well for collision detection, too.

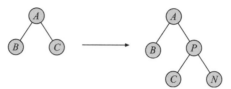

Figure 14.7. On the left, a binary tree with three nodes is shown. We assume that only one primitive is stored at each leaf. Now we wish to insert a new node, named N. This node has a *Bounding Volume* (BV) and a primitive that that BV encloses. Therefore, the node will be inserted as a leaf node. In this example, say we find that the total tree volume is smaller if we insert N at the node called C (rather than at B). Then a new parent node P is created that encloses both C and the new node N.

The top-down approach, which is used by the majority of hierarchy construction algorithms, starts by finding a BV for all primitives of the model, which then acts as the root of the tree. Then a divide-and-conquer strategy is applied, where the BV is first split into k or fewer parts. For each such part, all included primitives are found, and then a BV is created in the same manner as for the root, i.e., the hierarchy is created recursively. It is most common to find some axis along which the primitives should be split, and then to find a good split point on this axis. Note that a potential advantage of the top-down approach is that a hierarchy can be created lazily, i.e., on an as-needed basis. This means that we construct the hierarchy only for those parts of the scene where it is actually needed. But since this building process is performed during runtime, whenever a part of the hierarchy is created, the performance may go down significantly. This is not acceptable for applications such as games and VR with real-time requirements, but may be a great time saver for off-line calculations such as path planning, animation, and more.

One challenge for CD algorithms is to find tight-fitting bounding volumes and hierarchy construction methods that create balanced and efficient trees. Note that balanced trees are expected to perform best on average in all cases, since the depth of every leaf is the same (or almost the same). This means that it takes an equal amount of time to traverse the hierarchy down to any leaf (i.e., a primitive), and that the time of a collision query will not vary depending on which leaves are accessed. In this sense, a balanced tree is optimal. However, this does not mean that it is best for all inputs. For example, if part of a model will seldom or never be queried for a collision, then those parts can be located deep in an unbalanced tree, so that the parts that are queried most often are closer to the root [284].[3]

---

[3]In some ways, this is similar to Huffman coding, where symbols that occur often are coded with a smaller number of bits than are symbols that occur more infrequently.

14.3.2   Collision Testing between Hierarchies

Usually there are two different situations that the user wants to detect at different times. First, she might only be interested in whether or not the two models collide, and then the method may terminate whenever a pair of triangles has been found to overlap. Second, she might want all pairs of overlapping triangles reported. The solution to the first problem is called *collision detection*, while the solution to the second is called *collision determination*. Here, pseudocode is given that solves the first problem. The second situation can be solved with small alterations of the given code, and will be discussed later on.

A and B are two nodes in the model hierarchies, which at the first call are the roots of the models. A_{BV} and B_{BV} are used to access the BV of the appropriate node. As can be expected, the code recursively calls itself, since the model hierarchies are k-ary trees.

```
      FindFirstHitCD(A, B)
      returns ({TRUE, FALSE});
 1:   if(isLeaf(A) and isLeaf(B))
 2:       for each triangle pair T_A ∈ A_c and T_B ∈ B_c
 3:           if(overlap(T_A, T_B)) return TRUE;
 4:   else if(isNotLeaf(A) and isNotLeaf(B))
 5:       if(Volume(A) > Volume(B))
 6:           for each child C_A ∈ A_c
 7:               FindFirstHitCD(C_A, B)
 8:       else
 9:           for each child C_B ∈ B_c
10:               FindFirstHitCD(A, C_B)
11:   else if(isLeaf(A) and isNotLeaf(B))
12:       for each child C_B ∈ B_c
13:           FindFirstHitCD(C_B, A)
14:   else
15:       for each child C_A ∈ A_c
16:           FindFirstHitCD(C_A, B)
17:   return FALSE;
```

As can be seen in the above pseudocode, there are portions of code that could be shared, but it is presented like this to show how the algorithm works. Some lines deserve some attention. Lines 2–3 take care of the case where both nodes are leaves. Lines 5–10 handle the case where both nodes are internal nodes. The consequence of the comparison Volume(A) > Volume(B) is that the node with the largest volume is descended. The idea behind such a test is to get the same tree traversal for the calls **FindFirstHitCD**(A, B) and for **FindFirstHitCD**(B, A), so that traversal becomes deterministic. Perhaps even more important is that this tends to give better performance, as the largest box is traversed first at each step. Another idea is to alternate between descending A and B. This avoids the volume computation, and so could be faster. Alternatively, the volume can be precomputed for rigid bodies, but this requires extra memory per node. Also, note that this pseudocode involves only BV/BV tests and triangle/triangle tests. However, when a leaf from one tree and an internal node from the other are encountered, it is possible to directly use a triangle/BV test instead of descending into the tree with the internal node. Such a change may reduce the size of the BVH, since each triangle then does not need a BV. In a balanced binary tree, there are about as many leaves as internal nodes, which means that half the BVs (the ones around triangles in the leaves) can be eliminated. By removing the BVs around the leaves, pruning may improve. For example, with BVs around the leaves, a BV/BV test is performed before reaching the triangles. Without BVs around the leaves, the BV/BV test is replaced by a BV/triangle test, which may terminate the test earlier than the BV/BV test, since the triangle is part of the geometry of the model.

To find all pairs of triangles that collide, the above pseudocode is modified in the following way. The pairs of triangles that the algorithm finds are stored in a list, L, which begins empty. Then Line 3 requires modification: If the test is passed, the program should add the triangle pair to L (instead of returning). Line 17, should return **FALSE** if L is empty; otherwise, it should return **TRUE** and the list L.

14.3.3   Cost Function

The function t in Equation 14.5 below was first introduced (in a slightly different form, without the last term) as a framework for evaluating the performance of hierarchical BV structures in the context of acceleration algorithms for ray tracing [797]. It has since been used to evaluate the performance of CD algorithms as well [283], and it has been augmented by the last term to include a new cost specific to some systems [433, 445] that might have a significant impact on performance. This cost results from the fact that if a model is undergoing a rigid-body motion, then its BV and parts or all of its hierarchy might have to be recomputed, depending on the motion and the choice of BV.

$$t = n_v c_v + n_p c_p + n_u c_u \qquad (14.5)$$

Here, the parameters are:

n_v : number of BV/BV overlap tests
c_v : cost for a BV/BV overlap test
n_p : number of primitive pairs tested for overlap
c_p : cost for testing whether two primitives overlap
n_u : number of BVs updated due to the model's motion
c_u : cost for updating a BV

Creating a better hierarchical decomposition of a model would result in lower values of n_v, n_p, and n_u. Creating better methods for determining whether two BVs or two triangles overlap would lower c_v and c_p. However, these are often conflicting goals, because changing the type of BV in order to use a faster overlap test usually means that we get looser-fitting volumes.

Examples of different bounding volumes that have been used in the past are spheres [373], axis-aligned bounding boxes (AABBs) [349, 762], oriented bounding boxes (OBBs) [283], k-DOPs (discrete oriented polytopes) [433, 442, 833], pie slices [44], spherical shells [445, 446] (which provide a good fit for Bézier patches), line swept spheres (LSSs), rectangle swept spheres (RSSs) [471], and QuOSPOs (which combines the advantages of OBBs and k-DOPs) [326]. Spheres are the fastest to transform, and the overlap test is also fast, but they provide quite a poor fit. AABBs normally provide a better fit and a fast overlap test, and they are a good choice if there is a large amount of axially aligned geometry in a model (as is the case in most architectural models). OBBs have a much better fit, but slower overlap tests. The fit of the k-DOPs are determined by the parameter k—higher values of k give a better fit, slower overlap testing, and poorer transform speed.

There are obviously many parameters to fine tune in order to get good performance, which is the goal of the following two sections on the OBBTree and k-DOPTree. Both have their own strengths and weaknesses.

14.4   OBBTree

At SIGGRAPH 96, Gottschalk et al. [283] presented a paper called "OBB-Tree: A Hierarchical Structure for Rapid Interference Detection," which has strongly influenced further research on CD algorithms.[4] Their approach and their parameters will be treated thoroughly in this section.

The OBBTree was designed to perform especially well if *parallel close proximity*, where two surfaces are very close and nearly parallel, is found during collision detection. For such tests, the OBBTree performed better than the k-DOPTree [433]. These kinds of situations often occur in tolerance analysis and in virtual prototyping.

Choice of Bounding Volume

As the name of the *OBBTree* algorithm implies, the bounding volume used is the oriented bounding box, the OBB. One reason for this is that both the AABB (axis-aligned bounding box) and the sphere, which were commonly used in previous CD algorithms, provide quite a poor fit in general. That is, they contain much empty space compared to the geometry they are holding. The convergence of the OBB to the underlying geometry of the models was generally better than that for either AABBs or spheres. Another reason was that the authors developed a new method for determining whether two OBBs overlap. This new method is about a magnitude faster than previous methods. The speed of this test results in part from the fact that the OBBs are transformed so that one of them becomes an AABB centered around the origin. The actual transform (presented below in Section 14.4) takes 63 operations, and the OBB/OBB test may exit early due to one of the 15 axis tests. After the transformation, an exit after the first axis test takes 17 operations, and an exit after the last axis would take 180 operations.[5] OBB/OBB overlap testing is treated in Section 13.12.5.

In terms of the performance evaluation framework of Section 14.3.3, the above reasoning means that n_v and n_p are lower for OBBs than for AABBs and spheres.

Van den Bergen has suggested a simple technique for speeding up the overlap test between two OBBs [762, 764]: Simply skip the last nine axis tests that correspond to a direction perpendicular to one edge of the first OBB and one edge of the second OBB. This test is often referred to as *SAT lite*. Geometrically, this can be thought of as doing two AABB/AABB tests, where the first test is done in the coordinate system of the first OBB and the other is done in the coordinate system of the other. This is illustrated in Figure 14.8. The shortened OBB/OBB test (which omits the last nine axis tests) will sometimes report two disjoint OBBs as overlapping.

---

[4]In 1981, Ballard [37] did similar work in two dimensions for computing intersections between curves, so his work was a precursor to the OBBTree.

[5]Extra arithmetic error testing would take nine extra operations.

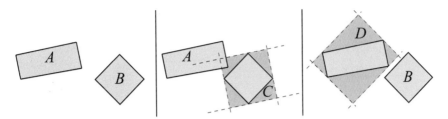

Figure 14.8. At the left are two OBBs (A and B) that are to be tested for overlap with an OBB/OBB overlap test that omits the last nine axis tests. If this is interpreted geometrically, then the OBB/OBB overlap test is approximated with two AABB-AABB overlap tests. The middle illustration shows how B is bounded by an AABB in the coordinate system of A. C and A overlap, so the test continues on the right. Here, A is enclosed with an AABB in the coordinate system of B. B and D are reported not to overlap. So, testing ends here. However, in three dimensions, D and B could overlap as well, and still A and B need not overlap due to the remaining axis tests. In such cases, A and B would erroneously be reported to overlap.

In these cases, the recursion in the OBBTree will go deeper than necessary. The reason for using such extensive recursion is that it was found that these last nine axis tests culled away only a small proportion of the overlaps. The net result was that the average performance was improved by skipping these tests. Van den Bergen's technique has been implemented in a collision detection package called SOLID [762, 763, 764], which also handles deformable objects.

Hierarchy Building

The basic data structure is a binary tree with each internal node holding an OBB (see Section 13.2 for a definition) and each external (leaf) node holding only one triangle. The top-down approach developed by Gottschalk et al. for creating the hierarchy is divided into finding a tight-fitting OBB for a polygon soup and then splitting this along one axis of the OBB, which also categorizes the triangles into two groups. For each of these groups, a new OBB is computed. The creation of OBBs is treated in Section 13.3.

After we have computed an OBB for a set of triangles, the volume and the triangles should be split and formed into two new OBBs. Gottschalk et al. use a strategy that takes the longest axis of the box and splits it into two parts of the same length. An illustration of this procedure is shown in Figure 14.9. A plane that contains the center of the box and has the longest box axis for its normal is thus used to partition the triangles into two subgroups. A triangle that crosses this plane is assigned to the group that contains its centroid. If the longest axis cannot be subdivided (in

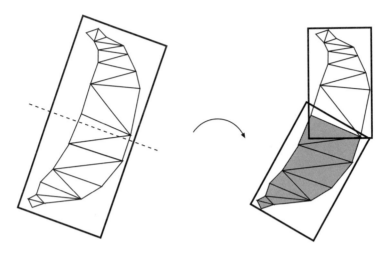

Figure 14.9. This figure shows how a set of geometry with its OBB is split along the longest axis of the OBB, at the split point marked by the dashed line. Then the geometry is partitioned into two subgroups, and an OBB is found for each of them. This procedure is repeated recursively in order to build the OBBTree.

the rare case that all centroids of all triangles are located on the dividing plane), the other axes are tried in diminishing order.

For each of the subgroups, the matrix method presented in Section 13.3 is used to compute (sub-) OBBs. Gottschalk et al. also point out that, if the OBB is instead split at the median center point, then balanced trees are obtained, which in a sense are optimal.

Since the computation of the convex hull takes $O(n \log n)$ and the depth of a binary tree is $O(\log n)$, the total running time for the creation of an OBBTree is $O(n \log^2 n)$.

Handling Rigid-Body Motions

In the OBBTree hierarchy, each OBB, A, is stored together with a rigid-body transformation (a rotation matrix $\mathbf{R}$ and a translation vector $\mathbf{t}$) matrix $\mathbf{M}_A$. This matrix holds the relative orientation and position of the OBB with respect to its parent.

Now, assume that we start to test two OBBs, A and B, against each other. The overlap test between A and B should then be done in the coordinate system of one of the OBBs. Let us say that we decide to do the test in A's coordinate system. In this way, A is an AABB (in its own coordinate system) centered around the origin. The idea is then to transform B into A's coordinate system. This is done with the matrix below, which first transforms B into its own position and orientation (with $\mathbf{M}_B$) and then into A's coordinate system (with the inverse of A's transform, $\mathbf{M}_A^{-1}$).

$$\mathbf{T}_{AB} = \mathbf{M}_A^{-1}\mathbf{M}_B \tag{14.6}$$

The OBB/OBB overlap test takes as input a matrix consisting of a 3×3 rotation matrix $\mathbf{R}$ and a translation vector $\mathbf{t}$, which hold the orientation and position of B with respect to A (see Section 13.12.5), so $\mathbf{T}_{AB}$ is decomposed as below.

$$\mathbf{T}_{AB} = \left(\begin{array}{cc} \mathbf{R} & \mathbf{t} \\ \mathbf{0}^T & 0 \end{array} \right) \tag{14.7}$$

Now, assume that A and B overlap, and that we want to descend into A's child called C. A smart technique for doing this is presented here. We choose to do the test in C's coordinate system. The idea is then to transform B into A's coordinate system (with $\mathbf{T}_{AB}$) and then transform that into the coordinate system of C (using $\mathbf{M}_C^{-1}$). This is done with the following matrix, which is then used as the input to the OBB/OBB overlap test:

$$\mathbf{T}_{CB} = \mathbf{M}_C^{-1}\mathbf{T}_{AB}. \tag{14.8}$$

This procedure is then used recursively to test all OBBs.

Miscellaneous

The **FindFirstHitCD** pseudocode for collision detection between two hierarchical trees, as presented in Section 14.3.2, can be used on two trees created with the above algorithms. All that needs to be exchanged is the `overlap()` function, which should point to a routine that tests two OBBs for overlap.

All algorithms involved in OBBTree have been implemented in a free software package called *RAPID* (Robust and Accurate Polygon Interference Detection) [283].

14.5 *k*-DOPTree

Another variant of hierarchical collision detection is presented here [350, 433]. More information about it can be found in Klosowski's Ph.D. thesis [434]. In the spirit of the OBBTree, we call this the k-DOPTree algorithm, since the BV used is a k-DOP. To recap, a k-DOP is the volume formed by the intersection of a set of slabs. See Section 13.2 for the full definition of a k-DOP, and Section 13.12.4 for k-DOP overlap testing.

Choice of Bounding Volume

The rationale behind choosing the k-DOP as the BV for the CD hierarchy is that it has both a faster BV/BV overlap test than the OBB and a tighter fit. The overlap test is faster because the directions of the planes of the k-DOP are fixed.

Of course, this only holds in nonextreme cases, i.e., for reasonable values of k. As k grows, the k-DOP tends to resemble the convex hull, which is the tightest-fitting convex BV. The k-DOP is not always tighter than the OBB, however. For example, if a triangle is bounded by a well-aligned OBB, then we get a rectangle in three dimensions, which is a fairly good bound. For a k-DOP, we can get a worse fit, since the triangle may be badly aligned with respect to the chosen directions.

For k-DOPs, there is a cost for updating the BVs of the moving models. That is, n_u (the number of BVs updated due to motion) and c_u (the cost for updating a BV) affect the total cost function for performance evaluation. This was not the case for the OBB, since the motion transform is an integral part of the OBB/OBB overlap test.

What happens to n_v (the number of overlap tests performed) in comparison to the OBBTree is hard to say, since this is highly scenario-dependent. But at least the k-DOP performs better in terms of tighter-fitting BVs, i.e., having a lower n_v, than both spheres and AABBs (which are simple k-DOPs, and so any k-DOP with $k > 6$ is bound to have a tighter fit). 6-DOPs (AABBs), 14-DOPs, 18-DOPs, and 26-DOPs were tested in order to find a good compromise between the BV tightness (affecting n_v, n_p, and n_u) and the BV/BV overlap cost (c_v).

It was found that $k = 18$ gave the best execution times for several different scenarios [433]. The choice of normals for $k = 18$ (and for the other k-values as well) was made with efficiency in mind. In addition to the three normals of an AABB, the sum of two normals of the AABB was used. An example is $(\pm 1, \pm 1, 0)$. These sort of planes cut off edges from a box.

The normals of the AABB give six planes, and the sum of two normals gives an additional twelve planes, resulting in a 18-DOP. For a 26-DOP, the other normals are $(\pm 1, \pm 1, \pm 1)$, that is, planes that cut off the corners of a box. An additional eight planes are obtained from these. This selection of normals makes the projection of the vertices onto the normals (an operation involved in the creation of a k-DOP) extremely cheap. This is because only additions and subtractions need to be computed, thanks to the fact that the elements of the unnormalized normals are either zero or ± 1. An example of a two-dimensional 8-DOP is shown on the left in Figure 14.10.

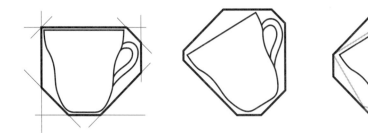

Figure 14.10. This illustrates how the approximation method handles rotating objects. The left figure shows an 8-DOP for a tea cup, and the middle figure shows a rotated version of the tea cup, and a best-fit 8-DOP for the rotated object. However, the amount of computation involved can be costly. The approximation method transforms the initial 8-DOP in the left figure, and a new 8-DOP for the transformed 8-DOP is found, as shown in the right figure. The previous 8-DOP of the tea cup appears in gray.

Hierarchy Building

As was mentioned above, Klosowski et al. show that the binary tree is optimal in some ways, and so the k-DOPTree also uses a binary tree. The main difference between it and the OBBTree is that the leaves may contain an arbitrary number of triangles.[6] For static models, the (maximum) number of triangles allowed was one per leaf, and for dynamic (moving) models it was 40 per leaf. The reason for this difference is that it is expensive to transform the k-DOPs.

The creation of the hierarchy is based on a top-down approach. The topic of finding a minimal k-DOP is treated in Section 13.3. When it comes to splitting the k-DOP into two subvolumes, four methods have been investigated [433] for the selection of one of the main axes, x, y, or z:

1. *Min Sum* selects the axis that minimizes the sum of the subvolumes.

2. *Min Max* selects the axis that minimizes the larger of the two subvolumes.

3. *Splatter* computes the variances of the projections of the centroids of the triangles onto each axis and selects the axis that yields the largest variance.

4. *Longest Side* simply selects the axis along which the BV is longest.

---

[6]The particular implementation of the OBBTree called RAPID [283] allows only one triangle per leaf, but the code could easily be extended to handle more than one.

The most profitable method was found to be Splatter, since it performed well both when constructing the hierarchy and when detecting collisions.

Along the axis selected by the Splatter method, a point must be chosen where the k-DOP is to be split. While it is easy to imagine that the best method would be to split at the median of the centroid coordinates along the split axis, experimental results show that the mean of the centroid coordinates performed better. The depth of the k-DOPTree was usually higher when using the mean (i.e., the tree was more unbalanced), but the BVs were tighter, resulting in shorter collision detection times [348, 433]. After a split point has been determined, each triangle is put in the respective subvolume in which its centroid lies.

Updating the k-DOPTree Due to a Rigid-Body Motion

Since the orientations of the planes of the k-DOPs are fixed, a rigid-body motion of an object makes the hierarchy invalid (translations can be handled, but not rotations), and therefore, it must be rebuilt or updated in some way.

Klosowski et al. [433] proposed two ways of updating the k-DOPs fairly efficiently, while maintaining the same structure of the hierarchy. The methods are called the *approximation method* and *hill climbing*. The approximation method allows the algorithm to avoid recomputing a new k-DOP for the transformed geometry from scratch by using the original k-DOP. Instead of reforming a k-DOP from the transformed vertex locations for the geometry, vertex locations at the corners of the original k-DOP are transformed and used. This results in less work if there are fewer vertices in the k-DOP than in the geometry it contains. This procedure is depicted in Figure 14.10. Note that the size of the k-DOP often grows with this technique, making for a worse fit of the underlying geometry.

The hill climbing method requires additional storage, since it requires the convex hull of the geometry that the current node contains. At each frame, local updates are made to a new best-fit k-DOP for the geometry. A local update tests whether a vertex that was maximal (i.e., furthest out) along one of the k-DOP's normals is still maximal. This is done by checking the neighboring vertices recursively. If one of the neighbors is now maximal, it is selected to form the new k-DOP.

The hill climbing method is the more expensive of the two, but it also gives a tighter BV. Therefore, since the root of the tree is the most frequently visited node, the root is recomputed using the hill climbing method, and its children are recomputed using the approximation method. The results were found to be worse when the hill climbing method was used for any additional nodes.

14.6   A Multiple Objects CD System

Consider an old-style clock consisting of springs and cog-wheels. Say this clock is represented as a detailed, three-dimensional model in the computer. Now imagine that the clock's movements are to be simulated using collision detection. The spring is wound and the clock's motion is simulated as collisions are detected and responses are generated. Such a system would require collision detection between possibly hundreds of pairs of objects. The previously described algorithms that detect collisions between only one pair of objects (two-body collision detection). A brute-force search of all possible collision pairs is incredibly inefficient and so is impractical under these circumstances.

Here, we will describe a two-level collision detection system [130, 375, 497] that is targeted at large-scale environments with multiple objects in motion. The first level of this system reports potential collisions among all the objects in the environment. These results are then sent to the second level, which performs exact collision detection between each pair of objects. Any of the algorithms from Sections 14.4 and 14.5 (or any other method that detects collisions between two objects, for that matter) can be used for this task.

14.6.1   The First-Level CD

In order to minimize the number of calls to the second-level system (that is, to report as few potential object/object collisions as possible), each object is enclosed in a BV and some algorithm finds all BV/BV pairs that overlap.

A simple approach is to use an axis-aligned bounding box (AABB) for each object. To avoid recomputing this AABB for an object undergoing rigid-body motion, the AABB is adjusted to be a *fixed cube* large enough to contain the object in any arbitrary orientation. Dynamically sized boxes have also been investigated [130, 375], but their performance was found to be poorer.[7] The fixed cubes are used to determine rapidly which pairs of objects are totally disjoint in terms of these bounding volumes.

Instead of fixed cubes, spheres can be used. This is reasonable, since the sphere is the perfect BV with which to enclose an object at any orientation. An algorithm for spheres is presented by Kim et al. [426]. Yet another approach is to use the convex hull or any other convex polyhedron, using for example the Lin-Canny algorithm [495, 496] or the V-clip [553] instead

---

[7]For long, skinny objects, dynamically sized AABBs may be faster.

of fixed cubes. In the next section, we focus on fixed cubes. An entirely different method is to use the loose octree presented in Section 9.1.3.

Sweep-and-Prune

The fixed cubes are used in a *sweep-and-prune* technique [496, 809] that exploits the *temporal coherence* most often found in virtual environments. Temporal coherence means that objects undergo small (if any) changes in their position and orientation from frame to frame (and so it is also called *frame-to-frame coherence*).

Lin [496] points out that the overlapping bounding box problem in three dimensions can be solved in $O(n \log^2 n + k)$ time (where k is the number of pairwise overlaps), but it can be improved upon by exploiting coherence and so be reduced to $O(n + k)$.

If two AABBs overlap, then all three one-dimensional intervals (formed by start and end points of AABBs) in each main axis direction must also overlap. Here, we will describe how all overlaps of a number of one-dimensional intervals can be detected efficiently when the frame-to-frame coherency is high (which is what we can expect in a reasonable application). Given that solution, the three-dimensional problem for AABBs is solved by using the one-dimensional algorithm for each of the three main axes.

Assume that n intervals (along a particular axis) are represented by s_i and e_i where $s_i < e_i$ and $0 \le i < n$. These values are sorted in one list in increasing order. This list is then swept from start to end. When a start point s_i is encountered, the corresponding interval is put into an active interval list. When an endpoint is encountered, the corresponding interval is removed from the active list. Now, if the start point of an interval is encountered while there are intervals in the active list, then the encountered interval overlaps all intervals in the list. This is shown in Figure 14.11.

This procedure would take $O(n \log n)$ to sort all the intervals, plus $O(n)$ to sweep the list and $O(k)$ to report k overlapping intervals, resulting in an $O(n \log n + k)$ algorithm. However, due to temporal coherence, the lists are not expected to change very much from frame to frame, and so a *bubble sort* or *insertion sort* [437] can be used with great efficiency after the first pass has taken place. These sorting algorithms sort nearly-sorted lists in an expected time of $O(n)$.

Insertion sort works by building up the sorted sequence incrementally. We start with the first number in the list. If we consider only this entry, then the list is sorted. Next, we add the second entry. If the second entry is smaller than the first, then we change places of the first and the second entries; otherwise we leave them be. We continue to add entries, and we

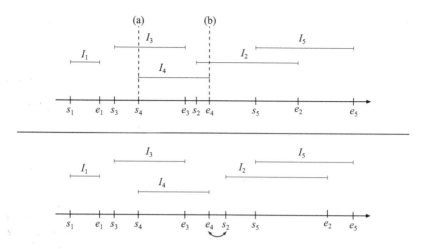

Figure 14.11. At the top, the interval I_4 is encountered (at the point marked (a)) when there is only one interval in the active list (I_3), so it is concluded that I_4 and I_3 overlap. When I_2 is encountered, I_4 is still in the active list (since e_4 has not been encountered yet), and so I_4 and I_2 also overlap. When e_4 is encountered, I_4 is removed (at the point marked (b)) from the active list. At the bottom, I_2 has moved to the right, and when the insertion sort finds that s_2 and e_4 need to change places, it can also be concluded that I_2 and I_4 do not overlap any longer. *(Illustration after Witkin et al. [809].)*

change the places of the entries until the list is sorted. This procedure is repeated for all objects that we want to sort, and the result is a sorted list.

To use temporal coherence to our advantage, we keep a boolean for each interval pair. A specific boolean is TRUE if the pair overlaps and FALSE otherwise. The values of the booleans are initialized at the first step of the algorithm when the first sorting is done. Assume that a pair of intervals were overlapping in the previous frame and so their boolean was TRUE. Now, if the start point of one interval exchanges places with the end point of the other interval, then the status of this interval pair is inverted, which in this case means that their boolean is then FALSE and they do not overlap anymore. The same goes in the other direction, i.e., if a boolean was FALSE, then it becomes TRUE when one start point changes place with one end point. This is also illustrated in Figure 14.11.

So we can create a sorted list of intervals for all three main axes and use the above algorithm to find overlapping intervals for each axis. If all three intervals for a pair overlap, their AABBs (which the intervals represent) also overlap; otherwise, they do not.

Keeping track of the overlap status changes takes $O(n + e_x + e_y + e_z)$, where e_i is the number of swaps along the i-axis [496]. In the worst case, the number of swaps, in each direction, takes $O(n^2)$ time with a small constant. However, the expected time is linear, which results in an $O(n+k)$-expected-time sweep-and-prune algorithm, where, again, k is the number of pairwise overlaps. This makes for fast overlap detection of the fixed cubes.

14.6.2 Summary

The outline of the collision detection system is summarized below, and depicted in Figure 14.12.

- First, using the sweep-and-prune algorithm, all pairs of objects whose fixed cubes overlap are detected and stored in the pair list.

- Second, the object pairs are sent to exact collision detection algorithms, such as OBBTree or k-DOPTree.

- Finally, the results from collision detection are forwarded and taken care of by the application, so that action (collision response) can be taken.

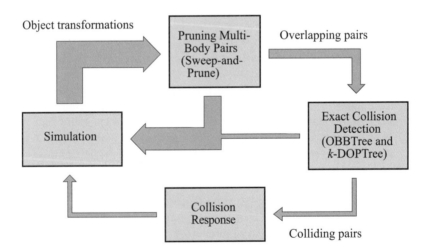

Figure 14.12. The outline of the collision detection system. The overlapping object pairs found by the sweep-and-prune technique are reported to the exact CD system, which, in turn, reports true collisions to a part of the system that should compute the collision response. Finally, all objects are treated by the simulation, where objects get their transforms, for example. *(After Cohen et al. [130].)*

14.7 Miscellaneous Topics

In this section, short introductions will be given for a number of different topics of interest: an acceleration technique called front tracking, time-critical collision detection, distance queries, collision detection of arbitrarily deformable models, and finally, collision response.

14.7.1 Front Tracking

Here we will present an advanced type of caching mechanism that uses temporal coherence for speeding up collision queries. It can be applied to any CD system that uses hierarchies of bounding volumes. Klosowski [434] first published a simple version of this idea. This was then generalized by Li and Chen [493], and later Ehmann and Lin independently developed a similar algorithm [206].

Before the algorithm is described, we present a simple analysis of what happens when two bounding volumes hierarchies (BVHs) are tested against each other. Two BVHs are shown to the left in Figure 14.13, with three and seven nodes. The right part of this figure shows the *BV test tree* [471]. This tree is a representation of what happens when two BV trees are tested against each other. Each node in the BV test tree is a test between a node in each tree. Not all nodes overlap when testing two BVs against each

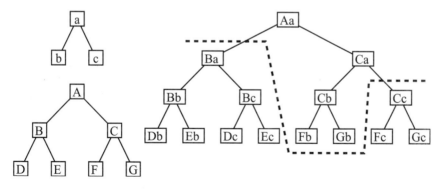

Figure 14.13. To the left are two bounding volumes hierarchies. To the right is the BV test tree. Nodes in this tree represent testing two nodes in the trees to the left. For example, the topmost node "Aa" denotes that the two roots are tested against each other. Note that the entire tree is shown here, even though testing may be terminated before reaching the leaves.

other, and so the dashed line illustrates where the overlapping borders the
nonoverlapping pairs. That is, above this line each pair of nodes overlap,
and below it they are disjoint. For example, node "C" overlaps "b," so the
node "Cb" is above the line; node "C" does not overlap "c," so the node
"Cc" is below.

As the name reveals, the algorithm keeps track of a *front*, and this
front is the dashed line in in Figure 14.13. By storing this front for the
next frame, testing can start just above the front, thereby saving traversal
time at the upper parts of the trees. The effect is the same as starting from
the root of the BV test tree. Obviously, the BV test tree will not be the
same from frame to frame. If more nodes are found to overlap, then the
BV test tree grows, and the front is lowered. If a node is not overlapping
any longer, then the front has to be raised. Ehmann and Lin [206] found
that it is more efficient to raise the front only one level at the time, even
though this does not keep the front fully updated. This sort of speed-up
technique is of most use when the BV/BV test is expensive, as the cost of
updating the front decreased compared to traversing above the front.

Another, much simpler type of caching mechanism can be used if only
one intersection needs to be found. Store the node, N, in the BV test tree
that previously gave an intersection. Then start the testing with the node
just above N. If the objects move slowly, then it is likely that the same
node will give a collision next frame too. If those objects do not overlap
any longer, then testing restarts at the root or at the front, if front tracking
is used.

14.7.2   Time-Critical Collision Detection

Assume that a certain rendering engine is rendering a scene in 7 ms when
the viewer looks at a single wall, but that the rendering takes 15 ms when
the viewer is looking down a long corridor. Clearly, this will give very different frame rates, which is usually disturbing to the user. One rendering
algorithm that attempts to achieve constant frame rate is presented in Section 9.8.3. Here, another approach, called *time-critical collision detection*,
is taken, which can be used if the application uses CD as well. It is called
"time-critical" because the CD algorithm is given a certain time frame, say
9 ms, to complete its task, and it must finish within this time. Another
reason to use such algorithms for CD is that it is very important for the
perceived causality [606, 607], e.g., detecting whether one object causes
another to move. So, returning to our example, assume that we set the
goal that each frame (including CD) should take at most 20 ms, that is,

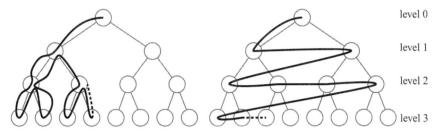

Figure 14.14. Depth-first (left) versus breadth-first (right) traversal. Depth-first traversal is often used in collision detection when traversing the bounding volume hierarchies, but for time-critical CD, breadth-first traversal is used.

50 frames per second. With a time-critical collision detection algorithm, we can see to it that the collision detection part of the rendering engine uses what time is left, up to 20 ms. For example, if a frame uses 15 ms for rendering, the CD part can use only 5 ms.

The following algorithm was introduced by Hubbard [373]. The idea is to traverse the bounding volume hierarchies in *breadth-first* order. This means that all nodes at one level in the tree are visited before descending to the next level. This is in contrast to *depth-first traversal*, which traverses the shortest way to the leaves. These two traversals are illustrated in Figure 14.14. The reason for using breadth-first traversal is that both the left and the right subtree of a node are visited, which means that BVs which together enclose the entire object are visited. With depth-first traversal, we might only visit the left subtree because the algorithm might run out of time. When we do not know whether we have time to traverse the whole tree, it is at least better to traverse a little of both subtrees.

The algorithm first finds all pairs of objects whose BVs overlap, using, for example, the algorithm in Section 14.6.1. These pairs are put in a queue, called Q. The next phase starts by taking out the first BV pair from the queue. Their children BVs are tested against each other and if they overlap, the children pairs are put at the end of the queue. Then the testing continues with the next BV pair in the queue, until either the queue is empty (in which case all of the tree has been traversed) or until we run out of time [373].

Another related approach is to give each BV pair a priority and sort the queue on this priority [178]. This priority can be based on factors such as visibility, eccentricity, distance, etc. Dingliana and O'Sullivan describe algorithms for computing approximate collision response and approximate collision contact determination. This is needed for time-critical CD since the time may run out before the tree traversal has finished.

14.7.3   Distance Queries

In certain applications one wants to test whether an object is at least a certain distance from an environment. For example, when designing new cars, there has to be enough space for different sized passengers to be able to seat themselves comfortably. Therefore, a virtual human of different sizes can be tried against the car seat and the car, to see if he can be seated without bumping into the car. Preferably, the passengers should be able to seat themselves and still be at least, say, 10 cm apart from the car. This sort of testing is called *tolerance verification*. This can be used for *path planning*, i.e., how an object's collision-free path from one point to another can be determined algorithmically. Given the acceleration and velocity of an object, the minimum distance can be used to estimate a lower bound on the time to impact. In this way, collision detection can be avoided until that time [496]. Another related query is of the penetration depth, that is, finding out how far two objects have moved into each other. This distance can be used to move the objects back just enough so that they do not penetrate any longer, and then an appropriate collision response can be computed at that point.

One of the first practical approaches that compute the minimum distance between convex polyhedra is called *GJK*, after its inventors; Gilbert, Johnson and Keerthi [257]. An overview of this algorithm will be given in this section. This algorithm computes the minimum distance between two convex objects, A and B. To do this, the *difference object* (sometimes called the *sum object*) between A and B is used [763]:

$$A - B = \{\mathbf{x} - \mathbf{y} : \mathbf{x} \in A, \mathbf{y} \in B). \qquad (14.9)$$

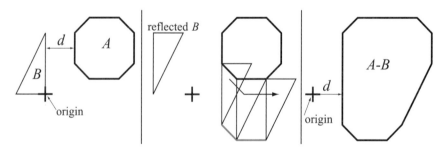

Figure 14.15. To the left, two convex objects A and B are shown. To construct $A - B$, first move A and B so that one reference point is at the origin (already done at the left). Then B is reflected, as shown in the middle, and the chosen reference point on B is put on the surface of A and then the reflected B is swept around A. This creates $A - B$, to the right. The minimum distance, d, is shown both on the left and the right.

This is also called the *Minowksi sum* of A and B. All differences $\mathbf{x} - \mathbf{y}$ are treated as a point set, which forms a convex object. An example of such a difference is shown in Figure 14.15, which also explains how to mentally build such a difference object.

The idea of GJK is that instead of computing the minimum distance between A and B, the minimum distance between $A - B$ and the origin is computed. These two distances can be shown to be equivalent. The algorithm is visualized in Figure 14.16. Note that if the origin is inside $A - B$ then A and B overlap.

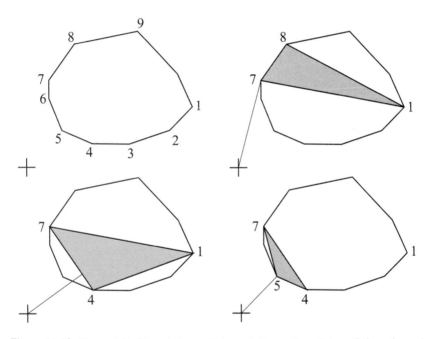

Figure 14.16. Upper left: The minimum distance between the origin and the polygon is to be computed. Upper right: An arbitrary triangle is chosen as a starting point for the algorithm, and the minimum distance to that triangle is computed. Vertex 7 is closest. Lower left: In the next step, all vertices are projected onto the line from the origin to vertex 7, and the closest vertex replaces the one in the triangle which is farthest away on this projection. Thus vertex 4 replaces vertex 8. The closest point on this triangle is then found, which is located on the edge from vertex 4 to 7. Lower right: The vertices are projected onto the line from the origin to the closest point from the previous step, and vertex 5 thus replaces vertex 1, which is farthest away on the projection. Vertex 5 is the closest point on this triangle, and when the vertices are projected on the line to vertex 5, we find that vertex 5 is the closest point overall. This completes the iteration. At this time the closest point on the triangle is found, which also happens to be vertex 5. This point is returned. *(Illustration after Jiménez et al. [395].)*

The algorithm starts from an arbitrary simplex in the polyhedron. A simplex is the simplest primitive in the respective dimension, so it is a triangle in two dimensions, and a tetrahedron in three dimensions. Then the minimum distance from the origin to a point on this simplex is computed. Van den Bergen shows how this can be done by solving a set of linear equations [763, 764]. A vector is then formed starting at the origin and ending at the nearest point. All vertices of the polyhedron are projected onto this vector, and the one with the smallest projection distance from the origin is chosen to be a new vertex in the updated simplex. Since a new vertex is added to the simplex, an existing vertex in the simplex must be removed. The one whose projection is farthest away is deleted. At this point, the minimum distance to the updated simplex is computed, and the algorithm iterates through all vertices again until the algorithm cannot update the simplex any longer. The algorithm terminates in a finite number of steps for two polyhedra [257]. The performance of this algorithm can be improved using many techniques, such as incremental computation and caching [763].

Van den Bergen describes a fast and robust implementation of GJK [763, 764]. GJK can also be extended to compute penetration depth [111, 765]. GJK is not the only algorithm for computing minimum distance; there are many others, such as the Lin-Canny algorithm [495], V-Clip [553], PQP [471] SWIFT [205], and SWIFT++ [206].

14.7.4   Deformable Models

So far, the main focus of this section has been on either static models or rigid-body animated models. Obviously, there are other sorts of motion, such as waves on the water or a piece of cloth swaying in the wind. This type of motion is generally not possible to describe using rigid bodies, and instead, one can treat each vertex as being an independent vector function over time. Collision detection for such models is generally more expensive, and some initial research is presented here.

Assuming that the mesh connectivity stays the same for an object during deformation, it is possible to design clever algorithms that exploit this. Such deformation is what would happen to a piece of cloth in the wind (unless it is torn apart somehow). As a preprocess, an initial hierarchical bounding volume (BV) tree is built. Instead of actually rebuilding the tree when deformation has taken place, the bounding volumes are simply refitted to the deformed geometry [472, 762]. By using AABBs, which are fast to recompute, this operation is pretty efficient (as compared to OBBs).

However, in general, any type of BV can be used. Van den Bergen organizes his tree so that all BVs are allocated and placed in an array, where a node always is placed so that its index is lower than its child nodes [762, 764]. In this way, a bottom-up update can be done by traversing the array from the end backwards, recomputing each BV at each node. This means that the BVs of the leaves are recomputed first, and then their parents' BVs are recomputed using the newly computed BVs, and so on back to the root of the tree. This sort of refit operation is reported to be about ten times as fast as rebuilding the tree from scratch [762].

However, it has been noted that, in general, few BVs in a tree need to be updated. This is because most of them are not used during a collision query. A hybrid top-down/bottom-up tree update has therefore been proposed [472]. The idea is to use a bottom-up update for the higher levels (including the root), which means that only the upper BVs will be updated each frame. The rationale for this is that the upper levels often prune away most geometry. These updated upper levels are tested for overlap with the other tree (also possibly deforming and updated). For nodes that do not overlap, we can skip the updating of their subtrees, and so save much effort. On the other hand, for nodes that do overlap, a top-down strategy is used for updating nodes in their subtrees as they are needed during a tree traversal. Bottom-up could also be used for these, but top-down was found to be more effective [472]. Good results were achieved when the first $n/2$ upper levels were updated with a bottom-up method, and the lower $n/2$ levels with a top-down method. This is shown in Figure 14.17. To update a node top-down, the node records which vertices its entire subtree

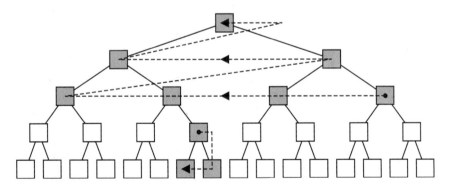

Figure 14.17. The hybrid bottom-up/top-down tree update method. The upper levels are updated using a bottom-up strategy, and only those nodes deeper down in the tree that are reached during a tree traversal are updated using a top-down method.

holds, and this list is traversed and a minimal BV is computed. When using top-down update, overlap testing is done as soon as a BV has been updated, so that the traversal can be terminated if no overlap is found. This, again, gives more efficiency. Initial tests show that this method is four to five times faster than van den Bergen's method [472].

Another more general method for deformable objects first computes minimal AABBs around two objects to be tested for collision [720]. If they overlap, the overlap AABB region is computed, which simply is the intersection volume of the AABBs. It is only inside this overlap region that a collision can occur. A list of all triangles inside this region is created. An octree (see Section 9.1.3) that surrounds the entire scene is then used. The idea is then to insert triangles into the octree's nodes, and if triangles from both objects are found in a leaf node, then these triangles are tested against each other. Several optimizations are possible. First, the octree does not need to be built explicitly. When a node gets a list of triangles, the triangles are tested against the eight children nodes, and eight new triangle lists are created. This recursion ends at the leaves, where triangle/triangle testing can take place. Second, this recursion can end any time the triangle list has triangles from only one of the objects. To avoid testing a triangle pair more than once, a checklist is kept that tracks the tested pairs. The efficiency of this method may break down when an overlap region is very large, or there are many triangles in an overlap region.

14.7.5 Collision Response

Collision response is the action that should be taken to avoid (abnormal) interpenetration of objects. Assume, for example, that a sphere is moving towards a cube. When the sphere first hits the cube, which is determined by collision detection algorithms, we would like the sphere to change its trajectory (e.g., velocity direction), so it appears that they collided. This is the task of *collision response* techniques, which has been and still is the subject of intensive research [40, 177, 303, 551, 569, 809]. It is a complex topic, and in this section only the simplest technique will be presented.

In Section 13.17.3, a technique for computing the exact time of collision between a sphere and a plane was presented. Here we will explain what happens to the sphere's motion at the time of collision.

Assume that a sphere is moving towards a plane. The velocity vector is $\mathbf{v}$, and the plane is $\pi : \mathbf{n} \cdot \mathbf{x} + d = 0$, where $\mathbf{n}$ is normalized. This is shown in Figure 14.18. To compute the simplest response, we represent the velocity vector as:

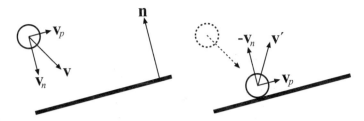

Figure 14.18. Collision response for a sphere approaching a plane. To the left the velocity vector $\mathbf{v}$ is divided into two components, $\mathbf{v}_n$, and $\mathbf{v}_p$. To the right, perfectly elastic (bouncy) collision is shown, where the new velocity is $\mathbf{v}' = \mathbf{v}_p - \mathbf{v}_n$. For a less elastic collision, the length of $-\mathbf{v}_n$ could be decreased.

$$\mathbf{v} = \mathbf{v}_n + \mathbf{v}_p, \quad \text{where}$$
$$\mathbf{v}_n = (\mathbf{v} \cdot \mathbf{n})\mathbf{n}, \quad (14.10)$$
$$\mathbf{v}_p = \mathbf{v} - \mathbf{v}_n.$$

With this representation, the velocity vector, $\mathbf{v}'$, after the collision is [460]:

$$\mathbf{v}' = \mathbf{v}_p - \mathbf{v}_n. \quad (14.11)$$

Here, we have assumed that the response was totally elastic. This means that no kinetic energy is lost, and thus that the response is "perfectly bouncy" [809]. Now, normally the ball is deformed slightly at collision, and some energy transformed into heat, so some energy is lost. This is described with a coefficient of *restitution*, k (often also denoted ϵ). The velocity parallel to the plane, $\mathbf{v}_p$, remains unchanged, while $\mathbf{v}_n$ is dampened with $k \in [0, 1]$:

$$\mathbf{v}' = \mathbf{v}_p - k\mathbf{v}_n. \quad (14.12)$$

As k gets smaller, more and more energy is lost, and the collision appears less and less bouncy. At $k = 0$, the motion after collision is parallel to the plane, so the ball appears to roll on the plane.

More sophisticated collision response is based on physics, and involves creating a system of equations that is solved using an *Ordinary Differential Equation* (ODE) solver. In such algorithms, a point of collision and a normal at this point is needed. The interested reader should consult the SIGGRAPH course notes by Witkin et al. [809] and the paper by Dingliana et al. [177]. Also, O'Sullivan and Dingliana present experiments that show that it is hard for a human to judge whether a collision response is correct [606, 607]. This is especially true when more dimensions are involved (i.e., it is easier in one dimension than in three). To produce a real-time algorithm, they found that when there was not time enough to compute an accurate response, a random collision response could be used. These were found to be as believable as more accurate responses.

Further Reading and Resources

See this book's website, http://www.realtimerendering.com/, for the latest information and free software in this rapidly evolving field. More information on spatial data structures can be found in Section 9.1. Even more information can be found in Samet's books [669, 670]. An extensive survey of collision detection algorithms was presented by Lin and Gottschalk [498] in 1998. More recent surveys are given by Jiménez and Torras [395], and by O'Sullivan et al. [608]. Schneider and Eberly present algorithms for computing the distance between many different primitives in their book on geometrical tools [688].

The OBBTree algorithm has been extended by Eberly to handle dynamic collision detection [199]. This work is briefly described in *IEEE CG&A* [65]. Algorithms for collision detection of extremely large models (millions of triangles) have been presented by Wilson et al. [803]. They combine BVHs of spheres, AABBs, and OBBs, with a data structure called the overlap graph, lazy creation of BVHs, temporal coherence, and more, into a system called *IMMPACT*. Storing a bounding volume hierarchy may use much memory, and so Gomez presents some methods for compressing an AABB tree [276].

Another method for transforming the k-DOPs is presented by Zachmann [833]. This resembles the approximation method in that a transformed k-DOP is enclosed in a new k-DOP which is aligned with the one that it is tested against. Konečný presents an efficient method for performing this operation using linear programming techniques [442].

Frisken et al. [241] present a framework for soft bodies, where collisions, impact forces, and contact determination can be computed efficiently. Their framework is based on *Adaptively sampled Distance Fields* (ADFs), which is a relatively new shape representation [240].

Baraff and Witkin [41] and Hughes et al. [376] present collision detection algorithms for objects undergoing polynomial deformation. Another more general system for arbitrary deformable objects is presented by Ganovelli et al. [248]. Related to his are algorithms for response and collision detection for cloth. This is treated by Baraff and Witkin [42], Courshesnes et al. [146], and Volino and Magnenat-Thalmann [777, 778]. Another complex phenomenon is (human) hair. Hadap and Magnenat-Thalmann [299] treat hair as a continuum, which makes it possible to simulate hair relatively quickly. Hecker has a set of four theoretical and practical tutorials on collision response and the physics involved [337, 338, 339, 340]. Lander also has a good introduction to the physics of collision response for accurately simulating a pool table [461].

Distance queries have been extended to handle concave objects by Quinlan [639], and Ehmann and Lin also handle concave objects by decomposing an object into convex parts [206]. Kawachi and Suzuki present another algorithm for computing the minimum distance between concave parts [412]. Hoff et al. [361] describe how graphics hardware can be used to efficiently compute intersection, minimum distances, contact points and normals, and penetration depth in two dimensions. This work also presents an overview of related research that uses graphics hardware.

Chapter 15
Graphics Hardware

"Within the next few years, there will be single-chip graphics devices more powerful and versatile than any graphics system that has ever been built, at any price."
–David Kirk, 1998

Despite the fact that graphics hardware is evolving at a rapid pace, there are some general concepts and architectures that are still commonly used in its design. Our goal in this chapter is to give an understanding of the various hardware elements of a graphics system and how they relate to one another. Other parts of the book discuss various hardware elements in terms of their use with particular algorithms. Here, we discuss hardware on its own terms. We begin by discussing how the contents of the color buffer gets displayed on the monitor. The various different buffers that can be a part of a real-time rendering system are then discussed. After that, perspective-correct interpolation is described. We continue with an overview of graphics architecture concepts, followed by three case studies of specific graphics systems.

15.1 Buffers and Buffering

15.1.1 A Simple Display System

In Section 2.4, we saw that the colors of the pixels are located in a color buffer. Visible primitives affect these pixels. Here, we will use a simple model to describe how the contents of the color buffer end up on the monitor (or any other device). The memory of the frame buffer may be located in the same memory as the CPU uses for its tasks, in dedicated frame-buffer memory, or in a dedicated memory that is shared between buffers and

669

Frame Buffer

**Output Device
(e.g. monitor)**

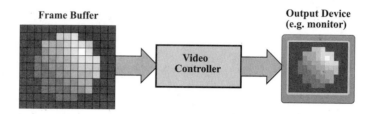

**Video
Controller**

Figure 15.1. A simple display system: the color buffer is scanned by the video controller, which fetches the colors of the pixels. These colors are in turn used to control the intensities on the output device.

textures. The color buffer is a part of the frame buffer. It is in some way connected to a *video controller*, which, in turn, is connected to the monitor. This is illustrated in Figure 15.1. The video controller is also called a *Digital-to-Analog Converter* (DAC), since the digital pixel value is converted to an analog equivalent for the monitor. Because every pixel must be read for each frame and sent through digital-to-analog conversion, this system must be able to deal with high bandwidths. Gamma correction (see Section 4.7) should be done before the data reaches the DAC.

The rate at which a monitor updates the image is typically between 60 and 120 times per second (Hertz). The job of the video controller is to scan through the color buffer, scanline by scanline, at the same rate as the monitor, and to do this in synchronization with the beam of the monitor. During a single refresh of the image, the colors of the pixels in the color buffer are used to control the intensities of the monitor beam. Note that the electron beam usually moves in a left-to-right and up-to-down manner. Because of this, the beam does not contribute to the image on the screen when it moves from the right side to the left. This is called the *horizontal retrace*. Related to this is the *line rate* or *horizontal refresh rate*, the amount of time it takes to complete one entire left-right-left cycle. The *vertical retrace* is the movement of the beam from the bottom to the upper left corner, i.e., its return to position to begin the next frame. This is shown in Figure 15.2. The *vertical refresh rate* is the number of times per second the monitor performs this process. Most viewers notice flicker at rates less than 72 Hz (see page 345 for more information on this).

EXAMPLE: MONITOR TIMING The VESA (Video Electronics Standards Association) specifies standard monitor timings. The VESA standard for a 1280×1024 resolution display at 75 Hz is an example. At 75 Hz, the screen updates once every 13.33 milliseconds. The standard specifies a *frame size*,

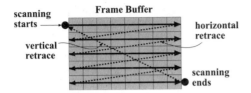

Figure 15.2. The horizontal and vertical retraces of a monitor. The color buffer shown here has five scanlines of pixels. The scanning of the lines starts at the upper left corner and proceeds one scanline at a time. At the end of a scanline it stops scanning and moves to the line below the current line. This passage is called horizontal retrace. When the bottom right corner is reached, the scanning ends and moves back to the upper left corner in order to be able to scan the next frame. This movement is called vertical retrace.

which defines the relationship between the resolution and retrace times. The frame size for a 1280×1024 resolution screen is 1688×1066. This size is related to the *pixel clock*, which is the rate at which pixels are refreshed. The pixel clock is $1688 \times 1066 \times 75$ Hz, or 135 MegaHertz (MHz). This is about 7.4 nanoseconds per pixel. The *line rate*, which is the monitor's frame rate times the number of scanlines, is then $75 \times 1066 = 79,950$ lines per second. The frame size can be used to derive the vertical retrace time. To get the vertical *sync length*, subtract the vertical resolution from the vertical frame size, that is, $1066 - 1024 = 42$. So the vertical retrace takes the same amount of time as drawing 42 lines on the screen. This gives $42 \times 1688 \times 7.4$ nanoseconds, or about 525 microseconds for the vertical retrace to occur. □

Related to this topic is interlacing. Computer monitors are typically noninterlaced, or what is commonly known as *progressive scan*. In television, the horizontal lines are interlaced, so that during one vertical refresh, the odd numbered lines are drawn, and during the next one, the even numbered lines are drawn. Filtering computer animation for television is nontrivial. Snyder et al. [723] discuss one way to tackle the problem. More recently, Dawson [161] discusses this topic, as well as television color issues. A related, obsolete method of achieving additional acceleration for PC graphics accelerators is to use *scanline interleave* (SLI) mode. In this scheme from (the now defunct) 3dfx, two chipsets run in parallel; one handles the odd scanlines, the other the even.

15.1.2 The Color Buffer

The color buffer usually has a few color modes, based on the number of bytes of depth. These modes include:

- High color: two bytes per pixel, of which 15 or 16 bits are used for the color, giving 32,768 or 65,536 colors, respectively.

- True color or RGB color: three or four bytes per pixel, of which 24 bits are used for the color, giving $16,777,216 \approx 16.8$ million different colors.

Other modes exist, but these are the two main modes used in real-time graphics on most systems. High color has a speed advantage over true color. This is because two bytes of memory per pixel may usually be accessed more quickly than three or four bytes per pixel.

The high color mode has 16 bits of color resolution to use. Typically, this amount is split into at least 5 bits each for red, green, and blue. This leaves one bit, which is usually given to the green channel, resulting in a 5-6-5 division. The green channel is chosen because it has the largest luminance effect on the eye, and so requires greater precision. This division yields 32 or 64 equally spaced, fixed levels of color per channel. An alternate division is 5-5-5-1, where the single bit is not used, or possibly used for the alpha channel.

With 32 or 64 levels of color, it is possible to discern differences in adjacent color levels. For example, a smoothly shaded Gouraud triangle may become shaded with contours as the color jumps from level to level across the surface; see Figure 15.3. The human visual system further increases this problem due to a perceptual phenomenon called *Mach banding* [264, 316]. This problem is usually termed *banding* or *contouring* [631]. Placing a texture on a banded surface can help mask the problem [230]. Dithering [45, 235] also lessens the effect, so most modern graphics systems support it. For many applications, high color mode can be adequate.

True color uses 24 bits of RGB[1] color, one byte per color channel. Internally, these colors may be stored as 24 or 32 bits. A 32-bit representation

Figure 15.3. As the rectangle is shaded from white to black, banding appears. Although each grayscale bar has a solid intensity level, each can appear to be darker on the left and lighter on the right due to Mach banding.

---

[1]On PC systems, the ordering is often reversed to BGR.

can be present for speed purposes, because various hardware commands are optimized for groups of four bytes (or larger). The extra 8 bits can also be used to store an alpha channel (see Section 4.5), giving the pixel an RGBA value. The 24-bit color (no alpha) representation is also called the *packed pixel format*, which can save frame buffer memory in comparison to its 32-bit, unpacked counterpart.

Using 24 bits of color is almost always acceptable for real-time rendering. It is still possible to see banding of colors, but much less likely than with only 16 bits. Gamma correction can also affect the number of color levels (see Section 4.7). Note that when using multipass techniques to increase the quality of the images, it is better to have more precision in the color buffer (i.e., more than eight bits per color component). If the precision is too low, then quantization effects may be visible and annoying to the viewer.

This quantization problem is one of the main arguments for more bits per channel. For example, some machines [568] compute color internally as 12 bits or more, since the additional bits are useful for image storage, compositing, gamma correction, image processing, etc. Only 8 bits per channel are displayed, but various banding problems are avoided by this approach.

It is often the case that an API supports higher-precision colors than the underlying hardware does. For example, in OpenGL the RGBA values can be numbers between 0.0 and 1.0, and the floating point representations of these then have essentially 24 bits of precision (i.e., the mantissa) per channel. The hardware rounds off to the nearest available color, or uses a more sophisticated technique, such as dithering, in order to approximate these colors.

In image file formats, you can see a mirroring of the various color buffer architectures [577]. GIF is an indexed look-up table format, in which 256 colors are selected out of all possible 24-bit colors. TIFF and PNG support look-up tables and true color. Targa has 16- and 32-bit modes. The successive versions of the Windows BMP format are a study in the evolution of the PC color buffer.

In any color mode, we may also think of the image as consisting of a set of color planes. For example, a true color system has 24 color planes. Some high-end CAD systems also support overlay planes, which are normally one to eight bits of independent color data that are stored separately. One color or bit of the overlay plane is used to denote that the pixel is transparent. This overlay plane can be drawn to in a manner similar to the color buffer. The hardware places any image in this overlay plane in front of the underlying color buffer on the monitor. The overlay plane is useful for a number of operations, such as menus and other user interface elements, object highlighting, cursors, heads-up displays, etc. The advantage is that such elements can be changed without affecting (and requiring the renderer to refresh) the underlying scene.

15.1.3   Z-Buffering and W-Buffering

As we saw in Section 2.4, the Z-buffer (also called the depth buffer) can be used to resolve visibility. This kind of buffer typically has 24 bits per pixel. For orthographic viewing, the corresponding world space distance values are proportional to the z-value, and so the depth resolution is uniform. For example, say the world space distance between the near and far planes is 100 meters, and the Z-buffer stores 16 bits per pixel. This means that the distance between any adjacent depth values is the same, 100 meters $/2^{16}$, i.e., about 1.5 millimeters.

However, for perspective viewing this is not the case. Instead, the distribution is nonuniform, and the resolution is finer at the lower depth values (see Figure 3.17 on page 66). The distribution is also highly dependent on the near and far values of the projection. Setting the near value as far out as possible without clipping gives better overall resolution in the viewed range. Bringing the far plane in does not help much at all. See page 266 for more information on this topic. Depth resolution is important because it helps avoid rendering errors. For example, say you modelled a sheet of paper and placed it on a desk, ever so slightly above the desk's surface.[2] With error in the least significant bits of the z-depths computed for the desk and paper, the desk can poke through the paper at various spots. A higher depth precision can help eliminate such problems. Subpixel addressing, in which the position within the pixel's cell is used for the location of endpoints (vs. using the center of the pixel), also has a major effect on correct Z-buffer primitive ordering [474].

After applying the perspective transform (Equations 3.68–3.70), a point $\mathbf{v} = (v_x, v_y, v_z, v_w)$ is obtained. Next, division by v_w is done so that $(v_x/v_w, v_y/v_w, v_z/v_w, 1)$. The value v_z/v_w is mapped from its valid range (e.g., $[0, 1]$ for DirectX) to the range $[0, 2^b - 1]$ and is stored in the Z-buffer, where b is the number of bits. The characteristics of the perspective transform matrix result in greater precision for objects closer to the viewer (see

---

[2]If the paper were placed exactly at the same height as the desk, i.e., the paper and desk were made coplanar, then there would be no right answer. Sometimes called *z-fighting*, this problem is due to poor modeling and cannot be resolved by better z precision.

page 65). This is especially true when there is a large difference between the near and the far values. When the near value is close to the far value, the precision tends to be uniform over the depth. To return to the paper and desk example, this change in precision can mean that as the viewer moves farther away from the paper, the desk poke-through problem occurs more frequently.

An alternate hardware architecture is called W-buffering [79]. This technique stores the w-value after the perspective transform, which is essentially the eye space depth, scaled. Here, the precision of the depth value is always uniform for all depths. Blinn offers a detailed comparison of Z-buffering and W-buffering [79]. One of the greatest advantages of using a W-buffer over the Z-buffer is that less care is needed to set the near and far planes in order to maximize the precision. This is due to the uniform depth precision of the W-buffer. The W-buffer is getting used less and less, and one proposal for DirectX 9 is that it be deprecated.

15.1.4   Single, Double, and Triple Buffering

In Section 2.4, we mentioned that double buffering is used in order for the viewer not to see the actual rendering of the primitives. Here, we will describe single, double, and even triple buffering.

Assume that we have only a single buffer. This buffer has to be the one that is currently shown to the viewer. As polygons for a frame are drawn, we will see more and more of them as the monitor refreshes—an unconvincing effect. Even if our frame rate is equal to the monitor's update rate, single buffering has problems. If we decide to clear the buffer or draw a large polygon, then we will briefly be able to see the actual partial changes to the color buffer as the beam of the monitor passes those areas that are being drawn. Sometimes called tearing, because the image displayed looks as if it were briefly ripped in two, this is not a desirable feature for real-time graphics.[3] Single buffering is useful, however, in other contexts. For example, when a drawing area is updated very infrequently then single buffering may be sufficient. This is often the case when a small image appears in a window. That buffer is usually redrawn only when another window has covered the image and is suddenly moved so that the image should be visible. Single buffering is also useful for optimizing the pipeline (see Section 10.4).

---

[3]On some systems, like the old Amiga, you could actually test where the beam was and so avoid drawing there. Thus, some real-time graphics can work fine with single buffering.

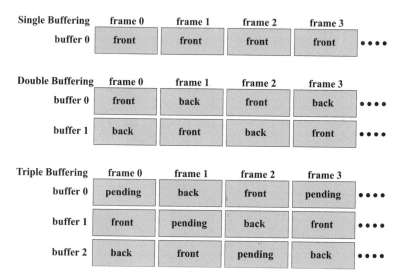

Figure 15.4. For single buffering, the front buffer is always shown. For double buffering, buffer 0 is first in front and buffer 1 is in the back. Then they swap from front to back and vice versa for each frame. Triple buffering works by having a pending buffer as well. Here, a buffer is first cleared, and rendering to it is begun (pending). Second, the system continues to use the buffer for rendering until the image has been completed (back). Finally, the buffer is shown (front).

To avoid the visibility problem, double buffering is commonly used. In this scheme, a finished image is shown in the *front buffer*, while an off-screen *back buffer* contains the scene that is currently being drawn. The back buffer and the front buffer are then swapped by the graphics driver, typically during vertical retrace to avoid tearing. The swap does not have to occur during retrace; instantly swapping is useful for benchmarking a rendering system, but is also used in many applications because it maximizes frame rate. Immediately after the swap, the (new) back buffer is then the recipient of graphics commands, and the new front buffer is shown to the user. This process is shown in Figure 15.4. For applications that control the whole screen, the swap is normally implemented on PCs using a *color buffer flipping* technique [148], also known as *page flipping*. This means that the front buffer is associated with the address of a special register. This address points to the pixel at the position $(0,0)$, which may be at the lower or upper left corner. When buffers are swapped, the address of the register is changed to the address of the back buffer. Panning the screen is easily done by writing to the register. For windowed applications, the common way to implement swapping on the PC is to use a technique called *BLT swapping* [148] or, simply, *blitting*. For this method there is one and only one piece of memory that is always displayed, often called the video RAM. To do a swap of the back buffer, which may reside in the host memory or in any other video memory, a piece of hardware called the BitBLT engine copies the contents of the back buffer into the front buffer.

The double buffer can be augmented with a second back buffer, which we call the *pending buffer*. This is called *triple buffering* [527]. The pending buffer is similar to the back buffer in that it is also off-screen, and in that it can be modified while the front buffer is being displayed. The pending buffer becomes part of a three-buffer cycle. During one frame, the pending buffer can be accessed. At the next swap, it becomes the back buffer, where the rendering is completed. Then it becomes the front buffer and is shown to the viewer. At the next swap, the buffer again turns into a pending buffer. This course of events is visualized at the bottom of Figure 15.4.

Triple buffering has a number of advantages over double buffering. First, the system can access the pending buffer while waiting for the vertical retrace. With double buffering, a swap can stall the graphics pipeline. While waiting for the vertical retrace so a swap can take place, a double-buffered construction must simply be kept waiting. This is so because the front buffer must be shown to the viewer, and the back buffer must remain unchanged because it has a finished image in it, waiting to be shown. If swapping is accomplished with blitting, triple buffering offers additional rendering time by allowing draw access to the pending buffer during this transfer time. A related advantage is that clearing the buffer can take significant time on some systems, and so while the pending buffer is being cleared, the back buffer can be accessed in parallel. These advantages make the load better balanced, the major reason to use triple buffering. Minor variations in image generation time can radically affect the frame rate when using double buffering. For example, if images are generated in less than 1/60th of a second and a monitor's update rate is 60 Hz, both double and triple buffering will display 60 new images a second. If images later take slightly longer than 1/60th of a second to generate, double buffering (without tearing) can display only 30 new images per second. Triple buffering does not get stalled and so allows the display of nearly 60 new images a second. See Section 10.4 for more on load balancing. Note also that all buffering schemes have different latencies. Single buffering has none (though it is subject to tearing), double buffering has at least one frame of latency, while triple buffering has at least two frames of latency.

The idea of triple buffering is good in theory, but there are some limitations and disadvantages. An additional color buffer must be allocated for the pending buffer, which consumes additional memory. Also, the latency increases up to one entire frame, which delays the reaction to user inputs, such as keystrokes and mouse or joystick moves. This happens because these user events are deferred after the rendering begins in the pending buffer. Triple buffering can easily be exploited if there is direct hardware support for it, or if there is the ability to allocate your own buffers. DirectX supports triple buffering, while OpenGL does not.

In theory, more than three buffers could be used. If the amount of time to compute a frame varies considerably, more buffers give more balance and an overall higher display rate, at the cost of more potential latency. To generalize, multibuffering can be thought of as a ring structure. There is a rendering pointer and a display pointer, each pointing at a different buffer. The rendering pointer leads the display pointer, moving to the next buffer when the current rendering buffer is done being computed. The only rule is that the display pointer should never be the same as the rendering pointer.

15.1.5 Stereo Buffers

Some hardware also has support for stereo rendering, in which two images are used in order to make objects look more three-dimensional. With two eyes, the visual system takes two views, and in combining them, retrieves depth information. This ability is called *stereopsis* or *stereo vision* [235, 264]. The idea behind stereo vision is to render two images, one for the left eye and one for the right eye (as shown in Figure 15.5), and then use some technique that ensures that the human viewer experiences a depth in the rendered image. These two images are called the *stereo pair*. One common method for creating stereo vision is to generate two images, one in red and one in green (or cyan, by rendering to both the blue and green channels), composite these images, then view the result with red-green glasses. In this case, only a normal single display buffer is needed, but display of color is problematic. For color images, the solution can be as simple as having two small screens, one in front of each (human) eye, in a head-mounted display. Another hardware solution is the use of shutter glasses, in which only one eye is allowed to view the screen at a time. Two different views can be displayed by rapidly alternating between eyes and synchronizing with the monitor [152].

For these latter forms of stereography, two separate display buffers are needed. When viewing is to take place in real time, double buffering is used together with stereo rendering. In this case, there have to be two front and two back buffers (one set for each eye), so the color buffer memory requirement doubles.

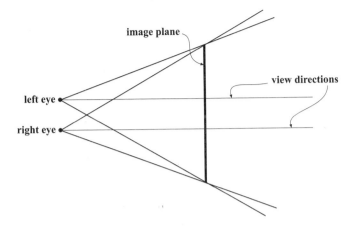

Figure 15.5. Stereo rendering. Note that the image plane is shared between the two frustums, and that the frustums are asymmetric. Such rendering would be used on, for example, a stereo monitor. Shutter glasses could use separate image planes for each eye.

15.1.6 Stencil and Accumulation Buffering

The stencil and accumulation buffers were first described in Section 2.4. The sizes of these buffers are important to hardware designers. Most often both buffers are of the same screen resolution (but not bit depth) as the color buffer. This is so because it is desirable to use the accumulation to add and subtract images from the color buffer, and the stencil buffer must be able to mask off certain parts of the color buffer.

The stencil buffer typically has between one and eight bits for each pixel. With one bit, you can create simple masking, and with more bits, you can create more complex effects such as general shadow volumes (see Section 6.12.3). The standard configuration on newer accelerators is 8 bits, paired with the 24 bits of the Z-buffer to make a word.

The accumulation buffer has a higher range than the color buffer, and so typically has more bits than the color buffer. Now, assume a particular accumulation buffer has twice as many bits as the color buffer, which is a common design choice. A color buffer of 24 bits per pixel (8 bits per color channel) would imply an accumulation buffer of 48 bits per pixel (16 bits per color channel). With 48 bits per pixel in the accumulation buffer, 256 images can be added together without loss of precision. Accumulation buffers with 8 bits per color channel are possible, and may be used by shifting down the images to be accumulated, but the quality will suffer due to lost bits. The accumulation buffer can be used to create effects such as depth of field, antialiasing, and motion blur.

15.1.7 T-Buffering

This buffer's function is explained in depth beginning on page 94. The T-buffer is like the accumulation buffer, in that effects can be generated by the same idea of merging individual images. However, instead of accumulating results to a single higher precision image, a number of 8 bits per channel images are stored and combined by video hardware to generate the final image. These separate images are generated by 2, 4, or more separate rasterizer pipelines. Antialiasing can be done in parallel by defining a different screen pixel shift for each pipeline. The main weakness of the T-buffer is hardware cost, since most of the hardware pipeline must be duplicated for each unit acting in parallel. 3dfx was the first and last hardware vendor to implement the T-buffer.

15.1.8 Buffer Memory

Here, a simple example will be given on how much memory is needed for the different buffers in a graphics system. Assume that we have a color buffer of 1280×1024 pixels with true colors, i.e., 8 bits per color channel. This would require $1280 \times 1024 \times 3 = 3.75$ megabytes (MB). Using double buffering doubles this value to 7.5 MB. Also, let us say that the Z-buffer has 24 bits per pixel. The Z-buffer would then need 3.75 MB of memory. Assume that we have a stencil buffer of 8 bits per pixel and an accumulation buffer of 48 bits per pixel. This alone would require 7 bytes per pixel, which is equal to 8.75 MB. This system would therefore require $7.5 + 8.75 + 3.75 = 20$ MB of memory for these buffers. Stereo buffers would double the color buffer size, and an alpha value would add an additional one byte per pixel (1.25 MB) of memory. Note that under all circumstances, only one Z-buffer is needed, since it is always paired with the color buffer active for rendering and thus never displayed.

15.2 Perspective-Correct Interpolation

The fundamentals of how perspective-correct interpolation is done in a rasterizer will briefly be described here. This is important, as it forms the basis of how rasterization is done so that textures look and behave correctly on primitives. As we have seen, each primitive vertex, $\mathbf{v}$, is perspectively projected using any of Equations 3.68-3.70. A projected vertex, $\mathbf{p} = (p_x w, p_y w, p_z w, w)$, is obtained. We use $w = p_w$ here to simplify the presentation. After division by w we obtain $(p_x, p_y, p_z, 1)$. Recall that $-1 \leq p_z \leq 1$ for the OpenGL perspective transform. However, the stored z-value in the Z-buffer is in $[0, 2^b - 1]$, where b is the number of bits in the Z-buffer. This is achieved with a simple translation and scale of p_z. Also, each vertex has a set of other parameters associated with it, e.g., texture coordinates (u, v), fog, and a color, $\mathbf{c}$.

The screen position (p_x, p_y, p_z) can be correctly interpolated linearly over the triangle, with no need for adjustment. In practice, this is often done by computing delta slopes: $\frac{\Delta z}{\Delta x}$ and $\frac{\Delta z}{\Delta y}$. These slopes represent how much the p_z value differs between two adjacent pixels in the x- and y-directions, respectively. Only a simple addition is needed to update the p_z value when moving from one pixel to its neighbor. However, it is important to realize that the colors and especially texture coordinates cannot normally be linearly interpolated. The result is that improper foreshortening due to the perspective effect will be achieved. See Figure 15.6 for a comparison. To solve this, Heckbert and Moreton [332] and Blinn [75] show that $1/w$ and $(u/w, v/w)$ can be linearly interpolated. Then the interpolated texture coordinates are divided by the interpolated $1/w$ to get the correct texture location. That is, $(u/w, v/w)/(1/w) = (u, v)$. This type of interpolation is called *hyperbolic interpolation*, because a graph of the interpolated value versus position forms a hyperbola. It is also called *rational linear interpolation*, because a numerator and denominator are linearly interpolated.

As an example, assume a triangle should be rasterized, and that each vertex is:

Figure 15.6. A textured quadrilateral consists of two triangles. To the left, linear interpolation is used over each triangle, and to the right, perspective-correct interpolation is used. Notice how linear interpolation ruins the three-dimensional effect.

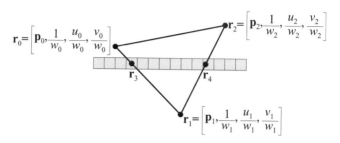

Figure 15.7. A triangle being rasterized. The vectors $\mathbf{r}_i$ are linearly interpolated over the triangle.

$$\mathbf{r}_i = \left[\mathbf{p}_i, \frac{1}{w_i}, \frac{u_i}{w_i}, \frac{v_i}{w_i}\right]. \tag{15.1}$$

Here, $\mathbf{p}_i = (p_{ix}, p_{iy}, p_{iz})$ is the point after projection and division by its w-component, which is denoted w_i. The (u_i, v_i) are texture coordinates at the vertices. This is shown in Figure 15.7. To find the coordinates of a pixel on the horizontal scanline shown in gray, one must first linearly interpolate $\mathbf{r}_0$ and $\mathbf{r}_1$ to get $\mathbf{r}_3$, and also linearly interpolate $\mathbf{r}_2$ and $\mathbf{r}_1$ to get $\mathbf{r}_4$. Then linear interpolation of $\mathbf{r}_3$ and $\mathbf{r}_4$ can be used to find a $\mathbf{r}$ vertex for each pixel on the gray scanline. The interpolated $\mathbf{p}$-values are correct as is. The other interpolated surface values $(u/w, v/w)$ are multiplied by a computed value w to obtain (u, v). To obtain w itself the linearly interpolated value $1/w$ is used, with a division done per pixel to compute $w = 1/(1/w)$.

This implementation of the interpolation is only one choice. Another possibility is to compute delta slopes for texture interpolation: $\Delta(u/w)/\Delta x$, $\Delta(u/w)/\Delta y$, $\Delta(v/w)/\Delta x$, $\Delta(v/w)/\Delta y$, $\Delta(1/w)/\Delta x$, and $\Delta(1/w)/\Delta y$. Again, the u/w, v/w, and $1/w$ values can be updated with only additions between neighboring pixels, and then the texture coordinates (u, v) are computed as before.

An in-depth discussion of perspective-correct interpolation is provided by Blinn [75, 76, 79].

15.3 Architecture

In this section, we will first present a general architecture for a real-time computer graphics system. The geometry and rasterizer stages, as well as a texture cache mechanism, will also be discussed here. Bandwidth and memory are important components in a graphics architecture, and related to this is latency. These topics are discussed in Section 15.3.2–15.3.4. To reduce bandwidth requirements, the Z-buffer can be compressed, and occlusion culling can be done. Such algorithms are treated in Section 15.3.5. Finally, we will describe three real-world graphics systems on a fairly high level.

15.3.1 General

Graphics accelerators have generally evolved from the end of the pipeline backward. For example, the first PC accelerators did little more than draw interpolated or textured spans of pixels rapidly. Triangle setup was then added in 1996 by the first credible accelerator, the 3Dfx Voodoo 1. NVIDIA introduced geometry stage acceleration, known as hardware *Transform and Lighting* (T&L), with the GeForce256 in 1999 [238]. However, the fixed function implementation limited the usefulness of this hardware stage. With the introduction of vertex and pixel shaders, graphics hardware has both the speed and programmability needed to overcome purely software renderers in essentially all areas. The modern accelerator is often called a *Graphics Processing Unit* (GPU) because of these capabilities.

The host is the computer system without any graphics hardware, i.e., it is a system with CPU(s), memory, buses, etc. Applications run on the host, i.e., on the CPU(s). The geometry pipeline stage may be performed on the host, or it may be hardware-accelerated, or both. Some CPUs have support for geometry acceleration on the chip. For example, the Intel Pentium IV has streaming, *Single-instruction/Multiple-data* (SIMD) extensions, called SSE 2, that work in parallel on vectors. Alternately, if there is geometry stage acceleration on the graphics hardware, which is the norm today, then this reduces the workload on the CPU. Finally, the rasterizer is always hardware-accelerated. The interface between the application and the graphics hardware is called a *driver*.

Pipelining and Parallelization

There are two major ways to achieve fast processing in graphics hardware, namely pipelining and parallelism. These techniques are most often used in conjunction with each other. See Section 2.1 for the basics of pipelining. When discussing pipelining in this section, we do not mean the conceptual or the functional stages, but rather the pipeline stages, i.e., the actual blocks built in silicon that are executed in parallel. It is worth repeating that dividing a certain function (for example, the lighting computation of a vertex) into n pipeline stages ideally gives a speedup of n. In general, graphics hardware for polygon rendering is much simpler to pipeline than a CPU. For example, the Intel Pentium IV has 20 pipeline stages, which should be compared to NVIDIA's GeForce3, which has 600–800 stages (depending on which path is taken). The reasons for this are many, including that most of the GPU is data-driven, while the CPU is operation-driven, that pixels are rendered independent of each other, there are very few branches, and much of the functionality is fixed.

The clock frequency of a CPU is often much higher than that of a graphics accelerator, but this hardly touches the huge advantage modern accelerators have over the CPU when used correctly. CPUs typically have much higher clock frequencies because, among other reasons, CPU designers spend much more time on optimizing the blocks. One reason for this is because CPUs have tens of pipeline stages compared to hundreds or thousands for GPUs. Also, for GPUs the clock frequency is most often not the bottleneck—rather, memory bandwidth is.[4] Another reason why graphics algorithms can run fast in hardware is that it is relatively simple to predict what memory accesses will be done, and so efficient memory prefetching can be achieved. The majority of memory accesses are reads, which also simplifies and improves performance. Also note that a CPU cannot tolerate long latencies (when an instruction is executed, the result is usually desired immediately), whereas a graphics accelerator can tolerate longer latencies as long as sufficiently many primitives can be rendered per second. In addition, in the beginning of the 21st century, the most complex GPUs surpassed the most complex PC CPUs in terms of number of transistors. In conclusion, if the same chip area is used to build a dedicated graphics accelerator as a standard CPU, then hardware rendering is about 100 times faster than using software rendering with the CPU [515].

The other way of achieving faster graphics is to parallelize, and this can be done in both the geometry and the rasterizer stages. The idea is to compute multiple results simultaneously and then merge these at a later stage. In general, a parallel graphics architecture has the appearance shown in Figure 15.8. The result of the graphics database traversal is sent to a number of *Geometry units* (G's) that work in parallel. Together, these geometry units do the geometry-stage work of the rendering pipeline (see Section 2.3), and forward their results to a set of *Rasterizer units* (R's), which together implement the rasterizer stage in the rendering pipeline.

However, since multiple results are computed in parallel, some kind of sorting must be done so that the parallel units together render the image

---

[4]In fact, memory bandwidth is most often the bottleneck for CPUs as well. However, CPU company marketing departments have found that a high clock frequency number is what sells best.

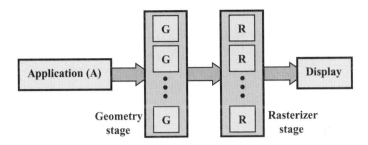

Figure 15.8. The general architecture for a high-performance, parallel computer graphics architecture. Each geometry unit (G) processes (i.e., transforms, projects, etc.) a portion of the geometry to be rendered, and each rasterizer unit (R) takes care of a portion of the pixel calculations.

that the user intended. Specifically, the sorting is that from model space to screen space (see Section 2.3.1 and 2.4). Molnar et al. [566] present a taxonomy for parallel architectures based on where in the parallel rendering pipeline the sort occurs. Eldridge et al. [207] present a slight variation of this taxonomy, and we follow their notation here. The sort can occur anywhere in the pipeline, which gives rise to four different classes of parallel architectures, as shown in Figure 15.9. These are called *Sort-First, Sort-*

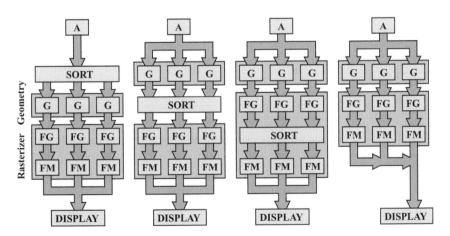

Figure 15.9. Taxonomy of parallel graphics architectures. A is the application, G is the geometry stage, then follows the rasterizer comprised of FG, which is *Fragment Generation,* and FM, which is *Fragment Merging.* The architectures are (left to right): Sort-First, Sort-Middle, Sort-Last Fragment, and Sort-Last Image. *(Illustration after Eldridge et al. [207].)*

Middle, Sort-Last Fragment, and *Sort-Last Image*. The rasterizer stage is comprised of two internal stages, namely, *Fragment Generation* (FG), and *Fragment Merge* (FM). FG generates the actual locations inside a primitive, and forwards these to FM, which merges the result with the Z-buffer. Texturing is not shown, but is, in general, done either at the end of FG, or in the beginning of FM. Also note that there may be, for example, twice as many FGs as there are geometry units. Any configuration is possible.

A Sort-First based architecture sorts primitives before the geometry stage. The strategy is to divide the screen into a set of regions, and the primitives inside a region is sent to the pipeline that "owns" that region. This is the least explored architecture [208, 566], and so is not described further here.

Both the InfiniteReality (see Section 15.3.7) and the KYRO (see Section 15.3.8) are variations of Sort-Middle. The idea here is to spread the work arbitrarily and reasonably evenly among the geometry units. Also, each rasterizer unit is responsible for a screen space region, here called a *tile*. This may be a rectangular region of pixels, or a set of scanlines, or some other interleaved pattern (e.g., every eighth pixel). After the geometry stage, the screen-space location of each primitive is known, and so the primitive can be directed to the rasterizer units (FGs and FMs) that are responsible for that tile. Note that a transformed triangle may be sent to several rasterizer units if the triangle overlaps more than one tile.

The Sort-Last Fragment architecture sorts the fragments after fragment generation (FG) and before fragment merge (FM). An example is the Xbox architecture described in Section 15.3.6. Just like Sort-Middle, primitives are spread as evenly as possible across the geometry units. One advantage with Sort-Last Fragment is that there will not be any overlap, meaning that a generated fragment is sent to only one FM, which is optimal. However, it may be hard to balance fragment generation work. For example, assume that a set of large polygons happens to be sent down to one FG unit. The FG unit will have to generate all the fragments on these polygons, but the fragments are then sorted to the FM units responsible for the respective pixels. Therefore, imbalance is likely to occur for such cases [208].

Finally, the Sort-Last Image architecture sorts after the entire rasterizer stage (FG and FM). PixelFlow [565, 220] is one such example. This architecture can be seen as a set of independent pipelines. The primitives are spread across the pipelines, and each pipeline renders an image with depth. In a final composition stage, all the images are merged with respect to its Z-buffers. The PixelFlow architecture is also interesting because it used *deferred shading*, meaning that it textured and shaded only visible fragments. The graphics group at Stanford has developed a system called

WireGL for high performance graphics using a cluster of commodity graphics accelerators [378, 733]. This is another example of a Sort-Last Image architecture. It should be noted that Sort-Last Image cannot fully implement an API such as OpenGL, because OpenGL requires that primitives are rendered in the order they are sent.

Eldridge et al. [207, 208] present "Pomegranate," a Sort-Everywhere architecture. Briefly, it inserts sort stages between the geometry stage and the fragment generators (FGs), between FGs and fragment mergers (FMs), and between FMs and the display. The work is therefore kept more balanced as the system scales (i.e., as more pipelines are added). The sorting stages are implemented as a high-speed network with point-to-point links. Simulations showed nearly linear speedup as more pipelines are added.

All the components in a graphics system (host, geometry processing, and rasterization) connected together give us a multiprocessing system. For such systems there are two problems that are well-known, and almost always associated with multiprocessing: *load balancing* and *communications* [148]. FIFO (first-in, first-out) queues are often inserted into many different places in the pipeline, so that jobs can be queued in order to avoid stalling parts of the pipeline. For example, the InfiniteReality (Section 15.3.7) has a FIFO between the geometry and the rasterizer stage. It can hold $65,536$ vertices. The different sort-architectures described above have different load balancing advantages and disadvantages. Consult Eldridge's Ph.D. thesis [208] or the paper by Molnar et al. [566] for more on these. The programmer can also affect the load balance; techniques for doing so are discussed in Chapter 10. Communications can be a problem if the bandwidth of the buses is too low, or used unwisely. Therefore, it is of extreme importance to design a graphics system so that the bottleneck does not occur in any of the buses, e.g., the bus from the host to the graphics hardware. Bandwidth is discussed in Section 15.3.3.

Next, the geometry stage, the rasterizer stage, and a texture caching mechanism with prefetching will be described.

The Geometry Stage

As mentioned before, the geometry stage can be located on the host, on special geometry acceleration hardware, or on both. It is most common to implement it in dedicated hardware today. This special hardware can be implemented on a custom chip, pipelined, and parallelized. This usually gives the best performance and the best cost per gate, but once it has been implemented, there is not much flexibility. Thus, such implementations are called *fixed-function*. To obtain more flexibility from the programmer's perspective, programmability has been introduced in the geometry stage. A vertex shader (see Section 6.5) is a small program that can be sent down to the geometry stage. This program is then executed for each vertex sent to it. Each vertex shader unit can be implemented in custom hardware as a limited form of a CPU.

The Rasterizer Stage

The rasterizer must be implemented on custom chip(s) for the sake of speed. The first step in rasterization is *triangle setup*, which computes various deltas and slopes from the vertex information. Such computation is needed in order to rasterize the primitive and do interpolation. Color and depth are interpolated over the primitive. If there is a texture associated with the primitive, then texture coordinates are interpolated and the texture applied. Some hardware supports interpolating two colors, allowing a separate specular color [600] to avoid the weakening of this component's effect when texturing. Interpolation is not always linear; see Section 15.2.

Primitive setup and interpolation produces a fragment, which is simply data for a pixel covered by a primitive, i.e., its depth, alpha value, color, etc. The rasterizer in modern hardware is also programmable (see Section 6.6). With this data, fragment processing is performed. These tests include, in order of execution:

- Texture interpolation, which interpolates texture coordinates in perspective, and fetches the filtered texels.

- Color interpolation, which interpolates one or more colors and sums them.

- Fog, which can blend a fragment with a fog color.

- The alpha test; If alpha is 0, the fragment is not visible at all.

- The stencil test, which may mask the fragment depending on the contents of the stencil buffer.

- The depth test, which determines whether the fragment is visible by comparing its depth to the stored depth value.

- Alpha blending, which can blend the fragment's data with the original pixel's data.

- Dithering, to make the color look better with a 15- or 16-bit display mode.

Note that some rasterizer chips support only triangles, and do not support points and lines directly—these primitives are rendered by drawing rectangles representing them. Also, rasterizers use subpixel addressing to help avoid holes and overlaps caused by T-vertices (see Section 11.2.2) [474]. This technique also helps avoid having objects poke through one another, as discussed in Section 15.1.3. Subpixel addressing also helps eliminate the shifting and snapping of objects and textures as the viewer moves through a scene. This effect can be seen on older hardware, and early three-dimensional game consoles such as the Playstation and Nintendo 64.

Texture Caching and Prefetching

The performance increase in terms of pure computations has grown exponentially for many years. However, the latency and bandwidth of memory accesses have not increased nearly as fast. In addition, the trend is to use more and more textures per primitive. In fact, reading from texture memory is often the main consumer of bandwidth [12]. Therefore, when reading out texels from memory, care must be taken to reduce the used bandwidth and to hide latency. To save bandwidth, most architectures use caches at various places in the pipeline, and to hide latency, a technique called prefetching is often used. These two techniques combined will be described here in a texturing system.

Caching is implemented with a small on-chip memory, where the result of recent texture reads are stored and access is very fast. Texture caching was first investigated by Hakura and Gupta [313]. If neighboring pixels need to access the same or closely located texels, then it is likely to find these in the cache. This is what is done for standard CPUs as well. However, reading texels into the cache takes time, and most often entire cache blocks (e.g., 32 bytes) are read in at once. So, if a texel is not in the cache, it may take relatively long before it can be found there. Therefore, caching is often combined with prefetching, with excellent results.

Igehy et al. [381] suggest the architecture illustrated in Figure 15.10. The basic function is as follows. The rasterizer unit produces fragments that should be textured. The part of the fragment that is not related to texturing is sent to the fragment FIFO (first-in, first out) for use later. The fragment also includes a set of addresses of texels needed to filter that fragment, and these are sent to a cache tag unit. This checks whether the texels with those addresses are in the cache. If a texel is not in the cache, then the cache tags are updated with a cache address of the wanted texel, and the cache address sent to the fragment FIFO. However, at this point, the texel is not in the cache, so a request must also be sent to the request FIFO, which sends these requests in order to the texture memory. If the

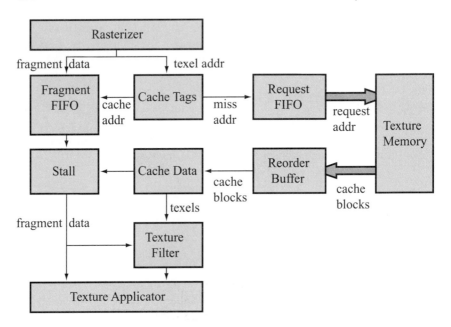

Figure 15.10. A texture prefetching architecture. *(Illustration after Igehy et al. [381].)*

texel is in the cache, its cache address is sent to the fragment FIFO. Cache blocks arrive from the texture memory to the reorder buffer, whose task is to order the blocks so that they arrive to the cache in the order that they were requested. The fragment FIFO holds a list of fragments, with a set of cache addresses containing the texels needed to do texture filtering for that fragment. The fragment on its way out from the fragment FIFO stalls until all texels are available in the texture cache. When the stall is resolved, the texels are sent to a unit that computes the filtered texel. Finally, this is forwarded to the unit that applies it to the fragment.

Simulation shows that such a system could attain 97 percent of the performance of a system with no latency at all.

More about this architecture and texture memory organization can be found in the paper by Igehy et al. [381], where they show that a certain blocking scheme for storing the textures reduces miss rate in the cache. Several researchers have also shown that the texture cache miss rate is reduced by doing rasterization in a tiled fashion, i.e., one rasterizes all the pixels inside, say, an 8×8 tile at a time [315, 381, 533]. In another study, Igehy et al. [382] investigate parallel texture caching schemes for use with parallel rasterization.

15.3.2 Memory Architecture

Here, we will mention a few different architectures that have been used for memory layout. The SGI O2 and the Xbox (Section 15.3.6) use a *Unified Memory Architecture*(UMA), which means that the graphics accelerator can use any part of the host memory for textures and different kinds of buffers [420]. An example of UMA is shown in Figure 15.12 on page 697. As can be seen both the CPU and the graphics accelerator uses the same memory, and thus also the same bus. A somewhat less unified layout is to have dedicated memory on the graphics card, which can then be used for textures and buffers in any way desired, but cannot be used directly by the CPU. This is the approach taken by the KYRO architecture (Section 15.3.8), which uses a local memory for scene data and for textures. The InfiniteReality [568] (see Section 15.3.7) also uses a nonunified memory architecture, and due to its scalable nature, it has to replicate the texture memory across each rasterizer.

15.3.3 Port and Bus Bandwidth

A port is a channel for sending data between two devices, and a bus is a shared channel for sending data among more than two devices. Bandwidth is the term used to describe throughput of data over the port or bus, and is measured in bytes per second, b/s. Ports and buses are important in computer graphics architecture because, simply put, they "glue" together different building blocks. Also important is that bandwidth is a scarce resource, and so a careful design and analysis must be done before building a graphics system. An example of a port is one that connects the CPU with the graphics accelerator, such as the Accelerated Graphics Port (AGP) used in PCs. 2Since ports and buses both provide data transfer capabilities, ports are often referred to as buses, a convention we will follow here.

When it comes to sending data to the graphics hardware over the bus, there are two methods—*push* and *pull*. The pull method works by writing data to the system memory. The graphics hardware can then *pull* data from those memory locations during an entire frame. This is also called *Direct Memory Access* (DMA), since the graphics hardware is allowed to directly access the memory and thus bypass the CPU. This is possible because a certain region of memory is locked by the graphics hardware, meaning that the CPU cannot use that region until it is unlocked. In general, DMA allows the GPU to work faster, and frees CPU time. The AGP can be used to pull data in this way, because it has a direct path from the graphics accelerator to the system memory. Thus, the AGP can be used to access, for example, triangle data and textures in system memory. Since AGP is a dedicated port connecting only the CPU and the graphics accelerator, memory accesses are very fast. This is the main reason why vertex buffers are so fast. Another nice property of AGP is that queries can be pipelined, so that several queries can be requested before results return. AGP 4× allows for peak rates of 1067 Mbytes/second. The upcoming AGP 3.0 specification improves this figure to 2.1 Gbytes/second.

The *push* method writes data to the graphics hardware. Since the push method writes the data only once per frame, there is more memory bandwidth available for the application than with the pull method, where first the CPU writes data, and then the accelerator reads it. However, when using the push method, you may need large FIFO queues on the graphics cards in order to get a balanced system. To reach peak performance on modern graphics hardware, the pull method is most often the way to go. This is especially true for data that is static in memory (but which may be animated using vertex shaders). Dynamic data involves extra synchronization overhead. That said, things change, and the best method to use depends on the circumstances and the hardware itself.

Next, we will present a simplified view of bandwidth between the CPU and the graphics hardware, and memory bandwidth. We say simplified, because there are many factors, such as caching and DMA, that are hard to take into account. In Figure 15.12 on page 697, an example of a system bus, from CPU to GPU, and a memory bus, from GPU to memory, are shown.

Now, let us discuss the bandwidth used and delivered in the memory subsystem. The common case of how to write a pixel is that one must first read the Z-buffer at that pixel (ZR). If the z-test is passed, then the z-value (ZW) and color buffer must be overwritten (CW). For blending operations, one may also need to read the color buffer (CR), but we assume this is not part of the common case. Since most scenes are textured, one or more *Texture Reads* (TR) may also occur. Our average case assumes that two TRs with trilinear mipmapping are done per pixel, and that each TR costs $8 \times 3 = 24$ bytes. Also assume that each of ZR, ZW, CW, and CR, use 32 bits (4 bytes) in a memory access. So, a common pixel sums to:

$$ZR + ZW + CW + 2 \times TR = 60 \text{ bytes per pixel.} \qquad (15.2)$$

Sixty bytes per pixel may seem small, but put in a real context, it is not. Assume we render at 60 frames per second with 1280×1024 resolution.

This gives:

$$60 \times 1280 \times 1024 \times 60 \text{ bytes/s} \approx 4.5 \text{ Gbytes/s}. \qquad (15.3)$$

Four and a half Gbytes per second may again not seem like much, and, in fact, it is not. However, this is not truly a realistic case either. We have assumed that each pixel is written only once, i.e., has a depth complexity of one. A more realistic number would be, say, 4, which means that we would need 18 Gbytes per second in the worst case.

Next, assume that the clock of the memory system is running at 300 MHz. Also, assume that a type of memory called DDRAM is used. 256 bits can be accessed per clock from DDRAM, as opposed to 128 bits for SDRAM. Using DDRAM gives:

$$300\text{Mhz} \times \frac{256}{8} \approx 9.6 \text{ Gbytes/s}. \qquad (15.4)$$

Unfortunately, $18 > 9.6$, and so it seems that in the system presented here, the memory subsystem would be the bottleneck. Then, in addition, the screen resolution could be increased, even more textures could be accessed, better texture filtering (costs more memory accesses) could be used, multisampling or supersampling may be used, etc. On top of that, the usage of bandwidth is never 100% in a real system. It should now be clear that memory bandwidth is extremely important in a computer graphics system, and that care must be taken when designing the memory subsystem. However, it is not as bad as it sounds. There are many techniques for reducing the number of memory accesses, including a texture cache with prefetching, texture compression, and the techniques in Section 15.3.5. Another technique often used, is to put several memory banks that can be accessed in parallel. This also increases the bandwidth delivered by the memory system.

Now, let us take a look at the bus bandwidth from the CPU to the GPU. Assume a vertex needs 32 bytes (3×4 for position, 3×4 for normal, and 2×4 for texture coordinates). Then, using an indexed vertex array, an additional 6 bytes per triangle is needed to index into the vertices. For large closed triangle meshes, the number of triangles is about twice the number of vertices (see Equation 11.7 on page 459). This gives $(32+6\times2)/2 = 22$ bytes per triangle. Assuming a goal of 150 million triangles per second should be handled, gives 3.3 Gbytes per second just for sending the triangles from the CPU to the graphics hardware.

The conclusion is that the needed bus bandwidth in graphics system is huge, and that one should design the buses with the target performance in mind.

15.3.4   Latency

In general, the latency is the time between making the query and receiving the result. As an example, one may ask for the value at a certain address in memory, and the time it takes from the query to getting the result is the latency. In a pipelined system with n pipeline stages, it takes at least n clock cycles to get through the entire pipeline, and the latency is thus n clock cycles. In some contexts, latency is a lesser problem. For example, the GeForce3 accelerator has 600–800 pipeline stages and is clocked at 233 MHz. For simplicity, assume 700 pipeline stages are used on average, and that one can get through the entire pipeline in 700 clock cycles (which is ideal). This gives $700/(233 \cdot 10^6) \approx 3 \cdot 10^{-6}$ seconds $= 3$ microseconds (μs). Now assume that we want to render the scene at 50 Hz. This gives $1/50 = 20$ milliseconds (ms) per frame. Since 3 μs is much smaller than 20 ms (about four magnitudes), it is possible to pass through the entire pipeline many times per frame. More importantly, due to the pipelined design, results will be generated every clock cycle, that is, 233 million times per second. On top of that, as we have seen, the architectures are often parallelized. So, in terms of rendering, this sort of latency is not often much of a problem.

However, sometimes it is desirable to read back data from the rendering pipeline, and in such cases, latency can really hurt performance. The major reason is that reading back results is often done with the PCI interface, while writing to the pipeline is done with the much faster AGP interface. So, to read back a 256×256 square of the Z-buffer, Maughan shows that it takes approximately 1 ms [524]. Given that we have perhaps 20 ms to render the entire scene, this is just not feasible in many applications. Instead, one should try to avoid any sort of read backs from the accelerator, if real-time performance is required. Another example of a read back is the occlusion query, which also has a relatively long latency. See Section 9.7.4. It should also be emphasized that when data is read back from the accelerator, the pipeline often has to be flushed before the read. During this time, the CPU is idle.

15.3.5   Z-Compression and Occlusion Culling

As can be seen in Equation 15.2, bandwidth traffic can be high even though a rendered triangle is invisible. This is because texturing is expensive and is done before the depth test. A hardware implementation of a basic type of occlusion culling can also help in avoiding texture accesses and other tests.

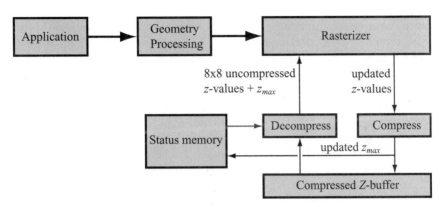

Figure 15.11. Block diagram of hardware techniques for fast clear of the Z-buffer, compression of Z-buffer, and occlusion culling.

If occlusion culling and texture caches can decrease texture bandwidth significantly, then the remaining main bandwidth consumer is the Z-buffer. Techniques for compressing and rapidly clearing the contents of the Z-buffer can reduce this use of bandwidth. Occlusion culling, compression, and rapid clears are presented together here because they are typically implemented in the same subsystem in hardware.

Central to these algorithms is on-chip storage, which we call *status memory*, with additional information for tiles of pixels in the Z-buffer. A block diagram of this algorithm is shown in Figure 15.11. Each element in the status memory stores the status of an 8×8 tile of pixels in the frame buffer. This includes a state and the maximum z-value, z_{max}, for the tile. As will be seen later, the z_{max} can be used for occlusion culling. The state of each tile can be either *compressed*, *uncompressed*, or *cleared*. These are used to implement a fast clear and compression of the Z-buffer. When the system issues a clear of the Z-buffer, the state of each tile is set to *cleared* and the frame buffer is not touched. When the rasterizer needs to read the cleared Z-buffer, the *decompressor* unit first checks the state, sees that the tile is cleared, and so can send a Z-buffer with all values set to z_{far} (the clear value) without reading and uncompressing the actual Z-buffer. In this way, access to the Z-buffer itself is minimized, so saving bandwidth. If the state is not cleared, then the Z-buffer for that tile has to be read. When the rasterizer has finished writing new z-values to the tile, it is sent to the *compressor*, where an attempt is made at compressing it, and a new z_{max} is computed. This z_{max} is sent to the status memory. If compression succeeded, the tile's state is set to *compressed* and the data is sent a compressed form. Otherwise, it is sent uncompressed and the state is set to *uncompressed*. Combined, fast Z-clear and Z-compression give about a 25% increase in frame rate for ATI's Radeon series [570].

The ATI Radeon uses a *Differential Pulse Code Modulation* (DPCM) scheme for compressing the 8×8 tiles [570]. This type of algorithm is good when there is a great deal of coherence in the data to be compressed. This is often the case for the contents of the Z-buffer, as a triangle tends to cover many pixels, and objects consist of adjacent triangles. The compression rate is about 4:1, i.e., 75% of the bandwidth is saved. Compression is out of the scope of this book—the interested reader should consult Gonzalez and Woods' book [277].

To perform occlusion culling, the rasterizer fetches the z_{max} for each 8×8 tile it processes, and it uses this value to exit the pipeline early for occluded pixels. Several different implementations are possible, each with its own advantages and disadvantages:

- The minimum z-value of the three vertices of a triangle can be used to test against the z_{max}. This is not very accurate, but it has little overhead.

- Since rasterization often is done on a tile basis [533] (e.g., 8×8-tiles) we can test the four corners of the tile the triangle is in. If these four z-values for the triangle's plane are larger than z_{max}, then the entire tile can be skipped.

- The depth test can be done per pixel against z_{max}.

If one or a combination of these are implemented, texturing and testing against the Z-buffer can be avoided for most occluded pixels on rasterized primitives, and so a significant performance boost can be expected. If the tile or pixel is determined to not be occluded, then processing continues as normal. As always, occlusion culling benefits from rendering front to back. See Section 10.3.3 for more information on how to optimize the rasterization stage. Since this type of occlusion culling is done in the rasterizer stage, it does not help if the application is transform-limited.

Both NVIDIA's GeForce3 and ATI's Radeon series implement all techniques in this section in some fashion. This occlusion culling hardware can be of great benefit to multipass algorithms (see Section 5.4). The first pass establishes the z_{max} values. Succeeding passes use all the z_{max}-values, which gives almost perfect occlusion culling for hidden triangles. Given that pixel shaders are often expensive to evaluate, it can be profitable to render an extra pass at the beginning purely to establish the Z-buffer and

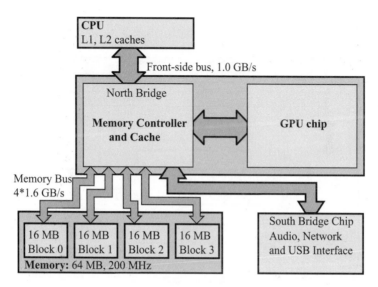

Figure 15.12. Xbox unified memory architecture (UMA). *(Illustration after Abrash [3].)*

z_{max}-values in advance. The GeForce3 also implements the occlusion query technique presented in Section 9.7.4, where the faces of a bounding volume (e.g., box) can be tested against the current Z-buffer and the hardware queried to find out whether the faces are visible.

15.3.6 Case Study: Xbox

The Xbox is a game console built by Microsoft and NVIDIA. It is based on a *Unified Memory Architecture* (UMA), as shown in Figure 15.12. As can be seen, the memory is divided into four blocks, and all the blocks can be accessed in parallel, for higher bandwidth. Here, we will focus mostly on the right part of the middle block, namely, the GPU (graphics processing unit). It should be pointed out that the GPU of the Xbox is essentially an extended GeForce3 accelerator, and that the CPU is a 733 MHz Intel Pentium III. Therefore, the whole system resembles a standard PC with a graphics accelerator. The block diagram of the GPU is shown in Figure 15.13.

The geometry stage of the Xbox, located on the top half of Figure 15.13, supports programmable vertex shaders. It has two vertex shader (geometry units) units that execute the same program in parallel on two different

System Memory Bus

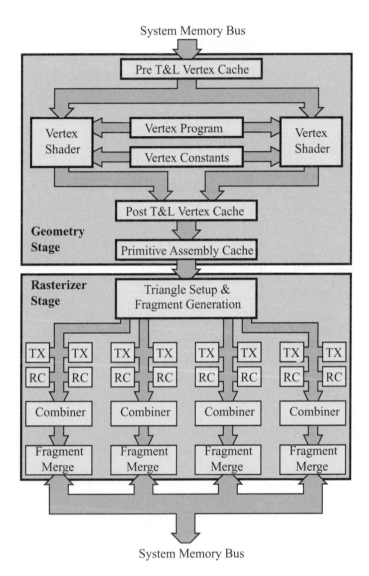

Figure 15.13. Xbox GPU. TX is short for *Texture Unit*, and RC means *Register Combiner*.

vertices, which effectively doubles the throughput. These units also access the same vertex shader constants. A vertex shader unit is basically a small SIMD CPU that can execute the instructions of a vertex program. Therefore, its design resembles that of a pipelined CPU. However, it cannot execute branches, which simplifies the design considerably. The geometry stage also implements a fixed-function vertex shader and a higher order surface unit that, for example, can tessellate Bézier surfaces. These are not shown in the block diagram, and omitted from the discussion here.

There are three caches in the geometry stage. The cache before the vertex shader units is called *Pre T&L* (*Transform and Lighting*), and the one immediately after the vertex shader units is called *Post T&L*. Pre T&L has 4 kilobytes of storage, and Post T&L has, in practice, storage for roughly 16 vertices. The task of the Pre T&L vertex cache is to avoid redundant memory fetches. When using the pull method, and a vertex that is needed for a triangle can be found in the Pre T&L vertex cache, the memory fetch for that vertex data can be avoided. The Post T&L vertex cache, on the other hand, is there to avoid processing the same vertex with the vertex shader more than once. This can happen because a vertex is, on average, shared by six other triangles. Both these caches can improve performance tremendously. Due to the memory requirements of a shaded vertex, located in the Post T&L vertex cache, it may take quite some time to fetch it from that cache. Therefore, a *Primitive Assembly* cache is inserted after the Post T&L vertex cache. This cache can store only three fully shaded vertices, and its task is to avoid fetches from the Post T&L vertex cache. For example, when rendering a triangle strip, two vertices from the previous triangle are used along with another new vertex to create a new triangle. If those two vertices already are located in the Primitive Assembly cache, then only one vertex is fetched from the Post T&L. It should be noted, however, as with all caches, hit rate is not perfect, so when the desired data is not in the cache, it needs to be fetched or recomputed.

As mentioned in Section 15.3.1, the first part of the rasterizer stage is the triangle setup. When all the vertices for a triangle have been assembled in the Primitive Assembly cache, they are forwarded to triangle setup. This block also generates all the fragments that are inside a triangle. Therefore, the Xbox is a Sort-Last Fragment architecture. Such fragments are then forwarded to the four pixel shader pipelines (rasterizer units), each of which is programmable. Fragments are generated in 2×2 regions, and may only belong to the same triangle. So, every fragment inside the 2×2 region may not be inside the triangle, meaning that at most, three pixel shader pipelines may be idle. This idleness can occur only for regions that intersect the triangle edges, but not the interior. See McCormack et al.'s paper [533] for different rasterization strategies. The memory for the color and Z-buffer is also recommended to be set to be tiled. Each tile for the Xbox is 256 bytes wide and 16 scanlines high. Together, the union of a set of tiles may form the color buffer, for example. Tiled memory improves page coherence during fragment generation. A page is a kilobyte of continuous memory, and at most, four pages can be opened in each memory block (see Figure 15.12). The reason for the desire to improve page locality is that hits within a page are cheaper than hits outside a page. Inside the triangle setup and fragment generation block, occlusion culling as described in Section 15.3.5 is also executed. This may terminate the entire processing of 4×4 fragments in one clock cycle.

When a fragment reaches a pixel shader pipeline, it is first processed by two *texture units* (TX). These can be run twice with feedback for a single fragment, resulting in a total of four texture unit operations. The texels are retrieved from an 8 kilobyte texture cache (not shown in Figure 15.13), which may send requests over the system memory bus. See Section 15.3.1 for more information on texture caching. *Texture swizzling* is a technique that can be used on the Xbox to improve the texture cache performance and page locality. Assume that the texture coordinates has been transformed to fixed point numbers: (u, v), where each of u and v have n bits. The bit with number i of u is denoted u_i. Then the remapping of (u, v) to a swizzled texture address is:

$$\text{texaddr}(u, v) = \text{texbaseaddr}$$
$$+ (v_{n-1}u_{n-1}u_{n-2}v_{n-2} \ldots v_2 u_2 v_1 u_1 v_0 u_0) * \text{texelsize}.$$
$$(15.5)$$

Here, texelsize is the number of bytes occupied by one texel. The advantage of this remapping is that it gives rise to the texel order shown in Figure 15.14. As can be seen, this is a space-filling curve, and these are known to improve coherency. In this case, the curve is two-dimensional since textures normally are too. See Section 11.4.4 for more on space-filling curves.

The produced values from the texture units, together with two constant values per stage and values from two general interpolators (commonly used for diffuse and specular colors), are then fed to the *Register Combiners* (RCs). There are two physical RCs per pixel shader pipeline, and these can be executed four times, resulting in, at most, eight RC operations per fragment. The combiner unit takes the resulting values that are output from the TXs, RCs, interpolators, and a fog interpolator, and combines them into the final color of the fragment. This is forwarded to the

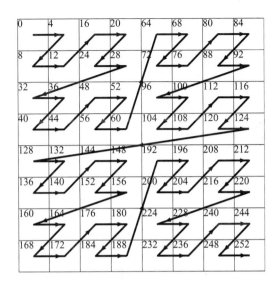

Figure 15.14. Texture swizzling increases coherency of texel memory accesses. Note that texel size here is four bytes, and that the texel address is shown in each texels upper left corner.

Fragment Merge (FM) unit, whose task is to merge it with the color and Z-buffer. Thus it is here that alpha blending, depth testing, stencil testing, alpha testing, and writing to the color buffer and the Z-buffer occurs. Z-compression and decompression are also handled here. Both the color buffer and Z-buffer can be configured to have a tiled memory architecture, which is recommended for better coherency.

15.3.7   Case Study: InfiniteReality

The maximum configuration of the InfiniteReality graphics system [106, 420, 568] from SGI will be studied here. This is a well-documented and highly parallelized *Sort-Middle* architecture. The VISUALIZE fx graphics system [692] is roughly similar to the InfiniteReality, but it does not exploit parallelism as much. The InfiniteReality architecture is shown in Figure 15.15.

We will study the geometry stage and the raster memory board of the InfiniteReality architecture.

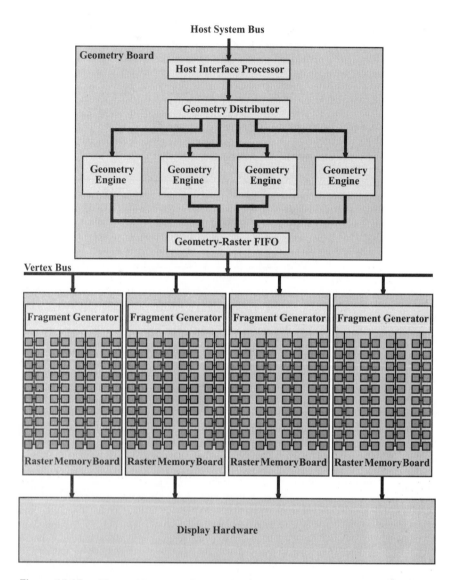

Figure 15.15. The architecture of the InfiniteReality graphics hardware from SGI. *(After Montrym et al. [568].)*

Geometry Stage

The geometry stage consists of a *Host Interface Processor* (HIP), a *geometry distributor*, *geometry engines*, and a FIFO queue at the end. The main task of the HIP is to see to it that the rest of the graphics system has work to do. To help with this task, two different ways of supporting display lists (see page 425) are implemented. First, compiled display lists can be pulled (see Section 15.3.3) from the host memory using DMA (direct memory access). This greatly reduces the load on the host. Second, the HIP has 16 MB of memory, of which 15 MB are available as a cache for display lists. This storage is used as much as possible, but the system goes back to the pull method when the cache is full. Since the cache avoids pulling data from the host, caching is much faster. If display lists are not used, then per-vertex data can be sent from the host to the HIP.

After passing through the HIP, the data is sent to the geometry distributor. This unit passes data to the geometry engines in a least-busy fashion. This was found to be better than round-robin, since the data loads tend to vary from one time to another. In the geometry distributor, each graphics command is also associated with a number. This is so the FIFO can recreate the order of the primitives as required by, for example, OpenGL [568].

The *Geometry Engines* (GEs) are implemented using a semi-custom ASIC (*Application-specific Integrated Circuit*). Since a vertex consists of three coordinates (x, y, z), and each must be processed geometrically, the heart of a GE is three *Floating-point Cores* (FPCs) that execute in a SIMD (*Single-instruction/Multiple-data*) arrangement. This means that each GE can process the three coordinates of a three-dimensional vertex in parallel. Each FPC has an ALU (*Arithmetic Logic Unit*), a multiplier, and a 32-word register file with two read and two write ports. The whole FPC is implemented as a four-stage pipeline. These three FPCs per GE share an on-chip memory of 2560 words (32 bits). This piece of memory holds the state of OpenGL, but is also used for scratch computations and for queuing incoming vertex data. The main idea behind this construction is to make a cost-efficient architecture with high performance. After the vertices have been processed by the FPCs, a floating-to-fixed-point conversion takes place.

The results from the GEs are then sent to the geometry-raster FIFO, which merges the streams from the GEs into one stream and sees to it that the graphic commands are in the same order as they were issued. The FIFO can hold a maximum of 65, 536 vertices. The merged stream is then written to the vertex bus, as shown in Figure 15.15.

To exploit the bandwidth of the vertex bus, only the screen-space vertex information is sent here. All data on this bus is broadcast to the fragment generators on the raster memory board.

Raster Memory Board

Each raster memory board has a single fragment generator, a copy of the entire texture memory, and 80 image engines that control the frame-buffer memory. The fragment generator receives and assembles vertex data from the vertex bus. Then, scan conversion is performed by evaluating the plane equations (from the triangle setup) rather than doing interpolation over the primitives [626]. This requires less setup, but more computations per pixel [568]. The reason for this design choice was that the trend in many areas is toward many small triangles, so setup time becomes a significant part of the rasterization process. The fragment generator also calculates texel addresses, texture filtering, mipmap level of detail, color, and depth interpolation. Fog and combination with the interpolated color is also taken care of here.

Fragments are then output by the fragment generators and distributed equally among the 80 image engines on the raster memory board. To balance the workload across the image engines, each fragment generator is responsible for several vertical, two-pixel-wide lines. The scan conversion completes all pixels in such a two-pixel-wide vertical line before proceeding to the next line for every primitive. To avoid fill-rate limitations for large primitives, all image engines must be responsible for part of each vertical line that its fragment generator owns. Also, all image engines must appear equally on each horizontal line. So, for four raster memory boards with a total of 320 image engines (80 per raster memory board), the image engine tiling pattern is 320×80 pixels [568].

Display Hardware

Each image engine drives a signal to the display hardware. The display hardware can drive up to eight different display output channels, and each has a video timing generator, dynamic video resize hardware (described in Section 10.3.3), gamma correction, and digital-to-analog conversion. It also has a 32,768 entry color index, and the color components are maintained at 12 bits per component.

Extra Features

The InfiniteReality graphics system supports drawing of the primitives with the multisample antialiasing technique presented in Section 4.4.2, using four or eight samples per pixel. It also has hardware support for pipeline instrumentation, which is extremely valuable when optimizing an application. This hardware can be used to find out whether an application is fill-limited, or either transform- or CPU-limited. There is also hardware support for texture loading and paging. For extremely large textures, there is hardware-supported clipmapping [568, 741], that is discussed briefly in Section 5.3.

15.3.8 Case Study: KYRO

The KYRO architecture (implemented in the KYRO II accelerator) is significantly different from both the Xbox and the InfiniteReality. It is based on the cost-effective PowerVR architecture, which is a tile-based rendering algorithm implemented in hardware. The first tile-based graphics hardware was the *Pixel-Planes 5* from UNC [244], and that system has some similarities to KYRO.

The screen is divided up into rectangular tiles of the same size. The tile size for KYRO II is 32×16 fragments, but can in theory be any size. Rendering is done on a tile basis, that is, each tile is independently rendered. This means that only a back buffer, Z-buffer, and stencil buffer of the same size as the tile is needed. Therefore, this small amount of memory can be located on the graphics chip, and so access to it is extremely fast (compared to doing external memory accesses). Still, front and back buffers of the entire screen are needed in order to display a rendered image and provide double buffering. However, tile-based architectures can render single buffered, i.e., without a back buffer. In this case, completed tiles are directly copied into the front buffer instead of the back buffer. Single buffering is not viable on immediate mode architectures as they render polygons when received, which will cause flashing. The rationale for this tiled architecture is that memory bandwidth is a scarce resource, and by putting much of the frame buffer memory on-chip, this bottleneck is seriously reduced. The KYRO II uses about one third of the memory bandwidth compared to conventional rendering.

An overview of the architecture can be seen in Figure 15.16. The main building blocks are the *Tile Accelerator* (TA), the *Image Synthesis Processor* (ISP), and *the Texture and Shading Processor* (TSP). Each of these will be discussed in turn. Note that geometry processing (transform and lighting) on KYRO II is done on the CPU, but this could be added to the front end of the hardware.

For performance reasons it is best if the data for the entire scene is sent to the KYRO before rendering begins. When the TA receives a rendering

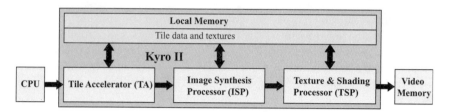

Figure 15.16. An overview of the tile-based KYRO architecture.

primitive from the CPU, it finds the tile or tiles the primitive overlaps. Thus, each tile has a list of primitives inside or overlapping it. It is only these primitives that need to be rendered for that tile. When all rendering primitives, render states, and textures have been received, the TA starts preparing a tile for efficient rendering. This includes creating triangle strips on the fly. When a tile has been processed the result is put in the local memory. The ISP is notified and can itself fetch the appropriate data from the local memory. The ISP then processes that tile while in parallel the TA prepares the next tile.

The ISP implements the Z-buffer and the stencil buffer of the tile, and also handles occlusion culling (similar to the technique discussed in Section 15.3.5). The Z-buffer is particularly interesting because it is implemented using true floating point arithmetic, instead of fixed-point. It is also possible to automatically sort semi-transparent polygons, so that transparency is rendered correctly. This would offload work from the CPU. However, this was not implemented in KYRO II. For efficient occlusion culling, the ISP rasterizes the triangles sent to it and performs depth testing per-pixel on one line consisting of 32 pixels in parallel. The reason for putting the depth testing this early in the pipeline is that everything that is invisible (occluded) should be eliminated early on. It is getting more and more important to do depth testing before shading and texturing, as these operations are getting more and more complex (and thus expensive). Texturing typically dominates bandwidth usage for nontrivial shaders. For example, the KYRO II can handle eight multitextures. Accessing all of these is expensive, and if this can be avoided, the bandwidth savings will be great.

Doing shading and texturing after depth testing means that shading and texturing is done only once per pixel. This is called deferred shading [244, 565]. Since changing to a different texture is expensive, the ISP groups spans of pixels that use the same texture before sending them on to the TSP. Note also that the ISP can write the stencil buffer and the Z-buffer of the tile to the local memory. This means that the entire Z-buffer and stencil buffer can be available after the entire scene has been rendered. This can be useful for shadow mapping, for example.

The TSP handles shading and texturing for visible fragments. The pipeline for texturing is duplicated, so that two pixels can be textured simultaneously. Eight texture stages are supported, and multitexturing is implemented using only one texturing unit (per texturing pipeline) that can be used eight times with feedback from the previous time it was used. As such, it can be seen as an accumulation buffer that is used for texturing and blending. Texture data is fetched from the local memory, and there is a texture cache on-chip for faster access to coherent data.

The architecture for KYRO also has advantages when performing full-scene antialiasing (see Section 4.4.2). 2×2, 1×2, and 2×1 supersampling is supported. To implement, say, 2×2 supersampling, the image is normally rendered at twice the resolution both horizontally and vertically. Then it is scaled down and filtered. KYRO, on the other hand, does not need a frame buffer four times as large. This is because the frame buffer only stores the final results. By rendering a 32×16 tile, scaling and filtering can then be done to 16×8 before writing to video memory. However, four times as many tiles need to be rendered in this way.

An advantage of tile-based rendering hardware is that it is inherently designed for rendering in parallel. For example, more ISPs and TSPs could be added to the pipeline for faster rendering. Note that the bottleneck in the system may change as this is done. A disadvantage of tile-based rendering hardware is that the entire scene data needs to be sent to the graphics hardware and stored in local memory. This places an upper limit on how large a scene can be rendered. Three megabytes of memory is enough for over $30,000$ triangles. This depends on several factors, such as, triangle size, the distribution on the screen, and more. Note that more complex scenes can be rendered with a multipass approach. Assume that in the first pass $30,000$ triangles are rendered, and the Z-buffer is saved out to the local memory. Now, in the second pass, another $30,000$ triangles are rendered, but before the ISP starts processing a tile, the Z-buffer for that tile is read into the ISP from the local memory. This multipass method comes at a cost of more bandwidth usage. Another disadvantage is that the accumulation buffer is not available for the entire screen after finishing a frame.

Xie and Shantz describe a tiled architecture for occlusion culling that somewhat resembles that of KYRO [832]. However, they build a visibility mask only when "enough" coverage information has been accumulated, and they do the visibility tests hierarchically.

15.3.9   Other Architectures

There are many other three-dimensional graphics architectures that have been proposed and built over the years. Two major systems, *Pixel-Planes* and *PixelFlow*, have been designed and built by the graphics group at the University of North Carolina, Chapel Hill. Pixel-Planes was built in the late 1980s [244], and was a Sort-Middle architecture with tile-based rendering. PixelFlow [220, 565, 567] was an example of a Sort-Last Image architecture with deferred shading and programmable shading. Recently, the group at UNC also has developed the *WarpEngine* [629], which is a rendering architecture for image-based rendering. The primitives used are images with depth. Owens et al. describe a stream architecture for polygon rendering, where a number of small, flexible processors are connected in a pipeline [609]. This architecture can be software programmed at all pipeline stages, giving high flexibility. The *SHARP* architecture developed at Stanford uses ray tracing as its rendering algorithm [12].

Further Reading and Resources

A great resource is the set of course notes on computer graphics architectures by Akeley and Hanrahan [12]. The annual *SIGGRAPH* and *SIG-GRAPH/Eurographics Workshop on Graphics Hardware* conference proceedings are good sources for more information, as are *IEEE Computer Graphics and Applications* and other journals. The OpenGL Advanced Techniques course notes [536] discuss ways of creating stereo pairs, and are available on the web.

Check this book's website, http://www.realtimerendering.com/, for information on benchmarking tests and results, as well as other hardware-related links.

Chapter 16
The Future

"Prediction is difficult, especially of the future."
–Niels Bohr

"The best way to predict the future is to create it."
–Alan Kay

"I program my home computer,
beam myself into the future."
–Kraftwerk

There are two parts to the future: you and everything else. This chapter is about both of these. First, there will be the obligatory predictions, some of which may even come true. More important is the second part of this chapter, which is about some places for you to go next. It is something of an extended Further Reading and Resources section, but also discusses ways to proceed from here—sources of information, conferences, programming tools, etc.

16.1   Everything Else

There have been roughly four stages so far for graphics accelerators [12]. The first generation was wireframe displays, the second was shaded solids, and the third was texture mapping. With the introduction of a programmable pipeline, the fourth generation began in 2001.

So, when will we be able to generate in real time an animated film such as 2001's *Monsters Inc.* by Pixar or *Shrek* by PDI? One answer is: decades. Generating an average frame of *Monsters Inc.* takes eleven hours, and requires about a gigabyte of geometric data and a gigabyte of texture data. To reach a minimum real-time rate of 12 frames per second, this means a speed-up of about 500,000 times is needed. Moore's Law gives an acceleration rate of 2 times every 1.5 years or, more usefully, about 10 times every 5 years [719]. This puts real-time *Monsters* at around 33 years out, the year 2034. It might take longer to get there—Moore's Law may fail in the long run, for whatever reasons.

However, that is the software-only prediction. Consumer-level (i.e., game) graphics accelerators have been more than doubling their speed each year [12], and are predicted to continue to do so in the near future. This rate gives an increase of about 50 every 5 years, versus Moore's Law's 10. In fact, the future is mostly here, at least for some scenes in some films. At *SIGGRAPH 2001*, Square USA and NVIDIA showed high-resolution scenes from the computer generated film *Final Fantasy* on a workstation. Instead of 90 minutes per frame, it updated at more than ten frames per second. See Plate I following page 274. NVIDIA claims that 80 percent of the scenes of the film could be rendered at interactive rates, though with fewer samples per pixel.[1] In another sense, the future has already passed: video consoles have rendered cinematic cut-scenes in games for years. The future in this case is a matter of degree, not possibility.

Graphics help sell games, and games help sell chips. One of the best features of real-time rendering from a chipmaker's marketing perspective is that graphics eats huge amounts of processing power and other resources. There are a few directions of growth. One is frame rate. Once a rate of about 85 Hz is reached, faster speeds are mostly irrelevant to the visual system. That said, as monitors become larger and brighter, they will need faster refresh rates. Another area for growth is monitor resolution. IBM's Bertha LCD display offers 3840 × 2400 resolution, with 200 dots per inch (dpi). A resolution of 1200 dpi, 36 times the Bertha LCD display's density, is offered by many printer companies today. A third area is bits per pixel. For color display, 24 bits is likely to hold as the norm for some time to come, but more bits can be used. For example, a 32 bit per pixel frame buffer does not have to be split 8/8/8/8; color configurations such as 11/11/10 are certainly feasible.[2] However, there are perceptual limits to all of these directions of growth.

The direction that is essentially unbounded is scene complexity. By complexity, we mean both the number of objects in a scene and the way these objects are rendered. Ignoring all other directions for growth, this

---

[1] This can include samples in time, to generate motion blur, samples on the camera lens, to generate depth-of-field, multisamples, to reduce jaggies, shadow map samples, texture samples, and sample points on subdivision surfaces and other primitives.

[2] At press time, Matrox announced their Parhelia accelerator, which has a 10/10/10/2 split.

single factor makes graphics a bottomless pit for processing power to fill. Depth complexity of scenes will rise, primitives will get smaller, illumination models will become more complex, and so on. First, build a model of the place where you are right now down to the tiniest details, and then create shaders that create a photorealistic rendering of that environment. Then, model the surroundings with the same detail. Keep moving outwards. Soon, any real-time rendering system will be a nonreal-time system.

So, we promised some predictions. "Faster and better," is a simple one to make. Hardware can do anything software can, what matters is the cost/benefit ratio of committing an algorithm to silicon. The programmable portion of the accelerator currently focuses on manipulating individual vertices and fragments. It is clear that graphics accelerators are now starting to provide support for surface modeling and animation. Bump and displacement maps and curved surface support are two features that have important consequences for model representation. So programmable surface generation on the accelerator is a definite trend. In the area of animation, capabilities such as vertex blending and vertex shaders accelerate the display of precomputed sequences. Researchers have looked upon the graphics accelerator as a SIMD machine, since the accelerator is so much faster for some tasks than the CPU. As accelerators continue to become more flexible and faster, algorithms in such fields as physical simulation and artificial intelligence are finding a home in the pipeline.

Kurt Akeley, one of the founders of SGI and now at Stanford and NVIDIA, predicts that the fifth generation of graphics hardware will tackle head-on such issues as shadows, ray tracing, and other global illumination techniques [12]. Initial research into CPU-side interactive ray tracing has been encouraging, though there are serious issues to resolve concerning accessing data in a cache coherent fashion [784]. The way in which special purpose features are added to peripheral hardware, which then later gets folded into the main CPU, is referred to as the *Wheel of Reincarnation* [578]. The interesting question is whether the hardware pipeline will evolve to perform more general algorithms by itself, will complement the CPU's capabilities, or will take a different evolutionary path altogether. See Plate XXXIII following page 562. The scene has ray traced quality, yet no rays were harmed in the making of this image.

16.2 You

So, while you and your children's children are waiting for ray tracing to take over the world, what do you do in the meantime? Program, of course: Discover new algorithms, create applications, design new hardware, or whatever else you enjoy doing. In this section, we cover various resources we have found to be useful in keeping on top of the field of real-time rendering.

This book does not exist in a vacuum; it draws upon a huge number of sources of information. If you are interested in a particular algorithm, track down the original sources. Journal and conference articles in computer graphics are usually not utterly mysterious. Go and get them. Most recent articles are available for download from the authors, and services such as the *ACM Digital Library* have a huge amount of new and older information available at reasonable subscription rates.

There are many resources that can help you keep abreast of the field. In the area of research, the *SIGGRAPH Proceedings* is a premier venue for new ideas, but hardly the only one. Other technical gatherings, such as the various *Eurographics* conferences and workshops, the *Symposium on Interactive 3D Graphics*, and the *Graphics Interface* conference, publish a significant amount of material relevant to real-time rendering. Particularly noteworthy are the *Eurographics Workshop on Rendering* and the *ACM SIGGRAPH/Eurographics Workshop on Graphics Hardware*. Of course, one of the best ways to stay in touch is actually to attend these conferences. There are also many excellent field-specific conferences, such as the *Game Developers Conference* (GDC).

There are a number of journals that publish technical articles, such as *IEEE Computer Graphics and Applications*, the *journal of graphics tools*, *ACM Transactions on Graphics*, and *IEEE Transactions on Visualization and Computer Graphics*, to mention a few. In recent years, *Game Developer* magazine has become an important source of information for high-quality tutorials and practical information about new techniques.

We refer you one last time to our website for links to online resources at: http://www.realtimerendering.com/. There you will find many other resources, such as lists of recommended and new books, as well as pointers to frequently asked questions lists and developer mailing lists. Some information on the web is available nowhere else, and there is a huge amount of useful material out there.

In the past few pages, you have been flooded with resources to explore and ideas to learn more about. Our last words of advice are to go and do it. The field of real-time computer graphics is continually evolving, and new ideas and features are appearing at an increasing rate. There are many combinations of techniques that have only begun to be explored. Even areas that seem old and well-established are worth revisiting; computer architectures change, and what worked (or did not work) a few years ago may no longer apply. What makes real-time rendering a qualitatively different field from other areas of computer graphics is that it provides different tools and has different goals. Today, hardware-accelerated shading, filtering, stencil buffering, and other operations change the relative costs of algorithms and so change our ways of doing things.

This edition comes 28 years after one of the milestone papers in the field of computer graphics, "A Characterization of Ten Hidden-Surface Algorithms" by Sutherland, Sproull, and Schumacker, published in 1974 [739]. Their 55-page paper is an incredibly thorough comparison of 10 different algorithms. What is interesting is that the algorithm described as "ridiculously expensive," the brute-force technique not even dignified with a researcher's name and mentioned only in the appendices, is what is now called the Z-buffer.[3] This eleventh hidden surface technique won out because it was easy to implement in hardware and because memory densities went up and costs went down. The research done by Sutherland et al. was perfectly valid for its time. As conditions change, so do the algorithms. It will be exciting to see what happens in the decades to come. How will it feel when we look back on this current era of rendering technology? No one knows, and each person can have a significant effect on the way the future turns out. There is no one future, no course that must occur. You create it.

---

[3]In fairness, Sutherland was the advisor of the inventor of the Z-buffer, Ed Catmull, whose thesis discussing this concept would be published a few months later [115].

Appendix A
Some Linear Algebra

BOOK I. DEFINITIONS.

A point is that which has no part.
A line is a breadthless length.
The extremities of a line are points.
A straight line is a line which lies evenly with the points
     on itself.
      –The first four definitions from Elements by Euclid [214]

This appendix deals with the fundamental concepts of linear algebra that are of greatest use for computer graphics. Our presentation will not be as mathematically abstract and general as these kinds of descriptions often are, but will rather concentrate on what is relevant to our context. For the inexperienced reader, it can be seen as a short introduction to the topic, and for the more experienced one, it may serve as a review, if needed.

We will start with an introduction to the Euclidean spaces. This may feel abstract at first, but in the section that follows, these concepts are connected to geometry, bases, and matrices. So bite the bullet during the first section, and reap the reward in the rest of the appendix, and in many of the other chapters of this book.

If you are uncertain about the notation used in this book, take a look at Section 1.2.

A.1 The Euclidean Space

The n-dimensional real Euclidean space is denoted $\mathbb{R}^n$. A vector $\mathbf{v}$ in this space is an n-tuple, that is, an ordered list of real numbers:[1]

---

[1]Note that the subscripts start at 0 and end at $n - 1$, a numbering system that follows the indexing of arrays in many programming languages, such as C and C++. This makes it easier to convert from formula to code. Some computer graphics books and linear algebra books start at 1 and end at n.

$$\mathbf{v} \in \mathbb{R}^n \Longleftrightarrow \mathbf{v} = \begin{pmatrix} v_0 \\ v_1 \\ \vdots \\ v_{n-1} \end{pmatrix} \text{ with } v_i \in \mathbb{R}, \ i = 0, \dots, n-1. \quad\quad \text{(A.1)}$$

The vector can also be presented as a row vector, but most computer graphics book use column vectors, in what is called the column-major form. We call $v_0, \dots, v_{n-1}$ the elements, the coefficients, or the components of the vector $\mathbf{v}$. All bold lowercase letters are vectors that belong to $\mathbb{R}^n$, and italicized lowercase letters are scalars that belong to $\mathbb{R}$. For vectors in Euclidean space there exist two operators, *addition* and *multiplication by a scalar*, which work as might be expected:

$$\mathbf{u} + \mathbf{v} = \begin{pmatrix} u_0 \\ u_1 \\ \vdots \\ u_{n-1} \end{pmatrix} + \begin{pmatrix} v_0 \\ v_1 \\ \vdots \\ v_{n-1} \end{pmatrix} = \begin{pmatrix} u_0 + v_0 \\ u_1 + v_1 \\ \vdots \\ u_{n-1} + v_{n-1} \end{pmatrix} \in \mathbb{R}^n \quad \textbf{(addition)}$$

$$\text{(A.2)}$$

and

$$a\mathbf{u} = \begin{pmatrix} au_0 \\ au_1 \\ \vdots \\ au_{n-1} \end{pmatrix} \in \mathbb{R}^n \quad\quad \textbf{(multiplication by a scalar)}. \quad \text{(A.3)}$$

The $\in \mathbb{R}^n$ simply means that addition and multiplication by a scalar yields vectors of the same space. As can be seen, addition is done componentwise, and multiplication is done by multiplying all elements in the vector with the scalar a.

Now, we will present a series of rules that hold for the Euclidean space.[2] Addition of vectors in the Euclidean space also works as might be expected:

$$(i) \quad (\mathbf{u} + \mathbf{v}) + \mathbf{w} = \mathbf{u} + (\mathbf{v} + \mathbf{w}) \quad \textbf{(associativity)}$$

$$\text{(A.4)}$$

$$(ii) \quad \mathbf{u} + \mathbf{v} = \mathbf{v} + \mathbf{u} \quad\quad\quad\quad \textbf{(commutativity)}.$$

There is a unique vector, called the zero vector, which is $\mathbf{0} = (0, 0, \dots, 0)$ with n zeros, such that:

$$(iii) \quad \mathbf{0} + \mathbf{v} = \mathbf{v} \quad \textbf{(zero identity)}. \quad\quad\quad \text{(A.5)}$$

---

[2] Actually, these are the definition of the Euclidean space.

There is also a unique vector $-\mathbf{v} = (-v_0, -v_1, \ldots, -v_{n-1})$ such that:

$$(iv) \quad \mathbf{v} + (-\mathbf{v}) = \mathbf{0} \quad \textbf{(additive inverse)}. \tag{A.6}$$

Rules for multiplication by a scalar work as follows:

$(i) \quad (ab)\mathbf{u} = a(b\mathbf{u})$

$(ii) \quad (a + b)\mathbf{u} = a\mathbf{u} + b\mathbf{u} \quad \textbf{(distributive law)}$

$(iii) \quad a(\mathbf{u} + \mathbf{v}) = a\mathbf{u} + a\mathbf{v} \quad \textbf{(distributive law)}$

$(iv) \quad 1\mathbf{u} = \mathbf{u}.$

$$\tag{A.7}$$

For the Euclidean space we may also compute the *dot product*[3] of two vectors $\mathbf{u}$ and $\mathbf{v}$. The dot product is denoted $\mathbf{u} \cdot \mathbf{v}$, and its definition is shown below:

$$\mathbf{u} \cdot \mathbf{v} = \sum_{i=0}^{n-1} u_i v_i \quad \textbf{(dot product)}. \tag{A.8}$$

For the dot product we have the rules:

$(i) \quad \mathbf{u} \cdot \mathbf{u} \geq 0$, with $\mathbf{u} \cdot \mathbf{u} = 0$ if and only if $\mathbf{u} = (0, 0, \ldots, 0) = \mathbf{0}$

$(ii) \quad (\mathbf{u} + \mathbf{v}) \cdot \mathbf{w} = \mathbf{u} \cdot \mathbf{w} + \mathbf{v} \cdot \mathbf{w}$

$(iii) \quad (a\mathbf{u}) \cdot \mathbf{v} = a(\mathbf{u} \cdot \mathbf{v})$

$(iv) \quad \mathbf{u} \cdot \mathbf{v} = \mathbf{v} \cdot \mathbf{u} \quad \textbf{(commutativity)}$

$(v) \quad \mathbf{u} \cdot \mathbf{v} = 0 \Longleftrightarrow \mathbf{u} \perp \mathbf{v}.$

$$\tag{A.9}$$

The last formula means that if the dot product is zero then the vectors are orthogonal (perpendicular). The norm of a vector, denoted $\|\mathbf{u}\|$, is a nonnegative number that can be expressed using the dot product:

$$\|\mathbf{u}\| = \sqrt{\mathbf{u} \cdot \mathbf{u}} = \sqrt{\left(\sum_{i=0}^{n-1} u_i^2 \right)} \quad \textbf{(norm)}. \tag{A.10}$$

---

[3] Also called *inner (dot) product* or *scalar product*.

The following rules hold for the norm:

(i) $||\mathbf{u}|| = 0 \iff \mathbf{u} = (0, 0, \ldots, 0) = \mathbf{0}$

(ii) $||a\mathbf{u}|| = |a| \, ||\mathbf{u}||$

(iii) $||\mathbf{u} + \mathbf{v}|| \leq ||\mathbf{u}|| + ||\mathbf{v}||$ **(triangle inequality)**

(iv) $|\mathbf{u} \cdot \mathbf{v}| \leq ||\mathbf{u}|| \, ||\mathbf{v}||$ **(Cauchy–Schwartz inequality)**.

$$\text{(A.11)}$$

The next section shows how we can use the theory in this section by interpreting everything geometrically.

A.2   Geometrical Interpretation

Here, we will interpret the vectors (from the previous section) geometrically. For this, we first need to introduce the concepts of *linear independence* and the *basis*.[4]

If the only scalars to satisfy Equation A.12 are $v_0 = v_1 = \ldots = v_{n-1} = 0$, then the vectors, $\mathbf{u}_0, \ldots \mathbf{u}_{n-1}$, are said to be linearly independent. Otherwise, the vectors are linearly dependent.

$$v_0 \mathbf{u}_0 + \cdots + v_{n-1} \mathbf{u}_{n-1} = 0 \tag{A.12}$$

For example, the vectors $\mathbf{u}_0 = (4, 3)$ and $\mathbf{u}_1 = (8, 6)$ are *not* linearly independent, since $v_0 = 2$ and $v_1 = -1$ (among others) satisfy Equation A.12.

If a set of n vectors, $\mathbf{u}_0, \ldots, \mathbf{u}_{n-1} \in \mathbb{R}^n$, is linearly independent and any vector $\mathbf{v} \in \mathbb{R}^n$ can be written as

$$\mathbf{v} = \sum_{i=0}^{n-1} v_i \mathbf{u}_i, \tag{A.13}$$

then the vectors $\mathbf{u}_0, \ldots, \mathbf{u}_{n-1}$ are said to span the Euclidean space $\mathbb{R}^n$. If, in addition, $v_0, \ldots, v_{n-1}$ are uniquely determined by $\mathbf{v}$ for all $\mathbf{v} \in \mathbb{R}^n$, then $\mathbf{u}_0, \ldots, \mathbf{u}_{n-1}$ is called a basis of $\mathbb{R}^n$. What this means is that every vector can be described uniquely by n scalars $(v_0, v_1, \ldots, v_{n-1})$ and the basis vectors $\mathbf{u}_0, \ldots, \mathbf{u}_{n-1}$. As a consequence, basis vectors can never be

---

[4]Note that the concepts of linear independence and the basis can be used without any geometry.

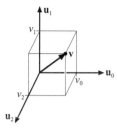

Figure A.1. A three-dimensional vector $\mathbf{v} = (v_0, v_1, v_2)$ expressed in the basis formed by $\mathbf{u}_0, \mathbf{u}_1, \mathbf{u}_2$ in $\mathbb{R}^3$. Note that this is a right-handed system.

parallel (because they would then be linearly dependent). The dimension of the space is n, if n is the largest number of linearly independent vectors in the space.

An example of a linearly independent basis is $\mathbf{u}_0 = (4, 3)$ and $\mathbf{u}_1 = (2, 6)$. This spans the Euclidean space, as any vector can be expressed as a unique combination of these two vectors. For example, $(-5, -6)$ is described by $v_0 = -1$ and $v_1 = -0.5$ and no other combinations of v_0 and v_1.

Now, if the basis is implicit (i.e., does not need to be stated), then $\mathbf{v}$ can be described as:

$$\mathbf{v} = \begin{pmatrix} v_0 \\ v_1 \\ \vdots \\ v_{n-1} \end{pmatrix}, \tag{A.14}$$

which is exactly the same vector description as in Expression A.1, and so this is the one-to-one mapping of the vectors in Section A.1 onto geometrical vectors.[5] An illustration of a three-dimensional vector is shown in Figure A.1. A vector $\mathbf{v}$ can either be interpreted as a point in space or as a directed line segment (i.e., a direction vector). All rules from Section A.1 apply in the geometrical sense, too. For example, the addition and the scaling operators from Equation A.2 are visualized in Figure A.2. A basis can also have different "handedness." A three-dimensional, right-handed basis is one in which the x-axis is along the thumb, the y-axis is along index-finger, and the z-axis is along the middle finger. If this is done with the left hand, a left-handed basis is obtained. See page 727 for a more formal definition of "handedness."

---

[5]In mathematics, this is called an isomorphism.

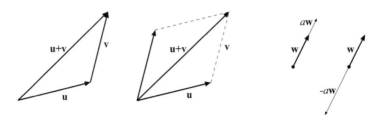

Figure A.2. Vector-vector addition is shown in the two figures on the left. They are called the head-to-tail axiom and the parallelogram rule. The two rightmost figures show scalar-vector multiplication for a positive and a negative scalar, a and $-a$, respectively.

The norm of a vector (see Equation A.10) can be thought of as the length of the vector. To create a vector of unit length, i.e., of length one, the vector has to be normalized. This can be done by dividing by the length of the vector: $\mathbf{q} = \frac{1}{||\mathbf{p}||}\mathbf{p}$, where $\mathbf{q}$ is the normalized vector, which also is called a unit vector.

For $\mathbb{R}^2$ and $\mathbb{R}^3$, or two- and three-dimensional space, the dot product can also be expressed as below, which is equivalent to Expression A.8.

$$\mathbf{u} \cdot \mathbf{v} = ||\mathbf{u}|| \, ||\mathbf{v}|| \cos \phi \quad \textbf{(dot product)} \qquad (A.15)$$

Here, ϕ (shown at the left in Figure A.3) is the smallest angle between $\mathbf{u}$ and $\mathbf{v}$. Several conclusions can be drawn from the sign of the dot product. First, $\mathbf{u} \cdot \mathbf{v} = 0 \Leftrightarrow \mathbf{u} \perp \mathbf{v}$, i.e., $\mathbf{u}$ and $\mathbf{v}$ are orthogonal (perpendicular) if their dot product is zero. Second, if $\mathbf{u} \cdot \mathbf{v} > 0$, then it is easily seen that $0 \le \phi < \frac{\pi}{2}$, and likewise if $\mathbf{u} \cdot \mathbf{v} < 0$ then $\frac{\pi}{2} < \phi \le \pi$.

Now we will go back to the study of basis for a while, and introduce a special kind of basis that is said to be *orthonormal*. For such a basis, consisting of the basis vectors $\mathbf{u}_0, \ldots, \mathbf{u}_{n-1}$, the following must hold:

$$\mathbf{u}_i \cdot \mathbf{u}_j = \begin{cases} 0, & i \ne j \\ 1, & i = j. \end{cases} \qquad (A.16)$$

This means that every basis vector must have a length of one, i.e., $||\mathbf{u}_i|| = 1$, and also that each pair of basis vectors must be orthogonal, i.e., the angle between them must be $\pi/2$ radians (90°). In this book, we will mostly use two- and three-dimensional orthonormal bases. If the basis vectors are mutually perpendicular, but not of unit length, then the basis is called *orthogonal*.

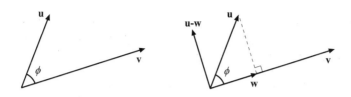

Figure A.3. The left figure shows the notation and geometric situation for the dot product. In the rightmost figure, orthographic projection is shown. The vector **u** is orthogonally (perpendicularly) projected onto **v** to yield **w**.

Let $\mathbf{p} = (p_0, \ldots, p_{n-1})$, then for an orthonormal basis it can also be shown that $p_i = \mathbf{p} \cdot \mathbf{u}_i$. This means that if you have a vector $\mathbf{p}$ and a basis (with the basis vectors $\mathbf{u}_0, \ldots, \mathbf{u}_{n-1}$), then you can easily get the elements of that vector in that basis by taking the dot product between the vector and each of the basis vectors. The most common basis is called the standard basis, where the basis vectors are denoted $\mathbf{e}_i$. The ith basis vector has zeroes everywhere except in position i, which holds a one. For three dimensions, this means $\mathbf{e}_0 = (1,0,0)$, $\mathbf{e}_1 = (0,1,0)$, and $\mathbf{e}_2 = (0,0,1)$. We also denote these vectors $\mathbf{e}_x$, $\mathbf{e}_y$, and $\mathbf{e}_z$, since they are what we normally call the x-, the y-, and the z-axes.

A very useful property of the dot product is that it can be used to project a vector orthogonally onto another vector. This orthogonal projection (vector), $\mathbf{w}$, of a vector $\mathbf{u}$ onto a vector $\mathbf{v}$ is depicted on the right in Figure A.3.

For arbitrary vectors $\mathbf{u}$ and $\mathbf{v}$, $\mathbf{w}$ is determined by

$$\mathbf{w} = \left(\frac{\mathbf{u} \cdot \mathbf{v}}{||\mathbf{v}||^2}\right)\mathbf{v} = \left(\frac{\mathbf{u} \cdot \mathbf{v}}{\mathbf{v} \cdot \mathbf{v}}\right)\mathbf{v} = t\mathbf{v}, \qquad (A.17)$$

where t is a scalar. The reader is encouraged to verify that Expression A.17 is indeed correct, which is quite easily done by inspection and the use of Equation A.15. The projection also gives us an orthogonal decomposition of $\mathbf{u}$, which is divided into two parts, $\mathbf{w}$ and $(\mathbf{u} - \mathbf{w})$. It can be shown that $\mathbf{w} \perp (\mathbf{u} - \mathbf{w})$, and of course $\mathbf{u} = \mathbf{w} + (\mathbf{u} - \mathbf{w})$ holds. An additional observation is that if $\mathbf{v}$ is normalized, then the projection is $\mathbf{w} = (\mathbf{u} \cdot \mathbf{v})\mathbf{v}$. This means that $||\mathbf{w}|| = |\mathbf{u} \cdot \mathbf{v}|$, i.e., the length of $\mathbf{w}$ is the absolute value of the dot product between $\mathbf{u}$ and $\mathbf{v}$.

Figure A.4. The geometry involved in the cross product.

Cross Product

The cross product, also called the vector product, and the previously introduced dot product are two very important operations on vectors.

The cross product in $\mathbb{R}^3$ of two vectors, $\mathbf{u}$ and $\mathbf{v}$, denoted by $\mathbf{w} = \mathbf{u} \times \mathbf{v}$, is defined by a unique vector $\mathbf{w}$ with the following properties:

- $||\mathbf{w}|| = ||\mathbf{u} \times \mathbf{v}|| = ||\mathbf{u}||\,||\mathbf{v}|| \sin \phi$, where ϕ is, again, the smallest angle between $\mathbf{u}$ and $\mathbf{v}$. See Figure A.4.

- $\mathbf{w} \perp \mathbf{u}$ and $\mathbf{w} \perp \mathbf{v}$.

- $\mathbf{u}$, $\mathbf{v}$, $\mathbf{w}$ form a right-handed system.

From this definition, it is deduced that $\mathbf{u} \times \mathbf{v} = \mathbf{0}$ if and only if $\mathbf{u} \parallel \mathbf{v}$ (i.e., $\mathbf{u}$ and $\mathbf{v}$ are parallel), since then $\sin \phi = 0$. The cross product also comes equipped with the following laws of calculation, among others:

$$\mathbf{u} \times \mathbf{v} = -\mathbf{v} \times \mathbf{u} \qquad\qquad \textbf{(anti-commutativity)}$$

$$(a\mathbf{u} + b\mathbf{v}) \times \mathbf{w} = a(\mathbf{u} \times \mathbf{w}) + b(\mathbf{v} \times \mathbf{w}) \quad \textbf{(linearity)}$$

$$\left.\begin{array}{rl} (\mathbf{u} \times \mathbf{v}) \cdot \mathbf{w} = & (\mathbf{v} \times \mathbf{w}) \cdot \mathbf{u} \\ = & (\mathbf{w} \times \mathbf{u}) \cdot \mathbf{v} = -(\mathbf{v} \times \mathbf{u}) \cdot \mathbf{w} \\ = & -(\mathbf{u} \times \mathbf{w}) \cdot \mathbf{v} = -(\mathbf{w} \times \mathbf{v}) \cdot \mathbf{u} \end{array}\right\} \quad \textbf{(scalar triple product)}$$

$$\mathbf{u} \times (\mathbf{v} \times \mathbf{w}) = (\mathbf{u} \cdot \mathbf{w})\mathbf{v} - (\mathbf{u} \cdot \mathbf{v})\mathbf{w} \qquad \textbf{(vector triple product)}$$
$$\text{(A.18)}$$

From these laws, it is obvious that the order of the operands is crucial in getting correct results from the calculations.

For three-dimensional vectors, $\mathbf{u}$ and $\mathbf{v}$, in an orthonormal basis, the cross product is computed according to Equation A.19.

$$\mathbf{w} = \begin{pmatrix} w_x \\ w_y \\ w_z \end{pmatrix} = \mathbf{u} \times \mathbf{v} = \begin{pmatrix} u_y v_z - u_z v_y \\ u_z v_x - u_x v_z \\ u_x v_y - u_y v_x \end{pmatrix} \qquad \text{(A.19)}$$

A method called Sarrus's scheme, which is simple to remember, can be used to derive this formula:

$$
\begin{array}{cccccc}
+ & + & + & - & - & - \\
\searrow & \searrow & \searrow & \swarrow & \swarrow & \swarrow \\
\mathbf{e}_x & \mathbf{e}_y & \mathbf{e}_z & \mathbf{e}_x & \mathbf{e}_y & \mathbf{e}_z \\
u_x & u_y & u_z & u_x & u_y & u_z \\
v_x & v_y & v_z & v_x & v_y & v_z
\end{array}
\qquad (A.20)
$$

To use the scheme, follow the diagonal arrows, and for each arrow, generate a term by multiplying the elements along the direction of the arrow and giving the product the sign associated with that arrow. The result, shown below, is the formula presented above.

$$\mathbf{u} \times \mathbf{v} = +\mathbf{e}_x(u_y v_z) + \mathbf{e}_y(u_z v_x) + \mathbf{e}_z(u_x v_y) - \mathbf{e}_x(u_z v_y) - \mathbf{e}_y(u_x v_z) - \mathbf{e}_z(u_y v_x)$$

A.3 Matrices

This section presents the definitions concerning matrices and some common, useful operations on them. Even though this presentation is (mostly) for arbitrarily sized matrices, square matrices of the sizes 2×2, 3×3, and 4×4 will be used in the chapters of this book. Note that Chapter 3 deals with transforms represented by matrices.

A.3.1 Definitions and Operations

A matrix, $\mathbf{M}$, can be used as a tool for manipulating vectors and points. $\mathbf{M}$ is described by $p \times q$ scalars (complex numbers are an alternative, but not relevant here), m_{ij}, $0 \le i < p - 1$, $0 \le j < q - 1$, ordered in a rectangular fashion (with p rows and q columns) as shown in Equation A.21.

$$
\mathbf{M} = \begin{pmatrix}
m_{00} & m_{01} & \cdots & m_{0,q-1} \\
m_{10} & m_{11} & \cdots & m_{1,q-1} \\
\vdots & \vdots & \ddots & \vdots \\
m_{p-1,0} & m_{p-1,1} & \cdots & m_{p-1,q-1}
\end{pmatrix} = [m_{ij}]
\qquad (A.21)
$$

The notation $[m_{ij}]$ will be used in the equations below and is merely a shorter way of describing a matrix. There is a special matrix called the *unit matrix*, $\mathbf{I}$, which contains ones in the diagonal and zeros elsewhere. This is also called the *identity matrix*. Equation A.22 shows its general appearance. This is the matrix-form counterpart of the scalar number one.

$$\mathbf{I} = \begin{pmatrix} 1 & 0 & 0 & \cdots & 0 & 0 \\ 0 & 1 & 0 & \cdots & 0 & 0 \\ \vdots & \vdots & \vdots & \ddots & \vdots & \vdots \\ 0 & 0 & 0 & \cdots & 1 & 0 \\ 0 & 0 & 0 & \cdots & 0 & 1 \end{pmatrix} \tag{A.22}$$

Next, the most ordinary operations on matrices will be reviewed.

Matrix-Matrix Addition

Adding two matrices, say $\mathbf{M}$ and $\mathbf{N}$, is possible only for equal-sized matrices and is defined as

$$\mathbf{M} + \mathbf{N} = [m_{ij}] + [n_{ij}] = [m_{ij} + n_{ij}], \tag{A.23}$$

that is, componentwise addition, very similar to vector-vector addition. The resulting matrix is of the same size as the operands. The following operations are valid for matrix-matrix addition: $i)$ $(\mathbf{L} + \mathbf{M}) + \mathbf{N} = \mathbf{L} + (\mathbf{M} + \mathbf{N})$, $ii)$ $\mathbf{M} + \mathbf{N} = \mathbf{N} + \mathbf{M}$, $iii)$ $\mathbf{M} + \mathbf{0} = \mathbf{M}$, $iv)$ $\mathbf{M} - \mathbf{M} = \mathbf{0}$, which are all very easy to prove.

Scalar-Matrix Multiplication

A scalar a and a matrix, $\mathbf{M}$, can be multiplied to form a new matrix of the same size as $\mathbf{M}$, which is computed by $\mathbf{T} = a\mathbf{M} = [am_{ij}]$. $\mathbf{T}$ and $\mathbf{M}$ are of the same size, and these trivial rules apply: $i)$ $0\mathbf{M} = \mathbf{0}$, $ii)$ $1\mathbf{M} = \mathbf{M}$, $iii)$ $a(b\mathbf{M}) = (ab)\mathbf{M}$, $iv)$ $a\mathbf{0} = \mathbf{0}$, $v)$ $(a + b)\mathbf{M} = a\mathbf{M} + b\mathbf{M}$, $vi)$ $a(\mathbf{M} + \mathbf{N}) = a\mathbf{M} + a\mathbf{N}$.

Transpose of a Matrix

$\mathbf{M}^T$ is the notation for the transpose of $\mathbf{M} = [m_{ij}]$, and the definition is $\mathbf{M}^T = [m_{ji}]$, i.e., the columns become rows and the rows become columns. For the transpose operator, we have: $i)$ $(a\mathbf{M})^T = a\mathbf{M}^T$, $ii)$ $(\mathbf{M} + \mathbf{N})^T = \mathbf{M}^T + \mathbf{N}^T$, $iii)$ $(\mathbf{M}^T)^T = \mathbf{M}$, $iv)$ $(\mathbf{M}\mathbf{N})^T = \mathbf{N}^T\mathbf{M}^T$.

Trace of a Matrix

The trace of a matrix, denoted $\mathrm{tr}(\mathbf{M})$, is simply the sum of the diagonal elements of a square matrix, as shown below.

$$\mathrm{tr}(\mathbf{M}) = \sum_{i=0}^{n-1} m_{ii} \tag{A.24}$$

Matrix-Matrix Multiplication

This operation, denoted $\mathbf{MN}$ between $\mathbf{M}$ and $\mathbf{N}$, is defined only if $\mathbf{M}$ is of size $p \times q$ and $\mathbf{N}$ is of size $q \times r$, in which case the result, $\mathbf{T}$, becomes a $p \times r$ sized matrix. Mathematically, the operation is as shown below, for the matrices named above.

$$
\mathbf{T} = \mathbf{MN} = \begin{pmatrix} m_{00} & \cdots & m_{0,q-1} \\ \vdots & \ddots & \vdots \\ m_{p-1,0} & \cdots & m_{p-1,q-1} \end{pmatrix} \begin{pmatrix} n_{00} & \cdots & n_{0,r-1} \\ \vdots & \ddots & \vdots \\ n_{q-1,0} & \cdots & n_{q-1,r-1} \end{pmatrix}
$$

$$
= \begin{pmatrix} \sum_{i=0}^{q-1} m_{0,i} n_{i,0} & \cdots & \sum_{i=0}^{q-1} m_{0,i} n_{i,r-1} \\ \vdots & \ddots & \vdots \\ \sum_{i=0}^{q-1} m_{p-1,i} n_{i,0} & \cdots & \sum_{i=0}^{q-1} m_{p-1,i} n_{i,r-1} \end{pmatrix}
$$

$$(A.25)$$

In other words, each row of $\mathbf{M}$ and column of $\mathbf{N}$ are combined using a dot product, and the result placed in the corresponding row and column element. The elements of $\mathbf{T}$ are computed as $t_{ij} = \sum_{k=0}^{q-1} m_{i,k} n_{k,j}$, which can also be expressed as $t_{ij} = \mathbf{m}_{i,} \cdot \mathbf{n}_{,j}$, that is, using the dot product and the matrix-vector indexing from Section 1.2.1. Note also that an $n \times 1$ matrix, $\mathbf{S} = (s_{00} \ s_{10} \ \cdots \ s_{n-1,0})^T$, is very similar to an n-tuple vector. If seen as such, then matrix-vector multiplication, between $\mathbf{M}$ ($p \times q$) and $\mathbf{v}$ (q-tuple), can be derived from the definition of matrix-matrix multiplication. This is shown in Equation A.26, resulting in a new vector, $\mathbf{w}$.

$$
\mathbf{w} = \mathbf{Mv} = \begin{pmatrix} m_{00} & \cdots & m_{0,q-1} \\ \vdots & \ddots & \vdots \\ m_{p-1,0} & \cdots & m_{p-1,q-1} \end{pmatrix} \begin{pmatrix} v_0 \\ \vdots \\ v_{p-1} \end{pmatrix}
$$

$$
= \begin{pmatrix} \sum_{k=0}^{q-1} m_{0,k} v_k \\ \vdots \\ \sum_{k=0}^{q-1} m_{p-1,k} v_k \end{pmatrix} = \begin{pmatrix} \mathbf{m}_0, \cdot \mathbf{v} \\ \vdots \\ \mathbf{m}_{p-1}, \cdot \mathbf{v} \end{pmatrix} = \begin{pmatrix} w_0 \\ \vdots \\ w_{p-1} \end{pmatrix}
$$

$$(A.26)$$

These three rules hold for the matrix-matrix multiplication: i) $(\mathbf{LM})\mathbf{N} = \mathbf{L}(\mathbf{MN})$, ii) $(\mathbf{L} + \mathbf{M})\mathbf{N} = \mathbf{LN} + \mathbf{MN}$, iii) $\mathbf{MI} = \mathbf{IM} = \mathbf{M}$. Also, in general $\mathbf{MN} \neq \mathbf{NM}$, if the dimensions of the matrices are the same. This means that some pairs of matrices do commute, but usually they do not.

Determinant of a Matrix

The determinant is defined only for square matrices, and in the general case, the definition is recursive or defined via permutations [478]. Here, the focus will be on determinants for 2×2 and 3×3 matrices, since those are the only ones usually needed in computer graphics.

The determinant of $\mathbf{M}$, written $|\mathbf{M}|$, for these matrices appears in Equation A.27 and A.28.

$$|\mathbf{M}| = \begin{vmatrix} m_{00} & m_{01} \\ m_{10} & m_{11} \end{vmatrix} = m_{00}m_{11} - m_{01}m_{10} \tag{A.27}$$

$$|\mathbf{M}| = \begin{vmatrix} m_{00} & m_{01} & m_{02} \\ m_{10} & m_{11} & m_{12} \\ m_{20} & m_{21} & m_{22} \end{vmatrix} \tag{A.28}$$
$$= m_{00}m_{11}m_{22} + m_{01}m_{12}m_{20} + m_{02}m_{10}m_{21}$$
$$- m_{02}m_{11}m_{20} - m_{01}m_{10}m_{22} - m_{00}m_{12}m_{21}$$

In these two equations, a certain pattern can be distinguished: the positive terms are the elements multiplied in the diagonals from the top downwards to the right and the negative terms are the elements in the diagonals from the top downwards to the left, where a diagonal continues on the opposite side if an edge is crossed. Note that if the top row in $\mathbf{M}$ is replaced by $\mathbf{e}_x \quad \mathbf{e}_y \quad \mathbf{e}_z$, the middle row by $u_x \quad u_y \quad u_z$, and the bottom row by $v_x \quad v_y \quad v_z$, the cross product $\mathbf{u} \times \mathbf{v}$ is obtained according to Sarrus's scheme (see Section A.2 on the cross product).

Another useful way to compute the determinant for 3×3 matrices is to use the dot and the cross product as in Equation A.29, which is reminiscent of the column vector indexing introduced in Section 1.2.1.

$$|\mathbf{M}| = |\mathbf{m}_{,0} \quad \mathbf{m}_{,1} \quad \mathbf{m}_{,2}| = |\mathbf{m}_x \quad \mathbf{m}_y \quad \mathbf{m}_z| = (\mathbf{m}_x \times \mathbf{m}_y) \cdot \mathbf{m}_z \tag{A.29}$$

The following notation is also used for determinants:

$$|\mathbf{M}| = \det(\mathbf{M}) = \det(\mathbf{m}_x, \mathbf{m}_y, \mathbf{m}_z). \tag{A.30}$$

Observe that the scalar triple product from Equation A.18 can be applied to Equation A.29; that is, if the vectors are rotated, the determinant remains unchanged, but changing the places of two vectors will change the sign of the determinant.

If $n \times n$ is the size of $\mathbf{M}$, then the following apply to determinant calculations: $i)$ $|\mathbf{M}^{-1}| = 1/|\mathbf{M}|$, $ii)$ $|\mathbf{MN}| = |\mathbf{M}|\,|\mathbf{N}|$, $iii)$ $|a\mathbf{M}| = a^n|\mathbf{M}|$, $iv)$ $|\mathbf{M}^T| = |\mathbf{M}|$. Also, if all elements of one row (or one column) are multiplied by a scalar, a, then $a|\mathbf{M}|$ is obtained, and if two rows (or columns) coincide (i.e., the cross product between them is zero), then $|\mathbf{M}| = 0$. The same result is obtained if any row or column is composed entirely of zeroes.

The orientation of a basis can be determined via determinants. A basis is said to form a right-handed system, also called a positively oriented basis, if its determinant is positive. The standard basis has this property, since $|\mathbf{e}_x \ \mathbf{e}_y \ \mathbf{e}_z| = (\mathbf{e}_x \times \mathbf{e}_y) \cdot \mathbf{e}_z = (0, 0, 1) \cdot \mathbf{e}_z = \mathbf{e}_z \cdot \mathbf{e}_z = 1 > 0$. If the determinant is negative, the basis is called negatively oriented or is said to be forming a left-handed system.

Some geometrical interpretations of the determinant are given in Section A.5.

Adjoints

The adjoint[6] is another form of a matrix that can sometimes be useful, as seen in Section 3.1.7 and below, where the inverse of a matrix is computed. We start by defining the subdeterminant (also called cofactor) $d_{ij}^{\mathbf{M}}$ of an $n \times n$ matrix $\mathbf{M}$ as the determinant that is obtained by deleting row i and column j and then taking the determinant of the resulting $(n-1) \times (n-1)$ matrix. An example of computing the subdeterminant $d_{02}^{\mathbf{M}}$ of a 3×3 matrix is shown in Equation A.31.

$$d_{02}^{\mathbf{M}} = \begin{vmatrix} m_{10} & m_{11} \\ m_{20} & m_{21} \end{vmatrix} \tag{A.31}$$

For a 3×3 matrix, the adjoint is then

$$\mathrm{adj}(\mathbf{M}) = \begin{pmatrix} d_{00} & -d_{10} & d_{20} \\ -d_{01} & d_{11} & -d_{21} \\ d_{02} & -d_{12} & d_{22} \end{pmatrix}, \tag{A.32}$$

where we have left out the superscript $\mathbf{M}$ of the subdeterminants for clarity. Note the signs and the order in which the subdeterminants appear. If we want to compute the adjoint $\mathbf{A}$ of an arbitrary sized matrix $\mathbf{M}$, then the component at position (i, j) is:

$$[a_{ij}] = \left[(-1)^{(i+j)} d_{ji}^{\mathbf{M}} \right]. \tag{A.33}$$

---

[6]Sometimes the adjoint has another definition than the one presented here, i.e., the adjoint of a matrix $\mathbf{M} = [m_{ij}]$ is denoted $\mathbf{M}^* = [\overline{m_{ji}}]$, where $\overline{m_{ji}}$ is the complex conjugate.

Inverse of a Matrix

The multiplicative inverse of a matrix, $\mathbf{M}$, denoted $\mathbf{M}^{-1}$, which is dealt with here, exists only for square matrices with $|\mathbf{M}| \neq 0$. If all elements of the matrix under consideration are real scalars, then it suffices to show that $\mathbf{MN} = \mathbf{I}$ and $\mathbf{NM} = \mathbf{I}$, where then $\mathbf{N} = \mathbf{M}^{-1}$. The problem can also be stated thus: If $\mathbf{u} = \mathbf{Mv}$ and a matrix $\mathbf{N}$ exists such that $\mathbf{v} = \mathbf{Nu}$, then $\mathbf{N} = \mathbf{M}^{-1}$.

The inverse of a matrix can be computed either implicitly or explicitly. If the inverse is to be used several times, then it is more economical to compute $\mathbf{M}^{-1}$ explicitly, i.e., to get a representation of the inverse as an array of $n \times n$ real numbers. On the other hand, if only a linear system of the type $\mathbf{u} = \mathbf{Mv}$ needs to be solved (for $\mathbf{v}$), then an implicit method, like *Cramer's rule*, can be used. For a linear system of the type $\mathbf{Mv} = \mathbf{0}$, $|\mathbf{M}| = 0$ is a requirement if there is to be a solution, $\mathbf{v}$.

Using Cramer's rule to solve $\mathbf{u} = \mathbf{Mv}$ gives $\mathbf{v} = \mathbf{M}^{-1}\mathbf{u}$, but not $\mathbf{M}^{-1}$ explicitly. Equation A.34 shows the general solution for the elements of $\mathbf{v}$.

$$v_i = \frac{d_i}{|\mathbf{M}|}$$

$$\text{(A.34)}$$

$$d_i = |\mathbf{m}_{,0} \quad \mathbf{m}_{,1} \quad \cdots \quad \mathbf{m}_{,i-1} \quad \mathbf{u} \quad \mathbf{m}_{,i+1} \quad \cdots \quad \mathbf{m}_{,n-1}|$$

The terms d_i are thus computed as $|\mathbf{M}|$, but column i is replaced by $\mathbf{u}$. For a 3×3, system the solution obtained by Cramer's rule is presented below:

$$\mathbf{v} = \begin{pmatrix} v_x \\ v_y \\ v_z \end{pmatrix} = \frac{1}{|\mathbf{M}|} \begin{pmatrix} \det(\mathbf{u}, \mathbf{m}_y, \mathbf{m}_z) \\ \det(\mathbf{m}_x, \mathbf{u}, \mathbf{m}_z) \\ \det(\mathbf{m}_x, \mathbf{m}_y, \mathbf{u}) \end{pmatrix}. \qquad \text{(A.35)}$$

Many terms in this equation can be factorized using the scalar triple product rule and then reused for faster calculation. For example, this is done in Section 13.7 when computing the intersection between a ray and a triangle.

For a 2×2 matrix, $\mathbf{M}$, the explicit solution is given by Equation A.36, and as can be seen, it is very simple to implement, since $|\mathbf{M}| = m_{00}m_{11} - m_{01}m_{10}$.

$$\mathbf{M}^{-1} = \frac{1}{|\mathbf{M}|} \begin{pmatrix} m_{11} & -m_{01} \\ -m_{10} & m_{00} \end{pmatrix} \qquad \text{(A.36)}$$

For the general case, the adjoint from the previous section can be used:

$$\mathbf{M}^{-1} = \frac{1}{|\mathbf{M}|} \text{adj}(\mathbf{M}). \qquad \text{(A.37)}$$

In fact, this is Cramer's rule expressed differently to get the inverse matrix explicitly.

However, for larger sizes than 4×4, there are no simple formulae, and Cramer's rule also becomes infeasible for matrices larger than 4×4. Gaussian elimination is then the method of preference, and it can be used to solve for $\mathbf{u} = \mathbf{Mv} \Rightarrow \mathbf{v} = \mathbf{M}^{-1}\mathbf{u}$—that is, an implicit solution, as is the case for Cramer's rule. But Gaussian elimination can also be used to compute the matrix $\mathbf{M}^{-1}$ explicitly. Consider the system in Equation A.38, where $\mathbf{u}$ and $\mathbf{v}$ are arbitrary vectors of the same dimension as $\mathbf{M}$ and $\mathbf{I}$ (the identity matrix).

$$\mathbf{Mu} = \mathbf{Iv} \tag{A.38}$$

Performing Gaussian elimination on this system until $\mathbf{M}$ has been transformed into the identity matrix $\mathbf{I}$ means that the right side identity matrix has become the inverse $\mathbf{M}^{-1}$. Thus, $\mathbf{u}$ and $\mathbf{v}$ are, in fact, not of any particular use; they are merely means for expressing Equation A.38 in a mathematically sound way.

LU decomposition is another method that can be used to compute the inverse efficiently. However, a discussion of Gaussian elimination and LU decomposition is beyond the scope of this text. Virtually any book on linear algebra [477, 478] or numerical methods books, such as the one by Press et al. [635], describe these methods.

Some important rules of computation for the inverse of matrices are:
$i)$ $(\mathbf{M}^{-1})^T = (\mathbf{M}^T)^{-1}$, $\quad ii)$ $(\mathbf{MN})^{-1} = \mathbf{N}^{-1}\mathbf{M}^{-1}$.

Eigenvalue and Eigenvector Computation

The solution to the *eigenvalue* problem has a large range of uses. For example, one application area is the computation of tight bounding volumes (see Section 14.4). The problem is stated as follows:

$$\mathbf{Ax} = \lambda\mathbf{x}, \tag{A.39}$$

where λ is a scalar.[7] The matrix $\mathbf{A}$ has to be square (say of size $n \times n$), and $\mathbf{x} \neq \mathbf{0}$, then, if $\mathbf{x}$ fulfills the above equation, $\mathbf{x}$ is said to be an *eigenvector* to $\mathbf{A}$, and λ is its belonging *eigenvalue*. Rearranging the terms of Equation A.39 yields Equation A.40.

$$(\lambda\mathbf{I} - \mathbf{A})\mathbf{x} = \mathbf{0} \tag{A.40}$$

This equation has a solution if and only if $p_A(\lambda) = \det(\lambda\mathbf{I} - \mathbf{A}) = 0$, where the function $p_A(\lambda)$ is called the characteristic polynomial to $\mathbf{A}$. The

---

[7]We use λ (even though this is not consistent with our notation) because that is what most texts use.

eigenvalues, $\lambda_0, \ldots, \lambda_{n_1}$, are thus solutions to $p_A(\lambda) = 0$. Focus for a while on a particular eigenvalue λ_i to $\mathbf{A}$. Then $\mathbf{x}_i$ is its corresponding eigenvector if $(\lambda_i \mathbf{I} - \mathbf{A})\mathbf{x}_i = 0$, which means that once the eigenvalues have been found, the eigenvectors can be found via Gaussian elimination.

Some theoretical results of great use are: i) $\operatorname{tr}(\mathbf{A}) = \sum_{i=0}^{n-1} a_{ii} = \sum_{i=0}^{n-1} \lambda_i$, ii) $\det(\mathbf{A}) = \prod_{i=0}^{n-1} \lambda_i$, iii) if $\mathbf{A}$ is real (consists of only real values) and is symmetric, i.e., $\mathbf{A} = \mathbf{A}^T$, then its eigenvalues are real and the different eigenvectors are orthogonal.

Orthogonal Matrices

Here, we will shed some light on the concept of an orthogonal matrix, its properties, and its characteristics. A square matrix, $\mathbf{M}$, with only real elements is orthogonal if and only if $\mathbf{M}\mathbf{M}^T = \mathbf{M}^T\mathbf{M} = \mathbf{I}$. That is, when multiplied by its transpose, it yields the identity matrix.

The orthogonality of a matrix, $\mathbf{M}$, has some significant implications such as: i) $|\mathbf{M}| = \pm 1$, ii) $\mathbf{M}^{-1} = \mathbf{M}^T$, iii) $\mathbf{M}^T$ is also orthogonal, iv) $||\mathbf{M}\mathbf{u}|| = ||\mathbf{u}||$, v) $\mathbf{M}\mathbf{u} \perp \mathbf{M}\mathbf{v} \Leftrightarrow \mathbf{u} \perp \mathbf{v}$, vi) if $\mathbf{M}$ and $\mathbf{N}$ are orthogonal, so is $\mathbf{M}\mathbf{N}$.

The standard basis is orthonormal because the basis vectors are mutually orthogonal and of length one. Using the standard basis as a matrix, we can show that the matrix is orthogonal:[8] $\mathbf{E} = (\mathbf{e}_x \quad \mathbf{e}_y \quad \mathbf{e}_z) = \mathbf{I}$, and $\mathbf{I}^T\mathbf{I} = \mathbf{I}$.

To clear up some possible confusion, an orthogonal matrix is not the same as an orthogonal vector set (basis). A set of vectors may be mutually perpendicular, and so be called an orthogonal vector set. But, if these are bound together as a set of row or column vectors making a matrix, this does not automatically make the matrix orthogonal. An orthogonal matrix's transpose must be its inverse. An orthonormal vector set (basis), on the other hand, always forms an orthogonal matrix if the vectors are inserted into the matrix as a set of rows or columns. A better term for an orthogonal matrix would be an orthonormal matrix, since it is always composed of an orthonormal basis, but even mathematics is not always logical.

A.3.2 Change of Base

Assume we have a vector, $\mathbf{v}$, in the standard basis (see Section 1.2.1), described by the coordinate axes $\mathbf{e}_x$, $\mathbf{e}_y$, and $\mathbf{e}_z$. Furthermore, we have another coordinate system described by the arbitrary basis vectors $\mathbf{f}_x$, $\mathbf{f}_y$,

---

[8]Note that the basis is orthonormal, but the matrix is orthogonal, though they mean the same thing.

and $\mathbf{f}_z$ (which must be noncoplanar, i.e., $|\mathbf{f}_x \ \mathbf{f}_y \ \mathbf{f}_z| \neq 0$). How can $\mathbf{v}$ be expressed uniquely in the basis described by $\mathbf{f}_x$, $\mathbf{f}_y$, and $\mathbf{f}_z$? The solution is [477]:

$$\mathbf{F}\mathbf{w} = (\ \mathbf{f}_x \ \ \mathbf{f}_y \ \ \mathbf{f}_z \ )\mathbf{w} = \mathbf{v}$$
$$\Longleftrightarrow \tag{A.41}$$
$$\mathbf{w} = \mathbf{F}^{-1}\mathbf{v}$$

where $\mathbf{w}$ is $\mathbf{v}$ expressed in the new basis, described by $\mathbf{F}$.

A special situation occurs if the matrix $\mathbf{F}$ is orthogonal, which implies that the inverse is easily obtained by $\mathbf{F}^{-1} = \mathbf{F}^T$. Therefore, Equation A.41 simplifies to Equation A.42.

$$\mathbf{w} = \mathbf{F}^T\mathbf{v} = \begin{pmatrix} \mathbf{f}_x^T \\ \mathbf{f}_y^T \\ \mathbf{f}_z^T \end{pmatrix} \mathbf{v} \tag{A.42}$$

Orthogonal coordinate system changes are the most common ones in the context of computer graphics.

A.4 Homogeneous Notation

This section is probably the most important in this chapter, since it influences many areas of computer graphics and is almost never treated in a common linear algebra book.

A point describes a location in space, while a vector describes a direction and has no location. Using 3×3 matrices (or 2×2 for two dimensions), it is possible to perform linear transformations such as rotations, scalings, and shears on coordinates. However, translation cannot be performed using such matrices. This lack is unimportant for vectors, for which translation has no meaning, but translation is meaningful for points.

Homogeneous notation is useful for transforming both vectors and points, and includes the ability to perform translation only on points. It augments 3×3 matrices to the size of 4×4, and three-dimensional points and vectors get one more element. So a homogeneous vector is $\mathbf{p} = (p_x, p_y, p_z, p_w)$. As will soon be made clear, $p_w = 1$ for points, and $p_w = 0$ for vectors. For projections, other values can be used for p_w (see Section 3.5). When $p_w \neq 0$ and $p_w \neq 1$, then the actual point is obtained through *homogenization*, where all components are divided by p_w. This means the point $(p_x/p_w, p_y/p_w, p_z/p_w, 1)$ is obtained.

Equation A.43 shows how a 3×3 matrix, $\mathbf{M}$, is augmented (in the simplest case) into the homogeneous form.

$$\mathbf{M}_{4 \times 4} = \begin{pmatrix} m_{00} & m_{01} & m_{02} & 0 \\ m_{10} & m_{11} & m_{12} & 0 \\ m_{20} & m_{21} & m_{22} & 0 \\ 0 & 0 & 0 & 1 \end{pmatrix} \tag{A.43}$$

Rotation, scaling, and shear matrices can replace $\mathbf{M}$ in the equation above, and affect both vectors and points, as they should. A translation, however, uses the additional elements of the augmented matrix to obtain the goal of the foundation. A typical translation matrix, $\mathbf{T}$, which translates a point by a vector, $\mathbf{t}$, is shown in Equation A.44.

$$\mathbf{T} = \begin{pmatrix} 1 & 0 & 0 & t_x \\ 0 & 1 & 0 & t_y \\ 0 & 0 & 1 & t_z \\ 0 & 0 & 0 & 1 \end{pmatrix}. \tag{A.44}$$

It is quickly verified that a vector $\mathbf{v} = (v_x, v_y, v_z, 0)$ is unaffected by the $\mathbf{Tv}$ transform due to the fact that its last element is 0. If the point $\mathbf{p} = (p_x, p_y, p_z, 1)$ is transformed as $\mathbf{Tp}$, the result is $(p_x + t_x, p_y + t_y, p_z + t_z, 1)$, i.e., $\mathbf{p}$ translated by $\mathbf{t}$.

Matrix-matrix multiplications (and thus concatenations of homogeneous matrices) and matrix-vector multiplications are carried out precisely as usual, and therefore the foundation has been established as desired. In Chapter 3, many kinds of different homogeneous transforms will be introduced and thoroughly dissected.

A.5 Geometry

This section is concerned with presenting some useful geometrical techniques that are used extensively in, for example, Chapter 13.

A.5.1 Lines

Two-Dimensional Lines

For two-dimensional lines, there are two main mathematical descriptions: the implicit form and the explicit form. The latter is parametric, and a typical equation for it is Equation A.45:

$$\mathbf{r}(t) = \mathbf{o} + t\mathbf{d}. \tag{A.45}$$

Here, $\mathbf{o}$ is a point on the line, $\mathbf{d}$ is the direction vector of the line, and t is a parameter that can be used to generate different points, $\mathbf{r}$, on the line.[9]

The implicit form is different in that it cannot generate points explicitly. Assume, instead, that on our line of interest, called L, any point can be described by $\mathbf{p} = (p_x, p_y) = (x, y)$, where the latter coordinate notation is used only in Equation A.46, because this is the line equation form that most people learn first.

$$ax + by + c = 0 \tag{A.46}$$

For $\mathbf{p}$ to lie on the line L, it must fulfill the above equation. Now, if the constants a and b are combined into a vector $\mathbf{n} = (n_x, n_y) = (a, b)$, then Equation A.46 can be expressed using the dot product as

$$\mathbf{n} \cdot \mathbf{p} + c = 0. \tag{A.47}$$

A common task is, naturally, to compute the constants of a line. Looking at Figure A.5 and using its notation, we may see that one way of describing L would be $\mathbf{n} \cdot (\mathbf{p} - \mathbf{q}) = 0$, where $\mathbf{q}$ is another point on the line. Thus, $\mathbf{n}$ must be perpendicular to the line direction, i.e., $\mathbf{n} = (\mathbf{p} - \mathbf{q})^{\perp} = (-(p_y - q_y), p_x - q_x) = (a, b)$, and $c = -\mathbf{q} \cdot \mathbf{n}$. Then, given two points on L, $\mathbf{n} = (a, b)$ and c can be calculated.

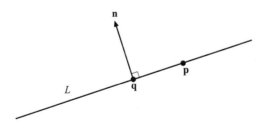

Figure A.5. Notation used for the implicit form of a two-dimensional line equation. L is the line, $\mathbf{p}$ and $\mathbf{q}$ are points on the line, and $\mathbf{n}$ is a vector perpendicular to the direction of L.

---

[9]The points are named $\mathbf{r}$ here because in other chapters the line is usually referred to as a ray.

Rewriting Equation A.47 as a function, $f(\mathbf{p}) = \mathbf{n} \cdot \mathbf{p} + c$, allows some very useful properties to be derived. Nothing is now assumed about $\mathbf{p}$; it can be any point in the two-dimensional plane. First, if again $\mathbf{q} \in L$, the following holds:

1. $f(\mathbf{p}) = 0 \Longleftrightarrow \mathbf{p} \in L$.

2. $f(\mathbf{p}) > 0 \Longleftrightarrow \mathbf{p}$ lies on the same side of the line as the point $\mathbf{q} + \mathbf{n}$.

3. $f(\mathbf{p}) < 0 \Longleftrightarrow \mathbf{p}$ lies on the same side of the line as the point $\mathbf{q} - \mathbf{n}$.

This test is usually called a *half-plane test* and is used in, for example, some point-in-polygon routines (see Section 13.8). Second, $f(\mathbf{p})$ happens to be a measure for the perpendicular distance from $\mathbf{p}$ to L. In fact, it turns out that the *signed distance*, f_s, is found by using Equation A.48.

$$f_s(\mathbf{p}) = \frac{f(\mathbf{p})}{||\mathbf{n}||} \tag{A.48}$$

If $||\mathbf{n}|| = 1$, that is, $\mathbf{n}$ is normalized, then $f_s(\mathbf{p}) = f(\mathbf{p})$.

Three-Dimensional Lines

In three dimensions, the implicit form of a line is often expressed as the intersection between two nonparallel planes. An explicit form is shown in Equation A.49. This equation is heavily used in computing the intersection between a line (or ray) and a three-dimensional surface.

$$\mathbf{r}(t) = \mathbf{o} + t\mathbf{d} \tag{A.49}$$

This is exactly the same equation used for the two-dimensional line, except that the points and the direction vector are now three-dimensional.

The distance from a point $\mathbf{p}$ to $\mathbf{r}(t)$ can be computed by first projecting $\mathbf{p}$ onto $\mathbf{r}(t)$, using Equation A.17. Assuming $\mathbf{d}$ is normalized, this is done by computing the vector $\mathbf{w} = ((\mathbf{p} - \mathbf{o}) \cdot \mathbf{d})\mathbf{d}$. Then the sought-for distance is $||(\mathbf{p} - \mathbf{o}) - \mathbf{w}||$.

A.5.2   Planes

Since the three-dimensional plane is a natural extension of the two-dimensional line, it can be expected that the plane has similar properties as the line. In fact, any hyperplane, which is the name for a plane of an arbitrary dimension, has these similar characteristics. Here, the discussion will be limited to the three-dimensional plane.

First, the plane can be described in both explicit and implicit form. Equation A.50 shows the explicit form of the three-dimensional plane.

$$\mathbf{p}(u, v) = \mathbf{o} + u\mathbf{s} + v\mathbf{t} \tag{A.50}$$

Here, $\mathbf{o}$ is a point lying on the plane, $\mathbf{s}$ and $\mathbf{t}$ are direction vectors that span the plane (i.e., they are noncollinear), and u and v are parameters that generate different points on the plane. The normal of this plane is $\mathbf{s} \times \mathbf{t}$.

The implicit equation for the plane, called π, shown in Equation A.51, is identical to Equation A.47, with the exception that the plane equation is augmented with an extra dimension, and c has been renamed to d.

$$\mathbf{n} \cdot \mathbf{p} + d = 0 \tag{A.51}$$

Again, $\mathbf{n}$ is the normal of the plane, $\mathbf{p}$ is any point on the plane, and d is a constant that determines part of the position of the plane. As was shown above, the normal can be computed using two direction vectors, but it can naturally also be obtained from three noncollinear points, $\mathbf{u}$, $\mathbf{v}$, and $\mathbf{w}$, lying on the plane, as $\mathbf{n} = (\mathbf{u} - \mathbf{w}) \times (\mathbf{v} - \mathbf{w})$. Given $\mathbf{n}$ and a point $\mathbf{q}$ on the plane, the constant is computed as $d = -\mathbf{n} \cdot \mathbf{q}$. The half-plane test is equally valid. By denoting $f(\mathbf{p}) = \mathbf{n} \cdot \mathbf{p} + d$, the same conclusions can be drawn as for the two-dimensional line; that is:

1. $f(\mathbf{p}) = 0 \Longleftrightarrow \mathbf{p} \in \pi$.

2. $f(\mathbf{p}) > 0 \Longleftrightarrow \mathbf{p}$ lies on the same side of the plane as the point $\mathbf{q} + \mathbf{n}$.

3. $f(\mathbf{p}) < 0 \Longleftrightarrow \mathbf{p}$ lies on the same side of the plane as the point $\mathbf{q} - \mathbf{n}$.

The signed distance from an arbitrary point $\mathbf{p}$ to π is obtained by exchanging the two-dimensional parts of Equation A.48 for their three-dimensional counterparts for the plane. Also, it is very easy to interpret the meaning of d using the signed distance formula. This requires inserting the origin, $\mathbf{0}$, into that formula; $f_s(\mathbf{0}) = d$, which means that d is the shortest (signed) distance from the origin to the plane.

A.5.3 Convex Hull

For a set of points, the *convex hull* is defined as the smallest set that satisfies the condition that the straight line between any two points in the set is totally included in the set as well. This holds for any dimension.

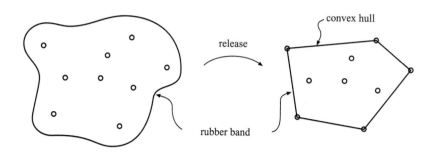

Figure A.6. The rubberband/nail scheme in action. The left figure shows the rubber band before it has been released and the right figure shows the result after. Then the rubber band is a representation of the convex hull of the nails.

In two dimensions, the construction of the convex hull is intuitively illustrated by the rubberband/nail scheme. Imagine that the points are nails in a table, and that a rubber band is held in such a way that its interior includes all nails. The rubber band is then released, and now the rubber band is, in fact, the convex hull of the nails. This is illustrated in Figure A.6.

The convex hull has many areas of use; the construction of bounding volumes is one. The convex hull is, by its definition, the smallest convex volume for a set of points, and is therefore attractive for those computations. Algorithms for computing the convex hull in two and three dimensions can be found in, for example, books by de Berg et al. [56] or O'Rourke [605]. A fast algorithm, called *QuickHull*, is presented by Barber et al. [43].

A.5.4   Miscellaneous

Area Calculation

A parallelogram defined by two vectors, **u** and **v**, starting at the origin, trivially has the area $||\mathbf{u} \times \mathbf{v}|| = ||\mathbf{u}||\,||\mathbf{v}|| \sin \phi$, as shown in Figure A.7.

If the parallelogram is divided by a line from **u** to **v**, two triangles are formed. This means that the area of each triangle is half the area of the parallelogram. So, if a triangle is given by three points, say **p**, **q**, and **r**, its area is:

$$\text{Area}(\triangle \mathbf{pqr}) = \frac{1}{2}||(\mathbf{p} - \mathbf{r}) \times (\mathbf{q} - \mathbf{r})||. \tag{A.52}$$

The signed area of a general two-dimensional polygon can be computed by [605, 660]:

$$\text{Area}(P) = \frac{1}{2} \sum_{i=0}^{n-1} (x_i y_{i+1} - y_i x_{i+1}), \tag{A.53}$$

where n is the number of vertices, and where i is modulo n, so that $x_n = x_0$, etc. This area can be computed with fewer multiplies and potentially more accuracy (though needing a wider range of indices for each term) by the following formula [738]:

$$\text{Area}(P) = \frac{1}{2} \sum_{i=0}^{n-1} (x_i(y_{i+1} - y_{i-1})). \tag{A.54}$$

Volume Calculation

The scalar triple product, from Equation A.18, is sometimes also called the volume formula. Three vectors, $\mathbf{u}$, $\mathbf{v}$ and $\mathbf{w}$, starting at the origin, form a solid, called a parallelepiped, whose volume is given by the equation below. The volume and the notation are depicted in Figure A.7.

$$\text{Volume}(\mathbf{u}, \mathbf{v}, \mathbf{w}) = (\mathbf{u} \times \mathbf{v}) \cdot \mathbf{w} = \det(\mathbf{u}, \mathbf{v}, \mathbf{w}) \tag{A.55}$$

This is a positive value only if the vectors form a positively oriented basis. The formula intuitively explains why the determinant of three vectors is zero if the vectors do not span the entire space $\mathbb{R}^3$: In that case, the volume is zero, meaning that the vectors must lie in the same plane (or one or more of them may be the zero vector).

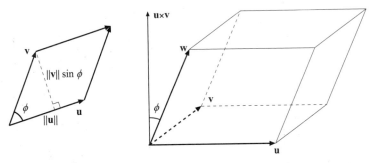

Figure A.7. Left figure: A parallelogram whose area is computed by multiplying the length of the base ($\|\mathbf{u}\|$) with the height ($\|\mathbf{v}\| \sin \phi$). Right figure: The volume of a parallelepiped is given by $(\mathbf{u} \times \mathbf{v}) \cdot \mathbf{w}$.

Further Reading and Resources

For a more thorough treatment of linear algebra, the reader is directed to, for example, the books by Lawson [477] and Lax [478]. Hutson and Pym's book [379] gives an in-depth treatment of all kinds of spaces (and more). A lighter read is Farin and Hansford's *The Geometry Toolbox* [225], which builds up a geometric understanding for transforms, eigenvalues, and much else.

The 30th edition of the *CRC Standard Mathematical Tables and Formulas* [846] is a recent major update of this classic reference. Much of the material in this appendix is included, as well as a huge amount of other mathematical knowledge.

Appendix B
Trigonometry

"Life is good for only two things, discovering mathematics and teaching mathematics."

–Siméon Poisson

This appendix is intended to be a reference to some simple laws of trigonometry as well as some more sophisticated ones. The laws of trigonometry are particularly important tools in computer graphics. One example of their usefulness is that they provide ways to simplify equations and thereby to increase speed.

B.1 Definitions

According to Figure B.1, where $\mathbf{p} = (p_x, p_y)$ is a unit vector, i.e., $||\mathbf{p}|| = 1$, the fundamental trigonometric functions, sin, cos, and tan, are defined by Equation B.1.

$$
\boxed{
\begin{array}{l}
\textbf{Fundamental trigonometric functions :} \\[1em]
\sin\phi = p_y \\[1em]
\cos\phi = p_x \\[1em]
\tan\phi = \dfrac{\sin\phi}{\cos\phi} = \dfrac{p_y}{p_x}
\end{array}
}
\tag{B.1}
$$

The sin, cos, and tan functions can be expanded into MacLaurin series as shown in Equation B.2. MacLaurin series are a special case of the

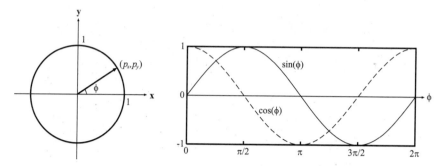

Figure B.1. The geometry for the definition of the sin, cos, and tan functions is shown to the left. The right-hand part of the figure shows $p_x = \cos\phi$ and $p_y' = \cos\phi$, which together traces out the circle.

more general Taylor series. A Taylor series is an expansion about an arbitrary point, while a MacLaurin series always is developed around $x = 0$. MacLaurin series are beneficial because they clarify the origins of some of the derivatives (shown in Equation set B.4).

MacLaurin series :

$$\sin\phi = \phi - \frac{\phi^3}{3!} + \frac{\phi^5}{5!} - \frac{\phi^7}{7!} + \cdots + (-1)^n \frac{\phi^{2n+1}}{(2n+1)!} + \cdots$$

$$\cos\phi = 1 - \frac{\phi^2}{2!} + \frac{\phi^4}{4!} - \frac{\phi^6}{6!} + \cdots + (-1)^n \frac{\phi^{2n}}{(2n)!} + \cdots$$

$$\tan\phi = \phi + \frac{\phi^3}{3} + \frac{2\phi^5}{15} + \cdots + (-1)^{n-1} \frac{2^{2n}(2^{2n}-1)}{(2n)!} B_{2n}\phi^{2n-1} + \cdots$$

$$(B.2)$$

The two first series hold for $-\infty < \phi < \infty$, the last one for $-\pi/2 < \phi < \pi/2$ and B_n is the nth Bernoulli number.[1]

The inverses of the trigonometric functions, arcsin, arccos, and arctan, are defined as in Equation B.3.

---

[1]The Bernoulli numbers can be generated with a recursive formula, where $B_0 = 1$ and then for $k > 1$, $\sum_{j=0}^{k-1} \binom{k}{j} B_j = 0$.

> **Inverses of trigonometric functions :**
>
> $$p_y = \sin\phi \Leftrightarrow \phi = \arcsin p_y, \quad -1 \le p_y \le 1, \quad -\frac{\pi}{2} \le \phi \le \frac{\pi}{2}$$
>
> $$p_x = \cos\phi \Leftrightarrow \phi = \arccos p_x, \quad -1 \le p_x \le 1, \quad 0 \le \phi \le \pi$$
>
> $$\frac{p_y}{p_x} = \tan\phi \Leftrightarrow \phi = \arctan\frac{p_y}{p_x}, \quad -\infty \le \frac{p_y}{p_x} \le \infty, \quad -\frac{\pi}{2} \le \phi \le \frac{\pi}{2}$$

(B.3)

The derivatives of the trigonometric functions and their inverses are summarized below.

> **Trigonometric derivatives :**
>
> $$\frac{d\sin\phi}{d\phi} = \cos\phi$$
>
> $$\frac{d\cos\phi}{d\phi} = -\sin\phi$$
>
> $$\frac{d\tan\phi}{d\phi} = \frac{1}{\cos^2\phi} = 1 + \tan^2\phi$$
>
> $$\frac{d\arcsin t}{dt} = \frac{1}{\sqrt{1-t^2}}$$
>
> $$\frac{d\arccos t}{dt} = -\frac{1}{\sqrt{1-t^2}}$$
>
> $$\frac{d\arctan t}{dt} = \frac{1}{1+t^2}$$

(B.4)

B.2 Trigonometric Laws and Formulae

We begin with some fundamental laws about right triangles. To use the notation from Figure B.2, the following laws apply:

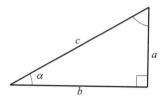

Figure B.2. A right triangle and its notation.

$$
\boxed{
\begin{array}{l}
\textbf{Right triangle laws :} \\[2mm]
\sin \alpha = \dfrac{a}{c} \\[4mm]
\cos \alpha = \dfrac{b}{c} \\[4mm]
\tan \alpha = \dfrac{\sin \alpha}{\cos \alpha} = \dfrac{a}{b}
\end{array}
}
\qquad \text{(B.5)}
$$

$$
\boxed{\textbf{Pythagorean relation :} \quad c^2 = a^2 + b^2} \qquad \text{(B.6)}
$$

For arbitrarily angled triangles, the following well-known rules are valid, using the notation from Figure B.3.

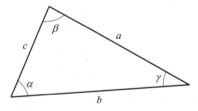

Figure B.3. An arbitrarily angled triangle and its notation.

$$\textbf{Law of sines :} \quad \frac{\sin \alpha}{a} = \frac{\sin \beta}{b} = \frac{\sin \gamma}{c}$$

$$\textbf{Law of cosines :} \quad c^2 = a^2 + b^2 - 2ab \cos \gamma$$

$$\textbf{Law of tangents :} \quad \frac{a+b}{a-b} = \frac{\tan \dfrac{\alpha + \beta}{2}}{\tan \dfrac{\alpha - \beta}{2}}$$

(B.7)

Named after their inventors, the following two formulae are also valid for arbitrarily angled triangles.

$$\textbf{Newton's formula :} \quad \frac{b+c}{a} = \frac{\cos \dfrac{\beta - \gamma}{2}}{\sin \dfrac{\alpha}{2}}$$

$$\textbf{Mollweide's formula :} \quad \frac{b-c}{a} = \frac{\sin \dfrac{\beta - \gamma}{2}}{\cos \dfrac{\alpha}{2}}$$

(B.8)

The definition of the trigonometric functions (Equation B.1) together with the Pythagorean relation (Equation B.6) trivially gives the *trigonometric identity*:

$$\boxed{\textbf{Trigonometric identity :} \quad \cos^2 \phi + \sin^2 \phi = 1} \qquad \text{(B.9)}$$

Here follow some laws that can be exploited to simplify equations and thereby make their implementation more efficient.

Double angle relations :

$$\sin 2\phi = 2 \sin \phi \cos \phi = \frac{2 \tan \phi}{1 + \tan^2 \phi}$$

$$\cos 2\phi = \cos^2 \phi - \sin^2 \phi = 1 - 2 \sin^2 \phi = 2 \cos^2 \phi - 1 = \frac{1 - \tan^2 \phi}{1 + \tan^2 \phi}$$

$$\tan 2\phi = \frac{2 \tan \phi}{1 - \tan^2 \phi}$$

(B.10)

Extensions of the laws above are called the *multiple angle relations*, shown below.

Multiple angle relations :

$$\sin(n\phi) = 2\sin((n-1)\phi)\cos\phi - \sin((n-2)\phi)$$

$$\cos(n\phi) = 2\cos((n-1)\phi)\cos\phi - \cos((n-2)\phi)$$

$$\tan(n\phi) = \frac{\tan((n-1)\phi) + \tan\phi}{1 - \tan((n-1)\phi)\tan\phi}$$

(B.11)

Equations B.12 and B.13 show a collection of laws that we call the *angle sum* and *angle difference relations*.

Angle sum relations :

$$\sin(\phi + \rho) = \sin\phi\cos\rho + \cos\phi\sin\rho$$

$$\cos(\phi + \rho) = \cos\phi\cos\rho - \sin\phi\sin\rho$$

$$\tan(\phi + \rho) = \frac{\tan\phi + \tan\rho}{1 - \tan\phi\tan\rho}$$

(B.12)

Angle difference relations :

$$\sin(\phi - \rho) = \sin\phi\cos\rho - \cos\phi\sin\rho$$

$$\cos(\phi - \rho) = \cos\phi\cos\rho + \sin\phi\sin\rho$$

$$\tan(\phi - \rho) = \frac{\tan\phi - \tan\rho}{1 + \tan\phi\tan\rho}$$

(B.13)

Next follow the *product relations*.

Product relations :

$$\sin \phi \sin \rho = \frac{1}{2}(\cos(\phi - \rho) - \cos(\phi + \rho))$$

$$\cos \phi \cos \rho = \frac{1}{2}(\cos(\phi - \rho) + \cos(\phi + \rho))$$ (B.14)

$$\sin \phi \cos \rho = \frac{1}{2}(\sin(\phi - \rho) + \sin(\phi + \rho))$$

The formulae in Equations B.15 and B.16 go under the names *function sums and differences* and *half-angle relations*.

Function sums and differences :

$$\sin \phi + \sin \rho = 2 \sin \frac{\phi + \rho}{2} \cos \frac{\phi - \rho}{2}$$

$$\cos \phi + \cos \rho = 2 \cos \frac{\phi + \rho}{2} \cos \frac{\phi - \rho}{2}$$

$$\tan \phi + \tan \rho = \frac{\sin(\phi + \rho)}{\cos \phi \cos \rho}$$ (B.15)

$$\sin \phi - \sin \rho = 2 \cos \frac{\phi + \rho}{2} \sin \frac{\phi - \rho}{2}$$

$$\cos \phi - \cos \rho = -2 \sin \frac{\phi + \rho}{2} \sin \frac{\phi - \rho}{2}$$

$$\tan \phi - \tan \rho = \frac{\sin(\phi - \rho)}{\cos \phi \cos \rho}$$

Half-angle relations :

$$\sin \frac{\phi}{2} = \pm \sqrt{\frac{1 - \cos \phi}{2}}$$

$$\cos \frac{\phi}{2} = \pm \sqrt{\frac{1 + \cos \phi}{2}}$$

(B.16)

$$\tan \frac{\phi}{2} = \pm \sqrt{\frac{1 - \cos \phi}{1 + \cos \phi}} = \frac{1 - \cos \phi}{\sin \phi} = \frac{\sin \phi}{1 + \cos \phi}$$

Further Reading and Resources

The first chapter of *Graphics Gems* [261] provides other geometric relationships that are useful in computer graphics. The 30th edition of the *CRC Standard Mathematical Tables and Formulas* [846] includes the formulae in this appendix and much more.

References

[1] "Wildcat's SuperScene Antialiasing," 2001. http://www.3dlabs.com/product/technology/superscene_antialiasing.htm Cited on p. 100

[2] Abrash, Michael, *Michael Abrash's Graphics Programming Black Book, Special Edition*, The Coriolis Group, Inc., Scottsdale, Arizona, 1997. http://www.ddj.com/articles/2001/0165/0165f/0165f.htm Cited on p. 141, 150, 351, 403, 410, 415

[3] Abrash, Michael, "Inside Xbox Graphics," *Dr. Dobb's Journal*, pp. 21–26, August 2000. http://www.ddj.com/documents/s=882/ddj0008a/0008a.htm Cited on p. 697

[4] Agrawala, Maneesh, Ravi Ramamoorthi, Alan Heirich, and Laurent Moll, "Efficient Image-Based Methods for Rendering Soft Shadows," *Computer Graphics (SIGGRAPH 2000 Proceedings)*, pp. 375–384, July 2000. http://graphics.stanford.edu/papers/shadows/ Cited on p. 273

[5] Aila, T., and V. Miettinen, *Umbra Reference Manual*, Hybrid Holding Ltd., Helsinki, Finland, October 2000. http://www.hybrid.fi/umbra/download.html Cited on p. 372, 388, 403

[6] Airey, John M., John H. Rohlf, and Frederick P. Brooks Jr., "Towards Image Realism with Interactive Update Rates in Complex Virtual Building Environments," *Computer Graphics (1990 Symposium on Interactive 3D Graphics)*, vol. 24, no. 2, pp. 41–50, March 1990. Cited on p. 365, 444

[7] Airey, John M., *Increasing Update Rates in the Building Walkthrough System with Automatic Model-Space Subdivision and Potentially Visible Set Calculations*, Ph.D. Thesis, Technical Report TR90-027, Department of Computer Science, University of North Carolina at Chapel Hill, July 1990. Cited on p. 365

[8] Akeley, K., and T. Jermoluk, "High-Performance Polygon Rendering," *Computer Graphics (SIGGRAPH '88 Proceedings)*, pp. 239–246, August 1988. Cited on p. 20

[9] Akeley, Kurt, "The Silicon Graphics 4D/240GTX Superworkstation," *IEEE Computer Graphics and Applications*, vol. 9, no. 4, pp. 71–83, July 1989. Cited on p. 14, 428

[10] Akeley, K., P. Haeberli, and D. Burns, tomesh.c, a C-program on the *SGI Developer's Toolbox CD*, 1990. Cited on p. 460

[11] Akeley, Kurt, "RealityEngine Graphics," *Computer Graphics (SIGGRAPH 93 Proceedings)*, pp. 109–116, August 1993. Cited on p. 93, 424, 428

[12] Akeley, Kurt, and Pat Hanrahan, "Real-Time Graphics Architectures", Course CS448A Notes, Fall 2001. http://graphics.stanford.edu/courses/cs448a-01-fall/ Cited on p. 689, 708, 709, 710, 711

[13] Akenine-Möller, Tomas, "Fast 3D Triangle-Box Overlap Testing," *journal of graphics tools*, vol. 6, no. 1, pp. 29–33, 2001. http://www.acm.org/jgt/papers/AkenineMoller01/ Cited on p. 596, 597

[14] Aliaga, D., J. Cohen, H. Zhang, R. Bastos, T. Hudson, and C. Erikson, "Power Plant Walkthrough: An Integrated System for Massive Model Rendering," Technical Report TR no. 97-018, Computer Science Department, University of North Carolina at Chapel Hill, 1997. ftp://ftp.cs.unc.edu/pub/publications/techreports/FILE.html Cited on p. 401

[15] Aliaga, D., J. Cohen, A. Wilson, H. Zhang, C. Erikson, K. Hoff, T. Hudson, W. Stürzlinger, E. Baker, R. Bastos, M. Whitton, F. Brooks Jr., and D. Manocha, "A Framework for the Real-Time Walkthrough of Massive Models," Technical Report UNC TR no. 98-013, Computer Science Department, University of North Carolina at Chapel Hill, 1998. ftp://ftp.cs.unc.edu/pub/publications/techreports/FILE.html Cited on p. 401

[16] Aliaga, D., J. Cohen, A. Wilson, E. Baker, H. Zhang, C. Erikson, K. Hoff, T. Hudson, W. Stürzlinger, R. Bastos, M. Whitton, F. Brooks, and D. Manocha, "MMR: An Interactive Massive Model Rendering System Using Geometric and Image-Based Acceleration," *Proceedings 1999 Symposium on Interactive 3D Graphics*, pp. 199–206, April 1999. Cited on p. 401

[17] Aliaga, Daniel G., and Anselmo Lastra, "Automatic Image Placement to Provide A Guaranteed Frame Rate," *Computer Graphics (SIGGRAPH 1999 Proceedings)*, pp. 307–316, August 1999. Cited on p. 325, 337

[18] Aliaga, Daniel, Jonathan Cohen, Thomas Funkhouser, Subodh Kumar, Ming C. Lin, David Luebke, Dinesh Manocha, and Andrew Wilson, "Interactive Walkthrough of Large Geometric Datasets," *Course 18 notes at SIGGRAPH 2000*, 2000. http://www.cs.unc.edu/~geom/SIG00_COURSE/ Cited on p. 401

[19] Andújar, Carlos, Carlos Saona-Vázquez, Isabel Navazo, and Pere Brunet, "Integrating Occlusion Culling and Levels of Detail through Hardly-Visible Sets," *Proceedings of Eurographics 2000*, vol. 19, no. 3, pp. 499–506, 2000. http://www.lsi.upc.es/~andujar/ Cited on p. 377

[20] Ankrum, Dennis R., "Viewing Distance at Computer Workstations," *WorkPlace Ergonomics*, pp. 10–12, Sept./Oct. 1996. http://www.ur-net.com/office-ergo/viewing.htm Cited on p. 64

[21] Antonio, Franklin, "Faster Line Segment Intersection," in David Kirk, ed., *Graphics Gems III*, Academic Press, pp. 199–202, 1992. http://www.graphicsgems.org/ Cited on p. 617, 618

[22] Apodaca, Anthony A., and Larry Gritz, *Advanced RenderMan: Creating CGI for Motion Pictures*, Morgan Kaufmann Publishers, Inc., San Francisco, 1999. Cited on p. 71, 232, 287

[23] Appel, Andrew W., with Maia Ginsburg, *Modern Compiler Implementation in C*, Cambridge University Press, 1998. Cited on p. 414, 436

[24] Arenberg, Jeff, "Re: Ray/Triangle Intersection with Barycentric Coordinates," in Eric Haines, ed., *Ray Tracing News*, vol. 1, no. 11, November 1988. http://www.acm.org/tog/resources/RTNews/html/rtnews5b.html Cited on p. 580

[25] Arkin, Esther M., Martin Held, Joseph S. B. Mitchell, and Steven S. Skiena, "Hamiltonian Triangulations for Fast Rendering," *The Visual Computer*, vol. 12, no. 9, pp. 429–444, 1996. Cited on p. 458

[26] Arvo, James, "Backward Ray Tracing," *SIGGRAPH '86 Developments in Ray Tracing course notes*, 1986. Cited on p. 150

[27] Arvo, James, "A Simple Method for Box-Sphere Intersection Testing," in Andrew S. Glassner, ed., *Graphics Gems*, Academic Press, pp. 335–339, 1990. http://www.graphicsgems.org/ Cited on p. 599, 609

[28] Arvo, James, "Ray Tracing with Meta-Hierarchies," *SIGGRAPH '90 Advanced Topics in Ray Tracing course notes*, Volume 24, 1990. http://www.cs.caltech.edu/~arvo/papers.html Cited on p. 564

[29] Arvo, James, ed., *Graphics Gems II*, Academic Press, 1991. http://www.graphicsgems.org/ Cited on p. 66, 435, 629

[30] Ashdown, Ian, *Radiosity: A Programmer's Perspective*, John Wiley & Sons, Inc., 1994. Cited on p. 183, 185, 278, 287

[31] Ashdown, Ian, *Eigenvector Radiosity*, M.Sc. Thesis, Department of Computer Science, University of British Columbia. http://www.cs.ubc.ca/labs/imager/th/ashdown.msc.2001.html Cited on p. 281

[32] Ashikhmin, Michael, Simon Premože, and Peter Shirley, "A Microfacet-Based BRDF Generator," *Computer Graphics (SIGGRAPH 2000 Proceedings)*, pp. 67–74, July 2000. Cited on p. 198, 200

[33] Assarsson, Ulf, and Tomas Möller, "Optimized View Frustum Culling Algorithms for Bounding Boxes," *journal of graphics tools*, vol. 5, no. 1, pp. 9–22, 2000. http://www.ce.chalmers.se/staff/uffe Cited on p. 365, 403, 587, 608, 610, 613

[34] ATI developer web site. http://www.ati.com/na/pages/resource_centre/dev_rel/devrel.html Cited on p. 231, 287

[35] Badouel, Didier, *An Efficient Ray-Polygon Intersection*, in *Graphics Gems*, ed. Andrew S. Glassner, Academic Press, pp. 390–393, 1990. http://www.graphicsgems.org/ Cited on p. 582

[36] Baldwin, Dave, *OpenGL 2.0 Shading Language White Paper*. Issue 1.2, February 2002. http://www.3dlabs.com/support/developer/ogl2 Cited on p. 234

[37] Ballard, Dana H., "Strip Trees: A Hierarchical Representation for Curves," *Graphics and Image Processing*, vol. 24, no. 5, pp. 310–321, May 1981. Cited on p. 646

[38] Banks, David, "Illumination in Diverse Codimensions," *Computer Graphics (SIGGRAPH 94 Proceedings)*, pp. 327–334, July 1994. `http://www.icase.edu/Dienst/UI/2.0/Describe/ncstrl.icase/TR-94-6` Cited on p. 201, 213

[39] Barad, Haim, Mark Atkins, Or Gerlitz, and Daniel Goehring, "Real-Time Procedural Texturing Techniques Using MMX," *Gamasutra*, May 1, 1998. `http://www.gamasutra.com/features/19980501/mmxtexturing_01.htm` Cited on p. 411

[40] Baraff, D., "Curved Surfaces and Coherence for Non-Penetrating Rigid Body Simulation," *Computer Graphics (SIGGRAPH '90 Proceedings)*, pp. 19–28, August 1990. Cited on p. 664

[41] Baraff, D., and A. Witkin, "Dynamic Simulation of Non-Penetrating Flexible Objects," *Computer Graphics (SIGGRAPH '92 Proceedings)*, pp. 303–308, July 1992. Cited on p. 666

[42] Baraff, David, and Andrew Witkin, "Large Steps in Cloth Simulation," *Computer Graphics (SIGGRAPH 98 Proceedings)*, pp. 43–54, July 1998. Cited on p. 666

[43] Barber, C.B., D.P. Dobkin, and H. Huhdanpaa, "The Quickhull Algorithm for Convex Hull," Geometry Center Technical Report GCG53, July 1993. `http://www.geom.umn.edu/software/qhull/` Cited on p. 566, 736

[44] Barequet, G., B. Chazelle, L.J. Guibas, J.S.B. Mitchell, and A. Tal, "BOX-TREE: A Hierarchical Representation for Surfaces in 3D," in *Proceedings of Eurographics '96*, pp. 387–396, 1996. Cited on p. 641, 645

[45] Barkans, Anthony C., "Color Recovery: True-Color 8-Bit Interactive Graphics," *IEEE Computer Graphics and Applications*, vol. 17, no. 1, pp. 67–77, Jan./Feb. 1997. Cited on p. 672

[46] Barkans, Anthony C., "High-Quality Rendering Using the Talisman Architecture," *ACM SIGGRAPH/Eurographics Workshop on Graphics Hardware* Los Angeles, CA, pp. 79–88, August 1997. Cited on p. 141, 316

[47] Bartels, Richard H., John C. Beatty, and Brian A. Barsky, *An Introduction to Splinges for use in Computer Graphics & and Geometric Modeling*, Morgan Kaufmann Publishers, San Mateo, CA, 1987. Cited on p. 529, 530, 555

[48] Bartz, Dirk, James T. Klosowski, and Dirk Staneker, "*k*-DOPs as Tighter Bounding Volumes for Better Occlusion Performance," *Visual Proceedings (SIGGRAPH 2001)*, p. 213, August 2001. Cited on p. 382

[49] Bar-Yehuda, Reuven, and Craig Gotsman, "Time/Space Tradeoffs for Polygon Mesh Rendering," *ACM Transactions on Graphics*, vol. 15, no. 2, pp. 141–152, April 1996. Cited on p. 456

[50] Bastos, Rui, Kenneth Hoff, William Wynn, and Anselmo Lastra, "Increased Photorealism for Interactive Architectural Walkthroughs," *Proceedings 1999 Symposium on Interactive 3D Graphics*, pp. 183–190, April 1999. Cited on p. 79, 212, 244

[51] Baum, Daniel R., Stephen Mann, Kevin P. Smith, and James M. Winget, "Making Radiosity Usable: Automatic Preprocessing and Meshing Techniques for the Generation of Accurate Radiosity Solutions," *Computer Graphics (SIGGRAPH '91 Proceedings)*, pp. 51–60, July 1991. Cited on p. 447

[52] Beaudoin, Philippe, and Juan Guardado, "A Non-Integer Power Function on the Pixel Shader," in Engel, Wolfgang, ed., *ShaderX*, Wordware, May 2002. http://www.shaderx.com/ Cited on p. 226, 227

[53] Bec, Xavier, "Faster Refraction Formula, and Transmission Color Filtering," in Eric Haines, ed., *Ray Tracing News*, vol. 10, no. 1, January 1997. http://www.acm.org/tog/resources/RTNews/html/rtnv10n1.html Cited on p. 246

[54] Beers, Andrew C., Maneesh Agrawala, and Navin Chaddha, "Rendering from Compressed Textures," *Computer Graphics (SIGGRAPH 96 Proceedings)*, pp. 373–378, August 1996. Cited on p. 142

[55] Bennebroek K., I. Ernst, H. Rüsseler, and O. Wittig, "Design principles of hardware-based phong shading and bump-mapping," *Computers & Graphics*, vol. 21 no. 2, pp. 143–149, March 1997. Cited on p. 176, 181

[56] de Berg, M., M. van Kreveld, M. Overmars, and O. Schwarzkopf, *Computational Geometry—Algorithms and Applications*, second edition, Springer-Verlag, Berlin, 2000. Cited on p. 442, 443, 459, 583, 736

[57] Bergman, L. D., H. Fuchs, E. Grant, and S. Spach, "Image Rendering by Adaptive Refinement," *Computer Graphics (SIGGRAPH '86 Proceedings)*, pp. 29–37, August 1986. Cited on p. 100, 340

[58] Bestimt, Jason, and Bryant Freitag, "Real-Time Shadow Casting Using Shadow Volumes," *Gamasutra*, Nov. 1999. http://www.gamasutra.com/features/19991115/bestimt_freitag_03.htm Cited on p. 264

[59] Bier, Eric A., and Kenneth R. Sloan, Jr., "Two-Part Texture Mapping," *IEEE Computer Graphics and Applications*, vol. 6, no. 9, pp. 40–53, September 1986. Cited on p. 120, 125

[60] Biermann, Henning, Adi Levin, and Denis Zorin, "Piecewise Smooth Subdivision Surface with Normal Control," *Computer Graphics (SIGGRAPH 2000 Proceedings)*, pp. 113–120, July 2000. Cited on p. 546, 555

[61] Bigos, Andrew, "Avoiding Buffer Clears," *journal of graphics tools*, vol. 1, no. 1, pp. 19–20, 1996. Cited on p. 420

[62] Bilodeau, Bill, with Mike Songy, "Real Time Shadows," *Creativity '99*, Creative Labs Inc. sponsored game developer conferences, Los Angeles, California, and Surrey, England, May 1999. Cited on p. 264

[63] Birn, Jeremy, *Digital Lighting & Rendering*, New Riders Publishing, 2000. http://www.3drender.com/ Cited on p. 81

[64] Bischoff, Stephan, Leif P. Kobbelt, and Hans-Peter Seidel, "Towards Hardware Implementation of Loop Subdivision," *ACM SIGGRAPH/Eurographics Workshop on Graphics Hardware*, pp. 41–50, 2000. http://www.mpi-sb.mpg.de/~kobbelt/publist.html Cited on p. 555

[65] Bishop, L., D. Eberly, T. Whitted, M. Finch, and M. Shantz, "Designing a PC Game Engine," *IEEE Computer Graphics and Applications*, pp. 46–53, Jan./Feb. 1998. http://computer.org/cga/cg1998/g1toc.htm Cited on p. 610, 613, 620, 666

[66] Bittner, Jiří, and Jan Přikryl, "Exact Regional Visibility using Line Space Partitioning," Technical Report TR-186-2-01-06, Institute of Computer Graphics and Algorithms, Vienna University of Technology, March 2001 Cited on p. 371, 389

[67] Bittner, Jiří, Peter Wonka, and Michael Wimmer, "Visibility Preprocessing for Urban Scenes using Line Space Subdivision," *Pacific Graphics 2001*, pp. 276–284, October 2001. Cited on p. 371

[68] Blinn, J.F., and M.E. Newell, "Texture and reflection in computer generated images," *Communications of the ACM*, vol. 19, no. 10, pp. 542–547, October 1976. Cited on p. 153, 154, 181

[69] Blinn, James F., "Models of Light Reflection for Computer Synthesized Pictures," *ACM Computer Graphics (SIGGRAPH '77 Proceedings)*, pp. 192–198, July 1977. Cited on p. 77, 79

[70] Blinn, James, "Simulation of wrinkled surfaces," *Computer Graphics (SIGGRAPH '78 Proceedings)*, pp. 286–292, August 1978. Cited on p. 84, 166, 548

[71] Blinn, James F., "A Generalization of Algebraic Surface Drawing," *ACM Transactions on Graphics*, vol. 1, no. 3, pp. 235–256, 1982. Cited on p. 526

[72] Blinn, Jim, "Me and My (Fake) Shadow," *IEEE Computer Graphics and Applications*, vol. 8, no. 1, pp. 82–86, January 1988. Also collected in [76]. Cited on p. 250, 253

[73] Blinn, Jim, "Dirty Pixels," *IEEE Computer Graphics and Applications*, vol. 9, no. 4, pp. 100–105, July 1989. Also collected in [77]. Cited on p. 114

[74] Blinn, Jim, "A Trip Down the Graphics Pipeline: Line Clipping," *IEEE Computer Graphics and Applications*, vol. 11, no. 1, pp. 98–105, January 1991. Also collected in [76]. Cited on p. 17

[75] Blinn, Jim, "Hyperbolic Interpolation," *IEEE Computer Graphics and Applications*, vol. 12, no. 4, pp. 89–94, July 1992. Also collected in [76]. Cited on p. 681, 682

[76] Blinn, Jim, *Jim Blinn's Corner: A Trip Down the Graphics Pipeline*, Morgan Kaufmann Publishers, Inc., San Francisco, 1996. Cited on p. 24, 360, 682, 752

[77] Blinn, Jim, *Jim Blinn's Corner: Dirty Pixels*, Morgan Kaufmann Publishers, Inc., San Francisco, 1998. Cited on p. 114, 752

[78] Blinn, Jim, "A Ghost in a Snowstorm," *IEEE Computer Graphics and Applications*, vol. 18, no. 1, pp. 79–84, Jan/Feb 1998. Cited on p. 112

[79] Blinn, Jim, "W Pleasure, W Fun," *IEEE Computer Graphics and Applications*, vol. 18, no. 3, pp. 78–82, May/June 1998. Cited on p. 675, 682

[80] Blinn, Jim, "Optimizing C++ Vector Expressions," *IEEE Computer Graphics & Applications*, vol. 20, no. 4, pp. 97–203, 2000. Cited on p. 413

[81] Bloom, Charles, "The Genesis Terrain Renderer Technology," Dec. 1999. http://www.cbloom.com/3d Cited on p. 479

[82] Bloom, Charles, "Algorithm for Fast Animating Subdivision Surfaces," May 2000. http://www.cbloom.com/3d Cited on p. 552

[83] Bloom, Charles, "The Poly Pipeline," July 2000. http://www.cbloom.com/3d Cited on p. 215

[84] Bloom, Charles, "View Independent Progressive Meshes (VIPM)," June 2000. http://www.cbloom.com/3d Cited on p. 472, 474, 477, 479

[85] Bloom, Charles, "VIPM Advanced Topics," Oct. 2000. http://www.cbloom.com/3d Cited on p. 394, 475

[86] Bloom, Charles, "Advanced Techniques in Shadow Mapping," June 2001. http://www.cbloom.com/3d Cited on p. 261, 275, 276

[87] Bloomenthal, Jules, "Polygonization of Implicit Surfaces," *Computer-Aided Geometric Design*, vol. 5, no. 4, pp. 341–355, 1988. Cited on p. 527
http://www.unchainedgeometry.com/jbloom/papers/index.html

[88] Bloomenthal, Jules, "An Implicit Surface Polygonizer," in Paul S. Heckbert, ed., *Graphics Gems IV*, Academic Press, pp. 324–349, 1994. http://www.unchainedgeometry.com/jbloom/papers/index.html, http://www.graphicsgems.org/ Cited on p. 527

[89] Bloomenthal, Jules, ed., *Introduction to Implicit Surfaces*, Morgan Kaufmann Publishers, Inc., San Francisco, 1997. Cited on p. 343, 439, 526, 527, 555, 561

[90] Blow, Jonathan, "Implementing a Texture Caching System," *Game Developer*, vol. 5, no. 4, pp. 46–56, April 1998. Cited on p. 141, 142

[91] Blow, Jonathan, "Terrain Rendering at High Levels of Detail," *Game Developers Conference*, San Jose, March 2000. http://www.bolt-action.com/dl_papers.html Cited on p. 477

[92] Blow, Jonathan, "Mipmapping, Part 1," *Game Developer*, vol. 8, no. 12, pp. 13–17, Dec. 2001. http://www.gdmag.com/code.htm Cited on p. 134

[93] Blow, Jonathan, "Mipmapping, Part 2," *Game Developer*, vol. 9, no. 1, pp. 16–19, Jan. 2002. http://www.gdmag.com/code.htm Cited on p. 134

[94] Bobic, Nick, "Advanced Collision Detection Techniques," *Gamasutra*, March 2000. http://www.gamasutra.com/features/20000330/bobic_01.htm Cited on p. 627, 628

[95] Bogomjakov, Alexander, and Craig Gotsman, "Universal Rendering Sequences for Transparent Vertex Caching of Progressive Meshes," *Graphics Interface 2001*, Ottawa, Canada, pp. 81–90, June 2001. http://www.graphicsinterface.org/ Cited on p. 463

[96] Bolz, Jeffrey, and Peter Schröder, "Rapid Evaluation of Catmull-Clark Subdivision Surfaces," *7th International Conference on 3D Web Technology*, February 2002. http://multires.caltech.edu/pubs/fastsubd Cited on p. 552, 553

[97] Booth, Rick, *Inner Loops*, Addison-Wesley, Reading, Massachusetts, 1997. Cited on p. 411, 413, 415

[98] Brennan, Chris, "Accurate Environment Mapped Reflections and Refractions by Adjusting for Object Distance," in Engel, Wolfgang, ed., *ShaderX*, Wordware, May 2002. http://www.shaderx.com/ Cited on p. 247, 269

[99] Brennan, Chris, "Diffuse Cube Mapping," in Engel, Wolfgang, ed., *ShaderX*, Wordware, May 2002. http://www.shaderx.com/ Cited on p. 212

[100] Brennan, Chris, "Shadow Volume Extrusion using a Vertex Shader," in Engel, Wolfgang, ed., *ShaderX*, Wordware, May 2002. http://www.shaderx.com/ Cited on p. 268

[101] Bresenham, J.E., "Algorithm for Computer Control of a Digital Plotter," *IBM Systems Journal*, vol. 4, no. 1, pp. 25–30, 1965. Cited on p. 9

[102] Brickhill, David, "Practical Implementation Techniques for Multiresolution Subdivision Surfaces," *Game Developers Conference*, pp. 131–135, March 2001. http://www.gdconf.com/archives/proceedings/2001/prog_papers.html Cited on p. 552

[103] Brinkmann, Ron, *The Art and Science of Digital Compositing*, Morgan Kaufmann Publishers Inc., San Francisco, 1999. Cited on p. 102, 104, 105

[104] Brotman, Lynne Shapiro, and Norman Badler, "Generating Soft Shadows with a Depth Buffer Algorithm," *IEEE Computer Graphics & Applications*, vol. 4, no. 10, pp. 71–81, 1984 Cited on p. 269

[105] Buchanan, J.W., and M.C. Sousa, "The edge buffer: A Data Structure for Easy Silhouette Rendering," *Proceedings of the First International Symposium on Non-photorealistic Animation and Rendering (NPAR)*, pp. 39–42, June 2000. http://www.red3d.com/cwr/npr/ Cited on p. 301

[106] Burwell, John M., "Redefining High Performance Computer Image Generation," Proceedings of the IMAGE Conference, Scottsdale, Arizona, June 1996. Cited on p. 420, 701

[107] Bushnell, Jim, and Jason L. Mitchell, "Advanced Mulitexturing Practice with DirectX 6 and OpenGL," *Game Developers Conference*, March, 1999. http://www.users.qwest.net/~jlmitchell1/ Cited on p. 164

[108] Cabral, Brian, Marc Olano, and Phillip Nemec, "Reflection Space Image Based Rendering," *Computer Graphics (SIGGRAPH 99 Proceedings)*, pp. 165–170, August 1999. http://www.sgi.com/software/clearcoat/tech_info.html Cited on p. 209

[109] *cacheprof*, http://www.cacheprof.org/ Cited on p. 412

[110] Calver, Dean, "Vertex Decompression Using Vertex Shaders," in Engel, Wolfgang, ed., *ShaderX*, Wordware, May 2002. http://www.shaderx.com/ Cited on p. 416

[111] Cameron, S., "Enhancing GJK: Computing Minimum and Penetration Distance Between Convex Polyhedra," *International Conference on Robotics and Automation*, pp. 3112–3117, 1997. http://users.comlab.ox.ac.uk/stephen.cameron/distances.html Cited on p. 662

[112] Card, Drew, and Jason L. Mitchell, "Non-Photorealistic Rendering with Pixel and Vertex Shaders," in Engel, Wolfgang, ed., *ShaderX*, Wordware, May 2002. http://www.shaderx.com/ Cited on p. 290, 291, 299, 300, 301, 302, 306

[113] Carpenter, Loren, "The A-buffer, an Antialiased Hidden Surface Method," *Computer Graphics (SIGGRAPH '84 Proceedings)*, pp. 103–108, July 1984. Cited on p. 94

[114] Catmull, E., and R. Rom, "A Class of Local Interpolating Splines," *Computer Aided Geometric Design*, edited by R. Barnhill and R. Riesenfeld, Academic Press, pp. 317–326, 1974. Cited on p. 495

[115] Catmull, E. E., *A Subdivision Algorithm for Computer Display fo Curved Surfaces*, Ph.D. Thesis, University of Utah, December 1974. Cited on p. 515, 713

[116] Catmull, Edwin, "Computer Display of Curved Surfaces," *Proceedings of the IEEE Conference on Computer Graphics, Pattern Recognition and Data Structures*, Los Angeles, pp. 11–17, May 1975. Cited on p. 20

[117] Catmull, E., and J. Clark, "Recursively Generated B-Spline Surfaces on Arbitrary Topological Meshes," *Computer-Aided Design*, vol. 10, no. 6, pp. 350–355, September 1978. Cited on p. 543, 545

[118] Chaikin, G., "An Algorithm for High Speed Curve Generation," *Computer Graphics and Image Processing*, vol. 4, no. 3, 1974. Cited on p. 528

[119] Chang, Chun-Fa, Gary Bishop, Anselmo Lastra, "LDI Tree: A Hierarchical Representation for Image-based Rendering," *Computer Graphics (SIGGRAPH 99 Proceedings)*, pp. 291–298, August, 1999. Cited on p. 334

[120] Chambers, Mike, "Occlusion Culling," *nV News web site*, July 2001. http://www.nvnews.net/previews/geforce3/occlusion_culling.shtml Cited on p. 423

[121] Chen, S. E., "Quicktime VR - An Image-Based Approach to Virtual Environment Navigation," *Computer Graphics (SIGGRAPH 95 Proceedings)*, pp. 29–38, August 1995. Cited on p. 316

[122] Chhugani, Jatin, and Subodh Kumar, "View-dependent Adaptive Tessellation of Spline Surfaces," *Proceedings 2001 Symposium on Interactive 3D Graphics*, pp. 59–62 March 2001. Cited on p. 522

[123] Chow, Mike M., "Using Strips for Higher Game Performance," Presentation at *Meltdown X99*. Cited on p. 460

[124] Chung, A.J., and A.J. Field, "A Simple Recursive Tessellator for Adaptive Surface Triangulation," *journal of graphics tools*, vol. 5, no. 3, pp. 1–9, 2000. Cited on p. 516, 518

[125] Cignoni, P., C. Montani, and R. Scopigno, "Triangulating Convex Polygons Having T-Vertices," *journal of graphics tools*, vol. 1, no. 2, pp. 1–4, 1996. Cited on p. 447

[126] Clark, James H., "Hierarchical Geometric Models for Visible Surface Algorithms," *Communications of the ACM*, vol. 19, no. 10, pp. 547–554, October 1976. Cited on p. 363

[127] Clay, Sharon R., "Optimization for Real-Time Graphics Applications," Silicon Graphics Inc., February 1996. http://www.sgi.com/software/performer/presentations/tune_wp.pdf Cited on p. 428

[128] *CodeAnalyst*, AMD Corporation, http://www.amd.com/ Cited on p. 407, 436

[129] Coelho, Rohan, and Maher Hawash, *DirectX, RDX, RSZ, and MMX Technology*, Addison-Wesley, Reading, Massachusetts, 1998. Includes VTune evaluation version. New chapters 24 and 25 are available online at http://www.awl.com Cited on p. 315, 435

[130] Cohen, Jonathan D., Ming C. Lin, Dinesh Manocha, and Madhave Ponamgi, "I-COLLIDE: An Interactive and Exact Collision Detection System for Large-Scaled Environments," *Proceedings 1995 Symposium on Interactive 3D Graphics*, pp. 189–196, 1995. http://www.cs.unc.edu/~geom/ Cited on p. 653, 656

[131] Cohen, Jonathan D., Marc Olano, and Dinesh Manocha, "Appearance-Preserving Simplification," *Computer Graphics (SIGGRAPH 98 Proceedings)*, pp. 115–122, July 1998. http://www.cs.unc.edu/~geom/APS/ Cited on p. 171, 468

[132] Cohen, Jonathan, Chris Tchou, Tim Hawkins, and Paul Debevec, "Realtime High Dynamic Range Texture Mapping," *12th Eurographics Workshop on Rendering*, pp. 309–316, June 2001. http://www.debevec.org/~debevec/Publications/ Cited on p. 213

[133] Cohen, Michael F., and John R. Wallace, *Radiosity and Realistic Image Synthesis*, Academic Press Professional, Boston, 1993. Cited on p. 183, 186, 278, 279, 440

[134] Cohen-Or, Daniel, Yiorgos Chrysanthou, Frédo Durand, Ned Greene, Vladlen Kulton, and Cláudio T. Silva, "Visibility, Problems, Techniques and Applications," *Course 30 notes at SIGGRAPH 2001*, 2001. Cited on p. 403, 768

[135] Cohen-Or, Daniel, Yiorgos Chrysanthou, Cláudio T. Silva, and Frédo Durand, "A Survey of Visibility for Walkthrough Applications," accepted for publication, *IEEE Transactions on Visualization and Computer Graphics*, 2002. Cited on p. 358, 403

[136] Cok, Keith, Roger Corron, Bob Kuehne, Thomas True, "Developing Efficient Graphics Software: The Yin and Yang of Graphics," *Course 6 notes at SIGGRAPH 2000*, 2000. http://www.sgi.com/software/opengl/advanced00/notes/00_yin_yang.pdf Cited on p. 410, 420, 424

[137] Columbia-Utrecht Reflectance and Texture Database (CUReT). http://www.cs.columbia.edu/CAVE/curet/ Cited on p. 202

[138] Cook, Robert L., and Kenneth E. Torrance, "A Reflectance Model for Computer Graphics," *Computer Graphics (SIGGRAPH '81 Proceedings)*, pp. 307–316, July 1981. Cited on p. 195, 199, 200, 204

[139] Cook, Robert L., and Kenneth E. Torrance, "A Reflectance Model for Computer Graphics," *ACM Transactions on Graphics*, vol. 1, no. 1, pp. 7–24, January 1982. Cited on p. 195, 199, 200

[140] Cook, Robert L., "Shade Trees," *Computer Graphics (SIGGRAPH '84 Proceedings)*, pp. 223–231, July 1984. Cited on p. 176, 232, 233, 469, 547

[141] Cook, Robert L., "Stochastic Sampling in Computer Graphics," *ACM Transactions on Graphics*, vol. 5, no. 1, pp. 51–72, January 1986. Cited on p. 100

[142] Cook, Robert L., Loren Carpenter, and Edwin Catmull, "The Reyes Image Rendering Architecture," *Computer Graphics (SIGGRAPH '87 Proceedings)*, pp. 95–102, July 1987. Cited on p. 71

[143] Coorg, S., and S. Teller, "Real-Time Occlusion Culling for Models with Large Occluders," *Proceedings 1997 Symposium on Interactive 3D Graphics*, pp. 83–90, April 1997. Cited on p. 397

[144] Cornell University Program of Computer Graphics Measurement Data. http://www.graphics.cornell.edu/online/measurements/ Cited on p. 202

[145] Cormen, T.H., C.E. Leiserson, and R. Rivest, *Introduction to Algorithms*, MIT Press, Inc., Cambridge, Massachusetts, 1990. Cited on p. 347, 356, 363, 460

[146] Courshesnes, Martin, Pascal Volino, and Nadia Magnenat Thalmann, "Versatile and Efficient Techniques for Simulating Cloth and Other Deformable Objects," *Computer Graphics (SIGGRAPH 95 Proceedings)*, pp. 137–144, August 1995. Cited on p. 666

[147] Cox, Michael, and Pat Hanrahan, "Pixel Merging for Object-Parallel Rendering: a Distributed Snooping Algorithm", *ACM SIGGRAPH Symposium on Parallel Rendering*, pp. 49–56, Nov. 1993. Cited on p. 422

[148] Cox, Michael, David Sprague, John Danskin, Rich Ehlers, Brian Hook, Bill Lorensen, and Gary Tarolli, "Developing High-Performance Graphics Applications for the PC Platform," *Course 29 notes at SIGGRAPH 98*, 1998. Cited on p. 145, 424, 676, 677, 687

[149] Cripe, Brian and Thomas Gaskins, "The DirectModel Toolkit: Meeting the 3D Graphics Needs of Technical Applications," *Hewlett-Packard Journal*, pp. 19–27, May 1998. http://www.hp.com/hpj/98may/ma98a3.htm Cited on p. 345

[150] Crow, Franklin C., "Shadow Algorithms for Computer Graphics," *Computer Graphics (SIGGRAPH '77 Proceedings)*, pp. 242–248, July 1977. Cited on p. 261

[151] Crow, Franklin C., "Summed-Area Tables for Texture Mapping," *Computer Graphics (SIGGRAPH '84 Proceedings)*, pp. 207–212, July 1984. Cited on p. 137

[152] Cruz-Neira, Carolina, Daniel J. Sandin, and Thomas A. DeFanti, "Surround-screen Projection-based Virtual Reality: The Design and Implementation of the CAVE," *Computer Graphics (SIGGRAPH 93 Proceedings)*, pp. 135–142, August 1993. http://www.ee.iastate.edu/~cruz/sig93.paper.html Cited on p. 63, 678

[153] Culler, David E., and Jaswinder Pal Singh, with Anoop Gupta, *Parallel Computer Architecture: A Hardware/Software Approach*, Morgan Kaufmann Publishers Inc., San Francisco, 1998. Cited on p. 434, 436

[154] Cunnif, R., "Visualize fx Graphics Scalable Architechture," *Hot3D Proceedings, ACM SIGGRAPH/Eurographics Workshop on Graphics Hardware*, Switzerland, August 2000. Cited on p. 382

[155] Cunningham, Steve, "3D Viewing and Rotation using Orthonormal Bases," in Andrew S. Glassner, ed., *Graphics Gems*, Academic Press, pp. 516–521, 1990. http://www.graphicsgems.org/ Cited on p. 42

[156] Curtis, Cassidy, "Loose and Sketchy Animation," *SIGGRAPH 98 Technical Sketch*, p. 317, 1998. http://www.cs.washington.edu/homes/cassidy/loose/ Cited on p. 307

[157] Cychosz, J.M. and W.N. Waggenspack Jr., "Intersecting a Ray with a Cylinder," in Paul S. Heckbert, ed., *Graphics Gems IV*, Academic Press, pp. 356–365, 1994. http://www.graphicsgems.org/ Cited on p. 572

[158] Cyrus, M., and J. Beck, "Generalized two- and three-dimensional clipping," *Computers and Graphics*, vol. 3, pp. 23–28, 1978. Cited on p. 572

[159] Dam, Erik B., Martin Koch, and Martin Lillholm, "Quaternions, Interpolation and Animation," Technical Report DIKU-TR-98/5, Department of Computer Science, University of Copenhagen, July 1998. http://ftp.diku.dk/students/myth/quat.html Cited on p. 50

[160] Davis, Douglass, William Ribarsky, T.Y. Kiang, Nickolas Faust, and Sean Ho, "Real-Time Visualization of Scalably Large Collections of Heterogeneous Objects," *IEEE Visualization*, pp. 437–440, 1999. Cited on p. 401

[161] Dawson, Bruce, "What Happened to My Colours!?!" *Game Developers Conference*, pp. 251–268, March 2001. http://www.gdconf.com/archives/proceedings/2001/prog_papers.html Cited on p. 193, 671

[162] Debevec, Paul E., "Rendering Synthetic Objects into Real Scenes: Bridging Traditional and Image-Based Graphics with Global Illumination and High Dynamic Range Photography," *Computer Graphics (SIGGRAPH 98 Proceedings)*, pp. 189–198, July 1998. http://www.debevec.org/~debevec/Research/IBL/ Cited on p. 159, 212

[163] Decaudin, Philippe, "Cartoon-Looking Rendering of 3D-Scenes," Technical Report INRIA 2919, Université de Technologie de Compiègne, France, June 1996. Cited on p. 299, 300

[164] Decoret, Xavier, Gernot Schaufler, François Sillion, and Julie Dorsey, "Multi-layered Impostors for Accelerated Rendering," *Proceedings of Eurographics '99*, vol. 18, no. 3, pp. 61–72, 1999. Cited on p. 336

[165] Deering, Michael F., and Scott R. Nelson, "Leo: A System for Cost Effective 3D Shaded Graphics," *Computer Graphics (SIGGRAPH 93 Proceedings)*, pp. 101–108, August 1993. Cited on p. 456

[166] Deering, Michael, "Geometry Compression," *Computer Graphics (SIGGRAPH 95 Proceedings)*, pp. 13–20, August 1995. Cited on p. 416

[167] DeLoura, Mark A., "An In-Depth Look at Bicubic Bézier Surfaces", *Gamasutra*, October 1999. `http://www.gamasutra.com/features/19991027/deloura_01.htm` Cited on p. 516

[168] DeLoura, Mark, ed., *Game Programming Gems*, Charles River Media, 2000. Cited on p. 435

[169] DeLoura, Mark, ed., *Game Programming Gems II*, Charles River Media, 2001. Cited on p. 287, 435

[170] DeLoura, Mark, ed., *Game Programming Gems III*, Charles River Media, 2002. Cited on p. 287, 435

[171] DeRose, T., M. Kass, and T. Truong, "Subdivision Surfaces in Character Animation," *Computer Graphics (SIGGRAPH 98 Proceedings)*, pp. 85–94, July 1998. Cited on p. 543, 547, 550

[172] Diefenbach, Paul J., "Pipeline Rendering: Interaction and Realism through Hardware-based Multi-pass Rendering," Ph.D. Thesis, University of Pennsylvania, 1996. `http://www.cis.upenn.edu/~diefenba/home.html` Cited on p. 247, 286

[173] Diefenbach, Paul J., and Norman I. Badler, "Multi-Pass Pipeline Rendering: Realism for Dynamic Environments," *Proceedings 1997 Symposium on Interactive 3D Graphics*, pp. 59–70, April 1997. `http://www.cis.upenn.edu/~diefenba/home.html` Cited on p. 103, 144, 163, 233, 243

[174] Dietrich, Sim, "Attenuation Maps," in Mark DeLoura, ed., *Game Programming Gems*, Charles River Media, pp. 543–548, 2000. Cited on p. 108, 152, 171

[175] Dietrich, Sim, "Hardware Bump Mapping," in Mark DeLoura, ed., *Game Programming Gems*, Charles River Media, pp. 555–561, 2000. Cited on p. 168, 170, 173

[176] Dietrich, D. Sim, Jr., "Practical Priority Buffer Shadows," in Mark DeLoura, ed., *Game Programming Gems 2*, Charles River Media, pp. 481–487, 2001. Cited on p. 274, 275

[177] Dingliana, John, and Carol O'Sullivan, "Graceful Degradation of Collision Handling in Physically Based Animation," *Computer Graphics Forum* (Proceedings of Eurographics 2000), vol. 19, no. 3, pp. 239–247, 2000. Cited on p. 664, 665

[178] Dingliana, John, and Carol O'Sullivan, "Collisions and Adaptive Level of Detail," *Visual Proceedings (SIGGRAPH 2001)*, p. 156, August 2001. Cited on p. 659

[179] Dippé, Mark A. Z., and Erling Henry Wold, "Antialiasing Through Stochastic Sampling," *Computer Graphics (SIGGRAPH '85 Proceedings)*, pp. 69–78, July 1985. Cited on p. 100

[180] "DirectX 8.1 SDK," Microsoft, 2001. `http://msdn.microsoft.com/directx` Cited on p. 69, 107, 141, 143, 146, 216, 318, 466

[181] Do Carmo, Manfred P., *Differential Geometry of Curves and Surfaces*, Prentice-Hall, Inc., Englewoods Cliffs, New Jersey, 1976. Cited on p. 50

[182] Dobashi, Yoshinori, Kazufumi Kaneda, Hideo Yamashita, Tsuyoshi Okita, and Tomoyuki Nishita, "A Simple, Efficient Method for Realistic Animation of Clouds," *Computer Graphics (SIGGRAPH 2000 Proceedings)*, pp. 19–28, July 2000. Cited on p. 322

[183] Doo, D., and M. Sabin, "Behaviour of Recursive Division Surfaces Near Extraordinary Points," *Computer-Aided Design*, vol. 10, no. 6, pp. 356–360, September 1978. Cited on p. 543

[184] Dougan, Carl, "The Parallel Transport Frame," in Mark DeLoura, ed., *Game Programming Gems 2*, Charles River Media, pp. 215–219, 2001. Cited on p. 66

[185] Downs, Laura, Tomas Möller, and Carlo Séquin, "Occlusion Horizons for Driving through Urban Scenery," *Proceedings 2001 Symposium on Interactive 3D Graphics*, pp. 121–124, March 2001. Cited on p. 373, 376

[186] Duchaineau, Mark A., Murray Wolinsky, David E. Sigeti, Mark C. Miller, Charles Aldrich, and Mark B. Mineev-Weinstein, "ROAMing Terrain: Real-time Optimally Adapting Meshes," *IEEE Visualization '97*, pp. 81–88, 1997. Cited on p. 476

[187] Duff, Tom, "Compositing 3-D Rendered Images," *Computer Graphics (SIGGRAPH '85 Proceedings)*, pp. 41–44, July 1985. Cited on p. 102

[188] Dumont, Reynald, Fabio Pellacini, and James A. Ferwerda, "A Perceptually-Based Texture Caching Algorithm for Hardware-Based Rendering," *12th Eurographics Workshop on Rendering*, pp. 246–253, June 2001. http://www.graphics.cornell.edu/pubs/2001/DPF01.html Cited on p. 142

[189] Durand, Frédo, George Drettakis, and Claude Puech, "The Visibility Skeleton: A Powerful and Efficient Multi-Purpose Global Visibility Tool," *Computer Graphics (SIGGRAPH 97 Proceedings)*, pp. 89–100, August 1997. http://graphics.lcs.mit.edu/~fredo/ Cited on p. 403

[190] Durand, Frédo, George Drettakis, and Claude Puech, "The 3D Visibility Complex: a unified data–structure for global visibility of scenes of polygons and smooth objects," *Canadian Conference on Computational Geometry*, pp. 153–158, August 1997. http://graphics.lcs.mit.edu/~fredo/ Cited on p. 403

[191] Durand, Frédo, *3D Visibility: Analytical Study and Applications*, Ph.D. Thesis, Université Joseph Fourier, Grenoble, July 1999. Cited on p. 403

[192] Durand, Frédo, and Julie Dorsey, "Interactive Tone Mapping," *11th Eurographics Workshop on Rendering*, pp. 219–230, 2000. http://graphics.lcs.mit.edu/~fredo/ Cited on p. 194, 277

[193] Durand, Frédo, George Drettakis, Joëlle Thollot, and Claude Puech, "Conservative Visibility Preprocessing Using Extended Projections," *Computer Graphics (SIGGRAPH 2000 Proceedings)*, pp. 239–248, July 2000. Cited on p. 388

[194] Dutré, Philip, *Global Illumination Compendium*, 1999. http://www.graphics.cornell.edu/~phil/GI/ Cited on p. 193, 200, 286

[195] Dutré, Philip, Kavita Bala, and Philippe Bekaert, *Advanced Global Illumination*. A K Peters Ltd., 2002. Cited on p. 286

[196] Duttweiler, Craig R., "Mapping Texels to Pixels in D3D," NVIDIA White Paper, April 2000. http://developer.nvidia.com/view.asp?IO= Mapping_texels_Pixels Cited on p. 342

[197] Dyn, Nira, David Levin, and John A. Gregory, "A 4-point Interpolatory Subdivision Scheme for Curve Design," *Computer Aided Geometric Design*, vol. 4, no. 4, pp. 257–268, 1987. Cited on p. 529, 530, 539

[198] Dyn, Nira, David Levin, and John A. Gregory, "A Butterfly Subdivision Scheme for Surface Interpolation with Tension Control," *ACM Transactions on Graphics*, vol. 9, no. 2, pp. 160–169, April 1990. Cited on p. 537

[199] Eberly, David, *3D Game Engine Design: A Practical Approach to Real-Time Computer Graphics*, Morgan Kaufmann Publishers Inc., San Francisco, 2000. http://www.magic-software.com/ Cited on p. 51, 109, 357, 479, 519, 522, 565, 567, 572, 620, 628, 629, 666

[200] Eberly, David, "Testing for Intersection of Convex Objects: The Method of Separating Axes," Technical Report, Magic Software, 2001. http:// www.magic-software.com/Documentation/MethodOfSeparatingAxes.pdf Cited on p. 627, 628

[201] Ebert, David S., John Hart, Bill Mark, F. Kenton Musgrave, Darwyn Peachey, Ken Perlin, and Steven Worley, *Texturing and Modeling: A Procedural Approach*, third edition, Morgan-Kaufmann, 2002. Cited on p. 126, 179, 308

[202] Eccles, Allen, "The Diamond Monster 3Dfx Voodoo 1," Gamespy Hall of Fame, 2000. http://www.gamespy.com/halloffame/october00/voodoo1/ Cited on p. 1

[203] Eckel, George, *IRIS Performer Programmer's Guide*, Silicon Graphics Inc., 1997. http://www.sgi.com/software/performer/manuals.html Cited on p. 422

[204] Eckstein, Ilya, Vitaly Surazhsky, Craig Gotsman, "Texture Mapping with Hard Constraints," *Computer Graphics Forum*, (Proceedings of Eurographics 2001), vol. 20, no. 3, pp. 95–104, 2001. www.cs.technion.ac.il/ ~gotsman/AmendedPubl/TextureMapping/TextureMapping.pdf Cited on p. 123

[205] Ehmann, Stephen A., and Ming C. Lin, "Accelerated Proximity Queries Between Convex Polyhedra Using Multi-Level Voronoi Marching," *IEEE/RSJ International Conference on Intelligent Robots and Systems 2000*, pp. 2101–2106, 2000. http://www.cs.unc.edu/~geom/SWIFT Cited on p. 662

[206] Ehmann, Stephen A., and Ming C. Lin, "Accurate and Fast Proximity Queries Between Polyhedra Using Convex Surface Decomposition," *Computer Graphics Forum* (Proceedings of Eurographics 2001), vol. 20, no. 3, pp. C500–C510, 2001. http://www.cs.unc.edu/~geom/SWIFT++ Cited on p. 657, 658, 662, 667

[207] Eldridge, Matthew, Homan Igehy, and Pat Hanrahan, "Pomegranate: A Fully Scalable Graphics Architecture," *Computer Graphics (SIGGRAPH 2001 Proceedings)*, pp. 443–454, July 2000. vol. 11, no. 6, pp. 290–296, 1995. Cited on p. 685, 687

[208] Eldridge, Matthew, *Designing Graphics Architectures around Scalability and Communication*, Ph.D. Thesis, Stanford University, June 2001. Cited on p. 686, 687

[209] Elinas, Pantelis, and Wolfgang Stuerzlinger, "Real-time Rendering of 3D Clouds," *journal of graphics tools*, vol. 5, no. 4, pp. 33–45, 2000. Cited on p. 322

[210] Engel, Wolfgang, ed., *ShaderX*, Wordware, May 2002. http://www.shaderx.com/ Cited on p. xii, 216, 231, 287

[211] Eriksson, Carl, Dinesh Manocha, William V. Baxter III, *Proceedings 2001 Symposium on Interactive 3D Graphics*, pp. 111–120, March 2001. Cited on p. 401

[212] Ernst, I., D. Jackel, H. Russeler, and O. Wittig, "Hardware Supported Bump Mapping: A step towards higher quality real-time rendering," *10th Eurographics Workshop on Graphics Hardware*, pp. 63–70, 1995. Cited on p. 176

[213] Ernst, I., H. Russeler, H. Schulz, and O. Wittig, "Gouraud Bump Mapping," *ACM SIGGRAPH/Eurographics Workshop on Graphics Hardware*, pp. 47–53, August 1998. Cited on p. 176

[214] Euclid (original translation by Heiberg, with introduction and commentary by Sir Thomas L. Heath), *The Thirteen Books of EUCLID'S ELEMENTS*, Second Edition, Revised with Additions, Volume I (Books I, II), Dover Publications, Inc., 1956. Cited on p. 715

[215] Everitt, Cass, "One-Pass Silhouette Rendering with GeForce and GeForce2," NVIDIA White Paper, June 2000. http://developer.nvidia.com Cited on p. 295

[216] Everitt, Cass, "Interactive Order-Independent Transparency," NVIDIA White Paper, May 2001. http://developer.nvidia.com Cited on p. 104, 273

[217] Everitt, Cass, Ashu Rege, and Cem Cebenoyan, "Hardware Shadow Mapping," NVIDIA White Paper, December 2001. http://developer.nvidia.com Cited on p. 272

[218] Everitt, Cass, and Mark Kilgard, "Practical and Robust Stenciled Shadow Volumes for Hardware-Accelerated Rendering," NVIDIA White Paper, March 2002. http://developer.nvidia.com Cited on p. 263, 265

[219] Ewins, Jon P., Marcus D. Waller, Martin White, and Paul F. Lister, "MIP-Map Level Selection for Texture Mapping," *IEEE Transactions on Visualization and Computer Graphics*, vol. 4, no. 4, pp. 317–329, Oct.–Dec. 1998. Cited on p. 135

[220] Eyles, J., S. Molnar, J. Poulton, T. Greer, A. Lastra, N. England, and L. Westover, "PixelFlow: The Realization," *ACM SIGGRAPH/Eurographics*

Workshop on Graphics Hardware Los Angeles, CA, pp. 57–68, August 1997. Cited on p. 686, 708

[221] Fairchild, Mark D. and David R. Wyble, "Colorimetric Characterization of the Apple Studio Display (Flat Panel LCD)," Technical Report, RIT Munsell Color Science Laboratory, July, 1998. `http://www.cis.rit.edu/research/mcsl/research/reports.shtml` Cited on p. 112

[222] Falby, John S., Michael J. Zyda, David R. Pratt, and Randy L. Mackey, "NPSNET: Hierarchical Data Structures for Real-Time Three-Dimensional Visual Simulation," *Computers & Graphics*, vol. 17, no. 1, pp 65—69, 1993. Cited on p. 401

[223] Farin, Gerald, "Triangular Bernstein-Bézier Patches," *Computer Aided Geometric Design*, vol. 3, no. 2, pp. 83–127, 1986. Cited on p. 506, 555

[224] Farin, Gerald, *Curves and Surfaces for Computer Aided Geometric Design—A Practical Guide*, Fourth Edition (First Edition, 1988), Academic Press Inc., 1996. Cited on p. 482, 484, 485, 489, 491, 500, 502, 503, 506, 510, 512, 529, 530, 555

[225] Farin, Gerald E., and Dianne Hansford, *The Geometry Toolbox for Graphics and Modeling*, A K Peters Ltd., 1998. `http://eros.cagd.eas.asu.edu/~farin/gbook/gbook.html` Cited on p. 66, 479, 629, 738

[226] Farin, Gerald E., *NURBS: From Projective Geometry to Practical Use*, 2nd edition, A K Peters Ltd., 1999. Cited on p. 555

[227] Farin, Gerald, and Dianne Hansford, *The Essentials of CAGD*, A K Peters Ltd., 2000. Cited on p. 555

[228] Fedkiw, Ronald, Jos Stam, and Henrik Wann Jensen, "Visual Simulation of Smoke," *Computer Graphics (SIGGRAPH 2001 Proceedings)*, pp. 15–22, August 2001. `http://www.dgp.toronto.edu/people/stam/reality/Research/pub.html` Cited on p. 342

[229] Fernando, Randima, Sebastian Fernandez, Kavita Bala, and Donald P. Greenberg, "Adaptive Shadow Maps," *Computer Graphics (SIGGRAPH 2001 Proceedings)*, pp. 387–390, August 2001. `http://www.graphics.cornell.edu/pubs/2001/FFBG01.html` Cited on p. 273

[230] Ferwerda, James, "Elements of early vision for computer graphics," *IEEE Computer Graphics and Applications*, vol. 21, no. 5, pp. 22–33, September/October 2001. `http://www.graphics.cornell.edu/~jaf/publications/publications.html` Cited on p. 194, 259, 672

[231] de Figueiredo, L.H., "Adaptive Sampling of Parametric Curves," in Alan Paeth, ed., *Graphics Gems V*, Academic Press, pp. 173–178, 1995. `http://www.graphicsgems.org/` Cited on p. 519

[232] Fisher, F., and A. Woo, "R.E versus N.H Specular Highlights," in Paul S. Heckbert, ed., *Graphics Gems IV*, Academic Press, pp. 388–400, 1994. Cited on p. 77

[233] Flavell, Andrew, "Run Time Mip-Map Filtering," *Game Developer*, vol. 5, no. 11, pp. 34–43, November 1998. `http://www.gdmag.com/code.htm` Cited on p. 135, 136

[234] Foley, J.D., A. van Dam, S.K. Feiner, J.H. Hughes, and R.L. Philips, *Introduction to Computer Graphics*, Addison-Wesley, Reading, Massachusetts, 1994. Cited on p. 32, 66

[235] Foley, J.D., A. van Dam, S.K. Feiner, and J.H. Hughes, *Computer Graphics: Principles and Practice, Second Edition in C*, Second Edition, Addison-Wesley, Reading, Massachusetts, 1996. Cited on p. 32, 50, 66, 114, 193, 495, 672, 678

[236] Forsyth, Tom, "Comparison of VIPM Methods," in Mark DeLoura, ed., *Game Programming Gems 2*, Charles River Media, pp. 363–376, 2001. Cited on p. 394, 466, 471, 472, 475, 479

[237] Forsyth, Tom, "Impostors: Adding Clutter," in Mark DeLoura, ed., *Game Programming Gems 2*, Charles River Media, pp. 488–496, 2001. Cited on p. 325, 327, 329

[238] Fosner, Ron, "All Aboard Hardware T & L," *Game Developer*, vol. 7, no. 4, pp. 30–41, April 2000. Cited on p. 163, 683

[239] Freitas, Jorge, "Simulated Real-Time Lighting Using Vertex Color Interpolation," in Mark DeLoura, ed., *Game Programming Gems*, Charles River Media, pp. 535–542, 2000. Cited on p. 418

[240] Frisken, Sarah, Ronald N. Perry, Alyn P. Rockwood, and Thouis R. Jones, "Adaptively Sampled Distance Fields: A General Representation of Shape for Computer Graphics," *Computer Graphics (SIGGRAPH 2000 Proceedings)*, pp. 249–254, July 2000. Cited on p. 666

[241] Frisken, Sarah, and Ronald N. Perry, "A Computationally Efficient Framework for Modeling Soft Body Impact," *Visual Proceedings (SIGGRAPH 2001)*, p. 160, August 2001. Cited on p. 666

[242] Fuchs, H., Z.M. Kedem, and B.F. Naylor, "On Visible Surface Generation by A Priori Tree Structures," *Computer Graphics (SIGGRAPH '80 Proceedings)*, pp. 124–133, July 1980. Cited on p. 351, 352

[243] Fuchs, H., G.D. Abram, and E.D. Grant, "Near Real-Time Shaded Display of Rigid Objects," *Computer Graphics (SIGGRAPH '89 Proceedings)*, pp. 65–72, July 1983. Cited on p. 351

[244] Fuchs, H., J. Poulton, J. Eyles, T. Greer, J. Goldfeather, D. Ellsworth, S. Molnar, G. Turk, B. Tebbs, and L. Israel, "Pixel-Planes 5: A Heterogeneous Multiprocessor Graphics System Using Processor-Enhanced Memories," *Computer Graphics (SIGGRAPH '89 Proceedings)*, pp. 79–88, July 1989. Cited on p. 7, 705, 706, 708

[245] Funkhouser, Thomas A., and Carlo H. Séquin, "Adaptive Display Algorithm for Interactive Frame Rates During Visualization of Complex Virtual Environments," *Computer Graphics (SIGGRAPH 93 Proceedings)*, pp. 247–254, August 1993. http://www.cs.princeton.edu/~funk/ Cited on p. 337, 398, 399, 400, 401, 475

[246] Funkhouser, Thomas A., *Database and Display Algorithms for Interactive Visualization of Architectural Models*, Ph.D. Thesis, University of California, Berkeley, 1993. http://www.cs.princeton.edu/~funk/ Cited on p. 400, 433

[247] *Game Development Algorithms* mailing list archives. `http://lists.sourceforge.net/lists/listinfo/gdalgorithms-list/` Cited on p. 142, 263

[248] Ganovelli, Fabio, John Dingliana, and Carol O'Sullivan, "BucketTree: Improving Collision Detection between Deformable Objects," *Spring Conference in Computer Graphics (SCCG2000)*, pp. 156–163, 2000. Cited on p. 666

[249] Garland, Michael, and Paul S. Heckbert, "Fast Polygonal Approximation of Terrains and Height Fields," Technical Report CMU-CS-95-181, Carnegie Mellon University, 1995. `http://graphics.cs.uiuc.edu/~garland/papers.html` Cited on p. 476

[250] Garland, Michael, and Paul S. Heckbert, "Surface Simplification Using Quadric Error Metrics," *Proceedings of SIGGRAPH 97*, pp. 209-216, August 1997. `http://graphics.cs.uiuc.edu/~garland/papers.html` Cited on p. 472

[251] Garland, Michael, and Paul S. Heckbert, "Simplifying Surfaces with Color and Texture using Quadric Error Metrics," *IEEE Visualization 98*, pp. 263–269, July 1998. `http://graphics.cs.uiuc.edu/~garland/papers.html` Cited on p. 471, 472, 479

[252] Garland, Michael, "Quadric-Based Polygonal Surface Simplification," Ph.D. thesis, Technical Report CMU-CS-99-105, Carnegie Mellon University, 1999. `http://graphics.cs.uiuc.edu/~garland/papers.html` Cited on p. 474

[253] Geczy, George, "2D Programming in a 3D World: Developing a 2D Game Engine Using DirectX 8 Direct3D," *Gamasutra*, June 2001. `http://www.gamasutra.com/features/20010629/geczy_01.htm` Cited on p. 314, 315

[254] Gershbein, Reid, and Pat Hanrahan, "A Fast Relighting Engine for Interactive Cinematic Lighting Design," *Computer Graphics (SIGGRAPH 2000 Proceedings)*, pp. 353–358, July 2000. `http://graphics.stanford.edu/papers/fastlight/` Cited on p. 340

[255] Giegl, Markus, and Michael Wimmer, "Unpopping: Solving the Image-Space Blend Problem", submitted to *journal of graphics tools*, Special Issue on Hardware-Accelerated Rendering Techniques, 2002. Cited on p. 391

[256] Gigus, Z., J. Canny, and R. Seidel, "Efficiently Computing and Representing Aspect Graphs of Polyedral Objects," *IEEE Transactions On Pattern Analysis and Machine Intelligence*, vol. 13, no. 6, pp. 542–551, 1991. Cited on p. 358

[257] Gilbert, E., D. Johnson, and S. Keerthi, "A Fast Procedure for Computing the Distance between Complex Objects in Three-Dimensional Space," *IEEE Journal of Robotics and Automation*, vol. 4, no. 2, pp. 193–203, April 1988. Cited on p. 660, 662

[258] Ginsburg, Dan, and Dave Gosselin, "Dynamic Per-Pixel Lighting Techniques," in Mark DeLoura, ed., *Game Programming Gems 2*, Charles River Media, pp. 452–462, 2001. Cited on p. 152, 167, 171, 172, 176

[259] Girshick, Ahna, Victoria Interrante, Steve Haker, and Todd Lemoine, "Line Direction Matters: An Argument for the Use of Principal Directions in 3D Line Drawings," *Proceedings of the First International Symposium on Non-photorealistic Animation and Rendering (NPAR)*, pp. 43–52, June 2000. http://www.cs.umn.edu/Research/graphics/ Cited on p. 307

[260] Glassner, Andrew S., ed., *An Introduction to Ray Tracing*, Academic Press Inc., London, 1989. Cited on p. 86, 99, 153, 283, 287, 629

[261] Glassner, Andrew S., ed., *Graphics Gems*, Academic Press, 1990. http://www.graphicsgems.org/ Cited on p. 66, 435, 629, 746

[262] Glassner, Andrew S., "Computing Surface Normals for 3D Models," Andrew S. Glassner, ed., *Graphics Gems*, Academic Press, pp. 562–566, 1990. Cited on p. 452

[263] Glassner, Andrew, "Building Vertex Normals from an Unstructured Polygon List," in Paul S. Heckbert, ed., *Graphics Gems IV*, Academic Press, pp. 60–73, 1994. Cited on p. 450, 452

[264] Glassner, Andrew S., *Principles of Digital Image Synthesis*, vol. 1, Morgan Kaufmann Publishers Inc., San Francisco, 1995. Cited on p. 71, 114, 194, 286, 672, 678

[265] Glassner, Andrew S., *Principles of Digital Image Synthesis*, vol. 2, Morgan Kaufmann Publishers Inc., San Francisco, 1995. Cited on p. 79, 114, 183, 185, 189, 194, 196, 199, 200, 286

[266] Goldman, Ronald, "Intersection of Three Planes," in Andrew S. Glassner, ed., *Graphics Gems*, Academic Press, p. 305, 1990. Cited on p. 619

[267] Goldman, Ronald, "Intersection of Two Lines in Three-Space," in Andrew S. Glassner, ed., *Graphics Gems*, Academic Press, p. 304, 1990. Cited on p. 619

[268] Goldman, Ronald, "Matrices and Transformations," in Andrew S. Glassner, ed., *Graphics Gems*, Academic Press, pp. 472–475, 1990. Cited on p. 43

[269] Goldman, Ronald, "Some Properties of Bézier Curves," in Andrew S. Glassner, ed., *Graphics Gems*, Academic Press, pp. 587–593, 1990. Cited on p. 486

[270] Goldman, Ronald, "Recovering the Data from the Transformation Matrix," in James Arvo, ed., *Graphics Gems II*, Academic Press, pp. 324–331, 1991. Cited on p. 42

[271] Goldman, Ronald, "Decomposing Linear and Affine Transformations," in David Kirk, ed., *Graphics Gems III*, Academic Press, pp. 108–116, 1992. Cited on p. 42

[272] Goldman, Ronald, "Identities for the Univariate and Bivariate Bernstein Basis Functions," in Alan Paeth, ed., *Graphics Gems V*, Academic Press, pp. 149–162, 1995. http://www.graphicsgems.org/ Cited on p. 555

[273] Goldsmith, Jeffrey, and John Salmon, "Automatic Creation of Object Hierarchies for Ray Tracing," *IEEE Computer Graphics and Applications*, vol. 7, no. 5, pp. 14–20, May 1987. Cited on p. 641

[274] Golub, Gene, and Charles Van Loan, *Matrix Computations*, Third Edition, Johns Hopkins University Press, 1996. Cited on p. 66

[275] Gomez, Miguel, "Simple Intersection Tests for Games," *Gamasutra*, October 1999. http://gamasutra.com/features/19991018/Gomez_1.htm Cited on p. 622

[276] Gomez, Miguel, "Compressed Axis-Aligned Bounding Box Trees," in Mark DeLoura, ed., *Game Programming Gems 2*, Charles River Media, pp. 388–393, 2001. Cited on p. 666

[277] Gonzalez, Rafael C., and Richard E. Woods, *Digital Image Processing*, Third Edition, Addison-Wesley, Reading, Massachusetts, 1992. Cited on p. 85, 300, 696

[278] Gooch, Amy, Bruce Gooch, Peter Shirley, and Elaine Cohen, "A Non-Photorealistic Lighting Model for Automatic Technical Illustration," *Computer Graphics (SIGGRAPH 98 Proceedings)*, pp. 447–452, July 1998. http://www.cs.utah.edu/npr/utah_papers.html Cited on p. 290, 303

[279] Gooch, Bruce, Peter-Pike J. Sloan, Amy Gooch, Peter Shirley, and Richard Riesenfeld, "Interactive Technical Illustration," *Proceedings 1999 Symposium on Interactive 3D Graphics*, pp. 31–38, April 1999. http://www.cs.utah.edu/npr/utah_papers.html Cited on p. 257, 290, 293, 303

[280] Gooch, Bruce or Amy, and Amy or Bruce Gooch, *Non-Photorealistic Rendering*, A K Peters Ltd., 2001. http://www.cs.utah.edu/~gooch/book.html Cited on p. 289, 303, 312

[281] Gordon, Dan, and Shuhong Chen, "Front-to-back display of BSP trees," *IEEE Computer Graphics and Applications*, vol. 11, no. 5, pp. 79–85, September 1991. Cited on p. 351

[282] Gortler, Steven J., Radek Grzeszczuk, Richard Szeliski, and Michael F. Cohen, "The Lumigraph," *Computer Graphics (SIGGRAPH 96 Proceedings)*, pp. 43–54, August, 1996. http://www.research.microsoft.com/~cohen/ Cited on p. 317

[283] Gottschalk, S., M.C. Lin, and D. Manocha, "OBBTree: A Hierarchical Structure for Rapid Interference Detection," *Computer Graphics (SIGGRAPH 96 Proceedings)*, pp. 171–180, August, 1996. http://www.cs.unc.edu/~geom/OBB/OBBT.html Cited on p. 563, 566, 602, 603, 605, 633, 644, 645, 649, 651

[284] Gottschalk, Stefan, *Collision Queries using Oriented Bounding Boxes*, Ph.D. Thesis, Department of Computer Science, University of North Carolina at Chapel Hill, 1999. Cited on p. 565, 566, 602, 605, 642

[285] Gouraud, H., "Continuous shading of curved surfaces," *IEEE Transactions on Computers*, vol. C-20, pp. 623–629, June 1971. Cited on p. 16, 70, 181

[286] Green, D., and D. Hatch, "Fast Polygon-Cube Intersection Testing," in Alan Paeth, ed., *Graphics Gems V*, Academic Press, pp. 375–379, 1995. http://www.graphicsgems.org/ Cited on p. 596

[287] Greene, Ned, "Environment Mapping and Other Applications of World Projections," *IEEE Computer Graphics and Applications*, vol. 6, no. 11, pp. 21–29, November 1986. Cited on p. 75, 156, 206, 210

[288] Greene, Ned, Michael Kass, and Gavin Miller, "Hierarchical Z-Buffer Visibility," *Computer Graphics (SIGGRAPH 93 Proceedings)*, pp. 231–238, August 1993. Cited on p. 381, 383, 384, 385

[289] Greene, Ned, "Detecting Intersection of a Rectangular Solid and a Convex Polyhedron," in Paul S. Heckbert, ed., *Graphics Gems IV*, Academic Press, pp. 74–82, 1994. Cited on p. 563

[290] Greene, Ned, and Michael Kass, "Error-Bounded Antialiased Rendering of Complex Environments," *Computer Graphics (SIGGRAPH 94 Proceedings)*, pp. 59–66, July 1994. Cited on p. 403

[291] Greene, Ned, *Hierarchical Rendering of Complex Environments*, Ph.D. Thesis, University of California at Santa Cruz, Report No. UCSC-CRL-95-27, June 1995. Cited on p. 383, 384

[292] Greene, Ned, "Hierarchical Polygon Tiling with Coverage Masks," *Computer Graphics (SIGGRAPH 96 Proceedings)*, pp. 65–74, August 1996. Cited on p. 385

[293] Greene, Ned, "Occlusion Culling with Optimized Hierarchical Z-Buffering," appears in *Course 30 notes at SIGGRAPH 2001: Visibility, Problems, Techniques and Applications* [134], 2001. Cited on p. 385

[294] Gregory, Arthur, Ming C. Lin, Stefan Gottschalk, and Russell Taylor, "H-Collide: A Framework for Fast and Accurate Collision Detection for Haptic Interaction," *Proceedings of Virtual Reality Conference 1999*, pp. 38–45, 1999. Cited on p. 576

[295] Gribb, Gil, and Klaus Hartmann, "Fast Extraction of Viewing Frustum Planes from the World-View-Projection Matrix," June 2001. http://www2.ravensoft.com/users/ggribb/plane\%20extraction.pdf Cited on p. 614

[296] Guenter, Brian, Todd Knoblock, and Erik Ruf, "Specializing Shaders," *Computer Graphics (SIGGRAPH 95 Proceedings)*, pp. 343–350, August 1995. http://research.microsoft.com/~guenter/ Cited on p. 340

[297] Gumhold, Stefan, and Wolfgang Straßer, "Real Time Compression of Triangle Mesh Connectivity," *Computer Graphics (SIGGRAPH 98 Proceedings)*, pp. 133–140, August 1998. Cited on p. 460

[298] Guymon, Mel, "Pyro-Techniques: Playing with Fire," *Game Developer*, vol. 7, no. 2, pp. 23–27, Feb. 2000. Cited on p. 322

[299] Hadap, Sunil, and Nadia Magnenat-Thalmann, "Modeling Dynamic Hair as a Continuum," *Computer Graphics Forum* (Proceedings of Eurographics 2001), vol. 20, no. 3, pp. 329–338, 2001. Cited on p. 666

[300] Haeberli, P., and K. Akeley, "The Accumulation Buffer: Hardware Support for High-Quality Rendering," *Computer Graphics (SIGGRAPH '90 Proceedings)*, pp. 309–318, August 1990. Cited on p. 22, 93, 236, 237

[301] Haeberli, Paul, and Mark Segal, "Texture Mapping as a Fundamental Drawing Primitive," *4th Eurographics Workshop on Rendering*, pp. 259–266, 1993. http://www.sgi.com/grafica/texmap/index.html Cited on p. 127, 148, 157, 178

[302] Hagen, Margaret A., "How to Make a Visually Realistic 3D Display," *Computer Graphics*, vol. 25, no. 2, pp. 76–81, April 1991. Cited on p. 321

[303] Hahn, James K., "Realistic Animation of Rigid Bodies," *Computer Graphics (SIGGRAPH '88 Proceedings)*, pp. 299–308, 1988. Cited on p. 664

[304] Haines, Eric, ed., *The Ray Tracing News.* http://www.raytracingnews.org Cited on p. 287

[305] Haines, Eric, "Essential Ray Tracing Algorithms," Chapter 2 in Andrew Glassner, ed., *An Introduction to Ray Tracing*, Academic Press Inc., London, 1989. Cited on p. 570, 572, 574, 584

[306] Haines, Eric, "Fast Ray-Convex Polyhedron Intersection," in James Arvo, ed., *Graphics Gems II*, Academic Press, pp. 247–250, 1991. http://www.graphicsgems.org/ Cited on p. 575

[307] Haines, Eric, "Point in Polygon Strategies," in Paul S. Heckbert, ed., *Graphics Gems IV*, Academic Press, pp. 24–46, 1994. http://www.erichaines.com/ptinpoly/ Cited on p. 578, 583, 584, 585, 586

[308] Haines, Eric, and John Wallace, "Shaft Culling for Efficient Ray-Traced Radiosity," in P. Brunet and F.W. Jansen, eds., *Photorealistic Rendering in Computer Graphics (Proceedings of the Second Eurographics Workshop on Rendering)*, Springer-Verlag, pp. 122–138, 1994. http://www.acm.org/tog/editors/erich/ Cited on p. 587, 588, 616

[309] Haines, Eric, and Steven Worley, "Fast, Low-Memory Z-buffering when Performing Medium-Quality Rendering," *journal of graphics tools*, vol. 1, no. 3, pp. 1–6, 1996. Cited on p. 233

[310] Haines, Eric, "The Curse of the Monkey's Paw," in Eric Haines, ed., *Ray Tracing News*, vol. 10, no. 2, June 1997. http://www.acm.org/tog/resources/RTNews/html/rtnv10n2.html Cited on p. 446

[311] Haines, Eric, "A Shaft Culling Tool," *journal of graphics tools*, vol. 5, no. 1, pp. 23–26, 2000. http://www.acm.org/jgt/papers/Haines00/ Cited on p. 616

[312] Haines, Eric, "Soft Planar Shadows Using Plateaus," *journal of graphics tools*, vol. 6, no. 1, pp. 19–27, 2001. http://www.acm.org/jgt/papers/Haines01/ Cited on p. 259

[313] Hakura, Ziyad S., and Anoop Gupta, "The Design and Analysis of a Cache Architecture for Texture Mapping," *24th International Symposium of Computer Architecture (ISCA)*, pp. 108–120, June 1997. Cited on p. 689

[314] Hakura, Ziyad S., John M. Snyder, and Jerome E. Lengyel, "Parameterized Environment Maps," *Proceedings 2001 Symposium on Interactive 3D Graphics*, pp. 203–208, March 2001. Cited on p. 164

[315] Hakura, Ziyad S., and John M. Snyder, "Realistic Reflections and Refractions on Graphics Hardware With Hybrid Rendering and Layered Environment Maps," *12th Eurographics Workshop on Rendering*, pp. 286–297, 2001. http://graphics.stanford.edu/papers/hybridrendering/ Cited on p. 278, 690

[316] Hall, Roy, *Illumination and Color in Computer Generated Imagery*, Springer-Verlag, 1989. Cited on p. 68, 71, 79, 114, 198, 199, 672

[317] Hall, Tim, "A how to for using OpenGL to Render Mirrors," *comp.graphics.api.opengl* newsgroup, August 1996. Cited on p. 242, 243

[318] Halstead, Mark, Michal Kass, and Tony DeRose, "Efficient, Fair Interpolation using Catmull-Clark Surfaces," *Computer Graphics (SIGGRAPH 93 Proceedings)*, pp. 35–44, August 1994. Cited on p. 544, 545

[319] Hanrahan, Pat, "A Survey of Ray-Surface Intersection Algorithms," Chapter 3 in Andrew Glassner, ed. *An Introduction to Ray Tracing*, Academic Press Inc., London, 1989. Cited on p. 35

[320] Hanrahan, P., and P. Haeberli, "Direct WYSIWYG Painting and Texturing on 3D Shapes," *Computer Graphics (SIGGRAPH '90 Proceedings)*, pp. 215–223, August 1990. Cited on p. 558

[321] Hapke, B., "A Theoretical Photometric Function for the Lunar Surface," *J. Geophysical Research*, vol. 68, no. 15, 1 August 1963. Cited on p. 198

[322] Harris, Mark J., and Anselmo Lastra, "Real-Time Cloud Rendering," *Proceedings of Eurographics 2001*, Vol. 20, No. 3, pp. 76–84, September 2001. http://www.cs.unc.edu/~harrism/clouds/ Cited on p. 278, 322

[323] Hart, Evan, Dave Gosselin, and John Isidoro, "Vertex Shading with Direct3D and OpenGL," *Game Developers Conference*, San Jose, March 2001. http://www.ati.com/na/pages/resource_centre/dev_rel/techpapers.html Cited on p. 268, 297, 308

[324] Hart, John C., Nate Carr, Masaki Kameya, Stephen A. Tibbitts, and Terrance J. Coleman, "Antialiased Parameterized Solid Texturing Simplified for Consumer-Level Hardware Implementation," *ACM SIGGRAPH/Eurographics Workshop on Graphics Hardware*, pp. 45–53, Aug. 1999. http://graphics.cs.uiuc.edu/~jch/papers/apst.pdf Cited on p. 127

[325] Hart, John C., "Perlin Noise Pixel Shaders," *ACM SIGGRAPH/Eurographics Workshop on Graphics Hardware*, pp. 87–94, August 2001. http://graphics.cs.uiuc.edu/~jch/papers/pixelnoise.pdf Cited on p. 127

[326] He, Taosong, "Fast Collision Detection Using QuOSPO Trees," *Proceedings 1999 Symposium on Interactive 3D Graphics*, pp. 55–62, April 1999. Cited on p. 645

[327] He, Xiao D., Kenneth E. Torrance, François X. Sillion, and Donald P. Greenberg, "A Comprehensive Physical Model for Light Reflection," *Computer Graphics (SIGGRAPH '91 Proceedings)*, pp. 175–186, July 1991. Cited on p. 200, 201

[328] Hearn, Donald, and M. Pauline Baker, *Computer Graphics*, Second Edition, Prentice-Hall, Inc., Englewoods Cliffs, New Jersey, 1994. Cited on p. 17, 66, 109

[329] Heckbert, Paul, "Survey of Texture Mapping," *IEEE Computer Graphics and Applications*, vol. 6, no. 11, pp. 56–67, November 1986. http://www.cs.cmu.edu/~ph/ Cited on p. 178

[330] Heckbert, Paul S., "Fundamentals of Texture Mapping and Image Warping," Report No. 516, Computer Science Division, University of California, Berkeley, June 1989. `http://www.cs.cmu.edu/~ph/` Cited on p. 127, 137, 139, 141, 178, 445, 446

[331] Heckbert, Paul S., "Adaptive Radiosity Textures for Bidirectional Ray Tracing," *Computer Graphics (SIGGRAPH '90 Proceedings)*, pp. 145–154, August 1990. Cited on p. 150

[332] Heckbert, Paul S., and Henry P. Moreton, "Interpolation for Polygon Texture Mapping and Shading," *State of the Art in Computer Graphics: Visualization and Modeling*, Springer-Verlag, pp. 101–111, 1991. Cited on p. 681

[333] Heckbert, Paul S., ed., *Graphics Gems IV*, Academic Press, 1994. `http://www.graphicsgems.org/` Cited on p. 66, 435, 629

[334] Heckbert, Paul S., "A Minimal Ray Tracer," Heckbert, Paul S., ed., *Graphics Gems IV*, Academic Press, pp. 375–381, 1994. `http://www.graphicsgems.org/` Cited on p. 282

[335] Heckbert, Paul S., and Michael Herf, *Simulating Soft Shadows with Graphics Hardware*, Technical Report CMU-CS-97-104, Carnegie Mellon University, January 1997. `http://www.cs.cmu.edu/~ph/shadow.html` Cited on p. 254, 255, 257

[336] Hecker, Chris, "More Compiler Results, and What To Do About It," *Game Developer*, pp. 14–21, August/September 1996. `http://www.d6.com/users/checker/misctech.htm` Cited on p. 414

[337] Hecker, Chris, "Physics, The Next Frontier," *Game Developer*, pp. 12–20, October/November 1996. `http://www.d6.com/users/checker/dynamics.htm` Cited on p. 667

[338] Hecker, Chris, "Physics, Part 2: Angular Effects," *Game Developer*, pp. 14–22, December/January 1997. `http://www.d6.com/users/checker/dynamics.htm` Cited on p. 667

[339] Hecker, Chris, "Physics, Part 3: Collision Response," *Game Developer*, pp. 11–18, February/March 1997. `http://www.d6.com/users/checker/dynamics.htm` Cited on p. 667

[340] Hecker, Chris, "Physics, Part 4: The Third Dimension," *Game Developer*, pp. 15–26, June 1997. `http://www.d6.com/users/checker/dynamics.htm` Cited on p. 667

[341] Heidmann, Tim, "Real shadows, real time," *Iris Universe*, No. 18, pp. 23–31, Silicon Graphics Inc., November 1991. Cited on p. 261, 262

[342] Heidrich, Wolfgang, and Hans-Peter Seidel, "View-independent Environment Maps," *ACM SIGGRAPH/Eurographics Workshop on Graphics Hardware*, pp. 39–45, August 1998. Cited on p. 161, 171

[343] Heidrich, Wolfgang, and Hans-Peter Seidel, "Efficient Rendering of Anisotropic Surfaces Using Computer Graphics Hardware," *Image and Multidimensional Digital Signal Processing Workshop (IMDSP)*, 1998. `http://www.cs.ubc.ca/~heidrich/Papers/` Cited on p. 178, 201

[344] Heidrich, Wolfgang, Rüdifer Westermann, Hans-Peter Seidel, and Thomas Ertl, "Applications of Pixel Textures in Visualization and Realistic Image Synthesis," *Proceedings 1999 Symposium on Interactive 3D Graphics*, pp. 127–134, April 1999. http://www.cs.ubc.ca/~heidrich/Papers/ Cited on p. 108, 176, 178, 231, 271

[345] Heidrich, Wolfgang, and Hans-Peter Seidel, "Realistic, Hardware-accelerated Shading and Lighting," *Computer Graphics (SIGGRAPH 99 Proceedings)*, pp. 171–178, August 1999. http://www.cs.ubc.ca/~heidrich/Papers/ Cited on p. 79, 161, 171, 176, 178, 207, 208, 213, 226

[346] Heidrich, Wolfgang, Stefan Brabec, and Hans-Peter Seidel, "Soft Shadow Maps for Linear Lights," *11th Eurographics Workshop on Rendering*, pp. 269–280, 2000. http://www.cs.ubc.ca/~heidrich/Papers/ Cited on p. 273

[347] Heidrich, Wolfgang, Katja Daubert, Jan Kautz, and Hans-Peter Seidel, "Illuminating Micro Geometry Based on Precomputed Visibility," *Computer Graphics (SIGGRAPH 2000 Proceedings)*, pp. 455–464, July 2000. http://www.cs.ubc.ca/~heidrich/Papers/ Cited on p. 168

[348] Held, M., J.T. Klosowski, and J.S.B. Mitchell, "Speed Comparison of Generalized Bounding Box Hierarchies," Technical Report, Department of Applied Math, SUNY Stony Brook, 1995. Cited on p. 652

[349] Held, M., J.T. Klosowski, and J.S.B. Mitchell, "Evaluation of Collision Detection Methods for Virtual Reality Fly-Throughs," *Proceedings of the 7th Canadian Conference on Computational Geometry*, pp. 205–210, 1995. Cited on p. 645

[350] Held, M., J.T. Klosowski, and J.S.B. Mitchell, "Real-Time Collision Detection for Motion Simulation within Complex Environments," *Visual Proceedings (SIGGRAPH 96)*, p. 151, August 1996. Cited on p. 649

[351] Held, Martin, "ERIT—A Collection of Efficient and Reliable Intersection Tests," *journal of graphics tools*, vol. 2, no. 4, pp. 25–44, 1997. http://www.acm.org/jgt/papers/Held97 Cited on p. 572, 590, 594, 595, 596

[352] Held, Martin, "FIST: Fast Industrial-Strength Triangulation," submitted for publication, 1998. http://www.cosy.sbg.ac.at/~held/publications.html Cited on p. 442

[353] Helman, James L., "Architecture and Performance of Entertainment Systems," *SIGGRAPH 94 Course Notes: Designing Real-Time Graphics for Entertainment*, July 1994. Cited on p. 345

[354] Hennessy, John L., and David A. Patterson, *Computer Architecture: A Quantitative Approach*, Second Edition, Morgan Kaufmann Publishers, 1996. Cited on p. 10, 405, 410, 419

[355] Herf, M., and P.S. Heckbert, "Fast Soft Shadows," *Visual Proceedings (SIGGRAPH 96)*, p. 145, August 1996. Cited on p. 254

[356] Herrell, Russ, Joe Baldwin, and Chris Wilcox, "High-Quality Polygon Edging," *IEEE Computer Graphics and Applications*, vol. 15, no. 4, pp. 68–74, July 1995. Cited on p. 309, 310

[357] Hertzmann, Aaron, "Introduction to 3D Non-Photorealistic Rendering: Silhouettes and Outlines," *SIGGRAPH 99 Non-Photorealistic Rendering course notes*, 1999. http://www.mrl.nyu.edu/~hertzman/hertzmann-intro3d.pdf Cited on p. 300, 303

[358] Hill, Steve, "A Simple Fast Memory Allocator," in David Kirk, ed., *Graphics Gems III*, Academic Press, pp. 49–50, 1992. http://www.graphicsgems.org/ Cited on p. 415

[359] Hill, F.S., Jr., "The Pleasures of 'Perp Dot' Products," in Paul S. Heckbert, ed., *Graphics Gems IV*, Academic Press, pp. 138–148, 1994. Cited on p. 5, 616

[360] Hoff., Kenneth E., III, "A Faster Overlap Test for a Plane and a Bounding Box," 1996. http://www.cs.unc.edu/~hoff/research/vfculler/boxplane.html Cited on p. 587, 589

[361] Hoff, Kenneth E., III, Andrew Zaferakis, Ming Lin, and Dinesh Manocha, "Fast and Simple 2D Geometric Proximity Queries Using Graphics Hardware," *Proceedings 2001 Symposium on Interactive 3D Graphics*, pp. 145–148, March 2001. Cited on p. 667

[362] Hoffman, Naty, and Kenny Mitchell, "Photorealistic Terrain Lighting in Real Time," *Game Developer*, vol. 8, no. 7, pp. 32–41, July 2001. More detailed version in *Game Developers Conference*, pp. 357–367, March 2001. http://www.gdconf.com/archives/proceedings/2001/prog_papers.html Cited on p. 150, 176, 250, 282

[363] Hook, Brian, "Multipass Rendering and the Magic of Alpha Blending," *Game Developer*, vol. 4, no. 5, pp. 12–19, August 1997. Cited on p. 150, 337

[364] Hoppe, H., T. DeRose, T. Duchamp, M. Halstead, H. Jin, J. McDonald, J. Schweitzer, and W. Stuetzle, "Piecewise Smooth Surface Reconstruction," *Computer Graphics (SIGGRAPH 94 Proceedings)*, pp. 295–302, July 1994. Cited on p. 533, 536, 545

[365] Hoppe, Hugues, "Progressive Meshes," *Computer Graphics (SIGGRAPH 96 Proceedings)*, pp. 99–108, August 1996. http://research.microsoft.com/~hoppe/ Cited on p. 394, 471, 474, 475

[366] Hoppe, Hugues, "View-Dependent Refinement of Progressive Meshes," *Computer Graphics (SIGGRAPH 97 Proceedings)*, pp. 189–198, August 1997. http://research.microsoft.com/~hoppe/ Cited on p. 476, 520, 522

[367] Hoppe, Hugues, "Efficient Implementation of Progressive Meshes," *Computers and Graphics*, vol. 22, no. 1, pp. 27–36, 1998. http://research.microsoft.com/~hoppe/ Cited on p. 454, 472

[368] Hoppe, Hugues, "Smooth View-Dependent Level-of-Detail Control and Its Application to Terrain Rendering," *IEEE Visualization 1998*, pp. 35–42, Oct. 1998. http://research.microsoft.com/~hoppe/ Cited on p. 476

[369] Hoppe, Hugues, "Optimization of Mesh Locality for Transparent Vertex Caching," *Computer Graphics (SIGGRAPH 99 Proceedings)*, pp. 269–276, August 1999. http://research.microsoft.com/~hoppe/ Cited on p. 456, 462

[370] Hoppe, Hugues, "New Quadric Metric for Simplifying Meshes with Appearance Attributes," *IEEE Visualization 1999*, pp. 59–66, October 1999. http://research.microsoft.com/~hoppe/ Cited on p. 474

[371] Hoschek, Josef, and Dieter Lasser, *Fundamentals of Computer Aided Geometric Design*, A.K. Peters Ltd., 1993. Cited on p. 482, 485, 489, 502, 512, 529, 555

[372] Hourcade, J.C., and A. Nicolas, "Algorithms for Antialiased Cast Shadows," *Computers and Graphics*, vol. 9, no. 3, pp. 259–265, 1985. Cited on p. 273

[373] Hubbard, Philip M., "Approximating Polyhedra with Spheres for Time-Critical Collision Detection," *ACM Transactions on Graphics*, vol. 15, no. 3, pp. 179–210, 1996. Cited on p. 598, 645, 659

[374] Huddy, Richard, "The Efficient Use of Vertex Buffers," NVIDIA White Paper, November 2000. http://developer.nvidia.com Cited on p. 465, 466, 468

[375] Hudson, T., M. Lin, J. Cohen, S. Gottschalk, and D. Manocha, "V-COLLIDE: Accelerated collision detection for VRML," *Proceedings of VRML '97*, Monterey, California, February 1997. Cited on p. 653

[376] Hughes, M., M. Lin, D. Manocha, and C. Dimattia, "Efficient and Accurate Interference Detection for Polynomial Deformation," *Proceedings of Computer Animation*, Geneva, Switzerland, pp. 155–166, 1996. Cited on p. 666

[377] Hughes, John F., and Tomas Möller, "Building an Orthonormal Basis from a Unit Vector," *journal of graphics tools*, vol. 4, no. 4, pp. 33–35, 1999. http://www.acm.org/jgt/papers/HughesMoller99/

[378] Humphreys, Greg, Matthew Eldridge, Ian Buck, Gordon Stoll, Matthew Everett, and Pat Hanrahan "WireGL: A Scalable Graphics System for Clusters," *Computer Graphics (SIGGRAPH 2001 Proceedings)*, pp. 129–140, August 2001. http://graphics.stanford.edu/software/wiregl/ Cited on p. 43, 318 Cited on p. 687

[379] Hutson, V., and J.S. Pym, *Applications of Functional Analysis and Operator Theory*, Academic Press, London, 1980. Cited on p. 738

[380] Igehy, Homan, Gordon Stoll, and Pat Hanrahan, "The Design of a Parallel Graphics Interface," *Computer Graphics (SIGGRAPH 98 Proceedings)*, pp. 141–150, July 1998. http://graphics.stanford.edu/papers/parallel_api/ Cited on p. 436

[381] Igehy, Homan, Matthew Eldridge, and Kekoa Proudfoot, "Prefetching in a Texture Cache Architecture," *ACM SIGGRAPH/Eurographics Workshop on Graphics Hardware*, pp. 133–142, August 1998. Cited on p. 689, 690

[382] Igehy, Homan, Matthew Eldridge, and Pat Hanrahan, "Parallel Texture Caching," *ACM SIGGRAPH/Eurographics Workshop on Graphics Hardware*, pp. 95–106, August 1999. Cited on p. 690

[383] Ikedo, T., and J. Ma, "The Truga001: A Scalable Rendering Processor," *IEEE Computer Graphics and Applications*, vol. 18, no. 2, pp. 59–79,

March/April 1998. `http://computer.org/cga/cg1998/g2toc.htm` Cited on p. 176

[384] *Streaming SIMD Extensions—Inverse of 4x4 Matrix*, Order Number 245043-001, Intel Corporation, March 1999. `http://developer.intel.com/vtune/compilers/cpp/matrix_lib.htm` Cited on p. 37

[385] *Iris Graphics Library Programming Guide*, Silicon Graphics Inc., 1991. Cited on p. 456

[386] Isidoro, John, Alex Vlachos, and Chris Brennan, "Rendering Ocean Water," in Engel, Wolfgang, ed., *ShaderX*, Wordware, May 2002. `http://www.shaderx.com/` Cited on p. 218, 247

[387] Isidoro, John, and Chris Brennan, "Per-Pixel Strand Based Anisotropic Lighting," in Engel, Wolfgang, ed., *ShaderX*, Wordware, May 2002. `http://www.shaderx.com/` Cited on p. 213

[388] Ivanov, D., and Ye. Kuzmin, "Color Distribution – A New Approach to Texture Compression," *Proceedings of Eurographics 2000*, vol. 19, no. 3, pp. C283–C289, 2000. Cited on p. 144

[389] James, Adam, *Binary Space Partitioning for Accelerated Hidden Surface Removal and Rendering of Static Environments*, Ph.D. Thesis, University of East Anglia, August 1999. Cited on p. 352, 403

[390] James, Greg, "Operations for Hardware Accelerated Procedural Texture Animation," in Mark DeLoura, ed., *Game Programming Gems 2*, Charles River Media, pp. 497–509, 2001. Cited on p. 341, 342

[391] Jaquays, Paul, and Brian Hook, *Quake 3: Arena Shader Manual, Revision 12*, December 1999. `http://graphics.stanford.edu/courses/cs448-00-spring/readings.html` Cited on p. 233

[392] Jensen, Henrik Wann, *Realistic Image Synthesis Using Photon Mapping*, A.K. Peters Ltd., 2001. Cited on p. 277

[393] Jensen, Henrik Wann, Stephen R. Marschner, Marc Levoy, and Pat Hanrahan, "A Practical Model for Subsurface Light Transport," *Computer Graphics (SIGGRAPH 2001 Proceedings)*, pp. 511–518, August 2001. Cited on p. 196

[394] Jensen, Lasse Staff, and Robert Golias, "Deep-Water Animation and Rendering," *Gamasutra*, Sept. 2001. `http://www.gamasutra.com/gdce/jensen/jensen_03.htm` Cited on p. 231, 247

[395] Jiménez, P., and Thomas C. Torras, "3D Collision Detection: A Survey," *Computers & Graphics*, vol. 25, pp. 269–285, 2001. Cited on p. 661, 666

[396] Johannsen, Andreas, and Michael B. Carter, "Clustered Backface Culling," *journal of graphics tools*, vol. 3, no. 1, pp. 1–14, 1998. Cited on p. 363

[397] Jouppi, Norman P., and Chun-Fa Chang, "Z^3: An Economical Hardware Technique for High-Quality Antialiasing and Transparency," *ACM SIGGRAPH/Eurographics Workshop on Graphics Hardware*, pp. 85–93, August 1999. `http://research.compaq.com/wrl/people/jouppi/Z3.html` Cited on p. 96, 97, 99

[398] Joy, Kenneth I., *On-Line Geometric Modeling Notes*, `http://graphics.cs.ucdavis.edu/CAGDNotes/` Cited on p. 530

[399] Junkins, Stephen, and Allen Hux, "Subdividing Reality: Employing Subdivision Surfaces for Real-Time Scalable 3D," *Game Developers Conference proceedings*, 2000. Cited on p. 550

[400] Kajiya, James T., "Anisotropic Reflection Models," *Computer Graphics (SIGGRAPH '85 Proceedings)*, pp. 15–21, July 1985. Cited on p. 469

[401] Kajiya, James T., "The Rendering Equation," *Computer Graphics (SIGGRAPH '86 Proceedings)*, pp. 143–150, August 1986. Cited on p. 277, 284

[402] Kaplan, Matthew, Bruce Gooch, and Elaine Cohen, "Interactive Artistic Rendering," *Proceedings of the First International Symposium on Non-photorealistic Animation and Rendering (NPAR)*, pp. 67–74, June 2000. `http://www.cs.utah.edu/npr/utah_papers.html` Cited on p. 304, 307

[403] Karkanis, Tasso, and A. James Stewart, "Curvature-Dependent Triangulation of Implicit Surfaces," *IEEE Computer Graphics and Applications*, vol. 22, no. 2, pp. 60–69, March 2001. Cited on p. 527

[404] Karypis, George, and Vipin Kumar, "A Fast and High Quality Multilevel Scheme for Partitioning Irregular Graphs," *SIAM Journal on Scientific Computing*, vol. 20, no. 1, pp. 359–392, 1998. `http://www-users.cs.umn.edu/~karypis/metis/` Cited on p. 464

[405] Kautz, Jan, and M.D. McCool, "Interactive Rendering with Arbitrary BRDFs using Separable Approximations," *10th Eurographics Workshop on Rendering*, pp. 281–292, June 1999. `http://www.mpi-sb.mpg.de/~jnkautz/publications` Cited on p. 204

[406] Kautz, Jan, and M.D. McCool, "Approximation of Glossy Reflection with Prefiltered Environment Maps," *Graphics Interface 2000*, pp. 119–126, May 2000. `http://www.mpi-sb.mpg.de/~jnkautz/publications` Cited on p. 209

[407] Kautz, Jan, P.-P. Vázquez, W. Heidrich, and H.-P. Seidel, "A Unified Approach to Prefiltered Environment Maps," *11th Eurographics Workshop on Rendering*, pp. 185–196, June 2000. `http://www.mpi-sb.mpg.de/~jnkautz/publications` Cited on p. 209, 213

[408] Kautz, Jan, and Hans-Peter Seidel, "Towards Interactive Bump Mapping with Anisotropic Shift-Variant BRDFs," *ACM SIGGRAPH/Eurographics Workshop on Graphics Hardware*, pp. 51–58, 2000. `http://www.mpi-sb.mpg.de/~jnkautz/projects/anisobumpmaps/` Cited on p. 201, 202, 226

[409] Kautz, Jan, Chris Wynn, Jonathan Blow, Chris Blasband, Anis Ahmad, and Michael McCool, "Achieving Real-Time Realistic Reflectance, Part 1" *Game Developer*, vol. 8, no. 1, pp. 32–37, January 2001. Cited on p. 176, 196, 202

[410] Kautz, Jan, Chris Wynn, Jonathan Blow, Chris Blasband, Anis Ahmad, and Michael McCool, "Achieving Real-Time Realistic Reflectance, Part 2" *Game Developer*, vol. 8, no. 2, pp. 38–44, February 2001. `http://www.gdmag.com/code.htm` Cited on p. 161, 178, 204, 205, 206

[411] Kautz, Jan, and Hans-Peter Seidel, "Hardware Accelerated Displacement Mapping for Image Based Rendering," *Graphics Interface 2001*, pp. 61–70, May 2001. Cited on p. 344

[412] Kawachi, Katsuaki, and Hirosama Suzuki, "Distance Computation between Non-convex Polyhedra at Short Range Based on Discrete Voronoi Regions," *IEEE Geometric Modeling and Processing*, pp. 123–128, April 2000. Cited on p. 667

[413] Kay, T.L., and J.T. Kajiya, "Ray Tracing Complex Scenes," *Computer Graphics (SIGGRAPH '86 Proceedings)*, pp. 269–278, August 1986. Cited on p. 572, 575

[414] Keating, Brett, "Efficient Shadow Antialiasing using an A-buffer," *journal of graphics tools*, vol. 4, no. 3, pp. 23-33, 1999. Cited on p. 273

[415] Keller, Alexander, and Wolfgang Heidrich, "Interleaved Sampling," *12th Eurographics Workshop on Rendering*, pp. 266–273, 2001. http://www.cs.ubc.ca/labs/imager/tr/keller.2001a.html Cited on p. 100

[416] Kelley, Michael, Kirk Gould, Brent Pease, Stephanie Winner, and Alex Yen, "Hardware Accelerated Rendering of CSG and Transparency," *Computer Graphics (SIGGRAPH 94 Proceedings)*, pp. 177–184, July 1994. Cited on p. 103

[417] Kempf, Renate, and Jed Hartman, *OpenGL on Silicon Graphics Systems*, Silicon Graphics Inc., 1998. Cited on p. 408, 424, 435

[418] Kershaw, Kathleen, *A Generalized Texture-Mapping Pipeline*, M.S. Thesis, Program of Computer Graphics, Cornell University, Ithaca, New York, 1992. Cited on p. 118, 120

[419] Kilgard, Mark, "Fast OpenGL-rendering of Lens Flares," http://www.opengl.org/developers/code/mjktips/lensflare/ Cited on p. 330

[420] Kilgard, Mark J., "Realizing OpenGL: Two Implementations of One Architecture," *ACM SIGGRAPH/Eurographics Workshop on Graphics Hardware*, Los Angeles, California, pp. 45–55, August 1997. Cited on p. 691, 701

[421] Kilgard, Mark J., "Creating Reflections and Shadows Using Stencil Buffers," *Game Developers Conference*, NVIDIA slideset, 1999. http://developer.nvidia.com Cited on p. 423

[422] Kilgard, Mark J., "A Practical and Robust Bump-mapping Technique for Today's GPUs," *Game Developers Conference*, NVIDIA White Paper, 2000. http://developer.nvidia.com Cited on p. 168, 170, 171, 172, 173, 174, 176

[423] Kilgard, Mark J., "Shadow Mapping with Today's OpenGL Hardware," *Game Developers Conference*, 2001. http://developer.nvidia.com Cited on p. 271

[424] Kilgard, Mark J., "More Advanced Hardware Rendering Techniques," *Game Developers Conference*, 2001. http://developer.nvidia.com Cited on p. 264

[425] Kilgard, Mark J., "Shadow Mapping with Today's OpenGL Hardware," *CEDEC*, 2001. http://developer.nvidia.com Cited on p. 271, 272

[426] Kim, Dong-Jin, Leonidas J. Guibas, and Sung-Yong Shin, "Fast Collision Detection Among Multiple Moving Spheres," *IEEE Transactions on Visualization and Computer Graphics*, vol. 4, no. 3., July/September 1998. Cited on p. 653

[427] King, Yossarian, "Never Let 'Em See You Pop—Issues in Geometric Level of Detail Selection," in Mark DeLoura, ed., *Game Programming Gems*, Charles River Media, pp. 432–438, 2000. Cited on p. 398, 399

[428] King, Yossarian, "2D Lens Flare," in Mark DeLoura, ed., *Game Programming Gems*, Charles River Media, pp. 515–518, 2000. Cited on p. 330

[429] King, Yossarian, "Ground-Plane Shadows," in Mark DeLoura, ed., *Game Programming Gems*, Charles River Media, pp. 562–566, 2000. Cited on p. 253

[430] Kirk, David B., and Douglas Voorhies, "The Rendering Architecture of the DN-10000VS," *Computer Graphics (SIGGRAPH '90 Proceedings)*, pp. 299–307, August 1990. Cited on p. 135

[431] Kirk, David, ed., *Graphics Gems III*, Academic Press, 1992. http://www.graphicsgems.org/ Cited on p. 66, 435, 629

[432] Klein, Allison W., Wilmot Li, Michael M. Kazhdan, Wagner T. Corrêa, Adam Finkelstein, and Thomas A. Funkhouser, "Non-Photorealistic Virtual Environments," *Computer Graphics (SIGGRAPH 2000 Proceedings)*, pp. 527–534, July 2000. Cited on p. 304, 306

[433] Klosowski, J.T., M. Held, J.S.B. Mitchell, H. Sowizral, and K. Zikan, "Efficient Collision Detection Using Bounding Volume Hierarchies of k-DOPs," *IEEE Transactions on Visualization and Computer Graphics*, vol. 4, no. 1, 1998. Cited on p. 600, 601, 641, 644, 645, 646, 649, 650, 651, 652

[434] Klosowski, James T., '*Efficient Collision Detection for Interactive 3D Graphics and Virtual Environments*, Ph.D. Thesis, State University of New York at Stony Brook, May 1998. Cited on p. 649, 657

[435] Klosowski, James T., and Cláudio T. Silva, "The Prioritized-Layered Projection Algorithm for Visible Set Estimation," *IEEE Transactions on Visualization and Computer Graphics*, vol. 6, no. 2, pp. 108–123, April/June 2000. Cited on p. 383

[436] Klosowski, James T., and Cláudio T. Silva, "Efficient Conservative Visibility Culling Using The Prioritized-Layered Projection Algorithm," *IEEE Transactions on Visualization and Computer Graphics*, vol. 7, no. 4, pp. 365–379, 2001. Cited on p. 383

[437] Knuth, Donald E., *The Art of Computer Programming: Sorting and Searching*, vol. 3, Second Edition, Addison-Wesley, Reading, Massachusetts, 1998. Cited on p. 654

[438] Kobbelt, Leif, "$\sqrt{3}$-Subdivision," *Computer Graphics (SIGGRAPH 2000 Proceedings)*, pp. 103–112, July 2000. Cited on p. 532, 542, 543, 554, 555

[439] Kochanek, Doris H.U., and Richard H. Bartels, "Interpolating Splines with Local Tension, Continuity, and Bias Control," *Computer Graphics (SIG-GRAPH '84 Proceedings)*, pp. 33–41, July 1984. Cited on p. 494, 495

[440] Koltun, Vladlen, Yiorgos Chrysanthou, and Daniel Cohen-Or, "Virtual Occluders: An Efficient Intermediate PVS representation," *11th Eurographics Workshop on Rendering*, pp. 59–70, 2000. Cited on p. 379

[441] Koltun, Vladlen, Yiorgos Chrysanthou, and Daniel Cohen-Or, "Hardware-Accelerated From-Region Visibility using a Dual Ray Space," *12th Eurographics Workshop on Rendering*, pp. 204–214, 2001. http://www.math.tau.ac.il/~vladlen/ Cited on p. 371, 389

[442] Konečný, Petr, *Bounding Volumes in Computer Graphics*, M.S. Thesis, Faculty of Informatics, Masaryk University, Brno, April 1998. http://www.fi.muni.cz/~pekon/ Cited on p. 645, 666

[443] Kovach, Peter, "Inside Direct3D: Stencil Buffers," *Gamasutra*, August 2000. http://www.gamasutra.com/features/20000807/kovach_01.htm Cited on p. 337

[444] Krishnamurthy, V., and M. Levoy, "Fitting Smooth Surfaces to Dense Polygon Meshes," *Computer Graphics (SIGGRAPH 96 Proceedings)*, pp. 313–324, August, 1996. Cited on p. 547

[445] Krishnan, S., A. Pattekar, M.C. Lin, and D. Manocha, "Spherical Shell: A Higher Order Bounding Volume for Fast Proximity Queries," *Proceedings of Third International Workshop on Algorithmic Foundations of Robotics*, pp. 122–136, 1998. http://www.cs.unc.edu/~dm/ Cited on p. 482, 644, 645

[446] Krishnan, S., M. Gopi, M. Lin, D. Manocha, and A. Pattekar, "Rapid and Accurate Contact Determination between Spline Models using ShellTrees," *Proceedings of Eurographics '98*, vol. 17, no. 3, pp. C315–C326, 1998. http://www.cs.unc.edu/~dm/ Cited on p. 482, 645

[447] Kumar, Subodh, and Dinesh Manocha, "Hierarchical Visibility Culling for Spline Models," *Graphics Interface 96*, Toronto, Canada, pp. 142–150, May 1996. ftp://ftp.cs.unc.edu/pub/publications/techreports/FILE.html Cited on p. 363

[448] Kumar, S., D. Manocha, B. Garrett, and M. Lin, "Hierarchical Back-Face Computation," *Proceedings of Eurographics Rendering Workshop 1996*, pp. 235–244, June 1996. Cited on p. 362

[449] Labsik, U., and G. Greiner, "Interpolatory $\sqrt{3}$-Subdivision," *Computer Graphics Forum (Proceedings of Eurographics 2000)*, vol. 19, no. 3, pp. 131–138, 2000. Cited on p. 555

[450] Lacroute, Philippe, and Marc Levoy, "Fast Volume Rendering Using a Shear-Warp Factorization of the Viewing Transformation," *Computer Graphics (SIGGRAPH 94 Proceedings)*, pp. 451–458, July 1994. http://www-graphics.stanford.edu/papers/shear/ Cited on p. 343

[451] Lafortune, Eric P. F., Sing-Choong Foo, Kenneth E. Torrance, and Donald P. Greenberg, "Non-Linear Approximation of Reflectance Functions,"

Computer Graphics (SIGGRAPH 97 Proceedings), pp. 117–126, August 1997. http://www.graphics.cornell.edu/pubs/1997/LFTG97.html Cited on p. 201, 202

[452] Laidlaw, D.H., W.B. Trumbore, and J. Hughes, "Constructive Solid Geometry for Polyhedral Objects," *Computer Graphics (SIGGRAPH '86 Proceedings)*, pp. 161–168, August 1986. Cited on p. 591

[453] Lake, Adam, Carl Marshall, Marc Harris, and Marc Blackstein, "Stylized Rendering Techniques for Scalable Real-time Animation," *Proceedings of the First International Symposium on Non-photorealistic Animation and Rendering (NPAR)*, pp. 13–20, June 2000. http://developer.intel.com/ial/3dsoftware/doc.htm Cited on p. 290, 303, 304

[454] Lake, Adam, "Cartoon Rendering Using Texture Mapping and Programmable Vertex Shaders," in Mark DeLoura, ed., *Game Programming Gems 2*, Charles River Media, pp. 444–451, 2001. Cited on p. 290, 291

[455] Lake, Adam, "Programmable Vertex Shader Compiler," in Mark DeLoura, ed., *Game Programming Gems 3*, Charles River Media, 2002. Cited on p. 287

[456] Lambert, J. H., *Photometria*, 1760. English translation by D. L. DiLaura, Illuminating Engineering Society of North America, 2001. Cited on p. 187

[457] Lander, Jeff, "Slashing Through Real-Time Character Animation," *Game Developer*, vol. 5, no. 4, pp. 13–15, April 1998. http://www.gdmag.com/code.htm Cited on p. 53

[458] Lander, Jeff, "Skin Them Bones: Game Programming for the Web Generation," *Game Developer*, vol. 5, no. 5, pp. 11–16, May 1998. http://www.gdmag.com/code.htm Cited on p. 53

[459] Lander, Jeff, "The Ocean Spray in Your Face," *Game Developer*, vol. 5, no. 7, pp. 13–19, July 1998. http://www.gdmag.com/code.htm Cited on p. 331

[460] Lander, Jeff, "Collision Response: Bouncy, Trouncy, Fun," *Game Developer*, vol. 6, no. 3, pp. 15–19, March 1999. http://www.gamasutra.com/features/20000208/lander_01.htm Cited on p. 665

[461] Lander, Jeff, "Physics on the Back of a Cocktail Napkin," *Game Developer*, vol. 6, no. 9, pp. 17–21, September 1999. http://www.gamasutra.com/features/20000516/lander_01.htm Cited on p. 667

[462] Lander, Jeff, "Under the Shade of the Rendering Tree," *Game Developer Magazine*, vol. 7, no. 2, pp. 17–21, Feb. 2000. http://www.gdmag.com/code.htm Cited on p. 290, 295, 304, 312

[463] Lander, Jeff, "Shades of Disney: Opaquing a 3D World," *Game Developer Magazine*, vol. 7, no. 3, pp. 15–20, March 2000. Cited on p. 290, 312

[464] Lander, Jeff, "Return to Cartoon Central," *Game Developer Magazine*, vol. 7, no. 8, pp. 9–14, August 2000. http://www.gdmag.com/code.htm Cited on p. 305, 312

[465] Lander, Jeff, "That's a Wrap: Texture Mapping Methods," *Game Developer Magazine*, vol. 7, no. 10, pp. 21–26, October 2000. http://www.gdmag.com/code.htm Cited on p. 120, 123, 156

[466] Lander, Jeff, "Haunted Trees for Halloween," *Game Developer Magazine*, vol. 7, no. 11, pp. 17–21, November 2000. http://www.gdmag.com/code. htm Cited on p. 559

[467] Lander, Jeff, "Graphics Programming and the Tower of Babel," *Game Developer*, vol. 8, no. 3, pp. 13–16, March 2001. http://www.gdmag.com/ code.htm Cited on p. 291, 312

[468] Lander, Jeff, "A Heaping Pile of Pirate Booty," *Game Developer*, vol. 8, no. 4, pp. 22–30, April 2001. Cited on p. 53, 56

[469] Lander, Jeff, "Images from Deep in the Programmer's Cave," *Game Developer*, vol. 8, no. 5, pp. 23–28, May 2001. http://www.gdmag.com/code.htm Cited on p. 292, 301, 307, 312

[470] Lander, Jeff, "The Era of Post-Photorealism," *Game Developer*, vol. 8, no. 6, pp. 18–22, June 2001. Cited on p. 304, 312

[471] Larsen, E., S. Gottschalk, M. Lin, and D. Manocha, "Fast proximity queries with swept sphere volumes," Technical Report TR99-018, Department of Computer Science, University of North Carolina, 1999. http://www.cs. unc.edu/~geom/SSV Cited on p. 629, 645, 657, 662

[472] Larsson, Thomas, and Tomas Akenine-Möller, "Collision Detection for Continuously Deforming Bodies," *Eurographics 2001*, short presentation, pp. 325–333, September 2001. Cited on p. 348, 662, 663, 664

[473] Lastra, Anselmo, Steven Molnar, Marc Olano, and Yulan Wang, "Real-Time Programmable Shading," *Proceedings 1995 Symposium on Interactive 3D Graphics*, pp. 59–66, April 1995. Cited on p. 232

[474] Lathrop, Olin, David Kirk, and Doug Voorhies, "Accurate Rendering by Subpixel Addressing," *IEEE Computer Graphics and Applications*, vol. 10, no. 5, pp. 45–53, September 1990. Cited on p. 447, 674, 689

[475] Laur, David, and Pat Hanrahan, "Hierarchical Splatting: A Progressive Refinement Algorithm for Volume Rendering," *Computer Graphics (SIGGRAPH '91 Proceedings)*, pp. 285–288, July 1991. Cited on p. 343

[476] Law, Fei-Ah, and Tiow-Seng Tan, "Preprocessing Occlusion for Real-Time Selective Refinement," *Proceedings 1999 Symposium on Interactive 3D Graphics*, pp. 47–53, April 1999. Cited on p. 386

[477] Lawson, Terry, *Linear Algebra*, John Wiley & Sons, Inc., 1996. Cited on p. 729, 731, 738

[478] Lax, Peter D., *Linear Algebra*, John Wiley & Sons, Inc., 1997. Cited on p. 28, 726, 729, 738

[479] Lee, Aaron, Henry Moreton, and Hugues Hoppe, "Displaced Subdivision Surfaces," *Computer Graphics (SIGGRAPH 2000 Proceedings)*, pp. 85–94, July 2000. Cited on p. 470, 547, 548, 549

[480] Lee, Aaron, "Building Your Own Subdivision Surfaces," *Gamasutra*, September 8, 2000. http://www.gamasutra.com/features/20000908/lee_01. htm Cited on p. 470

[481] Leed, Yuan-Chung, and Chein-Wei Jen, "Improved Quadratic Normal Vector Interpolation for Realistic Shading," *The Visual Computer*, vol. 17, no. 6, pp. 337–352, 2001. Cited on p. 508

[482] Legakis, Justin, "Fast Multi-Layer Fog," *Conference Abstracts and Applications (SIGGRAPH 98)*, p. 266, July 1998. Cited on p. 108

[483] LeGrand, Scott, "Compendium of Vertex Shader Tricks," in Engel, Wolfgang, ed., *ShaderX*, Wordware, May 2002. http://www.shaderx.com/ Cited on p. 331

[484] Lengyel, Eric, "A Fast Cylinder-Frustum Intersection Test," in Mark DeLoura, ed., *Game Programming Gems*, Charles River Media, pp. 380–389, 2000. Cited on p. 611

[485] Lengyel, Jed, and John Snyder, "Rendering With Coherent Layers," *Computer Graphics (SIGGRAPH 97 Proceedings)*, pp. 233–242, August 1997. http://www.research.microsoft.com/~jedl/ Cited on p. 316

[486] Lengyel, Jerome, "The Convergence of Graphics and Vision," *Computer*, pp. 46–53, July 1998. http://www.research.microsoft.com/~jedl/ Cited on p. 314, 344

[487] Lengyel, Jerome, "Real-Time Fur," *11th Eurographics Workshop on Rendering*, pp. 243–256, June 2000. http://www.research.microsoft.com/~jedl/ Cited on p. 201, 308, 344, 469

[488] Lengyel, Jed, Emil Praun, Adam Finkelstein, and Hugues Hoppe, "Real-Time Fur over Arbitrary Surfaces," *Proceedings 2001 Symposium on Interactive 3D Graphics*, pp. 59–62 March 2001. http://www.research.microsoft.com/~jedl/ Cited on p. 308, 469

[489] Levoy, Marc, and Turner Whitted, *The Use of Points as a Display Primitive*, Technical Report 85-022, Computer Science Department, University of North Carolina at Chapel Hill, January, 1985. Cited on p. 401

[490] Levoy, Marc, and Pat Hanrahan, "Light Field Rendering," *Computer Graphics (SIGGRAPH 96 Proceedings)*, pp. 31–42, August, 1996. http://www-graphics.stanford.edu/papers/light/ Cited on p. 317

[491] Levoy, Marc, Kari Pulli, Brian Curless, Szymon Rusinkiewicz, David Koller, Lucas Pereira, Matt Ginzton, Sean Anderson, James Davis, Jeremy Ginsberg, and Jonathan Shade, "The Digital Michelangelo Project: 3D scanning of large statues," *Computer Graphics (SIGGRAPH 2000 Proceedings)*, pp. 131–144, July 2000. Cited on p. 402

[492] Lewis, J.P., Matt Cordner, and Nickson Fong, "Pose Space Deformation: A Unified Approach to Shape Interpolation and Skeleton-Driven Deformation," *Computer Graphics (SIGGRAPH 2000 Proceedings)*, pp. 165–172, July 2000. Cited on p. 53, 57, 66

[493] Li, Tsai-Yen, and Jin-Shin Chen, "Incremental 3D Collision Detection with Hierarchical Data Structures," *Virtual Reality Software and Technology'98 (VRST'98)*, pp. 139–144, November 1998. Cited on p. 657

[494] Lien, Sheue-Ling, Michael Shantz, and Vaughan Pratt, "Adaptive Forward Differencing for Rendering Curves and Surfaces," *Computer Graphics (SIGGRAPH '87 Proceedings)*, pp. 111–118, July 1987. Cited on p. 514

[495] Lin, M.C., and J. Canny, "Efficient algorithms for incremental distance computation," *IEEE Conference on Robotics and Automation*, pp. 1008–1014, 1991. Cited on p. 653, 662

[496] Lin, M.C., *Efficient Collision Detection for Animation and Robotics*, Ph.D. Thesis, University of California, Berkeley, 1993. Cited on p. 653, 654, 655, 660

[497] Lin, M.C., D. Manocha, J. Cohen, and S. Gottschalk, "Collision Detection: Algorithms and Applications," *Proceedings of Algorithms for Robotics Motion and Manipulation*, Jean-Paul Laumond and M. Overmars, eds., A.K. Peters Ltd., pp. 129–142, 1996. Cited on p. 653

[498] Lin, M.C., and S. Gottschalk, "Collision Detection between Geometric Models: A Survey," *Proceedings of IMA Conference on Mathematics of Surfaces*, 1998. http://www.cs.unc.edu/~dm/ Cited on p. 666

[499] Lindholm, Erik, Mark Kilgard, and Henry Moreton, "A User-Programmable Vertex Engine," *Computer Graphics (SIGGRAPH 2001 Proceedings)*, pp. 149–158, August 2001. Cited on p. 215, 217, 284

[500] Lindstrom, P., D. Koller, W. Ribarsky, L.F. Hodges, N. Faust, and G.A. Turner, "Real-Time, Continuous Level of Detail Rendering of Height Fields," *Computer Graphics (SIGGRAPH 96 Proceedings)*, pp. 109–118, August 1996. Cited on p. 476, 522

[501] Lindstrom, Peter, and Greg Turk, "Image-Driven Simplification," *ACM Transactions on Graphics*, vol. 19, no. 3, pp. 204–241, July 2000. http://www.cc.gatech.edu/gvu/people/peter.lindstrom/ Cited on p. 474

[502] Lokovic, Tom, and Eric Veach, "Deep Shadow Maps," *Computer Graphics (SIGGRAPH 2000 Proceedings)*, pp. 385–392, July 2000. http://graphics.stanford.edu/papers/deepshadows/ Cited on p. 273

[503] Loop, C., *Smooth Subdivision Based on Triangles*, Master's Thesis, Department of Mathematics, University of Utah, August 1987. http://www.research.microsoft.com/~cloop/ Cited on p. 533, 535, 536, 537

[504] Lorensen, William E., and Harvey E. Cline, "Marching Cubes: A High Resolution 3D Surface Construction Algorithm," *Computer Graphics (SIGGRAPH '87 Proceedings)*, pp. 163–169, July 1987. Cited on p. 527

[505] Luebke, David P., and Chris Georges, "Portals and Mirrors: Simple, Fast Evaluation of Potentially Visible Sets," *Proceedings 1995 Symposium on Interactive 3D Graphics*, pp. 105–106, April 1995. Cited on p. 366

[506] Luebke, David P., "A Developer's Survey of Polygonal Simplification Algorithms," *IEEE Computer Graphics & Applications*, vol. 21, no. 3, pp. 24–35, May/June 2001. http://www.cs.virginia.edu/~luebke/publications/pdf/cg+a.2001.pdf Cited on p. 479

[507] Luebke, David, Martin Reddy, Jonathan Cohen, Amitabh Varshney, Benjamin Watson, and Robert Huebner, "Advanced Issues in Level of Detail," *Course 41 notes at SIGGRAPH 2001*, 2001. Cited on p. 390, 403, 470, 472, 475

[508] Maciel, P., and P. Shirley, "Visual Navigation of Large Environments Using Textured Clusters," *Proceedings 1995 Symposium on Interactive 3D Graphics*, pp. 96–102, 1995. `ftp://ftp.cs.indiana.edu/pub/shirley/interactive95.ps.Z` Cited on p. 325, 400, 469

[509] Macri, Dean, "Fast AGP Writes for Dynamic Vertex Data," *Game Developer*, pp. 36–42, May 2001. Cited on p. 407, 411

[510] Magnenat-Thalmann, Nadia, Richard Laperrière, and Daniel Thalmann, "Joint-Dependent Local Deformations for Hand Animation and Object Grasping", *Graphics Interface '88*, pp. 26–33, June 1988. Cited on p. 53

[511] Maillot, Patrick-Giles, "Using Quaternions for Coding 3D Transformations," in Andrew S. Glassner, ed., *Graphics Gems*, Academic Press, pp. 498–515, 1990. `http://www.graphicsgems.org/` Cited on p. 45

[512] Maillot, Jérôme, and Jos Stam, "A Unified Subdivision Scheme for Polygonal Modeling," *Proceedings of Eurographics 2001*, Vol. 20, No. 3, pp. 471–479, September 2001. `http://www.dgp.utoronto.ca/people/stam/reality/Research/pub.html` Cited on p. 537

[513] Malzbender, Tom, Dan Gelb, and Hans Wolters, "Polynomial Texture Maps," *Computer Graphics (SIGGRAPH 2001 Proceedings)*, pp. 519–528, August 2001. Cited on p. 168

[514] Mammen, Abraham, "Transparency and Antialiasing Algorithms Implemented with the Virtual Pixel Maps Technique," *IEEE Computer Graphics & Applications*, vol. 9, no. 4, pp. 43–55, July 1989. Cited on p. 93, 97, 103

[515] Mark, Bill, "Background and Future of Real-Time Procedural Shading," in *Approaches for Procedural Shading on Graphics Hardware*, SIGGRAPH 2000 course 27 notes, July 2000. Cited on p. 684

[516] Mark, William R., and Kekoa Proudfoot, "The F-Buffer: A Rasterization-Order FIFO Buffer for Multi-Pass Rendering," *ACM SIGGRAPH/Eurographics Workshop on Graphics Hardware*, pp. 57–63, August 2001. `http://graphics.stanford.edu/projects/shading/pubs/hwws2001-fbuffer/` Cited on p. 104

[517] Markosian, Lee, Michael A. Kowalski, Samuel J. Trychin, Lubomir D. Bourdev, Daniel Goldstein, and John F. Hughes, "Real-Time Nonphotorealistic Rendering," *Computer Graphics (SIGGRAPH 97 Proceedings)*, pp. 415–420, August 1997. `http://www.cs.brown.edu/research/graphics/research/npr/home.html` Cited on p. 302

[518] Markosian, Lee, Barbara J. Meier, Michael A. Kowalski, Loring S. Holden, J.D. Northrup, and John F. Hughes, "Art-based Rendering with Continuous Levels of Detail," *Proceedings of the First International Symposium on Non-photorealistic Animation and Rendering (NPAR)*, pp. 59–66, June 2000. `http://www.cs.brown.edu/research/graphics/research/art/graftal/` Cited on p. 304, 307

[519] Marschner, Stephen R., Stephen H. Westin, Eric P.F. Lafortune, and Kenneth E. Torrance, "Image-based Bidirectional Reflectance Distribution Function Measurement," *Applied Optics*, vol. 39, no. 16, June 2000. `http://www.graphics.cornell.edu/pubs/2000/MWLT00.html` Cited on p. 202

[520] Marselas, Herbert, "Optimizing Vertex Submission for OpenGL," in Mark DeLoura, ed., *Game Programming Gems*, Charles River Media, pp. 353–360, 2000. Cited on p. 465, 468

[521] Marshall, Carl S., "Cartoon Rendering: Real-time Silhouette Edge Detection and Rendering," in Mark DeLoura, ed., *Game Programming Gems 2*, Charles River Media, pp. 436–443, 2001. Cited on p. 294, 301

[522] Mason, Ashton E. W., and Edwin H. Blake, "Automatic Hierarchical Level Of Detail Optimization in Computer Animation," *Computer Graphics Forum*, vol. 16, no. 3, pp. 191–199, 1997. Cited on p. 401

[523] Maughan, Chris, and Matthias Wloka, "Vertex Shader Introduction," NVIDIA White Paper, May 2001. http://developer.nvidia.com Cited on p. 215, 216

[524] Maughan, Chris, "Texture Masking for Faster Lens Flare," in Mark DeLoura, ed., *Game Programming Gems 2*, Charles River Media, pp. 474–480, 2001. Cited on p. 331, 694

[525] Max, Nelson, "Weights for Computing Vertex Normals from Facet Normals," *journal of graphics tools*, vol. 4, no. 2, pp. 1–6, 1999. Cited on p. 452

[526] "Maxima for Symbolic Computation Program," http://www.ma.utexas.edu/maxima.html Cited on p. 629

[527] McCabe, Dan, and John Brothers, "DirectX 6 Texture Map Compression," *Game Developer*, vol. 5, no. 8, pp. 42–46, August 1998. http://www.gdmag.com/code.htm Cited on p. 143, 677

[528] McCloud, Scott, *Understanding Comics: The Invisible Art*, Harper Perennial, 1994. Cited on p. 290, 312

[529] McCool, Michael D., "SMASH: A Next-Generation API for Programmable Graphics Accelerators," Technical Report CS-2000-14, University of Waterloo, August 2000. http://www.cgl.uwaterloo.ca/Projects/rendering/Papers/smash.pdf Cited on p. 287

[530] McCool, Michael D., Jason Ang, and Anis Ahmad, "Homomorphic Factorization of BRDFs for High-performance Rendering," *Computer Graphics (SIGGRAPH 2001 Proceedings)*, pp. 171–178, August 2001. http://www.cgl.uwaterloo.ca/Projects/rendering/Papers/ Cited on p. 178, 200, 202, 204, 215, 219, 287

[531] McCormack, Joel, Bob McNamara, Christopher Gianos, Larry Seiler, Norman P. Jouppi, Ken Corell, Todd Dutton, and John Zurawski, "Implementing Neon: A 256-Bit Graphics Accelerator," *IEEE Micro*, vol. 19, no. 2, pp. 58–69, March/April 1999. http://www.research.digital.com/wrl/publications/abstracts/98.1.html Cited on p. 135

[532] McCormack, Joel, Ronald Perry, Keith I. Farkas, and Norman P. Jouppi, "Feline: Fast Elliptical Lines for Anisotropic Texture Mapping," *Computer Graphics (SIGGRAPH 99 Proceedings)*, pp. 243–250, August 1999. http://www.research.compaq.com/wrl/techreports/abstracts/99.1.html Cited on p. 141

[533] McCormack, Joel, and Robert McNamara, "Tiled Polygon Traversal Using Half-Plane Edge Functions," *ACM SIGGRAPH/Eurographics Workshop on Graphics Hardware*, pp. 15–22, 2000. Cited on p. 690, 696, 700

[534] McCuskey, Mason, "Using 3D Hardware for 2D Sprite Effects," in Mark DeLoura, ed., *Game Programming Gems*, Charles River Media, pp. 519–523, 2000. Cited on p. 315

[535] McMillan, Leonard, and Gary Bishop, "Plenoptic Modeling: An Image-Based Rendering System," *Computer Graphics (SIGGRAPH 95 Proceedings)*, pp. 39–46, August 1995. http://graphics.lcs.mit.edu/~mcmillan/Publications/plenoptic.html Cited on p. 187

[536] McReynolds, Tom, David Blythe, Brad Grantham, and Scott Nelson, *SIGGRAPH 99 Advanced Graphics Programming Techniques Using OpenGL course notes*, 1999. www.opengl.org/developers/code/sig99/index.html Cited on p. 92, 103, 126, 137, 141, 148, 151, 152, 159, 163, 168, 171, 178, 237, 243, 260, 264, 308, 309, 310, 311, 312, 318, 331, 343, 344, 424, 425, 444, 708

[537] McVoy, Larry, and Carl Staelin, "lmbench: Portable tools for performance analysis," *Proceedings of the USENIX 1996 Annual Technical Conference*, San Diego, pp. 120–133, January 1996. http://www.bitmover.com/lmbench/ Cited on p. 415

[538] Meißner, Michael, Dirk Bartz, Tobias Hüttner, Gordon Müller, and Jens Einighammer, *Generation of Subdivision Hierarchies for Efficient Occlusion Culling of Large Polygonal Models*, Technical Report WSI-99-13, WSI/GRIS, University of Tbingen, 1999 Cited on p. 382

[539] Meißner, M., D. Bartz, R. Günther, W. Straßer, "Visibility Driven Rasterization," *Computer Graphics Forum*, Vol. 20, No. 4, pp 283–293, 2001. Cited on p. 385

[540] Melax, Stan, "A Simple, Fast, and Effective Polygon Reduction Algorithm," *Game Developer*, vol. 5, no. 11, pp. 44–49, November 1998. http://www.melax.com/polychop/ Cited on p. 394, 471, 472, 475

[541] Melax, Stan, "The Shortest Arc Quaternion," in Mark DeLoura, ed., *Game Programming Gems*, Charles River Media, pp. 214–218, 2000. Cited on p. 52

[542] Melax, Stan, "Dynamic Plane Shifting BSP Traversal," *Graphics Interface 2000*, Canada, pp. 213–220, May 2000. http://www.graphicsinterface.org/ Cited on p. 634, 636, 638

[543] Melax, Stan, "BSP Collision Detection as Used in MDK2 and NeverWinter Nights," *Gamasutra*, March 2001. http://www.gamasutra.com/features/20010324/melax_01.htm Cited on p. 634

[544] Meyer, Alexandre, and Fabrice Neyret, "Interactive Volumetric Textures," *9th Eurographics Workshop on Rendering*, pp. 157–168, July 1998. http://www-imagis.imag.fr/Membres/Fabrice.Neyret/publis/EWR98-eng.html Cited on p. 334, 344

[545] Meyer, Alexandre, Fabrice Neyret, and Pierre Poulin, "Interactive Rendering of Trees with Shading and Shadows," *12th Eurographics Workshop on Rendering*, pp. 182–195, June 2001. http://www-imagis.imag. fr/Publications/2001/MNP01/index.gb.html Cited on p. 149, 324, 337

[546] Miano, John, *Compressed Image File Formats: JPEG, PNG, GIF, XBM, BMP*, Addison-Wesley, Reading, Massachusetts, 1999. Cited on p. 143

[547] Microsoft Corp., "Advanced Shading and Lighting," *Meltdown 2001*, July 2001. http://www.microsoft.com/mscorp/corpevents/meltdown2001/ presentations.asp Cited on p. 111, 168, 171, 212, 231, 284

[548] Miller, Gene S., and C. Robert Hoffman, "Illumination and Reflection Maps: Simulated Objects in Simulated and Real Environments," *SIGGRAPH '84 Advanced Computer Graphics Animation course notes*, 1984. http://www.debevec.org/ReflectionMapping Cited on p. 158

[549] Miller, Gavin, Mark Halstead, and Michael Clifton, "On-the-Fly Texture Computation for Real-Time Surface Shading," *IEEE Computer Graphics and Applications*, vol. 18, no. 2, pp. 44–58, March/April 1998. http:// computer.org/cga/cg1998/g2toc.htm Cited on p. 176

[550] Miné, Antoine, and Fabrice Neyret, "Perlin Textures in Real Time using OpenGL," Technical Report RR-3713, INRIA, France, June 1999. http: //www-imagis.imag.fr/Publications/1999/MN99/ Cited on p. 126

[551] Mirtich, Brian, and John Canny, "Impulse-Based Simulation of Rigid-Bodies," *Proceedings 1995 Symposium on Interactive 3D Graphics*, pp. 181–188, 1995. Cited on p. 664

[552] Mirtich, Brian, "Fast and Accurate Computation of Polyhedral Mass Properties," *journal of graphics tools*, vol. 1, no. 2, pp. 31–50, 1996. http://www.acm.org/jgt/papers/Mirtich96/ Cited on p. 593

[553] Mirtich, Brian, "V-Clip: fast and robust polyhedral collision detection," *ACM Transactions on Graphics*, vol. 17, no. 3, July 1998. http://www. merl.com/projects/vclip/ Cited on p. 653, 662

[554] Mitchell, Jason L., "Optimizing Direct3D Applications for Hardware Acceleration," *Gamasutra*, December 5, 1997. http://www.gamasutra.com/ features/19971205/mitchell_01.htm Cited on p. 424

[555] Mitchell, Jason L., Michael Tatro, and Ian Bullard, "Multitexturing in DirectX 6," *Game Developer*, vol. 5, no. 9, pp. 33–37, September 1998. http://www.gamasutra.com/features/programming/19981009/ multitexturing_01.htm Cited on p. 148, 163

[556] Mitchell, Jason L., "Advanced Vertex and Pixel Shader Techniques," *European Game Developers Conference*, London, September 2001. http: //www.users.qwest.net/~jlmitchell1/ Cited on p. 227, 231, 341

[557] Mitchell, Jason L. "Image Processing with Pixel Shaders in Direct3D," in Engel, Wolfgang, ed., *ShaderX*, Wordware, May 2002. http://www. shaderx.com/ Cited on p. 299, 341

[558] Mitchell, Kenny, "Real-Time Full Scene Anti-Aliasing for PCs and Consoles," *Game Developers Conference*, pp. 537–543, March 2001. http://

www.gdconf.com/archives/proceedings/2001/prog_papers.html Cited on p. 93, 114, 237

[559] Mohr, Alex, and Michael Gleicher, "Non-Invasive, Interactive, Stylized Rendering," *Proceedings 2001 Symposium on Interactive 3D Graphics*, pp. 59–62 March 2001. http://www.cs.wisc.edu/graphics/Gallery/Stylized/ Cited on p. 307

[560] Möller, Tomas, and Ben Trumbore, "Fast, Minimum Storage Ray-Triangle Intersection," *journal of graphics tools*, vol. 2, no. 1, pp. 21–28, 1997. http://www.acm.org/jgt/papers/MollerTrumbore97/ Cited on p. 578, 581, 582, 593

[561] Möller, Tomas, "A Fast Triangle-Triangle Intersection Test," *journal of graphics tools*, vol. 2, no. 2, pp. 25–30, 1997. http://www.acm.org/jgt/papers/Moller97/ Cited on p. 590, 594, 596

[562] Möller, Tomas, *Real-Time Algorithms and Intersection Test Methods for Computer Graphics*, Ph.D. Thesis, Technology, Technical Report No. 341, Department of Computer Engineering, Chalmers University of Technology, October 1998. Cited on p. 240

[563] Möller, Tomas, and John F. Hughes, "Efficiently Building a Matrix to Rotate One Vector to Another," *journal of graphics tools*, vol. 4, no. 4, pp. 1–4, 1999. http://www.acm.org/jgt/papers/MollerHughes99/ Cited on p. 52

[564] Molnar, Steven, "Efficient Supersampling Antialiasing for High-Performance Architectures," TR91-023, Department of Computer Science, The University of North Carolina at Chapel Hill, 1991. http://www.cs.unc.edu/Research/tech-report.html Cited on p. 100, 340

[565] Molnar, S., J. Eyles, and J. Poulton, "PixelFlow: High-Speed Rendering Using Image Composition," *Computer Graphics (SIGGRAPH '92 Proceedings)*, pp. 231–240, July 1992. Cited on p. 686, 706, 708

[566] Molnar, S., M. Cox, D. Ellsworth, and H. Fuchs, "A Sorting Classification of Parallel Rendering," *IEEE Computer Graphics and Applications*, vol. 14, no. 4, pp. 23–32, July 1994. Cited on p. 685, 686, 687

[567] Molnar, S., "The PixelFlow Texture and Image Subsystem," in the *Proceedings of the 10th Eurographics Workshop on Graphics Hardware*, Maastricht, Netherlands, pp. 3–13, August 28–29, 1995. Cited on p. 708

[568] Montrym, J., D. Baum, D. Dignam, and C. Migdal, "InfiniteReality: A Real-Time Graphics System," *Computer Graphics (SIGGRAPH 97 Proceedings)*, pp. 293–302, August 1997. Cited on p. 84, 99, 142, 144, 420, 673, 691, 701, 702, 703, 704, 705

[569] Moore, Matthew, and Jane Wilhelms, "Collision Detection and Response for Computer Animation," *Computer Graphics (SIGGRAPH '88 Proceedings)*, pp. 289–298, August 1988. Cited on p. 664

[570] Morein, Steve, "ATI Radeon HyperZ Technology," *ACM SIGGRAPH/Eurographics Workshop on Graphics Hardware*, Hot3D Proceedings, Switzerland, August 2000. Cited on p. 422, 696

[571] Moreton, Henry P., and Carlo H. Séquin, "Functional Optimization for Fair Surface Design," *Computer Graphics (SIGGRAPH '92 Proceedings)*, pp. 167–176, July 1992. Cited on p. 536

[572] Moreton, Henry, "Watertight Tessellation using Forward Differencing," *ACM SIGGRAPH/Eurographics Workshop on Graphics Hardware*, pp. 25–132, August 2001. Cited on p. 514, 522, 523, 524

[573] Mortenson, Michael E., *Geometric Modeling*, Second Edition, John Wiley & Sons, 1997. Cited on p. 482, 555

[574] Muchnick, Steven, *Advanced Compiler Design and Implementation*, Morgan Kaufmann Publishers, San Francisco, 1997. Cited on p. 436

[575] Mueller, Carl, "Architectures of Image Generators for Flight Simulators," TR95-015, Department of Computer Science, The University of North Carolina at Chapel Hill, 1995. http://www.cs.unc.edu/Research/tech-report.html Cited on p. 101

[576] Müller, Kerstin, and Sven Havemann, "Subdivision Surface Tesselation on the Fly using a versatile Mesh Data Structure," *Computer Graphics Forum* (Proceedings of Eurographics 2000), Vol. 19, No. 3, pp. 151–159, 2000. http://www.cg.cs.tu-bs.de/v3d2/pubs Cited on p. 554

[577] Murray, James D., and William VanRyper, *Encyclopedia of Graphics File Formats*, Second Edition, O'Reilly & Associates, 1996. http://www.ora.com/centers/gff/index.htm Cited on p. 105, 143, 440, 479, 673

[578] Myer, T.H., and I.E. Sutherland, "On the Design of Display Processors," *Communications of the ACM*, vol. 11, no. 6, pp. 410–414, June 1968. Cited on p. 711

[579] Nagy, Gabor, "Real-Time Shadows on Complex Objects," in Mark DeLoura, ed., *Game Programming Gems*, Charles River Media, pp. 567–580, 2000. Cited on p. 260

[580] Nagy, Gabor, "Convincing-Looking Glass for Games," in Mark DeLoura, ed., *Game Programming Gems*, Charles River Media, pp. 586–593, 2000. Cited on p. 102, 103

[581] Narkhede, Atul, and Dinesh Manocha, "Fast Polygon Triangulation Based on Seidel's Algorithm," Paeth, Alan W., ed., *Graphics Gems V*, Academic Press, pp. 394–397, 1995. Improved code at: http://www.cs.unc.edu/~dm/CODE/GEM/chapter.html Cited on p. 443, 479

[582] Naylor, B., J. Amanatides, and W. Thibault, "Merging BSP Trees Yield Polyhedral Modeling Results," *Computer Graphics (SIGGRAPH '89 Proceedings)*, pp. 115–124, July 1989. Cited on p. 420

[583] Nelson, Scott R., "Twelve characteristics of correct antialiased lines," *journal of graphics tools*, vol. 1, no. 4, pp. 1–20, 1996. http://www.acm.org/jgt/papers/Nelson96/ Cited on p. 92, 112

[584] Nelson, Scott R., "High quality hardware line antialiasing," *journal of graphics tools*, vol. 2, no. 1, pp. 29–46, 1997. http://www.acm.org/jgt/papers/Nelson97/ Cited on p. 92

[585] Nicodemus, F.E., J.C. Richmond, J.J. Hsia, I.W. Ginsberg, and T. Limperis, "Geometric Considerations and Nomenclature for Reflectance," National Bureau of Standards (US), October 1977. Cited on p. 194, 196

[586] Nielsen, Kasper Høy, *Real-Time Hardware-Based Photorealistic Rendering*, Master's Thesis, Informatics and Mathematical Modeling, The Technical University of Denmark, 2000. Cited on p. 243

[587] Nishita, Tomoyuki, Thomas W. Sederberg, and Masanori Kakimoto, "Ray Tracing Trimmed Rational Surface Patches," *Computer Graphics (SIGGRAPH '90 Proceedings)*, pp. 337–345, August 1990. Cited on p. 583

[588] Nguyen, Hubert, "Casting Shadows on Volumes," *Game Developer*, vol. 6, no. 3, pp. 44–53, March 1999. Cited on p. 260

[589] Northrup, J.D., and Lee Markosian, "Artistic Silhouettes: A Hybrid Approach," *Proceedings of the First International Symposium on Non-photorealistic Animation and Rendering (NPAR)*, pp. 31–37, June 2000. http://www.cs.brown.edu/research/graphics/research/art/artistic-sils/ Cited on p. 303

[590] NVIDIA developer web site. http://developer.nvidia.com/ Cited on p. 173, 231, 287

[591] NVIDIA Corporation, "HRAA: High-Resolution Antialiasing through Multisampling," Technical Brief, 2001. http://www.nvidia.com/docs/IO/83/ATT/HRAA.pdf Cited on p. 98

[592] NVIDIA Corporation, "NVIDIA Accuview Technology: High-Resolution Antialiasing Subsystem," Technical Brief, 2002. http://www.nvidia.com/docs/lo/1451/SUPP/accuview.final.pdf Cited on p. 99

[593] Ofek, E., and A. Rappoport, "Interactive Reflections on Curved Objects," *Computer Graphics (SIGGRAPH 98 Proceedings)*, pp. 333–342, July 1998. Cited on p. 240, 243, 245

[594] Olano, Marc, and Michael North, "Normal Distribution Mapping," UNC Chapel Hill Computer Science Technical Report 97-041, 1997. http://www.cs.unc.edu/~olano/papers/ndm/ Cited on p. 172

[595] Olano, Marc, and Anselmo Lastra, "A Shading Language on Graphics Hardware: The PixelFlow Shading System," *Computer Graphics (SIGGRAPH 98 Proceedings)*, pp. 159–168, July 1998. http://www.cs.unc.edu/~pxfl/papers/pxflshading.pdf Cited on p. 232

[596] Olano, Marc, John Hart, Wolfgang Heidrich, and Michael McCool, *Real-Time Shading*, A K Peters Ltd., 2002. Cited on p. 287

[597] Oliveira, Gustavo, "Refractive Texture Mapping, Part Two," *Gamasutra*, November 2000. http://www.gamasutra.com/features/20001117/oliveira_01.htm Cited on p. 246, 247

[598] Oliveira, Manuel M., Gary Bishop, and David McAllister, "Relief Texture Mapping," *Computer Graphics (SIGGRAPH 2000 Proceedings)*, pp. 359–368, July 2000. Cited on p. 334

[599] Omohundro, Stephen M., "Five Balltree Construction Algorithms," Technical Report no. 89-063, International Computer Science Institute, 1989. http://www.icsi.berkeley.edu/techreports/ Cited on p. 641

[600] OpenGL Architecture Review Board, J. Neider, T. Davis, and M. Woo, *OpenGL Programming Guide*, Third Edition, Addison-Wesley, Reading, Massachusetts, 1999. Cited on p. 123, 124, 127, 141, 425, 456, 479, 688

[601] OpenGL Architecture Review Board, *OpenGL Reference Manual*, Third Edition, Addison-Wesley, Reading, Massachusetts, 1999. Cited on p. 61, 69

[602] *OpenGL Optimizer Programmer's Guide: An Open API for Large-Model Visualization*, Silicon Graphics Inc., 1997. http://www.sgi.com/software/optimizer/ Cited on p. 178

[603] *OpenGL Volumizer Programmer's Guide*, Silicon Graphics Inc., 1998. http://www.sgi.com/software/volumizer/tech_info.html Cited on p. 343

[604] Oren, Michael, and Shree K. Nayar, "Generalization of Lambert's Reflectance Model," *Computer Graphics (SIGGRAPH 94 Proceedings)*, pp. 239–246, July 1994. http://www.cs.columbia.edu/~oren/ Cited on p. 200

[605] O'Rourke, Joseph, *Computational Geometry in C*, Second Edition, Cambridge University Press, Cambridge, 1998. ftp://cs.smith.edu/pub/compgeom/ Cited on p. 442, 443, 583, 736, 737

[606] O'Sullivan, Carol, and John Dingliana, "Real vs. Approximate Collisions: When Can We Tell the Difference?," *Visual Proceedings (SIGGRAPH 2001)*, p. 249, August 2001. Cited on p. 658, 665

[607] O'Sullivan, Carol, and John Dingliana, "Collisions and Perception," *ACM Transactions on Graphics*, vol. 20, no. 3, pp. 151–168, 2001. Cited on p. 658, 665

[608] O'Sullivan, Carol, John Dingliana, Fabio Ganovelli, and Garet Bradshaw, "T6: Collision Handling for Virtual Environments," *Eurographics 2001 Tutorial proceedings*, 2001 Cited on p. 666

[609] Owens, John D., William J. Dally, Ujval J. Kapasi, Scott Rixner, Peter Mattson, Ben Mowery, "Polygon Rendering on a Stream Architecture," *ACM SIGGRAPH/Eurographics Workshop on Graphics Hardware*, pp. 23–32, 2000. Cited on p. 708

[610] Paeth, Alan W., ed., *Graphics Gems V*, Academic Press, 1995. http://www.graphicsgems.org/ Cited on p. 66, 435, 629

[611] Pagán, Tito, "Efficient UV Mapping of Complex Models," *Game Developer*, vol. 8, no. 8, pp. 28–34, August 2001. Cited on p. 120, 123

[612] Pallister, Kim, "'Ups and Downs' of Bump Mapping with DirectX 6," *Gamasutra*, June 1999. http://www.gamasutra.com/features/19990604/bump_01.htm Cited on p. 168, 174

[613] Pallister, Kim, "Rendering to Texture Surfaces Using DirectX7," *Gamasutra*, November 1999. http://www.gamasutra.com/features/19991112/pallister_01.htm Cited on p. 223, 257, 326

[614] Pallister, Kim, and Dean Macri, "Building Scalable 3D Games for the PC," *Gamasutra*, November 1999. http://www.gamasutra.com/features/19991124/pallistermacri_01.htm Cited on p. 146, 470

[615] Pallister, Kim, "Generating Procedural Clouds Using 3D Hardware," in Mark DeLoura, ed., *Game Programming Gems 2*, Charles River Media, pp. 463–473, 2001. Cited on p. 322

[616] Pattanaik, S., J. Tumblin, H. Yee, and D. Greenberg, "Time-Dependent Visual Adaptation for Fast, Realistic Image Display," *Computer Graphics (SIGGRAPH 2000 Proceedings)*, pp. 47–54, July 2000. Cited on p. 194

[617] Paul, Richard P.C., *Robot Manipulators: Mathematics, Programming, and Control*, MIT Press, Cambridge, Mass., 1981. Cited on p. 40

[618] Peercy, M., J. Airey, and B. Cabral, "Efficient Bump Mapping Hardware," *Computer Graphics (SIGGRAPH 97 Proceedings)*, pp. 303–306, August 1997. Cited on p. 176

[619] Peercy, Mark S., Marc Olano, John Airey, and P. Jeffrey Ungar, "Interactive Multi-Pass Programmable Shading," *Computer Graphics (SIGGRAPH 2000 Proceedings)*, pp. 425–432, July 2000. Cited on p. 145, 173, 233

[620] Pfister, Hans-Peter, Matthias Zwicker, Jeroen van Barr, and Markus Gross, "Surfels: Surface Elements as Rendering Primitives," *Computer Graphics (SIGGRAPH 2000 Proceedings)*, pp. 335–342, July 2000. Cited on p. 402

[621] Phong, Bui Tuong, "Illumination for Computer Generated Pictures," *Communications of the ACM*, vol. 18, no. 6, pp. 311–317, June 1975. Cited on p. 70, 76, 181

[622] Poulin, P., and A. Fournier, "A Model for Anisotropic Reflection," *Computer Graphics (SIGGRAPH '90 Proceedings)*, pp. 273–282, August 1990. Cited on p. 201

[623] Proudfoot, Kekoa, "Version 5 Real-Time Shading Language Description," *Game Developers Conference*, pp. 131–135, March 2001. http://www.gdconf.com/archives/proceedings/2001/prog_papers.html Cited on p. 287

[624] Proudfoot, Kekoa, William R. Mark, Svetoslav Tzvetkov, and Pat Hanrahan, "A Real-Time Procedural Shading System for Programmable Graphics Hardware," *Computer Graphics (SIGGRAPH 2001 Proceedings)*, pp. 159–170, August 2001. http://graphics.stanford.edu/projects/shading/pubs/sig2001/ Cited on p. 145, 220, 234

[625] Piegl, L., and W. Tiller, *The NURBS Book*, Springer-Verlag, Berlin/Heidelberg, Second Edition, 1997. Cited on p. 555

[626] Pineda, Juan, "A Parallel Algorithm for Polygon Rasterization," *Computer Graphics (SIGGRAPH '88 Proceedings)*, pp. 17–20, August 1988. Cited on p. 704

[627] Piponi, Dan, and George Borshukov, "Seamless Texture Mapping of Subdivision Surfaces by Model Pelting and Texture Blending," *Computer Graphics (SIGGRAPH 2000 Proceedings)*, pp. 471–478, July 2000. Cited on p. 550

[628] Pletinckx, Daniel, "Quaternion calculus as a basic tools in computer graphics," *The Visual Computer*, vol. 5, pp. 2–13, 1989. Cited on p. 66

[629] Popescu, Voicu, John Eyles, Anselmo Lastra, Joshua Steinhurst, Nick England, and Lars Nyland, "The WarpEngine: An Architecture for the Post-Polygonal Age," *Computer Graphics (SIGGRAPH 2000 Proceedings)*, pp. 433–442, July 2000. http://www.cs.unc.edu/~ibr/projects/HQWarping/HighQualityWarping.html Cited on p. 708

[630] Porter, Thomas, and Tom Duff, "Compositing digital images," *Computer Graphics (SIGGRAPH '84 Proceedings)*, pp. 253–259, July 1984. Cited on p. 102, 104

[631] Poynton, Charles, *A Technical Introduction to Digital Video*, John Wiley & Sons, Inc., pp. 91–114, 1996. http://www.inforamp.net/~poynton/Poynton-colour.html Cited on p. 109, 110, 111, 115, 193, 672

[632] Praun, Emil, Adam Finkelstein, and Hugues Hoppe, "Lapped Textures," *Computer Graphics (SIGGRAPH 2000 Proceedings)*, pp. 465–470, July 2000. Cited on p. 123, 306

[633] Praun, Emil, Hugues Hoppe, Matthew Webb, and Adam Finkelstein, "Real-time Hatching," *Computer Graphics (SIGGRAPH 2001 Proceedings)*, pp. 581–586, August 2001. Cited on p. 305, 306

[634] Preparata, F.P., and M.I. Shamos, *Computational Geometry: An Introduction*, Springer-Verlag, 1985. Cited on p. 443, 583

[635] Press, William H., Saul A. Teukolsky, William T. Vetterling, and Brian P. Flannery, "Numerical Recipes in C," Cambridge University Press, Cambridge, 1992. http://www.nr.com Cited on p. 564, 567, 623, 729

[636] Proakis, John G., and Dimitris G. Manolakis, *Digital Signal Processing: Principles, Algorithms, and Applications*, Third Edition, Macmillan Publishing Co., 1995. Cited on p. 85, 87, 89, 91

[637] Pulli, Kari, and Mark Segal, "Fast Rendering of Subdivision Surfaces," *7th Eurographics Workshop on Rendering*, pp. 61–70, June 1996. Cited on p. 555

[638] Purcell, Timothy J., Ian Buck, William R. Mark, and Pat Hanrahan, "Ray Tracing on Programmable Graphics Hardware," *Computer Graphics (SIGGRAPH 2002 Proceedings)*, July 2002. Cited on p. 286

[639] Quinlan, S., "Efficient distance computation between non-convex objects," *IEEE Conference on Robotics and Automation*, pp. 3324–3329, 1994. Cited on p. 667

[640] Rafferty, Matthew, Daniel Aliaga, Voicu Popescu, and Anselmo Lastra, "Images for Accelerating Architectural Walkthroughs," *IEEE Computer Graphics and Applications*, vol. 18, no. 6, pp. 38–45, Nov./Dec. 1998. Cited on p. 337

[641] Ramamoorthi, Ravi, and Pat Hanrahan, "An Efficient Representation for Irradiance Environment Maps," *Computer Graphics (SIGGRAPH 2001 Proceedings)*, pp. 497–500, August 2001. http://graphics.stanford.edu/papers/envmap/ Cited on p. 210, 211

[642] Ranck, Steven, "Motif-Based Static Lighting," in Mark DeLoura, ed., *Game Programming Gems*, Charles River Media, pp. 524–534, 2000. Cited on p. 418

[643] Raskar, Ramesh, and Michael Cohen, "Image Precision Silhouette Edges," *Proceedings 1999 Symposium on Interactive 3D Graphics*, pp. 135–140, April 1999. http://www.cs.unc.edu/~raskar/NPR/ Cited on p. 295, 296, 297

[644] Raskar, Ramesh, "Hardware Support for Non-photorealistic Rendering," *ACM SIGGRAPH/Eurographics Workshop on Graphics Hardware*, pp. 41–46, 2001. http://www.cs.unc.edu/~raskar/HWWS/ Cited on p. 297, 298, 299

[645] Ratcliff, John W., "Sphere Trees for Fast Visibility Culling, Ray Tracing, and Range Searching," in Mark DeLoura, ed., *Game Programming Gems 2*, Charles River Media, pp. 384–387, 2001. Cited on p. 349

[646] Reddy, Martin, *Perceptually Modulated Level of Detail for Virtual Environments*, Ph.D. Thesis, University of Edinburgh, 1997 Cited on p. 399

[647] Reeves, William T., "Particle Systems—A Technique for Modeling a Class of Fuzzy Objects," *ACM Transactions on Graphics*, vol. 2, no. 2, pp. 91–108, April 1983. Cited on p. 331

[648] Reeves, William T., and Ricki Blau, "Approximate and Probabilistic Algorithms for Shading and Rendering Structured Particle Systems," *Computer Graphics (SIGGRAPH '85 Proceedings)*, pp. 313–322, July 1985. Cited on p. 331

[649] Reeves, William T., David H. Salesin, and Robert L. Cook, "Rendering Antialiased Shadows with Depth Maps," *Computer Graphics (SIGGRAPH '87 Proceedings)*, pp. 283–291, July 1987. Cited on p. 272

[650] Reif, Ulrich, "A Unified Approach to Subdivision Algorithms Near Extraordinary Vertices," *Computer Aided Geometric Design*, vol. 12, no. 2, pp. 153–174, 1995. Cited on p. 555

[651] Reynolds, Craig, *Stylized Depiction in Computer Graphics* web site. http://www.red3d.com/cwr/npr/ Cited on p. 312

[652] Rhodes, Graham, "Fast, Robust Intersection of 3D Line Segments," in Mark DeLoura, ed., *Game Programming Gems 2*, Charles River Media, pp. 191–204, 2001. Cited on p. 619

[653] Ritter, Jack, "An Efficient Bounding Sphere," in Andrew S. Glassner, ed., *Graphics Gems*, Academic Press, pp. 301–303, 1990. http://www.graphicsgems.org/ Cited on p. 565

[654] Rockwood, Alyn, and Peter Chambers, "Interactive Curves and Surfaces: A Multimedia Tutorial on CAGD," Morgan Kaufmann Publishers, Inc., San Francisco, 1996 Cited on p. 482

[655] Roettger, Stefan, Alexander Irión, and Thomas Ertl, "Shadow Volumes Revisited," *10th International Conference in Central Europe on Computer Graphics, Visualization and Computer Vision 2002 (WSCG)*, pp. 373–379. http://wwwvis.informatik.uni-stuttgart.de/ger/research/pub/pub2002/roettgerWSCG02.pdf Cited on p. 263

[656] Rogers, David F., *Mathematical Elements for Computer Graphics*, Second Edition, McGraw-Hill, 1989. Cited on p. 66, 373, 555

[657] Rogers, David F., *Procedural Elements for Computer Graphics*, Second Edition, McGraw-Hill, 1998. Cited on p. 9, 20, 178, 442

[658] Rogers, David F., *An Introduction to NURBS: With Historical Perspective*, Morgan Kaufmann Publishers, 2000. Cited on p. 555

[659] Rohlf, J., and J. Helman, "IRIS Performer: A High Performance Multiprocessing Toolkit for Real-Time 3D Graphics," *Computer Graphics (SIGGRAPH 94 Proceedings)*, pp. 381–394, July 1994. Cited on p. 398, 431, 433, 434

[660] Rokne, Jon, "The Area of a Simple Polygon," in James Arvo, ed., *Graphics Gems II*, Academic Press, pp. 5–6, 1991. Cited on p. 737

[661] Rossignac, J., and M. van Emmerik, M., "Hidden contours on a framebuffer," *Proceedings 7th Eurographics Workshop on Computer Graphics Hardware*, pp. 188–204, 1992. Cited on p. 295

[662] Rule, Keith, *3D Graphics File Formats: A Programmer's Reference*, Addison-Wesley, Reading, Massachusetts, 1996. http://www.europa.com/~keithr/ Cited on p. 440, 479

[663] Rundberg, Peter, *An Optimized Collision Detection Algorithm*, M.S. Thesis, Department of Computer Engineering, Chalmers University of Technology, Gothenburg, 1999. http://www.ce.chalmers.se/staff/biff/exjobb/ Cited on p. 606

[664] Rusinkiewicz, Szymon, "A Survey of BRDF Representation for Computer Graphics," written for CS348C, Stanford University, 1997. http://www.cs.princeton.edu/~smr/ Cited on p. 182, 196, 202

[665] Rusinkiewicz, Szymon, and Marc Levoy, "QSplat: A Multiresolution Point Rendering System for Large Meshes," *Computer Graphics (SIGGRAPH 2000 Proceedings)*, pp. 343–352, July 2000. http://www.cs.princeton.edu/~smr/ Cited on p. 402

[666] "S3TC DirectX 6.0 Standard Texture Compression," S3 Inc., 1998. http://www.s3.com/savage3d/s3tc.htm Cited on p. 143

[667] Sagan, Hans, *Space-Filling Curves*, Springer-Verlag, 1994. Cited on p. 463

[668] Saito, Takafumi, and Tokiichiro Takahashi, "Comprehensible Rendering of 3-D Shapes," *Computer Graphics (SIGGRAPH '90 Proceedings)*, pp. 197–206, August 1990. Cited on p. 299

[669] Samet, Hanan, *Applications of Spatial Data Structures: Computer Graphics, Image Processing and GIS*, Addison-Wesley, Reading, Massachusetts, 1989. Cited on p. 353, 403, 666

[670] Samet, Hanan, *The Design and Analysis of Spatial Data Structures*, Addison-Wesley, Reading, Massachusetts, 1989. Cited on p. 351, 353, 364, 403, 666

[671] Samosky, Joseph, *SectionView: A system for interactively specifying and visualizing sections through three-dimensional medical image data*, M.S. Thesis, Department of Electrical Engineering and Computer Science, Massachusetts Institute of Technology, 1993. Cited on p. 584

[672] Sander, Pedro V., Xianfeng Gu, Steven J. Gortler, Hugues Hoppe, and John Snyder, "Silhouette Clipping," *Computer Graphics (SIGGRAPH 2000 Proceedings)*, pp. 327–334, July 2000. Cited on p. 363, 468

[673] Sander, Pedro V., John Snyder, Steven J. Gortler, and Hugues Hoppe, "Texture Mapping Progressive Meshes," *Computer Graphics (SIGGRAPH 2001 Proceedings)*, pp. 409–416, August 2001. Cited on p. 166, 468, 475

[674] Schaufler, Gernot, "Dynamically Generated Impostors," *GI Workshop on "Modeling - Virtual Worlds - Distributed Graphics,"* D.W. Fellner, ed., Infix Verlag, pp. 129–135, November 1995. http://www.gup.uni-linz.ac.at:8001/staff/schaufler/papers/ Cited on p. 326, 327, 328

[675] Schaufler, G., and W. Stürzlinger, "A Three Dimensional Image Cache for Virtual Reality," in *Proceedings of Eurographics '96*, pp. 227–236, 1996. http://www.gup.uni-linz.ac.at:8001/staff/schaufler/papers/ Cited on p. 328, 335

[676] Schaufler, Gernot, "Exploiting Frame to Frame Coherence in a Virtual Reality System," *VRAIS '96*, Santa Clara, California, pp. 95–102, April 1996. http://www.gup.uni-linz.ac.at:8001/staff/schaufler/papers/ Cited on p. 337

[677] Schaufler, Gernot, "Nailboards: A Rendering Primitive for Image Caching in Dynamic Scenes," *Eurographics Rendering Workshop 1997*, pp. 151–162, 1997. http://www.gup.uni-linz.ac.at:8001/staff/schaufler/papers/ Cited on p. 332, 333

[678] Schaufler, Gernot, "Per-Object Image Warping with Layered Impostors," *9th Eurographics Workshop on Rendering*, pp. 145–156, June–July 1998. http://www.gup.uni-linz.ac.at:8001/staff/schaufler/papers/ Cited on p. 334, 337

[679] Schaufler, Gernot, Julie Dorsey, Xavier Decoret, and François Sillion, "Conservative Volumetric Visibility with Occluder Fusion," *Computer Graphics (SIGGRAPH 2000 Proceedings)*, pp. 229–238, July 2000. Cited on p. 379, 380, 381

[680] Scheib, Vincent, "Introduction to Demos & The Demo Scene," *Gamasutra*, February 2001. http://www.gamasutra.com/features/20010216/scheib_01.htm Cited on p. 284

[681] Schilling, Andreas, and Wolfgang Straßer, "EXACT: Algorithm and Hardware Architecture for an Improved A-buffer," *Computer Graphics (SIGGRAPH 93 Proceedings)*, pp. 85–92, August 1993. Cited on p. 97

[682] Schilling, Andreas, G. Knittel, and Wolfgang Straßer, "Texram: A Smart Memory for Texturing," *IEEE Computer Graphics and Applications*, vol. 16, no. 3, pp. 32–41, May 1996. Cited on p. 141, 176

[683] Schlag, John, "Using Geometric Constructions to Interpolate Orientations with Quaternions," in James Arvo, ed., *Graphics Gems II*, Academic Press, pp. 377–380, 1991. Cited on p. 66

[684] Schlag, John, "Fast Embossing Effects on Raster Image Data," in Paul S. Heckbert, ed., *Graphics Gems IV*, Academic Press, pp. 433–437, 1994. http://www.graphicsgems.org/ Cited on p. 167, 168

[685] Schlick, Christophe, "A Fast Alternative to Phong's Specular Model," in Paul S. Heckbert, ed., *Graphics Gems IV*, Academic Press, pp. 385–387, 1994. Cited on p. 79

[686] Schlick, Christophe, "An Inexpensive BDRF Model for Physically based Rendering," *Eurographics'94*, published in *Computer Graphics Forum*, vol. 13, no. 3, Sept. 1994, pp. 149–162. http://dept-info.labri.u-bordeaux. fr/~schlick/DOC/eur2.html Cited on p. 231

[687] Schmalstieg, Dieter, and Robert F. Tobler, "Fast Projected Area Computation for Three-Dimensional Bounding Boxes," *journal of graphics tools*, vol. 4, no. 2, pp. 37–43, 1999. Cited on p. 397

[688] Schneider, Philip, and David Eberly, *Geometry Tools for Computer Graphics* (tentative title), Morgan-Kaufmann Press, 2002. Cited on p. 442, 443, 479, 628, 666

[689] Schorn, Peter and Frederick Fisher, "Testing the Convexity of Polygon," in Paul S. Heckbert, ed., *Graphics Gems IV*, Academic Press, pp. 7–15, 1994. http://www.graphicsgems.org/ Cited on p. 443, 457, 479

[690] Schroeder, Tim, "Collision Detection Using Ray Casting," *Game Developer*, vol. 8, no. 8, pp. 50–56, August 2001. http://www.gdmag.com/code. htm Cited on p. 572, 598, 620, 624, 625, 626, 635

[691] Schumacher, Dale A., "General Filtered Image Rescaling," in David Kirk, ed., *Graphics Gems III*, Academic Press, pp. 8–16, 1992. http://www. graphicsgems.org/ Cited on p. 134, 259

[692] Scott, N., D. Olsen, and E. Gannett, "An Overview of the VISUALIZE fx Graphics Accelerator Hardware," *Hewlett-Packard Journal*, pp. 28–34, May 1998. http://www.hp.com/hpj/98may/ma98a4.htm Cited on p. 381, 382, 701

[693] Sears, Chris, "The Elements of Cache Programming Style," *Proceedings of the 4th Annual Linux Showcase and Conference*, October 2000. http://www.usenix.org/publications/library/proceedings/ als2000/full_papers/sears/sears_html/ Cited on p. 412

[694] Segal, M., C. Korobkin, R. van Widenfelt, J. Foran, and P. Haeberli, "Fast Shadows and Lighting Effects Using Texture Mapping," *Computer Graphics (SIGGRAPH '92 Proceedings)*, pp. 249–252, July 1992. Cited on p. 123, 151, 260, 271

[695] Segal, Mark, and Kurt Akeley, *The OpenGL Graphics System: A Specification (Version 1.2.1)*, Editor (v1.1): Chris Frazier, Editor (v1.2): Jon Leech, March 1998. http://www.opengl.org/ Cited on p. 146

[696] Shade, J., D. Lischinski, D. Salesin, T. DeRose, and J. Snyder, "Hierarchical Image Caching for Accelerated Walkthroughs of Complex Environments," *Computer Graphics (SIGGRAPH 96 Proceedings)*, pp. 75–82, August 1996. http://www.cs.washington.edu/research/grail/pub/ abstracts.html Cited on p. 335, 336

[697] Shade, J., Steven Gortler, Li-Wei He, and Richard Szeliski, "Layered Depth Images," *Computer Graphics (SIGGRAPH 98 Proceedings)*, pp. 231–242, July 1998. http://www.research.microsoft.com/MSRSIGGRAPH/ 1998/ldi.htm Cited on p. 334

[698] Shankel, Jason, "Rendering Distant Scenery with Skyboxes," in Mark De-Loura, ed., *Game Programming Gems 2*, Charles River Media, pp. 416–420, 2001. Cited on p. 338

[699] Sharp, Brian, "Implementing Curved Surface Geometry," *Game Developer*, vol. 6, no. 6, pp. 42–53, June 1999. Cited on p. 522

[700] Sharp, Brian, "Subdivision Surface Theory," *Game Developer*, vol. 7, no. 1, pp. 34–42, January 2000. http://www.gamasutra.com/features/20000411/sharp_01.htm Cited on p. 540, 541, 555

[701] Sharp, Brian, "Implementing Subdivision Surface Theory," *Game Developer*, vol. 7, no. 2, pp. 40–45, February 2000. http://www.gamasutra.com/features/20000425/sharp_01.htm Cited on p. 539, 541, 550, 555

[702] Shene, Ching-Kuang, "Computing the Intersection of a Line and a Cylinder," in Paul S. Heckbert, ed., *Graphics Gems IV*, Academic Press, pp. 353–355, 1994. Cited on p. 572

[703] Shene, Ching-Kuang, "Computing the Intersection of a Line and a Cone," in Alan Paeth, ed., *Graphics Gems V*, Academic Press, pp. 227–231, 1995. Cited on p. 572

[704] Shirley, Peter, *Physically Based Lighting Calculations for Computer Graphics*, Ph.D. Thesis, University of Illinois at Urbana Champaign, December 1990. http://www.cs.utah.edu/~shirley/papers/thesis/ Cited on p. 99, 114

[705] Shirley, Peter, *Realistic Ray Tracing*, A.K. Peters Ltd., 2000. Cited on p. 153, 284, 287

[706] Shirman, Leon A., and Salim S. Abi-Ezzi, "The Cone of Normals Technique for Fast Processing of Curved Patches," *Proceedings of Eurographics '93*, vol. 12, no. 3, pp. 261–272, 1993. Cited on p. 361, 362

[707] Shoemake, Ken, "Animating Rotation with Quaternion Curves," *Computer Graphics (SIGGRAPH '85 Proceedings)*, pp. 245–254, July 1985. Cited on p. 38, 44, 48, 51

[708] Shoemake, Ken, "Quaternions and 4×4 Matrices," in James Arvo, ed., *Graphics Gems II*, Academic Press, pp. 351–354, 1991. Cited on p. 48, 49

[709] Shoemake, Ken, "Polar Matrix Decomposition," in Paul S. Heckbert, ed., *Graphics Gems IV*, Academic Press, pp. 207–221, 1994. http://www.graphicsgems.org/ Cited on p. 42

[710] Shoemake, Ken, "Euler Angle Conversion," in Paul S. Heckbert, ed., *Graphics Gems IV*, Academic Press, pp. 222–229, 1994. http://www.graphicsgems.org/ Cited on p. 37, 40

[711] Sillion, François, and Claude Puech, *Radiosity and Global Illumination*, Morgan Kaufmann Publishers, Inc., San Francisco, 1994. Cited on p. 183, 278, 279, 440

[712] Sillion, François, G. Drettakis, and B. Bodelet, "Efficient Impostor Manipulation for Real-Time Visualization of Urban Scenery," *Computer Graphics Forum*, vol. 16, no. 3, pp. 207–218, 1997. Cited on p. 336

[713] Skiena, Steven, *The Algorithm Design Manual*, Springer Verlag, 1997. http://www.cs.sunysb.edu/~algorith/ Cited on p. 472

[714] Sloan, Peter-Pike, Michael F. Cohen, and Steven J. Gortler, "Time Critical Lumigraph Rendering," *Proceedings 1997 Symposium on Interactive 3D Graphics*, pp. 17–23, April 1997. Cited on p. 318

[715] Sloan, Peter-Pike J., and Michael F. Cohen, "Interactive Horizon Mapping," *11th Eurographics Workshop on Rendering*, pp. 281–286, June 2000. http://research.microsoft.com/~cohen/ Cited on p. 168

[716] Smith, Alvy Ray, *Digital Filtering Tutorial for Computer Graphics*, Technical Memo 27, revised March 1983. http://www.alvyray.com/ Cited on p. 91

[717] Smith, Alvy Ray, "A Pixel is Not a Little Square, a Pixel is Not a Little Square, a Pixel is Not a Little Square! (And a Voxel is Not a Little Cube)," Technical Memo 6, Microsoft Research, July 1995. http://www.alvyray.com/ Cited on p. 92, 98, 115

[718] Smith, Alvy Ray, and James F. Blinn, "Blue Screen Matting," *Computer Graphics (SIGGRAPH 96 Proceedings)*, pp. 259–268, August 1996. http://www.alvyray.com/ Cited on p. 105

[719] Smith, Alvy Ray, "The Stuff of Dreams," *Computer Graphics World*, pp. 27–29, July 1998. http://www.alvyray.com/ Cited on p. 710

[720] Smith, Andrew, Yoshifumi Kitamura, Haruo Takemura, and Fumio Kishino, "A Simple and Efficient Method for Accurate Collision Detection Among Deformable Polyhedral Objects in Arbitrary Motion," *IEEE Virtual Reality Annual International Symposium*, pp. 136–145, 1995. Cited on p. 664

[721] Smits, Brian, "Efficiency Issues for Ray Tracing," *journal of graphics tools*, vol. 3, no. 2, pp. 1–14, 1998. http://www.cs.utah.edu/~bes/papers/fastRT/paper.html Cited on p. 575

[722] Snook, Greg, "Simplified Terrain Using Interlocking Tiles," in Mark DeLoura, ed., *Game Programming Gems 2*, Charles River Media, pp. 377–383, 2001. Cited on p. 479

[723] Snyder, John, Ronen Barzel, and Steve Gabriel, "Motion Blur on Graphics Workstations," in David Kirk, ed., *Graphics Gems III*, Academic Press, pp. 374–382, 1992. http://www.graphicsgems.org/ Cited on p. 671

[724] Snyder, John, and Jed Lengyel, "Visibility Sorting and Compositing without Splitting for Image Layer Decompositions," *Computer Graphics (SIGGRAPH 98 Proceedings)*, pp. 219–230, July 1998. http://www.research.microsoft.com/~jedl/ Cited on p. 237, 316

[725] Soler, Cyril, and François Sillion, "Fast Calculation of Soft Shadow Textures Using Convolution," *Computer Graphics (SIGGRAPH 98 Proceedings)*, pp. 321–332, July 1998. http://www-imagis.imag.fr/Membres/Francois.Sillion/Papers/Index.html Cited on p. 259

[726] Spencer, Greg, Peter Shirley, Kurt Zimmerman, and Donald Greenberg, "Physically-Based Glare Effects for Digital Images," *Computer Graphics*

(SIGGRAPH 95 Proceedings), pp. 325–334, August 1995. http://www.cs.
utah.edu/~shirley/papers.html Cited on p. 329

[727] Stam, Jos, "Exact Evaluation of Catmull-Clark Subdivision Surfaces at
Arbitrary Parameter Values," *Computer Graphics (SIGGRAPH 98 Proceedings)*, pp. 395–404, July 1998. Cited on p. 555

[728] Stam, Jos, "Diffraction Shaders," *Computer Graphics (SIGGRAPH 99
Proceedings)*, pp. 101–110, August 1999. Cited on p. 199

[729] Stamminger, M., J. Haber, H. Schirmacher, and H.-P. Seidel, "Walkthroughs with Corrective Texturing," *11th Eurographics Workshop on
Rendering*, pp. 377–390, 2000. http://www.mpi-sb.mpg.de/~mcstammi/
corrtex.html Cited on p. 278

[730] Stewart, A.J., and M.S. Langer, "Towards Accurate Recovery of Shape
from Shading Under Diffuse Lighting," *IEEE Trans. on Pattern Analysis and Machine Intelligence*, Vol. 19, No. 9, Sept. 1997, pp. 1020–1025.
http://www.cs.queensu.ca/home/jstewart/papers/pami97.html Cited
on p. 282

[731] Stewart, A. James, "Tunneling for Triangle Strips in Continuous Level-
of-Detail Meshes," *Graphics Interface 2001*, Ottawa, Canada, pp. 91–100,
June 2001. http://www.graphicsinterface.org/ Cited on p. 233, 462

[732] Stokes, Michael, Matthew Anderson, Srinivasan Chandrasekar, and Ri-
cardo Motta, "A Standard Default Color Space for the Internet - sRGB,"
Version 1.10, Nov. 1996. http://www.color.org/sRGB.html Cited on
p. 110, 111

[733] Stoll, Gordon, Matthew Eldridge, Dan Patterson, Art Webb, Steven
Berman, Richard Levy, Chris Caywood, Milton Taveira, Steve Hunt, Pat
Hanrahan, "Lightning-2: A High-Performance Display Subsystem for PC
Clusters," *Computer Graphics (SIGGRAPH 2001 Proceedings)*, pp. 141–
148, August 2001. Cited on p. 687

[734] Stone, Maureen, "A Survey of Color for Computer Graphics," *Course 4
at SIGGRAPH 2001*, August 2001. http://www.stonesc.com/ Cited on
p. 194

[735] Strauss, Paul S., "A Realistic Lighting Model for Computer Animators,"
IEEE Computer Graphics and Applications, vol. 10, no. 6, pp. 56–64, November 1990. Cited on p. 73

[736] Stürzlinger, Wolfgang, and Rui Bastos, "Interactive Rendering of Glob-
ally Illuminated Glossy Scenes," *Rendering Techniques '97*, Eds. Dorsey,
Slusallek, Springer Verlag, pp. 93–102, June 1997. Cited on p. 278

[737] Sudarsky, Oded, and Craig Gotsman, "Dynamic Scene Occlusion Culling,"
IEEE Transactions on Visualization and Computer Graphics, vol. 5, no. 1,
pp. 13–29, January–March 1999. Cited on p. 389

[738] Sunday, Dan, "Area of Triangles and Polygons (2D and 3D)," Geom-
etryAlgorithms.com, 2001. http://geometryalgorithms.com/Archive/
algorithm_0101/ Cited on p. 737

[739] Sutherland, Ivan E., Robert F. Sproull, and Robert F. Schumacker, "A Characterization of Ten Hidden-Surface Algorithms," *Computing Surveys*, vol. 6, no. 1, March 1974. Cited on p. 713

[740] Svarovsky, Jan, "View-Independent Progressive Meshing," in Mark DeLoura, ed., *Game Programming Gems*, Charles River Media, pp. 454–464, 2000. Cited on p. 472, 475, 479

[741] Tanner, Christopher C., Christopher J. Migdal, and Michael T. Jones, "The Clipmap: A Virtual Mipmap," *Computer Graphics (SIGGRAPH 98 Proceedings)*, pp. 151–158, July 1998. Cited on p. 142, 705

[742] Tarini, M., P. Cignoni, C. Rocchini, and R. Scopigno, "Real Time, Accurate, Multi-Featured Rendering of Bump Mapped Surfaces," *Computer Graphics Forum* (Proceedings of Eurographics 2000), Vol. 19, No. 3, pp 119–130, 2000. http://www.eg.org/EG/CGF/Volume19/Issue3/paper140/paper140.pdf Cited on p. 176

[743] Taubin, Gabriel, and Jarek Rossignac, "Geometric Compression through Topological Surgery," *ACM Transactions on Graphics*, vol. 17, no. 2, April 1998. Cited on p. 462

[744] Taubin, Gabriel, André Guéziec, William Horn, and Francis Lazarus, "Progressive Forest Split Compression," *Computer Graphics (SIGGRAPH 98 Proceedings)*, pp. 123–132, July 1998. Cited on p. 471

[745] Teller, Seth J., and Carlo H. Séquin, "Visibility Preprocessing For Interactive Walkthroughs," *Computer Graphics (SIGGRAPH '91 Proceedings)*, pp. 61–69, July 1991. Cited on p. 365

[746] Teller, Seth J., *Visibility Computations in Densely Occluded Polyhedral Environments*, Ph.D. Thesis, Department of Computer Science, University of Berkeley, 1992. Cited on p. 365, 366

[747] Teller, Seth, and Pat Hanrahan, "Global Visibility Algorithms for Illumination Computations," *Computer Graphics (SIGGRAPH 94 Proceedings)*, pp. 443–450, July 1994. Cited on p. 365

[748] Tessman, Thant, "Casting Shadows on Flat Surfaces," *Iris Universe*, pp. 16–19, Winter 1989. Cited on p. 250

[749] Thomas, Spencer W., "Decomposing a Matrix into Simple Transformations," in James Arvo, ed., *Graphics Gems II*, Academic Press, pp. 320–323, 1991. http://www.graphicsgems.org/ Cited on p. 40, 42

[750] Thürmer, Grit, and Charles A. Wüthrich, "Computing Vertex Normals from Polygonal Facets," *journal of graphics tools*, vol. 3, no. 1, pp. 43–46, 1998. Cited on p. 452

[751] Tombesi, Marco, "3ds max Skin Exporter and Animation Toolkit," in Mark DeLoura, ed., *Game Programming Gems 2*, Charles River Media, pp. 141–152, 2001. Cited on p. 55

[752] Torborg, J., and J.T. Kajiya, "Talisman: Commodity Realtime 3D Graphics for the PC," *Computer Graphics (SIGGRAPH 96 Proceedings)*, pp. 353–363, August 1996. Cited on p. 273, 316

[753] Torrance, K., and E. Sparrow, "Theory for Off-Specular Reflection From Roughened Surfaces," *J. Optical Society of America*, Vol. 57, September 1967. Cited on p. 198

[754] Trendall, Chris, and A. James Stewart "General Calculations using Graphics Hardware with Applications to Interactive Caustics," *11th Eurographics Workshop on Rendering*, pp. 287–298, 2000. http://www.dgp.utoronto. ca/people/JamesStewart/papers/egwr00.html Cited on p. 247

[755] Tumblin, Jack, J.K. Hodgins, and B. Guenter, "Two Methods for Display of High Contrast Images," *ACM Transactions on Graphics*, Vol. 18, No. 1, pp. 56–94, January 1999. http://www.cs.northwestern.edu/~jet Cited on p. 194

[756] Turk, Greg, "Texture Synthesis on Surfaces," *Computer Graphics (SIGGRAPH 2001 Proceedings)*, pp. 347–354, August 2001. http://www.gvu.gatech.edu/people/faculty/greg.turk/texture_ surfaces/texture.html Cited on p. 126

[757] Turkowski, Ken, "Properties of Surface-Normal Transformations," in Andrew Glassner, ed., *Graphics Gems*, Academic Press, pp. 539–547, 1990. http://www.worldserver.com/turk/computergraphics/ index.html Cited on p. 35

[758] Turner, Bryan, "Real-Time Dynamic Level of Detail Terrain Rendering with ROAM," *Gamasutra*, April 2000. http://www.gamasutra.com/ features/20000403/turner_01.htm Cited on p. 476

[759] Ulrich, Thatcher, "Continuous LOD Terrain Meshing Using Adaptive Quadtrees," *Gamasutra*, February 2000. http://www.gamasutra.com/ features/20000228/ulrich_01.htm Cited on p. 479

[760] Ulrich, Thatcher, "Loose Octrees," in Mark DeLoura, ed., *Game Programming Gems*, Charles River Media, pp. 444–453, 2000. Cited on p. 354

[761] Upstill, S., *The RenderMan Companion: A Programmer's Guide to Realistic Computer Graphics*, Addison-Wesley, Reading, Massachusetts, 1990. Cited on p. 71, 176, 179, 232, 287

[762] van den Bergen, G., "Efficient Collision Detection of Complex Deformable Models Using AABB Trees," *journal of graphics tools*, vol. 2, no. 4, pp. 1–13, 1997. http://www.acm.org/jgt/papers/vanDenBergen97 Cited on p. 645, 646, 647, 662, 663

[763] van den Bergen, G., "A Fast and Robust GJK Implementation for Collision Detection of Convex Objects," *journal of graphics tools*, vol. 4, no. 2, pp. 7–25, 1999. http://www.acm.org/jgt/papers/vanDenBergen99 Cited on p. 647, 660, 662

[764] van den Bergen, Gino, *Collision Detection in Interactive 3D Computer Animation*, Ph.D. Thesis, Eindhoven University of Technology, 1999. Cited on p. 646, 647, 662, 663

[765] van den Bergen, Gino, "Proximity Queries and Penetration Depth Computation on 3D Game Objects," *Game Developers Conference*, pp. 821–837, March 2001. Cited on p. 662

[766] van der Burg, John, "Building an Advanced Particle System," *Gamasutra*, June 2000. http://www.gamasutra.com/features/20000623/vanderburg_01.htm Cited on p. 331

[767] van Overveld, C.V.A.M., and B. Wyvill, "Phong Normal Interpolation Revisited," *ACM Transaction on Graphics*, vol. 16, no. 4, pp. 397–419, October 1997. Cited on p. 507

[768] van Overveld, C.V.A.M., and B. Wyvill, "An Algorithm for Polygon Subdivision Based on Vertex Normals," *Computer Graphics International '97*, pp. 3–12, June 1997. Cited on p. 505

[769] Velho, Luiz, "Simple and Efficient Polygonization of Implicit Surfaces," *journal of graphics tools*, vol. 1, no. 2, pp. 5–24, 1996. Cited on p. 527

[770] Velho, Luiz, and Luiz Henrique de Figueiredo, "Optimal Adaptive Polygonal Approximation of Parametric Surfaces," Technical Report CS-96-23, University of Waterloo, 1996. Cited on p. 519

[771] *Virtual Terrain Project* web site. http://www.vterrain.org/ Cited on p. 344, 476, 479

[772] Vlachos, Alex, and Jason L. Mitchell, "Refraction Mapping in Liquid Containers," in Mark DeLoura, ed., *Game Programming Gems*, Charles River Media, pp. 594–600, 2000. Cited on p. 231, 247

[773] Vlachos, Alex, Jörg Peters, Chas Boyd, and Jason L. Mitchell, "Curved PN Triangles," *ACM Symposium on Interactive 3D Graphics 2001*, pp. 159–166, 2001. http://alex.vlachos.com/graphics/CurvedPNTriangles.pdf Cited on p. 504, 506, 507, 508

[774] Vlachos, Alex, and John Isidoro, "Smooth C^2 Quaternion-based Flythrough Paths," in Mark DeLoura, ed., *Game Programming Gems 2*, Charles River Media, pp. 220–227, 2001. Cited on p. 66

[775] Vlachos, Alex, "Approximating Fish Tank Refractions," in Mark DeLoura, ed., *Game Programming Gems 2*, Charles River Media, pp. 402–405, 2001. Cited on p. 247

[776] Vlachos, Alex, David Gosselin, and Jason L. Mitchell, "Self-Shadowing Characters," in Mark DeLoura, ed., *Game Programming Gems 2*, Charles River Media, pp. 421–424, 2001. Cited on p. 274, 275

[777] Volino, Pascal, and Nadia Magnenat Thalmann, "Collision and Self-Collision Detection: Efficient and Robust Solutions for Highly Deformable Surfaces," *Eurographics Workshop on Animation and Simulation '95*, pp. 55–65, September 1995. Cited on p. 666

[778] Volino, Pascal, and Nadia Magnenat Thalmann, "Implementing Fast Cloth Simulation with Collision Response," *Computer Graphics International 2000*, pp. 257–268, June 2000. Cited on p. 666

[779] Von Herzen, B., and A.H. Barr, "Accurate Triangulations of Deformed Intersecting Surfaces," *Computer Graphics (SIGGRAPH '87 Proceedings)*, pp. 103–110, July 1987. Cited on p. 519

[780] Voorhies, Douglas, "Space-Filling Curves and a Measure of Coherence," in James Arvo, ed., *Graphics Gems II*, Academic Press, pp. 26–30, 1991. Cited on p. 463

[781] International Standard ISO/IEC 14772-1:1997 (VRML). `http://www.vrml.org/` Cited on p. 41, 81

[782] *VTune Analyzer,* Intel Corporation, `http://www.intel.com/software/products/vtune/` Cited on p. 407, 435

[783] Wald, Ingo, Philipp Slusallek, and Carsten Benthin, "Interactive Distributed Ray-Tracing of Highly Complex Models," *12th Eurographics Workshop on Rendering,* pp. 274–285, 2001. `http://graphics.cs.uni-sb.de/Publications/index.html` Cited on p. 285

[784] Wald, Ingo, and Philipp Slusallek, "State-of-the-Art in Interactive Ray-Tracing," in *State of the Art Reports, EUROGRAPHICS 2001,* pp. 21–42, September 2001. `http://graphics.cs.uni-sb.de/Publications/index.html` Cited on p. 286, 711

[785] Wald, Ingo, Carsten Benthin, Markus Wagner, and Philipp Slusallek, "Interactive Rendering with Coherent Ray-Tracing," *Proceedings of Eurographics 2001,* vol. 20, no. 3, pp. 153–164, 2001. `http://graphics.cs.uni-sb.de/Publications/index.html` Cited on p. 285

[786] Walker, R., and J. Snoeyink, "Using CSG Representations of Polygons for Practical Point-in-Polygon Tests," *Visual Proceedings (SIGGRAPH 97),* p. 152, August 1997. Cited on p. 583

[787] Waller, Marcus D., Jon. P. Ewins, Martin White, and Paul F. Lister, "Efficient Coverage Mask Generation for Antialiasing," *IEEE Computer Graphics and Applications,* vol. 20, no. 6, pp. 86–93, Nov./Dec. 2000. Cited on p. 97

[788] Wallis, Bob, "Tutorial on Forward Differencing," in Andrew S. Glassner, ed., *Graphics Gems,* Academic Press, pp. 594–603, 1990. `http://www.graphicsgems.org/` Cited on p. 514

[789] Walter, Bruce, Gün Alppay, Eric P. F. Lafortune, Sebastian Fernandez, and Donald P. Greenberg, "Fitting Virtual Lights For Non-Diffuse Walkthroughs," *Computer Graphics (SIGGRAPH 97 Proceedings),* pp. 45–48, August 1997. `http://www.graphics.cornell.edu/~bjw/virtlite.html` Cited on p. 282

[790] Wanger, Leonard, "The effect of shadow quality on the perception of spatial relationships in computer generated imagery," *Computer Graphics (1992 Symposium on Interactive 3D Graphics),* vol. 25, no. 2, pp. 39–42, 1992. Cited on p. 250

[791] Ward, Gregory, "Measuring and Modeling Anisotropic Reflection," *Computer Graphics (SIGGRAPH '92 Proceedings),* pp. 265–272, July 1992. `http://radsite.lbl.gov/radiance/papers/sg92/paper.html` Cited on p. 201, 202

[792] Warren, Joe, and Henrik Weimer, *Subdivision Methods for Geometric Design: A Constructive Approach,* Morgan Kaufmann Publishers, Inc., 2001. Cited on p. 482, 529, 530, 532, 535, 537, 555

[793] Watt, Alan, and Mark Watt, *Advanced Animation and Rendering Techniques—Theory and Practice,* Addison-Wesley, 1992. Cited on p. 38, 66, 79, 85, 178, 248, 331, 555

[794] Watt, Alan, *3D Computer Graphics*, Second Edition, Addison-Wesley, 1993. Cited on p. 178, 331

[795] Watt, Alan, and Fabio Policarpo, *The Computer Image*, Addison-Wesley, 1998. Cited on p. 85, 87, 178

[796] Watt, Alan, and Fabio Policarpo, *3D Games: Real-Time Rendering and Software Technology*, Addison-Wesley, 2001. Cited on p. 178

[797] Weghorst, H., G. Hooper, and D. Greenberg, "Improved Computational Methods for Ray Tracing," *ACM Transactions on Graphics*, pp. 52–69, 1984. Cited on p. 644

[798] Welzl, Emo, "Smallest Enclosing Disks (Balls and Ellipsoids)," in H. Maurer, ed., *New Results and New Trends in Computer Science, LNCS 555*, 1991. Cited on p. 565

[799] Wernecke, Josie, *The Inventor Mentor*, Addison-Wesley, Reading, Massachusetts, 1994. Cited on p. 403

[800] Westover, Lee, "Footprint Evaluation for Volume Rendering," *Computer Graphics (SIGGRAPH '90 Proceedings)*, pp. 367–376, August 1990. Cited on p. 343

[801] Williams, Lance, "Casting Curved Shadows on Curved Surfaces," *Computer Graphics (SIGGRAPH '78 Proceedings)*, pp. 270–274, August 1978. Cited on p. 269

[802] Williams, Lance, "Pyramidal Parametrics," *Computer Graphics*, vol. 7, no. 3, pp. 1–11, July 1983. Cited on p. 133, 135, 158, 163

[803] Wilson, A, E. Larsen, D. Manocha, and M.C. Lin, "Partioning and Handling Massive Models for Interactive Collision Detection," *Proceedings of Eurographics 1999*, vol. 18, no. 3, pp. 319–329, 1999. Cited on p. 666

[804] Wimmer, Michael, and Dieter Schmalstieg, "Load balancing for smooth LODs," Technical Report TR-186-2-98-31, Institute of Computer Graphics and Algorithms, Vienna University of Technology, December 1998. ftp://ftp.cg.tuwien.ac.at/pub/TR/98/TR-186-2-98-31Paper.pdf Cited on p. 401

[805] Wimmer, Michael, Markus Giegl, and Dieter Schmalstieg, "Fast Walkthroughs with Image Caches and Ray Casting," *Computers & Graphics*, vol. 23, no. 6, pp. 831–838, 1999. Cited on p. 373

[806] Wimmer, Michael, Peter Wonka, and François Sillion, "Point-Based Impostors for Real-Time Visualization," *12th Eurographics Workshop on Rendering*, pp. 163–176, June 2001. Cited on p. 325, 337

[807] Wimmer, Michael, *Representing and Rendering Distant Objects for Real-Time Visualization*, Ph.D. Thesis, The Institute of Computer Graphics and Algorithms, Vienna University of Technology, June, 2001. Cited on p. 346

[808] Winner, Stephanie, Mike Kelley, Brent Pease, Bill Rivard, and Alex Yen, "Hardware Accelerated Rendering of Antialiasing Using a Modified A-Buffer Algorithm," *Computer Graphics (SIGGRAPH 97 Proceedings)*, pp. 307–316, August 1997. Cited on p. 93, 97

[809] Witkin, Andrew, David Baraff, and Michael Kass, "Physically Based Modeling," *Course 25 notes at SIGGRAPH 2001*, 2001. http://www.pixar.com/aboutpixar/research/pbm2001/ Cited on p. 654, 655, 664, 665

[810] Wloka, Matthias, and R. Zeleznik, "Interactive Real-Time Motion Blur," *The Visual Computer*, vol. 12, no. 6, pp. 283–295, 1996. http://www.cs.brown.edu/research/graphics/research/vrml/ Cited on p. 237

[811] Wloka, Matthias, "Implementation of 'Missing' Vertex Shader Instructions," NVIDIA White Paper, December 2000. http://developer.nvidia.com Cited on p. 216, 217

[812] Wloka, Matthias, "Implementing Motion Blur & Depth of Field using DirectX 8," *Meltdown 2001*, July 2001. http://www.microsoft.com/mscorp/corpevents/meltdown2001/presentations.asp Cited on p. 237

[813] Wolberg, George, *Digital Image Warping*, IEEE Computer Society Press, 1990. Cited on p. 85, 87, 98, 114, 148, 178

[814] Wonka, Peter, and Dieter Schmalstieg, "Occluder Shadows for Fast Walkthroughs of Urban Environments," *Computer Graphics Forum*, vol. 18, no. 3, pp. 51–60, 1999. Cited on p. 373

[815] Wonka, Peter, Michael Wimmer, and Dieter Schmalstieg, "Visibility Preprocessing with Occluder Fusion for Urban Walkthroughs," *11th Eurographics Workshop on Rendering*, pp. 71–82, 2000. Cited on p. 377

[816] Wonka, Peter, Michael Wimmer, and François X. Sillion, "Instant Visibility," *Proceedings of Eurographics 2001*, Vol. 20, No. 3, pp. 411–421, September 2001. Cited on p. 377, 378, 379

[817] Wonka, Peter, *Occlusion Culling for Real-Time Rendering of Urban Environments*, Ph.D. Thesis, The Institute of Computer Graphics and Algorithms, Vienna University of Technology, June, 2001. Cited on p. 377

[818] Woo, Andrew, "Fast Ray-Box Intersection," in Andrew Glassner, ed., *Graphics Gems*, Academic Press, pp. 395–396, 1990. http://www.graphicsgems.org/ Cited on p. 575, 576

[819] Woo, A., P. Poulin, and A. Fournier, "A Survey of Shadow Algorithms," *IEEE Computer Graphics and Applications*, vol. 10, no. 6, pp. 13–32, November 1990. Cited on p. 248

[820] Woo, Andrew, "The Shadow Depth Map Revisited," in David Kirk, ed., *Graphics Gems III*, Academic Press, pp. 338–342, 1992. http://www.graphicsgems.org/ Cited on p. 272, 273

[821] Woo, Andrew, Andrew Pearce, and Marc Ouellette, "It's Really Not a Rendering Bug, You See...," *IEEE Computer Graphics and Applications*, vol. 16, no. 5, pp. 21–25, September 1996. http://computer.org/cga/cg1996/g5toc.htm Cited on p. 78, 445

[822] Woodland, Ryan, "Filling the Gaps—Advanced Animation Using Stitching and Skinning," in Mark DeLoura, ed., *Game Programming Gems*, Charles River Media, pp. 476–483, 2000. Cited on p. 53, 55

[823] Woodland, Ryan, "Advanced Texturing Using Texture Coordinate Generation," in Mark DeLoura, ed., *Game Programming Gems*, Charles River Media, pp. 549–554, 2000. Cited on p. 148, 151

[824] Worley, Steve, and Eric Haines, "Bounding Areas for Ray/Polygon Intersection," in Eric Haines, ed., *Ray Tracing News*, vol. 6, no. 1, January 1993. http://www.acm.org/tog/resources/RTNews/html/rtnv6n1.html Cited on p. 583

[825] Wright, Richard, "Understanding and Using OpenGL Texture Objects," *Gamasutra*, July 23, 1999. http://www.gamasutra.com/features/19990723/opengl_texture_objects_01.htm Cited on p. 141, 142, 424

[826] Wu, David. Personal communication, 2002. Cited on p. 295, 298, 301, 302, 303

[827] Wyatt, Rob, "Hardware Accelerated Spherical Environment Mapping using Texture Matrices," *Gamasutra*, August 2000. http://www.gamasutra.com/features/20000811/wyatt_01.htm Cited on p. 160

[828] Wynn, Chris, "Real-Time BRDF-based Lighting using Cube-Maps," NVIDIA White Paper, 2001. http://developer.nvidia.com Cited on p. 204

[829] Wyvill, Brian, "Symmetric Double Step Line Algorithm," in Andrew S. Glassner, ed., *Graphics Gems*, Academic Press, pp. 101–104, 1990. http://www.graphicsgems.org/ Cited on p. 9

[830] Xia, Julie C., Jihad El-Sana, and Amitabh Varshney, "Adaptive Real-Time Level-of-detail-based Rendering for Polygonal Objects," *IEEE Transactions on Visualization and Computer Graphics*, vol. 3, no. 2, June 1997. Cited on p. 520

[831] Xiang, X., M. Held, and J.S.B. Mitchell, "Fast and Effective Stripification of Polygonal Surface Models," *Proceedings 1999 Symposium on Interactive 3D Graphics*, pp. 71–78, April 1999. http://www.cosy.sbg.ac.at/~held/projects/strips/strips.html Cited on p. 462, 464

[832] Xie, Feng, and Micheal Shantz, "Adaptive Hierarchical Visibility in a Tiled Architecture," *ACM SIGGRAPH/Eurographics Workshop on Graphics Hardware*, pp. 75–84, 1999. Cited on p. 707

[833] Zachmann, Gabriel, "Rapid Collision Detection by Dynamically Aligned DOP-Trees," *Proceedings of IEEE Virtual Reality Annual International Symposium—VRAIS '98*, Atlanta, Georgia, pp. 90–97, March 1998. Cited on p. 645, 666

[834] Zhang, Hansong, and Kenneth E. Hoff III, "Fast Backface Culling Using Normal Masks," in *Proceedings 1997 Symposium on Interactive 3D Graphics*, pp. 103–106, April 1997. Cited on p. 362

[835] Zhang, H., D. Manocha, T. Hudson, and K.E. Hoff III, "Visibility Culling using Hierarchical Occlusion Maps," *Computer Graphics (SIGGRAPH 97 Proceedings)*, pp. 77–88, August 1997. http://www.cs.unc.edu/~zhangh/hom.html Cited on p. 372, 386, 388

[836] Zhang, Hansong, *Effective Occlusion Culling for the Interactive Display of Arbitrary Models*, Ph.D. Thesis, Department of Computer Science, University of North Carolina at Chapel Hill, July 1998. Cited on p. 371, 386, 388, 433

[837] Zhang, Hansong, "Forward Shadow Mapping," *9th Eurographics Workshop on Rendering*, pp. 131–138, June–July 1998. `http://www.cs.unc.edu/~zhangh/shadow.html` Cited on p. 273

[838] Zhao, YouBing, Ji Zhou, JiaoBing Shi, and ZhiGeng Pan, "A Fast Algorithm For Large Scale Terrain Walkthrough," *International Conference on CAD & Graphics 2001*, China, 2001. `http://www.cad.zju.edu.cn/home/zhaoyb/` Cited on p. 479

[839] Zhukov, S., A. Iones, G. Kronin, "An Ambient Light Illumination Model," *9th Eurographics Workshop on Rendering*, pp. 45–56, June–July 1998. Cited on p. 284

[840] Zorin, Denis, Peter Schröder, and Wim Sweldens, "Interpolating Subdivision for Meshes with Arbitrary Topology," *Computer Graphics (SIGGRAPH 96 Proceedings)*, pp. 189–192, August 1996. Cited on p. 537, 539

[841] Zorin, Denis, C^k *Continuity of Subdivision Surfaces*, Caltech CS-TR-96-23, 1996. Cited on p. 555

[842] Zorin, Denis, Peter Schröder, and Wim Sweldens, "Interactive Multiresolution Mesh Editing," *Computer Graphics (SIGGRAPH 97 Proceedings)*, pp. 259–268, August 1997. Cited on p. 554

[843] Zorin, Denis, *Stationary Subdivision and Multiresolution Surface Representations*, Ph.D. thesis, Caltech CS-TR-97-32, 1997. Cited on p. 535, 537, 539, 541

[844] Zorin, Denis, "A Method for Analysis of C1-Continuity of Subdivision Surfaces," *SIAM Journal of Numerical Analysis*, vol. 37, no. 5, pp. 1677–1708, 2000. `http://mrl.nyu.edu/publications/method-analysis/` Cited on p. 555

[845] Zorin, Denis, Peter Schröder, Tony DeRose, Leif Kobbelt, Adi Levin, and Wim Sweldens, "Subdivision for Modeling and Animation," *Course notes at SIGGRAPH 2000*, 2000. `http://www.mrl.nyu.edu/~dzorin/sig00course/` Cited on p. 530, 532, 536, 537, 538, 539, 545, 551, 555

[846] Zwillinger, Dan, "CRC Standard Mathematical Tables and Formulas," 30th Edition, CRC Press, 1995. `http://freeabel.geom.umn.edu/docs/reference/CRC-formulas/` Cited on p. 738, 746

Index